CONCISE

EARTH
BOOK

WORLD ATLAS

GRAPHIC LEARNING

Published in the United States of America by Graphic
Learning International Publishing Corporation, Boulder,
Colorado.

The Concise EARTHBOOK ©
M.L. (Mert) Yockstick, Publisher

Designed, edited, drawn and reproduced by the
cartographers, geographers, artists and technicians
at ESSELTE MAP SERVICE.

Consultants for the United States Edition: James E. Davis
Sharryl Davis Hawke

Design Council: Turnbull & Company

Esselte Map Service AB (Sweden)
    (Title) Concise EARTHBOOK

    Includes Glossary and Index
    1. Atlases I. Title
    ISBN No. 0-87746-101-5

Printed in Sweden

11.95

The Concise edition of the EarthBook is designed to place the world at your fingertips. The Age of Information has brought a new perspective to the planet Earth. Space travel and satellite photography have inspired the new style of environmental mapping for the EarthBook that offers unique insight into the land use and life conditions of humans, animals and plants throughout the world.

Our city, state and country are slowly losing their prominence as our place of residence. The entire Earth is becoming our home. We are all related – distant relatives, sharing the Earth and its environments. This new age atlas brings this world home to you in a way that will nurture and strengthen our geographic literacy.

The Concise edition of the EarthBook gives you the world in a compact new size and format – places you want to locate, travel to or dream about.

M.L. (Mert) Yockstick
Publisher

READER INFORMATION

Reader information   8   **Legend**   9

NORTH AMERICA

North America, environment,   **Southern United States,**   24-25
flags   10-11   **Hawaii, Mexico**
Alaska   12-13   **South Eastern United States,**   26-27
incl. the Aleutian islands   **The Caribbean Archipelago**
Western Canada   14-15   The Bahamas, Cuba, Dominican
                                             Republic, Haiti, Jamaica
Northern Canada   16-17
                                             Central America and   28-29
Eastern Canada   18-19   **the West Indies**
Central, Western United State 20-21   Belize, The Caribbean Archipelago,
Eastern, United States   22-23   Costa Rica, Cuba, El Salvador, Guatemala,
                                             Honduras, Mexico, Nicaragua

SOUTH AMERICA

South America, environment,   **South America, central part**   34-35
flags   30-31   Bolivia, Brazil, Chile, Peru
South America, northern part 32-33   **South America, southern part**   36-37
Brazil, Colombia, Ecuador, Guyana,   Argentina, Bolivia, Brazil, Chile,
Panama, Peru, Surinam, Venezuela   Paraguay, Uruguay

EUROPE

Europe, environment, flags   38-39   **Spain, Italy, France**   44-45
British Isles and Central   **The Balkans**   46-47
Europe   40-41   Bulgaria, Cyprus, Greece, Hungary,
Belgium, Czechoslovakia, Federal   Romania, Turkey
Republic of Germany, German   **The Middle East**   48-49
Democratic Republic, Luxembourg,   Bahrain, Iran, Iraq, Israel, Jordan, Kuwait,
Netherlands, Poland   Lebanon, Qatar, Syria, United Arab Emirates
Northern Europe   42-43   **Western Soviet Union**   50-51
Denmark, Finland, Iceland, Norway,   European USSR, Western Siberia
Sweden

AFRICA

Africa, environment, flags   52-53   **West Africa**   58-59
North-West Africa   54-55   Benin, Burkina, Cameroon, Chad, Congo,
Algeria, Libya, Morocco, Mauretania,   Equatorial Guinea, Gabon, Ghana,
Niger, Tunisia   Guinea, Guinea-Bissau, Ivory Coast,
The Nile Valley and Arabia   56-57   Liberia, Mali, Niger, Nigeria, São Tomé
Bahrain, Egypt, Iraq, Israel, Jorda,   and Príncipe, Senegal, Sierra Leone,
Kuwait, Lebanon, Oman, Qatar, Saudi-   The Gambia, Togo
Arabia, Southern Yemen, Sudan, Syria,
United Arab Emirates, Yemen

East Africa   60-61
Central Africa, Ethiopia, Kenya, Sudan,
Tanzania, Uganda, Zaire

Southern Africa   62-63
Angola, Botswana, Comores, Madagascar,
Malawi, Mauritius, Mozambique,
Namibia, Lesotho, South Africa,
Swaziland, Zambia, Zimbabwe

ASIA

Asia, environment, flags   64-65

South West Asia   66-67
Afghanistan, Iran, Pakistan

Eastern soviet Union   68-69
Eastern Siberia, Mongolia

China and Japan   70-71
incl. Mongolia, North Korea, South
Korea, Taiwan

India and South East Asia   72-73
incl. Bangladesh, Bhutan, Burma,
Kampuchea, Laos, Nepal, Sri Lanka,
Thailand, Vietnam

The East Indies   74-75
Brunei, Indonesia, Malaysia,
Philippines

AUSTRALIA

**Australasia, environment,
flags**   76-77
Australia   78-79

New Guinea and New Zealand   80-81
Oceania   82-83
Melanesia, Micronesia, Polynesia

POLAR REGIONS

The Arctic, environment   84

The Antarctica, environment   85

THE WORLD

The World, environment   86-87
The World, political

The World, Time Zones   90-91
**Animals on the Egde of
Extinction**   92-93

STATISTICS

The World   94-95
North-America   96-100
South-America   101-105
Europe   106-113

Asia   114-123
Australia   122-125
Africa   126-136

INDEX

Index   137-215

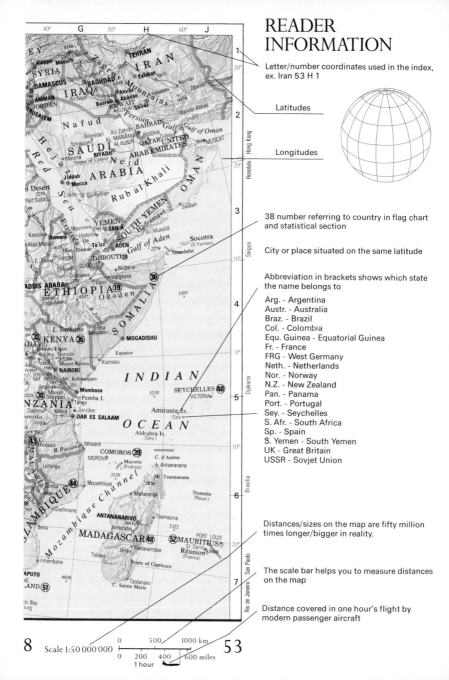

READER INFORMATION

Letter/number coordinates used in the index, ex. Iran 53 H 1

Latitudes

Longitudes

38 number referring to country in flag chart and statistical section

City or place situated on the same latitude

Abbreviation in brackets shows which state the name belongs to

Arg. - Argentina
Austr. - Australia
Braz. - Brazil
Col. - Colombia
Equ. Guinea - Equatorial Guinea
Fr. - France
FRG - West Germany
Neth. - Netherlands
Nor. - Norway
N.Z. - New Zealand
Pan. - Panama
Port. - Portugal
Sey. - Seychelles
S. Afr. - South Africa
Sp. - Spain
S. Yemen - South Yemen
UK - Great Britain
USSR - Sovjet Union

Distances/sizes on the map are fifty million times longer/bigger in reality.

The scale bar helps you to measure distances on the map

Distance covered in one hour's flight by modern passenger aircraft

Scale 1:50 000 000

0   500   1000 km

0   200   400   600 miles
1 hour

Symbols   Scale 1:10 000 000, 1:13 500 000   1:20 000 000

Bombay More than 5 000 000 inhabitants

Milano 1 000 000-5 000 000 inhabitants

Zürich 250 000-1 000 000 inhabitants

Dijon 100 000-250 000 inhabitants

Dover 25 000-100 000 inhabitants

Torquay Less than 25 000 inhabitants

Tachiumet Small sites

WIEN National capital

Atlanta State capital

———— Major road

———— Other road

- - - - Road under construction

———— Railway

- - - - Railway under construction

········ Train ferry

▬▬▬ National boundary

▪ ▪ ▪ ▪ Disputed national boundary

———— State boundary

- - - - Disputed state boundary

▬▬▬ Undefined boundary in the sea

˙4807 Height above sea-level in metres

'3068 Depth in metres

National park

∴ Niniveh Ruin

≍ Pass

KAINJI DAM Dam

- - - - Wadi

.... Canal

—|— Waterfalls

⌒⌒⌒ Reef

Symbols   Scale 1:30 000 000 1:50 000 000 1:54 000 000 1:60 000 000 1:75 000 000

Shanghai More than 5 000 000 inhabitants

Barcelona 1 000 000-5 000 000 inhabitants

Venice 250 000-1 000 000 inhabitants

Aberdeen 50 000-250 000 inhabitants

Beida Less than 50 000 inhabitants

Mawson Scientific station

CAIRO National capital

———— Major road

———— Railway

- - - - Railway under construction

▬▬▬ National boundary

▪ ▪ ▪ ▪ Disputed national boundary

———— State boundary

- - - - Disputed state boundary

▬▬▬ Undefined boundary in the sea

˙8848 Height above sea-level in metres

'11034 Depth in metres

2645 Thickness of ice cap

∴ Thebes Ruin

▷—|— Dam

- - - - Wadi

.... Canal

—|— Waterfalls

⌒⌒⌒ Reef

Colour Key

Tundra

Glacier

Coniferous forest

Mixed forest

Deciduous forest

Tropical rain forest

Chacos

Arable land

Grassland, pasture

Savanna

Steppe, semi-desert

Sand desert

Other desert

Mountain

Marshland

Salt lake

Intermittent lake

Salt desert, salt pan, dry lake

Lava plateau

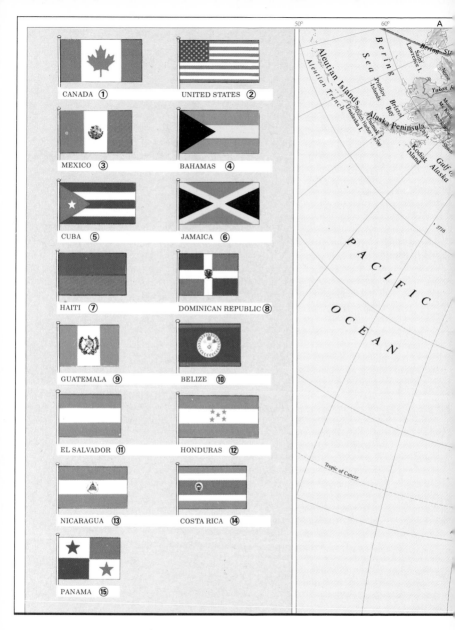

CANADA ①

UNITED STATES ②

MEXICO ③

BAHAMAS ④

CUBA ⑤

JAMAICA ⑥

HAITI ⑦

DOMINICAN REPUBLIC ⑧

GUATEMALA ⑨

BELIZE ⑩

EL SALVADOR ⑪

HONDURAS ⑫

NICARAGUA ⑬

COSTA RICA ⑭

PANAMA ⑮

50° 60° A

Bering Str

Bering Sea

Saint Lawrence I.

Aleutian Islands

Aleutian Trench

Pribilov Bristol Islands Bay.

Andrean Islands Unimak I.

Dutch Harbor, 6700

Unalaska I.

Alaska Peninsula

Kodiak Island

Yukon

Gulf of Alaska

· 3716

PACIFIC

OCEAN

Tropic of Cancer

10   NORTH AMERICA

1 foot = 0,30 m
1 meter = 3,28 feet

Scale 1:50 000 000

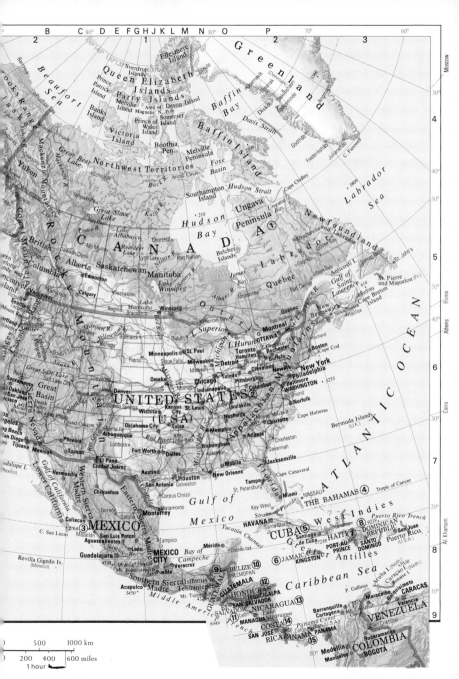

ALASKA
12

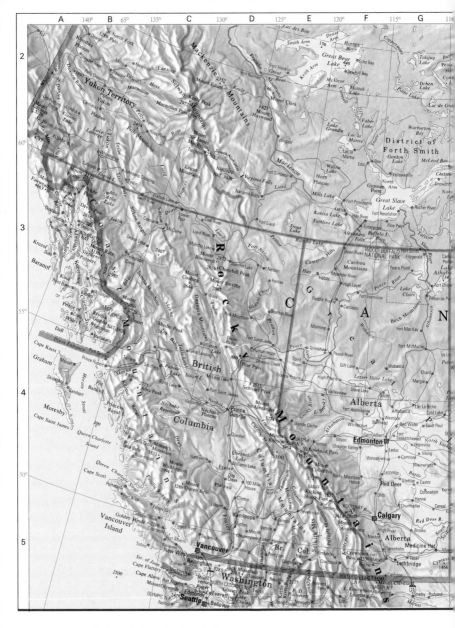

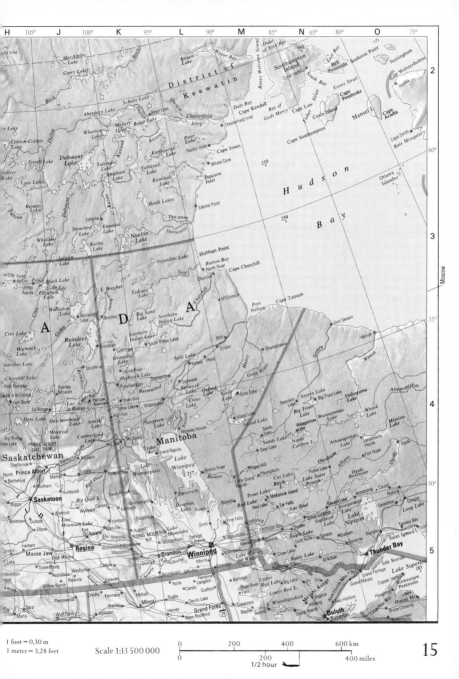

Scale 1:13 500 000

1 foot = 0,30 m
1 meter = 3,28 feet

0   200   400   600 km

0   200   400 miles
1/2 hour

15

NORTHERN CANADA

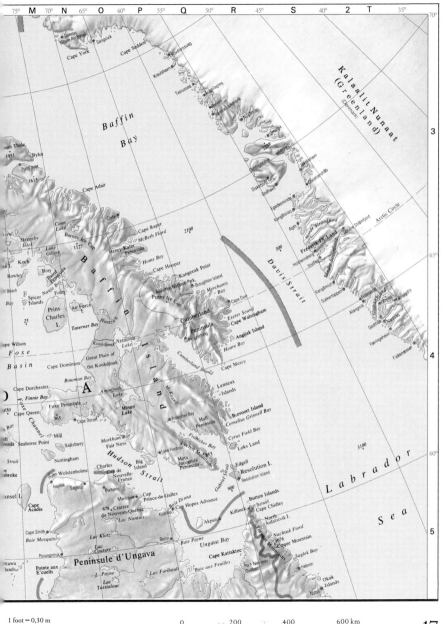

75° M 70° N 65° O 60° P 55° Q 50° R 45° S 40° 2 T 35° 70°

Dundas
Thule Air Base
Saundersvik
Cape York
Cape Seddon
Kullorssuaq
Kraulshavn

Baffin
Bay

Kalaalit Nunaat
(Greenland)
(Danmark)

Tasiussaq
Upernavik

Mount Thule
1951
Bylot
Point Inlet
1615
Cape Adair

Nuussuaq

Upernavik Kujalleq

Conn
Lake
Barnes Ice Cap
1127
Lake
Gillian
Cape Raper
2100
McBeth Fiord
Henry Kater
Peninsula
Home Bay
Cape Hooper
Kangeeak Point
Broughton Island

Arctic Circle

Umanaq

Diskofjord
Godhavn

Egedesminde
Kangâtsiaq
Agto

Mount Strømfjord
Frederik IX Land
Holsteinsborg
Søndre Strømfjord

65°

Steensby
Inlet
Koch
Bray
Penny Ice Cap
Auyuittuq National Park
Penny Ice Cap
Merchants
Bay
Cape Dyer

300

Davis Strait

Sukkertoppen
Kangilinnguit

Spicer
Islands
Foley

Cumberland
Peninsula
Exeter Sound
Cape Walsingham
Angikak Island

Atangmik

Godthåb · Nuuk

Prins
Charles
I.
Air Force
Taverner Bay
Hantzsch

Cape Wilson
Koukdjuak
Nettilling
Lake
Cumberland Sound
Cape Mercy
Hoare Bay

Frederikshåb

Faeringehavn

Fiskenæsset

Foxe
Cape Dominion
Great Plain of
the Kookdjuak
Bowman Bay

4

Basin

Cape Dorchester
Finnie Bay
Amadjuak
Lake

Lemieux
Islands

Foxe
Queen
Foxe Peninsula
365
Cape Dorset
Mingo
Lake
McKeand
Frobisher Bay
Hall
Peninsula
Brevoort Island
Cornelius Grinnell Bay
Cyrus Field Bay

3100

Seahorse Point
Mill
Salisbury
Markham Bay
Fair Ness
Frobisher Bay
Loks Land

60°

Nottingham
Charles
Cap de
Nouvelle-
France
Big
Island
Lake Harbour
Everett Mountains
553
Meta
Incognita
Peninsula
Edgell
Resolution I.
Resolution Island

Labrador

Cape Wolstenholme
Ivujivik
Saglouc

Hudson

Strait

Gabriel Strait
900

Button Islands
Cape Chidley
Killinek

Cape
Acadia

Purtuniq
Maricourt
Cap
Prince-de-Galles
Baie Diana
678 Cratère
du Nouveau-Québec
Lac Nantais
Koartac
Cap Hopes Advance
Akpatok

North
Aulatsivik I.
Nachvak Fiord
1676
Torngat Mountains
Torngat Mountains
Cirque Mountain

Cape Smith
Baie Mosquito
Lac Klotz
Lac
Couture

Bélino
Baie Payne

Ungava Bay
Port-Nouveau-
Québec

Sea

Saglek Bay
Hebron

Povungnituk
Pointe aux
E'cueils
L. Payne
Lac
Tassialouc

Peninsule d'Ungava

Lac Faribault
Baie aux Feuilles
Cape Kattaktoc

Okak
Islands
Nutak

5

1 foot = 0,30 m
1 meter = 3,28 feet

Scale 1:13 500 000

0   200   400   600 km
0   200   400 miles
200
1/2 hour

17

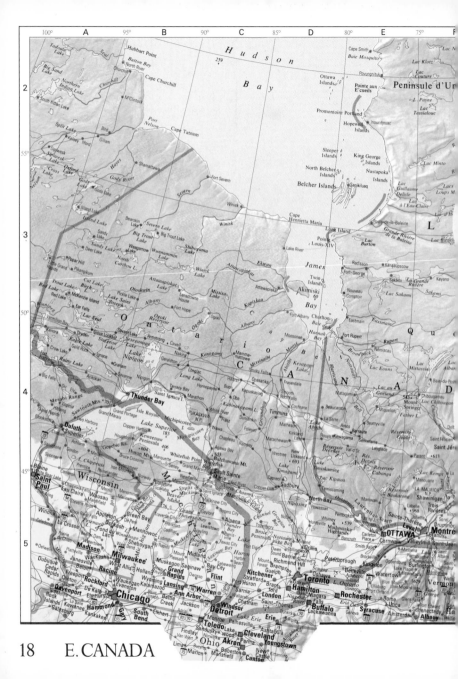

70°
G
65°
H
60°
J
55°
K
50°
L
2
3
4
5
55°
50°
45°
Moscow
Labrador Sea
Cap Hopes Advance
Koartac
Button Islands
Port Burwell
Killinek
Cape Chidley
Akpatok
North Aulatsivik I.
Bellin
Baie Payne
Ungava Bay
Nachvak Fiord
1676
Cirque Mountain
Torngat Mountains
Cape Kattaktoc
Baie aux Feuilles
Port-Nouveau-Québec
Saglek Bay
Hebron
3800
Fort-Chimo
Koksoak
George
Okak Islands
Nutak
719
1076
South Aulatsivik
Rivière à la Baleine
Lac Le Moyne
Nain
Tunungayualok
Davis Inlet
614
Wheeler
Kaguluk
Coast of Labrador
Caniapiscau
Lac Champdoré
Hopedale
Aillik
Makkovik
Cape Harrison
Lac Wakuach
Lac aux Goéland
Postville
Indian Harbour
Labrador
Kanairiktok
Groswater Bay
Schefferville
Attikamagen Lake
Caniapiscau
Lac Delorme
Rigolet
Sandwich Bay
Cartwright
Petitsikapau Lake
Smallwood Réservoir
Naskaupi
Mealy Mountains
1150
Separation Point
Domino
Lac Caniapiscau
Menihek Lakes
Livingston
North West River
L. Melville
Hawke Harbour
Goose Bay
Newfoundland and Labrador
Square Islands
Lac Bermen
Churchill Falls
Twin Falls
Churchill
Port Hope Simpson
Cape Charles
Battle Harbour
Nitchequon
Lac Opiscotéo
Lac Naocoçane
Ashuanipi
Labrador City
Atikonak Lake
Belle Isle
Cape Bauld
Saint Anthony
Ashuanipi Lake
Joseph Lake
938
Pitaga
Red Bay
Strait of Belle Isle
Laurentien
Monts Otish
1135
Eric
Vieux-Fort
Gagnon
777
Natashquan
Rivière du Petit-Mécatina
Saint Augustin
Saguenay
Grey Islands
300
Lac Plétipi
Réservoir Manicouagan
Waco
Roddickton
953
Moisie
Romaine
Baie-des-Moutons
Lac Musquaro
Port Saunders
Lac Manouane
White Bay
Manicouagan
Harrington Harbour
Daniel's Harbour
Long Range Mountains
Baie Verte
Notre Dame Bay
Fogo
Lac-Allard
Kégashka
Sept-Îles
Moisie
Magpie
Mingan
Havre Saint-Pierre
Natashquan
Romaine
Cape Freels
Wesleyville
Springdale
Trout River
806
Gros Morne
Deer Lake
Bishop's Falls
Botwood
Bonavista Bay
Bonavista
Détroit de Jacques-Cartier
Port-Cartier
Port-Ménier
312
Île d'Anticosti
Pointe de l'Est
Gander
Chute des-Passes
400
Grand Lake
Grand Falls
Port Blandford
Bay of Islands
Baie-Trinité
Pointe des Monts
Détroit d'Honguedo
Corner Brook
814
Stephenville
Newfoundland
Trinity Bay
Bay de Verde
Conception Bay
Réservoir Pipmouacan
Labrieville
Baie Comeau
Hauterive
Matane
Monts Chic-Chocs
Mont Jacques-Cartier
1268
Cap de Gaspé
Clarenville
376
Saint John's
Forestville
Saint Lawrence R.
Notre-Dame
Mont Joli
Péninsule de Gaspé
Gaspé
Percé
Cape Saint George
Saint George's Bay
Long Range Mountains
Saint Alban's
Harbour Grace
Wabana
Bay Bulls
Jonquière
Chicoutimi
Saguenay
Les Escoumins
Rimouski
Causapscal
New Richmond
Chandler
Cape Anguille
500
Burgeo
Ramea
Marystown
Placentia
Avalon Peninsula
Trois-Pistoles
Chaleur Bay
Balhousie
Gulf of Saint Lawrence
Cape Ray
Channel Port aux Basques
Harbour Breton
Fortune Bay
Burin Peninsula
Placentia Bay
Trepassey
La Malbaie
Rivière-du-Loup
Campbellton
Big Bald Mountain
820
Caraquet
Shippegan
Bathurst
Cabot Strait
Grand Bank
Miquelon
Saint Pierre
Saint Mary's Bay
Cape Race
Fort Kent
Edmundston
Saint Léonard
Île de la Madeleine
Cape North
562
Saint Pierre et Miquelon (France)
Beaupré
Montmagny
Québec
Lévis
Caribou
Perth-Andover
Newcastle
Chatham
Miramichi Bay
Prince Edward Island
CAPE BRETON HIGHLANDS N. P.
Cape Breton Island
600
Saint-John
Presque Isle
689
Peaked Mountain
New Brunswick
Saint John
Souris
Sydney Mines
Glace Bay
Sydney
Saint-Georges
Chesuncook L.
Sherman Station
Houlton
Woodstock
Moncton
Charlottetown
Cape Bear
Northumberland Strait
Bras d'Or Lake
Lac Mégantic
Moosehead L.
Fredericton
Oromocto
Grand Lake
Amherst
Pictou
Antigonish
Port Hawkesbury
1133
95
Danforth
Sussex
Springhill
New Glasgow
Strait of Canso
Canso
Greenville
Maine
Howland
Saint John
Truro
Bingham
Saint Stephen
Nova Scotia
Sheet Harbour
Skowhegan
Bangor
Eastport
Bay of Fundy
Windsor
Dartmouth
Waterville
New England
Grand Manan
Digby
Halifax
20
Augusta
Bar Harbor
ACADIA N.P.
Bridgewater
Lewiston
Bath
Penobscot Bay
Meteghan
Sable Island
2600
Portland
250
Yarmouth
Liverpool
Biddeford
Shelburne
Portsmouth
Gulf of Maine
Cape Sable
70
4100

1 foot = 0,30 m
1 meter = 3,28 feet

Scale 1:13 500 000

0 200 400 600 km
0 200 400 miles
1/2 hour

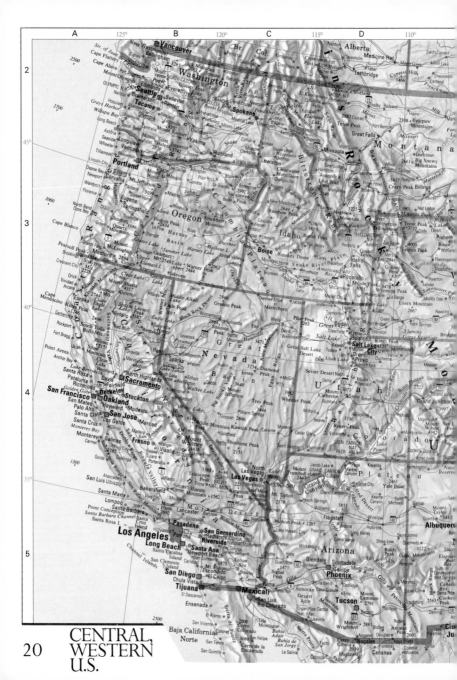

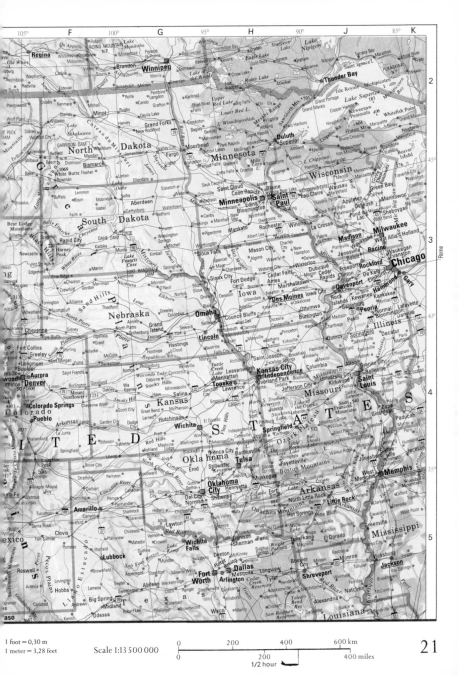

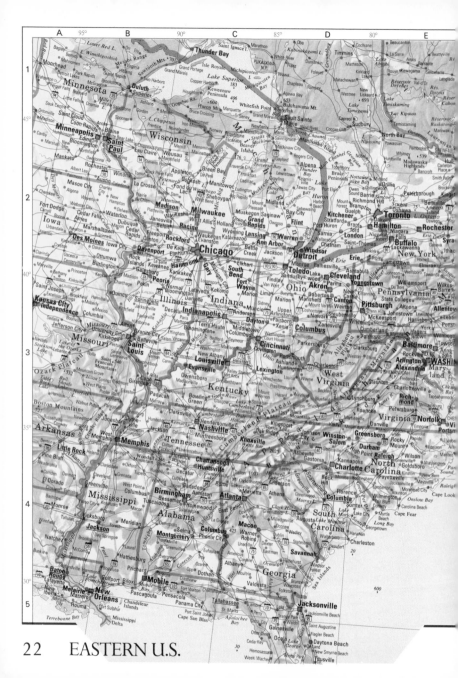

22 EASTERN U.S.

F   70°   G   65°   H   60°   J   55°

Dolbeau • St. Félicien
Jonquière • Forestville
Péninsule de Gaspé
Gulf of Saint Lawrence
500 Cape Ray
Cabot Strait
Saint Pierre et Miquelon (France)
Les Escoumins
Mont Joli • Perce
New Richmond Chandler
Île de la Madeleine
Cape North 562
Grand Bank
Saint Pierre
St. Siméon
Jonquière Saguenay
Chaleur Bay
Cape Breton HIGHLANDS N.P.
Cape Breton Island
Chicoutimi
Tadoussac
Campbellton Bathurst
Shippagan
Glace Bay 600
Burin Peninsula
Saint Jérôme
Dalhousie
Big Bald Mountain 820
Miramichi Bay
Bras d'Or Lake
Port aux Basques
+613
La Malbaie
Rivière-du-Loup
Edmundston
Miramichi
Prince Edward Island
Sydney
Lac Kempt
La Tuque
Kedgwick
St. Léonard
Newcastle
Charlottetown
Souris
Louisbourg
La Madeleine
Charles-bourg Québec
Perth-Andover
Chatham
Northumberland Strait
Cape Beat
Antigonish
New Glasgow
Strait of Canso
LA MAURICIE N.P.
Lévis
Woodstock
New Brunswick
Moncton
Amherst
Pictou
Canso
Shawinigan
689 Peakel Mountain
Grand Lake
Springhill
Truro
Trois Rivières
Chrsumcook
St. Georges Fredericton
Sussex
N o v a S c o t i a
968
Drummondville
Sherman Station
Sheet Harbour 20
Montreal
Moosehead L.
Saint John
Windsor
Dartmouth
Halifax
Sorel
Granby Saint-Jean
1679
Bar of Fundy
Bridgewater
Sherbrooke
Howland
Bangor
Eastport
Digby
Sable Island
2600
Vermont
Lake
Grand Manan
Yarmouth
Liverpool
Shelburne
Skowhegan
M a i n e
Bar Harbor
ACADIA N.P.
Meteghan
Champlain
1917 Mount Washington
Waterville
Augusta
New Hampshire
Farmington
Lewiston
Auburn
250
Cape Sable
70
New York
Concord
Portland
Portsmouth
Biddeford
Rochester
Gulf of Maine
Schenectady
Haverhill
Gloucester
Pittsfield
North Adams Lowell
Massachusetts Boston
Holyoke
Worcester
Springfield Cambridge
Rhode Island
Hartford
Provincetown
Connecticut
Fall River
Cape Cod Bay
New Bedford
Cape Cod
Waterbury
New London
Hyannis
15
New Haven Providence
Nantucket Sound
Bridgeport
Stamford Yonkers
Nantucket Island
Newark
New York
2600

Atlantic City
U N I T E D
S T A T E S
BRIDGE-TUNNEL

A T L A N T I C

4200

O C E A N

5500

Bermuda Islands (U.K.)
Hamilton

45°
Rome
40°
35°
30°
Cairo

1   2   3   4

1 foot = 0.30 m
1 meter = 3.28 feet
Scale 1:13 500 000

0   200   400   600 km
0   200   400 miles
1/2 hour

23

SOUTHERN U.S., HAWAII, MEXICO

Scale 1:10 000 000

| 0 | 100 | 200 | 300 | 400 km |

| 0 | 100 | 200 miles |

24   SOUTHERN U.S., HAWAII, MEXICO

1 foot = 0,30 m
1 meter = 3,28 feet

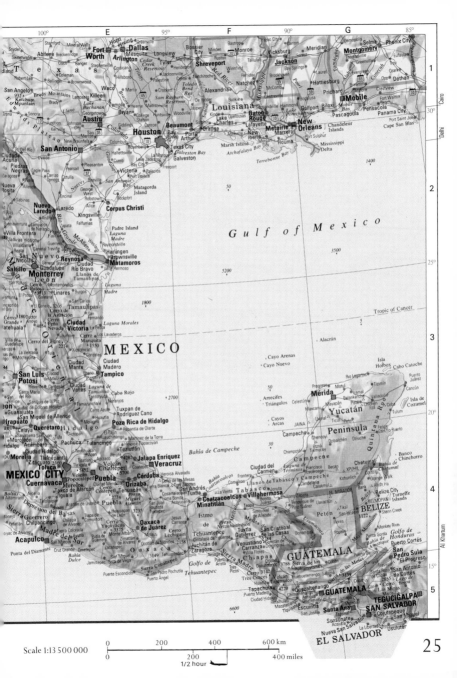

Scale 1:13 500 000

25

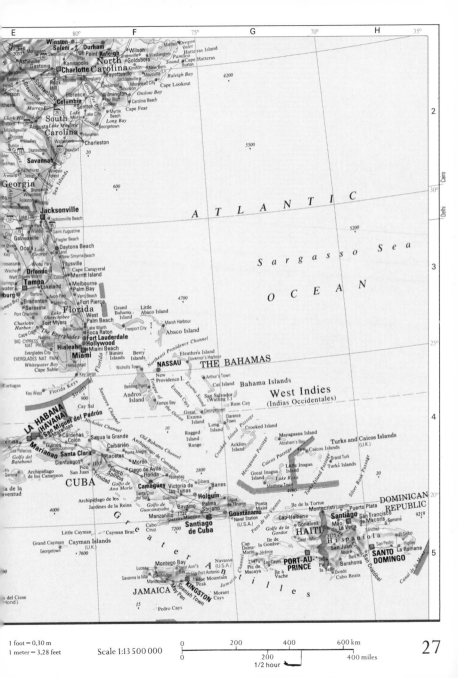

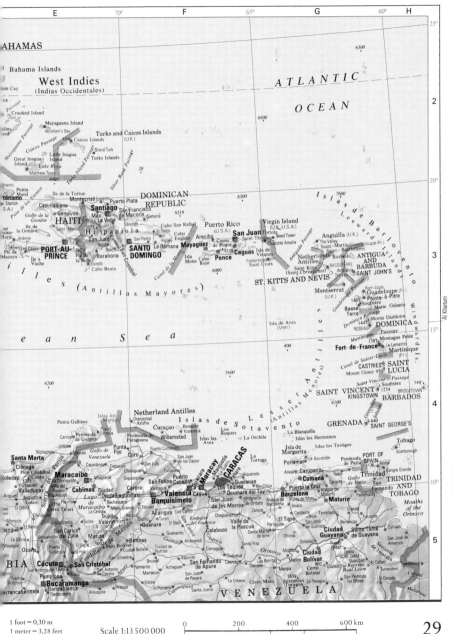

BAHAMAS

Bahama Islands
West Indies
(Indias Occidentales)

A T L A N T I C

O C E A N

6300

Crooked Island

6900

Mayaguana Island
Abraham's Bay
Turks and Caicos Islands
Caicos Islands (U.K.)
Grand Turk
Great Inagua Little Inagua Island
Island Island Turks Islands
Matthew Town Lake Rosa

Silver Bank Passage

20°

4400

Punta
Maisi
Cap-Haitien Montecristi Juperón
Golfe de la Santiago San Francisco
Gonâve Gonaïves Mao de Macoris Samaná
Ile de la HAITI La Vega
Gonâve San Marc Puerto Plata
PORT-AU- Hispaniola San Pedro
PRINCE Barahona Santo San Juan
Les Cayes La Romana

DOMINICAN
REPUBLIC

8300

9219

Islas de Barlovento

7600

Leeward Islands

Puerto Rico
(U.S.A.) **San Juan**
Arecibo
Cabo San Rafael
Cabo Engaño **Mayagüez**
Isla de
Mona **Ponce** **Caguas**
Cabo
Rojo Isla de
Vieques
6000 Frederiksted
Saint Croix

Virgin Island
(U.K.-U.S.A.)
Saint Thomas
Charlotte Amalie

Anguilla (U.K.)
The Valley
Saint-Martin (Guadeloupe-Fr.)
Netherlands Road Town
Antilles Barbuda **ANTIGUA**
Saint Kitts **AND**
(Saint Christopher) Antigua **BARBUDA**
BASSETERRE **SAINT JOHN'S**
ST. KITTS AND NEVIS

Al Khartum

i l l e s (Antillas Mayores)

Montserrat Port-Louis
(U.K.) **Guadeloupe** (Fr.)
1467 Pointe-à-Pitre
Basse- Marie Galante
Terre
1447 Morne Diablotin
ROSEAU **DOMINICA**

15°

Isla de Aves (Ven.)

e a n S e a

5600

Lesser Antilles (Antillas Menores)

Windward Islands

400

1397 Montagne Pelée
Martinique
Fort-de-France Le Lamentin
(Fr.)
Canal de Sainte-Lucie
CASTRIES **SAINT**
Mount Gimie 950 **LUCIA**
Soufrière

4200

Saint Vincent 1234 340°
SAINT VINCENT Soufrière **BARBADOS**
KINGSTOWN BRIDGETOWN

4100

GRENADA 840 **SAINT GEORGE'S**

4

Netherland Antilles
Punta Gallinas Islas los Oranjestad
Monjes Aruba Islas de Sotavento
Peninsula Curaçao Bonaire
de Guajira Kralendijk Islas las
Santa Marta Golfo de Willemstad Aves La Orchila
Ciénaga Venezuela Coro Islas los
Pico Cristóbal Puerto Cumarebo Roques
Colón Punta San Juan La Blanquilla
MARACAIBO Fijo de los Cayos La Islas los Hermanos
Cabimas Puerto Tortuga
Ciudad San Felipe Cabello **CARACAS** Isla de
Ojeda Ojeda **Maracay** Margarita
Lago La Asunción
de **Valencia** Los Teques Porlamar Islas los Testigos
Maracaibo **Barquisimeto** **Cagua** Guarenas Arava Carúpano
Los Morros Ocumare del Tuy **Cumaná**
Acarigua Río Chico **Barcelona** Puerto La Cruz
Valencia
El Tigre

Tobago
Scarborough

PORT OF
Peninsula **SPAIN** Arima
de Paria Sangre Grande
Trinidad
Golfo de Paria
Guiria **TRINIDAD**
San **AND**
Fernando **TOBAGO**

Mouths
of the
Orinoco

5

Ocaña Valledupar
Codazzi
Cúcuta Pamplona **San Cristóbal**
Bucaramanga
Floridablanca

Barinas

Orinoco
Ciudad
Ciudad Guayana
Bolívar
Cerro 807
Ciudad
Bolívar
Ciudad
Guayana Santo Tomé
de Guayana

San José de
Amacuro

V E N E Z U E L A

1 foot = 0.30 m
1 meter = 3.28 feet
Scale 1:13 500 000

0 200 400 600 km
0 200 400 miles
1/2 hour

29

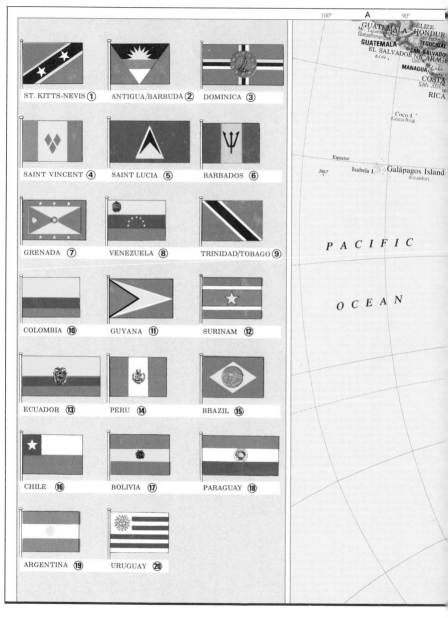

ST. KITTS-NEVIS ①　ANTIGUA/BARBUDA ②　DOMINICA ③

SAINT VINCENT ④　SAINT LUCIA ⑤　BARBADOS ⑥

GRENADA ⑦　VENEZUELA ⑧　TRINIDAD/TOBAGO ⑨

COLOMBIA ⑩　GUYANA ⑪　SURINAM ⑫

ECUADOR ⑬　PERU ⑭　BRAZIL ⑮

CHILE ⑯　BOLIVIA ⑰　PARAGUAY ⑱

ARGENTINA ⑲　URUGUAY ⑳

GUATEMALA　BELIZE
Mt. Tajumulco　San Pedro　HONDUR
Quezaltenango　TEGUCIGAL
GUATEMALA　SAN SALVADOR
EL SALVADOR　NICARAG
6,149　León
MANAGUA　Lake
COSTA
SAN JOSÉ
RICA

Coco I.
(Costa Rica)

Equator
3667　Isabela I.　Galápagos Island
(Ecuador)

P A C I F I C

O C E A N

1 foot = 0,30 m
1 meter = 3,28 feet

Scale 1:50 000 000

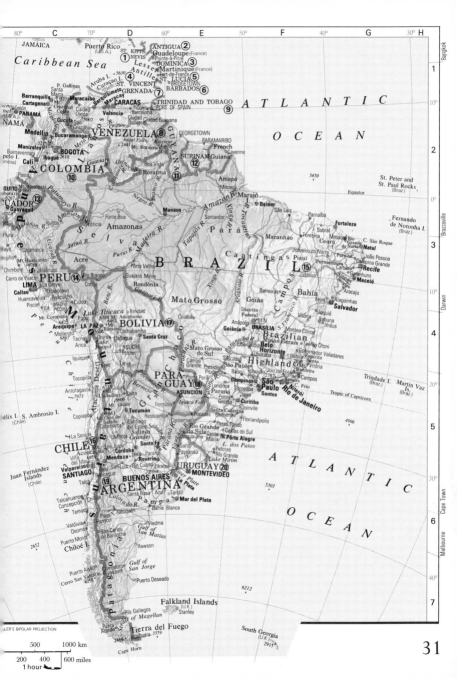

Bangkok

SAINT LUCIA
CASTRIES
SAINT
VINCENT BRIDGETOWN
KINGSTOWN BARBADOS
GRENADA
SAINT GEORGE'S
Tobago
Porlamar PORT OF TRINIDAD
SPAIN AND TOBAGO
Cumaná San Fernando
erto la Cruz Trinidad
rcelona
naco Pedernales
antaura Maturín
El Tigre Mouths of
Tucupita the Orinoco
Ciudad Barrancas
Guayana Santo Tomé
dad de Guayana
lívar Guasipati
Upata
Paragua Morawhanna
Represa Maburuma
Raúl Leoni Arakaka
Tumereng Towakaima Charity
El Dorado Kamaria Falls Suddie GEORGETOWN
Kamaria Falls Fort Wellington
Churún Merú Bartica New Amsterdam PARAMARIBO
(Angel Falls) Issano Rosignol Nieuw Nickerie Nieuw Amsterdam
La Gran Mahdia Linden Torsens Paranam Albina Iracoubo
Sabana Matthews Ridge Kwakoegron Brokopondo Sinnamary
Sierra Pacaraima Avanavero Ile du Diable (Devil's Island)
GUYANA Kourou
G Depósito SURINAM Saint-Elie Cayenne
u Uraricoera Julianatop Guisanbourg
a 1280 French Cabo Orange
Roraima Lethem Guiana Oiapoque
n Dadanawa Vila Velha
a Isherton Cunani
Pico Rondón Calçoene
1189 Amapá Ilha de
Caracaraí H Maracá
Vista Alegre i Amapá Cabo Norte
Catrimani g Jaripo
h Serra do Navio
Vila Conceição l Ferreira Gomes
Rio Branco a Pôrto Grande Mouths of
Barcelos Boiaçu n Macapá the Amazon
Carvoeiro d Canal do Norte
Aiuã s Arere Pôrto Santana
Chaves Soure Curuçá Salinópolis
Oriximiná Almeirim Carumu Bragança
Faro Monte Ilha Capanema
MANAUS Urucará Alegre Óbidos de Marajó Cametá Casanal
Manacapuru Itapiranga Curuçá Marajó Breves Belém Abaetetuba
Anori Maués Santarém Pôrto de Moz Irituia
Coari Parintins Altamira Tucuruí Baião Camiranga
Borba Itaituba Belo Monte Cajuapara Pinheiro
Abufari Pimental Remansão Jatobá Açailândia Alto
Manicoré Trans-Amazon Iriri Turi
Santa Maria highway Marabá Imperatriz Barra do
dos Marmelos Jacareacanga Araguatins Corda
Humaitá Entre Rios Pau d'Arco São Félix do Xingu Montes Grajaú
Pôrto Velho Praínha Conceição Altos
Jamari Sumaúma Barração do Araguaia Carolina
Ariquemes Nova Vida do Barreto Cachimbo Araguacema Pedro Afonso Balsas
Jaciparaná Aripuanã Piara Açu Lizarda
Caritianas Canéla Natividade
Guaporé Barão de Gurupi Peixe Gebués
Itenes Melgaço Pimenta Bueno Nhambiquara Juruena Lucas Barra do Pôrto Nacional Arraias
Rondônia Pôrto Artur Garças Taguatinga
Baures Vilhena Araguaia Alvorado Goiás Bahia
São Félix São Miguel do Araguaia
Puerto Villazón Parangatu
Mato Grosso Correntina

RONDÔNIA
BRAZIL
Pará
Maranhão
São Luís
Rosário
Bacabal
Caxias
Coroatá
Codó
Floriano
Presidente Dutra
Pastos Bons
Loreto
Bertolínia
Uruçuí
Canto do Burtí
Bom Jesus
Redenção da Gurguéia
Curralinho
Parnaguá
Pilão Arcado
Corrente
Santa Filomena
Caririaçu
Angical
Barreiras
Ibotirama
Xique-Xique
Barra
Bom Jesus da Lapa

Roraima
Boa Vista

ELA
Lesser Antilles
VENEZUELA

A T L A N T I C

O C E A N

Guiana Highlands

Serra Acaraí
Northern Perimeter Highway

Caatingas

Serra dos Carajás
Serra dos Gradaús
Serra do Estrondo
Tocantins
Araguaia
Serra do Roncador
Serra Formosa
Serra do Cachimbo
Serra do Tombador
Teles Pires
Xingu
Tapajós
Madeira
Rio Negro
Purus
Juruena
Arinos

Serra dos Parecís

São Francisco

Brazzaville

1 foot = 0,30 m
1 meter = 3,28 feet

Scale 1:20 000 000

0   200   400   600   800   1000 km
0   200   400   600 miles
1 hour

33

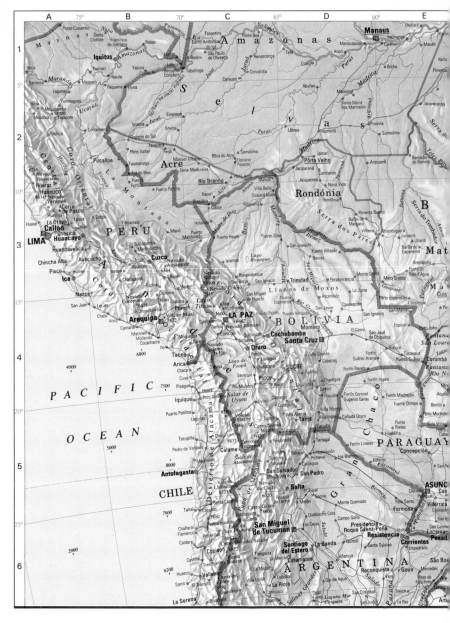

Brazzaville

Darwin

Antananarivo

Santarém · Altamira · Belo Monte
Vitória

Amazon Highway

Belo Horizonte

Iriri · Xingu

Serra dos Carajás

Carajás · Marabá

á r a

Conceição do Araguaia

Serra do Estrondo

Serra dos Gradaús

Cachimbo

Pará Açu

Serra do Roncador

Rio das Mortes

A Z I L

Goiás

Serra do Norte

Cuiabá

osso

Ministro João Alberto

Pindaíba

alto

Rondonópolis

Aragarças

Baús

Rio Verde de Mato Grosso

Camapuã

Campo Grande

Três Lagoas

Andradina

Dourados

Presidente Prudente

Paranaíba

Maringá

Paraná

Londrina

Cascavel

Ponta Grossa

Curitiba

Santa Catarina

Blumenau

Florianópolis

Lages

Grande do Sul

Caxias do Sul

Canoas

Pôrto Alegre

São Luís

Fortaleza

Parnaíba

Sobral

Ceará

Teresina

Piauí

Maranhão

Rio Grande do Norte

Natal

Campina Grande

Paraíba

João Pessoa

Olinda

Recife

Pernambuco

Caruaru

Alagoas

Maceió

Aracaju

Sergipe

Feira de Santana

Salvador

Bahía

Bahia

Campos

Ilhéus

Vitória da Conquista

Planalto do Brasil

BRASÍLIA · Distrito Federal

Goiânia

Planalto Central

Minas Gerais

Belo Horizonte

Uberlândia

Uberaba

Araxá

Governador Valadares

Espírito Santo

Vitória

Vila Velha

São Paulo

Ribeirão Prêto

Juiz de Fora

Campos

Nova Iguaçu

Petrópolis

Rio de Janeiro

Niterói

São Paulo

Campinas

Santo André

São Vicente

Santos

ATLANTIC OCEAN

ATLANTIC

Rio de Janeiro

oot = 0,30 m
meter = 3,28 feet

Scale 1:20 000 000

0 · 200 · 400 · 600 · 800 · 1000 km

0 · 200 · 400 · 600 miles

1 hour

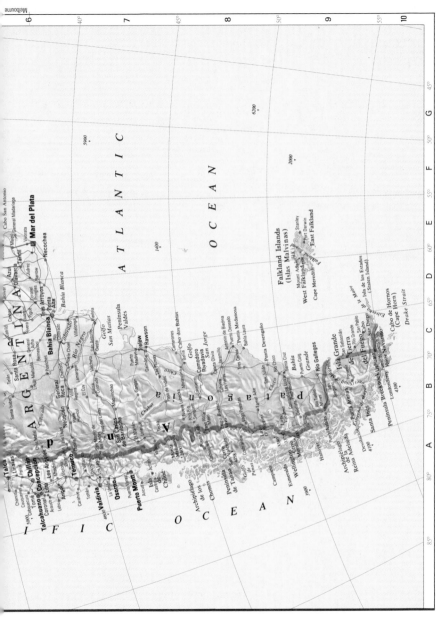

ARGENTINA

Mar del Plata

A T L A N T I C   O C E A N

Cabo San Antonio

Bahía Blanca

Neuquén

San Carlos
de Bariloche

P a t a g o n i a

Valdivia

Osorno

Puerto Montt

Temuco

Concepción

Talcahuano

Chillán

Talca

Península
Valdés

Trelew

Rawson

Golfo
San Matías

Golfo
San Jorge

Comodoro
Rivadavia

Río Gallegos

Isla
Grande

Tierra del Fuego

Cabo de Hornos
(Cape Horn)

Drake Strait

Estrecho de Magallanes

Punta Arenas

Falkland Islands
(Islas Malvinas)

West Falkland
East Falkland

Mount Adam
Port Stanley
Port Darwin
Cape Meredith

P A C I F I C   O C E A N

Archipiélago
de los
Chonos

Península
de Taitao

Golfo de
Penas

Archipiélago
de la
Reina Adelaida

Santa Inés

Península Brecknock

6200

5900

2000

1400

4300

4100

3900

4600

5000

foot = 0.30 m
meter = 3.28 feet

Scale 1:20 000 000

0   200   400   600   800   1000 km

0   200   400   600 miles

1 hour

37

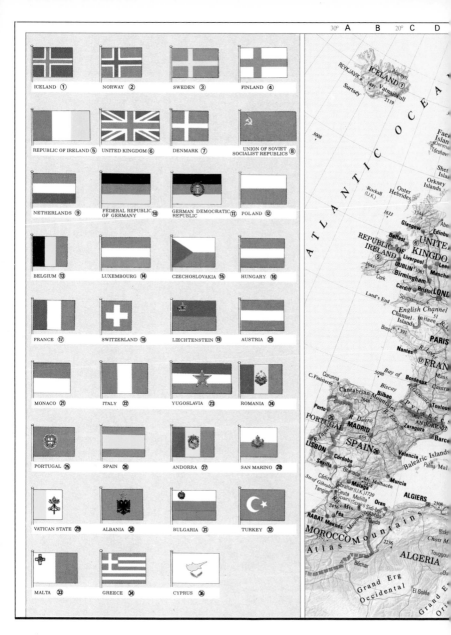

ICELAND ①
NORWAY ②
SWEDEN ③
FINLAND ④

REPUBLIC OF IRELAND ⑤
UNITED KINGDOM ⑥
DENMARK ⑦
UNION OF SOVIET SOCIALIST REPUBLICS ⑧

NETHERLANDS ⑨
FEDERAL REPUBLIC OF GERMANY ⑩
GERMAN DEMOCRATIC REPUBLIC ⑪
POLAND ⑫

BELGIUM ⑬
LUXEMBOURG ⑭
CZECHOSLOVAKIA ⑮
HUNGARY ⑯

FRANCE ⑰
SWITZERLAND ⑱
LIECHTENSTEIN ⑲
AUSTRIA ⑳

MONACO ㉑
ITALY ㉒
YUGOSLAVIA ㉓
ROMANIA ㉔

PORTUGAL ㉕
SPAIN ㉖
ANDORRA ㉗
SAN MARINO ㉘

VATICAN STATE ㉙
ALBANIA ㉚
BULGARIA ㉛
TURKEY ㉜

MALTA ㉝
GREECE ㉞
CYPRUS ㉟

foot = 0,30 m
meter = 3,28 feet

Scale 1:10 000 000

0   100   200   300   400   500 km

0   100   200   300 miles

1/2 hour

41

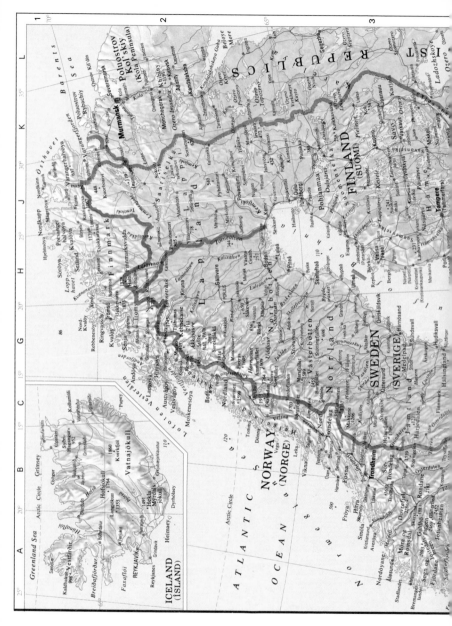

foot = 0,30 m
meter = 3,28 feet

Scale 1:10 000 000

| 0 | 100 | 200 | 300 | 400 | 500 km |

| 0 | 100 | 200 | 300 miles |

1/2 hour

43

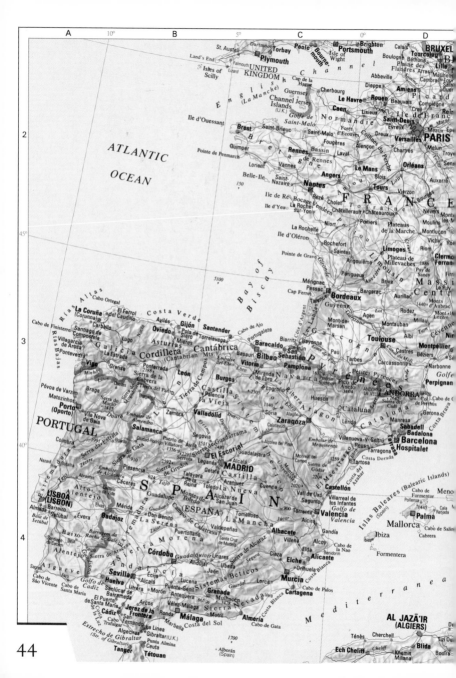

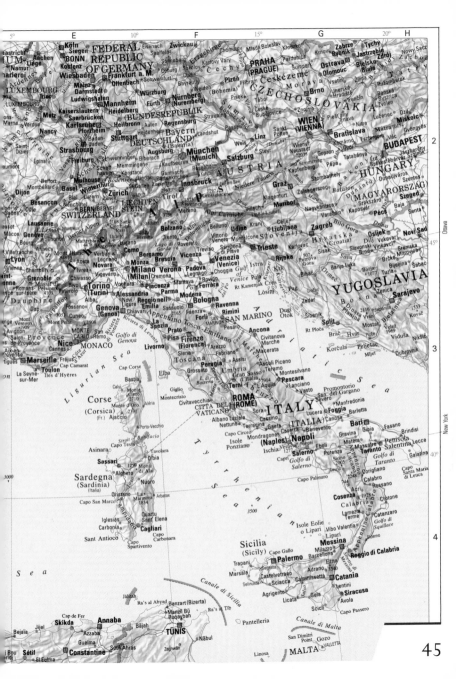

46   THE BALKANS

1 foot = 0,30 m
1 meter = 3,28 feet

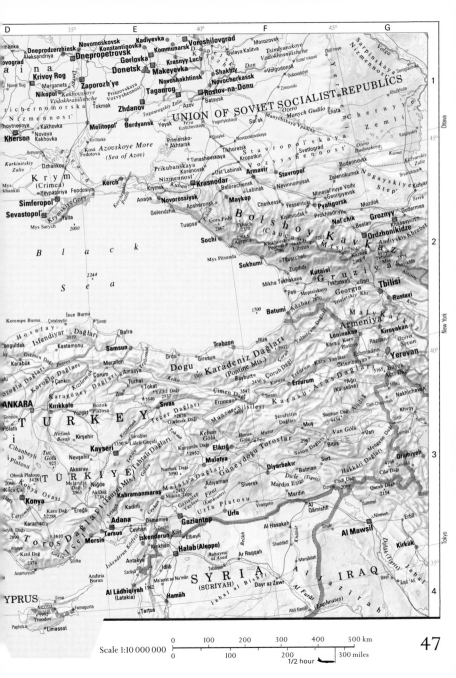

D   35°   E   40°   F   45°   G

UNION OF SOVIET SOCIALIST REPUBLICS

menka
Dneprodzerzhinsk • Novomoskovsk • Kadiyevka • Voroshilovgrad • Morozovsk
ovgrad
Dnepropetrovsk • Gorlovka • Kommunarsk • Krasnyy Luch • Belaya Kalitva • Tsimlyanskoye Vodokhranilishche
a i n a • Krivoy Rog • Donetsk • Makeyevka • Shakhty • Volgodonsk • Kotel'nikovo • Obil'noye • Sarpinskaya Nizmennost'
Novyy Bug • Nikopol • Zaporozh'ye • Novoshakhtinsk • Novocherkassk • Volga
Marganets • Konstantinovka • Taganrog • Rostov-na-Donu • Don • Serafimovich
Kakhovskoye • Priazovskaya • Bataysk • Azov • Zimovniki
Nizmennost' • Vodokhranilishche • Zhdanov • Ozero • C h e r n y y e
Melitopol' • Berdyansk • Yeysk • Manych-Gudilo • Elista • Z e m l i
Kherson • Novaya • Kosa • *Azovskoye More* • Primorsko- • Yegorlykskaya • Sal'sk • Manych • Manychskaya Vpadina • Kaspiyskiy
Kakhovka • Fedotova • (Sea of Azov) • Akhtarsk • Sosyka • Novopokrovskaya • Kuma • Kaspiyskoye
Karkinitskiy • Dzhankoy • Timashevskaya • Tikhoretsk • Stavropol'skaya • Svetlograd • Zaliv
Zaliv • Prikubanskaya • Ust'-Labinsk • V o z v y s h e n n o s t' • Budennovsk
Krym • Kerch' • Nizmennost' • Krasnodar • Belorechensk • Labinsk • Nevinnomyssk • Mineral'nyye Vody • Zelenokumsk • Nogayskiye • Kizlyar • Terek
(Crimea) • Anapa • Novorossiysk • Kuban' • Stavropol' • Georgiyevsk • Step'
Simferopol' • Yevpatoriya • Feodosiya • Apsheronsk • Maykop • Cherkessk • Yessentuki • Pyatigorsk • Mozdok
Sevastopol' • Yalta • Gelendzhik • Tuapse • Gora Fisht • Kislovodsk • Prokhladnyy • Nal'chik • Groznyy • Gudermes
Mys Sarych • Krymskiye Gory • 2000 • 2867 • **B o l s h o y** • Elbrus • Beslan • Ordzhonikidze • Andiyskiy Khrebet
Sochi • Agepsta • 3261 • **K a v k a z** • 5047 • Mta • Shatilde
Mys Pitsunda • Khukhorskiy Pereval • Kazbek • Tbulosi • Alazani
Sukhumi • Tkvarcheli • Zugdidi • Kutaisi • **Gruziya**
Mikha Tskhakaya • Tskhinvali • Gori
2244 • **B l a c k** • Poti • Mtsire Khr. • **Georgia** • Tbilisi
Batumi • Adzhar • Trialetskiy Khr. • Kura • Rustavi
S e a • 1700 • Mepistskaro • 2850 • **M a l y y**
İnce Burnu • Kerempe Burnu • Çatalzeytin • Sinop • Bafra • Trabzon • Rize • Yalnizcam Daglari • Leninakan • Kars • **Armeniya** • Kirovakan
Hosalay • Isfendiyar Daglari • Samsun • Ordu • Giresun • Çoruh • Kars Platosu • Echmiadzin • Ozero Sevan
onguldak • Dikmen Dagi • Devrez • Kastamonu • **Dogu Karadeniz Daglari** • 3937 • Oktemberyan • Yerevan
Karabük • Köroglu Dagi • Amasya • (Pontine Mts.) • 3305 • Çoruh Dagi • Kars Yaylasi • 5165 • Büyük • Agri Dagi
oroğlu Daglari • Merzifon • Zile • Kelkit • Çimen Dagi • 2430 • Erzurum • Terjan • (Karaköse)
ANKARA • Kırıkkale • Çorum • Turhal • Tokat • Yıldız Dağı • 3547 • Karasu • Karasu-Aras Daglari • Nakhichevan'
Gordion • Yozgat • Bozok • 1646 • **Sivas** • Erzincan • Karasu • 5008
Polatlı • Platosu • Kızılırmak • Teçer Daglari • Munzur Silsilesi • 3489 • Serafettin • Süphan Dagi
T U R K E Y • Kırşehir • Sarıoğlan • Tohma • Dağları • Muş • 4434 • Van Gölü • Van • Khvoy
Cihanbeyli • Tuz • Kayseri • 1350 • Laleli Geçidi • Keban • Hazar • Murat • Sason Daglari • 2967 • Bitlis • Qotur
ipatozu • a) • Gölü • Nevşehir • Tahtalı Daglari • Gölü • Gölü • Elâzığ • 2952 • Kurşunlu Dağı • Siirt • Hakkâri Daglari • Orumiyeh
Obruk Platosu • Melendiz • Niğde • **Türkiye** • Nurhak Dağı • Malatya • Diyarbakır • Batman • 4168 • Selvala
200k • Koca Çay • Dağı • 2963 • 3090 • Malatya Daglari • Adıyaman • Dicle • (Tigris) • Mardin Esigi • Çılo Dağı • Qarah Dagh • 2154
Konya • 3734 • 2453 • Firat • Siverek • Mardin • Sinjar • Nineveh • Erbil
Kara Dağ • Güneydoğu Toroslar • Milcan Tepe • Gaziantep • (Euphrates) • Al Qamishli • Dümmel
Karaman • 2288 • Ereğli • Kadirli • Göksu • Urfa Platosu • Urfa • Viranşehir • Al Hasakah • Dijlah (Tigris) • Jabal • Kirkük
cyık Dağı • Çarşamba • Osmaniye • 2 Çanch • **Adana** • Ceyhan • Kilis • Halab (Aleppo) • Al Mawşil
2800 • Silifke • Kızıl Dağ • **Mersin** • Tarsus • İskenderun • Kırıkhan • Belikh • Shaddadi • Marqādah
2374 • Göksu • İskenderun Körfezi • Antakya • İdlib • **S Y R I A** • Ar Raqqah • Al Jazirah • **I R A Q**
Andiria • (SÜRIYAH) • Tabaqah • Buhayrat al Asad
Burun • Al Lādhiqiyah • 1562 • Jabal al Bishri • Abū Kamāl • (Euphrates)
CYPRUS • Gima • (Latakia) • Hamāh • Ma'arrat an Nu'man • Dayr az Zawr
NICOSIA • Troodos • 1951 • Tartus • Sariya
Paphos • Limassol • Famagusta

Scale 1:10 000 000

0   100   200   300   400   500 km
0   100   200   300 miles
1/2 hour

47

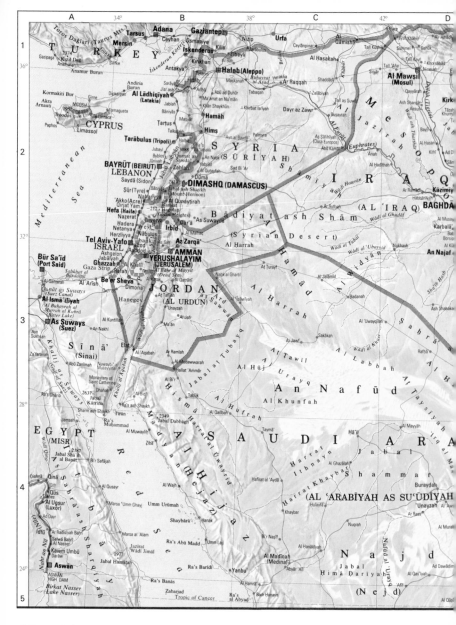

48 THE MIDDLE EAST

1 foot = 0,30 m
1 meter = 3,28 feet

Scale 1:10 000 000

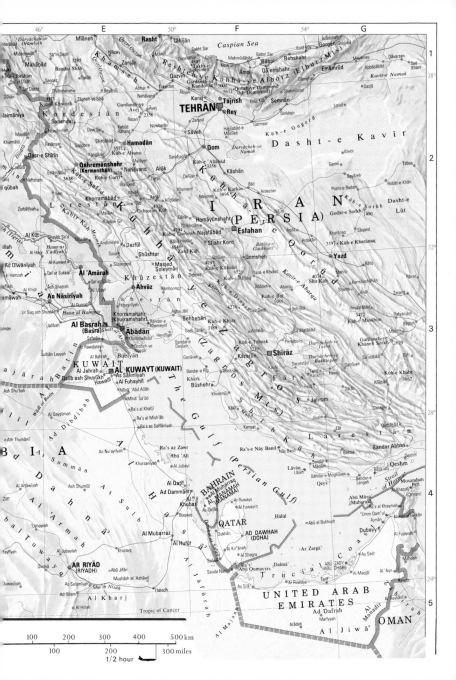

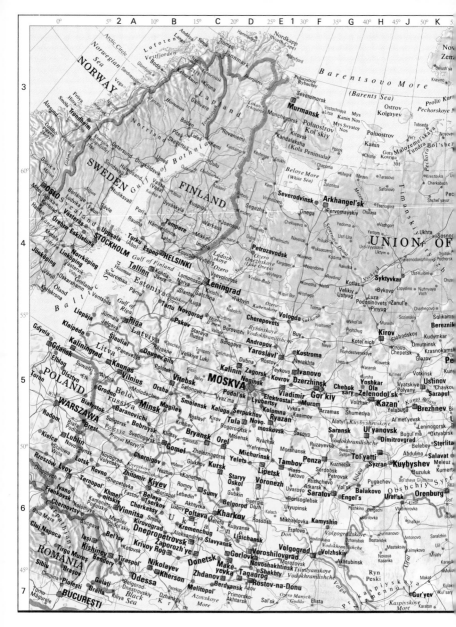

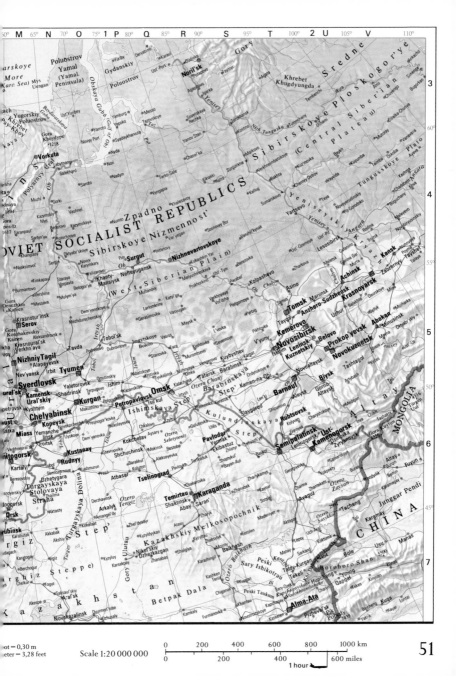

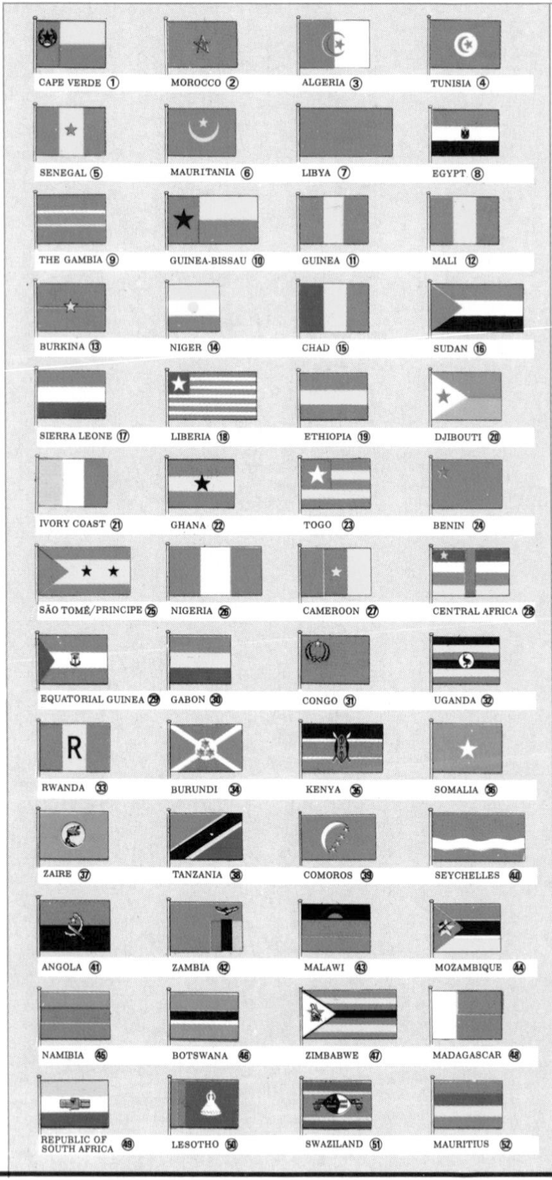
CAPE VERDE ①
MOROCCO ②
ALGERIA ③
TUNISIA ④
SENEGAL ⑤
MAURITANIA ⑥
LIBYA ⑦
EGYPT ⑧
THE GAMBIA ⑨
GUINEA-BISSAU ⑩
GUINEA ⑪
MALI ⑫
BURKINA ⑬
NIGER ⑭
CHAD ⑮
SUDAN ⑯
SIERRA LEONE ⑰
LIBERIA ⑱
ETHIOPIA ⑲
DJIBOUTI ⑳
IVORY COAST ㉑
GHANA ㉒
TOGO ㉓
BENIN ㉔
SÃO TOMÉ/PRINCIPE ㉕
NIGERIA ㉖
CAMEROON ㉗
CENTRAL AFRICA ㉘
EQUATORIAL GUINEA ㉙
GABON ㉚
CONGO ㉛
UGANDA ㉜
R
RWANDA ㉝
BURUNDI ㉞
KENYA ㉟
SOMALIA ㊱
ZAIRE ㊲
TANZANIA ㊳
COMOROS ㊴
SEYCHELLES ㊵
ANGOLA ㊶
ZAMBIA ㊷
MALAWI ㊸
MOZAMBIQUE ㊹
NAMIBIA ㊺
BOTSWANA ㊻
ZIMBABWE ㊼
MADAGASCAR ㊽
REPUBLIC OF SOUTH AFRICA ㊾
LESOTHO ㊿
SWAZILAND (51)
MAURITIUS (52)

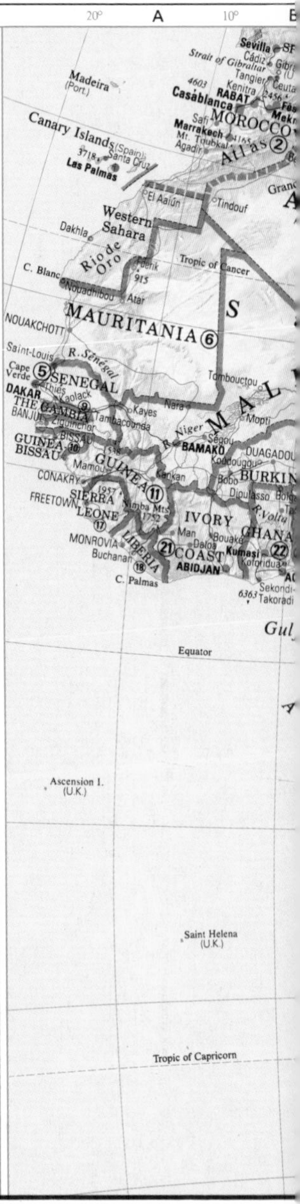
20°
A
10°
Madeira (Port.)
Canary Islands (Spain)
Santa Cruz
Las Palmas
Strait of Gibraltar
Sevilla
Cádiz
Tangier
Ceuta
Casablanca
RABAT
Marrakech
Mt. Toubkal
Agadir
Safi
MOROCCO ②
Atlas
El Aaiún
Tindouf
Western Sahara
Dakhla
Rio de Oro
C. Blanc
Nouadhibou
Atar
Tropic of Cancer
MAURITANIA ⑥
NOUAKCHOTT
Saint-Louis
R. Sénégal
Cape Verde
⑤ SENEGAL
DAKAR
Thies
Kaolack
THE GAMBIA ⑨
BANJUL
Ziguinchor
Tambacounda
Kayes
Nara
Tombouctou
MALI
Mopti
R. Niger
BAMAKO
Ségou
GUINEA-BISSAU ⑩
BISSAU
Mamou
GUINEA ⑪
Kankan
CONAKRY
SIERRA LEONE ⑰
FREETOWN
Bobo Dioulasso
OUAGADOU
Koudougou
BURKIN
MONROVIA
Buchanan
LIBERIA ⑱
C. Palmas
IVORY COAST ㉑
Man
Daloa
Bouaké
ABIDJAN
GHANA ㉒
Kumasi
Koforidua
Sekondi-Takoradi
Gul
Equator
Ascension I. (U.K.)
Saint Helena (U.K.)
Tropic of Capricorn

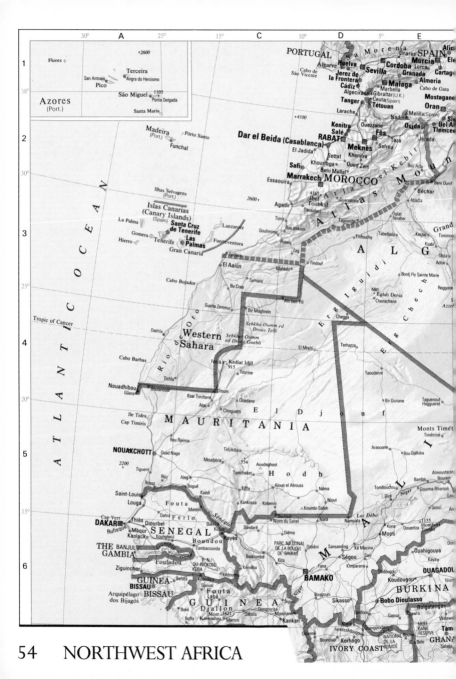

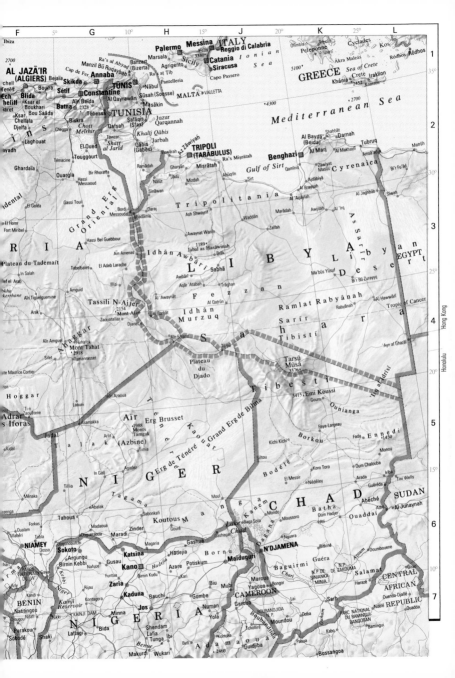

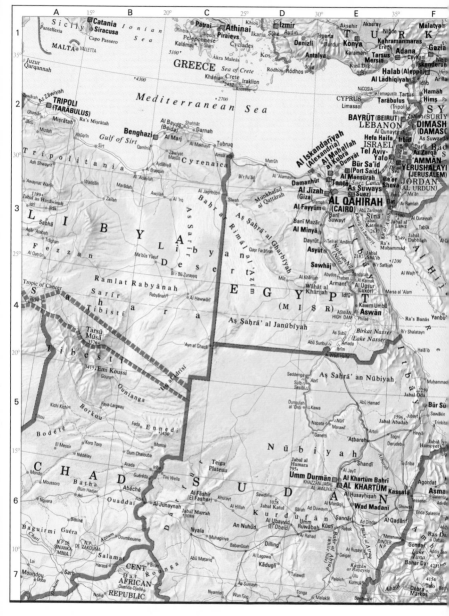

THE NILE VALLEY AND ARABIA

foot = 0,30 m
meter = 3,28 feet

Scale 1:20 000 000

0   200   400   600   800   1000 km

0   200   400   600 miles

1 hour

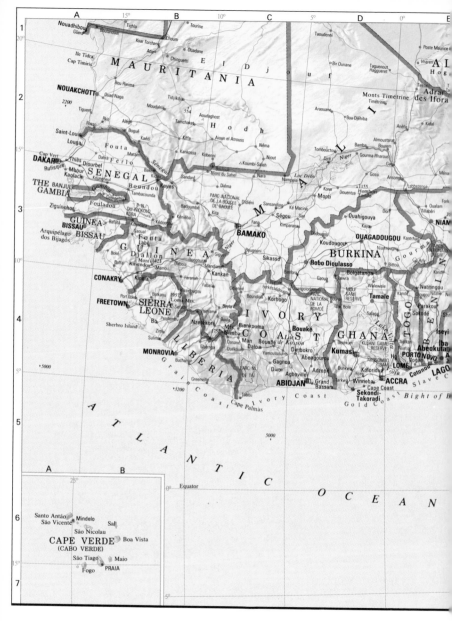

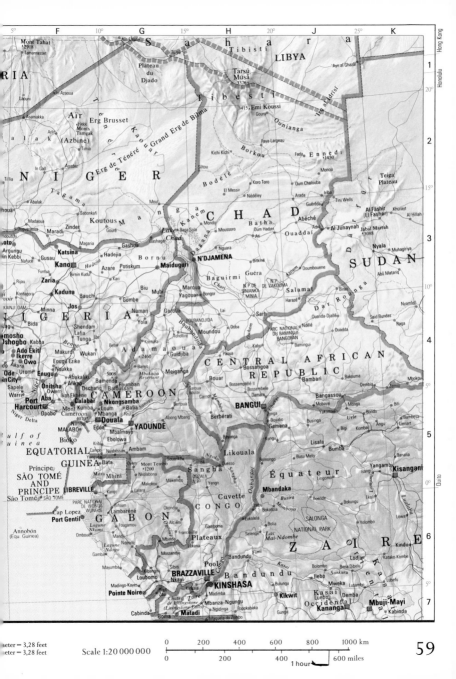

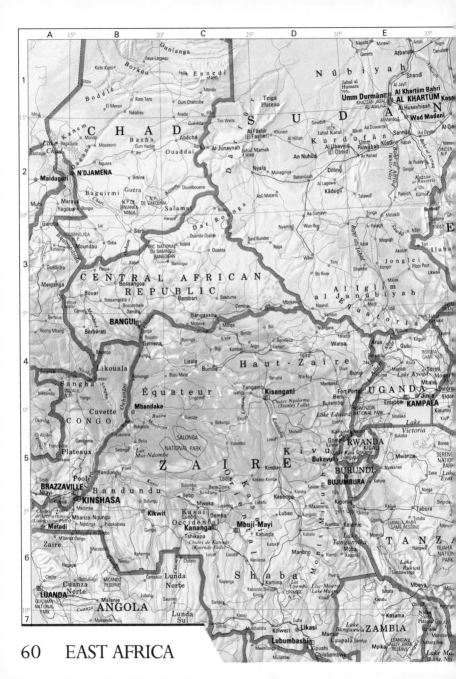

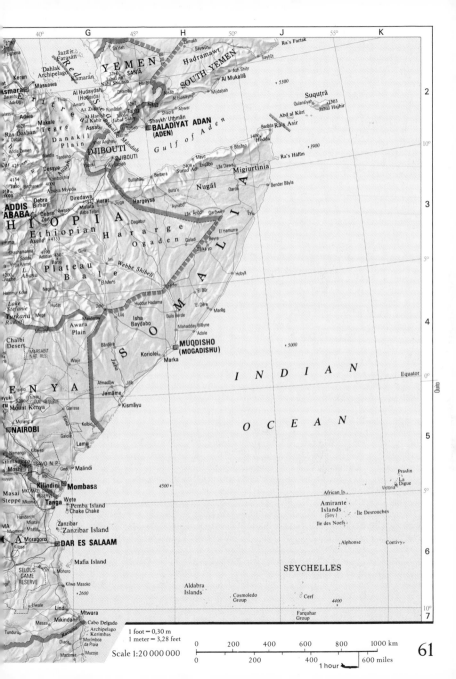

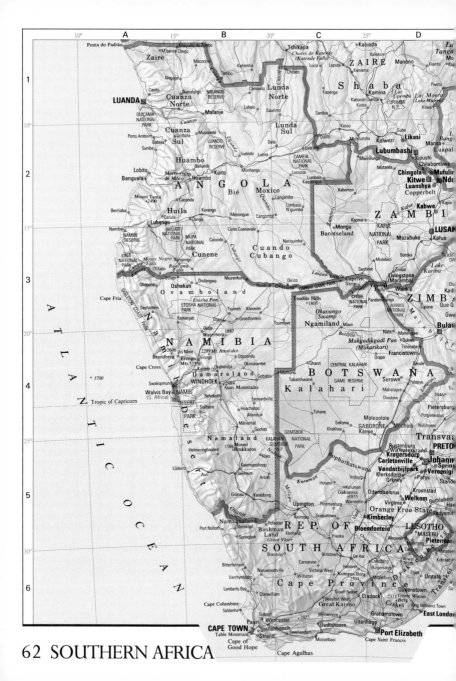

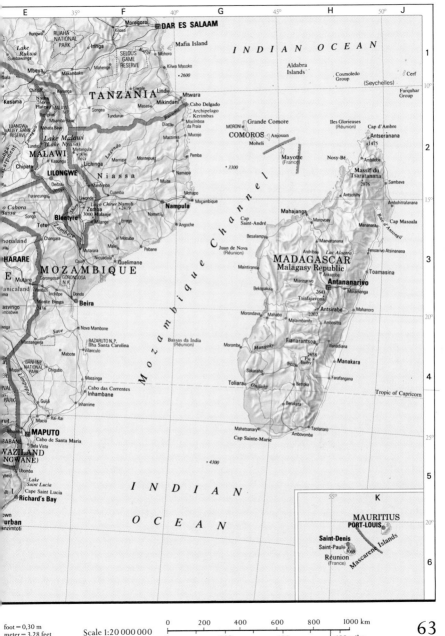

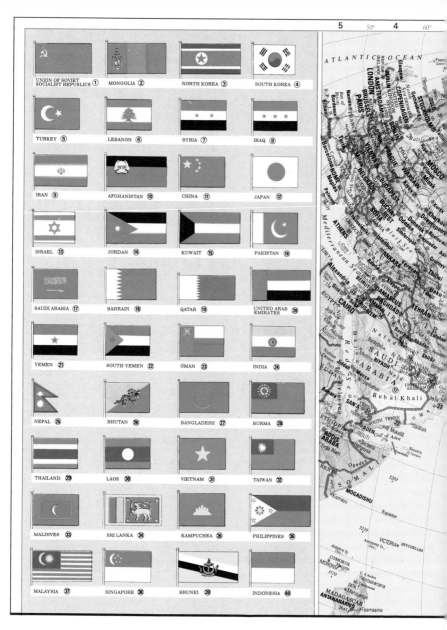

UNION OF SOVIET SOCIALIST REPUBLICS ①   MONGOLIA ②   NORTH KOREA ③   SOUTH KOREA ④

TURKEY ⑤   LEBANON ⑥   SYRIA ⑦   IRAQ ⑧

IRAN ⑨   AFGHANISTAN ⑩   CHINA ⑪   JAPAN ⑫

ISRAEL ⑬   JORDAN ⑭   KUWAIT ⑮   PAKISTAN ⑯

SAUDI ARABIA ⑰   BAHRAIN ⑱   QATAR ⑲   UNITED ARAB EMIRATES ⑳

YEMEN ㉑   SOUTH YEMEN ㉒   OMAN ㉓   INDIA ㉔

NEPAL ㉕   BHUTAN ㉖   BANGLADESH ㉗   BURMA ㉘

THAILAND ㉙   LAOS ㉚   VIETNAM ㉛   TAIWAN ㉜

MALDIVES ㉝   SRI LANKA ㉞   KAMPUCHEA ㉟   PHILIPPINES ㊱

MALAYSIA ㊲   SINGAPORE ㊳   BRUNEI ㊴   INDONESIA ㊵

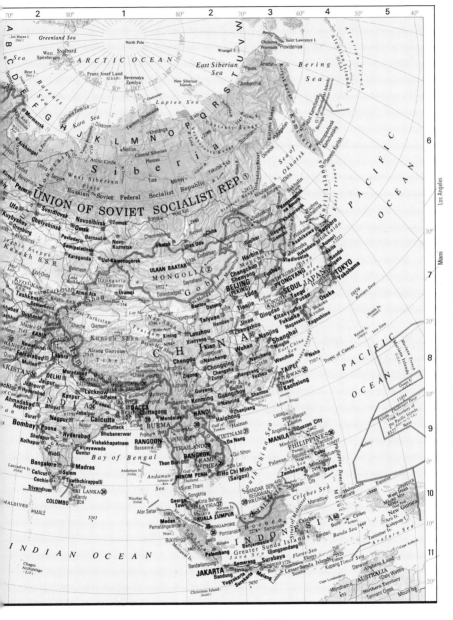

A
B
C
D
E
F
G
H
J
K
L
M
N
O
P
Q
R
S
T
U

6

7

8

9

10

11

Los Angeles
Miami

Greenland Sea
Jan Mayen I.
(Nor.)
West Spitsbergen
Svalbard
North Pole
Wrangel I.
Chukotski
Peninsula
Saint Lawrence I.
Providenija
Aleutian Islands
Bear I.
(Nor.)
Franz Josef Land
(U.S.S.R.)
Severnaya
Zemlya
New Siberian
Islands
Anadyr
Aleutian Trench

ARCTIC OCEAN

East Siberian
Sea

Bering
Sea

Barents
Sea
Murmansk
Kara Sea
Dikson
Laptev Sea
Ambarchik
Pevek
Koryak Range
Kamchatka

Arkhangel
Kola
Kirov
Vorkuta
Arctic Circle
Noril'sk
Central Siberian
Plateau
Tura
Cherskiy Range
Verkhoyansk Range
Sea of
Okhotsk
Sakhalin
Hokkaido

UNION OF SOVIET SOCIALIST REP.

Siberia

West Siberian
Plain
Russian Soviet Federal Socialist Republic

Perm
Ufa
Sverdlovsk
Chelyabinsk
Novosibirsk
Tomsk
Omsk
Barnaul
Novo-
Kuznetsk
Pavlodar
Semipalatinsk
Karaganda
Ust-Kamenogorsk

Kuybyshev
Orenburg
Aktyubinsk
Kazakh S.S.R.
Balkhash
Lake
Balkhash

Irkutsk
Ulan Ude
Bratsk
Ust-Kut
Chita
Komsomol'sk-
na-Amure
Blagoveshchensk
Khabarovsk
Vladivostok
Sapporo
Sea
of
Japan
Akita
Sendai

ULAAN BAATAR
MONGOLIA
Gobi
Harbin
Changchun
Shenyang
Fushun
TOKYO
Yokohama

BEIJING
(PEKING)
PYONGYANG
SEOUL
JAPAN
Tianjin
SOUTH KOREA
Pusan
Osaka
Kitakyushu
Fukuoka
Nagasaki
Kagoshima

Tashkent
Samarkand
Alma Ata
Tien Shan
Urumqi
Hami
Lanzhou
Xining
Taiyuan
Jinan
Qingdao
Yellow
Sea

KABUL
Islamabad
Rawalpindi
Lahore
Kunlun Shan
Tibet
Xizang Gaoyuan
Chengdu
Xi'an
Zhengzhou
Nanjing
Shanghai
East China
Sea
Tropic of Cancer

DELHI
Jaipur
Kanpur
Lucknow
Patna
KATHMANDU
Himalayas
CHINA
Chongqing
Wuhan
Changsha
Nanchang
Fuzhou
TAIPEI
TAIWAN
Kaohsiung

INDIA
Ahmadabad
Bhopal
Jabalpur
Nagpur
Calcutta
DACCA
BURMA
Guiyang
Kunming
Guangzhou
HONG KONG
Shantou
Zhanjiang

Bombay
Poona
Hyderabad
Vishakhapatnam
RANGOON
HANOI
Haiphong
Hainan
MANILA
Quezon City
PHILIPPINES

Bangalore
Madras
Bay of Bengal
THAILAND
BANGKOK
KAMPUCHEA
VIETNAM
Da Nang
South China
Sea
Cebu
Davao

COLOMBO
SRI LANKA
PHNOM PENH
Ho Chi Minh
(Saigon)
BRUNEI
BANDAR SERI
BEGAWAN

MALDIVES
MALE
George
Town
Kota Baharu
MALAYSIA
KUALA LUMPUR
SINGAPORE
Borneo
Celebes Sea
New Guinea

INDIAN OCEAN
Palembang
Greater Sunda Islands
INDONESIA
Banda Sea
Arafura Sea

JAKARTA
Bandung
Surabaya
Semarang
Yogyakarta
Lesser Sunda Islands
Bali
Timor
Kupang Timor Sea
Arnhem Land
AUSTRALIA
Northern Territory

Christmas Island
(Austr.)

PACIFIC
OCEAN

PACIFIC
OCEAN

foot = 0,30 m
meter = 3,28 feets
Scale 1:75 000 000
0   1000   2000 km
0 1 hour 400   800   1200 miles

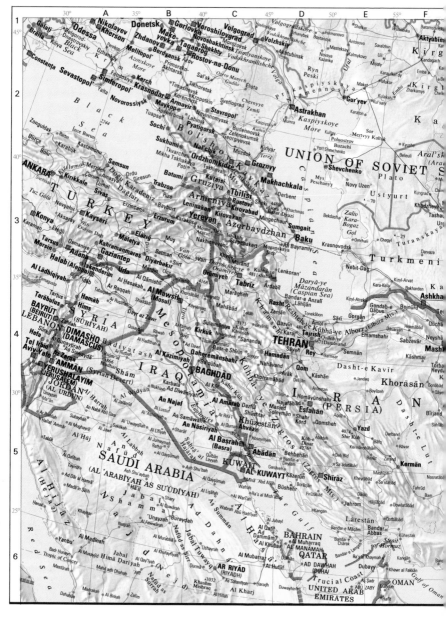

66   SOUTH WEST ASIA

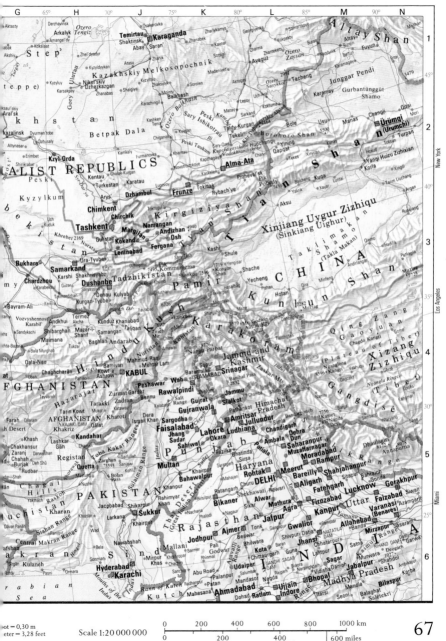

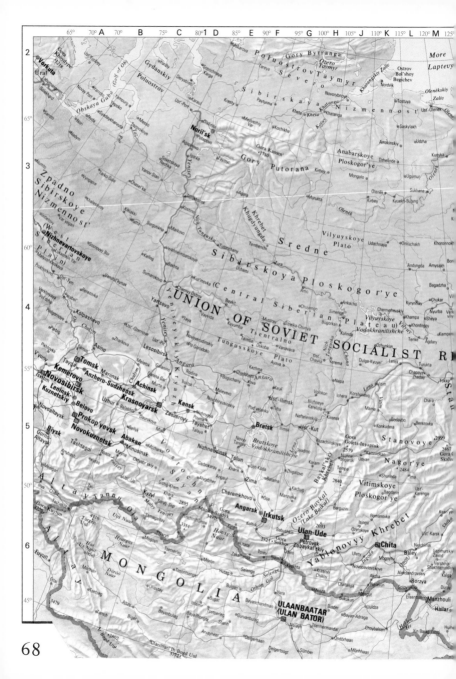

69

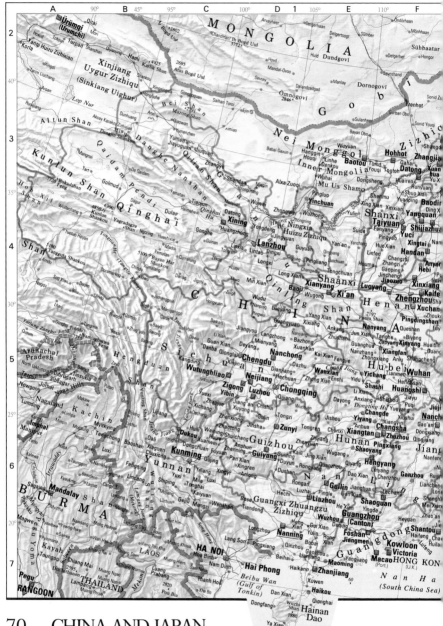

70 CHINA AND JAPAN

foot = 0,30 m
meter = 3,28 feet

Scale 1:20 000 000

| 0 | 200 | 400 | 600 | 800 | 1000 km |

| 0 | 200 | 400 | 600 miles |

1 hour

MALDIVES

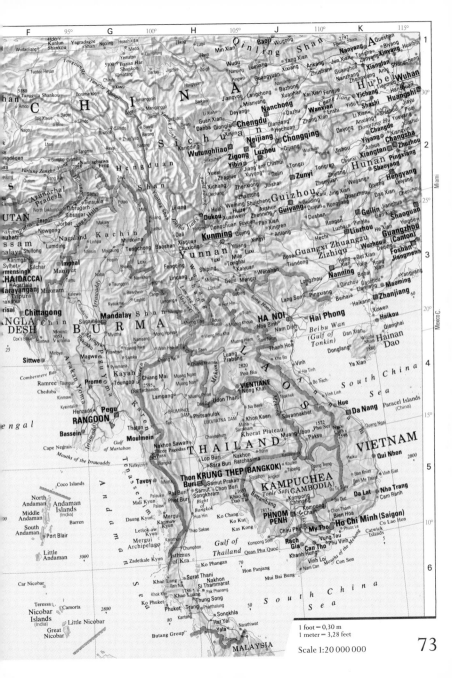

Scale 1:20 000 000

1 foot = 0,30 m
1 meter = 3,28 feet

73

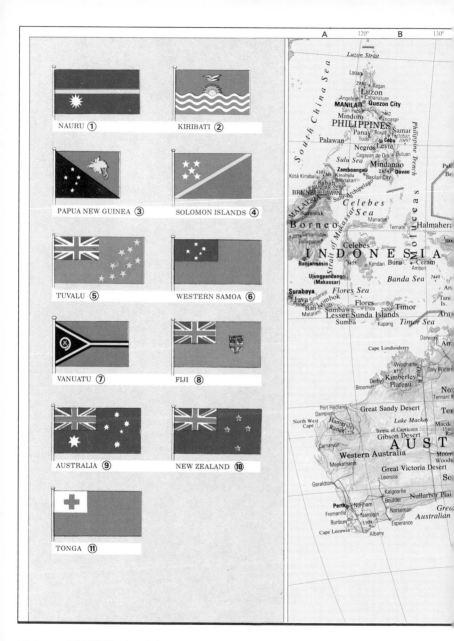

NAURU ①

KIRIBATI ②

PAPUA NEW GUINEA ③

SOLOMON ISLANDS ④

TUVALU ⑤

WESTERN SAMOA ⑥

VANUATU ⑦

FIJI ⑧

AUSTRALIA ⑨

NEW ZEALAND ⑩

TONGA ⑪

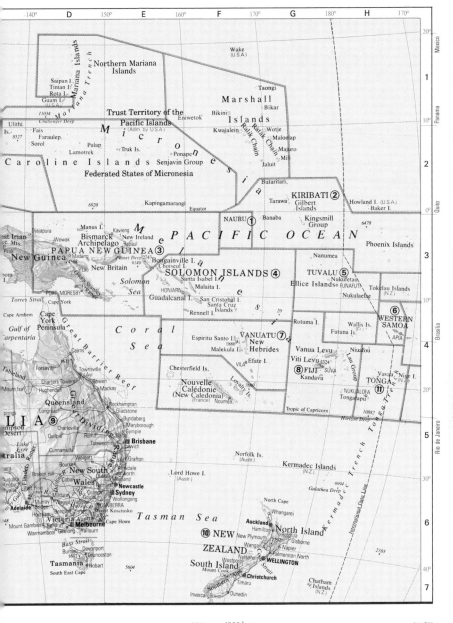

Scale 1:50 000 000

ot = 0,30 m
eter = 3,28 feet

| 0 | | 500 | | 1000 km |

| 0 | 200 | 400 | | 600 miles |
1 hour

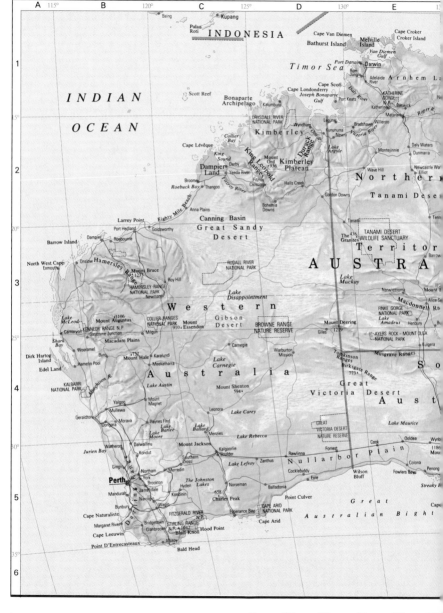

Scale 1:20 000 000

0	200	400	600	800	1000

0	200	400	600 r

1 hour

1 foot = 0,30 m
1 meter = 3,28 feet

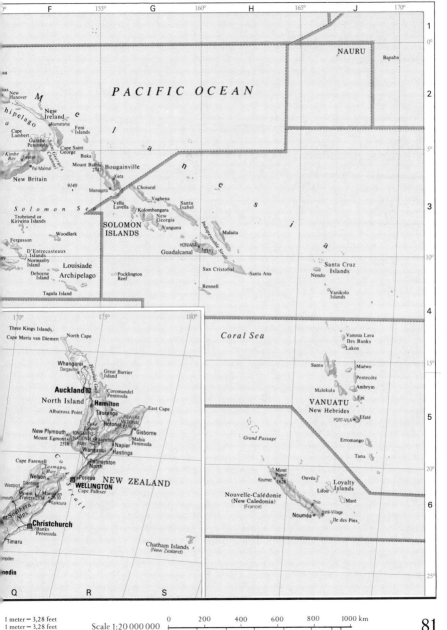

	F	155°	G	160°	H	165°	J	170°	

PACIFIC OCEAN

NAURU

Banaba

au

New Hanover

M e

l a n e s i a

Chipelago

New Ireland

Cape Lambert

Namatanai

Feni Islands

Gazelle Peninsula

Kimbe Bay

Ewasse

Pal Malmal

Saint George Channel

Cape Saint George

Buka

Mount Balbi 2743

Bougainville

Kieta

New Britain

9140

Mamagota

Choiseul

Vella Lavella

Vaghena

Santa Isabel

Kolombangara

New Georgia

Vangunu

Solomon Sea

Trobriand or Kiriwina Islands

Woodlark

SOLOMON ISLANDS

Malaita

Indispensable Strait

Fergusson

D'Entrecasteaux Islands

Normanby Island

Louisiade Archipelago

Deboyne Island

Pocklington Reef

HONIARA 2331

Guadalcanal

San Cristobal

Santa Ana

Santa Cruz Islands

Nendo

Tagula Island

Rennell

Vanikolo Islands

	170°		175°		180°				

Three Kings Islands

Cape Maria van Diemen

North Cape

Coral Sea

Vanoua Lava Iles Banks

Lakon

Whangarei

Dargaville

Great Barrier Island

Santo

Maéwo

Hauraki Gulf

Coromandel Peninsula

Pentecôte

Auckland

Hamilton

North Island

Malekula

Ambrym

Epi

Albatross Point

East Cape

VANUATU New Hebrides

New Plymouth

Mount Egmont 2518

Tauranga

Lake Rotorua

UREWERA NATIONAL PARK

Gisborne

Efaté

PORT-VILA

TONGARIRO NATIONAL PARK

Ruapehu 2797

Napier

Mahia Peninsula

Grand Passage

Erromango

Wanganui

Hastings

Tana

Cape Farewell

Tasman Bay

Palmerston North

Nelson

Porirua

NEW ZEALAND

Mont Panié 1628

Koumac

Ouvéa

Loyalty Islands

Lifou

Westport

WELLINGTON

Cook Strait

Cape Palliser

Nouvelle-Calédonie (New Caledonia) (France)

Thio

Maré

Mouth

Mount Travers 2338

2610

Glenhope

Kaikoura

Yaté-Village

Nouméa

Ile des Pins

or Southern Alps

Christchurch

Banks Peninsula

Chatham Islands (New Zealand)

Timaru

mpden

nedin

1 meter = 3,28 feet
1 meter = 3,28 feet

Scale 1:20 000 000

0	200	400	600	800	1000 km

0		200		400	600 miles

1 hour

81

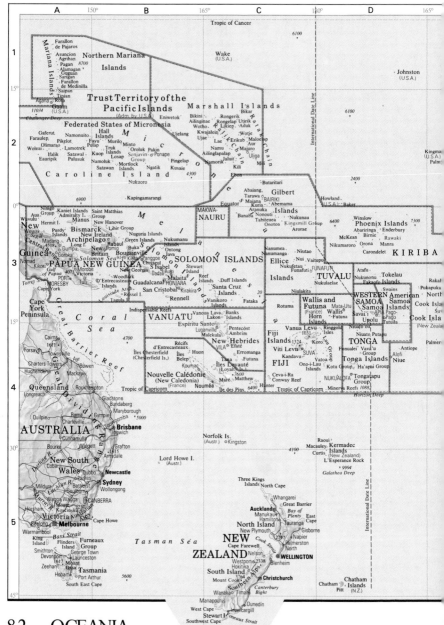

82 OCEANIA

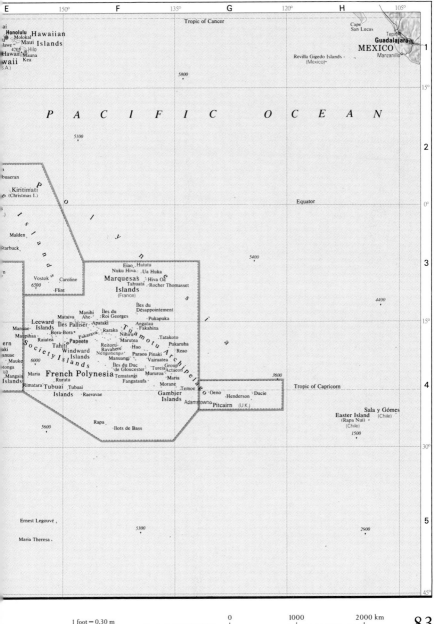

E　　150°　　F　　135°　　G　　120°　　H　　105°

Tropic of Cancer

Honolulu　Hawaiian
Molokai
Maui　Islands
4205　Hilo
Mauna
Hawaii　Kea
(U.S.A.)

Cape
San Lucas
Tepic
Guadalajara
MEXICO
Manzanillo

Revilla Gigedo Islands
(Mexico)

1

P　A　C　I　F　I　C　　　O　C　E　A　N

5800

15°

5100

2

buaeran
Kiritimati
(Christmas I.)

Equator

0°

Malden

Starbuck

5400

3

Eiao　Hatutu
Nuku Hiva　Ua Huka
Marquesas　Hiva Oa
Vostok　Caroline　Tahuata
6500　　Flint　　Islands　Rocher Thomasset
(France)

Îles du
Désappointement

4400

15°

Manihi
Mataiva　Ahe
Leeward　Îles Palliser　Apataki
Manuae　Islands
Bora-Bora
Mauphiaa　Raiatea　Fakarava
Maria　Tahiti　Papeete
Windward
6000　Islands
Mauke　　Reitoru
nuae　　　Ravahere
Mangaia　Maria　Rurutu
Islands　Rimatara　Tubuai　Tubuai
Islands　　Raevavae

Îles du
Roi Georges
Pukapuka
Angatau
Raraka　Nihiru　Fakahina
Marutea　Tatakoto
Hao　Pukaruha
Nengonengo　Paraoa　Pinaki　Reao
Manuangi　Vairaatea
Îles du Duc　Tureia
de Gloucester　Muroroa　Group
Tematangi　　Actaeon
Fangataufa　Maria
Morane
Temoe

3600

Tropic of Capricorn

Sala y Gómes
(Chile)
Easter Island
(Rapa Nui)
(Chile)
1500

4

French Polynesia

Gambier
Islands
Adamstown
Pitcairn　(U.K.)

Oeno
Henderson　Ducie

Rapa
5600　　Îlots de Bass

30°

Ernest Legouvé

Maria Theresa

5300

2900

5

45°

1 foot = 0,30 m
1 meter = 3,28 feet　　Scale 1:54 000 000

0　　　　1000　　　　2000 km
0　　400　　800　　1200 miles
1 hour

83

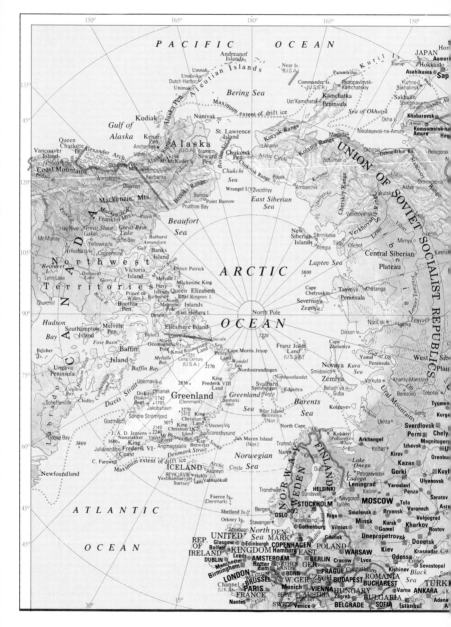

1 foot = 0,30 m
1 meter = 3,28 feet

Scale 1:60 000 00

ANTARCTICA 85

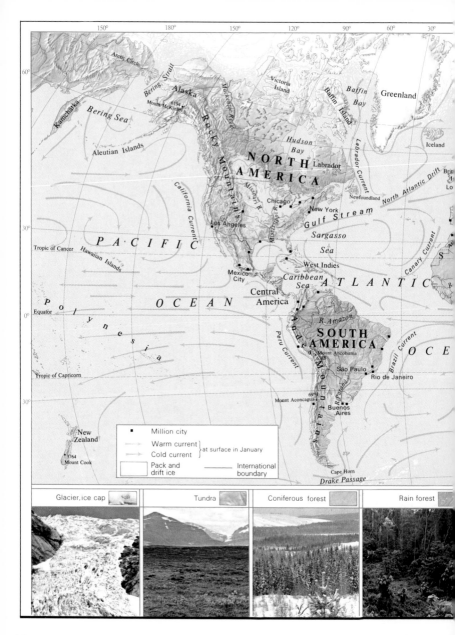

150°   180°   150°   120°   90°   60°   30°

Arctic Circle

Bering Strait

Kamchatka

Bering Sea

Alaska

Mount McKinley 6194

Aleutian Islands

Rocky Mountains

Mackenzie R.

Victoria Island

Baffin Island

Baffin Bay

Greenland

Iceland

Hudson Bay

NORTH AMERICA

Labrador

Labrador Current

North Atlantic Drift

Brit

Lo

Missouri R.

Chicago

Mississippi R.

New York

Newfoundland

California Current

Los Angeles

Gulf Stream

PACIFIC

Tropic of Cancer

Hawaiian Islands

Sargasso Sea

Canary Current

S

Mexico City

West Indies

Caribbean Sea

ATLANTIC

Central America

P

OCEAN

Equator

o

l

y

n

e

s

i

a

R. Amazon

SOUTH AMERICA

OCE

Peru Current

Mount Ancohuma 6388

Tropic of Capricorn

Andes Mountains

São Paulo

Brazil Current

R. Paraná

Rio de Janeiro

30°

Mount Aconcagua 6959

Buenos Aires

New Zealand

Mount Cook 3764

■   Million city

→   Warm current ⎫ at surface in January
→   Cold current   ⎭

☐   Pack and   ——— International
    drift ice   boundary

Cape Horn

Drake Passage

| Glacier, ice cap | Tundra | Coniferous forest | Rain forest |

86   THE WORLD

1 foot = 0,30 m
1 meter = 3,28 feet

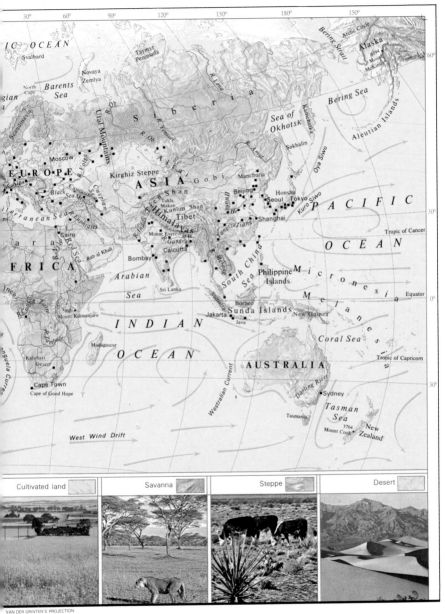

Scale 1:180 000 000
at the equator

VAN DER GRINTEN'S PROJECTION

0°	0 400 800 km	0 200 600 miles
30°		30°
60°	200 600 1000 km	60° 100 300 500 miles

Cultivated land   Savanna   Steppe   Desert

87

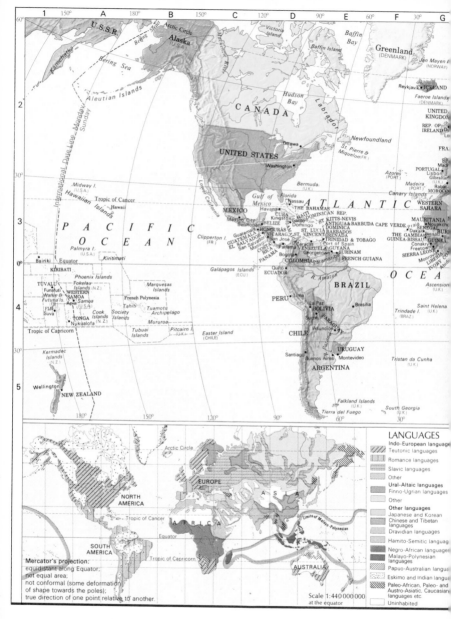

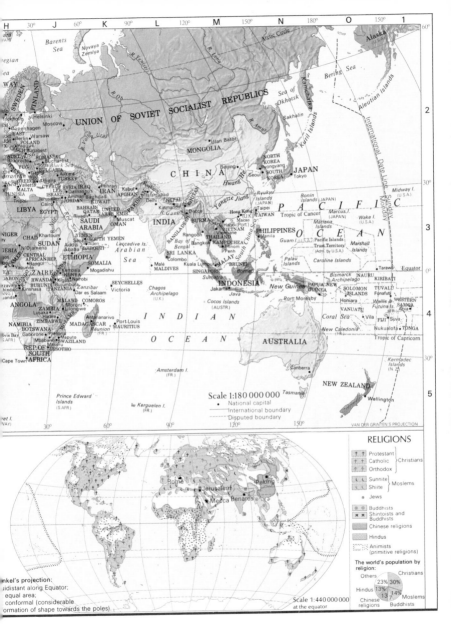

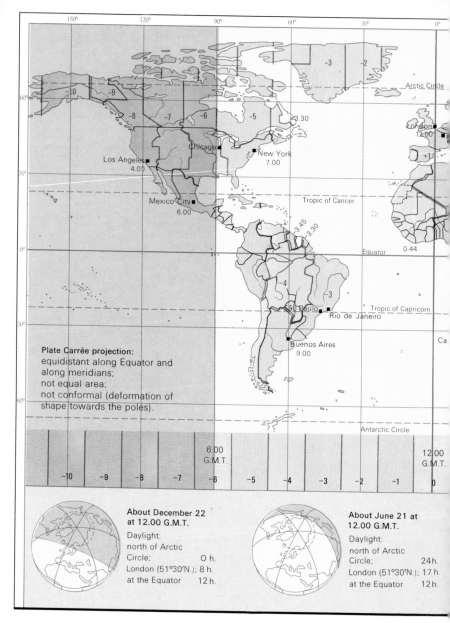

Plate Carrée projection:
equidistant along Equator and
along meridians;
not equal area;
not conformal (deformation of
shape towards the poles).

Arctic Circle

London
12.00

Tropic of Cancer

Equator   0.44

Tropic of Capricorn

Antarctic Circle

-10 -9 -8 -7 -6 -5 -4 -3 -2 -1 0

6.00
G.M.T.

12.00
G.M.T.

Chicago

New York
7.00

Los Angeles
4.00

Mexico City
6.00

São Paulo

Rio de Janeiro

Buenos Aires
9.00

About December 22
at 12.00 G.M.T.

Daylight:
north of Arctic
Circle;   0 h.
London (51°30′N.); 8 h.
at the Equator   12 h.

About June 21 at
12.00 G.M.T.

Daylight:
north of Arctic
Circle;   24 h.
London (51°30′N.); 17 h.
at the Equator   12 h.

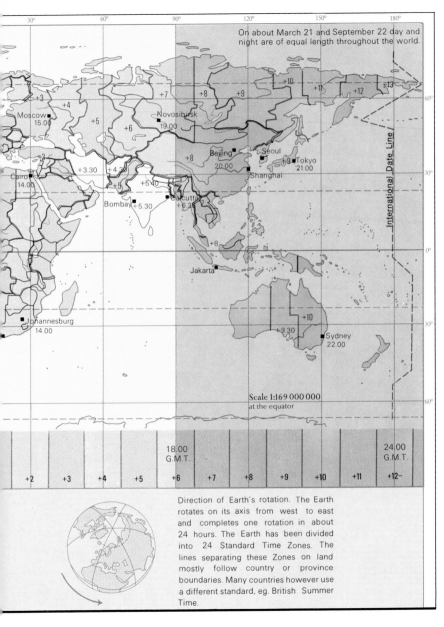

On about March 21 and September 22 day and night are of equal length throughout the world.

Moscow 15.00
+3
+4
+5
+6
+7
+8
+9
+10
+11
+12
+13

Novosibirsk 19.00

Beijing 20.00
Seoul
+9 Tokyo 21.00
Shanghai

Cairo 14.00
+2
+3.30
+4.30
+5
+5.40
Calcutta +6.30
Bombay +5.30

+8

Jakarta

+10
+9.30
Sydney 22.00

Johannesburg 14.00

International Date Line

Scale 1:169 000 000
at the equator

18.00 G.M.T.
24.00 G.M.T.

+2   +3   +4   +5   +6   +7   +8   +9   +10   +11   +12−

Direction of Earth's rotation. The Earth rotates on its axis from west to east and completes one rotation in about 24 hours. The Earth has been divided into 24 Standard Time Zones. The lines separating these Zones on land mostly follow country or province boundaries. Many countries however use a different standard, eg. British Summer Time.

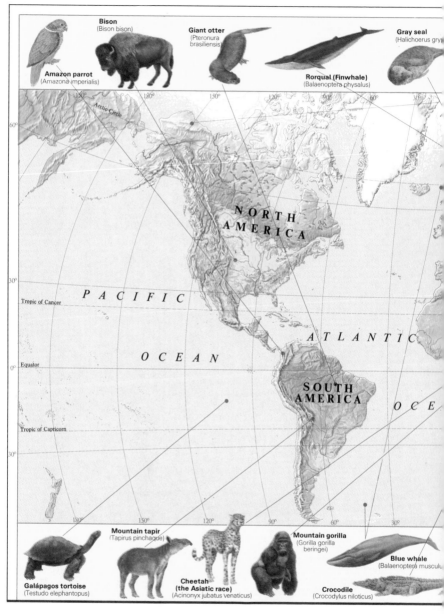

Amazon parrot
(Amazona imperialis)

Bison
(Bison bison)

Giant otter
(Pteronura brasiliensis)

Rorqual (Finwhale)
(Balaenoptera physalus)

Gray seal
(Halichoerus gryi)

NORTH AMERICA

PACIFIC

Tropic of Cancer

OCEAN

Equator

ATLANTIC

SOUTH AMERICA

OCE

Tropic of Capricorn

Galápagos tortoise
(Testudo elephantopus)

Mountain tapir
(Tapirus pinchaque)

Cheetah
(the Asiatic race)
(Acinonyx jubatus venaticus)

Mountain gorilla
(Gorilla gorilla beringei)

Crocodile
(Crocodylus niloticus)

Blue whale
(Balaenoptera musculu

92   ANIMALS ON THE EDGE OF EXTINCTION

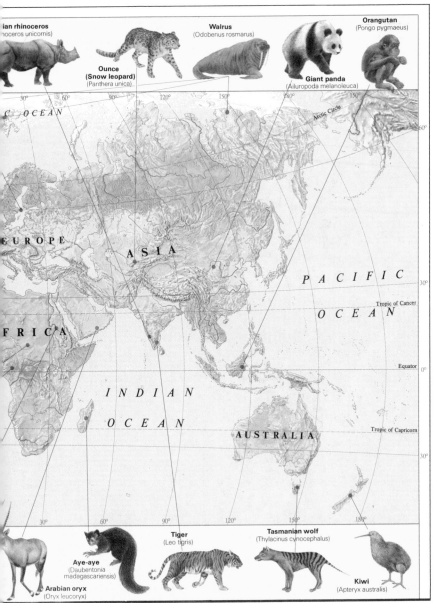

ian rhinoceros
(noceros unicornis)

**Ounce
(Snow leopard)**
(Panthera uncia)

Walrus
(Odobenus rosmarus)

Giant panda
(Ailuropoda melanoleuca)

Orangutan
(Pongo pygmaeus)

30°   60°   90°   120°   150°   Arctic Circle   150°   60°

C O C E A N

E U R O P E

A S I A

P A C I F I C

30°

Tropic of Cancer

O C E A N

F R I C A

Equator   0°

I N D I A N

O C E A N

AUSTRALIA

Tropic of Capricorn

30°

30°   60°   90°   120°   150°   180°

Aye-aye
(Daubentonia
madagascariensis)

Tiger
(Leo tigris)

Tasmanian wolf
(Thylacinus cynocephalus)

Arabian oryx
(Oryx leucoryx)

Kiwi
(Apteryx australis)

N DER GRINTEN'S PROJECTION

EARTH RECORDS

Area: 58,009,000 sq.mi. (150,243,000 km²)
(Land: 26%, Water: 71%, Ice: 3%)
Population: 4,025,281,000

Greenland

Mount McKinley

NORTH AMERICA

Great B[

Missouri   Lake Superior

Mississippi

Milwaukee Depth

Amazon

SOUTH AMERICA

Lago Titicaca

Cerro Aconcagua

Grande de Tierra
del Fuego

World's Longest Rivers
1.	Nile (Africa)	4,160 miles
2.	Amazon (South America)	4,080 miles
3.	Mississippi-Missouri (North America)	3,740 miles
4.	Yangtze (Asia)	3,720 miles
5.	Yenisey (Asia)	3,650 miles

Greatest Depth in each ocean
Arctic: North Polar Basin	18,040 ft.
Atlantic: Milwaukee Depth (Puerto Rico Trench)	30,238 ft.
Indian: Java Trench	24,436 ft.
Pacific: Challenger Deep (Mariana Trench)	36,192 ft.

Highest Mountain in each continent
Africa: Kilimanjaro	19,34C
(Antarctica Vinson Massif)	16,863
Asia: Mt. Everest	29,028
Europe: Mont Blanc	15,771
North America: Mount McKinley	20,321
Oceania: Puncak Jaya	16,502
South America: Cerro Aconcagua	22,831

Largest Island in each continent
Africa: Madagascar	227,000 sq
(Antarctica: Alexander 1)	16,700 sq
Asia: Borneo	285,000 sq
Europe: Great Britain	84,400 sq
North America: Greenland	823,000 sq
Oceania: New Guinea	305,000 sq
South America: Grande de Tierra del Fuego	18,700 sq

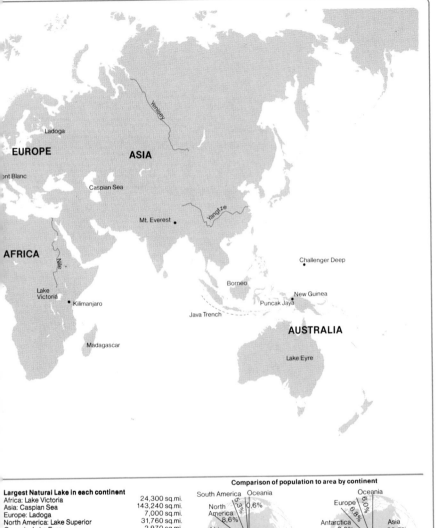

Ladoga

EUROPE

ASIA

Yenisey

ont Blanc

Caspian Sea

AFRICA

Nile

Mt. Everest •

Yangtze

Challenger Deep •

Lake
Victoria

• Kilimanjaro

Borneo

New Guinea

Puncak Jaya

Java Trench

AUSTRALIA

Madagascar

Lake Eyre

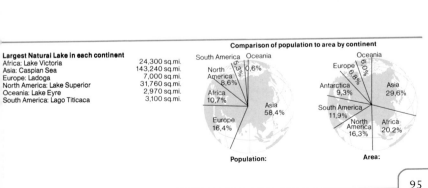

Largest Natural Lake in each continent

Africa: Lake Victoria	24,300 sq.mi.
Asia: Caspian Sea	143,240 sq.mi.
Europe: Ladoga	7,000 sq.mi.
North America: Lake Superior	31,760 sq.mi.
Oceania: Lake Eyre	2,970 sq.mi.
South America: Lago Titicaca	3,100 sq.mi.

Comparison of population to area by continent

Population:

South America 5,3% — Oceania 0,6%
North America 8,6%
Africa 10,7%
Asia 58,4%
Europe 16,4%

Area:

Oceania 6,0%
Europe 6,8%
Antarctica 9,3%
Asia 29,6%
South America 11,9%
North America 16,3%
Africa 20,2%

NORTH AMERICA

Area: 9,442,000 sq.mi. (24,454,000 km²)
Population: 346,418,000
Density of population per sq.mi.: 37

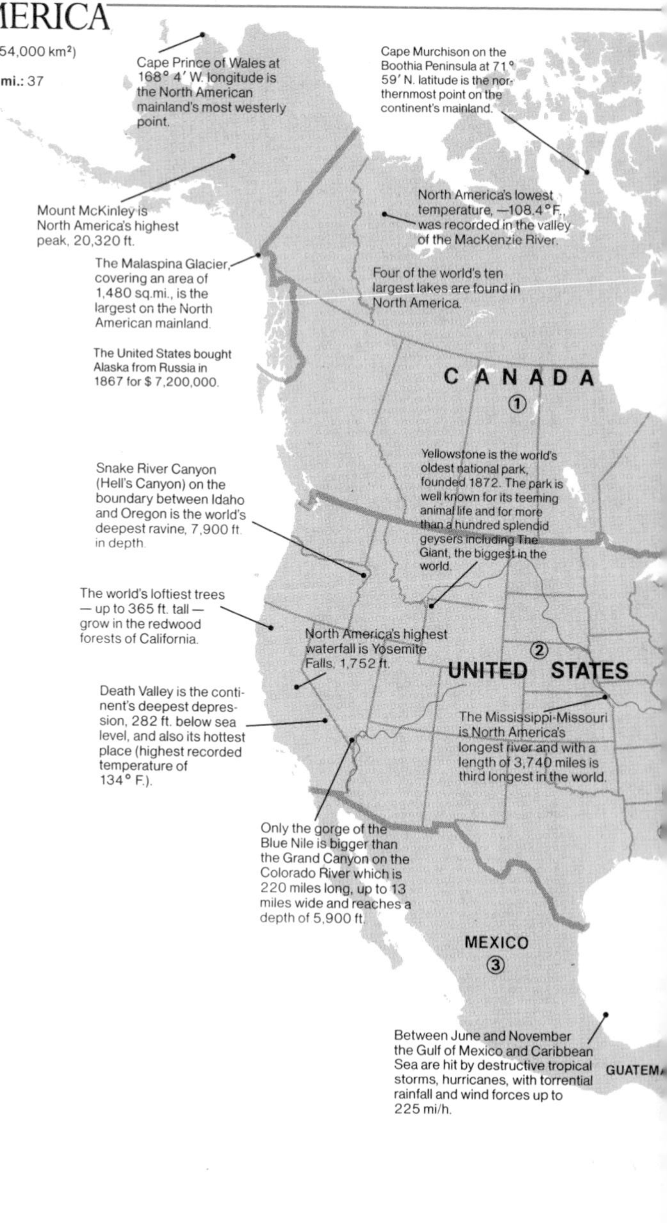

Cape Prince of Wales at 168° 4′ W. longitude is the North American mainland's most westerly point.

Cape Murchison on the Boothia Peninsula at 71° 59′ N. latitude is the northernmost point on the continent's mainland.

Mount McKinley is North America's highest peak, 20,320 ft.

North America's lowest temperature, −108.4° F., was recorded in the valley of the MacKenzie River.

The Malaspina Glacier, covering an area of 1,480 sq.mi., is the largest on the North American mainland.

Four of the world's ten largest lakes are found in North America.

The United States bought Alaska from Russia in 1867 for $ 7,200,000.

C A N A D A
①

Yellowstone is the world's oldest national park, founded 1872. The park is well known for its teeming animal life and for more than a hundred splendid geysers including The Giant, the biggest in the world.

Snake River Canyon (Hell's Canyon) on the boundary between Idaho and Oregon is the world's deepest ravine, 7,900 ft. in depth.

The world's loftiest trees — up to 365 ft. tall — grow in the redwood forests of California.

North America's highest waterfall is Yosemite Falls, 1,752 ft.

②

UNITED STATES

Death Valley is the continent's deepest depression, 282 ft. below sea level, and also its hottest place (highest recorded temperature of 134° F.).

The Mississippi-Missouri is North America's longest river and with a length of 3,740 miles is third longest in the world.

Only the gorge of the Blue Nile is bigger than the Grand Canyon on the Colorado River which is 220 miles long, up to 13 miles wide and reaches a depth of 5,900 ft.

MEXICO
③

Between June and November the Gulf of Mexico and Caribbean Sea are hit by destructive tropical storms, hurricanes, with torrential rainfall and wind forces up to 225 mi/h.

GUATEMA

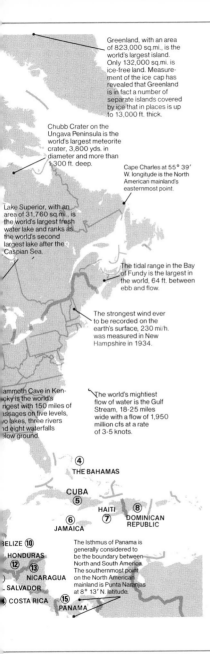

Greenland, with an area of 823,000 sq.mi., is the world's largest island. Only 132,000 sq.mi. is ice-free land. Measurement of the ice cap has revealed that Greenland is in fact a number of separate islands covered by ice that in places is up to 13,000 ft. thick.

Chubb Crater on the Ungava Peninsula is the world's largest meteorite crater, 3,800 yds. in diameter and more than 1,300 ft. deep.

Cape Charles at 55° 39' W. longitude is the North American mainland's easternmost point.

Lake Superior, with an area of 31,760 sq.mi., is the world's largest fresh water lake and ranks as the world's second largest lake after the Caspian Sea.

The tidal range in the Bay of Fundy is the largest in the world, 64 ft. between ebb and flow.

The strongest wind ever to be recorded on the earth's surface, 230 mi/h. was measured in New Hampshire in 1934.

Mammoth Cave in Kentucky is the world's largest with 150 miles of passages on five levels, two lakes, three rivers and eight waterfalls below ground.

The world's mightiest flow of water is the Gulf Stream, 18-25 miles wide with a flow of 1,950 million cfs at a rate of 3-5 knots.

④ THE BAHAMAS

CUBA ⑤

HAITI ⑧
⑥ ⑦ DOMINICAN
JAMAICA REPUBLIC

BELIZE ⑩

HONDURAS
⑫ ⑬
NICARAGUA
SALVADOR
COSTA RICA ⑮ PANAMA

The Isthmus of Panama is generally considered to be the boundary between North and South America. The southernmost point on the North American mainland is Punta Naranjas at 8° 13' N. latitude.

⑩ **BELIZE**

① **CANADA**

⑭ **COSTA RICA**

⑤ **CUBA**

⑧ **DOMINICAN REPUBLIC**

⑪ **EL SALVADOR**

⑨ **GUATEMALA**

⑦ **HAITI**

⑫ **HONDURAS**

⑥ **JAMAICA**

③ **MEXICO**

⑬ **NICARAGUA**

⑮ **PANAMA**

④ **THE BAHAMAS**

② **UNITED STATES**

① CANADA

Area: 3,851,809 sq.mi. (9,976,139 km²)
Population: 25,130,000
Population growth per annum: 1.5%
Life expectancy at birth: males 70 years, females 77 years
Literacy: 99%
Capital with population: Ottawa 295,000
Other important cities with population:
Montréal 1,000,000, Toronto 600,000, Calgary 595,000
Language: English, French
Religion: Roman Catholic (46%), Protestant (36%)
Currency: Canadian dollar = 100 cents

A nation that spans a continent, Canada is the world's second largest country. Halifax on the Atlantic is closer to Great Britain than to Vancouver on the Pacific. When the sun rises over Newfoundland it is still midnight in Yukon. The 55 ft tides in the Bay of Fundy are the world's greatest. Independent JUL 1, 1867.

② UNITED STATES
(United States of America)

Area: 3,615,122 sq.mi. (9,363,123 km²)
Population: 234,250,000
Population growth per annum: 0.9%
Life expectancy at birth: males 69 years, females 77 years
Literacy: 99%
Capital with population: Washington 638,000
Other important cities with population:
New York 7,100,000, Chicago 3,000,000,
Los Angeles 3,000,000
Language: English
Religion: Protestant (33%),Roman Catholic (23%),
Judaism (3%)
Currency: US dollar = 100 cents

U.S.A. is a powerful nation. The economic strength and military might of the nation can hardly be overestimated. It is the world's leading producer of most important commodities: oil, gas, coal, steel, paper. It is also found at the top of most lists of world records and extremes — and especially those of engineering feats. Independent JUL 4, 1776.

③ MEXICO
Estados Unidos Mexicanos
(United Mexican States)

Area: 761,605 sq.mi. (1,972,547 km²)
Population: 76,790,000
Population growth per annum: 3.0%
Life expectancy at birth: males 62 years, females 67 years
Literacy: 74 %
Capital with population: Mexico City 13,000,000
Other important cities with population:
Guadalajara 2,300,000, Monterrey 2,000,000
Language: Spanish
Religion: Roman Catholic
Currency: Mexican peso = 100 centavos

The center of power in Central America lies as before in Mexico. In the early 19th century, the Spanish viceroy ruled half of Northern America from here, and today the nation is ranked high among the powers of the Third World. The famous pyramids of Teotihuacán manifest the greatness of Mexico. Independent SEP 16, 1810.

④ THE BAHAMAS
(Commonwealth of the Bahamas)

Area: 5,380 sq.mi. (13,935 km²)
Population: 230,000
Population growth per annum: 3.7%
Life expectancy at birth: males 64 years, females 69 years
Literacy: 89 %
Capital with population: Nassau 139,000
Other important cities with population: Freeport 16,000
Language: English
Religion: Mainly Protestant
Currency: Bahamian dollar = 100 cents

A thousand coral reefs and not one but 700 coral islands in the sun. For the industrial eastern USA the beaches of the Bahamas are conveniently close — as Mediterranean shores are to northwestern Europe. Blue underwater caves attract scuba divers. Independent JUL 10, 1973.

⑤ CUBA
República de Cuba
(Republic of Cuba)

Area: 46,736 sq.mi. (121,046 km²)
Population: 10,000 000
Population growth per annum: 0.8%
Life expectancy at birth: males 71 years, females 74 years
Literacy: 96%
Capital with population: La Habana (Havana) 1,950,000
Other important cities with population:
Santiago de Cuba 565,000, Camagüey 480,000
Language: Spanish
Religion: Roman Catholic
Currency: Cuban peso = 100 centavos

The Sugar Island. Sugar and Cuba are now almost synonymous words, but it is a fact that the sugar cane was imported to Cuba from the Old World by the Spaniards. The Cubans themselves are also descendants of immigrants from the Old World: the Spaniards and their negro slaves. Independent DEC 10, 1898.

⑥ JAMAICA

Area: 4,244 sq.mi. (10,991 km²)
Population: 2,310,000
Population growth per annum: 1.4%
Life expectancy at birth: males 68 years, females 73 years
Literacy: 82%
Capital with population: Kingston 650,000
Other important cities with population:
St. Catherine 220,000, Clarendon 195,000
Language: English
Religion: Protestant (75%), Roman Catholic
Currency: Jamaica dollar = 100 cents

Pirate Island has become Island in the Sun and Land of the Rasta — as Fifteen men on a dead man's chest has been replaced by the inspired music of the Rastafarians. The bottle of rum is still available. Only scuba divers can today visit infamous Port Royal on the bottom of Kingston Bay. Independent AUG 6, 1962.

⑦ HAITI

République d'Haïti
(Republic of Haiti)

Area: 10,714 sq.mi. (27,750 km²)
Population: 5,200,000
Population growth per annum: 2.4%
Life expectancy at birth: males 49 years, females 52 years
Literacy: 23%
Capital with population: Port-au-Prince 460,000
Other important cities with population: Cap Haïtien 55,000
Language: French, Creole
Religion: Roman Catholic (66%), Protestant (11%)
Currency: Guorde = 100 centimes

*Historically the land of voodo, of mystery and magic. Officially
all are Roman Catholics, but the undercurrent of ancient
African religions is still strong here. Slaves who won their
freedom against Spanish, British and French armies created
here the world's first Negro republic. Independent JAN 1,
1804.*

⑧ DOMINICAN REPUBLIC

República Dominicana

Area: 18,703 sq.mi. (48,442 km²)
Population: 5,980,000
Population growth per annum: 2.6%
Life expectancy at birth: males 58 years, females 62 years
Literacy: 62%
Capital with population: Santo Domingo 1,300,000
Other important cities with population: Santiago
(de los Caballeros) 280,000, La Romana 90,000
Language: Spanish
Religion: Roman Catholic
Currency: RD peso = 100 centavos

*This is in all but name Columbus's country. Here lie his mortal re-
mains in a lead casket in the cathedral of Santo Domingo. The
city that he founded is the oldest European city in the New
World, and the island itself carries the name he gave it,
Hispaniola — "the Spanish (Island)". Independent FEB 27,
1844.*

⑨ GUATEMALA

República de Guatemala
(Republic of Guatemala)

Area: 42,042 sq.mi. (108,889 km²)
Population: 6,580,000
Population growth per annum: 3.0%
Life expectancy at birth: males 57 years, females 59 years
Literacy: 47%
Capital with population: Guatemala 1,300,000
Other important cities with population:
Quezaltenango 66,000
Language: Spanish, Indian dialects
Religion: Roman Catholic
Currency: Quetzal = 100 centavos

*A land of awe inspiring ruins and memories of its brilliant past
during the reign of the Mayas — of once glorious cities like
Tikal and Uaxactún. It is also a land of melodious place names
like Chichicastenango (a famous market town) and Sololá.
Independent 1821, 1839.*

⑩ BELIZE

Area: 8,867 sq.mi. (22,965 km²)
Population: 158 000
Population growth per annum: not available
Life expectancy at birth: 60 years
Literacy: 80%
Capital with population: Belmopan 2,900
Other important cities with population: Belize City 40,000
Language: English, Spanish
Religion: Roman Catholic (60%), Protestant
Currency: Belize dollar = 100 cents

*Belize is an anomaly — the only British enclave in Latin
America. The forests yield valuable timber — mahogany and
rosewood — and chicle latex, the original "gum" used for making chewing gum before the development of synthetic gum.
Independent SEP 21, 1981.*

⑪ EL SALVADOR

República de El Salvador
(Republic of El Salvador)

Area: 8,260 sq.mi. (21,393 km²)
Population: 5,300,000
Population growth per annum: 2.9%
Life expectancy at birth: males 60 years, females 65 years
Literacy: 40%
Capital with population: San Salvador 884,000
Other important cities with population: Santa Ana 210,000,
San Miguel 160,000
Language: Spanish
Religion: Roman Catholic
Currency: Colón = 100 centavos

*This is truly the land of volcanoes. The average distance be-
tween active volcanoes here is less than 19 miles! Politically the
nation is disrupted by even more serious eruptions of violence,
aggravated by outside interference. Independent 1839, 1841.*

⑫ HONDURAS

Repúr lica de Honduras
(Republic of Honduras)

Area: 43,277 sq.mi. (112,088 km²)
Population: 4,090,000
Population growth per annum: 3.8%
Life expectancy at birth: males 55 years, females 59 years
Literacy: 47%
Capital with population: Tegucigalpa 534,000
Other important cities with population:
San Pedro Sula 398,000, El Progreso 105,000
Language: Spanish
Religion: Roman Catholic
Currency: Lempira = 100 centavos

*The word banana republic must have been coined with Hon-
duras in mind. Bananas thrive in the fertile volcanic soil and the
warm, humid climate of the tropical coastlands. The forest
covers impressive Maya ruins, such as Copán. Independent
1821, NOV 5, 1838.*

⑬ NICARAGUA
República de Nicaragua
(Republic of Nicaragua)

Area: 57,143 sq.mi. (148,000 km²)
Population: 2,910,000
Population growth per annum: 3.3%
Life expectancy at birth: males 54 years, females 57 years
Literacy: 87%
Capital with population: Managua 615,000
Other important cities with population: León 160,000
Language: Spanish
Religion: Roman Catholic
Currency: Córdoba = 100 centavos

Nicaragua could be called a land of turmoil. Plagued by earth-quakes, revolutions, and counter-revolutions the people today are certainly longing for peace and quiet. Lake Nicaragua is said to contain people-eating sharks, trapped there when the former bay became a fresh water lake. Indep. 1821, 1838.

⑭ COSTA RICA
República de Costa Rica

Area: 19,600 sq.mi. (50,700 km²)
Population: 2,450,000
Population growth per annum: 2.4%
Life expectancy at birth: males 68 years, females 72 years
Literacy: 90%
Capital with population: San José 245,000
Other important cities with population: Alajuela 35,000
Language: Spanish
Religion: Roman Catholic
Currency: Colón = 100 céntimos

Costa Rica is known as the country that has no army, but the police are one of the world's best equipped! The lack of generals and colonels is in any case not the only cause for the peaceful, democratic development of the country during the last twenty-five years. Independent 1821, 1838.

⑮ PANAMA
República de Panamá
(Republic of Panamá)

Area: 30,134 sq.mi. (78,046 km²)
Population: 1,970,000
Population growth per annum: 2.5%
Life expectancy at birth: males 68 years, females 72 years
Literacy: 85%
Capital with population: Panamá 389,000
Other important cities with population: Colón 80,000
Language: Spanish
Religion: Roman Catholic
Currency: Balboa = 100 centimes

Panama is known all over the Seven Seas. Few know that the word means 'abundance of fish' but many know the quartered tricolor flag that is flown over many ships (as a flag of 'conve-nience') — and all know of the Canal that every year carries over 10,000 large ships between the Atlantic and the Pacific. Independent 1819, NOV 3, 1903.

SOUTH AMERICA

Area: 6,887,000 sq.mi. (17,838,000 km²)
Population: 214,684,000
Density of population per sq.mi.: 31

① SAINT KITTS NEVIS

④ SAINT VINC

⑦ GRENA

⑧ VENEZUELA

⑩ COLOMBIA

Punta Gallinas at 12° 28′ N. latitude is the most northerly point on the South American mainland.

ECUADOR ⑬
At 81° 20′ W. longitude Punta Pariñas is the westernmost point on the mainland of South America.

Ocean-going ships can reach as far as Iquitos, 2,300 miles from the mouth of the Amazon.

⑭ PERU

The world's most exten-sive lowland is part of Amazon Basin with the largest rain forests, the selvas, covering som 1.9 million sq.mi.

South America's largest lake is Lago Titicaca, 3,100 sq.mi. Situated at 12,507 ft. above sea level it is one of the world's highest bodies of water.

South America's high active volcano is Guallatiri, 19,880 ft (latest eruption in 1

⑰ BOLIV

In relation to the surround-ings the Andes are the world's highest mountain range. Over a distance of 300 miles the surface drops from peaks around 23,000 ft. high to nearly 26,000 ft. deep in the Peru-Chile Trench, a dif-ference of over 48,000 ft.!

Calama in the Atacar Desert is probably the driest spot on earth, because no precipita has ever been recorde there.

South America's highest mountain, Cerro Acon-cagua, reaches 22,831 ft. above sea level.

ARGENT
⑲

CHILE
⑯

One of the few passes through the mighty wall of the Andes is the Uspallata (Paso de la Cumbre). 12,600 ft. high.

Glacier de Patagonia, covering more than 1,550 sq.mi., is the conti-nent's largest.

Cabo Froward at 53° 54′ S. latitude is the South American mainland's southernmost point.

GUA (AND BARBUDA)

INICA ③

T LUCIA ⑤

BADOS

⑨
IDAD

AGO

Discovered in 1935 the Angel Falls in the
Roraima Mountains are highest in the world.
The total fall is 3,215 ft. with the greatest single
drop of 2,640 ft.

YANA

SURINAM
⑫

The waters from the
Amazon can clearly be
distinguished 200 miles
out into the Atlantic
Ocean.

The Amazon is the longest river in South America
(4,080 miles from source to mouth) and is the world's
second longest. The drainage basin is the largest in
the world and covers 2.37 million sq.mi. and the river
flow is greater than any other (6,180,000 cfs.)

BRAZIL
⑮

Cabo Branco at 34° 36′
W. longitude is the South
American mainland's
most easterly point.

RAGUAY

The Iguazu Falls are the
mightiest in South
America. The falls are
divided by forested
islands over a width of
3,200 yds. with two falls
totalling a height of
230 ft.

⑳
URUGUAY

e deepest depression
South America is
alinas Grandes on
ninsula Valdes, 115 ft.
low sea level.

a Grande de Tierra del
ego is the continent's
gest island (18,700
.mi.)

Most southerly point in
South America is Cape
Horn at 55° 59′s.
latitude.

② ANTIGUA (AND BARBUDA)

⑲ ARGENTINA

⑥ BARBADOS

⑰ BOLIVIA

⑮ BRAZIL

⑯ CHILE

⑩ COLOMBIA

③ DOMINICA

⑬ ECUADOR

⑦ GRENADA

⑪ GUYANA

⑱ PARAGUAY

⑭ PERU

① SAINT KITTS-NEVIS

⑤ SAINT LUCIA

④ SAINT VINCENT

⑫ SURINAM

⑨ TRINIDAD AND TOBAGO

⑳ URUGUAY

⑧ VENEZUELA

① SAINT KITTS-NEVIS
(Sovereign Democratic Federal State)

Area: 101 sq.mi. (261 km²)
Population: 45,000
Population growth per annum: not available
Life expectancy at birth: not available
Literacy: not available
Capital with population: Basseterre 15,000
Other important cities with population: none
Language: English
Religion: Protestant (76%), Roman Catholic (8%)
Currency: EC-dollar = 100 cents

St. Kitts cultivates tourists and sugar. The pleasant climate in the trade wind tropics favors both of the main industries. Palms and beaches correspond to the common "image" of the Caribbean. Independent SEP 19, 1983.

② ANTIGUA (AND BARBUDA)

Area: 170 sq.mi. (442 km²)
Population: 79,000
Population growth per annum: not available
Life expectancy at birth: not available
Literacy: not available
Capital with population: Saint Johns 25,000
Other important cities with population: none
Language: English
Religion: Christian (predominantly Church of England)
Currency: East Caribbean dollar = 100 cents

Antigua and Barbuda are names known to collectors of stamps, to naval strategy planners, some students of colonial history and a few in the sugar trade, and of course, to the proud and independent islanders of the Lesser Antilles. Ind. NOV 1, 1981.

③ DOMINICA
(Commonwealth of Dominica)

Area: 290 sq.mi. (751 km²)
Population: 82,000
Population growth per annum: 2.7%
Life expectancy at birth: males 57 years, females 59 years
Literacy: not available
Capital with population: Roseau 20,000
Other important cities with population: none
Language: English, French patois
Religion: Roman Catholic
Currency: French franc = 100 centimes

Dominica can be called the only Caribbean country among all the Caribbean lands. Only here still lives a sizeable remnant of the once dreaded Carib Indians — whose name is perpetuated in the equally dreadful word cannibal. Indep. NOV 3, 1978.

④ SAINT VINCENT (AND THE GRENADINES)

Area: 150 sq.mi. (389 km²)
Population: 123,000
Population growth per annum: 5.9%
Life expectancy at birth: males 59 years, females 60 years
Literacy: 95 %
Capital with population: Kingstown 33,000
Other important cities with population: none
Language: English
Religion: Protestant (75%), Roman Catholic (13%)
Currency: EC-dollar = 100 cents

Many different kinds of fruit are grown on the islands — coconuts, mangoes, avocados, guavas just to mention a few, but not the pomegranates used for making grenadine syrup (an ingredient of many cocktails). Most of the 600 volcanic Grenadine Islands belong to St. Vincent. Ind. OCT 27, 1979.

⑤ SAINT LUCIA

Area: 238 sq.mi. (616 km²)
Population: 127,000
Population growth per annum: 1.8%
Life expectancy at birth: males 65 years, females 70 years
Literacy: 78%
Capital with population: Castries 45,000
Other important cities with population: none
Language: English, French patois
Religion: Roman Catholic
Currency: EC-dollar = 100 cents

Bananas, cocoa and coconuts are the chief products of St. Lucia instead of sugar as on most other Antillean Islands. A growing number of tourists are discovering the pleasant beaches of St. Lucia. Independent FEB 22, 1979.

⑥ BARBADOS

Area: 166 sq.mi. (431 km²)
Population: 250,000
Population growth per annum: 1.4%
Life expectancy at birth: males 68 years, females 73 years
Literacy: 97%
Capital with population: Bridgetown 7,500
Other important cities with population: none
Language: English
Religion: Protestant
Currency: Barbados dollar = 100 cents

Tourists and sugar cane thrive here on the most easterly of the Windward Islands. The gentle trade winds blow with a constant 16-20 fts. to keep the surf rolling in and the sky clear of clouds. Independent NOV 30, 1966.

⑦ GRENADA
(State of Grenada)

Area: 133 sq.mi. (344 km²)
Population: 115,000
Population growth per annum: 1.0%
Life expectancy at birth: 69 years
Literacy: 85%
Capital with population: Saint George's 7,500
Other important cities with population: none
Language: English
Religion: Roman Catholic
Currency: E C dollar = 100 cents

Grenada is one of the "spice islands" of the world. It produces more than one third of the nutmeg on the world market. In the world of the super powers Grenada has also had an importance without relation to its tiny size. Independent FEB 7, 1974.

⑩ COLOMBIA
República de Colombia
(Republic of Colombia)

Area: 440,829 sq.mi. (1,141,748 km²)
Population: 27,410,000
Population growth per annum: 2.1%
Life expectancy at birth: males 60 years, females 65 years
Literacy: 82%
Capital with population: Bogotá 4,900,000
Other important cities with population:
Medellín 1,800,000, Cali 1,200,000, Barranquilla 900,000
Language: Spanish
Religion: Roman Catholic
Currency: Colombian peso = 100 centavos

Colombia may have been the legendary land of El Dorado — the gold-covered king. Today it could be called the land of green gold — as 90% of all emeralds in the world come from mines in Colombia. However high quality coffee is the country's main export product. Independent DEC 17, 1819.

⑧ VENEZUELA
República de Venezuela
(Republic of Venezuela)

Area: 352,144 sq.mi. (912,050 km²)
Population: 15,260,000
Population growth per annum: 3.5%
Life expectancy at birth: males 64 years, females 69 years
Literacy: 86%
Capital with population: Caracas 2,700,000
Other important cities with population:
Maracaibo 845,000, Barquismeto 459,000
Language: Spanish
Religion: Roman Catholic
Currency: Bolivar = 100 céntimos

Venice has been called a floating city, and Venezuela — "little Venice" — a land floating on oil. Over 4,000 oil drilling derricks stand now in the shallow waters of the Maracaibo lagoon like the houses on stilts that gave the country its name. In the southeast the Angel Falls, highest in the world, plunge 3,214 ft. down. Independent 1821, 1830.

⑪ GUYANA
(Cooperative Republic of Guyana)

Area: 83,000 sq.mi. (215,000 km²)
Population: 830,000
Population growth per annum: 2.2%
Life expectancy at birth: males 67 years, females 72 years
Literacy: 85%
Capital with population: Georgetown 187,000
Other important cities with population: none
Language: English, Hindi, Creole
Religion: Hindu (37%), Protestant (32%),
Roman Catholic (13%), Islam (9%)
Currency: Guyana dollar = 100 cents

Guyana is an East Indian country in the West Indies, as the major part of the inhabitants are descendants of immigrants from India. Of all the world's waterfalls only nine are higher than the near 1,640 ft. high uninterrupted cascades of the King George VI Falls, north of the Roraima Plateau. Indep. MAY 26, 1966.

⑨ TRINIDAD AND TOBAGO

Area: 1,980 sq.mi. (5,128 km²)
Population: 1,160,000
Population growth per annum: 1.5%
Life expectancy at birth: males 66 years, females 72 years
Literacy: 92%
Capital with population: Port of Spain 56 000
Other important cities with population:
San Fernando 40,000
Language: English, Spanish
Religion: Roman Catholic (31%), Protestant (26%),
Hindu (23%), Moslem (6%)
Currency: Trinidad and Tobago dollar = 100 cents

A melting pot where everything is transformed. Cultures , traditions, and people from five continents have been mixed and combined under the sun of Trinidad. A different melting pot, an "inexhaustible" lake of asphalt, Pitch Lake, is unique in the world. Independent AUG 31, 1962.

⑫ SURINAM

Area: 63,251 sq.mi. (163,820 km²)
Population: 370,000
Population growth per annum: 1.3%
Life expectancy at birth: males 65 years, females 70 years
Literacy: 80%
Capital with population: Paramaribo 68,000
Other important cities with population: none
Language: Dutch
Religion: Hindu (29%), Protestant (20%), Moslem (19%),
Roman Catholic (18%) .
Currency: Suriname guilder or florin = 100 cents

A country for $ 24? In a deal with Britain in the 15th century the Dutch acquired this British colony in exchange for New Amsterdam — later better known as the city of New York — in turn bought for $24. 90% of today's Surinam is covered with dense rainforest. Independent NOV 25, 1975.

⑬ ECUADOR

República del Ecuador
(Republic of Ecuador)

Area: 109,484 sq.mi. (283,561 km²),
   (disputed area 190,807 km² not included)
Population: 8,810,000
Population growth per annum: 3.0%
Life expectancy at birth: males 58 years, females 62 years
Literacy: 84%
Capital with population: Quito 920,000
Other important cities with population:
   Guaqaquil 1,300,000, Cuenca 270,000
Language: Spanish, Quechuan, Jivaroan
Religion: Predominantly Roman Catholic
Currency: Sucre = 100 centavos

A "heavy" item in Ecuador's export statistics is featherweight balsa timber. The Spanish word balsa denotes both raft and the timber, lighter than cork. The Indians used it for building sailing rafts as early as prehistoric times. The logs for Heyerdahl's famous Kon-Tiki were cut in Ecuador in 1947. Independent MAY 13, 1830.

⑭ PERU

República del Perú
(Republic of Peru)

Area: 496,225 sq.mi. (1,285,216 km²)
Population: 18,300,000
Population growth per annum: 2.7%
Life expectancy at birth: males 56 years, females 59 years
Literacy: 72%
Capital with population: Lima 3,100,000
Other important cities with population: Callao 300,000
Language: Spanish, Quechua, Aymarà
Religion: Roman Catholic
Currency: Sol = 100 centavos

The Inca's land of gold and silver was turned into a land of guano and fishmeal. The conquistadores stripped the land of its immense treasures of golden artwork. The stone buildings of Machu Picchu's breath-taking eagle's nest-city still remain — hidden and forgotten for five centuries until discovered by Hiram Bingham in 1911. Independent JUL 28, 1821.

⑮ BRAZIL

Repuíblica Federativa do Brasil
(Federative Republic of Brazil)

Area: 3,286,488 sq.mi. (8,511,965 km²)
Population: 120,000,000
Population growth per annum: 2.4%
Life expectancy at birth: males 60 years, females 64 years
Literacy: 68%
Capital with population: Brasilia 410,000,
   (Federal district 1,200,000)
Other important cities with population:
   São Paulo 7,000,000, Rio de Janeiro 5,100,000
Language: Portuguese
Religion: Roman Catholic (89%), Protestant (7%)
Currency: Cruzeiro = 100 centavos

Only four countries in the world are larger than Brazil. The mighty Amazon carries more water than any other river (6,180,000 cfs. at the mouth) and is navigable for ocean-going ships up to Iquitos, 2,300 mi. from the sea. Brasilia, created by president Kubitscheck and architects Oscar Niemeyer and Lúcio Costa, became capital in 1960. Indep. SEP 7, 1822.

⑯ CHILE

República de Chile
(Republic of Chile)

Area: 292,258 sq.mi. (756,945 km²)
Population: 11,490,000
Population growth per annum: 1.7%
Life expectancy at birth: males 62 years, females 69 years
Literacy: 90%
Capital with population: Santiago 3,450,000
Other important cities with population:
   Viña del Mar 300,000, Varpariso 270,000
Language: Spanish
Religion: Predominantly Roman Catholic
Currency: Chilean peso = 100 centavos

The "narrowest" country in the world, Chile, is nearly twenty-five times longer than it is wide (110 × 2,700 mi.) and stretches from the tropics down to the stormy Cape Horn in the "Furious Fifties". At Calama in the Atacama Desert no rainfall has ever been recorded. Independent SEP 18, 1810.

⑰ BOLIVIA

República de Bolivia
(Republic of Bolivia)

Area: 424,164 sq.mi. (1,098,580 km²)
Population: 5,900,000
Population growth per annum: 2.6%
Life expectancy at birth: males 47 years, females 51 years
Literacy: 75%
Capital with population: La Paz 650,000 and Sucre 65,000
Other important cities with population:
   Santa Cruz 260,000, Cochabamba 200,000
Language: Spanish, Quechua (34%), Aymará (25%)
Religion: Roman Catholic
Currency: Bolivian peso = 100 centavos

Tin mining is the main source of wealth in land-locked Bolivia. Most of the population live on the dry, cold tablelands, higher than many peaks in the European Alps. Lake Titicaca, shared with Peru, is the world's highest (12,507 ft.) navigable body of water. Independent AUG 6, 1825.

⑱ PARAGUAY

República del Paraguay
(Republic of Paraguay)

Area: 157,048 sq.mi. (406,752 km²)
Population: 3,000,000
Population growth per annum: 3.3%
Life expectancy at birth: males 62 years, females 66 years
Literacy: 82%
Capital with population: Asunción 460,000
Other important cities with population: Caaguazu 73,000
Language: Spanish, Guarani (90%)
Religion: Roman Catholic
Currency: Guarani = 100 céntimos

Here one man's will is, and has been, law — by unbroken tradition from Jesuit times. The pope was replaced by the King of Spain, he in turn by the founding dictator "El Supremo" and so on. General Alfredo Stroessner seized power in 1954. The Iguaçu falls of the Parana cascade 270 ft. over a width of 2,5 mi. between hundreds of forest islands. Independent MAY 14, 1811.

⑲ ARGENTINA
República Argentina
(Argentine Republic)

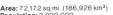

Area: 1,072,514 sq.mi. (2,777,815 km²)
Population: 27,950,000
Population growth per annum: 1.3%
Life expectancy at birth: males 66 years, females 73 years
Literacy: 94 %
Capital with population: Buenos Aires 2,900,000,
  (Greater Buenos Aires 9,900,000)
Other important cities with population: Córdoba 970,000,
  Rosario 880,000, Mendoza 600,000
Language: Spanish
Religion: Roman Catholic
Currency: Arg. peso = 100 centavos

The home of the tango and the gaucho, Argentina is a Europe in miniature. It is situated on southern latitudes, and it was populated by settlers from all over Europe. It has the continent's highest peak, Aconcagua, and its lowest spot, Salinas Grandes on the Peninsula Valdés, 115 ft. below sea level. Independent MAR 25, 1810.

⑳ URUGUAY
República Oriental del Uruguay
(Oriental Republic of Uruguay)

Area: 72,172 sq.mi. (186,926 km²)
Population: 2,990,000
Population growth per annum: 0.6%
Life expectancy at birth: males 66 years, females 73 years
Literacy: 94%
Capital with population: Montevideo 1,362,000
Other important cities with population: Salto 80,000,
  Paysandá 80,000
Language: Spanish
Religion: Roman Catholic
Currency: Nuevo peso (new peso) = 100 centésimos

A country of rolling grasslands with grazing cattle and cultivated fields. As in other agricultural lands, more people live in the capital than in all the other towns put together. Independent AUG. 25, 1825.

EUROPE

Area: 3,956,000 sq.mi. (10,245,000 km²)
Population: 660,476,000
Density of population per sq.mi. 167

The North Atlantic West Wind Drift together with prevailing westerly winds gives Northern Europe a climate about 41°F. warmer than the average for these latitudes.

The European mainland most northerly point is Nordkinn at 71° 8′ N. latitude. North Cape is an impressive rocky promontory on the neighboring island of Magerøy which has its most northerly point at Knivskjellodden.

① ICELAND

All the world's geysers are named after Geysir in Haukadalur, Europe's largest geyser which at irregular intervals, but usually once a day, throws a column of boiling water some 100 ft. in the air (maximum height 230 ft.)

Vatnajökull is Europe's largest glacier with an area of about 3,250 sq.mi.

② NORWAY

Sognefjorden (135 miles in length) is Europe's longest inlet.

③ SWEDEN

④ FINLAND

Ladoga with an area 7,000 sq.mi. is Europe largest lake.

⑧ UNION

Europe's largest island is Great Britain which, with an area of 84,400 sq.mi., ranks seventh in the world.

⑤ REPUBLIC OF IRELAND

⑥ UNITED KINGDOM

⑦ DENMARK

Agricultural land covers 40% of Europe. No other continent is so intensively utilized.

Europe lies on the Prime Meridian, which divides the earth into Eastern and Western hemispheres.

⑨ NETHERLANDS

GERMAN

⑩ FEDERAL REPUBLIC OF GERMANY

⑪ DEMOCRATIC REPUBLIC

⑫ POLAND

⑬ BELGIUM

At St. Malo the difference between ebb and flow is 50 ft., the greatest tidal range in Europe.

⑭ LUXEMBOURG

⑮ CZECHOSLOVAKIA

Cabo da Roca at 9° 31′ W. longitude is the westernmost point on the European mainland.

⑰ FRANCE

⑲ LIECHTENSTEIN

⑱ SWITZERLAND

⑳ AUSTRIA

Mont Blanc is Europe's highest mountain.

⑯ HUNGARY

㉔ ROMANIA

㉓ YUGOSLAVIA

PORTUGAL
㉕

ANDORRA
㉗

㉑ MONACO

㉘ SAN MARINO

BULGARIA

㉖ SPAIN

㉙ VATICAN STATE

㉒ ITALY

㉛

TURKEY
㉜

Europe's highest temperature, 123.8° F., has been recorded at Sevilla.

㉚ ALBANIA

Punta Marroqui at 36° 0′ N. latitude is the most southerly point on the European mainland.

㉞ GREECE

The highest active volcano in Europe is Etna which last erupted in 1984.

㉝ MALTA

① ICELAND
Lýðveldið Island
(Republic of Iceland)

Area: 39,698 sq.mi. (102,819 km²)
Population: 240,000
Population growth per annum: 1.1%
Life expectancy at birth: males 73 years, females 79 years
Literacy: 99.9%
Capital with population: Reykjavik 87,000
Other important cities with population: Akureyri 14,000
Language: Icelandic
Religion: Protestant
Currency: Króna = 100 aurar

The Island of the Norse sagas, Iceland's "althingi" claims to be the world's oldest parliament, enacting laws since 930. The Icelanders kept the old Norse myths and sagas alive by oral tradition until Snorri Sturluson collected them in his epic Edda. A sight to be seen is the world famous Geysir. Independent 930, JUN 17, 1944.

② NORWAY
Kongeriket Norge
(Kingdom of Norway)

Area: 149,411 sq.mi. (386,974 km²),
(including Svalbard and Jan Mayen)
Population: 4,130,000
Population growth per annum: 0.4%
Life expectancy at birth: males 72 years, females 78 years
Literacy: 99%
Capital with population: Oslo 447,000
Other important cities with population: Bergen 207,000, Trondheim 134,000
Language: Norwegian
Religion: Protestant
Currency: Norwegian krone = 100 öre

Norway, proclaimed "The land of the Midnight Sun", might rather be called the Land of Fiords. These spectacular inlets between vertical mountain walls dissect Norway, and have made the Norwegians a people who sail and fish. The Sogne Fiord is 136,7 mi. long — Europe's longest. Independent 1905.

③ SWEDEN
Konungariket Sverige
(Kingdom of Sweden)

Area: 173,732 sq.mi. (449,964 km²)
Population: 8,350,000
Population growth per annum: 0.2%
Life expectancy at birth: males 72 years, females 79 years
Literacy: 99%
Capital with population: Stockholm 651,000
(metropolitan area 1,409, 000)
Other important cities with population: Göteborg 424,000 Malmö 230,000
Language: Swedish
Religion: Protestant
Currency: Swedish krona = 100 öre

The metallurgical industry that gave the world "Swedish steel" has traditions that reach beyond the Viking Age. The world's oldest company, Stora, chartered in 1280, is still working the mine of Falun, that produced the copper that once made Sweden a great power.

④ FINLAND
Suomen Tasavalta — Republiken Finland
— (Republic of Finland)

Area: 130,128 sq.mi. (337,032 km²)
Population: 4,870 000
Population growth per annum: 0.6%
Life expectancy at birth: males 69 years, females 77 years
Literacy: 99%
Capital with population: Helsinki (Helsingfors) 484,000
Other important cities with population: Tampere (Tammerfors) 170.000, Turku (Åbo) 165,000
Language: Finnish, Swedish
Religion: Protestant
Currency: Markka (mark) = 100 penniä (penni)

The "land of a thousand lakes" (actually almost a hundred thousand) has also become known as "the land that pays its debts" — by repaying not only U.S. loans but also a huge war indemnity to the Soviet Union after World War II. Exporting high quality manufactured goods to East and West has brought prosperity to the Finns. Independent MAR 29, 1809, DEC 6, 1917.

⑤ REPUBLIC OF IRELAND
Eire

Area: 27,136 sq.mi. (70,283 km²)
Population: 3,440,000
Population growth per annum: 1.1%
Life expectancy at birth: males 70 years, females 75 years
Literacy: 99%
Capital with population: Dublin 526,000
Other important cities with population: Cork 150,000, Limerick 76,000
Language: Irish, English
Religion: Roman Catholic
Currency: Irish pound (punt Eirennach) = 100 pighne

"The Emerald Isle" is perhaps most famous for its people — for boisterous bards, for poets and playwrights and Irish Eyes — but also for Irish coffee, whiskey and Guinness beer. Ireland justly prides itself also on the Book of Kells — and maybe more reluctantly for the Blarney Stone, kissed by many. Independent 1916, 1922.

⑥ UNITED KINGDOM AND NORTHERN IRELAND

Area: 94,250 sq.mi (244,104 km²)
Population: 56,780,000
Population growth per annum: — 0.1%
Life expectancy at birth: males 70 years, females 76 years
Literacy: 99%
Capital with population: London 6,755,000
Other important cities with population: Birmingham 1,013,000, Leeds 714,000, Sheffield 543,000
Language: English
Religion: Protestant, Roman Catholic, Moslem
Currency: British pound = 100 pence

Britannia ruled the waves for over three hundred years, and finally gracefully resigned from the role of "peacekeeper" after the Pax Britannica had been broken by two world wars. The sun may have set over the Empire, but it still shines on the Union Jack in many places all over the world.

⑦ DENMARK

Kongeriget Danmark
(Kingdom of Denmark)

Area: 16,629 sq.mi. (43.069 km²)
Population: 5,112,000
Population growth per annum: 0.2%
Life expectancy at birth: males 71 years, females 77 years
Literacy: 99%
Capital with population: Köbenhavn (Copenhagen) 483,000, (Greater Copenhagen 1,400,000)
Other important cities with population: Aarhus 250,000, Odense 170,000
Language: Danish
Religion: Protestant (Lutheran)
Currency: Danish krone = 100 øre

Danish kings have ruled not only all of Scandinavia but also England. Today no other country has larger overseas territories. They include the world's largest island, Greenland. Friendly Denmark now serves as an important link between the Nordic countries and the rest of Europe, especially the E.E.C.

⑧ UNION OF SOVIET SOCIALIST REPUBLICS

Soyuz Sovyetskikh
Sotsialisticheskikh Respublik

Area: 8,649,500 sq.mi. (22,402,200 km²)
Population: 276,300,000
Population growth per annum: 0.9 %
Life expectancy at birth: males 65 years, females 74 years
Literacy: 99%
Capital with population: Moskva (Moscow) 8,537,000
Other important cities with population:
Leningrad 4,800,000, Baku 1,660,000,
Kuybyshev 1,250,000
Language: Slavic (Russian, Ukrainian, Byelorussian, Polish), Altaic (Turkush, etc.) Other Indo-European, Uralian, Caucasian.
Religion: Orthodox, Moslem
Currency: Rubel = 100 kopek

The U.S.S.R. is a country that is almost a continent not only in size, but also in diversity. It covers 1/6 of the Earth's land area, and is larger than South America. 75% is traditionally considered to be part of Asia, but 75% of its people live in the European part. In comprises 120 different peoples, dominated by the Russians.

⑨ NETHERLANDS

Koninkrijk der Nederlanden
(Kingdom of the Netherlands)

Area: 16,042 sq.mi. (41,548 km²)
Population: 14,395,000
Population growth per annum: 0.6%
Life expectancy at birth: males 72 years, females 78 years
Literacy: 99%
Capital with population: Amsterdam 994,000
Other important cities with population:
Rotterdam 1,025,500, S-Gravenhage (The Hague) 672,000
Language: Dutch
Religion: Roman Catholic (40%), Protestant (35%)
Currency: Guilder = 100 cents

More than one third of the country lies below sea level. Some Dutch say that 'God created the world, except the Netherlands, which we had to create ourselves'. This task was begun in the 15th century, when they learned to reclaim their slowly sinking land from the encroaching sea. Independent APR 19, 1839.

⑩ FEDERAL REPUBLIC OF GERMANY

Bundesrepublik Deutschland

Area: 96,018 sq.mi. (248,687 km²)
Population: 61,420,000
Population growth per annum: − 0.3 %
Life expectancy at birth: males 69 years, females 75 years
Literacy: 99%
Capital with population: Bonn 293,000
Other important cities with population: Berlin 1,860,000, Hamburg 1,620,000, Munich 1,285,000
Language: German
Religion: Protestant (49%), Roman Catholic (45%)
Currency: D-mark = 100 pfennig

Like the mythical Phoenix, West Germany has miraculously sprung from the pyre of total defeat and destruction since 1945. In economic and industrial importance the western half of divided Germany now ranks fourth in the world. The Grand Tour must include the Rhine valley with its castles and vineyards. Independent SEP 6, 1949.

⑪ GERMAN DEMOCRATIC REPUBLIC

Deutsche Demokratische Republik

Area: 41,827 sq.mi. (108,333 km²)
Population: 16,700,000
Population growth per annum: 0%
Life expectancy at birth: males 69 years, females 75 years
Literacy: 99%
Capital with population: Berlin 1,185,000
Other important cities with population: Leipzig 560,000, Dresden 525,000, Karl-Marx-Stadt 320,000
Language: German
Religion: Protestant (80%)
Currency: Mark (of the GDR) = 100 pfennig

The republic is a divided nation with a divided capital. The fears and the rivalries of the victorious powers after World War II prevented the reestablishment of a German "Reich". Thus part of the old capital, Berlin, is now a West German enclave, by road and railway over 100 miles inside East Germany. Independent OCT 7, 1949.

⑫ POLAND

Polska Rzeczpospolita Ludowa
(Polish Peoples Republic)

Area: 120,727 sq.mi. (312,683 km²)
Population: 36,400,000
Population growth per annum: 1.0 %
Life expectancy at birth: males 67 years, females 75 years
Literacy: 98%
Capital with population: Warsaw 1,630,000
Other important cities with population: Łódź 850,000 Kraków 725,000
Language: Polish
Religion: Roman Catholic
Currency: Zloty = 100 groszy

The Polish people do not give up. Time and again conquering armies have swept over Poland and divided the spoils. After World War II the Soviet Union pushed the land westwards over former German land, annexing 1/3 of pre-war Poland in the east. Independent 966, NOV 10, 1918.

⑬ BELGIUM
Royaume de Belgique —
Koninkrijk België
(Kingdom of Belgium)

Area: 11,783 sq.mi.(30,519 km²)
Population: 9,850 000
Population growth per annum: 0.1%
Life expectancy at birth: males 69 years, females 75 years
Literacy: 98%
Capital with population: Bruxelles (Brussels) 980,000
Other important cities with population:
Antwerpen 490,000, Gent 240,000
Language: Flemish (Dutch), French, German
Religion: Roman Catholic
Currency: Belgian franc = 100 centimes

*The country at "the crossroads of Western Europe" is
dominated by the capital Brussels. Brussels is also the capital of
the E.E.C. The difficulties in uniting Europe are mirrored in the
Belgian nation. The Dutch-speaking Flemings and French-
speaking Walloons stick together against others, but often
quarrel amongst themselves. Independent OCT 4, 1830.*

⑭ LUXEMBOURG
Grand-Duché Luxembourg
(Grand Duchy of Luxembourg)

Area: 998 sq.mi. (2,586 km²)
Population: 366,000
Population growth per annum: —0.04%
Life expectancy at birth: males 68 years, females 75 years
Literacy: 100%
Capital with population: Luxembourg 79,000
Other important cities with population: none
Language: Luxemburgish, French, German
Religion: Roman Catholic (94%)
Currency: Luxembourg franc = 100 centimes

*Historically Luxembourg has always had strong ties with one or
another of its neighbors while maintaining independence in
form if not in fact. It also formed some sort of a nucleus for the
Coal and Steel Union that evolved into the E.E.C. Indep. 1866.*

⑮ CZECHOSLOVAKIA
Československá Socialistická
Republika
(Czechoslovak Socialist Republic)

Area: 49,370 sq.mi. (127,869 km²)
Population: 15,400 000
Population growth per annum: 0.7%
Life expectancy at birth: males 67 years, females 74 years
Literacy: 99%
Capital with population: Praha (Prague) 1,185,000
Other important cities with population: Bratislava 395,000,
Brno 380,000
Language: Czech, Slovak
Religion: Roman Catholic (55%), Protestant (10%)
Currency: Koruna = 100 haléřu

*Haseks fictionary "Good soldier Schweik" in many ways
epitomizes the survival instincts of his fellow citizens. Both
Czechs and Slovaks have always striven for freedom, but
throughout the centuries have been forced to bow to foreign
rule. Mining and manufacturing have a long history in
Czechoslovakia. Independent OCT 28, 1918.*

⑯ HUNGARY
Magyar Népköztársaság
(Hungarian People's Republic)

Area: 35,920 sq.mi. (93,032 km²)
Population: 10,680,000
Population growth per annum: 0.4%
Life expectancy at birth: males 67 years, females 73 years
Literacy: 98%
Capital with population: Budapest 2,064,000
Other important cities with population:
Debrecen 205,000, Miskolc 212,000
Language: Hungarian (Magyar)
Religion: Roman Catholic (65%), Protestant (25%)
Currency: Forint = 100 fillèr

*Hungary is in many ways an enclave in Eastern Europe — a
Finno-Ugric nation surrounded by Slav neighbors, a land of
plains, the famous puszta, and rolling hills, encircled by higher
mountain lands — and, within limits, more prosperous and
"capitalistic" than the other Soviet satellites. Independent 1001.*

⑰ FRANCE
République Française
(French Republic)

Area: 211,208 sq.mi. (547,026 km²)
Population: 54,539,000
Population growth per annum: 0.3%
Life expectancy at birth: males 70 years, females 78 years
Literacy: 99%
Capital with population: Paris 2,320,000
(Greater Paris 8,550,000)
Other important cities with population: Marseille 915,000,
Lyon 465,000
Language: French
Religion: Roman Catholic (90%) Islam (4%)
Currency: French franc = 100 centimes

*France is one of the great powers of the world. The French
language is still the language of diplomacy. France is culturally
the world's leading nation, and most former French colonies remain members of the French Commonwealth. France is also the
leading European nation on the space frontier. National day:
JULY 14, (1789)*

⑱ SWITZERLAND
Schweiz - Suisse - Svizzera
(Swiss Confederation)

Area: 15,943 sq.mi. (41,293 km²)
Population: 6,400,000
Population growth per annum: 0.2 %
Life expectancy at birth: males 72 years, females 78 years
Literacy: 99%
Capital with population: Bern 144,000
Other important cities with population: Zürich 363,000,
Basel 180,000
Language: German, French, Italian, Romansch
Religion: Roman Catholic (49%), Protestant (48%)
Currency: Swiss franc = 100 centimes (rappen)

*The Financial Pole of the world is claimed to be situated in
some undefined spot in Zürich. Through centuries of neutrality
and economic stability, Switzerland has grown into a global
center of banking. Besides quality watches, tourism somehow
seems to have been invented in this land of few natural
resources. Independent AUG 1, 1291.*

⑲ LIECHTENSTEIN
Fürstentum Liechtenstein
(Principality of Liechtenstein)

Area: 62 sq.mi. (160 km²)
Population: 27,000
Population growth per annum: 7.0%
Life expectancy at birth: not available
Literacy: 100 %
Capital with population: Vaduz 5,000
Other important cities with population: none
Language: German
Religion: Roman Catholic
Currency: Swiss franc = 100 centimes

Liechtenstein epitomizes the notion "postage stamp state" — because of its size and its fame among collectors of stamps. It is also an anomaly, surviving from the times when Europe was divided among many princes and kings, before their realms were united into nations. Indep. MAY 3, 1342.

⑳ AUSTRIA
Republik Österreich
(Republic of Austria)

Area: 32,376 sq.mi. (83,855 km²)
Population: 7,550,000
Population growth per annum: —0.1%
Life expectancy at birth: males 68 years, females 75 years
Literacy: 98%
Capital with population: Wien (Vienna) 1,530,000
Other important cities with population: Graz 243,000, Linz 200,000
Language: German
Religion: Roman Catholic (89%), Protestant (6%)
Currency: Schilling = 100 groschen

Austria is the only state pledged both by law and treaties to neutrality. Vienna, for centuries the capital of the "Holy Roman Empire", the seat of the Hapsburg Emperors, still bears the imprint of bygone greatness, and remains the cultural capital of Central Europe. Indep. 1276, 1804, 1918, APR 27, 1945.

㉑ MONACO
Principauté de Monaco
(Principality of Monaco)

Area: 0,76 sq.mi. (1,95 km²)
Population: 27,000
Population growth per annum: —3.0%
Life expectancy at birth: males 70 years, females 78 years
Literacy: 99%
Capital with population: Monaco-Ville 1,700
Other important cities with population: none
Language: French, Monegasque
Religion: Roman Catholic
Currency: French-or Monegasque franc = 100 centimes

Monaco proves that gambling can pay, provided you run the bank! The Monte Carlo Casino has been the Mecca of gamblers since 1858 and also made Monaco a fashionable tourist resort. The citizens of microscopic Monaco do not pay income tax. Independent 1297.

㉒ ITALY
Repubblica Italiana
(Italian Republic)

Area: 116,320 sq.mi. (301,268 km²)
Population: 56,930,000
Population growth per annum: 0.4%
Life expectancy at birth: males 70 years, females 76 years
Literacy: 98%
Capital with population: Roma (Rome) 2,830,000
Other important cities with population: Milano 1,500,000, Napoli 1,200,000
Language: Italian
Religion: Roman Catholic
Currency: Lira = 100 centesimi

All roads lead to Rome, still the Eternal City — the city of the Pope, of the Sistine Chapel, of the Colosseum and innumerable monuments of Imperial Rome. But Italy is also the land of Saint Francis and Leonardo, of Pisa, Venice and Florence — and to-day of Milan, Torino and Cortina d'Ampezzo. Independent FEB 18, 1861.

㉓ YUGOSLAVIA
Socijalistička Federativna Republika Jugoslavija
(Socialist Federal Republ. of Yogoslavia)

Area: 98,766 sq.mi. (255,804 km²)
Population: 22,850,000
Population growth per annum: 0.9%
Life expectancy at birth: males 67 years, females 72 years
Literacy: 85%
Capital with population: Belgrade 1,407,000
Other important cities with population: Zagreb 1,175,000, Skopje 507,000, Ljubljana 305,000
Language: Serbo-Croatian, Macedonian, Slovenian, Albanian
Religion: Orthodox (41%), Roman Catholic (32%), Moslem (12%)
Currency: Yugoslavian dinar = 100 para

Few would in 1918 have placed any money on the survival of any country in the Balkan Peninsula and least of them all Yugoslavia with its mosaic of quarrelling religions — three — and combative peoples — five — speaking four different languages. Independent DEC 1, 1918.

㉔ ROMANIA
Republica Socialistă România
(Socialist Republic of Romania)

Area: 91,700 sq.mi. (237,500 km²)
Population: 22,600,000
Population growth per annum: 0.9%
Life expectancy at birth: males 68 years, females 73 years
Literacy: 98%
Capital with population: Bucuresti (Bucharest) 1,835,000
Other important cities with population: Constanța 285,000, Cluj-Napoca 271,000
Language: Romanian
Religion: Orthodox (70%), Roman Catholic (14%)
Currency: Leu = 100 bani

A land that is still Roman after almost two thousand years! Rome settled fertile Dacia and made an everlasting imprint. In spite of that, the frontier province was lost less than two centuries after conquest. The people today speak a language based on Latin. Transylvania is known for fictitious Count Dracula. Independent 1877.

㉕ PORTUGAL
República Portuguesa
(Republic of Portugal)

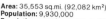

Area: 35,553 sq.mi. (92,082 km²)
Population: 9,930,000
Population growth per annum: 0.9%
Life expectancy at birth: males 66 years, females 74 years
Literacy: 80%
Capital with population: Lisboa (Lisbon) 818,000
Other important cities with population: Porto 330,000
Language: Portuguese
Religion: Roman Catholic
Currency: Escudo = 100 centavos

In spite of its small size, Portugal managed to become one of the world's great powers, and to acquire and retain a global empire for half a millennium. Portugal produces famous wines, such as madeira and port (from Oporto), and every second wine bottle in the world is sealed with Portuguese cork.

㉖ SPAIN
España
(Kingdom of Spain)

Area: 194,897 sq.mi. (504,782 km²)
Population: 38,220,000
Population growth per annum: 1.0 %
Life expectancy at birth: males 70 years, females 76 years
Literacy: 97%
Capital with population: Madrid 3,188,000
Other important cities with population:
  Barcelona 1,755,000, Seville 654,000,
  Zaragoza 600,000
Language: Spanish, Catalan, Basque
Religion: Roman Catholic
Currency: Spanish peseta = 100 céntimos

Proud Spain, once one of the world's great powers that sent the Great Armada to England in a bid to become master of the oceans, is today still the cultural leader in the Iberic World. It gave the world people such as Cervantes, Loyola, Goya, and Picasso.

㉗ ANDORRA
Principat d'Andorra
(Principality of Andorra)

Area: 175 sq.mi. (453 km²)
Population: 41,600
Population growth per annum: not available
Life expectancy at birth: males 70 years, females 76 years
Literacy: 100%
Capital with population: Andorra la Vella 10,500
Other important cities with population: none
Language: Catalan
Religion: Roman Catholic
Currency: French franc, Spanish peseta

Conducting trade between Spain and France is and has been the main business of this Pyrenean principality, jointly ruled by the Spanish Bishop of Urgel and the Head of State of France. Outside Andorra some call it smuggling. Tourism also benefits from the absence of customs duties. Independent 1278.

㉘ SAN MARINO
Repubblica di San Marino
(Republic of San Marino)

Area: 24 sq.mi. (61 km²)
Population: 22,000
Population growth per annum: not available
Life expectancy at birth: not available
Literacy: not available
Capital with population: San Marino 5,000
Other important cities with population: none
Language: Italian
Religion: Roman Catholic
Currency: Italian lira = 100 centesimi

The only surviving city state of medieval Italy, San Marino is still governed by two Capitani Reggenti, democratically elected for a period of only six months. Sale of postage stamps was an important industry, but is now dwarfed by the tourist trade. Over 3.5 million visit San Marino each year. Independent 1263.

㉙ VATICAN STATE
Stato della Citta del Vaticano

Area: 0,17 sq.mi. (0,44 km²)
Population: 1,000
Population growth per annum: —
Life expectancy at birth: —
Literacy: —
Capital with population: —
Other important cities with population: —
Language: Italian
Religion: Roman Catholic
Currency: Vatican City lira, Italian lira = 100 centesimi

The spiritual importance of the Pope is inversely proportionate to the size of his worldly domains, the world's smallest state. Relative to its size it certainly contains greater treasures of art than any other state in the world, such as the Sistine Chapel and the Pietà. Independent FEB 11, 1929.

㉚ ALBANIA
(People's Socialist
Republic of Albania)

Area: 11,100 sq. mi. (28,748 km²)
Population: 2,850 000
Population growth per annum: 2.4%
Life expectancy at birth: males 68 years, females 71 years
Literacy: 75%
Capital with population: Tirana 198,000
Other important cities with population: Shkodra 63,000
Language: Albanian
Religion: Religions are not allowed since 1967
Currency: Lek = 100 qindarka

A desire for self-sufficiency has turned Albania into a virtually unknown "white spot" on the map. This nation is Europe's only Moslem country, but has declared itself "the world's first atheist state". It is so dogmatically communist, that it has broken all ties with other communist countries. Independent NOV 11,1912.

㉛ BULGARIA
Narodna Republika Bulgarija
(Peoples Republic of Bulgaria)

Area: 42,823 sq. mi. (110,912 km²)
Population: 8,930,000
Population growth per annum: 0.6%
Life expectancy at birth: males 69 years, females 75 years
Literacy: 95%
Capital with population: Sofiya 1,080,000
Other important cities with population: Plovid 310,000,
Varna 260,000
Language: Bulgarian
Religion: Orthodox (85%), Moslem (13%)
Currency: Lev = 100 stótinki

*The Bulgarians do not forget that Russia helped to liberate their
country from Turkish rule that lasted for over five centuries. Today it is counted among the most loyal allies of the Soviet Union.
Europe's "vegetable and fruit garden" is also the tourist "Riviera"
of Eastern Europe. Independent SEPT 22, 1908.*

㉜ TURKEY
Türkiye Cumhuriyeti
(Republic of Turkey)

Area: 300,946 sq.mi. (779,452 km²)
Population: 48,000,000
Population growth per annum: 2.5%
Life expectancy at birth: males 58 years, females 63 years
Literacy: 70%
Capital with population: Ankara 1,877,000
Other important cities with population: Istanbul 2,773,000,
Izmir 758,000,
Language: Turkish
Religion: Moslem
Currency: Turkish lira = 100 kuruş

*The land that for centuries served as a link between Europe and
Asia now also provides the two continents with a physical link,
the huge bridge over the Bosporus. The world famous cathedral
of Hagia Sofia, built by emperor Justinian 532-537, was turned
into a mosque after the fall of Constantinople in 1453.*

㉝ MALTA
Repubblika Ta'Malta
(Republic of Malta)

Area: 122 sq.mi. (316 km²)
Population: 330,000
Population growth per annum: 0.9%
Life expectancy at birth: males 69 years, females 73 years
Literacy: 83%
Capital with population: Valletta 14,000
Other important cities with population: none
Language: Maltese, English
Religion: Roman Catholic
Currency: Lira Maltija (Maltese Lira) = 100 cents = 1000 mils

*For unprecedented valor during World War II the people of
Malta were collectively awarded the George Cross, Britain's
highest civilian decoration. Malta still proudly carries the cross
in its national flag. From 1530 to 1798 Malta was ruled by the
Knights Hospitallers — since known as the Knights of Malta.
Independent SEP 21, 1964.*

㉞ GREECE
Elliniki Dimokratia
(Hellenic Republic)

Area: 50,944 sq.mi. (131,944 km²)
Population: 9,750,000
Population growth per annum: 0.6%
Life expectancy at birth: males 71 years, females 75 years
Literacy: 95%
Capital with population: Athinai (Athens) 900,000
(Greater Athens 3,000,000)
Other important cities with population:
Thessaloniki 400,000, Pátrai 140,000
Language: Greek
Religion: Greek Orthodox (97%)
Currency: Drachma = 100 lepta

*The cradle of European civilization is now a member of the
E.E.C. and thus takes an active part in shaping the Europe of the
future. Greece may well have the world's largest merchant fleet
— even if few sail under Greek flag. Venerable Parthenon, temple of Pallas Athena, still crowns Athen's Acropolis.
Independent FEB 3, 1830.*

㉟ CYPRUS
Kypriaki Dimokratia —
Kibris Cumhuriyeti
(Republic of Cyprus)

Area: 3,572 sq.mi. (9,251 km²)
Population: 655,000
Population growth per annum: 0.4%
Life expectancy at birth: males 70 years, females 74 years
Literacy: 89%
Capital with population: Nicosia 161,000
Other important cities with population: Limassol 107,000,
Famagusta 40,000
Language: Greek, Turkish
Religion: Orthodox (77%)
Currency: Cyprus pound = 100 cents

*The very name of the metal copper is derived from the island's
original name, Kypros, as it in ancient times was the world's
leading producer of copper. The Greek goddess of love,
Aphrodite, was said to have been born here out of the surf. Actually Cyprus itself is a child of the sea, a part of former deep
ocean crust lifted high above sea level. Indep. AUG 16, 1960.*

ASIA

Area: 17,179,000 sq.mi. 44,493,000 km²)
Population: 2,349,048,000
Density of population per sq.mi.: 137

The Asian mainland's northernmost point is Cape Chelyuskin at 77° 44' N. latitude.

Lowest surface temperature in the northern hemisphere, −97.6° F., was recorded at Oymyakon.

Northeastern Siberia has the most extreme continental climate in the world. The variation between the warmest month of Summer (average temperature of up to 62.6° F.) and the coldest month of Winter (below −58° F.) is greater than anywhere else. Winter here is colder than in any other populated spot.

The coniferous forests of Siberia, the Taiga, are the most extensive in the world. The widestretched lowlands rank second after those of the Amazon Basin.

There is no clear, natural boundary between Asia and Europe which together form the Eurasian mainland. The boundary is usually drawn along the crest of the Ural Mountains then follows the Ural River to the Caspian Sea then to the Black Sea via the Manych Depression and the Sea of Azov.

① **UNION OF SOVIET SOCIALIST REPUBLICS**

The Ob drainage system of 1.2 million sq.mi. is the largest in Asia.

The deepest lake in the world is Lake Baykal, 6.365 ft.

Baba Burun at 26° 3' E. longitude is the Asian mainland's westernmost cape.

The Caspian Sea 143,240 sq.mi. is the largest lake in the world.

The deserts and steppes of Central Asia are the most extensive area of inland drainage in the world. They cover about a third of the continent.

② **MONGOLIA**

TURKEY ⑤

⑥ **LEBANON** ⑦
⑬ **ISRAEL** **SYRIA**
⑭ **JORDAN**
Asia's highest surface temperature, 122°F., has been recorded at Baghdad.

The Fedchenko Glacier is Asia's largest, 520 sq.mi.

The earth's largest variety of grass — bamboo can reach up to 130 ft length and up to a foot thickness in China.

Asia's and the world's deepest depression is the Dead Sea in the Jordan Valley. − 1,319 ft.

⑧ **IRAQ** ⑨ **IRAN**
⑮ **KUWAIT**

Tibet is the Roof of the World, 800,000 sq.mi. above 13,000 ft. altitude.

C H I N A
⑪

AFGHANISTAN ⑩

The Arabian Peninsula is the world's largest and extends over 965,000 sq.mi. (larger than Greenland).

⑱ **BAHRAIN**
⑲ **QATAR** ⑳
UNITED ARAB EMIRATES

PAKISTAN ⑯

Mount Everest (Qomolangma Feng) is the world's highest mountain, 29,030 ft.

NEPAL ㉕ ㉖ **BHUTAN**

The world's heaviest rainfall, 1,042 inches, was recorded at Cherrapunji in 1860-61.

SAUDI ARABIA ⑰

㉑ **YEMEN** **SOUTH YEMEN** ㉒ ㉓ **OMAN**

Himalaya is the world's highest mountain range with nine of the world's ten highest peaks and altogether fourteen reaching above 26,200 ft.

BANGLA-DESH ㉗ ㉘ **BURMA** ㉚ **LAOS**

INDIA ㉔

THAILAND ㉙

VIETNAM ㉛

KAMPUCHEA ㉟

In Summer the eastbound Southwest Monsoon Current replaces the westerly North Equatorial Current in the Indian Ocean, just as the South West Monsoon replaces the Northeast Trade Winds.

㉞ **SRI LANKA**

㉝ **MALDIVES**

Cape Buru at 1° 25'N. latitude is the southernmost point of the Asian mainland.

MALAYSIA ㊲

BR

SINGAPORE ㊳

114

Cape Dezhneva at 169° 45′ E. longitude is the most easterly point on the Asian mainland.

The world's lowest temperature, —88.3° C., was recorded in Antarctica in 1960.

Klyuchevskaya Sopka, 15.584 ft., is Asia's highest active volcano. The most recent eruption was in 1962.

The northern part of the Sea of Okhotsk is frozen over in February and March

The Sikhote-Alin Range was bombarded in 1947 by the greatest swarm of meteorites known to humankind, over 10,000 meteorites weighing together some 100 tons.

JAPAN

⑫ On the average Tokyo is shaken by an earthquake every week.

⌐RTH ⌐REA

⌐UTH ⌐REA ④

ongest river in Asia ⌐urth longest in the , is the Yangtze, ⌐0 miles.

The East Asian seas are hit by more than twenty typhoons (tropical storms) during the period September-November every year, the earth's most severely hit region.

⌐WAN

㊱ PHILIPPINES

Borneo, 285,000 sq.mi., is Asia's largest island and ranks third in the world.

⌐NESIA

⑩	AFGHANISTAN
⑱	BAHRAIN
㉗	BANGLADESH
㉖	BHUTAN
㊴	BRUNEI
㉘	BURMA
⑪	CHINA
㉔	INDIA
㊵	INDONESIA
⑨	IRAN
⑧	IRAQ
⑬	ISRAEL
⑫	JAPAN
⑭	JORDAN
㉟	KAMPUCHEA
⑮	KUWAIT
㉚	LAOS
⑥	LEBANON
㊲	MALAYSIA
㉝	MALDIVES
②	MONGOLIA
㉕	NEPAL
③	NORTH KOREA
㉓	OMAN
⑯	PAKISTAN
㊱	PHILIPPINES
⑲	QATAR
⑰	SAUDI ARABIA
㊳	SINGAPORE
④	SOUTH KOREA
㉒	SOUTH YEMEN
㉞	SRI LANKA
⑦	SYRIA
㉙	THAILAND
㉜	TAIWAN
⑤	TURKEY
①	UNION OF SOVIET SOCIALIST REPUBLICS
⑳	UNITED ARAB EMIRATES
㉛	VIETNAM
㉑	YEMEN

① UNION OF SOVIET SOCIALIST REPUBLICS
Soyuz Sovyetskikh Sotsialisticheskikh Respublik

Area: 8,649,500 sq.mi. (22,402,200 km²)
Population: 276,300,000
Population growth per annum: 0.9%
Life expectancy at birth: males 65 years, females 74 years
Literacy: 99%
Capital with population: Moskva (Moscow) 8,537,000
Other important cities with population:
Leningrad 4,800,000, Baku 1,660,000,
Kuybyshev 1,250,000
Language: Slavic (Russian, Ukrainian, Byelorussian, Polish), Uralian, Caucasian
Religion: Orthodox, Moslem
Currency: Rubel = 100 kopek

The U.S.S.R. is a country that is almost a continent not only in size, but also in diversity. It covers 1/6 of the Earth's land area, and is larger than South America. 75% is traditionally considered to be part of Asia, but 75% of its people live in the European part. It comprises 120 different peoples, dominated by the Russians.

② MONGOLIA
Bugd Nayramdakh Mongol Ard Uls
(Mongolian People's Republic)

Area: 604,000 sq.mi. (1,565,000 km²)
Population: 1,820,000
Population growth per annum: 2.9%
Life expectancy at birth: males 61 years, females 65 years
Literacy: 80%
Capital with population: Ulaanbaatar (Ulan Bator) 400,000
Other important cities with population: Darkhan 52,000
Language: Mongol, Russian, Chinese
Religion: Buddhist
Currency: Tugrik = 100 möngö

The home of Genghis Khan is now as then a land of unbroken horizons where trees are as rare as people on the windswept grasslands. The Mongols have now exchanged their horses for motor bikes, and so only disappear faster out of view. One third of Mongolia is part of the mighty Gobi Desert. Independent JAN 5, 1946.

③ NORTH KOREA
Chosun Minchu-chui Inmin
Konghwa-guk
(Democratic People's Republic of Korea)

Area: 47,142 sq.mi. (122,098 km²)
Population: 18,490,000
Population growth per annum: 3.2%
Life expectancy at birth: males 70 years, females 78 years
Literacy: 85%
Capital with population: P'yŏngyang 1,280,000
Other important cities with population: Hamhŭng 420,000,
Ch'ŏngjin 265,000
Language: Korean
Religion: Buddhist (activities discouraged)
Currency: Won = 100 chon

Korea is a victim of the 20th century. During the scramble for colonies it was annexed by Japan, and after the Japanese capitulation in 1945 it was divided into two zones of occupation by the U.S.A. and the U.S.S.R. along 38° N lat. The cold war began here and grew into a real war in 1950-53. Korea remains divided. Independent SEP 9, 1948.

④ SOUTH KOREA
Han Kook
(Republic of Korea)

Area: 38,221 sq.mi. (98,992 km²)
Population: 39,950,000
Population growth per annum: 1.6%
Life expectancy at birth: 68 years
Literacy: 92%
Capital with population: Sŏul (Seoul) 8,367,000
Other important cities with population: Pusan 3,160,000,
Taegu 1,607,000
Language: Korean
Religion: Buddhist, Confucianist, Christian
Currency: Won = 100 chon

In the shadow of China, the Korean people have managed to maintain a national identity — and true independence during most of their history — and also to achieve great cultural feats of their own. Here books were being printed as early as a thousand years ago. Independent AUG 15, 1948.

⑤ TURKEY
Türkiye Cumhuriyeti
(Republic of Turkey)

Area: 300,946 sq.mi. (779,452 km²)
Population: 48,000,000
Population growth per annum: 2.5%
Life expectancy at birth: males 58 years, females 63 years
Literacy: 70%
Capital with population: Ankara 1,877,000
Other important cities with population: İstanbul 2,773,000,
İzmir 758,000
Language: Turkish
Religion: Moslem
Currency: Turkish lira = 100 kuruş

The land that for centuries served as a link between Europe and Asia now also provides the two continents with a physical link, the huge bridge over the Bosporus. The world famous cathedral of Hagia Sofia, built by emperor Justinian 532-537, was turned into a mosque after the fall of Constantinople in 1453.

⑥ LEBANON
Al-Jumhouriya al-Lubnaniya
(Republic of Lebanon)

Area: 4,036 sq.mi. (10,452 km²)
Population: 3,500,000
Population growth per annum: 0.8%
Life expectancy at birth: males 63 years, females 67 years
Literacy: 75%
Capital with population: Bayrut (Beirūt) 702,000
Other important cities with population:
Tarābulus (Tripoli) 175,000
Language: Arabic
Religion: Moslem (50%), Christian (50%)
Currency: Lebanese pound = 100 piastres

Since Phoenician times international trade has been the blood of life here at the crossroads of the Levant, populated by fiercely proud clans from all over the Middle East. The lone cedar tree on the flag is almost the last remnant of the mighty forests that once covered Mt. Lebanon. Independent JAN 1, 1944.

⑦ SYRIA

Al-Jamhouriya al Arabia as-Souriya
(Syrian Arab Republic)

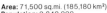

Area: 71,500 sq.mi. (185,180 km²)
Population: 9,840,000
Population growth per annum: 3.8%
Life expectancy at birth: males 63 years, females 66 years
Literacy: 65%
Capital with population: Dimashq (Damascus) 1,251,000
Other important cities with population:
  Halab (Aleppo) 1,525,000 Hims (Homs) 630,000
Language: Arabic
Religion: Moslem (88%), Christian
Currency: Syrian pound = 100 piaster

Long before Rome was founded all caravan trails and trade routes "of the world" converged on the capital of Syria, Damascus. Herod, St. Paul and Ibn Battuta as well as Alexander the Great, Julius Caesar and Genghis Khan have all passed through Damascus. Independent JAN 1, 1944.

⑧ IRAQ

Al Jumhouriya al 'Iraqia
(Republic of Iraq)

Area: 167,925 sq.mi. (434,924 km²)
Population: 14,000,000
Population growth per annum: 3.4%
Life expectancy at birth: males 54 years, females 57 years
Literacy: 70%
Capital with population: Baghdad 3,200,000
Other important cities with population: Al Başrah 400,000,
  Al Mawşil (Mosul) 350,000
Language: Arabic, Kurdish
Religion: Moslem (95%)
Currency: Iraqi dinar = 20 dirham = 1000 fils

The ancient "Land Between the Rivers", Mesopotamia, is today known as Iraq. The name is said to be derived from a word meaning "origin", a very apt name. Here the wheel and the plow were invented. Here the oldest maps and written records have been found as well as the oldest Codes of Law. Independent 1932.

⑨ IRAN

Jomhori-e-Islami-e-Irân
(Islamic Republic of Iran)

Area: 636,000 sq.mi. (1,648,000 km²)
Population: 43,830,000
Population growth per annum: 3.0%
Life expectancy at birth: males 53 years, females 54 years
Literacy: 48%
Capital with population: Tehrân 4,500,000
Other important cities with population: Esfahân 700,000,
  Mashhad 700,000
Language: Farsi (persian), Turkic languages, Kurdish
Religion: Shiá Moslems (93%)
Currency: Rial = 100 dinars

Through millennia Iran, previously called Persia, has influenced the history and culture of all people. Iran has nurtured Cyrus, Darius and Xerxes, Zoroaster, Firdawsi and Omar Khayyam — and ayatollah Khomeini. Iranians invented polo and developed chess.

⑩ AFGHANISTAN

De Afghanistan Democrateek
Jamhuriat
(Democratic Republic of Afganistan)

Area: 250,000 sq.mi. (647,497 km²)
Population: 17,500,000 (of which 23% are refugees outside
  the country)
Population growth per annum: 2.5%
Life expectancy at birth: males 40 years, females 41 years
Literacy: 10%
Capital with population: Kabul 900,000
Other important cities with population: Kandahar 180,000
  Herat 140,000
Language: Pushtu, Dari (Persian)
Religion: Islam (90% Sunni Moslems)
Currency: Afghani = 100 puls

The crossroads of Asia — and once more, a theater of war. Throughout history, conquering armies have marched through the green valleys beneath Afghanistan's forbidding mountains, but no one has ever been able to subjugate its warlike tribes, so fiercely independent, that they were not even united into an emirate before 1747. Independent 1747.

⑪ CHINA

(Peoples Republic of China)

Area: 3,692,000 sq.mi. (9,561,000 km²)
Population: 1,008,175,000
Population growth per annum: 1.4%
Life expectancy at birth: males 62 years, females 69 years
Literacy: 75%
Capital with population: Beijing (Peking) 5,550,000
Other important cities with population: Shanghai
  6,300,000, Tianjin 5,200,000, Shenyang 4,000,000
Language: Mandarin Chinese, Shanghai-, Canton-, Fukien-,
  Hakka- dialects, Tibetan, Vigus (Turkic)
Religion: Officially atheist, Confucianist, Buddhist, Taoist.
Currency: Yuan = 10 jiap = 100 fen

The length of the historical records of China are paralleled only by the Great Wall one of the greatest human-made structures (2,500 miles). China is the world's most populous nation and will without doubt be one of the superpowers of the future. Independent OCT 1, 1949.

⑫ JAPAN

Nippon (or Nihon)

Area: 145,855 sq.mi. (377,765 km²)
Population: 119,500,000
Population growth per annum: 0.9%
Life expectancy at birth: males 73 years, females 78 years
Literacy: 99%
Capital with population: Tôkyô 8,150,000
Other important cities with population:
  Yokohama 2,870,000 Nagoya 2,060,000,
  Kyôto 1,460,000
Language: Japanese
Religion: Buddhist, Shinto, Roman Catholic
Currency: Yen = 100 sen

Japan has learned to live with earthquakes. Minor tremors are registered more than twice a day, and on average the earth here trembles perceptibly once a week. Only a few cause damage to buildings, as houses here are either very light structures or built to resist even severe shocks.

⑬ ISRAEL
Medinat Israel — State of Israel

Area: 8,019 sq.mi. (20,770 km²)
Population: 4,150,000
Population growth per annum: 2.6%
Life expectancy at birth: males 71 years, females 73 years
Literacy: 88%
Capital with population: Yerushalayim (Jerusalem) 430,000
Other important cities with population:
   Tel Aviv-Yafo 330,000, Hefa (Haifa) 226,000
Language: Hebrew, Arabic
Religion: Judaism (85%), Moslem (11%)
Currency: Shekel = 100 agorot

The unprecedented rebirth of a land and a language after almost two thousand years must be considered a miracle. This fulfillment of ancient prophecies is due to the tenacity and spirit of the Jewish people. A majority of humankind considers Jerusalem holy. Independent MAY 14, 1948.

⑭ JORDAN
Al Mamlaka al Urduniya al Hashemiyah
(The Hashemite Kingdom of Jordan)

Area: 37,740 sq.mi. (incl. 2,270 sq.mi. on the West Bank)
   (97,740 km², incl. 5,880 km² on the West Bank)
Population: 3,500,000
Population growth per annum: 3.7%
Life expectancy at birth: males 58 years, females 62 years
Literacy: 58%
Capital with population: 'Ammän 1,230,000
Other important cities with population: Az Zarqä 270,000,
   Irbid 140,000
Language: Arabic
Religion: Moslem (80% Sunni Moslems)
Currency: Jordan dinar = 1000 fils

Once the rulers of the arid lands east of River Jordan controlled the trade routes across the desert, and accumulated wealth from the incense trade, as can be seen from the glory of the rose-red ruins of Petra. Independent MAR 22, 1946.

⑮ KUWAIT
Dowlat al Kuwait
(State of Kuwait)

Area: 6,880 sq.mi. (17,818 km²)
Population: 1,910,000
Population growth per annum: 6.0%
Life expectancy at birth: males 67 years, females 72 years
Literacy: 71%
Capital with population: Al Kuwayt (Kuwait) 280,000
Other important cities with population: none
Language: Arabic
Religion: Moslem (70% Sunni Moslems)
Currency: Kuwait dinar = 1000 fils

The name Kuwait today associates with oil and wealth. Once sturdy dhows sailing to far away African and East Indian ports brought renown to Kuwait. The real Sindbad the Sailor may have lived here. Independent JUN 19, 1961.

⑯ PAKISTAN
(Islamic Republic of Pakistan)

Area: 342,759 sq.mi. (887,747 km²)
Population: 89,000,000
Population growth per annum: 2.8%
Life expectancy at birth: males 52 years, females 50 years
Literacy: 23%
Capital with population: Islamabad 201,000
Other important cities with population: Karachi 5,103,000,
   Lahore 2,920,000, Faisalabad 1,092,000
Language: Urdu, Punjabi
Religion: Moslem (Sunni Moslems)
Currency: Pakistani rupie = 100 paisa

By peaceful agreement, but through tumultuous upheaval, the Islamic nation of Pakistan was created out of parts of former British India. Until 1971 it also comprised Bangladesh, 1,250 mi. away, then known as East Pakistan. Independent AUG 14, 1947.

⑰ SAUDI ARABIA
Al-Mamlaka-al- 'Arabiya as-Sa'udiya
(Kingdom of Saudi Arabia)

Area: 829,995 sq.mi. (2,149,690 km²)
Population: 8,400,000
Population growth per annum: 4.2%
Life expectancy at birth: males 52 years, females 55 years
Literacy: 15%
Capital with population: Ar Riyad (Riyadh) 670,000
Other important cities with population: Jiddah 561,000,
   Makkah (Mecca) 370,000
Language: Arabic
Religion: Moslem
Currency: Rial = 100 halalas

Like the genie released from Aladdin's oil lamp, the wealth of oil released from the rocks of the desert have brought fabulous palaces and gardens to its owners. Modern cities, industries, universities and highways have been created overnight. Independent SEP 20, 1932.

⑱ BAHRAIN
Mashyaka al Bahrayn
(State of Bahrain)

Area: 240 sq.mi. (622 km²)
Population: 380,000
Population growth per annum: 2.8%
Life expectancy at birth: males 64 years, females 68 years
Literacy: 40%
Capital with population: Al Manämah 122,000
Other important cities with population: Al Muharraq 62,000
Language: Arabic
Religion: Islam (Sunni Moslems)
Currency: Bahrain dinar = 100 fils

The popular joke, that Bahrain gas stations should give free fuel to every buyer of water for coolant, is of course not true. It reflects the lack of water that troubles oil-rich Bahrain. It will be solved by a pipeline following the giant causeway to the mainland. Independent AUG 15, 1971.

⑲ QATAR
Dawlat Qatar
(State of Qatar)

Area: 4,416 sq.mi. (11,437 km²)
Population: 260 000
Population growth per annum: 6.5%
Life expectancy at birth: males 55 years, females 58 years
Literacy: 40%
Capital with population: Ad Dawhah 190,000
Other important cities with population: none
Language: Arabic
Religion: Moslem
Currency: Riyal = 100 dirham

A black underground sea of oil has become the source of wealth to Qatar, instead of the Gulf's warm blue waters and its pearl oysters. Independent SEP 1, 1971.

⑳ UNITED ARAB EMIRATES
Al Imarat al Arabiya al Muttahida

Area: 35,560 sq.mi. (92,100 km²)
Population: 1,175,000
Population growth per annum: 7.3%
Life expectancy at birth: males 60 years, females 64 years
Literacy: 53%
Capital with population: Abū Ẓaby (Abu Dhabi) 240,000
Other important cities with population: Dubayy 278,000
Language: Arabic
Religion: Islam
Currency: UAE dirham = 100 fils

Pearl-fishing and clandestine trade (by some called smuggling) sustained the people on the Trucial Coast after the more lucrative slave trade was abolished by the Perpetual Maritime Truce Treaty, signed by Great Britain and the seven sheiks 1853. Oil has now brought prosperity. Independent DEC 2, 1971.

㉑ YEMEN
Al Jamhuriyah al Arabiya al Yamaniya
(Yemen Arab Republic)

Area: 75,300 sq.mi. (195,000 km²)
Population: 7,160,000
Population growth per annum: 2.3%
Life expectancy at birth: males 37 years, females 39 years
Literacy: 12%
Capital with population: Sanʿa 278,000
Other important cities with population: Hodeida 130,000, Taʿiz 120,000
Language: Arabic
Religion: Moslem
Currency: Yemen paper riyal = 100 rial

The Roman name for Yemen "Arabia Felix" or Lucky Arabia was more apt then than today. The old great dams filled up with silt and were destroyed by floods, and incense no longer fetches its weight in silver or gold.

㉒ SOUTH YEMEN
Jumhurijah al-Yemen al Dimuqratiya
al Shaʿabijah
(Peoples Democratic)

Area: 111,074 sq.mi. (287,682 km²)
Population: 2,030,000
Population growth per annum: 1.8%
Life expectancy at birth: males 40 years, females 42 years
Literacy: 25%
Capital with population: Baladīyat ʿAdan (Aden) 295,000
Other important cities with population: Al Mukallā 100,000
Language: Arabic
Religion: Moslem
Currency: South Yemen dinar = 1000 fils

This is the land of ancient skyscrapers. The high-rise buildings that form the skyline of Hadramaut are mainly built of mud bricks. They are 6-7 stories high, but seem higher as every story has 2 rows of windows.

㉓ OMAN
(Sultanate of Oman)

Area: 82,030 sq.mi. (212,457 km²)
Population: 1,500 000
Population growth per annum: 3.0%
Life expectancy at birth: males 46 years, females 48 years
Literacy: 20%
Capital with population: Masqat 50,000
Other important cities with population: none
Language: Arabic
Religion: Moslem
Currency: Rial = 1000 biazas

Like his rival, the King of Portugal, the Sultan of Oman once ruled over a far-flung transocean empire. The red flag of the Sultan flew over forts and trading posts on Asian and African coasts, such as Mombasa and Zanzibar.

㉔ INDIA
Bharat
(Republic of India)

Area: 1,229,454 sq.mi. (3,184,290 km²)
Population: 683,810,000
Population growth per annum: 2.0%
Life expectancy at birth: males 50 years, females 49 years
Literacy: 36%
Capital with population: Delhi 5,720,000
Other important cities with population:
Bombay 8,230,000, Calcutta 9,170,000,
Madras 4,280,000
Language: Hindi, English
Religion: Hindu (83%), Moslem (11%)
Currency: Rupee = 100 Paise

Like the images of Hindu gods that have several eyes, heads and arms (symbolizing their paradoxical nature), the subcontinent and nation of India has many diverse and contradictory features. India is the serene Taj Mahal in cool white marble, and Calcutta with its teeming millions, holy cows and also nuclear power. Independent JAN 26, 1950.

㉕ NEPAL

Sri Nepala Sarkar
(Kingdom of Nepal)

Area: 56,292 sq.mi. (145,391 km²)
Population: 16,100,000
Population growth per annum: 2.3%
Life expectancy at birth: males 43 years, females 44 years
Literacy: 20%
Capital with population: Katmandu 195,000
Other important cities with population: Patan 50,000
Language: Nepali, Indian Languages
Religion: Hindu (90%), Buddhist (7%)
Currency: Nepalese Rupee = 2 mohur = 100 paisa

By avoiding involvement in the affairs of the outside world the mountain kingdom of Nepal has like Switzerland managed to remain independent. Nepal shares with China the world's highest peak, Chomolungma, the "Goddess Mother of the World" to the Tibetans, since 1865 also known as Mt. Everest.

㉖ BHUTAN

Druk Gaykhab
(Kingdom of Bhutan)

Area: 17,992 sq.mi. (46,600 km²)
Population: 1,250,000
Population growth per annum: 2.2%
Life expectancy at birth: males 44 years, females 43 years
Literacy: 5%
Capital with population: Thimphu 21,000
Other important cities with population: none
Language: Dzongka, Nepali
Religion: Buddhist (70%), Hindu
Currency: Ngultrum = 100 chetrum (Indian rupee also used)

Bhutan's official name Druk Yul translates Land of the Dragon. This is an apt name, as the mountainous former hermit kingdom has many fairy-tale qualities . The only real dragons to be found are those on the national flags.

㉗ BANGLADESH

(Peoples Republic of Bangladesh)

Area: 55,598 sq.mi. (143,998 km²)
Population: 96,000,000
Population growth per annum: 2.8%
Life expectancy at birth: males 46 years, females 46 years
Literacy: 25%
Capital with population: Dhaka 3,500,000
Other important cities with population:
Chittagong 1,390,000,   Khulna 650,000
Language: Bengali, English
Religion: Islam (80%), Hindu
Currency: Taka = 100 poisha

The fertile delta lands of Ganges and Brahmaputra, created by floods, have long been more than overpopulated. Troubled by alternating droughts and torrential rains, poor Bangladesh is frequently plagued by hurricanes and devastating tidal floods. Independent DEC 20, 1971.

㉘ BURMA

Pyidaungsu Socialist Thammada
Myanma Naingngandaw
(Socialist Republic of the Union of Burma)

Area: 261,218 sq.mi. (676,552 km²)
Population: 35,310,000
Population growth per annum: 2.4%
Life expectancy at birth: males 51 years, females 54 years
Literacy: 78%
Capital with population: Rangoon 2,460,000
Other important cities with population: Mandalay 420,000, Bassein 360,000
Language: Burmese
Religion: Buddhist (85%)
Currency: Kyat = 100 pyas

Burma is still the land of the gilded pagodas, where time flows as slowly as the mighty Irrawaddy. In this land of yesterday veteran cars are in everyday use, and elephants haul teak logs to the rivers. Burma's socialists have governed the country since 1948. Independent JAN 4, 1948.

㉙ THAILAND

Prathes Thai
(Kingdom of Thailand)

Area: 198,500 sq.mi. (514,000 km²)
Population: 50,000,000
Population growth per annum: 2.3%
Life expectancy at birth: males 58 years, females 63 years
Literacy: 84%
Capital with population: Krung Thep (Bangkok) 5,470,000
Other important cities with population: Chiang Mai 105,000
Language: Thai
Religion: Buddhist (93%), Moslem (4%)
Currency: Baht = 100 Satang

Thailand has throughout history managed to survive and maintain independence by deft diplomacy and careful observation of prevailing wind directions. Internally the king retains power in much the same way.

㉚ LAOS

(The Lao People's Democratic Republic)

Area: 91,400 sq.mi. (236,800 km²)
Population: 3,500,000
Population growth per annum: 2.4%
Life expectancy at birth: males 42 years, females 45 years
Literacy: 28%
Capital with population: Vientiane 120,000
Other important cities with population:
Luang Prabang 45,000
Language: Lao
Religion: Buddhist
Currency: Kip = 100 at

Reverence for royalty has always transcended life in Laos. A royal prince led the communists to victory in 1975 and abolished monarchy. Several hundred huge carved burial urns, presumably containing royal remains from prehistoric times, still dot the Plain of Jars. Independent JUL 20, 1954.

㉛ VIETNAM
Công Hòa Xã Hội Chu Nghĩa Việt Nam
(Socialist Republic of Vietnam)

Area: 127,242 sq.mi. (329,566 km²)
Population: 60,000,000
Population growth per annum: 2.3%
Life expectancy at birth: males 51 years, females 54 years
Literacy: 78%
Capital with population: Hanoi 2,570,000
Other important cities with population:
  Ho Chi Minh 3,500,000, Hai Phong 1,300,000
Language: Vietnamese, French, English
Religion: Buddhist
Currency: Dong = 10 hao = 10 xu

The proud and martial Vietnamese of the Red River basin have been called the Prussians of Indo-China. With military aid from the U.S.S.R and captured U.S. arms they have now become the strongest military power of South East Asia. Independent JUL 20, 1954.

㉜ TAIWAN
(Republic of China)

Area: 13,967 sq.mi. (36,174 km²)
Population: 18,800,000
Population growth per annum: 1.8%
Life expectancy at birth: males 70 years, females 75 years
Literacy: 89%
Capital with population: Taipei 2,400,000
Other important cities with population:
  Kaohsiung 1,260,000
Language: Chinese
Religion: Confucianist, Buddhist, Taoist
Currency: New Taiwan dollar = 100 cents

The Chinese governments in Peking and Taipei do agree in one important respect: There is only one China, and Taiwan is no more than a Chinese province. The main difference is that the authority of the rulers in Taipei does not extend to any part of ancient, mainland China proper.

㉝ MALDIVES
Divehi Jumhuriya
(Republic of Maldives)

Area: 115 sq.mi. (298 km²)
Population: 168,000
Population growth per annum: 2.9%
Life expectancy at birth: not available
Literacy: 36%
Capital with population: Malè 40,000
Other important cities with population: none
Language: Divehi
Religion: Moslem (Sunni Moslems)
Currency: Rufiyaa = 100 laaris

In the days when the dhows carried carpets, ivory and slaves over the Indian Ocean, the thousand coral islands of the Maldives lay at the crossroads of the ocean. Now even the names of the atolls, Tiladummati, Fadiffolu, Miladummadulu sound of long lost fame and tales of far away lands. Independent NOV 11, 1968.

㉞ SRI LANKA
(Democratic Socialist
Republic of Sri Lanka)

Area: 25,332 sq.mi. (65,610 km²)
Population: 14,850,000
Population growth per annum: 1.7%
Life expectancy at birth: males 64 years, females 67 years
Literacy: 84%
Capital with population: Colombo 586,000
Other important cities with population:
  Dehiwela-Mt. Lavinia 175,000, Moratuwa 136,000
Language: Sinhala, Tamil
Religion: Buddhist (70%), Hindu (17%), Christian, Moslem
Currency: Sri Lanka rupee = 100 cents

Sri Lanka is even today a land of legends. On the top of Adam's Peak there is a 5 ft long foot print, claimed to be left in the rock by Adam (or by Buddha, or Sheva, or St. Thomas according to preference). Independent 1947.

㉟ KAMPUCHEA
(Cambodian People's Republic)

Area: 69,898 sq.mi. (181,035 km²)
Population: 6,680,000
Population growth per annum: 2.9%
Life expectancy at birth: males 44 years, females 47 years
Literacy: 48%
Capital with population: Phnom Penh 500,000
Other important cities with population:
  Battambang 50,000
Language: Khmer
Religion: Buddhist
Currency: Riel = 100 sen

Clashing radical ideologies have once more made life only worse for everyone. Pleasant Kampuchea now lies in ruins like mighty remains from its glorious past. Famous Angkor, for over 500 years the capital of all Indochina, has so far been spared further destruction. Independent OCT 9, 1970.

㊱ PHILIPPINES
República de Filipinas ·
Republika ng Pilipinas
(Republic of the Philippines)

Area: 116,000 sq.mi. (300,000 km²)
Population: 53,350,000
Population growth per annum: 2.7%
Life expectancy at birth: males 59 years, females 62 years
Literacy: 88%
Capital with population: Manila 1,600,000
Other important cities with population:
  Quezon City 1,200,000, Davao 620,000, Cebu 500,000
Language: Pilipino, English, Spanish
Religion: Roman Catholic (80%), Islam (7%)
Currency: Philippine peso = 100 centavos

East and west meet in this island nation, east of the Asian mainland, west of the Pacific. The people of this fomer colony of Spain (1521-1899) and the United States (1899-1942) are of Malayo-Polynesian stock but speak Spanish, English and Pilipino. Most are Roman Catholics but some are Moslems. Independent JUL 4, 1946.

③⑦ MALAYSIA

Area: 127,317 sq.mi. (329,749 km²)
Population: 15,070,000
Population growth per annum: 2.5%
Life expectancy at birth: males 62 years, females 65 years
Literacy: 75%
Capital with population: Kuala Lumpur 450,000
Other important cities with population:
George Town 300,000, Ipoh 250,000
Language: Bahasa Malaysia, Chinese
Religion: Moslem 50%, Buddhist (26%), Hindu (9%)
Currency: Ringgit = 100 sen

In this land reigning rajahs (and sultans) each in turn serve five years as 'Supreme Head of State'. This unusual system of royal rotation has brought unity and stability to the geographically divided nation. In Sarawak the world's largest cave (2,300×1,000 ft.) has been found. Independent SEP 16, 1963

③⑧ SINGAPORE
(Republic of Singapore)

Area: 239 sq.mi. (618 km²)
Population: 2,530,000
Population growth per annum: 1.2%
Life expectancy at birth: males 69 years, females 73 years
Literacy: 84%
Capital with population: Singapore 2,350,000
Other important cities with population: none
Language: Chinese, Malay, Tamil, English
Religion: Buddhist, Taoist, Moslem, Hindu, Christian
Currency: Singapore-dollar = 100 cents

A modern City state, living off free enterprise trade and local manufacturing industries requiring skilled labor, Singapore survives without a hinterland. Independent AUG 9, 1965.

AUSTRALASIA

Area: 3,454,000 sq.mi. (8,945,000 km²)
Population: 23,446,000
Density of population per sq.mi.: 6.8

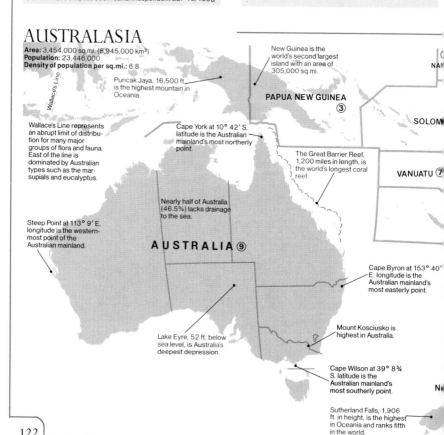

New Guinea is the world's second largest island with an area of 305,000 sq.mi.

Puncak Jaya, 16,500 ft. is the highest mountain in Oceania.

PAPUA NEW GUINEA ③

Wallace's Line represents an abrupt limit of distribution for many major groups of flora and fauna. East of the line is dominated by Australian types such as the marsupials and eucalyptus.

Cape York at 10° 42′ S. latitude is the Australian mainland's most northerly point.

The Great Barrier Reef, 1,200 miles in length, is the world's longest coral reef.

SOLOM

VANUATU ⑦

Nearly half of Australia (46.5%) lacks drainage to the sea.

Steep Point at 113° 9′ E. longitude is the westernmost point of the Australian mainland.

AUSTRALIA ⑨

Cape Byron at 153° 40′ E. longitude is the Australian mainland's most easterly point.

Mount Kosciusko is highest in Australia.

Lake Eyre, 52 ft. below sea level, is Australia's deepest depression.

Cape Wilson at 39° 8¾ S. latitude is the Australian mainland's most southerly point.

Sutherland Falls, 1,906 ft. in height, is the highest in Oceania and ranks fifth in the world.

㊴ BRUNEI

Area: 2,226 sq.mi. (5,765 km²)
Population: 213,000
Population growth per annum: not available
Life expectancy at birth: not available
Literacy: not available
Capital with population: Bandar Seri Begawan 51,000
Other important cities with population: none
Language: Malay, English
Religion: Moslem (64%), Buddhist, Christian
Currency: Brunei dollar = 100 cents

A land flowing with oil — where the citizens can use their own money to buy "milk and honey" — as they do not have to pay any income taxes! No wonder the Sultan of Brunei can continue to rule — with broad popular support. Independent DEC 31, 1983.

㊵ INDONESIA
Republik Indonesia
(Republic of Indonesia)

Area: 741,080 sq.mi. (1,919,400 km²)
Population: 158,000,000
Population growth per annum: 1.7%
Life expectancy at birth: males 46 years, females 49 years
Literacy: 64%
Capital with population: Jakarta 6,500,000
Other important cities with population:
  Surabaya 2,000,000   Bandung 1,500,000,
  Medan 1,400,000
Language: Bahasa Indonesia
Religion: Moslem (92%)
Currency: Rupiah = 100 sen

Panta rei (all flows) ought to be the motto of this nation of over 13,000 islands. No other state has so many active volcanoes. On Java alone there are 27. Here the island volcano of Krakatoa, 6,000 ft. high, disintegrated in 1883 in the most catastrophic eruption in history. Independent DEC 27, 1949.

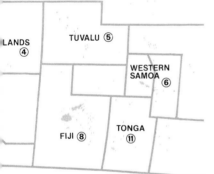

KIRIBATI ②

ISLANDS ④

TUVALU ⑤

WESTERN SAMOA ⑥

FIJI ⑧

TONGA ⑪

⑨ AUSTRALIA

⑧ FIJI

② KIRIBATI

① NAURU

⑩ NEW ZEALAND

③ PAPUA NEW GUINEA

④ SOLOMON ISLANDS

⑪ TONGA

⑤ TUVALU

⑦ VANUATU

⑥ WESTERN SAMOA

The area around Lake Taupo is a unique landscape of volcanic features such as bubbling mud cauldrons, hot springs, solfataras and fumaroles. The geyser Waimangu used to be the world's greatest, the column of water could reach as high as 1,500 ft.

EALAND ⑩

① NAURU
(Republic of Nauru)

Area: 8 sq.mi. (21.3 km²)
Population: 8,400
Population growth per annum: 1.5%
Life expectancy at birth: not available
Literacy: 99%
Capital with population: Yaren
Other important cities with population: none
Language: Nauruan, English
Religion: Protestant (60%), Roman Catholic (30%)
Currency: Australian dollar = 100 cents

It is easy to drive around all of Nauru in a car in less time that it takes for an astronaut to circle the Earth, as the total circumference is only 21 miles. Independent JUN 31, 1970. 1970.

② KIRIBATI
(Republic of Kiribati)

Area: 342 sq.mi. (886 km²)
Population: 60,000
Population growth per annum: not available
Life expectancy at birth: not available
Literacy: not available
Capital with population: Bairiki 20,000
Other important cities with population: none
Language: Kiribati, English
Religion: Protestant (50%), Roman Catholic (50%)
Currency: Australian dollar = 100 cents

No other nation is spread so thinly as Kiribati, with land size smaller than New York City scattered over an area wider than the contiguous United States! Kiribati always has two days, as it is divided by the date line. Independent JUL 12, 1979.

③ PAPUA NEW GUINEA

Area: 178,260 sq.mi. (461,691 km²)
Population: 3,260,000
Population growth per annum: 2.7%
Life expectancy at birth: males 51 years, females 50 years
Literacy: 32%
Capital with population: Port Moresby 124,000
Other important cities with population: Lae 62,000
Language: English, numerous local languages
Religion: Animist, Protestant, Roman Catholic
Currency: Kina = 100 toe

The official "Pidgin English" developed here during the last hundred years is quite a new language, using mainly English words. E.g. "Ars bilong diwai" means "roots" (Diwai is a melanesian word for tree, belong equals of — and ars is just the very bottom of anything.) Independent SEP 16, 1975.

④ SOLOMON ISLANDS

Area: 11,500 sq.mi. (29,785 km²)
Population: 258,000
Population growth per annum: 3.0%
Life expectancy at birth: not available
Literacy: not available
Capital with population: Honiara 24,000
Other important cities with population: none
Language: English, numerous local languages
Religion: Protestant (75%), Roman Catholic (19%)
Currency: Solomon Island dollar = 100 cents

The Solomon Islands suffered heavily during World War II during the battles of Guadalcanal and the Coral Sea. Yet some islands still profit from the spoils of war by exporting scrap iron. Independent JUL 7, 1978.

⑤ TUVALU

Area: 10 sq.mi. (24.6 km²)
Population: 7,300
Population growth per annum: 1.6%
Life expectancy at birth: males 57 years, females 59 years
Literacy: not available
Capital with population: Funafuti 2,100
Other important cities with population: none
Language: Samoan, English
Religion: Protestant
Currency: Australian dollar = 100 cents

Tuvalu comprises nine low coral atolls (formerly also called Lagoon or Ellice islands) in the very center of the island world of the South Pacific. In spite of the fact that an atoll can measure 6-12 mi. across its land area is almost negligible. Independent OCT 1, 1978.

⑥ WESTERN SAMOA
Samoa i Sisifo
(Independent State of
Western Samoa)

Area: 1,093 sq.mi. (2,831 km²)
Population: 156,000
Population growth per annum: 1.3%
Life expectancy at birth: not available
Literacy: 90%
Capital with population: Apia 33,200
Other important cities with population: none
Language: Samoan, English
Religion: Protestant (75%), Roman Catholic (22%)
Currency: Tala = 100 sene

Truly Polynesian Samoa is in many ways an incarnation of the South Sea Islands — complete with beaches and palms and friendly people, but it is at the same time a modern society with TV, colleges, and all the rest. Independent JAN 1, 1962.

⑦ VANUATU
(Republic of Vanuatu)

Area: 5,700 sq.mi. (14,763 km²)
Population: 117,000
Population growth per annum: 2.7%
Life expectancy at birth: not available
Literacy: not available
Capital with population: Vila 14,000
Other important cities with population: none
Language: Bislama, English, French
Religion: Protestant (68%), Roman Catholic (16%)
Currency: Vatu

Two colonial powers, France and Great Britain ruled the former Condominium of the New Hebrides in quaint harmony with strict and sometimes silly division of authority 1906-80. Independent JUL 30, 1980.

⑧ FIJI
(Dominion of Fiji)

Area: 7,095 sq.mi. (18,376 km²)
Population: 670,000
Population growth per annum: 1.8%
Life expectancy at birth: males 70 years, females 73%
Literacy: 75%
Capital with population: Suva 71,000
Other important cities with population: Lautoka 26,000
Language: English, Fijian, Hindustani
Religion: Christian (49%), Hindu (40%)
Currency: Fijian dollar = 100 cents

Volcanic soil, tropical sunshine and gentle trade winds bringing regular rainfall favor sugar cane cultivation. Sugar has become the major product of Fiji. Independent OCT 10, 1970.

⑨ AUSTRALIA
(Commonwealth of Australia)

Area: 2,967,909 sq.mi. (7,686,848 km²)
Population: 15,450,000
Population growth per annum: 1.2%
Life expectancy at birth: males 70 years, females 76 years
Literacy: 99%
Capital with population: Canberra 256,000
Other important cities with population: Sydney 3,281,000,
  Melbourne 2,804,000, Brisbane 1,090,000
Language: English, aboriginal languages
Religion: Christian Protestant (61%), Catholic (27%)
Currency: Australian dollar = 100 cents

The only land that is quite different, Australia comprises an entire continent with a quite different fauna and flora — eucalyptus trees and kangaroos, egg-laying mammals and koalas, the living teddy bears. The 1,200 mi. long Great Barrier Reef is the world's longest coral reef. Independent JAN 1, 1901.

⑩ NEW ZEALAND

Area: 103,747 sq.mi. (268,704 km²)
Population: 3,200,000
Population growth per annum: 1.1%
Life expectancy at birth: males 70 years, females 76 years
Literacy: 99%
Capital with population: Wellington 342,000
Other important cities with population: Auckland 864,000
  Christchurch 322,000
Language: English, Maori
Religion: Protestant
Currency: New Zealand dollar = 100 cents

Far from being the opposite of England, green and civilized New Zealand is at the Antipodes seen from Britain — that is exactly at the other side of the Earth. New Zealand is rich in beautiful scenery. Independent 1931.

⑪ TONGA
(Kingdom of Tonga)

Area: 289 sq.mi. (748 km²)
Population: 99,000
Population growth per annum: not available
Life expectancy at birth: not available
Literacy: not available
Capital with population: Niku'alofa 20,000
Other important cities with population: none
Language: English
Religion: Protestant (85%), Roman Catholic (15%)
Currency: Pa'anga = 100 seniti

The "Friendly Islands", Captain Cook's name for Tonga, are not easy to reach due to lack of good harbors. The island of Niuafo'ou has become known among philatelists as "Tin Can Island" because of the method used to collect and deliver mail. Independent JUN 4, 1970.

AFRICA

Area: 11,696,000 sq.mi. (30,293,000 km²)
Population: 431,209,000
Density of population per sq.mi.: 37

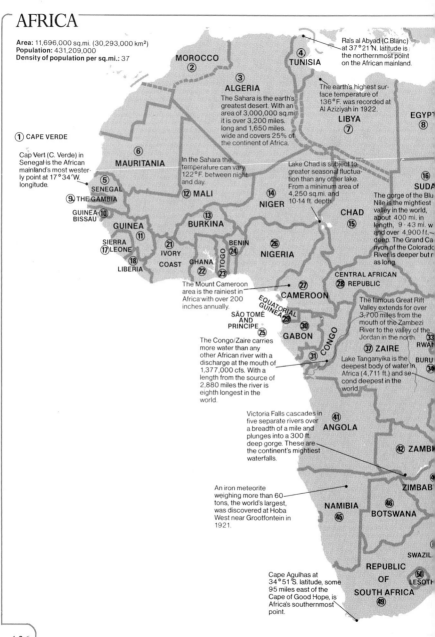

Ra's al Abyad (C.Blanc) at 37°21′N. latitude is the northernmost point on the African mainland.

The earth's highest surface temperature of 136°F. was recorded at Al Aziziyah in 1922.

MOROCCO ②

④ TUNISIA

③ ALGERIA

The Sahara is the earth's greatest desert. With an area of 3,000,000 sq.mi. it is over 3,200 miles. long and 1,650 miles. wide and covers 25% of the continent of Africa.

LIBYA ⑦

EGYPT ⑧

① CAPE VERDE

Cap Vert (C. Verde) in Senegal is the African mainland's most westerly point at 17°34′W. longitude.

MAURITANIA ⑥

In the Sahara the temperature can vary 122°F. between night and day.

⑤ SENEGAL

⑨ THE GAMBIA

GUINEA- ⑩ BISSAU

⑫ MALI

GUINEA ⑪

⑬ BURKINA

NIGER ⑭

Lake Chad is subject to greater seasonal fluctuation than any other lake. From a minimum area of 4,250 sq.mi. and 10-14 ft. depth.

CHAD ⑮

⑯ SUDAN

The gorge of the Blue Nile is the mightiest valley in the world, about 400 mi. in length, 9 - 43 mi. wide and over 4,900 ft. deep. The Grand Canyon of the Colorado River is deeper but not as long.

SIERRA ⑰ LEONE

⑱ LIBERIA

IVORY ㉑ COAST

GHANA ㉒

TOGO ㉓

BENIN ㉔

NIGERIA ㉖

The Mount Cameroon area is the rainiest in Africa with over 200 inches annually.

CAMEROON ㉗

CENTRAL AFRICAN ㉘ REPUBLIC

EQUATORIAL GUINEA ㉙

SÃO TOMÉ AND PRINCIPE ㉕

GABON ㉚

CONGO ㉛

The Congo/Zaire carries more water than any other African river with a discharge at the mouth of 1,377,000 cfs. With a length from the source of 2,880 miles the river is eighth longest in the world.

The famous Great Rift Valley extends for over 3,700 miles from the mouth of the Zambezi River to the valley of the Jordan in the north. ㉝

㊲ ZAIRE

RWANDA

Lake Tanganyika is the deepest body of water in Africa (4,711 ft.) and second deepest in the world.

BURUNDI ㉞

Victoria Falls cascades in five separate rivers over a breadth of a mile and plunges into a 300 ft. deep gorge. These are the continent's mightiest waterfalls.

ANGOLA ㊶

㊷ ZAMBIA

An iron meteorite weighing more than 60 tons, the world's largest, was discovered at Hoba West near Grootfontein in 1921.

ZIMBABWE

NAMIBIA ㊺

BOTSWANA ㊻

SWAZILAND

Cape Agulhas at 34°51′S. latitude, some 95 miles east of the Cape of Good Hope, is Africa's southernmost point.

REPUBLIC OF SOUTH AFRICA ㊾

LESOTHO ㊿

126

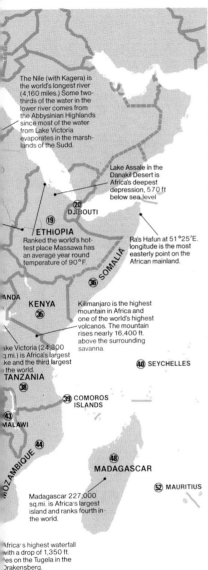

The Nile (with Kagera) is the world's longest river (4,160 miles.) Some two-thirds of the water in the lower river comes from the Abbysinian Highlands since most of the water from Lake Victoria evaporates in the marsh-lands of the Sudd.

Lake Assale in the Danakil Desert is Africa's deepest depression, 570 ft below sea level

DJIBOUTI

ETHIOPIA
Ranked the world's hottest place Massawa has an average year round temperature of 90°F.

Ra's Hafun at 51°25'E. longitude is the most easterly point on the African mainland.

SOMALIA

KENYA

Kilimanjaro is the highest mountain in Africa and one of the world's highest volcanos. The mountain rises nearly 16,400 ft. above the surrounding savanna.

Lake Victoria (24,300 q.mi.) is Africa's largest lake and the third largest in the world.

TANZANIA

COMOROS ISLANDS

MALAWI

MOZAMBIQUE

MADAGASCAR

MAURITIUS

Madagascar 227,000 sq.mi. is Africa's largest island and ranks fourth in the world.

Africa's highest waterfall with a drop of 1,350 ft. es on the Tugela in the Drakensberg.

③ ALGERIA
㊶ ANGOLA
㉔ BENIN
㊻ BOTSWANA
⑬ BURKINA
㉞ BURUNDI
㉗ CAMEROON
① CAPE VERDE
㉘ CENTRAL AFRICAN REP.
⑮ CHAD
㊴ COMOROS ISLANDS
㉛ CONGO
⑳ DJIBOUTI
⑧ EGYPT
㉙ EQUATORIAL GUINEA
⑲ ETHIOPIA
㉚ GABON
㉒ GHANA
⑪ GUINEA
⑩ GUINEA-BISSAU
㉑ IVORY COAST
㉟ KENYA
㊿ LESOTHO
⑱ LIBERIA
⑦ LIBYA
㊽ MADAGASCAR
㊸ MALAWI
⑫ MALI
⑥ MAURITANIA
㊼ MAURITIUS
② MOROCCO
㊹ MOZAMBIQUE
㊺ NAMIBIA
⑭ NIGER
㉖ NIGERIA
㊾ REPUBLIC OF SOUTH AFRICA
㉝ RWANDA
㉕ SÃO TOMÉ AND PRINCIPE

⑤ SENEGAL
㊵ SEYCHELLES
⑰ SIERRA LEONE
㊱ SOMALIA
⑯ SUDAN
㊿ SWAZILAND
㊳ TANZANIA
⑨ THE GAMBIA
㉓ TOGO
④ TUNISIA
㉜ UGANDA
㊲ ZAIRE
㊷ ZAMBIA
㊼ ZIMBABWE

127

① CAPE VERDE ISLAND
República de Cabo Verde
(Republic of Cape Verde)

Area: 1,557 sq.mi. (4,033 km²)
Population: 296,000
Population growth per annum: 1.7%
Life expectancy at birth: males 58 years, females 62 years
Literacy: 37%
Capital with population: Praia 38,000
Other important cities with population: Mindelo 40,000
Language: Portuguese, Crioulo
Religion: Roman Catholic
Currency: Escudo = 100 centavos

Heat and drought are two words that characterize the volcanic islands, named after a cape on the mainland, 360 mi. to the east. Salt is produced by evaporation , an industry with good natural prospects. Independent JUL 5, 1975.

② MOROCCO
Al-Mamlaka al-Maghrebia
(Kingdom of Morocco)

Area: 176,343 sq.mi. (458,730 km²)
Population: 21,160,000
Population growth per annum: 3.2%
Life expectancy at birth: males 54 years, females 57 years
Literacy: 24%
Capital with population: Rabat 440,000
Other important cities with population: Dar el Beida (Casablanca) 1,400,000, Marrakech 330,000
Language: Arabic, Berber
Religion: Moslem, (Sunni Moslems)
Currency: Dirham = 100 centimes

East and West meet in Morocco. For the "western" world it is a land of the Near East — and for the "eastern", Islamic world it is a land of the Maghreb, The West. The mosques and palaces of cities such as Marrakech and Fez are famous in the west as well as in the east. Independent MAR 28, 1956.

③ ALGERIA
al-Jumhuriya al -Jazairia ad-Dimuqratiya ash-Shabiya
(Democratic and Popular Republic of Algeria)

Area: 919,595 sq.mi. (2,381,740 km²)
Population: 21,460,000
Population growth per annum: 3.3%
Life expectancy at birth: males 54 years, females 56 years
Literacy: 46%
Capital with population: Al Jazāir(Algiers) 2,500,000
Other important cities with population: Oran 630,000, Constantine 385,000
Language: Arabic
Religion: Islam (Sunni Moslems)
Currency: Algerian dinar = 100 centimes

Four-fifths of the land is desert. The prosperous and fertile coastal area is just a thin gilt edge along the northern rim of the majestic Sahara. Covering more than 3 million sq.mi. (3,400 by 900 mi.) the Sahara is the world's greatest desert, so that the barren wastes of Algeria comprise only 25% of the Sahara! Independent JUL 3, 1962.

④ TUNISIA
Al-Djoumhouria Attunisia
(Republic of Tunisia)

Area: 63,378 sq.mi. (164,150 km²)
Population: 6,970,000
Population growth per annum: 2.5%
Life expectancy at birth: males 57 years, females 58 years
Literacy: 62%
Capital with population: Tunis 557,000
Other important cities with population: Sfax 232,000, Sousse 85,000
Language: Arabic
Religion: Moslem
Currency: Tunisian dinar = 100 millimes

A nation with many ties. Ties of history and culture link it forever to all its Mediterranean neighbors, and very strongly to France. Ties of language and blood bind it to the Arabic West, Maghreb. This is also the land of Carthage, that fought Rome for the hegemony of "the world". Independent MAR 20, 1956.

⑤ SENEGAL
République du Sénégal
(Republic of Senegal)

Area: 75,750 sq.mi. (196,,192 km²)
Population: 6,270,000
Population growth per annum: 2.6%
Life expectancy at birth: males 41 years, females 44 years
Literacy: 10%
Capital with population: Dakar 800,000
Other important cities with population: Thies 130,000, Kaolack 116,000
Language: French, tribal languages
Religion: Moslem (80%), Christian (10%), Animist
Currency: CFA-franc = 100 centimes

The Gateway to West Africa. The leading metropolis of the area, Dakar, is favored by a magnificent natural harbor. The location near Cap Vert, the most westerly point of the mainland made Dakar the natural staging post for transatlantic flights to South America until the 1960's. Independent AUG 20, 1960.

⑥ MAURITANIA
Republique Islamique de Mauritanie
(Islamic Republic of Mauritania)

Area: 398,000 sq.mi. (1,030,700 km²)
Population: 1,830,000
Population growth per annum: 2.8%
Life expectancy at birth: males 41 years, females 44 years
Literacy: 17%
Capital with population: Nouakchott 135,000
Other important cities with population: none
Language: French, Arabic
Religion: Moslem
Currency: Ouguiya = 5 khoum

For the Arabs and the Islamic World, Mauritania is the Far West, the Land of the Sunset. Only a fraction of the vast country is habitable, and the lack of water is a severe handicap to any development. Independent NOV 28, 1960.

⑦ LIBYA

Al-Jamahiriyah Al-Arabiya-Al Libya
Al-Shabiya Al-Ishtirakiya
(Socialist People's Libyan Arab Jamahiriya)

Area: 679,362 sq.mi. (1,759,540 km²)
Population: 3,500,000
Population growth per annum: 4.1%
Life expectancy at birth: males 54 years, females 57 years
Literacy: 40 %
Capital with population: Tripoli (Tarābulus) 860,000
Other important cities with population: Benghasi 300,000
Language: Arabic
Religion: Moslem
Currency: Libyan dinar = 1000 dirham

*Elusive Libya retains in our times some of the enigmatic
features of Africa. The central volcanic area, the Black Hills
that are clearly visible on space images of Africa, were recently mapped with the aid of satellite photos.*

⑧ EGYPT

Jumhuriyat Misr al-Arabiya
(Arab Republic of Egypt)

Area: 386,662 sq.mi. (1,001,449 km²)
Population: 46,000,000
Population growth per annum: 2.6%
Life expectancy at birth: males 54 years, females 56 years
Literacy: 40%
Capital with population: Al Qahirah (Cairo)9,000,000
Other important cities with population: Al Iskandarīyah
(Alexandria) 3,000,000, Al Jīzah (Giza) 2,000,000
Language: Arabic
Religion: Islam (Sunni Moslems 90%)
Currency: Egyptian pound = 100 piastres

*The whole of inhabitable Egypt is nothing but an oasis — total-
ly dependent on the water of the Nile. In general the width of
the cultivated and settled land is only 2-10 mi. Of the seven
wonders of the ancient world, Egypt had two, and even if the
Pharos has been destroyed, the Pyramids still stand. Independent FEB 28. 1922.*

⑨ THE GAMBIA

(Republic of The Gambia)

Area: 4,361 sq.mi. (11,295 km²)
Population: 700,000
Population growth per annum: 2.8%
Life expectancy at birth: males 39 years, females 43 years
Literacy: 12 %
Capital with population: Banjul 45,000
Other important cities with population: none
Language: English, Mandinka, Wolof
Religion: Moslem (85%), Christian, Animist
Currency: Dalasi = 100 bututs

*The land that is a river. This former British colonial enclave in-
side Senegal is now joined with Senegal in the Confederation
of Senegambia. Here Alex Haley found his roots, as described
in his bestseller. Independent FEB 18, 1965.*

⑩ GUINEA-BISSAU

(Republic of Guinea-Bissau)

Area: 13,948 sq.mi. (36,125 km²)
Population: 830,000
Population growth per annum: 1.7%
Life expectancy at birth: males 39 years, females 43 years
Literacy: 9%
Capital with population: Bissau 110,000
Other important cities with population: none
Language: Portuguese, Criolo
Religion: Tribal (50%), Moslem (38%), Christian (5%)
Currency: Guinea-Bissau peso = 100 centavos

*A new name heralds a new era. For more than 500 years this
land was known as Portuguese Guinea. No other land has
been a colony for so many years. Guinea Bissau has an excep-
tional un-African archipelago coast. Independent SEP 24,
1973.*

⑪ GUINEA

République populaire
et révolutionnaire de Guinée
(Republic of Guinea)

Area: 94,926 sq.mi. (245,857 km²)
Population: 5,410,000
Population growth per annum: 2.5%
Life expectancy at birth: males 42 years, females 45 years
Literacy: 48 %
Capital with population: Conakry
Other important cities with population: Kankan 100,000
Language: French, tribal languages
Religion: Moslem (75%), Tribal
Currency: Syli = 100 cauris

*The name Guinea rings with a chink of gold — since 1663,
when coins were struck in England out of pure 22 carat gold
from Guinea. In Britain prices can still be quoted in guineas.
Guinea still has natural resources that could bring prosperity to
this very poor country. Independent OCT 2, 1958.*

⑫ MALI

République du Mali
(Republic of Mali)

Area: 478,819 sq.mi. (1,240,142 km²)
Population: 7,720,000
Population growth per annum: 2.7%
Life expectancy at birth: males 44 years, females 44 years
Literacy: 10%
Capital with population: Bamako 405,000
Other important cities with population: Sègou 65,000
Language: French, Bambara
Religion: Moslem (65%), Animist (30%), Christian (5%)
Currency: Mali franc = 100 centimes

*Half Sahara and half Sahel, half desert and half savanna land,
Mali has been hard hit by years of drought. Once the kings of
Mali controlled the trade routes of the Sahara and the minarets
of fabled Timbuktu attracted both traders and adventurers to
cross the sand seas. Independent SEP 22, 1960.*

⑬ BURKINA

République de Burkina Faso
(People's Democratic Republic
of Burkina)

Area: 105,839 sq.mi. (274,122 km²)
Population: 6,700,000
Population growth per annum: 2.6%
Life expectancy at birth: males 42 years, females 45 years
Literacy: 7%
Capital with population: Ouagadougou 286,000
Other important cities with population:
Bobo Dioulasso 165,000
Language: French, Sudanic tribal languages
Religion: Animist (50%), Moslem (20%)
Currency: CFA-franc = 100 centimes

*A land at the mercy of the winds. The dreaded dry Harmattan
blowing from Sahara is a harbinger of death — the blessed
Guinea Monsoon from the south an angel of life with its
seasonal rain. The savanna lands here depend on a precarious
balance between precipitation and evaporation. Independent
AUG 5, 1960.*

⑭ NIGER

République du Niger
(Republic of Niger)

Area: 489,000 sq.mi. 1,267,000 km²)
Population: 6,270,000
Population growth per annum: 2.9%
Life expectancy at birth: males 41 years, females 44 years
Literacy: 5%
Capital with population: Niamey 225,000
Other important cities with population: Zinder 60,000
Language: French, Hausa, Djerma
Religion: Moslem (85%), Animist
Currency: CFA-franc = 100 centimes

*A name that is more of an incantation than a description. This is
a land-locked, dry and infertile part of Sahara, and the mighty
Niger crosses only a narrow corner. The Tuaregs still cross the
desert with salt caravans. Independent AUG 3, 1960.*

⑮ CHAD

République du Tchad
(Republic of Chad)

Area: 496,000 sq.mi. (1,284,000 km²)
Population: 5,120,000
Population growth per annum: 2.0%
Life expectancy at birth: males 39 years, females 41 years
Literacy: 15%
Capital with population: N'djamena 303,000
Other important cities with population: Moundou 66,000
Language: French, Arabic, Sudanese languages
Religion: Animist, Moslem (45%), Christian (5%)
Currency: CFA-franc = 100 centimes

*Land-locked Chad can be called a coastal land, as it is part of
the Sahel, "the coast" of the sand sea of Sahara. It is drained
to the shallow central basin of Lake Chad, the ever changing
lake that varies from 3,900-19,500 sq.mi. and from 3-13 ft.
in average depth. Independent AUG 11, 1960.*

⑯ SUDAN

Jamhuryat es-Sudan Al Democratia
(The Democratic Republic of Sudan)

Area: 967,494 sq.mi. (2,505,813 km²)
Population: 21,440,000
Population growth per annum: 2.8%
Life expectancy at birth: males 46 years, females 48 years
Literacy: 20 %
Capital with population: Al Khārṭum (Khartoum) 476,000,
(Metropolitan area 1,350,000)
Other important cities with population: Bur Sudan 207,000
Language: Arabic, various tribal languages
Religion: Moslem (70%) Christian, Animist
Currency: Sudanese pound = 100 piaster

*In Sudan there are two countries in one. There are the Islamic,
Arabic-speaking northern desert lands, and there are the
Christian, Nilotic southern savanna lands. In spite of the name,
most of the world's gum arabic comes from the acacia forests
of Sudan. Independent JAN 1, 1956.*

⑰ SIERRA LEONE

(Republic of Sierra Leone)

Area: 28,311 sq.mi. (73,326 km²)
Population: 3,350,000
Population growth per annum: 2.6%
Life expectancy at birth: males 44 years, females 48 years
Literacy: 15 %
Capital with population: Freetown 300,000
Other important cities with population: Makeni 1,000,000
Kenema 775,000
Language: English, tribal languages
Religion: Animist, Moslem (30%)
Currency: Leone = 100 cents

*A new homeland for freed slaves. Under British protection
repatriated slaves from Great Britain founded Freetown at one
of the few good natural harbors of West Africa back in 1787.
Later it was used as a settlement for Africans rescued from
slave ships. Sierra Leone became independent on APR 27,
1961.*

⑱ LIBERIA

(Republic of Liberia)

Area: 43,000 sq.mi. (111,369 km²)
Population: 1,900,000
Population growth per annum: 3.5%
Life expectancy at birth: males 52 years, females 54 years
Literacy: 24%
Capital with population: Monrovia 425,000
Other important cities with population: none
Language: English
Religion: Moslem (21%), Christian (35%), Traditional (43%)
Currency: Liberian dollar = 100 cents

*As the name implies, Liberia is a free nation, and has been
since it was established in 1822 for freed slaves from the USA.
In 1847 it became the continent's first independent republic
and remained so during the days of the "Scramble for Africa"
when this was divided into colonies.*

⑲ ETHIOPIA

Hebretesbawit Ityopia
(Socialist Ethiopia)

Area: 471,800 sq.mi. (1,221,900 km²)
Population: 42,020,000
Population growth per annum: 1.8%
Life expectancy at birth: males 38 years, females 41 years
Literacy: 8%
Capital with population: Addis Ababa 1,400,000
Other important cities with population: Asmara 45,000, Gondar 80,000
Language: Amharic, other Semitic and Hamitic languages, Arabic, English
Religion: Orthodox Christian (40%), Moslem (40%)
Currency: Ethiopian birr = 100 cents

The nation that is an archipelago on dry land. For centuries Ethiopia was a Christian island in a Moslem sea. It is still an archipelago of densely populated islands of high plateaus, separated by deep river gorges and hot lowlands — and a linguistic archipelago of over 70 ethnic groups.

⑳ DJIBOUTI

Jumhouriyya Djibouti
(Republic of Djibouti)

Area: 8,880 sq.mi. (23,000 km²)
Population: 340,000
Population growth per annum: 2.2%
Life expectancy at birth: 50 years
Literacy: 20%
Capital with population: Djibouti 150,000
Other important cities with population: Tadjourah
Language: French, Arabic
Religion: Islam
Currency: Djibouti franc = 100 centimes

The nation is a railway terminal — and vice versa. The entrepôt port would not and could not exist as an independent unity without the railway to Addis-Ababa. This railway was built in 1915 and has since served as the major link between central Ethiopia and the world. Independent JUN 27, 1977.

㉑ IVORY COAST

République de la Côte d'Ivoire
(Republic of Ivory Coast)

Area: 124,504 sq.mi. (322,464 km²)
Population: 8,500,000
Population growth per annum: 3.5%
Life expectancy at birth: males 44 years, females 48 years
Literacy: 24%
Capital with population: Abidjan 1,850,000
Other important cities with population: Bouaké 640,000, Man-Danané 450,000
Language: French, tribal languages
Religion: Moslem (15%), Christian (12%), Indigenous (63%)
Currency: CFA-franc = 100 centimes

The Cocoa Coast would be more apt but less poetic name for this land. Cocoa and coffee long ago replaced ivory and slaves as the staples of the Ivory Coast. No nation produces more cocoa. Other agricultural products are pineapples, bananas and palm oil. Independent AUG 7, 1960.

㉒ GHANA

(Republic of Ghana)

Area: 92,010 sq.mi. (238,305 km²)
Population: 12,210,000
Population growth per annum: 3.1%
Life expectancy at birth: males 47 years, females 50 years
Literacy: 30%
Capital with population: Accra 750,000
Other important cities with population: Sekondi-Takoradi 300,000,
Language: English, 50 tribal languages
Religion: Christian (42%), Traditional beliefs, Moslem (12%)
Currency: Cedi = 100 pesewas

The former Gold Coast is at the same time a historic truth and a fitting description. One man and his dreams brought first independence and then financial ruin to his once-prosperous country. Many foreign flags have flown over Gold Coast — Portuguese, Swedish, Danish, Dutch and British. Independent MAR 6, 1957.

㉓ TOGO

République Togolaise
(Republic of Togo)

Area: 21,925 sq.mi. (56,785 km²)
Population: 2,890,000
Population growth per annum: 2.7%
Life expectancy at birth: males 44 years, females 48 years
Literacy: 10%
Capital with population: Lomé 283,000
Other important cities with population: none
Language: French, tribal languages
Religion: Animist, Christian (25%), Moslem (10%)
Currency: CFA-franc = 100 centimes

An artificial nation. During the scramble for Africa, the Germans, like all other colonial powers just grabbed as much land as they could regardless of tribal, linguistic and other natural boundaries. Part of their colonial patchwork finally emerged as free Togo. Independent APR 27, 1960.

㉔ BENIN

République Populaire du Benin
(Peoples Republic of Benin)

Area: 43,484 sq.mi. (112,622 km²)
Population: 3,830,000
Population growth per annum: 3.0%
Life expectancy at birth: males 44 years, females 48 years
Literacy: 20%
Capital with population: Porto Novo 105,000
Other important cities with population: Cotonou 490,000
Language: French, local dialects
Religion: Roman Catholic, Islam, Animist
Currency: CFA-franc = 100 centimes

Coastal Benin is a country apart, with island-studded lagoons are neither sea nor land. Here the fishing villages were built on stilts to escape occasional floods and to give some protection against slavers. Independent AUG 1, 1960.

㉕ SÃO TOMÉ AND PRINCIPE

São Tomé e Principe
(Democratic Republic of Sao Tome and Principe)

Area: 372 sq.mi. (964 km²)
Population: 102,000
Population growth per annum: 3.4%
Life expectancy at birth: not available
Literacy: 50 %
Capital with population: São Tomé 20,000
Other important cities with population: none
Language: Portuguese
Religion: Roman Catholic
Currency: Dobra = 100 centimos

These tropical islands in the cool Benguela current are favored by fertile volcanic soil. At the turn of the century the were the world's leading producers of cocoa — but now others produce more. Coconuts and coffee are also grown. Independent JUL 12, 1975.

㉖ NIGERIA

(Federal Republic of Nigeria)

Area: 356,669 sq.mi. (923,768 km²)
Population: 82,390,000
Population growth per annum: 3.2%
Life expectancy at birth: males 46 years, females 49 years
Literacy: 25%
Capital with population: Lagos 1,061,000
Other important cities with population: Ibadan 850,000, Ogbomosho 435,000, Kano 400,000
Language: English, Hausa, Yoruba, Ibo
Religion: Moslem (55%), Christian (25%)
Currency: Naira = 100 kobo

Nigeria is Africa's most populous country in more than one sense. No other can match its over 80 millions and its over 250 linguistic groups (and tribes). It is hard to believe that this prosperous nation once was justly called "The White Man's Grave" (due to the coastal malaria swamps). Independent OCT 1, 1960.

㉗ CAMEROON

République du Cameroun
(United Republic of Cameroon)

Area: 183,569 sq.mi. (475,442 km²)
Population: 9,060,000
Population growth per annum: 2.3%
Life expectancy at birth: males 44 years, females 48 years
Literacy: 34%
Capital with population: Yaoundé 314,000
Other important cities with population: Douala 460,000
Language: English, French, Bantu, Sudanic
Religion: Moslem (25%), Roman Catholic (20%), Protestant (15%), Animist
Currency: CFA-franc = 100 centimes

An ethnic kaleidoscope, the country was a German colony, then two separate League of Nations mandates (French and British) before becoming a unitary republic. There are some two hundred different African ethnic groups. The famous Mt. Cameroon, that rises 13,350 ft. up from the sea, serves at times as a natural lighthouse. The volcano erupted as recently as 1959. Indep. JAN 1, 1960.

㉘ CENTRAL AFRICAN REPUBLIC

République Centrafricaine

Area: 240,535 sq.mi. (622,984 km²)
Population: 2,520,000
Population growth per annum: 2.7%
Life expectancy at birth: 44 years
Literacy: 20%
Capital with population: Bangui 390,000
Other important cities with population: Berbérati 95,000
Language: French, local dialects
Religion: Animist (57%), Roman Catholic (20%), Protestant (15%)
Currency: CFA-franc = 100 centimes

At this crossroads of Africa the savannas meet the rain forests and the Bantu peoples mingle with the nilo-saharan groups and others. Even the rivers are running in opposite directions: the Ubangi towards Congo, the Shari to Lake Chad. Indep. AUG 13, 1960.

㉙ EQUATORIAL GUINEA

República de Guinea Ecuatorial
(Republic of Equatorial)

Area: 10,831 sq.mi. (28,051 km²)
Population: 398,000
Population growth per annum: 2.3%
Life expectancy at birth: males 44 years, females 48 years
Literacy: 20%
Capital with population: Malabo 27,000
Other important cities with population: none
Language: Spanish, Fang, English
Religion: Roman Catholic (60%)
Currency: Ekuele = 100 céntimos

As an antithesis, a part of the mainland of Africa belongs to the main island of Equatorial Guinea. On Bioko the lingua franca has been pidgin English and on Pagalu Portuguese patois in spite of the fact that Spanish was the official language! Indep. OCT 12, 1968.

㉚ GABON

République Gabonaise
(Gabonese Republic)

Area: 103,347 sq.mi. (267,667 km²)
Population: 1,370,000
Population growth per annum: 1.0%
Life expectancy at birth: males 42 years, females 45 years
Literacy: 65%
Capital with population: Libreville 350,000
Other important cities with population: Port Gentil 78,000
Language: French, Bantu dialects
Religion: Roman Catholic (42%), Animist, Protestant
Currency: CFA-franc = 100 centimes

Like some brand names Gabon has become almost a household word, because of the widespread use of mahogany plywood for furniture and doors. In addition to timber, Gabon produces oil, manganese and uranium. Independent AUG 17, 1960.

㉛ CONGO

République Populaire du Congo
(Peoples Republic of the Congo)

Area: 132,000 sq.mi. (342,000 km²)
Population: 1,740 000
Population growth per annum: 2.6%
Life expectancy at birth: males 44 years, females 48 years
Literacy: 80%
Capital with population: Brazzaville 422,000
Other important cities with population:
    Pointe Noire 185,000
Language: French, bantu dialects
Religion: Animist (47%), Roman Catholic (40%),
    Protestant (12%)
Currency: CFA-franc = 100 centimes

*Without the Congo River there wouldn't be any Congo. The
sole reason for establishing the French colony north of the
great river was to explore and exploit as much as possible of
the basin (in competition with the Belgians). The name of the
capital still honors the founding explorer, de Brazza.
Independent AUG 15, 1960.*

㉜ UGANDA

(Republic of Uganda)

Area: 91,452 sq.mi. (236,860 km²)
Population: 14,000,000
Population growth per annum: 3.0%
Life expectancy at birth: males 51 years, females 54 years
Literacy: 25%
Capital with population: Kampala 340,000
Other important cities with population: none
Language: English, Swahili, tribal languages
Religion: Roman Catholic (35%), Protestant (25%),
    Moslem (10%), Animist
Currency: Uganda shilling = 100 cents

*Once and future Pearl of Africa? Here people demonstrated
once more that they are their own worst enemy in their
lust for power. The settling of the gem remains; fertile
lands with an abundance of water; and magnificent scenery;
the fabled Mountains of the Moon, the Ruwenzori; and the
source lakes of the Nile. Independent SEP 9, 1962.*

㉝ RWANDA

Republika y'u Rwanda
(Republic of Rwanda)

Area: 10,169 sq.mi. (26,338 km²)
Population: 5,650,000
Population growth per annum: 3.0%
Life expectancy at birth: males 44 years, females 48 years
Literacy: 37%
Capital with population: Kigali 157,000
Other important cities with population: none
Language: French, Kinyarwandu, Swahili
Religion: Animist, Roman Catholic (40%)
Currency: Rwanda franc = 100 centimes

*This tiny nation contains some spectacular features: some of
the true sources of the Nile, some of the last mountain gorillas
and some active volcanoes in the Virunga Mountains. Independent JUL 7, 1962.*

㉞ BURUNDI

(Republic of Burundi)

Area: 10,747 sq.mi. (27,834 km²)
Population: 4,560 000
Population growth per annum: 2.2%
Life expectancy at birth: males 39 years, females 43 years
Literacy: 25%
Capital with population: Bujumbura 160,000
Other important cities with population: none
Language: French, Kirundi
Religion: Roman Catholic 78%
Currency: Burundi franc = 100 centimes

*A free colony. The hamitic Tutsi established colonial rule over
the Hutu — the Bantu majority of the people as early as the
17th century. The Europeans came over two hundred years
later and left after seventy years. The Tutsi still rule Burundi.
Independent JUL 1, 1962.*

㉟ KENYA

Jamhuri ya Kenya
(Republic of Kenya)

Area: 224,961 sq.mi. (582,646 km²)
Population: 19,500,000
Population growth per annum: 4.0%
Life expectancy at birth: males 51 years, females 56 years
Literacy: 40 %
Capital with population: Nairobi 1,200,000
Other important cities with population: Mombasa 340,000,
    Kisumu 155,000
Language: Swahili, English
Religion: Protestant (37%), Roman Catholic (22%),
    Moslem (5%), Others
Currency: Kenya Shilling = 100 cents

*If there is a Safari Land in the world, it must be Kenya. The word
safari (from the Arabic word for travel) rings with adventure.
Here the adventurer's dreams may still be realized. In parks
such as famous Amboseli close-ups of lions can be taken
against the background of snow-capped Kilimanjaro.
Independent DEC 12, 1963.*

㊱ SOMALIA

Jamhuryadda Dimugradiga Somaliya
(Somali Democratic Republic)

Area: 246,199 sq.mi. (637,657 km²)
Population: 3,860,000
Population growth per annum: 7.9%
Life expectancy at birth: males 41 years, females 45 years
Literacy: 5%
Capital with population: Muqdisho 600,000
Other important cities with population: Hargeysa 150,000
Language: Somali
Religion: Moslem
Currency: Somali shilling = 100 centesimi

*The land of frankincense and myrrh — today as in the days of
ancient Egypt. Incense resins and carvings of aromatic
resinous wood are still an important product of this droughtrid-
den land of semideserts and dry savannas. Some of its proud
camel herders now farm irrigated lands. Independent JUL 1,
1960.*

㊲ ZAIRE
République du Zaïre
(Republic of Zaire)

Area: 905,746 sq.mi. (2,344,885 km²)
Population: 31,940,000
Population growth per annum: 2.8%
Life expectancy at birth: males 44 years, females 48 years
Literacy: males 40%, females 15%
Capital with population: Kinshasa 2,450,000
Other important cities with population: Kananga 705,000, Lubumbashi 455,000
Language: French, Bantu-an Sudan dialects
Religion: Roman Catholic 48%, Animist, Protestant (12%)
Currency: Zaire = 100 makuta

The heart of Africa. Within Zaire (former Belgian Congo) can be found sophisticated Kinshasa and rain forests with pygmy tribes, uranium and diamond mines as well as leaking river steamers, steaming rain forests but also prosperous farmland — and some 200 different ethnic groups. Independent JUN 30, 1960.

㊳ TANZANIA
(United Republic of Tanzania)

Area: 364,884 sq.mi. (945,050 km²)
Population: 19,730,000
Population growth per annum: 2.9%
Life expectancy at birth: 52 years
Literacy: 66%
Capital with population: Dar es Salaam 757,000
Other important cities with population: Zanzibar (Town) 111,000, Mwanza 111,000
Language: Swahili, English, local dialects
Religion: Animist, Christian (30%), Moslem (30%)
Currency: Tanzanian shilling = 100 cents

Arid Tanzania is full of natural wonders: The snow-capped, perfect volcanic cone on Mt Kilimanjaro, highest in Africa; Lake Victoria, third largest in the World; Lake Tanganyika, second deepest; the Serengeti Plains with the last primeval herds of wild animals; the serene Ngorongoro Crater.

㊴ COMORO ISLANDS
Republique fédérale islamique des Comores
(Federal Islamic Republic of the Comoros)

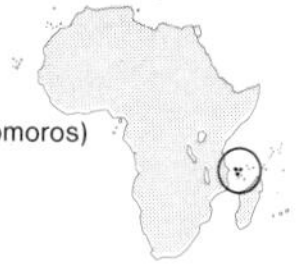

Area: 719 sq.mi. (1,862 km²)
Population: 370,000
Population growth per annum: 2.2%
Life expectancy at birth: males 47 years, females 45 years
Literacy: 15%
Capital with population: Moroni 25,000
Other important cities with population: none
Language: French, Arabic
Religion: Islam
Currency: CFA-franc = 100 centimes

Essence is the very essence of the economy of the Comoro Islands that produce exotic ilang-ilang, citronella and jasmine essences as well as vanilla extract and cloves. Independent JUL 6, 1975.

㊵ SEYCHELLES
(Republic of Seychelles)

Area: 171 sq.mi. (443 km²)
Population: 65,000
Population growth per annum: 3.1%
Life expectancy at birth: 66 years
Literacy: 60%
Capital with population: Victoria 14,000
Other important cities with population: none
Language: English, French, Creole
Religion: Roman Catholic (91%), Protestant (8%)
Currency: Seychelles rupee = 100 cents

The islands of the love fruit — the world's largest, the sea (or double) coconut. This gigantic fruit, that may weigh 50 pounds, contains 3-4 smooth bilobed nuts with unavoidable associations to the human body. They grow only on the Seychelles, and their origin was long a mystery. Independent JUN 29, 1976.

㊶ ANGOLA
República Popular de Angola
(People's Republic of Angola)

Area: 481,354 sq.mi. (1,246,700 km²)
Population: 7,770,000
Population growth per annum: 2.5%
Life expectancy at birth: males 40 years, females 43 years
Literacy: 20 %
Capital with population: Luanda 475,000
Other important cities with population: Huambo 62,000
Language: Portuguese, various Bantu languages
Religion: Roman Catholic, Animist
Currency: Kwanza = 100 lwei

Accessibility shaped the destiny of Angola. In contrast to other parts of Africa there are good harbors here and neither forbidding deserts nor feverish swamps bar the routes to the interior. Thus Angola became one of the first European colonies on the African mainland. Independent NOV 11, 1975.

㊷ ZAMBIA
(Republic of Zambia)

Area: 290,586 sq.mi. (752,620 km²)
Population: 6,240,000
Population growth per annum: 3.2%
Life expectancy at birth: males 47 years, females 50 years
Literacy: 54%
Capital with population: Lusaka 538,000
Other important cities with population: Kitwe 315,000, Ndola 285,000
Language: English, Bantu dialects
Religion: Christian (60%), Animist
Currency: Kwacha = 100 ngwee

A colony for less than 40 years! Here colonial rule was not established until 1924 (as the result of Cecil Rhodes's dream of extending British rule from the Cape to Cairo) but by 1964 the winds of change brought freedom to Zambia. The Victoria Falls are Zambia's most famous sight. Independent OCT 24, 1964.

㊸ MALAWI
(Republic of Malawi)

Area: 45,747 sq.mi. (118,484 km²)
Population: 6,100 000
Population growth per annum: 3.2%
Life expectancy at birth: males 44 years, females 48 years
Literacy: 25%
Capital with population: Lilongwe 103,000
Other important cities with population: Blantyre 220,000
Language: English, Chichewa
Religion: Animist, Christian (30%), Moslem (15%)
Currency: Kwacha = 100 tambala

A self-sufficient land of farmers, striving to build a better future. This is expressed also in their names for the units of currency. One kwacha (dawn) is divided into 100 tambalas (cockerels).

㊹ MOZAMBIQUE
República Popular de Moçambique
(People's Republic of Mozambique)

Area: 308,641 sq.mi. (799,380 km²)
Population: 13,140,000
Population growth per annum: 2.6%
Life expectancy at birth: males 44 years, females 48 years
Literacy: 14%
Capital with population: Maputo 755,000
Other important cities with population: Nampula 156,000 Beira 230,000
Language: Portuguese, Bantu languages
Religion: Roman Catholic (18%), Moslem (10%), Animist
Currency: Metical = 100 centavos

Geographical facts force "all-black" Mozambique to live in an uneasy partnership with white South Africa. Mozambique has water-power (Cabora Bassa, 1.4 GW.) and people-power but few minerals. South Africa needs contract workers and electricity in its mines. Independent JUN 15, 1975.

㊺ NAMIBIA (SOUTH-WEST AFRICA)
Namibia (Suidwes-Afrika)
(U.N. trusteeship, ruled by South Africa)

Area: 317,827 sq.mi. (823,168 km²)
Population: 1,040,000
Population growth per annum: not available
Life expectancy at birth: not available
Literacy: not available
Capital with population: Windhoek 89,000
Other important cities with population: none
Language: Afrikaans, English, German
Religion: Protestant (40%)
Currency: South African rand = 100 cents

Poor but potentially rich, a nation but yet kept in colonial bondage, Namibia awaits full freedom. This former German colony was given as a mandate under the auspices of the League of Nations in 1919. South Africa refuses to set Namibia free.

㊻ BOTSWANA
(Republic of Botswana)

Area: 231,805 sq.mi. (600,372 km²)
Population: 940,000
Population growth per annum: 2.8%
Life expectancy at birth: males 47 years, females 50 years
Literacy: 30%
Capital with population: Gaborone 79,000
Other important cities with population: Francistown 36,000
Language: English, Setswana
Religion: Indigenous beliefs (majority), Christian (15%)
Currency: Pula = 100 thebe

Land-locked Botswana lies in the center of the mountainbowl of southern Africa. Here lies the Kalahari desert and here the Cubango River loses itself in a maze of salt swamps and shallow lakes without outlet, such as famed Lake Ngami. Independent SEP 30, 1966.

㊼ ZIMBABWE

Area: 150,698 sq.mi. (390,308 km²)
Population: 7,530,000
Population growth per annum: 3.4%
Life expectancy at birth: males 52 years, females 55 years
Literacy: 45 %
Capital with population: Harare 656,000
Other important cities with population: Bulawayo 414,000, Chitungwiza 175,000
Language: English, Bantu dialects
Religion: Christian, Animist
Currency: Zimbabwe dollar = 100 cents

A nation with well-deserved pride. Zimbabwe is named after the impressive ruin-city that also is the firm foundation of the national spirit. These massive stone walls and towers were built more than a thousand years ago by Bantu kings — ancestors to the people of today's Zimbabwe. Independent APR 18, 1980.

㊽ MADAGASCAR
Repoblika Demokratika n'i Madagascar
(Democratic Republic of Madagascar)

Area: 226,658 sq.mi.(587,041 km²)
Population: 9,740,000
Population growth per annum: 2.6%
Life expectancy at birth: males 44 years, females 48 years
Literacy: 53%
Capital with population: Antananarivo 500,000
Other important cities with population: Toamasina 60,000
Language: Merina, French
Religion: Animist, Christian (40%), Moslem (10%)
Currency: Malagasy franc = 100 centimes

The fourth largest island of all — and in most aspects an Asian island. Geologically it is a segment of the same block as India, and the population is of Indo-Melanesian stock. The endemic wildlife comprises rare species, such as the bug-eyed aye-aye and the hedgehog-like tenrec.

㊾ REPUBLIC OF SOUTH AFRICA

Area: 473,291 sq.mi. (1,225,824 km²)
Population: 31,850,000
Population growth per annum: 2.8%
Life expectancy at birth: males 59 years, females 62 years
Literacy: Whites 98%, Asians 85%, Coloreds 75%, Africans (50%)
Capital with population: Cape Town 1,108,000 Pretoria 528,000
Other important cities with population: Johannesburg 1,540,000 Durban 506,000
Language: Afrikaans, English
Religion: Protestant, Roman Catholic
Currency: Rand = 100 cents

Humans are their own enemies in rich South Africa. The original natives, the bushmen, fled into the Kalahari desert at the arrival of the Bantu tribes and the original Dutch Boers. The peoples of South Africa are now torn apart by worsening racial conflicts, aggravated by the infamous Apartheid ideology. Independent MAY 31, 1910, 1931.

㊿ LESOTHO
(Kingdom of Lesotho)

Area: 11,720 sq.mi. (30,355 km²)
Population: 1,470,000
Population growth per annum: 2.4%
Life expectancy at birth: males 49 years, females 51 years
Literacy: 55%
Capital with population: Maseru 45,000
Other important cities with population: none
Language: Sesotho, English
Religion: Roman Catholic (40%), Protestant (40%)
Currency: Lote = 100 lisente

An encircled nation, but not a subjugated land. This free black enclave in "white" South Africa is a reminder to its neighbors that all people are created equal. Independent OCT 4, 1966.

㊼ SWAZILAND
(Kingdom of Swaziland)

Area: 6,705 sq.mi. (17,365 km²)
Population: 630,000
Population growth per annum: 2.8%
Life expectancy at birth: males 44 years, females 48 years
Literacy: 65%
Capital with population: Mbabane 23,000
Other important cities with population: none
Language: Swazi, English
Religion: Protestant (60%), Roman Catholic, Animist
Currency: Lilangeni = 100 cents

The proud Swazi people claim a history of five hundred years, but in their country their 'rights' are not older than those of their white neighbors on the other side of the Drakensberg Mountains. British protection kept Swaziland out of the Boer's hands. Independent SEP 6, 1968.

㊽ MAURITIUS

Area: 790 sq.mi. (2,045 km²)
Population: 990,000
Population growth per annum: 1.6%
Life expectancy at birth: males 61 years, females 67 years
Literacy: 61%
Capital with population: Port-Louis 150,000
Other important cities with population: Beau-Bassin (Rose Hill) 90,000
Language: English, French, Creole
Religion: Hindu (53%), Roman Catholic (25%), Moslem (16%)
Currency: Mauritius rupee = 100 cents

In relation to size no land on Earth has as many different languages — spoken by so many diverse ethnic groups: English (official), Hindi, Creole, Urdu, Tamil, French, Chinese, Arabic and a few African languages. Indep. MAR 12, 1968.

INDEX OF NAMES

After each name in this Index there are some numbers and letters. The number in **bold** type immediately after the name tells you which page to look at in the atlas. The letter and number after the page number tell you which grid square to look at. For example, suppose you look up Sacramento in the Index. You will see Sacramento **20** B4. So to find Sacramento you need to turn to page 20 and look in square B4.

A

Aachen **40** E 4
Aalen **41** F 5
Aa Sumayh **60** D 3
Aba **59** F 4
Abadab, Jabal **56** F 5
Åbādān **49** E 3
Åbādeh **49** F 3
Abadla **54** E 2
Abaetetuba **33** J 4
Abagnar Qi **71** G 2
Abaiang **82** C 2
Abakaliki **59** F 4
Abakan **68** F 5
Abalak **59** F 2
Abancay **34** B 3
Abant Silsilesi **46** D 2
Abariringa **82** D 3
Abarqu **49** F 3
Abarqu, Kavir-e **49** F 3
Abatskoye **51** O 4
Abay **51** O 6
Abaya, Lake **61** F 3
Abaza **68** F 5
Abbai **60** F 2
Abbāsābād **49** G 1
Abbeville **44** D 1
Abbeville (LA, U.S.A.) **25** F 2
Abbot Ice Shelf **85**
'Abd al Kūrī **61** J 2
Abdulino **50** K 5
Abéché **59** J 3
Abemama **82** C 2
Abengourou **58** D 4
Abeokuta **58** E 4
Aberdeen (S.D., U.S.A.) **21** G 2
Aberdeen (U.K.) **40** C 3
Aberdeen (WA, U.S.A.) **20** B 2
Aberdeen Lake **15** JK 2
Aberystwyth **40** C 4
Abha' **57** G 5
Abhar **49** E 1
Abidjan **58** CD 4
Abilene **21** G 5
Abitibi **18** D 3
Abkit **69** T 3
Åbo **43** H 3
Abong Abong, Gunung **74** A 3
Abong Mbang **59** G 5
Abraham's Bay **29** E 2
Abrantes **44** B 4
'Abri **56** E 4

Abruzzo **45** F 3
Absaroka Range **20** DE 2–3
Abū ad Duhūr **48** B 2
Abū al Bukhush **49** F 4
Abū 'Alī **49** E 4
Abu Dhabi **49** FG 4
Abufari **33** F 5
Abū Hadrīyah **66** D 5
Abū Hamad **56** E 5
Abū Jifān **49** E 4
Abū Kamāl **48** C 2
Abū Maţariq **56** D 6
Abū Mūsa' **49** G 4
Abunã (Brazil) **34** C 3
Abuqasr **66** BC 4
Abūqrin **55** J 2
Abū Qumayyis, Ra's **49** F 4
Abu Road **72** B 3
Abū Sunbul **56** E 4
Abuya Myeda **61** FG 2
Abū Zaby **57** J 4
Abū Zaby (United Arab Emirates) **49** FG 4
Abū Zanīmah **48** A 3
Abyad, Ra's al **48** BC 5
Abyār 'Alī **48** C 4
Abydos **56** E 3
Åbyek **49** F 2
Acadia, Cape **17** L 4
Acadia National Park **23** G 3
Açailândia **33** J 4
Acajutla **25** FG 5
Acámbaro **25** D 3–4
Acandí **28** D 5
Acaponeta **24** C 3
Acapulco **25** D 4
Acarai, Serra **33** G 3
Acaraú **35** HJ 1
Acari **35** J 2
Acarigua **32** E 2
Acatlán de Osorio **25** E 4
Acayucan **25** E 4
Accomac **22** E 3
Accra **58** DE 4
Acebuches **24** D 2
Achaguas **29** F 5
Achao **37** B 7
Achar **36** E 5
Achayvayam **69** VW 3
Achelóos **46** B 3
Achinsk **68** F 4
Acklins Island **29** E 2
Aconcagua, Cerro **36** BC 5
Acorizal **34** E 3–4

Acre (Brazil) **32** D 5
Acre (Brazil) **34** C 3
Acre (Israel) **48** B 2
Acri **45** G 4
Actopan **25** E 3
Ada (OK, U.S.A.) **21** G 5
Adaba **61** F 3
Adair, Bahia **20** D 5
Adak (AK, U.S.A.) **12** B 6
Adak (Sweden) **42** G 2
'Adale **61** H 4
Adam, Mount **37** DE 9
Adamantina **35** F 5
Adamaoua **59** G 4
Adams Bridge **72** CD 6
Adamstown **83** G 4
Adana **48** B 1
Adapazarı **46** D 2
Adare, Cape **85**
Adavale **79** GH 4
Aḍ Daḥnā' **49** DE 4
Ad Dammām **49** F 4
Ad Dār al Ḥamrā' **66** B 5
Ad Darb **57** G 5
Ad Dawādimī **48** D 4
Ad Dawhah **49** F 4
Ad Dawr **48** D 2
Ad Dayr **48** A 4
Ad Dibdibah **49** E 3
Ad Dilam **49** E 5
Ad Dindar **56** E 6
Addis Ababa **61** F 3
Addis Zemen **61** F 2
Ad Diwaniyah **49** D 3
Ad Duwaym **56** E 6
Adelaide Island **85**
Adelaide Peninsula **16** G 3
Adelaide River **78** E 1
Adélie Coast **85**
Adige **45** F 2
Adıgüzel Barajı **46** C 3
Adirondack Mountains **23** F 2
Adi Ugri **61** F 2
Adıyaman **47** E 3
Admiralty **13** L 4
Admiralty Island National Monument **13** L 4
Admiralty Islands **80** E 2
Admiralty Mountains **85**
Ado **58** E 4
Ado Ekiti **59** F 4
Adok **60** E 3
Adrano **45** F 4

Adrar **54** E 3
Adrar des Iforas **58** E 1–2
Adré **59** J 3
Adrian **22** D 2
Adriatic Sea **45** FG 3
Adwa **61** F 2
Adzhar **47** F 2
Adzopé **58** D 4
Aegean Sea **46** C 3
Afao, Mont **55** G 3
Afghanistan **67** GH 4
Afif **48** D 4–5
Afikpo **59** F 4
Afmadöw **61** G 4
Afognak **12** G 4
African Islands **61** J 5
Afyonkarahisar **46** D 3
Agabah, Khalij al **48** B 3
Agadez **59** F 2
Agadir **54** CD 2
Agalta, Sierra de **28** B 3
Agana **82** A 2
Agapitovo **51** R 2
Agartala **73** F 3
Agata **68** F 2
Agats **75** J 5
Agattu **12** A 5
Agawa Bay **18** D 4
Agboville **58** CD 4
Agdary **68** L 3
Agen **44** D 3
Agepsta **47** F 2
Agha Jārī **49** EF 3
Agordat **61** F 1
Agra **72** C 2
Ağrı **47** F 3
Agrigento **45** F 4
Agrihan **82** A 1
Agrinion **46** B 3
Agto **17** P 3
Água Clara **35** F 5
Aguadulce **32** BC 2
Agua Prieta **24** E 5
Águas Formosas **35** HJ 4
Aguililla **24** D 4
Agulhas, Cape **62** C 6
Aguscalientes **24** D 3
Agustín Codazzi **29** E 4–5
Ahaggar **55** FG 4
Ahe **83** F 3
Ahmadabad **72** B 3
Ahmadnagar **72** BC 4
Ahome **24** C 2
Ähtävänjoki **42** H 3

Ahväz 49 E 3
Ahvenanmaa 43 GH 3
Ahwar 57 H 6
Aihui 69 N 6
Aiken 22 D 4
Ailigandí 28 D 5
Ailinginae 82 BC 2
Ailinglapalap 82 C 2
Aillik 19 J 2
Ailuk 82 C 2
Aim 69 O 4
Ain Amenas 55 G 3
Aïn Amguel 55 FG 4
Aïn Beïda 55 G 1
Aïn Ezzane 55 H 4
Aïn Tiguelguemine 55 F 3
Aïoun el Atrouss 54 D 5
Aïr 59 F 2
Airao 33 F 4
Air Force Island 17 M 3
Aishihik 13 K 3
Aitape 80 D 2
Aitutaki 83 E 4
Aix-en-Provence 45 DE 3
Aiyaion Pélagos 46 C 3
Aizuwakamatsu 71 M 3
Ajaccio 45 E 3
Aj Bogd Uul 70 BC 2
'Ajmān 49 G 4
Ajmer 72 B 2
Ajo 20 D 5
Ajo, Cabo de 44 C 3
Akademii, Zaliv 69 P 5
Ak Dağ 46 C 3
Akespe 66 G 1
Akharnai 46 B 3
Akhisar 46 C 3
Akhtubinsk 50 J 6
Akhtyrka 50 FG 5
Akimiski 18 D 3
Akita 71 L 3
Akkabak 67 G 1
Akkajaure 42 G 2
'Akko 48 B 2
Aklavik 13 K 2
Akmenrags 43 H 4
Akobo 60 E 3
Akola 72 C 3
Akosombo Dam 58 E 4
Akpatok 17 N 4
Ákra Akritas 46 B 3
Akra Arnauti 48 A 2
Ákra Maleás 46 B 3
Ákra Spátha 46 B 3
Ákra Taínaron 46 B 3
Akritas, Ákra 46 B 3
Akron 22 D 2
Aksaray 47 D 3
Aksay Kazaku Zizhixian 70 B 3
Aksehir 46 D 3
Aksha 68 K 5
Akshiy 67 G 1
Aksu (China) 67 L 2

Aksu (Turkey) 46 D 3
Aktash 67 H 3
Aktasty 51 M 5
Aktogay 51 P 6
Aktyubinsk 51 L 5
Akun 12 D 5
Akure 59 F 4
Akureyri 42 B 2
Akutan 12 D 5
Ala, Monti di 45 E 3
Alabama 22 C 4
Alabama River 22 C 4
Al Abyad, Ra's 55 G 1
Alaçam Dağları 46 C 3
Alachakh 69 P 4
Alacrán 26 D 4
Aladağ 47 F 3
Alagoas 35 J 2
Alagoinhas 35 J 3
Alagon 44 C 3
Alajuela 28 C 4
Alakanuk 12 E 3
Alakurtti 42 K 2
Al 'Alamayn 56 D 2
Al Amādiyah 48 D 1
Alamagan 82 A 1
Al 'Amārah 49 E 3
Alamitos, Sierra de los 24 D 2
Alamogordo 20–21 E 5
Alamos 24 C 2
Alamos, Sierra 24 D 2
Alamosa 21 E 4
Ålands hav 43 G 3–4
Alanya 47 D 3
Alaotra, Lac 63 H 3
Alapaha River 22 D 4
Alapayevsk 51 M 4
Al' Aqabah 48 B 3
Al 'Aqaylah 55 J 2
Al Arabiyah as Su'udiyah 57 GH 4
Al 'Arīsh 48 A 3
Al 'Armah 49 DE 4
Al Artāwiyah 49 D 4
Al 'Āshūrīyah 66 C 4
Alaska 12 FH 2
Alaska, Gulf of 12 HJ 4
Alaska Peninsula 12 E 4
Alaska Range 12 GH 3
Alatna 12 G 2
Alatyr' 50 J 5
Alava, Cape 20 A 2
Al 'Awaynāt 55 H 3
Al'Awsajīyah 48 D 4
Al 'Ayn 49 G 4
Alazani 47 G 2
Alba 45 E 3
Al Bāb 48 B 1
Albacete 44 C 4
Al Badi' 57 H 4
Al Bahrah 49 E 3
Al Bahr al Mayyit 48 B 3
Alba Iulia 46 B 1
Albanel, Lac 18 F 3

Albania 46 AB 2
Albano Laziale 45 F 3
Albany (Australia) 78 B 5
Albany (GA, U.S.A.) 22 D 4
Albany (N.Y., U.S.A.) 23 F 2
Albany (Ontario, Can.) 18 D 3
Albany (OR, U.S.A.) 20 B 3
Al Barkāt 55 H 4
Al Basrah 49 E 3
Al Batin 49 E 3
Al Bāṭinah 57 K 4
Albatross Point 81 Q 8
Al Baydā' 55 K 2
Albemarle Sound 22 E 3
Albert, Lake 60 E 4
Alberta 14 FG 4
Albert Edward Bay 16 G 3
Albert Lake (OR, U.S.A.) 20 BC 3
Albert Lea 21 H 3
Albert Nile 60 E 4
Albi 44 D 3
Al Bid' 48 B 3
Albina 33 H 2
Al Bi'r 48 B 3
Al Birkah 66 C 6
Alborán 44 C 4
Ålborg 43 F 4
Al Brayqah 55 JK 3
Albu Ali 47 F 4
Al Buhayrah al Murrah al Ku- brā 48 A 3
Albuquerque 20 E 4
Albuquerque, Cayos de 28 C 4
Albury 79 H 6
Alcalá 44 C 3
Alcalá 44 B 4
Alcántara 33 K 4
Alcántara, Embalse de 44 B 4
Alcaraz, Sierra de 44 C 4
Alcázar de San Juan 44 C 4
Alcién 59 G 6
Alcira 44 C 4
Alcolea del Pinar 44 C 3
Alcoy 44 C 4
Aldabra Islands 61 H 6
Aldama 24 C 2
Aldan 69 O 3
Aldan 69 N 4
Aldanskoye Nagor'ye 69 MN 4
Aleg 54 C 5
Alegrete 36 E 4
Aleknagik 12 F 4
Aleksandriya (Ukraine, U.S.S.R.) 50 FG 6
Aleksandrovsk 51 M 4
Aleksandrovskiy 68 L 5
Aleksandrovsk-Sakhalinskiy 69 Q 5
Alekseyevka (Kazakhstan, U.S.S.R.) 51 O 5
Alekseyevo 69 R 1

Alençon 44 D 2
Aleppo 48 B 1
Aléria 45 E 3
Alès 44 D 3
Alessandria 45 E 3
Ålestrup 43 E 4
Ålesund 42 E 3
Aleutian Islands 12 AC 4
Aleutian Range 12 F 4
Aleution Islands 12 EG 4–5
Alexander Archipelago 13 K 4
Alexander Island 85
Alexandra 80 PQ 10
Alexandra Falls 14 F 2
Alexandria (Egypt) 56 DE 2
Alexandria (LA, U.S.A.) 25 H 5
Alexandria (MD, U.S.A.) 22 E 3
Alexandria (Romania)46 BC 2
Alexandroúpolis 46 C 2
Aleysk 51 Q 5
Al Fāshir 56 D 6
Al Fatḥah 66 C 3
Al Fayyūm 56 DE 3
Al Fuhayhil 49 E 3
Al Fujayrah 49 G 4
Al Furat 47 F 3–4
Al Fuwayrit 49 F 4
Algama 69 N 4
Alganskaya 69 WX 3
Algarve 44 B 4
Algeciras 44 B 4
Algeria 54–55 EF 3
Al Ghazālah 48 C 4
Alghero 45 E 3
Algiers 55 F 1
Algona 21 H 3
Al Hadhālīl 48–49 D 3
Al Hadīthah 48 CD 2
Al Hadīthah 66 C 4
Al Hamād 48 C 2–3
Al Hamrā' 48 C 5
Al Hanākiyah 48 C 4
Al Hanākiyah 57 G 4
Al Hanīsh al Kabīr 57 G 6
Al Harrah 48 BC 2
Al Harrah 48 C 3
Al Hasa 48 B 3
Al Hasā' 49 E 4
Al Hasakah 48 C 1
Al Hasan 48 D 2
Al Hawwāri 55 K 4
Al Hayy 49 DE 2
AlHijāz 56 F 3
Al Hijaz (Saudi Arabia) 48 B 4
Al Hillah 49 D 2
Al Hillah 49 E 5
Al Hillah 56 D 6
Al Hudaydah 57 G 6
Al Hufrah 48 BC 3–4
Al Hufūf 49 E 4
Al Hūj 48 C 3
Al Husayhiṣah 56 E 6
Al Huwaymi 57 H 6

Aliábád **49** G 3
Aliákmon **46** B 2
Ali Bayramly **66** DE 3
Alicante **44** C 4
Alice **25** E 2
Alice River **79** H 3
Alice Springs **78** E 3
Aligarh **72** C 2
Al Iglim al Janūbīyah **60** DE 3
Aligüdarz **49** E 2
Alijūq, Kūh-e **49** F 3
Al 'Iraq **48** D 2
Al 'Irq **55** K 3
Ali Sabjeh **61** G 2
Al 'Isāwiyah **48** B 3
Al Iskandariyah **56** DE 2
Aliskerovo **69** U 2
Al Ismā'īliyah **48** A 3
Alitak, Cape **12** FG 4
Aliwal North **62** D 6
Al Jafr **48** B 3
Al Jāfūrah **49** F 4–5
Al Jaghbūb **55** K 3
Al Jahrah **49** E 3
Al Jalāmīd **48** C 3
Al Jawf **48** C 3
Al Jayli **56** E 5
Al Jazā'ir **55** F 1
Al Jazīrah **47** F 3–4
Al Jiwā' **49** FG 5
Al Jīzah **56** DE 2
Al Jubayl **66** DE 5
Al Jubaylah **49** E 4
Al Jumaymah **66** C 5
Al Junaynah **56** C 6
Al Karak **48** B 3
Al Karnak **56** E 3
Al Kāzimīyah **48** D 2
Al Khalīl **48** B 3
Al Khāliş **49** D 2
Al Kharj **49** E 5
Al Kharţūm **56** EF 5
Al Kharţūm Baḥri **56** EF 5
Al Khaşab **49** G 4
Al Khidr **49** D 3
Al Khubar **49** F 4
Al Khufayfiyah **49** D 4
Al Khunfah **48** C 3
Al Kir'ānah **49** F 4
Al Kūfah **48** D 2
Al Kumayt **49** E 2–3
Al Kuntillah **48** B 3
Al Kūt **49** D 2
Al Kuwayt **49** E 3
Al Labbah **48** C 3
Al Lādhiqīyah **56** EF 1
Al Lagowa **56** D 6
Allahabad **72** D 2
Allakaket **12** G 2
Allakh-Yun' **69** P 3
Allegheny Mountains **22** DE 3
Allegheny Plateau **22** D 3
Allegheny River **22** E 2
Allende **25** D 2

Allentown **22** E 2
Alleppey **72** C 6
Alliance **21** F 3
Al Lifīyah **66** C 4
Al Liṣāfah **66** D 5
Al Lussuf **66** C 4
Alma **19** F 4
Alma-Ata **67** K 2
Almada **44** B 4
Al Madīnah **48** C 4
Al Mafraq **48** B 2
Al Maḥallah al Kubrā **56** E 2
Al Mahrah **57** J 5
Al Majann **49** F 5
Al Makhaylī **55** K 2
Al Manadīr **49** G 5
Al Manāmah **49** F 4
Al Manāmah **57** J 3
Al Manāqil **56** E 6
Al Manşūrah **56** E 2
Al Maqţá' **49** G 4
Al Marj **55** K 2
Al Mawşil **48** D 1
Al Mayyāh **48** D 4
Almeirim **33** H 4
Almenara **35** HJ 4
Almendra, Embalse de **44** B 3
Almería **44** C 4
Al'met'yevsk **50** K 4–5
Al Minyā **56** DE 3
Almirante Brown **85**
Almoustarat **58** D 2
Al Mubarraz **49** E 4
Al Mudawwarah **48** B 3
Al Mughayrā' **66** B 5
Al Muharraq **49** F 4
Al Mukallā **57** HJ 6
Al Murabbā' **48** D 4
Al Musayjid **66** BC 6
Al Musayyib **48** D 2
Al Muwaylih **48** B 4
Al Nasser **48** A 4
Alofi **82** D 4
Alongshan **69** M 5
Alor, Pulau **75** F 5
Alor Setar **74** AB 2
Alpena **22** D 2
Alphonse **61** J 6
Alpi Carniche **45** F 2
Alpi Dolomitiche **45** F 2
Alpine (TX, U.S.A.) **24** F 5
Alpine (WY, U.S.A.) **20** D 3
Al Qadārif **56** F 6
Al Qadīmah **57** F 4
Al Qāhirah **56** E 2
Al Qalibah **48** B 3
Al Qāmishlī **48** C 1
Al Qanţarah **48** A 3
Al Qatif **49** E 4
Al Qaţrānī **48** B 3
Al Qaţrūn **55** H 3
Al Qay'īyah **48** D 4
Al Qayrawān **55** GH 1
Al Qayşūmah **66** C 5

Al Qayşūmah (Saudi Arabia) **66** D 5
Al Qunayţirah **48** B 2
Al Qunfudhah **57** FG 5
Al Qurayyah **56** F 3
Al Qurnah **49** E 3
Al Qusayr **48** B 4
Al Qūşūrīyah **48** D 5
Al Qutayfah **48** B 2
Al Quwārah **66** C 5
Al Quwayīyah **49** D 4
Alsask **14** H 4
Alsek **13** K 3
Al Shagra **49** F 4
Altagracia de Orituco **29** F 5
Altamaha River **22** D 4
Altamira **33** H 4
Altamont **20** B 3
Altaqracia **29** E 4
Altar **24** D 5
Alta Shany **67** M 1
Altata **24** C 3
Altay (China) **67** M 1
Altay (Mongolia) **68** G 6
Altay (U.S.S.R.) **51** RS 5
Altiplanicie Mexicana **24** D 2
Altmark **41** F 4
Alto - Alentejo **44** B 4
Alto Garças **35** F 4
Alton (IL, U.S.A.) **21** H 4
Altoona **22** E 2
Alto Parnaíba **33** J 5
Alto Río Senguerr **37** BC 7–8
Alto Turi **33** J 4
Altun Ha **28** B 3
Altun Shan **70** AB 3
Alturas **20** B 3
Altus **21** G 5
Altynasar **67** G 1
Al Ubayyid **56** DE 6
Al Uqsur **48** A 4
Al Urayq (Saudi Arabia) **48** C 3
Al Urdun **48** B 3
Al 'Uwayqilah **48** CD 3
Al 'Uzayr **49** E 3
Alva (OK, U.S.A.) **21** G 4
Alvano, Kūh-e **49** E 2
Alvorado **35** G 3
Älvsbyn **42** H 2
Al Wajh **48** B 4
Alwar **72** C 2
Al Warī'ah **57** H 3
Al Widyān **48** C 3
Alxa Zuoqi **70** DE 3
Alygdzher **68** G 5
Alys-Khaya **69** P 2
Alytus **43** H 5
Amada **56** E 4
Amadjuak Lake **17** M 3–4
Amakinskiy **68** K 1
Amalfi (Colombia) **29** E 5
Amambaí **35** EF 5

Amami-ō-shima **71** JK 5
Amangel'dy **51** N 5
Amanzimtoti **63** E 6
Amapá **33** H 3
Amarillo **21** F 4
Amaro Leite **35** G 3
Amarti **61** G 2
Amasya **47** E 2
Amazar **68** LM 5
Amazonas **32–33** EF 4
Amazonas **33** H 4
Ambala **72** C 1
Ambam **59** G 5
Ambarchik **69** U 2
Ambato **32** C 4
Ambikapur **72** D 3
Ambilobe **63** H 2
Ambohitralanana **63** J 3
Ambon **75** G 4
Ambositra **63** H 4
Ambovombe **63** H 5
Ambre, Cap d' **63** HJ 2
Ambrim **82** C 4
Ambrym **81** J 5
Ambur **72** C 5
Amchitka **12** A 5
Amchitka Pass **12** AB 6
Amdo **70** B 4
Ameca **24** D 3
American Falls Reservoir
  20 D 3
American Highland **85**
American Samoa **82** D 3
Americus **22** D 4
Amery Ice Shelf **85**
Ames **21** H 3
Amga **69** O 3
Amguema **12** B 2
Amguid **55** G 3
Amhara **61** F 2
Amherst **19** H 4
Amherst Island **22** E 2
Amiens **44** D 2
Amindivi Islands **72** B 5
Amirante Islands **61** J 6
Amisk Lake **15** J 4
Amlia **12** C 6
'Ammān **48** B 3
Ammarfjället **42** G 2
Amo **68** H 3
Ámol **49** F 1
Amorgos **46** C 3
Amos **18** E 4
Amoy **71** G 6
Amravati **72** C 3
Amritsar **72** C 1
Amsá'ad **55** K 2
Amsterdam (Netherlands)
  40 DE 4
Amsterdam (N.Y., U.S.A.)
  23 F 2
Amu-Dar'ya **67** G 2
Amukta Pass **12** C 6
Amundsen Gulf **16** B 2

Amu – Arc

Amundsen-Scott **85**
Amundsen Sea **85**
Amuntai **74** E 4
Amur **69** P 5
Amysakh **68** L 2
Anabarskoye Ploskogor'ye **68** J 1–2
Anaco **33** F 2
Anaconda **20** D 2
Anadoli **46–47** CD 3
Anadyr **69** WX 3
Anadyrskaja Nizmennost **69** X 2
Anadyrskiy Zaliv **12** B 3
Anadyrskiy Zaliv **69** Y 3
Anadyrskoye Ploskogor'ye **69** VW 2
Ánah **48** C 2
Anáhuac **25** E 2
Anaimalai Hills **72** C 5
Anakapalle **72** D 4
Anaktuvuk Pass **12** G 2
Ana Maria, Golfo de **27** F 4
Anamur **48** A 1
Anamur Burun **48** A 2
Anamuryum **47** D 3
Anantapur **72** C 5
Anapa **47** E 2
Anápolis **35** G 4
Anár **49** G 3
Añatuya **36** D 4
Anchorage **12** H 3
Anchor Bay **20** B 4
Ancohuma **34** C 4
Ancona **45** F 3
Ancud **37** B 7
Anda **71** J 1
Andalucía **44** BC 4
Andaman Islands **73** F 5
Andaman Sea **73** G 5–6
Andarab **67** H 3
Anderson (IN, U.S.A.) **22** C 2–3
Anderson (N.W.T., Can.) **13** M 2
Anderson (S.C., U.S.A.) **22** D 4
Andes Mountains **31** C 2–6
Andfjorden **42** G 2
Andhra Pradesh **72** C 4
Andimeshk **49** E 2
Andiria Burun **47** D 3
Andirlangar **67** L 3
Andiyskiy Khrebet **47** G 2
Andizhan **67** J 2
Andkhui **67** GH 3
Andong **71** J 3
Andorra **44** D 3
Andorra la Vella **44** D 3
Andöya **42** G 2
Andradina **35** F 5
Andreanof Islands **12** BC 6
Andrews **24** F 5
Andriba **63** H 3

Andropov **50** G 4
Ándros **46** BC 3
Andros Island **27** F 4
Andselv **42** G 2
Andújar **44** C 4
Andyngda **68** L 2
Anéfis **58** E 2
Anegada Passage **29** G 3
Aneto, Pico de **44** D 3
Angar **75** H 4
Angara **68** F 4
Angarsk **68** H 5
Angatau **83** F 4
Angaul **68** GH 5
Ángel de la Guarda, Isla **24** B 2
Angeles **75** HJ 1
Angel Falls **33** F 2
Ängelholm **43** F 4
Ångermanälven **42** G 3
Angers **44** C 2
Angical **35** GH 3
Angijak Island **17** O 3
Angikuni Lake **15** K 2
Angkor **73** H 5
Anglesey **40** BC 4
Angmagssalik **84**
Angoche **63** G 3
Angol **37** B 6
Angola **62** BC 2
Angostura **24** C 2
Angoulême **44** D 2
Angu **60** C 4
Anguilla **29** G 3
Anguille, Cape **19** HJ 4
Anhua **70** F 5
Anhui **71** G 4
Aniak **12** F 3
Aniakchak National Monument and Preserve **12** F 4
Animas Peak **20** E 5
Anjou **44** CD 2
Anjouan **63** GH 2
Ankang **70** E 4
Ankara **47** D 2
Ankazobe **63** H 3
Anlong **70** E 5–6
Anlu **70** F 4
Ann, Cape **85**
Anna (IL, U.S.A.) **22** C 3
Annaba **55** G 1
An Nabk **48** B 2
An Nafūd **48** C 3
An Nāhiyah **57** G 2
Annai **33** G 3
An Najaf **48** D 2–3
An' Nakhi **48** AB 3
Annam **73** J 4–5
Annandale **79** H 3
Anna Plains **78** C 2
Annapolis **22** E 3
Annapurna **72** D 2
Ann Arbor **22** D 2
An Nāsirīyah **49** E 3

Annecy **45** E 2
Anniston **22** C 4
Annobón **59** F 6
An Nu'ayriyah **49** E 4
An Nuhūd **56** D 6
Anoka **21** H 2
Anori **33** F 4
Anqing **71** G 4
Anshan **71** H 2
Anshun **70** DE 5
Ansley **21** G 3
Ansongo **58** DE 2
Anta **34** B 3
Antakya **47** E 3
Antakya **48** B 1
Antalya Kórfezi **46** D 3
Antananarivo **63** H 3
Antarctic Peninsula **85**
Antequera **44** C 4
Anthony **24** E 5
Anticosti, Île de **19** H 4
Antigonish **19** H 4
Antigua **29** G 3
Antigua Guatemala **25** F 5
Antillas Mayores **29** EF 3
Antillas Menores **29** G 4
Antiope **82** D 4
Antipodes Islands **85**
Antlát **55** K 2
Antofagasta **34** B 5
Antofagasta de la Sierra **36** C 4
Antongil, Baie d' **63** HJ 3
Antonio de Biedma **37** CD 8
Antonovo **66** E 1
Antsirabe **63** H 3
Antsiranana **63** HJ 2
Antsohihy **63** H 2
Antwerpen **40** D 4
Anuradhapura **72** D 6
Anvik **12** E 3
Anxi **70** C 2
Anxiang **70** F 5
Anyang **70** FG 3
Anzhero-Sudzhensk **51** RS 4
Aomori **71** M 2
Aosta **45** E 2
Aoudaghost **54** CD 5
Aouinzt Legraa **54** D 3
Aoulef el Arab **54–55** F 3
Apalachee Bay **26** E 3
Apan **25** E 4
Apaporis **32** DE 3–4
Apataki **83** F 4
Apatity **42** K 2
Apatzingán **24** D 4
Apeldoorn **40** E 4
Api, Tanjung **74** C 3
Apia **82** D 3
Apizaco **25** E 4
Aporé **35** F 4
Appalachian Mountains **22** DF 2–3
Appenno Lucano **45** G 3–4

Appenno Tosco-Emiliano **45** F 3
Appleton **22** C 2
Apsheronsk **47** E 2
Apucarana **35** F 5
Apure **32** E 2
Apurimac **34** B 3
Aqär 'Atabah **55** H 3
Aqdá **49** F 2
Aquidauana **34** E 5
'Arabah, Wādi al **48** B 3
Arabestän **49** E 3
Arabian Sea **87**
Arabiyah as Su'udiyah **48** CD 4
Aracaju **35** J 3
Aracati **35** J 1
Araçatuba **35** FG 5
Aracena, Sierra de **44** B 4
Araçuai **35** H 4
Arad **46** B 1
Arada **59** J 2
'Arādah **49** F 5
Arafura Sea **75** HJ 5
Aragarças **35** F 4
Aragon **44** C 3
Araguacema **33** HJ 5
Aragua de Barcelona **29** FG 5
Aragua de Maturín **29** G 5
Aragua de Maturín **33** F 2
Araguaia **33** J 5
Araguaiana **35** F 4
Araguaína **33** J 5
Araguari **35** G 4
Araguatins **33** J 5
Arak (Algeria) **55** F 3
Aräk (Iran) **49** E 2
Arakaka **33** G 2
Arakan Yoma **73** FG 3–4
Aral'sk **67** G 1
Aral'skoye More **66–67** FG 2
Aramac **79** H 3
Arandai **75** H 4
Aranjuez **44** C 3–4
Aranos **62** B 4
Aranuka **82** C 3
Araouane **58** D 2
Arapiraca **35** J 2–3
Araquara **35** G 5
Arauá **35** J 3
Arauca **32** D 2
Arauco **37** B 6
Arauquita **29** E 5
Aravalli Range **72** B 2–3
Araxá **35** G 4
Araya **29** G 4
Arbatax **45** E 4
Arcata **20** B 3
Arcelia **24** D 4
Archer River National Park **79** G 1
Archipelago Kerimbas **63** G 2
Archipiélago de Camagüey **27** F 4

Archipiélago de Colón **32** B 6
Archipiélago de la Reina Adelaida **37** A 9
Archipiélago de los Canarreos **27** E 4
Archipiélago de los Chonos **37** AB 7–8
Archipiélago de los Jardinesde la Reina **27** EF 4
Arco (U.S.A.) **20** D 3
Arcos **44** B 4
Arctic Ocean **84**
Arctic Red River **13** L 2
Arctic Village **12** H 2
Arctowski **85**
Ardabīl **66** D 3
Ardakān **49** F 2
Ard as Sawwān **48** B 3
Ardennes **40** E 4
Ardestan **49** F 2
Ardmore **21** G 5
Arecibo **29** F 3
Areia Branca **35** J 1
Arena, Point **20** B 4
Arenápolis **34** E 3
Arequipa **34** B 4
Arere **33** H 4
Arezzo **45** F 3
Arga **69** R 2
Argan **70** A 2
Argentina **37** CD 6
Arges **46** C 2
Argolikós Kólpos **46** B 3
Argungu **59** EF 3
Argyle, Lake **78** D 2
Ar Horqin Qi **71** H 2
Århus **43** F 4
Arica (Chile) **34** B 4
Arica (Colombia) **32** D 4
Ariguaní **29** E 4
Ariguaní **32** C 1
Arīḥā **48** B 2
Arima (Trinidad and Tobago) **29** G 4
Arinos **34** E 3
Aripuanã **33** F 5
Aripuanã **33** FG 5
Ariquemes **33** F 5
Ariripina **35** HJ 2
Arismendi **29** F 5
Arizona (Argentina) **37** C 6
Arizona (U.S.A.) **20** D 5
Arjona **32** C 1
Arka **69** Q 3
Arkadelphia **21** H 5
Arkalyk **51** N 5
Arkansas **21** H 4
Arkansas City **21** G 4
Arkansas River **21** H 5
Arkhangel'sk **50** H 3
Arkhara **69** O 6
Arklow **40** B 4
Arles **45** D 3
Arlington (OR, U.S.A.) **20** C 2

Arlington (TX, U.S.A.) **21** G 5
Arlington (VA, U.S.A.) **22** E 3
Arlit **59** F 2
Arly **58** E 3
Armant **56** E 3
Armavir **47** F 1
Armenia **32** C 3
Armeniya **47** F 2
Armeria **24** D 4
Armidale **79** J 5
Armstrong **18** C 3
Armyansk **47** D 1
Arnauti, Akra **48** A 2
Arnawai **67** J 3
Arnhem **40** E 4
Arnhem, Cape **79** F 1
Aroab **62** B 5
Arorae **82** C 3
Arquipélago dos Bijagós **58** A 3
Ar Radīsīyah Baḥrī **48** A 4
Ar Rahad **56** E 6
Arraias **35** G 3
Ar Ramādī **48** D 2
Ar Ramlah **48** B 3
Arran **40** B 3
Ar Raqqafi **57** F 1
Ar Raqqah **48** C 2
Arras **44** D 1
Ar Rass **48** D 4
Ar Rawdatayn **49** E 3
Ar Rayhānī **49** G 5
Arrecifes Triángulos **25** F 3
Arriaga **25** F 4
Ar Rifāʿī **66** D 4
Ar Rimāl **57** J 4
Ar Riyād **49** E 4
Ar Rubʿ al Khālī **57** HJ 4–5
Ar Ruṣāfah **66** B 3
Ar Ruṣayriṣ **56** E 6
Ar Ruṭbah **48** C 2
Ar Ruways (Qatar) **49** F 4
Ar Ruways (United Arab Emirates) **49** F 4
Ārs **43** E 4
Arsen'yev **71** K 2
Årskogen **42** G 3
Arteaga **24** D 4
Artem **71** K 2
Artemisa **27** E 4
Artesia **21** F 5
Arthur's Town **27** F 4
Artic Circle **42** AB 2
Artigas **36** E 5
Artillery Lake **14** H 2
Artoli **56** E 5
Artybash **51** R 5
Artyk **69** R 3
Arua **60** E 4
Aruanã **35** F 3
Aruba, Isla **32** E 1
Arunachal **73** F 2
Arun Qi **69** M 6
Aruppukkottai **72** C 6

Arusha **61** F 5
Arvada **20** E 4
Arvayheer **70** D 1
Arvika **43** F 4
Arys' **67** H 2
Arzamas **50** H 4
Asahikawa **71** LM 2
Asamakka **59** F 2
Asansol **72** E 3
Asba Tafari **61** G 3
Ascensión **34** D 4
Ascoli Piceno **45** F 3
Aselle **61** F 3
Asha **51** L 5
Ashdod **48** B 3
Asheville **22** D 3
Ashgelon **48** B 3
Ashkhabad **66** FG 3
Ashland (KS, U.S.A.) **21** G 4
Ashland (KY, U.S.A.) **22** D 3
Ashland (OR, U.S.A.) **20** B 3
Ashland (WI, U.S.A.) **21** H 2
Ash Shabakah **48** D 3
Ash Sharqāt **48** D 2
Ash Shatrah (Iraq) **49** E 3
Ash Shiḥr **57** HJ 6
Ash Shinafīyah **49** D 3
Ash Shuʿaybah **66** C 5
Ash Shuʿbah **49** D 3
Ash Shumlūl **49** E 4
Ash Shwayrif **55** H 3
Ashtabula **22** D 2
Ashton **20** D 3
Ashuanipi **19** G 3
Ashuanipi Lake **19** G 3
Asinara **45** E 3
Asino **51** RS 4
Asir, Ra's **61** J 2
Asmara **61** F 1
Aspen **20** E 4
Aspermont **21** F 5
Aspurito **29** F 5
Assab **61** G 2
Aş Şadr **49** G 4
Aş Şaḥrā' al Gharbīyah **56** D 3
Aş Şaḥrā' al Janūbīyah **56** DE 4
Aş Şaḥrā' an Nūbīyah **56** EF 4
Aş Şaḥrā' ash Sharqīyah **48** AB 4
As Salamīyah **49** E 4
Aş Şālihīyah **48** C 2
As Sālimīyah **49** E 3
As Salmān **49** D 3
As Salt **48** B 2
Assam **73** F 2
As Samāwah **49** D 3
As Sarir **55** K 3
As Silā **49** F 4
Assiniboia **15** H 5
Assiniboine **15** K 5
Assiniboine, Mount **14** F 4

Assis **35** F 5
Assisi **45** F 3
As Subū' **56** E 4
Aş Şulb **49** E 4
Aş Şummān **49** DE 4
Assur **48** D 2
As Suwaydā' **48** B 2
As Suways **48** A 3
Astakh **69** P 2
Astipálaia **46** C 3
Astoria **20** B 2
Astrakhan **66** DE 1
Asturias **44** B 3
Asunción (Mariana Is.) **82** A 1
Asunción (Paraguay) **36** E 3–4
Aswān **48** A 4
Aswan High Dam **48** A 5
Asyūṭ **56** E 3
Atacama, Desierto de **34** C 5
Atacama, Salar de **34** C 5
Atafu **82** D 3
Atambua **75** F 5
Atangmik **17** Q 4
Atar **54** C 4
Atas Bogd Uul **70** C 2
Atascadero **20** B 4
Atasu **51** O 6
'Aṭbarah **56** E 5
Atbarah **56** EF 5
Atbasar **51** N 5
Atchafalaya Bay **25** F 2
Atchison **21** G 4
Athabasca (Alb., Can.) **14** G 3
Athabasca (Alb., Can.) **14** G 4
Athens (GA, U.S.A.) **22** D 4
Athens (Greece) **46** B 3
Athens (TN, U.S.A.) **22** D 3
Athínai **46** B 3
Ath Thumāmī **49** D 4
Ati **59** H 3
Atico **34** B 4
Atikokan **15** L 5
Atikonak Lake **19** H 3
Atka **12** C 6
Atka (AK, U.S.A.) **12** C 6
Atka (U.S.S.R.) **69** S 3
Atkarsk **50** H 5
Atkasuk **12** F 1
Atkinson (N.C., U.S.A.) **22** E 4
Atkinson (NE, U.S.A.) **21** G 3
Atlanta **22** CD 4
Atlantic (IA, U.S.A.) **21** H 3
Atlantic City **23** F 3
Atlantic Ocean **86**
Atlas el Kebir **54** DE 2
Atlas Mountains **54** DF 2
Atlin **13** L 4
Atlin Lake **13** L 4
Atmore **22** C 4
Atna Peak **13** M 5
Atoka **21** G 5
Atoyac de Alvarez **25** D 4
Ätran **43** F 4
Atrato **32** C 2

141

Atsy **75** J 5
At Tafilah **48** B 3
Aṭ Ṭā'if **57** G 4
Attawapiskat **18** CD 3
Attawapiskat **18** D 3
Attawapiskat Lake **18** C 3
At Tawil **48** C 3
Aṭ Ṭaysīyah **48** D 3–4
Aṭ Ṭīb, Ra's **55** H 1
Attikamagen Lake **19** G 3
Attu **12** A 5
Attu **12** A 5
At Turayf **48** C 3
At Turbah **57** G 6
Atuel **37** C 6
Atura **60** E 4
Aua **82** A 3
Auas Mountains **62** B 4
Aubry, Lake **13** M 2
Auburn (CA, U.S.A.) **20** B 4
Auburn (ME, U.S.A.) **23** F 2
Auburn (NE, U.S.A.) **21** G 3
Auckland **81** Q 8
Auckland Islands **85**
Aude **44** D 3
Augathella **79** H 4
Augsburg **41** F 5
Augusta (AR, U.S.A.) **21** H 4
Augusta (GA, U.S.A.) **22** D 4
Augusta (ME, U.S.A.) **23** G 3
Augustus, Mount **78** B 3
Auki **82** B 3
Aur **82** C 2
Aurangaband **72** C 4
Aurillac **44** D 3
Aurora (CO, U.S.A.) **21** F 4
Aus **62** B 5
Ausangate, Nevado **34** B 3
Aust-Agder **43** E 4
Austin (MN, U.S.A.) **21** H 3
Austin (NV, U.S.A.)**20** C 4
Austin (TX, U.S.A.) **25** G 5
Austin, Lake **78** B 4
Australia **78–79** CG 3
Australian Alps **79** H 6
Australian Capital Territory **79** H 6
Austria **45** F 2
Austvågöy **42** F 2
Autlán **24** D 4
Auvézère **44** D 2
Auxerre **44** D 2 Auyuittuq National Park **17** NO 3
Avalon Peninsula **19** K 4
Avanavero **33** G 3
Avarua **83** E 4
Avaz **66** FG 4
Avdhira **46** C 2
Ávej **49** E 2
Avellaneda **36** E 5
Averöya **42** E 3
Aves, Isla de **29** G 3
Avesta **43** G 3
Avignon **45** DE 3

Ávila **44** C 3
Avilés **44** B 3
Avola **45** G 4
Avon Park **27** E 3
Awara Plain **61** G 4
Awash **61** G 2
Awash **61** G 3
'Awaynat Wanin **55** H 3
Awbārī **55** H 3
Awjilah **55** K 3
Axel Heiberg Island **84**
Axios **46** B 2
Ayabaca **32** BC 4
Ayacucho **34** AB 3
Ayaguz **51** Q 6
Ayan **69** P 4
Ayanaka **69** V 3
Ayava **68** H 4
Ayaviri **34** BC 3
Aydın **46** C 3
Ayers Rock – Mount Olga National Park **78** E 4
Áyion Óros **46** B 2
Aylmer Lake **14** H 2
'Aynabo **61** H 3
'Ayn al Baydā' **48** BC 2
'Ayn al Ghazāl **55** K 4
Ayni **67** H 3
'Ayn Sukhnah **48** A 3
Ayon **69** V 1
Ayr (Australia) **79** H 2
Ayr (U.K.) **40** C 3
Aysary **51** O 5
Ayutla **25** E 4
Āzādshahr **49** G 1
Azamgarh **72** D 2
Azare **59** G 3
Azbine **59** F 2
Azerbaydzhan **66** D 2
Aznâ **49** E 2
Azores **54** A 1
Azoum **59** J 3
Azov **47** E 1
Azovskoye More **47** E 1
Aztec ruins **20** E 4
Azua **29** E 3
Azul **37** E 6
Az Zallāq **49** F 4
Az Zarqā' **49** F 4
Az Zarqā' **48** B 2
Az Zāwiyah **55** H 2
Az Zilfī **49** D 4
Az Zugar **57** G 6

B

Baba Burnu **46** D 2
Baba Burun **46** C 3
Bābā Heydar **49** F 2
Babahoyo **32** BC 4
Babai Gaxun **70** D 2
Bāb al Māndab **57** G 6
Babanūsah **56** D 6
Babar, Kepulauan **75** G 5

Babine **13** M 4
Babine Lake **13** M 5
Babo **75** H 4
Bābol **49** F 1
Babol Sar **49** F 1
Baborigame **24** C 2
Babushkin **68** J 5
Babylon **48** D 2
Bacabal **35** GH 1
Bacan, Pulau **75** G 4
Bacău **46** C 1
Bachaquero **29** E 5
Back **16** G 3
Bād **49** F 2
Badajoz **44** B 4
Badalona **44** D 3
Badanah **48** C 3
Baden-Baden **41** E 5
Badiraguato **24** C 2
Badiyat ash Shām **48** BC 2
Badlands **20** F 2
Badoumbé **58** B 3
Badr Hunayn **48** C 5
Badulla **72** D 6
Badzhal **69** OP 5
Baffata **58** B 3
Baffin Bay **84**
Baffin Island **17** MN 3
Bafia **59** G 5
Bafoussam **59** G 4
Bāfq **49** G 3
Bafra **47** E 2
Bāft **49** G 3
Bagadzha **68** L 3
Bagalkot **72** C 4
Baga Sola **59** GH 3
Bagdarin **68** K 5
Bagé **36** F 5
Baghdād **48** D 2
Bāghīn **49** G 3
Baghlan **67** H 3
Bagley **21** G 2
Bagua **32** C 5
Baguio **75** J 1
Baguirmi **59** H 3
Bahama Islands **29** E 2
Bahar Dar **61** F 2
Bahawalpur **67** J 5
Bahía (Argentina) **37** C 8
Bahía (Brazil) **35** H 3
Bahía Adair **20** D 5
Bahía Ballenas **24** B 2
Bahía Blanca **37** D 6
Bahía Chamela **24** C 4
Bahía Coatzacoalcos **25** F 4
Bahía Concepcíon **24** B 2
Bahía de Amatique **28** B 3
Bahia de Banderas **24** C 3
Bahía de Campeche **25** F 4
Bahía de Caráquez **32** B 4
Bahía de Chetumal **28** B 3
Bahía de Coronado **28** C 5
Bahía de La Paz **24** B 3

Bahia de Manzanillo **24** CD 4
Bahía de Parita **28** CD 5
Bahia de Petacalco **24** D 4
Bahía de Punta Gorda **28** C 4
Bahía de San Jorge **20** D 5
Bahia de San Quintin **20** C 5
Bahía de Santa Elena **28** B 4
Bahía de Santa María **24** C 2
Bahia de Tepoca **24** D 5
Bahía de Topolobampo **24** C 2
Bahia Dulce **25** E 4
Bahía Grande **37** C 9
Bahía Kino **24** B 2
Bahía Laura **37** CD 8
Bahia Magdalena **24** B 3
Bahía Rosario **24** A 2
Bahías, Cabo dos **37** CD 8
Bahía San Luis Gonzaga **24** B 2
Bahía Santa Ines **24** B 2
Bahía Sebastián Vizcaíno **24** B 2
Bahrain **49** F 4
Bahr al Abyaḍ **56** E 6
Bahr al Azraq **56** E 6
Bahr al Jabal **60** E 3
Bahr ar Rimāl al 'Aẓīm **56** CD 3
Baía de Setúbal **44** B 4
Baia Mare **46** B 1
Baião **33** J 4
Baicheng (Man. China) **71** H 1
Baicheng (Sink. Uig. China) **67** L 2
Baie aux Feuilles **19** G 2
Baie Comeau **19** G 4
Baie d'Antongil **63** HJ 3
Baie de Rupert **18** DE 3
Baie-des-Moutons **19** J 3
Baie Diana **17** N 4
Baie du Poste **18** F 3
Baie Mosquito **17** L 4
Baie Payne **19** G 2
Baie Trinité **19** G 4
Baie Verte **19** J 4
Bailang **68** M 6
Baile Átha Cliath **40** B 4
Bailundo **62** B 2
Baimuru **80** D 3
Bainbridge **22** D 4
Baing **75** F 6
Baingoin **72** E 1
Baiquan **69** N 6
Baird Inlet **12** E 3
Baird Mountains **12** E 2
Baird Peninsula **17** L 3
Bairiki **82** C 2
Bairin Zuoqi **71** GH 2
Baixo-Alentejo **44** B 4
Baiyü **70** C 4
Baja **46** A 1
Baja California Norte **24** C 5
Baja California Sur **24** B 2

Bakadzhitsite 46 C 2
Bakel 58 B 3
Baker 82 D 2
Baker (CA, U.S.A.) 20 C 4
Baker (MT, U.S.A.) 20 F 2
Baker (OR, U.S.A.) 20 C 3
Baker Lake 15 K 2
Baker Lake (N.W.T., Can.)
  15 K 2
Bakersfield 20 C 4
Bakhta 51 RS 3
Bakhta 51 RS 3
Bakhtegän, Daryächeh-ye
  49 FG 3
Bakony 46 A 1
Bakouma 60 C 3
Baku 66 DE 2
Balabac Strait 74 E 2
Balabakk, Ra's 48 B 2
Baladiyat 'Adan 57 H 6
Balaghat 72 D 3
Balakhta 68 F 4
Balakovo 50 J 5
Bala Murghab 67 G 3
Balasore 72 E 3
Balaton 46 A 1
Balboa 28 D 5
Balclutha 80 PQ 10
Balde 36 C 5
Bald Head 78 B 6
Baldy Peak 20 E 5
Bale 61 G 3
Balearic Islands 44 D 3
Baleia, Ponta da 35 J 4
Baleine, Grande Rivière de la
  18 E 2–3
Baleine, Rivière à la 19 G 2
Baley 68 L 5
Bali 74 D 5
Balıkesir 46 C 3
Balintang Channel 75 J 1
Balkan Mountains 46 C 2
Balkhash 51 OP 6
Balkhash, Ozero 51 P 6
Balladonia 78 C 5
Ballarat 79 G 6
Ballard, Lake 78 C 4
Ballenas, Bahía 24 B 2
Balleny Islands 85
Ballina 79 J 4
Ballinger 25 G 5
Balranald 79 G 5
Balsas 33 J 5
Balsas (Mexico) 25 E 4
Balsas, Rio 24 D 4
Baltic Sea 43 GH 4
Baltimore (MD, U.S.A.) 22 E 3
Baltiskaja Grjada 43 HJ 4–5
Baluchistan 66–67 G 5
Bam 66 F 5
Bamako 58 C 3
Bamba 58 D 2
Bambari 60 C 3
Bambesa 60 D 4

Bambesi 60 E 3
Bamenda 59 FG 4
Bamingui 60 C 3
Bamingui-Bangoran, Parc
  National du 60 BC 3
Bamiyan 67 H 4
Bampür 67 G 5
Banaba 81 J 2
Banalia 60 D 4
Banana 79 J 3
Banās, Ra's 48 B 5
Banās, Ra's 56 F 4
Banco Chinchorro 28 B 3
Banco de Serrana 28 D 4
Banco Quitasueño 28 C 4
Banco Serranilla 28 D 3
Bancroft 18 E 4
Banda 72 D 2
Banda Aceh 74 A 2
Bandar Abbas 49 G 4
Bandar-e-Anzalī 66 DE 3
Bandar-e Chārak 66 E 5
Bandar-e Deylam 66 E 4–5
Bandar-e Khomeyni 49 E 3
Bandar-e Lengeh 49 G 4
Bandar-e Māqām 49 F 4
Bandar-e Moghüyeh 49 FG 4
Bandar-e Rig 49 F 3
Bandarlampung 74 C 5
Bandarpunch 72 C 1
Bandar Seri Begawan 74 D 3
Bandar Shāh 49 E 1
Banda Sea 75 GH 5
Bandau 74 E 2
Band Boni 66 F 5
Bandeira 35 H 5
Bandeirante 35 FG 3
Bandirma 46 C 2
Bandundu 60 B 5
Bandung 74 C 5
Banes 27 F 4
Banff 14 F 4
Banff National Park 14 F 4
Banfora 58 CD 3
Bangalore 72 C 5
Bangassou 60 C 4
Bangeta, Mount 80 E 3
Banggai, Kepulauan 75 F 4
Bangko 74 B 4
Bangkok 73 H 5
Bangkok, Bight of 73 H 5
Bangladesh 73 F 3
Bangor (ME, U.S.A.) 23 G 3
Bangor (N. Ireland,
  U.K.)40 B 4
Bangsund 42 F 3
Bangui 60 B 4
Bangui Mogadishu 61 H 4
Banhine National Park 63 E 4
Baní 29 E 3
Banihal Pass 67 K 4
Banī Mazār 56 DE 3
Banī Suwayf 56 E 3
Bāniyās (Lebanon) 48 B 2

Bāniyās (Syria) 48 B 2
Banja Luka 45 G 3
Banjarmasin 74 DE 4
Banjul 58 A 3
Ban Kniet 73 J 5
Banks Island (Canada) 16 B 2
Banks Island (Queensland,
  Austr.) 79 G 1
Banks Islands 81 J 4
Banks Islands (Vanuatu)
  82 C 3
Banks Lake 20 C 2
Banks Peninsula 81 Q 9
Banks Strait 80 L 9
Ban Me Thuot 73 J 5
Bannu 67 J 4
Banská Bystrica 41 G 5
Banyo 59 G 4
Banyuwangi 74 D 5
Banzare Coast 85
Baoding 70 FG 3
Baoji 70 E 4
Baoqing 71 K 1
Baoshan 70 CD 5
Baotou 70 E 2
Baqen 70 B 4
Ba' qübah 49 D 2
Barabinsk 51 P 4
Barabinskaya Step' 51 P 5
Baracaldo 44 C 3
Bārah 56 E 6
Barahona 29 E 3
Barakkul' 51 N 5
Baramula 67 J 4
Baran 72 C 2
Barangbarang 75 EF 5
Baranoa 28 D 4
Baranof 13 K 4
Baranovichi 43 J 5
Barão de Capanema 34 E 3
Barão de Melgaco 34 D 3
Barbados 29 G 4
Barberton 22 D 2
Barbuda 29 G 3
Barcaldine 79 H 3
Barcellona 45 FG 4
Barcelona (Spain) 44 D 3
Barcelona (Venezuela) 33 F 2
Barcelos 33 F 4
Bardawil, Sabkhat al 48 A 3
Bārdère 61 G 4
Bardeskan 66 F 3
Barēda 61 J 2
Bareilly 72 C 2
Barentsovo More 50 GJ 1
Barents Sea 84
Barentu 61 F 1
Bārgå 42 G 2
Barga 72 D 1
Barguzin 68 J 5
Barhaj 72 D 2
Bar Harbor 23 G 3
Bari 45 G 3
Baridi, Ra's 48 B 4

Barim 57 G 6
Barinas 32 E 2
Baring, Cape 16 C 3
Barisal 73 F 3
Barisan, Pegunungan 74 B 4
Barito, Sungai 74 D 4
Barkå' 57 K 4
Barkam 70 D 4
Barkley, Lake 22 C 3
Barkly Tableland 79 F 2
Barlee, Lake 78 B 4
Barletta 45 G 3
Barmer 72 B 2
Barnaul 51 Q 5
Barnes Ice Cap 17 M 2–3
Barong 70 C 4
Barotseland 62 C 3
Barquisimeto 29 F 4–5
Barquisimeto 32 DE 1
Barra (Bahía, Brazil) 35 H 3
Barra (U.K.) 40 B 3
Barracão do Barreto 33 G 5
Barra do Corda 33 J 5
Barragem da Rocha de Galé
  44 B 4
Barra Head 40 B 3
Barranca 32 C 4
Barrancabermeja 32 D 2
Barrancas 29 G 5
Barrancas 33 F 2
Barranquilla 32 C 1
Barra Patuca 28 C 3
Barraute 18 E 4
Barreiras 35 G 3
Barreirinhas 35 H 1
Barreiro 44 B 4
Barreiros 35 JK 2
Barren 73 F 5
Barren Islands 12 G 4
Barrenitos 24 D 2
Barren Lands 16 EG 3
Barretos 35 G 4
Barrhead 14 G 4
Barrie 22 DE 2
Barrow (AK, U.S.A.) 12 F 1
Barrow (Argentina) 37 E 6
Barrow (Rep. of Ireland)
  40 B 4
Barrow, Point 12 F 1
Barrow Island 78 A 3
Barsi 72 C 4
Barstow 20 C 5
Bartica 33 G 2
Bartlesville 21 G 4
Bartow 27 E 3
Bāruni 72 E 2
Basauri 44 C 3
Basel 45 E 2
Bashi Haixia 71 H 6
Basilan City 75 F 2
Basílio 36 F 5
Baskatong, Réservoir 18 EF 4
Baskol' 51 P 5

Basra **49** E 3
Bassas da India **63** FG 4
Bassein **73** F 4
Basse Terre **29** G 3
Bassinde Rennes **44** C 2
Bass Strait **80** KL 8
Bastak **49** G 4
Bastia **45** E 3
Bastrop **21** H 5
Bata **59** F 5
Batabano, Golfo del **27** E 4
Batagay-Alyta **69** NO 2
Batama (U.S.S.R.) **68** H 5
Batamshinskiy **51** L 5
Batang **70** C 4
Batangas **75** F 1
Batang Hari **74** B 4
Bataysk **47** EF 1
Batchawana Mountain **18** D 4
Batemans Bay **79** J 6
Bath (ME, U.S.A.) **23** G 3
Batha **59** H 3
Bathalha **44** B 4
Bathurst (Canada) **19** G 4
Bathurst (N.S.W., Austr.)
  79 H 5
Bathurst, Cape **13** L 1
Bathurst Inlet **16** E 3
Bathurst Island (N.T., Austr.)
  78 D 1
Bathurst Island (The Arctic) **84**
Batin, Wadi al **49** DE 3
Batkanu **58** B 4
Batman **47** F 3
Batna **55** G 1
Batoka **62** D 3
Batomga **69** P 4
Baton Rouge **25** H 5
Batopilas **24** C 2
Battambang **73** H 5
Battle **14** G 4
Battle Creek **22** C 2
Battle Harbour **19** J 3
Battle Mountain **20** C 3
Batu **61** F 3
Batui **75** F 4
Batumi **47** F 2
Batu Puteh, Gunung **74** B 3
Baturité **35** J 1
Baubau **75** F 5
Bauchi **59** F 3
Bauld, Cape **19** J 3
Baures **34** D 3
Bauru **35** FG 5
Baús **35** F 4
Bavaria **41** F 5
Bavispe **24** E 5
Bawdwin **73** G 3
Baxoi **70** C 4
Bayamo **27** F 4
Bayan-Adraga **68** K 6
Bayan-Aul **51** P 5
Bayanbulag **68** G 6

Bayandzurh **68** J 6
Bayanga **60** B 4
Bayan Har Shankou **70** C 4
Bayanhongor **68** H 6
Bayan Obo **70** E 2
Bayäz **66** F 4
Bayäzeh **49** G 2
Bay Bulls **19** K 4
Bayburt **47** EF 2
Bay City (MI, U.S.A.) **22** D 2
Bay City (TX, U.S.A.) **25** E 2
Baydaratskaya Guba **51** N 2
Bay de Verde **19** K 4
Bayern **41** F 5
Bayji **48** D 2
Baykal'skiy Khrebet **68** J 4–5
Baykit **68** G 3
Bay of Bengal **72–73** EF 4
Bay of Biscay **44** C 2–3
Bay of Fundy **19** G 4–5
Bay of Gods Mercy **15** M 2
Bay of Islands **19** J 4
Bay of Plenty **82** C 5
Bayonne **44** C 3
Bayo Nuevo **28** D 3
Bayovar **32** B 5
Bayram-Ali **67** G 3
Bayreuth **41** F 5
Bayrüt **48** B 2
Bay Springs **21** HJ 5
Baytown **25** H 5–6
Bazarnyy Syzgan **50** J 5
Bazaruto National Park **63** F 4
Bazhong **70** E 4
Beach **20** F 2
Bear Cape **19** H 4
Bear Island **84**
Bear Lake **20** D 3
Bear Lodge Mountains
  21 EF 3
Bearpaw Mountains **20** E 2
Bearskin Lake **15** L 4
Beata, Cabo **29** E 3
Beatrice **21** G 3
Beatton **14** E 3
Beatton River **14** E 3
Beatty **20** C 4
Beattyville **18** E 4
Beaucanton **18** E 4
Beaufort **22** D 4
Beaufort (Malaysia) **74** E 2
Beaufort Sea **13** JL 1
Beaufort West **62** C 6
Beaumont (TX, U.S.A.) **21** H 5
Beaupré **18** F 4
Beausejour **15** K 4
Beauvais **44** D 2
Beaver (AK, U.S.A.) **12** H 2
Beaver (Sask., Can.)**15** H 4
Beaver (UT, U.S.A.) **20** D 4
Beaver Dam **22** C 2
Beaver Island **22** C 1
Beaverton **20** B 2
Beawar **72** BC 2

Beberibe **35** J 1
Becan **28** B 3
Béchar **54** E 2
Becharof Lake **12** F 4
Becharof National Monument
  12 F 4
Bechevin Bay **12** E 4
Beckley **22** D 3
Bedford (IN, U.S.A.) **22** C 3
Bedford (PA, U.S.A.) **22** E 2
Bedourie **79** F 3
Beech Grove **22** C 3
Be'er Sheva **48** B 3
Beeville **25** E 2
Bega **79** HJ 6
Begejski Kanal **46** B 1
Begna **43** E 3
Behbehän **49** F 3
Behring Point **27** F 4
Behshar **49** F 1
Bei'an **69** N 6
Beibu Wan **73** J 3
Beida **55** K 2
Beihai **70** E 6
Beijing **71** G 2
Beipiao **71** H 2
Beira **63** F 3
Beirut **48** B 2
Bei Shan **70** C 2
Beitbridge **62** DE 4
Beitstad **42** F 3
Beitun **67** M 1
Beja **44** B 4
Bejaïa **55** FG 1
Bekdash **66** E 2
Békéscsaba **46** B 1
Bekopaka **63** G 3
Bela **67** H 5
Belau **75** HJ 2
Bela Vista (Brazil) **34** E 5
Bela Vista (Mozambique)
  63 E 5
Belaya Kalitva **47** F 1
Belaya Tserkov **50** F 5–6
Belcher Islands **18** D 2
Belebey **50** K 5
Belém (Amazonas, Brazil)
  32 E 4
Belem (Mexico) **24** B 2
Belém (Pará, Brazil) **33** J 4
Belén **32** C 3
Belen (N.M., U.S.A.) **20** E 5
Belep, Îles **82** B 4
Beleuli **66** F 2
Belfast **40** B 4
Belfield **20** F 2
Belfort **45** E 2
Belgaum **72** BC 4
Belgium **40** DE 4
Belgorod **50** G 5
Belgorod-Dnestrovskiy
  46 CD 1
Belgrade **46** B 2
Beli **59** G 4

Belikh **48** C 1
Belitung, Pulau **74** C 4
Belize **28** B 3
Belize City **28** B 3
Belize River **28** B 3
Bel'kachi **69** O 4
Bell **18** E 4
Bella Bella **13** M 5
Bella Coola **13** M 5
Bellary **72** C 4
Bell Bay **16** K 2
Belle Fourche River **21** F 3
Belle Glade **27** E 3
Belle Ile **44** C 2
Belle Isle **19** JK 3
Belle Isle, Strait of **19** J 3
Belleville (IL, U.S.A.) **22** C 3
Belleville (KS, U.S.A.) **21** G 4
Belleville (Ontario, Can.)
  22 E 2
Bellevue (NE, U.S.A.)**21** G 3
Bellevue (WA, U.S.A.) **20** B 2
Bellin **17** M 4
Bellingham **20** B 2
Bellingshausen **85**
Bellingshausen Sea **85**
Bello **32** C 2
Bellot Strait **16** H 2
Bell Peninsula **16** K 4
Belluno **45** F 2
Bell Ville **36** D 5
Bellyk **68** F 5
Belmonte **35** J 4
Belmopan **28** B 3
Belogorsk (U.S.S.R.) **69** N 5
Belogor'ye **51** N 3
Belo Horizonte (Minas Gerais,
  Brazil) **35** H 4–5
Belo Horizonte (Pará, Brazil)
  33 H 5
Beloit **22** C 2
Belo Monta **33** H 4
Belorechensk **47** FG 2
Belorussiya **43** J 5
Belorusskaya **43** J 5
Belot, Lac **13** M 2
Belovo **51** R 5
Beloyarovo **69** NO 5
Beloye More**50** G 2
Belt'sy **46** C 1
Belush'ya Guba **50** KL 1
Belush'ya Guba **84**
Belyy **50** F 4
Bemidji **21** G 2
Bena Dibile **60** C 5
Benalla **79** H 6
Benares **72** D 2
Bend **20** B 3
Bender Bäyla **61** J 3
Bendery **46** C 1
Bendigo **79** GH 6
Benevento **45** FG 3
Bengal **72** E 3
Bengbu **71** G 4

Benghazi 55 J 2
Bengkulu 74 B 4
Benguela 62 A 2
Beni (Bolivia) 34 C 3
Beni (Zaire) 60 D 4
Benidorm 44 CD 4
Beni Mellal 54 D 2
Benin 58 E 3–4
Benin, Bight of 58 E 5
Benin City 59 EF 4
Beni Ounif 54 E 2
Benito Juárez 25 F 4
Benjamin Constant 32 D 4
Benkelman 21 F 3
Ben Nevis 40 BC 3
Benson 20 D 5
Bentiaba 62 A 2
Benton 21 H 5
Benue 59 F 4
Benxi 71 HJ 2
Beograd 46 B 2
Beraketa 63 H 4
Berati 46 A 2
Berau, Teluk 75 H 4
Berbera 61 H 2
Berbérati 60 B 4
Berchogur 66 FG 1
Berdichev 43 J 6
Berdigestyakh 69 MN 3
Berdyansk 47 E 1
Berekum 58 D 4
Berens 15 K 4
Berens River 15 K 4
Berezniki 50 KL 4
Berezovka (Russia, U.S.S.R.)
   51 Q 4
Berezovka (Russia, U.S.S.R.)
   68 L 4
Berezovo 51 N 3
Berezovskiy 51 LM 5
Bergamo (Italy) 45 EF 2
Bergamo (Turkey) 46 C 3
Bergen (F.R.G.) 41 F 4
Bergen (Norway) 43 DE 3
Bergerac 44 D 3
Bergö 42 H 3
Bergviken 42 G 3
Berhampore 72 E 3
Berhampur 72 DE 4
Bering Glacier 13 J 3
Bering Land Bridge National
   Preserve 12 E 2
Beringovskiy 69 XY 3
Bering Sea 65 UV 3–4
Bering Strait 12 CD 2–3
Berkakit 69 M 4
Berkeley 20 B 4
Berkner Island 85
Berlevåg 42 J 1
Berlin 41 F 4
Berlin (N.H., U.S.A.) 23 F 2
Bermejo (Argentina) 36 D 4
Bermejo (Argentina) 36 C 5
Bermen, Lac 19 G 3

Bermuda Islands 23 H 4
Bern 45 E 2
Bernalillo 20 E 4
Bernasconi 37 D 6
Bernburg 41 F 4
Berne 45 E 2
Berner Alpen 45 E 2
Bernina 45 E 2
Berry Islands 27 F 3
Bertolínia 35 H 2
Bertoua 59 G 5
Besalampy 63 G 3
Besançon 45 E 2
Besar, Gunung 74 E 4
Beskidy Zachodny 41 GH 5
Beslan 47 F 2
Besna Kobila 46 B 2
Bessarabiya 46 C 1
Bessemer 22 C 4
Bestobe 51 O 5
Beswick 78 E 1
Bethan (OK, U.S.A.) 21 G 4
Bethany 21 H 3
Bethel 12 E 3
Bethlehem 62 D 5
Béthune 44 D 1
Betong 73 H 6
Bet-Pak-Dala 51 NO 6
Betroka 63 H 4
Bettles 12 G 2
Beyänlü 49 E 1
Bey Dağları 46 CD 3
Beyla 58 C 4
Beyra 61 H 3
Beyşehir Gölü 46 D 3
Béziers 44 D 3
Bhadrakh 72 E 3
Bhadravati 72 C 5
Bhagalpur 72 E 3
Bhamo 73 G 3
Bhandara 72 CD 3
Bharuch 72 B 3
Bhatinda 72 BC 2
Bhatpara 72 E 3
Bhavnagar 72 B 3
Bhilwara 72 BC 2
Bhopal 72 C 3
Bhopalpatnam 72 D 4
Bhuban 72 E 3
Bhubaneswar 72 E 3
Bhumiphol Dam 73 GH 4
Bhusawal 72 C 3
Bhutan 73 F 2
Biak (Indonesia) 75 F 4
Biak (New Guinea) 75 J 4
Biak, Pulau 75 J 4
Biała Podlaska 41 H 4
Białystok 41 H 4
Biankouma 58 C 4
Biaora 72 C 3
Biarritz 44 C 3
Biberach 41 EF 5
Bicuari National Park 62 AB 3
Bida 59 F 4

Bidar 72 C 4
Biddeford 23 FG 2
Bidzhan 69 O 6
Bié 62 B 2
Biebrza 41 H 4
Biel 45 E 2
Bielefeld 41 E 4
Bielsko-Biała 41 G 5
Bien Hoa 73 J 5
Bienville, Lac 18 F 2
Bifoum 59 G 6
Big Bald Mountain 19 G 4
Big Belt Mountains 20 D 2
Big Bend National Park
   24 D 2
Big Cypress National
   Preserve 27 E 3
Big Delta 12 H 3
Biger 68 G 6
Big Falls 21 H 2
Biggar 15 H 4
Bighorn Basin 20 E 3
Bighorn Lake 20 E 3
Bighorn Mountains 20 E 3
Bighorn River 20 E 2
Bight of Bangkok 73 H 5
Bight of Benin 58 E 4
Bigi 60 C 4
Big Island 17 M 4
Big Quill Lake 15 J 4
Big Rapids 22 C 2
Big River 15 H 4
Big Sand Lake 15 K 3
Big Sheep Mountains
   20–21 E 2
Big Sioux 21 G 3
Big Smoky Valley 20 C 4
Big Snowy Mountains 20 E 2
Big Spring 24 F 5
Big Trout Lake 18 C 3
Big Trout Lake (Ontario, Can.)
   15 L 4
Bihač 45 G 3
Bihar 72 DE 2
Bijapur 72 C 4
Bijeljina 45 G 3
Bijiang 70 C 5
Bikaner 72 B 2
Bikar 82 C z
Bikin 69 O 6
Bikini 82 B 2
Bilaspur 72 D 3
Bilbao 44 C 3
Bili 60 D 4
Billings 20 E 2
Bilma, Grand Erg de 59 GH 2
Biloela 79 J 3
Bilogora 45 G 2
Biloxi 22 C 4
Bimini Islands 27 F 3
Binaiya, Gunung 75 G 4
Binder 68 K 6
Bindura 63 E 3
Bingara 79 J 4

Bingham 23 G 2
Binghamton 22 E 2
Binjai 74 A 3
Binnaway 79 H 5
Bintan, Pulau 74 B 3
Bintulu 74 D 3
Bira 69 P 6
Birao 60 C 2
Biratnagar 72 E 2
Bi'r Bū Zurayyq 55 K 3
Birch Creek 12 H 2
Birch Lake 15 L 4
Birch Mountains 14 G 3
Bird 15 L 3
Bi'r Fu'ād 56 D 2
Birjand 66 F 4
Birkat Nasser 48 A 5
Birkenhead 40 C 4
Birksgate Range 78 DE 4
Bîrlad 46 C 1
Birmingham (AL, U.S.A.)
   22 C 4
Birmingham (U.K.) 40 C 4
Bir Moghreim 54 C 3
Bi'r Nasif 48 C 4
Bi'r Safâjah 48 AB 4
Birnie 82 D 3
Birnin Kebbi 59 EF 3
Birnin Kudu 59 F 3
Birobidzhan 69 O 6
Bir Ounane 58 D 1
Bir Rhoraffa 55 G 2
Bi'r Shalatayn 56 F 4
Birsilpur 72 B 2
Birsk 50 L 4
Biru 70 B 4
Bisbee 20 DE 5
Biscad 46 B 1
Biscoe Islands 85
Bishop 20 C 4
Bishop's Falls 19 J 4
Biskra 55 G 2
Bismarck 20 F 2
Bismarck Archipelago
   80–81 EF 2
Bismarck Range 80 DE 2–3
Bismarck Sea 80 EF 2
Bison 20 F 2
Bissau 58 A 3
Bissett 15 K 4
Bistcho Lake 14 EF 3
Bistriţa 46 BC 1
Bitchana 61 F 2
Bitkiné 59 H 3
Bitlis 47 F 3
Bitola 46 B 2
Bitterfontein 62 B 6
Bitter Lake (Egypt) 48 A 3
Bitterroot Range 20 D 2–3
Biu 59 G 3
Biyang 70 F 4
Biysk 51 R 5
Bizerta → Banzart 55 GH 1
Bjerkvik 42 G 2

Bjesnica **46** A 2
Björkö **42** H 3
Björnöya **84**
Blackall **79** GH 3
Blackburn, Mount **13** J 3
Blackfoot **20** D 3
Black Hills **21** F 3
Black Lake **15** J 3
Black Mountain **22** D 3
Blackpool **40** C 4
Black Range **20** E 5
Black River Falls **21** HJ 3
Black Rock Desert **20** C 3
Black Sea **47** DE 2
Blackwell **21** G 4
Blåfjellhatten **42** F 3
Blagoevgrad **46** B 2
Blagoveshchensk **69** NO 5
Blaine **21** H 2
Blair **21** G 3
Blanco, Cape **20** AB 3
Blantyre **63** E 3
Blåskavlen **42** E 3
Blåvands Huk **43** E 4
Blekinge **43** FG 4
Blenheim **82** C 5
Blida **55** F 1
Blind River **18** D 4
Bloemfontein **62** CD 5
Blois **44** D 2
Blönduós **42** AB 2
Bloomington (IL, U.S.A.)
  22 C 2
Bloomington (IN, U.S.A.)
  22 C 3
Bloomington (MN, U.S.A.)
  21 H 3
Blosseville Coast **84**
Bluefield **22** D 3
Bluefields **28** C 4
Blue Mountain Lake **23** F 2
Blue Mountain Peak **28** D 3
Bluenose Lake **16** C 3
Blue Ridge **22** DE 3
Bluff Knoll **78** B 5
Blumenau **36** FG 4
Blythe **20** D 5
Blytheville **22** C 3
Bo **58** B 4
Boaco **28** B 4
Boa Vista (Cape Verde) **58** B 6
Boa Vista (Roraima, Brazil)
  33 F 3
Bobai **70** EF 6
Bobo Dioulasso **58** D 3
Bobruysk **43** J 5
Boby, Pic **63** H 4
Boca del Rio **24** C 2
Bôca do Acre **32** E 5
Boca Grande **29** GH 5
Bocaiúva **35** H 4
Boca Raton **27** F 3
Bocas del Toro **28** C 5

Bochum **41** E 4
Boconó **29** EF 5
Bodaybo **68** K 4
Bodélé **59** H 2
Boden **42** H 2
Bodensee **45** E 2
Bodö **42** F 2
Bo Duc **73** J 5
Boende **60** C 5
Boffa **58** B 3
Bogalusa **22** C 4
Boggeragh Mountains **40** B 4
Bogor **74** C 5
Bogoroditsk **50** G 5
Bogotá **32** D 3
Bogra **72** E 2–3
Boguchany **68** G 4
Bogué **54** C 5
Bo Hai **71** GH 3
Bohemia **41** F 5
Böhmerwald **41** F 5
Bohol **75** F 2
Bohol Sea **75** F 2
Boiaçu **33** F 4
Bois, Lac des **13** N 2
Boise **20** C 3
Boise City **21** F 4
Boise River **20** C 3
Boissevain **15** K 5
Bojnürd **66** F 3
Bojuro **36** F 5
Bokatola **60** B 5
Boké **58** B 3
Boknafjorden **43** E 4
Bokora Game Reserve **60** E 4
Bokpyin **74** A 1
Bokungu **60** C 5
Bolan Pass **67** H 5
Bole (China) **67** L 2
Bole (Ghana) **58** D 4
Bolesławiec **41** G 4
Bolgatanga **58** D 3
Boli **71** K 1
Bolia **60** B 5
Bolívar (Argentina) **37** D 6
Bolívar (Colombia) **32** C 3
Bolivia **34** CD 4
Bollon **79** H 4
Bologna **45** F 3
Bologoye **50** F 4
Bologur **69** O 3
Bolombo **60** C 5
Bolsena, Lago di **45** F 3
Bol'shaya Glushitsa **50** K 5
Bol'sheretsk **69** T 5
Bol'shezemel'skaya Tundra
  50 KM 2
Bolshoy Kavkaz **47** F 2
Bol'shoy Nimnyr **69** MN 4
Bol'shoy Shantar, Ostrov
  69 P 4–5
Bolsón de Mapimí **24** D 2
Bolton **40** C 4
Bolu **47** D 2

Bolzano **45** F 2
Boma **59** G 7
Bombay **72** B 4
Bomberai **75** H 4
Bom Jesus **35** H 2
Bom Jesus da Lapa **35** H 3
Bömlo **43** DE 4
Bomongo **60** B 4
Bom Retiro **36** G 4
Bona, Mount **13** J 3
Bonampak **25** F 4
Bonanza **28** C 4
Bonaparte Archipelago **78** C 1
Bonavista **19** K 4
Bonavista Bay **19** K 4
Bondo **60** C 4
Bondowoso **74** D 5
Bonete, Cerro **36** C 4
Bongor **59** H 3
Bonifacio, Strait of **45** E 3
Bonin Islands **65** R 7
Bonito **34** E 5
Bonn **41** E 4
Bonners Ferry **20** C 2
Bonnet Plume **13** L 2–3
Bonneville Saltflats **20** D 3
Bonobono **74** E 2
Boola **58** C 4
Boon **18** D 4
Boone **21** H 3
Boonville **21** H 4
Boothby, Cape **85**
Boothia, Gulf of **16** H 2
Boothia Peninsula **16** H 2
Bophuthatswana **62** C 5
Boquillagas del Carmen
  24 D 2
Bor **46** B 2
Bora-Bora **83** EF 4
Borah Peak **20** D 3
Borås **43** F 4
Borasambar **72** D 3
Borâzjân **49** F 3
Borba **33** G 4
Bordeaux **44** CD 3
Bordertown **79** G 6
Bordj Fly Sainte Marie **54** E 3
Bordj Messouda **55** G 2
Börgefjellet **42** F 2
Borisoglebsk **50** H 5
Borisov **43** J 5
Borispol **50** F 5
Bo River **60** D 3
Borja (Peru) **32** C 4
Borja (Yugoslavia) **46** A 2
Borkou **59** H 2
Borlänge **43** FG 3
Borneo **74** DE 3
Bornholm **43** F 5
Bornu **59** G 3
Borohoro Shan **67** L 2
Boroko **75** F 3
Borolgustakh **68** M 2
Borovichi **50** FG 4

Borroloola **79** F 2
Börselv **42** HJ 1
Borsippa **48** D 2
Boru **69** Q 1
Borüjen **49** F 3
Borüjerd **49** E 2
Borzya **68** L 5
Bösäso **61** H 2
Bose **70** E 6
Boshan **71** G 3
Boshnyakovo **69** Q 6
Boshuslän **43** F 4
Bosna **45** G 3
Bosporus **46** C 2
Bosque Bonito **24** E 5
Bossangoa **60** B 3
Bossembele **60** B 3
Bossemptélé II **60** B 3
Bossier City **21** H 5
Bostandyk **50** J 6
Boston (MA, U.S.A.) **23** F 2
Boston Mountains **21** H 4
Botletle **62** C 4
Botoşani **46** C 1
Bo Trach **73** J 4
Botswana **62** CD 4
Botucatu **35** G 5
Botwood **19** JK 4
Bouaflé **58** C 4
Bouaké **58** D 4
Bouar **60** B 3
Bou Arfa **54** E 2
Boubandjida **59** GH 4
Boubandjida National Park
  59 GH 4
Boucle de Baoulé, Parc
  National de la **58** C 3
Bou Djéhiba **58** D 2
Bougainville **81** G 3
Bougainville Reef **79** H 2
Bou Garfa **54** D 3
Bougouni **58** C 3
Bouïra **55** F 1
Bou Izakarn **54** D 3
Boulanouar **54** B 4
Boulder (U.S.A.) **21** F 3
Boulder (West Australia)
  78 C 5
Boulia **79** F 3
Boulouli **58** C 2
Bouna **58** D 4
Boundiali **58** C 4
Boundou **58** B 3
Boun Neua **73** H 3
Bountiful **20** D 3
Bounty Islands **85**
Bourem **58** D 2
Bourg **45** E 2
Bourges **44** D 2
Bourgogne **45** DE 2
Bou Rjeima **54** C 5
Bourke **79** H 4–5
Bournemouth **40** C 4
Bou Saâda **55** F 1

Bouvet Island **85**
Bow **14** G 4
Bowen (Argentina) **36** C 5
Bowen (Australia) **79** H 2
Bowling Green **22** C 3
Bowman **21** F 2
Bowman Bay **17** LM 3
Boxing **71** G 3
Boyabo **60** B 4
Boyne **40** B 4
Boyuibe **34** D 5
Bozeman **20** D 2
Bozok Platosu **47** DE 3
Brač **45** G 3
Bradenton **27** E 3
Bradford **40** C 4
Bradford (PA, U.S.A.) **22** E 2
Bradshaw **78** E 2
Brady **25** G 5
Brady Mountains **25** G 5
Braga **44** B 3
Bragança (Brazil) **33** J 4
Bragança (Portugal) **44** B 3
Bragina **69** X 3
Brahmaputra **73** F 2
Brai **17** L 3
Brăila **46** C 1
Brainerd **21** H 2
Bråk **55** H 3
Brampton **22** D 2
Brandberg **62** A 4
Brandenburg **41** F 4
Brandon **15** K 5
Brandvlei **62** BC 6
Brantford **22** D 2
Bras d'Or Lake **19** HJ 4
Brasil, Planalto do **35** H 4
Brasiléia **34** C 3
Brasília **35** G 4
Braşov **46** C 1
Brassey, Mount **78** E 3
Bratislava **41** G 5
Bratsk **68** H 4
Bratskoye Vodokhranilishche
  68 H 4
Bratslav **46** C 1
Brattleboro **23** F 2
Bratul Chilia **46** C 1
Braunschweig **41** F 4
Brawley **20** C 5
Brazil **34–35** EG 3
Brazo Casoquiare **32** E 3
Brazos River **25** G 5
Brazzaville **59** GH 6
Brčko **45** G 3
Breckenridge **21** G 5
Brecknock, Península **37** B 9
Breda **40** D 4
Bredbyn **42** G 3
Breiðafjörður **42** A 2
Brejo **35** H 1
Brekken **42** F 3
Bremangerlandet **42** D 3
Bremen **41** E 4

Bremerhaven **41** E 4
Bremerton **20** B 2
Brenner **45** F 2
Brescia **45** F 2
Brest **44** C 2
Bretagne **44** C 2
Breves **33** H 4
Brevoort Island **17** O 4
Brewster, Kap **84**
Brewton **22** C 4
Brezhnev **50** K 4
Bridgeport (CA, U.S.A.) **20** C 4
Bridgeport (CT, U.S.A.) **23** F 2
Bridger Peak **20** E 3
Bridgetown (Australia) **78** B 5
Bridgetown (Barbados)
  29 GH 4
Bridgewater **23** H 2
Brigham City **20** D 3
Brighton **40** D D 4
Brindisi **45** G 3
Brisbane **79** J 4
Bristol **40** C 4
Bristol (TN, U.S.A.) **22** D 3
Bristol Bay **12** EF 4
Bristol Channel **40** C D 4
British Columbia **14** DE 3–4
British Mountains **13** JK 2
Britstown **62** C 6
Brive **44** D 2
Brno **41** G 5
Broadback **18** E 3
Broadus **21** EF 2
Broadview **15** J 4
Brochet **15** J 3
Brockville **22** E 2
Broken Hill **79** G 5
Brokhovo **69** ST 4
Brokopondo **33** G 3
Brookfield **21** H 4
Brookhaven **25** H 5
Brookings (CA, U.S.A.) **20** B 3
Brookings (S.D., U.S.A.)
  21 G 3
Brooks **14** G 4
Brooks Range **12** FH 2
Brookston **21** H 2
Brookton **78** B 5
Broome **78** C 2
Broughton Island **17** O 3
Browne Range Nature
  Reserve **78** CD 3
Brownfield **21** F 5
Browning **20** D 2
Brown Lake **16** H 3
Brownsville **25** E 2
Brownwood **25** G 5
Bruce, Mount **78** B 3
Bruce Crossing **22** C 1
Bruce Peninsula **22** D 2
Brugge **40** D 4
Brumado **35** H 3
Bruneau **20** C 3
Brunei **74** D 2

Brunswick **22** D 4
Brus, Laguna de **28** C 3
Brusilovka **50** KL 5
Brusque **36** G 4
Bruxelles **40** D 4
Bruzual **29** F 5
Bryan **25** G 5
Bryan Coast **85**
Bryansk **50** F 5
Bryanskoye **47** G 2
Brzeg **41** G 4
Būbīyān **49** E 3
Bucaramanga **32** D 2
Buchanan **58** B 4
Buchanan, Lake (TX, U.S.A.)
  21 G 5
Bucharest → Bucureşti **46** C 2
Buckeye **20** D 5
Buckingham Bay **79** F 1
Buckland **12** E 2
Buco Zau **59** G 6
Bu Craa **54** C 3
Bucyrus **22** D 2
Budapest **46** AB 1
Budennovsk **47** F 2
Búðardalur **42** A 2
Buenaventura (Colombia)
  32 C 3
Buenaventura (Mexico)
  24 C 2
Buenavista **24** C 3
Buenos Aires **36** DE 5–6
Buenos Aires, Lago **37** B 8
Buffalo (N.W.T., Can.) **14** G 2
Buffalo (N.Y., U.S.A.) **22** E 2
Buffalo (OK, U.S.A.) **21** G 4
Buffalo (S.D., U.S.A.) **21** F 2
Buffalo (WY, U.S.A.) **20** E 3
Buffalo Lake **14** FG 2
Buffalo Narrows **14** H 3
Bug **41** H 4
Buga **32** C 3
Bugorkan **68** J 3
Bugøynes **42** J 2
Bugt **69** M 6
Bugul'ma **50** K 5
Buhayrat al Asad **47** E 3
Bujumbura **60** D 5
Buka **81** F 3
Bukadaban Feng **70** B 3
Bukavu **60** D 5
Bukhara **67** G 3
Bukit Gandadiwata **75** EF 4
Bukit Kambuno **75** EF 4
Bukit Masurai **74** B 4
Bukittinggi **74** AB 3–4
Bukoba **60** E 5
Bukukun **68** K 6
Būl, Kūh-e **49** F 3
Bulawayo **62** D 3–4
Buldana **72** C 3
Buldir **12** A 6
Bulgan **68** H 6
Bulgaria **46** C 2

Bullahär **61** G 2
Bullion Mountains **20** C 5
Bull Shoals Lake **21** H 4
Bulo Berde **61** H 4
Bulungu **60** B 5
Bumba **60** C 4
Bumbulan **75** F 3
Bunbury **78** B 5
Bunda **60** E 5
Bundaberg **79** J 3
Bunda Bunda **79** G 3
Bundesrepublik Deutschland
  41 EF 5
Bundooma **78** E 3
Bunia **60** DE 4
Bunkie **25** H 5
Buorkhaya, Guba **69** O 1
Buorkhaya, Mys **69** O 1
Buqayq **49** E 4
Buran **51** R 6
Bura'o **61** H 3
Burayda **48** D 4
Buraydah **57** G 3
Burdur **46** D 3
Burdwan **72** E 3
Bureinskiy, Khrebet **69** O 5
Bureya **69** O 5
Burgakhcha **69** Q 3
Burgas **46** C 2
Burgaski zaliv **46** C 2
Burgeo **19** J 4
Burgersdorp **62** D 6
Burgfjället **42** FG 3
Burgos (Mexico) **25** E 3
Burgos (Spain) **44** C 3
Burhanpur **72** C 3
Burica, Punta **28** C 5
Burin Peninsula **19** J 4
Burkhala **69** RS 3
Burkina **58** DE 3
Burley **20** D 3
Burlington (CO, U.S.A.) **21** F 4
Burlington (IA, U.S.A.) **21** H 3
Burlington (N.Y., U.S.A.)
  23 F 2
Burma **73** FG 3
Burmantovo **51** M 3
Burney **20** B 3
Burnie **80** L 9
Burns **20** C 3
Burnside **16** DE 3
Burns Lake **13** M 5
Burntwood **15** K 3
Burnu **46** D 3
Burqin **67** M 1
Burra **79** F 5
Bursa **46** C 2
Bur Sa'id **48** A 3
Bür Südän **56** F 5
Burton, Lac **18** E 3
Buru **75** G 4
Burundi **60** DE 5
Buşayrah **48** C 2
Büshehr **49** F 3

Bushman Land **62** BC 5
Businga **60** C 4
Busira **60** B 5
Buskerud **43** E 3
Busu Melo **60** C 4
Butang Group **73** G 6
Butaritari **82** C 2
Butembo **60** D 4
Butha Qi **69** M 6
Butte **20** D 2
Butt of Lewis **40** B 3
Button Bay **15** L 3
Button Islands **17** O 4
Butuan **75** G 2
Bu Tu Suay **73** J 5
Buxton **22** E 3
Buy **50** H 4
Büyük Ağrı Dağı **47** F 3
Buzachi, Poluostrov **66** E 1–2
Buzău **46** C 1
Buzuluk **50** K 5
Byblos **48** B 2
Bydgoszcz **41** G 4
Bygdeå **42** H 3
Bygdeträsket **42** GH 3
Byglandsfjord **43** E 4
Bykovo **50** J 3
Bykovskiy **69** NO 1
Bylot Island **84**
Byrd Station **85**
Byro **78** B 4
Byske **42** H 3
Byskeälven **42** GH 2
Bytom **41** G 4
Byuchennyakh **69** QR 3

C

Caaguazu **36** E 4
Cáatingas **35** GH 2–3
Caazapa **36** E 4
Caballo Res. **20** E 5
Cabanatuan **75** J 1
Cabezas **34** D 4
Cabimas **32** D 1
Cabinda **59** G 6–7
Cabinet Mountains **20** C 2
Cabo Barbas **54** B 4
Cabo Beata **29** E 3
Cabo Bojador **54** BC 3
Cabo Camarón **28** BC 3
Cabo Catoche **26** D 4
Cabo Corrientes **24** C 3
Cabo Corrientes **32** C 2
Cabo Cruz **28** D 3
Cabo das Correntes **63** F 4
Cabo de Ajo **44** C 3
Cabo de Creus **44** D 3
Cabo de Finisterre **44** B 3
Cabo de Formentor **44** D 3
Cabo de Gata **44** C 4
Cabo de Hornos **37** CD 10
Cabo de la Nao **44** D 4
Cabo Delgado **63** G 2

Cabo de Palos **44** C 4
Cabo de Salinas **44** D 4
Cabo de Santa Maria
  (Mozambique) **63** EF 5
Cabo de Santa Maria
  (Portugal) **44** B 4
Cabo de São Roque **35** JK 2
Cabo de São Vicente **44** B 4
Cabo dos Bahías **37** CD 8
Cabo Engaño **29** F 3
Cabo Francés **27** E 4
Cabo Frio **35** H 5
Cabo Gracias a Dios **28** C 3
Cabo Marzo **28** D 5
Cabonga, Réservoir **18** E 4
Cabo Norte **33** J 3
Cabo Orange **33** H 3
Cabo Ortegal **44** B 3
Caborca **24** D 5
Cabo Rojo (Mexico) **25** E 3
Cabo Rojo (Puerto Rico)
  29 F 3
Cabo San Antonio
  (Argentina) **37** E 6
Cabo San Antonio (Cuba)
  26 DE 4
Cabo San Diego **37** C 9
Cabo San Lucas **24** C 3
Cabo San Rafael **29** F 3
Cabo Santa Elena **28** B 4
Cabo Trafalgar **44** B 4
Cabot Strait **19** J 4
Cabo Verde **58** AB 6
Cabrera **44** D 4
Cabrera, Sierra de la **44** B 3
Cabruta **32** E 2
Caçador **36** F 4
Čačak **46** AB 2
Caceres (Brazil) **34** E 4
Cáceres (Colombia) **28** D 5
Cáceres (Spain) **44** B 4
Cachi, Nevado de **34** C 5
Cachimbo **33** H 5
Cachimbo, Serra do **33** G 5
Cachoeira **35** J 3
Cachoeira Alta **35** F 4
Cachoeira do Sul **36** F 5
Cachoeiro de Itapemirim
  35 HJ 5
Caconda **62** B 2
Cacula **62** A 2
Cadi, Sierra del **44** D 3
Cadillac **22** C 2
Cadiz (Philippines) **75** F 1
Cádiz (Spain) **44** B 4
Cadiz, Golfo de **44** B 4
Caen **44** C 2
Caetite **35** H 3
Cagayan de Oro **75** F 2
Cagayan Islands **75** F 2
Cagliari **45** E 4
Cagua **29** F 4
Caguas **29** F 3
Caia **63** EF 3

Caibarién **27** F 4
Caico **35** J 2
Caicos Islands **29** E 2
Caicos Passage **29** E 2
Cailloma **34** B 4
Cairns **79** H 2
Cairo **56** E 2
Caiundo **62** B 3
Cajamarca **32** C 5
Cajazeiras **35** J 2
Cajuapara **33** J 4
Calabar **59** F 4
Calabozo **32** E 2
Calabria **45** G 4
Calabro, Apennino **45** G 4
Calafate **37** B 9
Calais **40** D 4
Calakmul **25** F 4
Calama **34** C 5
Calamar **32** D 3
Calamian Group **75** E 1
Cala Ratjada **44** D 4
Calatayud **44** C 3
Calatrava, Campo de **44** C 4
Calbayog **75** FG 1
Calçoene **33** H 3
Calcutta **72** E 3
Caldas **32** C 2
Caldera **36** B 4
Caldwell **20** C 3
Caledonia **21** H 3
Caleta Olivia **37** C 8
Calgary **14** G 4
Cali **32** C 3
Calicut **72** BC 5
Caliente **20** D 4
California **20** BC 4
California, Golfo de
  24 DE 5–7
Caliiegua **34** CD 5
Callao **34** A 3
Caltanissetta **45** F 4
Calvi **45** E 3
Cama **28** C 4
Camaguán **29** F 5
Camagüey **27** F 4
Camagüey, Archipiélago de
  27 F 4
Camaná **34** B 4
Camapuã **35** F 4
Camaquã **36** F 5
Camarat, Cap **45** E 3
Camargo **34** C 5
Camarón, Cabo **28** BC 3
Camarones **37** CD 7
Camaxilo **62** B 1
Cambodia **73** HJ 5
Cambrai **44** D 1
Cambrian Mountains **40** C 4
Cambridge **40** D 4
Cambridge (ID, U.S.A.) **20** C 3
Cambridge (Jamaica) **28** D 3
Cambridge (MA, U.S.A.)
  23 F 2

Cambridge (MD, U.S.A.)
  22 E 3
Cambridge Bay **16** EF 3
Camden **21** H 5
Camden Bay **12** HJ 1
Cameia National Park **62** C 2
Cameron **21** H 2
Cameron Hills **14** F 3
Cameroon **59** FG 4
Cameroon, Mont **59** F 5
Cametá **33** HJ 4
Camiranga **33** J 4
Camiri **34** D 5
Camocim **35** H 1
Camooweal **79** F 2
Camorta **73** F 6
Campana, Isla **37** A 8
Campbell Island **85**
Campbell River **14** M 5
Campbellton **19** G 4
Camp Century **84**
Campeche **25** F 4
Campeche, Bahia de **25** F 4
Campidano **45** E 4
Campina Grande **35** J 2
Campinas **35** G 5
Campo **59** F 5
Campo Corral **32** DE 2
Campo de Calatrava **44** C 4
Campo Formoso **35** H 3
Campo Gallo **36** D 4
Campo Grande **35** F 5
Campo Maior **35** H 1
Campos **35** GH 3–4
Campos **35** H 5
Camp Verde **20** D 5
Cam Ranh **73** JK 5
Camrose **14** G 4
Camsell **13** O 3
Camsell Portage **14** GH 3
Ca Na **74** C 1
Canada **14–15**
Canadian **21** F 4
Canadian River **21** F 4
Canadian River North **21** G 4
Çanakkale **46** C 2
Çanakkale Boğazı **46** C 2–3
Canal de Ballenas **24** B 2
Canal de la Mona **29** F 3
Canal de Sainte-Lucie **29** F 4
Canal de Yucatán **26** D 4
Canal do Norte **33** H 3
Canal du Midi **44** D 3
Canale di Sicilia **45** F 4
Canale di Malta **45** F 4
Cananea **24** DE 5
Canary Islands **54** B 3
Canaveral, Cape **27** EF 3
Canavieiras **35** J 4
Canberra **79** H 6
Canby **21** G 3
Canchas **36** BC 4
Cancún **26** D 4
Candeias **35** J 3

Candelaria 25 F 4
Cando 21 G 2
Canéla 35 H 3
Cangamba 62 C 2
Cangombé 62 B 2
Cangyuan 70 C 6
Cangzhou 71 G 3
Caniapiscau 19 F 3
Caniapiscau, Lac 19 G 3
Canindé 35 J 1
Canipiscau 19 G 2
Çankırı 47 D 2
Cannanore 72 BC 5
Cannes 45 E 3
Canning Basin 78 C 2
Cann River 79 H 6
Canoas 36 F 4
Canon City 21 E 4
Canora 15 J 4
Canosa 45 G 3
Canso 19 H 4
Canso, Strait of 19 H 4
Cantabrian Mountains
   44 BC 3
Cantaura 33 F 2
Canterbury Bight 82 C 5
Can Tho 73 J 6
Canto do Buriti 35 H 2
Canton (China) 70 F 6
Canton (MS, U.S.A.) 21 HJ 5
Canton (OH, U.S.A.) 22 D 2
Cantwell 12 H 3
Canyon 21 F 4
Capanaparo 29 F 5
Capanema 33 J 4
Capão Bonito 35 G 5
Capatárida 29 E 4
Cap Camarat 45 E 3
Cap Corse 45 E 3
Cap Dame-Marie 29 E 3
Cap de Fer 55 G 1
Cap de Gaspé 19 H 4
Cap de la Hague 44 C 2
Cap-de-la-Madeleine
   18 F 4
Cap-de-Nouvelle France
   17 M 4
Cape Acadia 17 L 4
Cape Adare 85
Cape Agulhas 62 C 6
Cape Alava 20 A 2
Cape Alitak 12 FG 4
Cape Anguille 19 HJ 4
Cape Ann 85
Cape Arid 78 C 5
Cape Arid National Park
   78 C 5
Cape Arnhem 79 F 1
Cape Baring 16 C 3
Cape Bathurst 16 A 2
Cape Bauld 19 JK 3
Cape Bear 19 H 4
Cape Blanco 20 AB 3
Cape Boothby 85

Cape Breton Highlands Na-
   tional Park 19 H 4
Cape Breton Island 19 J 4
Cape Canaveral 27 EF 3
Cape Catastrophe 27 F 5–6
Cape Chapman 16 J 3
Cape Charles (Newfoundl.,
   Can.) 19 JK 3
Cape Charles (VA, U.S.A.) 22 E 3
Cape Chelyuskin 84
Cape Chidley 17 O 4
Cape Churchill 15 L 3
Cape Coast 58 DE 4
Cape Cod 23 G 3
Cape Cod Bay 23 FG 2
Cape Columbine 62 B 6
Cape Colville 16 H 3
Cape Comorin 72 C 6
Cape Constantine 12 EF 4
Cape Coral 27 E 3
Cape Cretin 80 E 3
Cape Croker 78 E 1
Cape Cross 62 A 4
Cape Dalhousie 13 L 1
Cape d'Ambre,Cape
   Bobraomby 63 HJ 2
Cape Darnley 85
Cape Dennison 85
Cape Dominion 17 L 3
Cape Dorchester 17 L 3
Cape Dorset 17 LM 4
Cape du Couedic 79 F 6
Cape Dyer 17 O 3
Cape Engaño 75 J 1
Cape Farewell 81 Q 9
Cape Fear 22 E 4
Cape Felix 16 G 3
Cape Finniss 78 E 5
Cape Flattery (WA, U.S.A.)
   20 B 2
Cape Freels 19 K 4
Cape Fria 62 A 3
Cape Girardeau 22 C 3
Cape Grim 80 K 9
Cape Halkett 12 G 1
Cape Harrison 19 J 3
Cape Hatteras 22–23 EF 3
Cape Henrietta Maria 18 D 2
Cape Hooper 17 N 3
Cape Hope 16 C 3
Cape Horn 37 CD 10
Cape Howe 79 J 6
Cape Jaffa 79 F 6
Cape Jones 15 L 2
Cape Kattaktoc 19 G 2
Cape Kellett 16 A 2
Cape Kendall 15 M 2
Cape Knox 13 L 5
Cape Krusenstern National
   Monument 12 E 2
Cape Lambert 81 F 2
Cape Lambton 16 AB 2
Cape Leeuwin 78 A 5
Cape Lévêque 78 C 2

Capelinha 35 H 4
Cape Lisburne 12 D 2
Cape Lisburne 12 DE 2
Cape Londonderry 78 D 1
Cape Lookout 22 E 4
Cape Low 15 MN 2
Cape Maria van Diemen
   81 PQ 7
Cape May 23 F 3
Cape Melville79 GH 1
Cape Mendocino 20 AB 3
Cape Mercy 17 O 4
Cape Meredith 37 D 9
Cape Michelsen 16 F 2
Cape Mohican 12 D 3
Cape Morris Jesup 84
Cape Naturaliste 78 A 5
Cape Negrais 73 F 4
Cape Newenham 12 E 4
Cape North (Nova Scotia,
   Can.) 19 H 4
Cape Norvegia 85
Cape of Good Hope 62 B 7
Cape Otway 79 G 6
Cape Palmas 58 C 5
Cape Parry 16 B 2
Cape Pembroke (Ontario,
   Can.) 17 K 4
Cape Poinsett 85
Cape Prince Alfred 16 M 1
Cape Prince of Wales 12 D 2
Cape Providence 80 OP 10
Cape Province 62 CD 6
Cape Queen 17 L 4
Cape Race 19 K 4
Cape Raper 17 N 3
Cape Ray 19 J 4
Cape Rodney 80 E 4
Cape Rodney (AK, U.S.A.)
   12 D 3
Cape Romanzof 12 D 3
Cape Sable 23 G 2
Cape Sable (FL, U.S.A.) 27 E 3
Cape Saint Francis 62 CD 6
Cape Saint George 19 HJ 4
Cape Saint George 81 F 2–3
Cape Saint James 13 L 5
Cape Saint Lucia 63 E 5
Cape San Blas 25 F 2
Cape Scott 13 M 5
Cape Scott 78 D 1
Cape Smith 17 L 4
Cape Southampton 15 MN 2
Cape Swinburne 16 FG 2
Cape Tatnam 15 LM 3
Cape Town 62 B 6
Cape Van Diemen 78 D 1
Cape Verde 58 AB 6
Cape Walsingham 17 O 3
Cape Wessel 79 F 1
Cape Wilson 17 KL 3
Cape Wrath 40 BC 3
Cape Wrottesley 16 B 2
Cape Yakataga 13 J 4

Cape York 79 G 1
Cape York Peninsula 79 G 1
Cape Zhelaniya 84
Cap Ferret 44 C 3
Cap-Haïtien 29 E 3
Cap Hopes Advance 17 N 4
Capitán Arturo Prat 85
Cap Lopez 59 F 6
Cap Masoala 63 J 3
Capo Carbonara 45 E 4
Capo Circeo 45 F 3
Capo Gallo 45 F 4
Capoompeta 79 J 4
Capo Palinuro 45 FG 4
Capo Passero 45 G 4
Capo San Marco 45 E 4
Capo Santa Maria di Leuca
   45 G 4
Capo Spartivento 45 E 4
Capo Testa 45 E 3
Cap Prince de Galles 17 M 4
Capreol 18 D 4
Capri 45 F 3
Capricorn Channel 79 J 3
Caprivi Game Park 62 C 3
Caprivi Strip 62 C 3
Cap Saint-André 63 G 3
Cap Sainte-Marie,Cap
   Vohimena 63 GH 5
Cap Timiris 54 B 5
Cap Vert 58 A 3
Cap Wolstenholme 17 L 4
Caquetá 32 D 4
Caracal 46 B 2
Caracarai 33 F 3
Caracas 32 E 1
Carahue 37 B 6
Carajás, Serra dos 33 H 4–5
Caraquet 19 H 4
Caratasca, Laguna de 28 C 3
Caratinga 35 H 4
Carauari 32 E 4
Carazinho 36 F 4
Carballo 44 B 3
Carbonara, Capo 45 E 4
Carbonia 45 E 4
Carcajou 14 F 3
Carcassonne 44 D 3
Carcross 13 K 3
Cárdenas (Cuba)27 E 4
Cárdenas (Mexico) 25 E 3
Cardiff 40 C 4
Cardigan 40 C 4
Cardston 14 G 5
Careiro 33 G 4
Carey 20 D 3
Carey, Lake 78 C 4
Caribbean Sea 28–29 DF 3
Cariboo Mountains (Br. Col.,
   Can.) 14 E 4
Caribou 23 G 2
Caribou Mountains (Alb.,
   Can.) 14 F 3
Carinhanha 35 H 3

Cariparé 35 G 3
Caripito 29 G 4
Caritianas 33 F 5
Carleton Place 18 E 4
Carletonville 62 D 5
Carlisle 40 C 4
Carlsbad (CA, U.S.A.) 20 C 5
Carlsbad (N.M., U.S.A.) 24 F 5
Carlyle 15 J 5
Carmacks 13 K 3
Carmel 20 B 4
Carmen, Isla 24 B 2
Carmi 22 C 3
Carnarvon (Australia) 78 A 3
Carnarvon (S. Africa) 62 C 6
Carnegie 78 C 4
Carnegie, Lake 78 C 4
Car Nicobar 73 F 6
Carnot 60 B 3
Carolina 33 J 5
Carolina Beach 22 E 4
Caroline 83 EF 3
Caroline Islands 82 AB 2
Carondelet 82 D 3
Carora 29 EF 4
Carpathians 46 BC 1
Carpáţii Meridionali 46 B 1–2
Carpentaria Gulf of 79 F 1
Carpina 35 J 2
Carribou Lake, North 15 L 4
Carrick-on-Shannon 40 B 4
Carrillo 24 D 2
Carrizal 32 D 1
Carrizal (Mexico) 20 E 5
Carrizos 24 E 5
Carrizo Springs 25 E 2
Carrizozo 21 E 5
Carroll 21 H 3
Carrollton 22 C 4
Çarşamba 47 D 3
Carson 20 B 2
Carson City 20 C 4
Cartagena (Colombia) 32 C 1
Cartagena (Spain) 44 C 4
Cartago (Costa Rica) 28 C 5
Carthage (MO, U.S.A.) 21 H 4
Carthago (IL, U.S.A.) 21 H 3
Cartwright 19 J 3
Caruaru 35 J 2
Carúpano 29 G 4
Carvoeiro 33 F 4
Casablanca 54 D 2
Casa Grande 20 D 5
Casbas 37 D 6
Cascade 20 C 3
Cascade Range 20 B 2–3
Cascavel 35 F 5
Caserta 45 F 3
Casey 85
Casino 79 J 4
Casma 32 C 5
Casper 20 E 3
Caspian Sea 66 DE 2–3
Cassiar 13 L 4

Cassiar Mountains 13 M 4
Cassino 45 F 3
Castanhal 33 J 4
Castaño 36 C 5
Castellón 44 CD 4
Castelo de Vide 44 B 4
Castelvetrano 45 F 4
Castilla (Chile) 36 B 4
Castilla (Peru) 32 BC 5
Castilla la Nueva 44 C 3–4
Castilla la Vieja 44 C 3
Castillos 36 F 5
Castlegar 14 F 5
Castor 14 G 4
Castres 44 D 3
Castries (Saint Lucia) 29 G 4
Castro 37 B 7
Catalão 35 G 4
Cataluna 44 D 3
Çatalzeytin 47 D 2
Catamarca 36 CD 4
Catanduanes 75 FG 1
Catanduva 35 G 5
Catania 45 G 4
Catanzaro 45 G 4
Catastrophe, Cape 79 F 6
Catbalogan 75 FG 1
Cateel 75 G 2
Catherine, Mount 20 D 4
Catinzaco 36 C 4
Cat Island 27 FG 4
Cat Lake 15 L 4
Catoche, Cabo 26 D 4
Catrilo 37 D 6
Catrimani 33 F 3
Catwick Islands 73 J 5–6
Caucasus Mountains 47 F 2
Cauquenes 37 B 6
Caura 33 F 2
Causapscal 19 G 4
Cavalcante 35 G 3
Cavell 18 C 3
Caxias (Amazonas, Brazil)
    32 D 4
Caxias (Maranhão, Brazil)
    35 H 1
Caxias do Sul 36 FG 4
Caxito 62 A 1
Cayenne 33 H 3
Cayman Brac 28 D 3
Cayman Islands 28 CD 3
Cayo Arenas 25 F 3
Cayo Nuevo 25 F 3
Cayos Arcas 25 F 3
Cayos de Albuquerque 28 C 4
Cayos de Roncador 28 D 4
Cayos Miskitos 28 C 4
Cay Sal 27 E 4
Ceará 35 HJ 1
Ceballos 24 D 2
Cebollar 36 C 4
Cebu 75 F 2
Čechy 41 F 4
Cedar City 20 D 4

Cedar Creek Reservoir 21 G 5
Cedar Falls 21 H 3
Cedar Key 27 E 3
Cedar Lake 15 JK 4
Cedar Rapids 21 H 3
Cedar River 21 H 3
Cedros, Isla 24 A 2
Celaya 25 D 3
Celebes 75 EF 4
Celebes Sea 75 F 3
Celestún 25 F 3
Celje 45 FG 2
Celle 41 F 4
Celtic Sea 40 B 4
Center 25 H 5
Centerville 21 H 3
Central, Cordilera (Colombia)
    32 C 2–3
Central, Cordillera (Peru)
    32 C 5
Central African Republic
    60 BC 3
Central Arctic District 16 EF 2
Centralia 20 B 2
Central Kalahari Game
    Reserve 62 C 4
Central Makran Range
    67 GH 5
Centralno Tungusskoye Plato
    68 GH 3–4
Central Range 80 D 2–3
Centreville 25 H 5
Cereal 14 G 4
Ceres 35 FG 4
Cereté 28 D 5
Cerf 61 J 6
Cerralvo, Isla 24 C 3
Cerra Viejo 24 D 5
Cerritos 25 DE 3
Cerro Aconcagua 36 BC 5
Cerro Agua Caliente 24 C 2
Cerro Ángel 24 D 3
Cerro Azul 25 E 3
Cerro Blanco 24 C 2
Cerro Bolívar 29 G 5
Cerro Bonete 36 C 4
Cerro Candelaria 24 D 3
Cerro Champaquí 36 D 5
Cerro Chirripó 28 C 5
Cerro Cibuta 24 D 5
Cerro Coatepetl 25 E 4
Cerro Colorado 20 C 5
Cerro de la Asunción 25 E 3
Cerro de la Encantada
    20 CD 5
Cerro de las Mesas 25 EF 4
Cerro del Tigre 25 DE 3
Cerro del Toro 36 C 4
Cerro de Pasco 34 A 3
Cerro de Punta 29 F 3
Cerro Desmoronado 24 CD 3
Cerro de Tocorpuri 34 C 5
Cerro Galán 36 C 4
Cerro Grande 25 D 3

Cerro La Ardilla 24–25 D 3
Cerro Las Casilas 24 C 3
Cerro Las Minas 28 B 4
Cerro Lechiguiri 25 E 4
Cerro Marahuaca 32 E 3
Cerro Mariquita 25 E 3
Cerro Mato 29 F 5
Cerro Mohinora 24 C 2
Cerro Murallón 37 B 8
Cerro Nuevo Mundo 34 C 5
Cerro Ojos del Salado 36 C 4
Cerro Peña Nevada 25 E 3
Cerro Potosí 25 D 2–3
Cerro Santiago 29 C 5
Cerro San Valentín 37 B 8
Cerro Tetari 29 E 5
Cerro Tres Cruces 25 F 4
Cerro Ventana 24 C 3
Cerro Yavi 32 E 2
Cerro Yucuyácua 25 E 4
Cerro Yumari 32 E 3
Cesano 45 F 3
České Budějovice 41 F 5
Českézemě 41 G 5
Cetteville 21 G 4
Ceuta 54 D 1
Ceva-i-Ra 82 C 4
Cévennes 44 D 3
Ceyhan (Turkey) 47 E 3
Ceyhan (Turkey) 47 E 3
Ceylanpınar 48 C 1
Chaca 34 B 4
Chachapoyas 32 C 5
Chad 59 HJ 3
Chad, Lake 59 G 3
Chãdegãn 49 F 2
Chadobets 68 GH 4
Chadron 21 F 3
Chagai Hills 67 G 5
Chagda 69 O 4
Chagdo Kangri 72 D 1
Chaghcharán 67 GH 4
Chagos Archipelago 65 K 10
Chaguaramas 29 F 5
Chagyl 66 F 2
Chahah Burjak 67 G 4
Chah Bahãr 67 G 5
Chaiyaphum 73 H 4
Chakari 62 D 3
Chake Chake 61 FG 6
Chakhansur 67 G 4
Chala 34 B 4
Chalbi Desert 61 F 4
Chaleur Bay 19 GH 4
Chalhuanca 34 B 3
Challapata 34 C 4
Challis 20 D 3
Châlons-sur-Marne 45 D 2
Chalon-sur-Saône 45 DE 2
Chãlũs 49 F 1
Chaman 67 H 4
Chamba 72 C 1
Chambery 45 E 2
Chamela 24 D 4

Chamical 36 C 5
Chamoli 72 CD 1
Chamouchouane 18 F 4
Champagne 45 DE 2
Champaquí, Cerro 36 D 5
Champdoré, Lac 19 G 2
Champlain, Lake 23 F 2
Champotón 25 F 4
Chana Liang 71 J 1
Chañaral 36 B 4
Chanco 37 B 6
Chandalar 12 H 2
Chandeleur Islands 25 F 2
Chandigarh 72 C 1
Chandler 19 H 4
Chandmanĭ 70 C 1
Chandpur 73 F 3
Chandrapur 72 C 3–4
Chanf 67 G 5
Changara 63 E 3
Changchun 71 J 2
Changde 70 F 5
Changji 67 M 2
Chang Jiang 70–71 EG 4
Changling 71 H 2
Changsha 70 F 5
Changwu 70 E 3
Changzhi 70 F 3
Channel Islands (U.K.) 40 C 5
Channel Islands (U.S.A.)
   20 C 5
Channel Port aux Basques
   19 J 4
Channing 21 F 4
Chantrey Inlet 16 G 3
Chaoyang 70 G 6
Chaoyang 71 GH 2
Chapala 24 D 3
Chapala, Lago de 24 D 3
Chapayev-Zheday 68 L 3–4
Chapleau 18 D 4
Chapman, Cape 16 J 3
Chapoma50 GH 2
Chapra 72 DE 2
Chara 68 L 4
Charagua 34 D 4
Charcas 25 D 3
Charcot Island 85
Chard 14 G 3
Chardzhou 67 G 3
Chari 59 H 3
Charity 33 G 2
Charkabozh 50 K 2
Charleroi 40 DE 4
Charles 17 M 4
Charles, Cape (Newfoundl.,
   Can.) 19 JK 3
Charlesbourg 19 F 4
Charles City 21 H 3
Charles Peak 78 C 5
Charleston (S.C., U.S.A.)
   22 E 4
Charleston (W.V., U.S.A.)
   22 D 3

Charleville 79 H 4
Charlotte 22 DE 3
Charlotte Amalie 29 G 3
Charlotte Harbor 27 E 3
Charlottesville 22 E 3
Charlottetown 19 H 4
Charlton 18 DE 3
Charlton (Australia) 79 G 6
Charters Towers 79 H 2–3
Chartres 44 D 2
Charyshskoye 51 Q 5
Chasel'ka 51 Q 2
Chatanga 68 K 6
Châteauroux 44 D 2
Châtellerault 44 CD 2
Chatham 81 S 9
Chatham (New Brunswick,
   Canada) 19 G 4
Chatham (Ontario, Can.)
   22 D 2
Chatham Strait 13 L 4
Chattahoochee 22 CD 4
Chattahoochee River 22 CD 4
Chattanooga 22 C 4
Chaumont 45 DE 2
Chau Phu 73 HJ 5
Chaves (Brazil) 33 H 4
Chaves (Portugal) 44 B 3
Chayatyn, Khrebet 69 P 5
Chaykovskiy 50 KL 4
Chazhegovo 50 K 3
Cheb 41 F 4
Cheboksary 50 J 4
Cheduba 73 F 4
Chegga 55 G 2
Chegytun 12 C 2
Cheju 71 J 4
Cheju-do 71 J 4
Chekhov 69 Q 6
Chekunda 69 O 5
Chekuyevo50 G 3
Chelan, Lake 20 B 2
Chelforó 37 C 6
Chelkar 66 F 1
Chełm 41 H 4
Chelmuzhi 50 G 3
Chelyabinsk 51 M 4
Chelyuskin, Cape 84
Chemult 20 B 3
Chenachane 54 E 3
Chencoyi 25 F 4
Chengde 71 G 2
Chengdu 70 DE 4
Chenxi 70 EF 5
Chenzhou 70 F 5
Chepen 32 C 5
Chepes 36 C 5
Cherbourg 44 C 2
Cherchell 55 F 1
Cheremkhovo 68 H 5
Cherepovets 50 G 4
Cherkassy 50 EF 6
Cherkessk 47 F 2
Chernigov 50 EF 5

Chernovtsy 46 C 1
Chernyakhovsk 43 H 5
Chernyshevskiy 68 K 3
Chernyye Zemli 47 G 1
Chernyy Ostrov 68 F 3
Cherokee 21 GH 3
Cherokees, Lake O' The
   21 H 4
Cherskogo, Khrebet 69 P 1–2
Chervonograd 43 H 5
Chervonoznamenka 46 CD 1
Chesapeake Bay 22 E 3
Chesapeake Bay Bridge-
   Tunnel 22–23 EF 3
Chesterfield Inlet 15 L 2
Chesterfield Inlet 15 LM 2
Chesterfield Islands 82 B 4
Chesuncook Lake 23 G 2
Chetumal 28 B 3
Chetumal, Bahia de 28 B 3
Cheulik 69 P 2
Cheyenne 21 F 3
Cheyenne River 21 F 3
Cheyenne Wells 21 F 4
Chhatarpur 72 C 3
Chiang Kham 73 H 4
Chiang Mai 73 G 4
Chiang Rai 73 G 4
Chiang Saen 73 H 3
Chiapas 25 F 4
Chiavari 45 E 3
Chiayi 71 H 6
Chiba 71 M 3
Chibagalakh 69 PQ 2
Chibit 51 R 5
Chibougamau 18 F 4
Chibougamau, Lac 18 F 4
Chicago 22 C 2
Chicapa 62 C 1
Chic-Chocs, Mounts 19 G 4
Chichagof 13 K 4
Chicheng 71 G 2
Chichén-Itzá 26 D 4
Chickasha 21 G 5
Chiclayo 32 B 5
Chico 37 C 7
Chico (CA, U.S.A.) 20 B 4
Chicoutimi 19 F 4
Chidley, Cape 17 O 4
Chifeng 71 G 2
Chiganak 51 O 6
Chignik 12 F 4
Chigorodó 32 C 2
Chigubo 63 E 4
Chihli, Gulf of 71 GH 3
Chihuahua 24 C 2
Chik Ballapur 72 C 5
Chikhacheva 69 R 1
Chilabombwe 62 D 2
Childress 21 F 5
Chile 37 B 5–6
Chilete 32 C 5
Chilipa de Alvarez 25 E 4

Chillán 37 B 6
Chillicothe (MO, U.S.A.)
   21 H 4
Chillicothe (OH, U.S.A.)
   22 D 3
Chiloé, Isla de 37 B 7
Chiloquin 20 B 3
Chilpancingo 25 DE 4
Chilwa, Lago 63 F 3
Chimaltenango 25 F 5
Chimbay 66 F 2
Chimborazo 32 C 4
Chimbote 32 C 5
Chimkent 67 H 2
Chin 73 F 3
China 70 DF 4
Chinandega 28 B 4
Chincha Alta 34 A 3
Chinchorro, Banco 28 B 3
Chindu 70 C 4
Chindwin 73 FG 3
Chinese Wall 70 E 3
Chingola 62 D 2
Chinguetti 54 C 4
Chinipas 24 C 2
Chinju 71 J 4
Chipata 63 E 2
Chippewa, Lake 21 H 2
Chippewa Falls 21 H 3
Chirchik 67 HJ 2
Chiriguaná 32 D 2
Chirikof 12 F 4
Chiriquí, Golfo de 32 B 2
Chiriqui Grande 178 B 2
Chishui 70 E 5
Chita 68 K 5
Chitado 62 A 3
Chitato 62 C 1
Chitina 13 J 3
Chitina 13 J 3
Chitipa 63 E 1
Chitral 67 J 3
Chitré 28 C 5
Chittagong 73 F 3
Chittaurgarh 72 BC 3
Chittoor 72 C 5
Chivasso 45 E 2
Chivay 34 B 4
Chizha 50 H 2
Chkalovo 51 O 5
Chobe National Park 62 C 3
Choele Choel 37 CD 6
Choggia 45 F 2
Choiseul 81 G 3
Choiseul 82 B 3
Choix 24 C 2
Chojnice 41 G 4
Cholet 44 C 2
Choluteca 28 B 4
Chomutov 41 F 4
Chona 68 J 3
Chon Buri 73 H 5
Ch'ŏngjin 71 JK 2
Ch'ŏngju 71 J 3

Chongqing 70 E 5
Chŏnju 71 J 3
Chonos, Archipiélago de los 37 AB 7–8
Chon Thanh 73 J 5
Chorzów 41 G 4
Chosica 34 A 3
Chos Malal 37 BC 6
Chotanagpur 72 DE 3
Chott Melrhir 55 G 2
Choum 54 C 4
Choybalsan 68 K 6
Christchurch 82 C 5
Christian Sound 13 KL 4
Christie Bay 14 G 2
Christmas Island 74 C 6
Chubut 37 C 7
Chudskoye Ozero 43 J 4
Chugach Mountains 12–13 HJ 3
Chuginadak 12 C 6
Chuhuichupa 24 C 2
Chukar 68 L 3
Chukchi Sea 12 CD 2
Chukchi Sea 84
Chuken 69 P 6
Chukotskiy, Mys 12 C 3
Chukotskiy Poluostrov 12 BC C 2
Chukotsk Peninsula 84
Chukotsk Range 84
Chulak-Kurgan 67 HJ 2
Chulasa 50 J 3
Chula Vista 20 C 5
Chulitna 12 H 3
Chulym 51 QR 4
Chulym 68 F 4
Chumikan 69 OP 5
Chumphon 73 GH 5
Ch'unch'ŏn 71 J 3
Chuquibamba 34 B 4
Chuquicamata 34 C 5
Chur 45 E 2
Churchill 15 KL 3
Churchill 19 H 3
Churchill (Man., Can.) 15 L 3
Churchill (Sask., Can.) 15 J 3
Churchill, Cape 15 L 3
Churchill Falls 19 H 3
Churchill Lake 14 H 3
Churchill Mountains 85
Churchill Peak 14 E 3
Churu 72 C 2
Churuguara 29 EF 4
Churún Merú 33 F 2
Chusovoy 51 L 4
Chusovskoy 50 L 3
Chute-des-Passes 19 F 4
Chutes de Katende (Katende Falls) 60 C 6
Chutes de Livingstone (Livingstone Falls) 60 A 6
Chutes Ngaliema (Stanley Falls) 60 D 4

Chuxiong 70 D 5
Chuyengo 68 HJ 3
Cianjur 74 C 5
Cibuta, Cerro 20 D 5
Cícero Dantas 35 J 3
Ciechanów 41 H 4
Ciego de Ávila 27 F 4
Ciénaga 32 D 1
Cienfuegos 27 E 4
Cieza 44 C 4
Cihanbeyli Platosu 47 D 3
Cihuatlán 24 D 4
Cilo Daği 47 F 3
Cimarron River 21 G 4
Çimen Daği 47 E 3
Cîmpia Bărăganului 46 C 1–2
Cîmpia Burnazului 46 C 2
Cîmpina 46 C 1
Cinca 44 D 3
Cincinatti 22 D 3
Cintalapa de Figueroa 25 F 4
Cinto, Monte 45 E 3
Circeo, Capo 45 F 3
Circle (AK, U.S.A.) 13 J 2
Circle (MT, U.S.A.) 21 E 2
Cirebon 74 C 5
Cirque Mountain 19 H 2
Cisco 25 G 5
Ciskei 62 D 6
Cisne, Islas del 28 C 3
Citlaltépetl, Volcán 25 E 4
Citta del Vaticano 45 F 3
Ciudad Acuña 25 D 2
Ciudad Altamirano 24 D 4
Ciudad Bolívar 33 F 2
Ciudad Bolivia 29 EF 5
Ciudad Camargo 24 C 2
Ciudad Cuauhtémoc 25 F 4
Ciudad de Dolores Hidalgo 25 DE 3
Ciudad del Carmen 25 F 4
Ciudad del Maíz 25 E 3
Ciudad de Nutrias 29 F 5
Ciudad de Rio Grande 24 D 3
Ciudad Guayana 33 F 2
Ciudad Guzmán 24 D 4
Ciudad Hidalgo (Mexico) 25 DE 4
Ciudad Hidalgo (Mexico) 25 F 5
Ciudad Juárez 24 E 5
Ciudad Lerdo 24 D 2
Ciudad Madero 25 E 3
Ciudad Mante 25 E 3
Ciudad Mendoza 25 E 4
Ciudad Obregón 24 C 2
Ciudad Ojeda 29 E 4
Ciudad Piar 29 G 5
Ciudad Río Bravo 25 E 2
Ciudad-Rodrigo 44 B 3
Ciudad Valles 25 E 3
Ciudad Victoria 25 E 3
Civitanova Marche 45 F 3
Civitavecchia 45 F 3

Cizre 47 F 3
Claire, Lake 14 G 3
Claire Coast 85
Claire Engle Lake 20 B 3
Clanwilliam 62 BC 6
Clarence Strait 13 L 4
Clarence Town 29 E 2
Clarendon 21 F 5
Clarenville 19 K 4
Claresholm 14 G 4
Clarinda 21 H 3
Clark, Lake 12 G 3
Clarke Range 79 H 2–3
Clark Fork 20 C 2
Clark Hill Lake 22 D 4
Clarksburg 22 DE 3
Clarksdale 21 H 5
Clarkston 20 C 2
Clarksville 22 C 3
Clay Belt 18 DE 3
Clearfield 20 D 3
Clear Lake 20 B 3
Clear Lake 20 B 4
Clearwater 27 E 3
Clearwater Mountains 20 C 2
Clermont 79 H 3
Clermont-Ferrand 44 D 2
Cleveland (MS, U.S.A.) 21 H 5
Cleveland (OH, U.S.A.) 22 D 2
Cleveland, Mount 20 D 2
Clifton 22 C 3
Clinton 14 E 4
Clinton (IA, U.S.A.) 21 H 3
Clinton (OK, U.S.A.) 21 G 4
Clinton-Colden Lake 14 H 2
Cloncurry 79 FG 3
Cloquet 21 H 2
Clorinda 36 E 4
Cloud Peak 20–21 E 3
Clovis 21 F 5
Cluj-Napoca 46 B 1
Clyde (N.W.T., Can.) 17 N 2
Cmi Drim 46 B 2
Cnossus 46 C 3
Coahuila 24 D 2
Coalcoman, Sierra de 24 D 4
Coalinga 20 B 4
Coal River 14 D 3
Coari 33 F 4
Coast Mountains 13 LM 4–5
Coast of Labrador 19 HJ 2–3
Coast Range (Queensland, Austr.) 79 J 4
Coast Range (U.S.A.) 20 B 3–4
Coatepec 25 E 4
Coats Island 16 K 4
Coats land 85
Coatzacoalcos 25 F 4
Coatzacoalcos, Bahia 25 F 4
Coba 26 D 4
Cobán 25 F 4
Cobar 79 H 5
Cobija 34 C 3

Cobquecura 37 B 6
Coburg 41 F 4
Cocachacra 34 B 4
Cochabamba 34 CD 4
Cochin 72 C 6
Cochrane 37 B 8
Cochrane (Man., Can.) 15 J 3
Cochrane (Ontario, Can.) 18 D 4
Cocklebiddy 78 D 5
Cocoa 27 E 3
Coco Islands 73 F 5
Coco o Segovia, Rio 28 BC 4
Cocula 24 D 3
Cod, Cape 23 G 3
Codó 35 H 1
Cody 20 E 3
Coetivy 61 JK 6
Coeur d'Alene 20 C 2
Coff's Harbour 79 J 5
Coihaique 37 B 8
Coimbatore 72 C 5
Coimbra 44 B 3
Cojimies 32 B 3
Cojutepeque 28 B 4
Colatina 35 HJ 4
Cold Bay 12 E 4
Col de Perthus 44 D 3
Cold Lake 14 G 4
Coleman 25 G 5
Colesberg 62 D 6
Colfax 20 C 2
Colima 24 D 4
College 12 H 3
College Station 25 G 5
Collier Bay 78 C 2
Collier Ranges National Park 78 B 3
Collines du Perche 44 D 2
Collingwood (Ontario, Can.) 22 E 2
Collinson Peninsula 16 F 2
Cololo, Nevado 34 C 4
Colombia 32 D 3
Colombo 72 C 6
Colón (Cuba) 27 E 4
Colón (Panamá) 32 C 2
Colón, Archipiélago de 32 B 6
Colona 78 E 5
Colonet 24 C 5
Colonia Las Heras 37 C 8
Colonia Morelos 24 E 5
Colorado (Argentina) 37 D 6
Colorado (U.S.A.) 21 EF 4
Colorado, Cerro (Mexico) 20 C 5
Colorado Plateau 20 DE 4
Colorado River (AZ, U.S.A.) 20 D 5
Colorado River (TX, U.S.A.) 25 G 5–6
Colorado Springs 21 F 4
Colotlán 24 D 3
Columbia 14 F 4

Columbia (MO, U.S.A.) **21** H 4
Columbia (S.C., U.S.A.) **22** D 4
Columbia (TN, U.S.A.) **22** C 3
Columbia (WA, U.S.A.)
    20 BC 2
Columbia, Mount **14** F 4
Columbia Falls **20** D 2
Columbia Mountains **14** EF 4
Columbia Plateau **20** C 3
Columbine, Cape **62** B 6
Columbus (GA, U.S.A.) **22** C 4
Columbus (IN, U.S.A.) **22** C 3
Columbus (MS, U.S.A.) **22** C 4
Columbus (NE, U.S.A.) **21** G 3
Columbus (OH, U.S.A.) **22** D 3
Columbus (TX, U.S.A.) **25** E 2
Colville **12** G 2
Colville, Cape **16** H 3
Colville Lake **13** MN 2
Colville Lake **13** MN 2
Comalcalco **25** F 4
Comandante Luis Piedra-
    buena **37** CD 8–9
Comayagua **28** B 4
Combarbala **36** B 5
Combermere Bay **73** F 4
Comitán de Dominguez
    25 F 4
Committee Bay **16** J 3
Como **45** E 2
Comodoro Rivadavia **37** C 8
Comondú **24** B 2
Comorin, Cape **72** C 6
Comoros **63** G 2
Compiègne **44** D 2
Conakry **58** B 4
Conceição do Araguaia
    33 HJ 5
Concepción (Bolivia) **34** D 4
Concepción (Chile) **37** B 6
Concepción (Paraguay) **34** E 5
Concepción, Bahía **24** B 2
Concepción del Oro **25** D 3
Concepción del Uruguay
    36 E 5
Conception, Point **20** B 5
Conception Bay **19** K 4
Conchos, Rio **24** CD 2
Concord **23** F 2
Concórdia (Amazonas, Brazil)
    32 E 4
Concordia (Argentina) **36** E 5
Concordia (KS, U.S.A.) **21** G 4
Concordia (Mexico) **24** C 3
Condon **20** C 2
Conecuh River **22** C 4
Conejo **24** B 3
Congo **59** H 6
Connaught **40** B 4
Connecticut **23** F 2
Connellsville **22** E 2
Conn Lake **17** M 2
Conrad **20** D 2
Conroe **25** G 5

Conselheiro Lafaiete **35** H 5
Con Son **73** J 6
Constanţa **46** C 2
Constantine **55** G 1
Constantine, Cape **12** F 4
Contamana **32** D 5
Contwoyto Lake **16** DE 3
Convención **29** E 5
Conway (AR, U.S.A.) **21** H 4
Conway (S.C., U.S.A.) **22** E 4
Conway Reef **82** C 4
Cook **78** E 5
Cook, Mount **82** C 5
Cook, Strait **82** C 5
Cookes Peak **20** E 5
Cook Inlet **12** G 3
Cook Islands **82** E 3
Cook Mountains **85**
Cook Strait **81** QR 9
Cooktown **79** H 2
Coolidge **20** D 5
Coon Rapids **21** H 2
Coosa River **22** C 4
Coos Bay **20** B 3
Copan **28** B 4
Copenhagen **43** F 4
Copiapó **36** BC 4
Copper **13** J 3
Copperbelt **62** D 2
Copper Center **12** H 3
Copper Cliff **18** D 4
Copper Harbor **22** C 1
Coppermine **16** CD 3
Coppermine **16** D 3
Coqên **72** E 1
Coquimbo **36** B 5
Coral Harbour **15** MN 2
Coral Sea **82** B 3–4
Coral Sea Islands Territory
    79 HJ 1–2
Corcaigh **40** B 4
Cordele **22** D 4
Cordillera Cantábrica **44** BC 3
Cordillera Central (Colombia)
    32 C 2–3
Cordillera Central (Dominican
    Rep.) **29** E 3
Cordillera Central (Peru)
    32 C 5
Cordillera Central
    (Philippines) **75** J 1
Cordillera de Mérida **29** E 5
Cordillera Isabella **28** BC 4
Cordillera Occidental
    (Colombia) **32** C 2–3
Cordillera Occidental (Peru)
    34 BC 3–4
Cordillera Oriental (Bolivia)
    34 CD 3–5
Cordillera Oriental (Colom-
    bia) **32** CD 2–3
Cordillera Real (Ecuador)
    32 C 4
Córdoba (Argentina) **36** D 5

Córdoba (Mexico) **25** E 4
Córdoba (Spain) **44** BC 4
Cordova (AK, U.S.A.) **12** H 3
Corfu **46** AB 3
Corigliano Calabro **45** G 4
Corinth (Greece) **46** B 3
Corinth (MS, U.S.A.) **22** C 4
Corinto **35** H 4
Cork **40** B 4
Çorlu **46** C 2
Cornelio **24** B 2
Cornélio Procópio **35** F 5
Cornelius Grinnel Bay **17** O 4
Corner Brook **19** J 4
Cornwall (Ontario, Can.)
    18 F 4
Coro **32** DE 1
Coroatá **35** H 1
Corocoro **34** C 4
Coromandel Coast **72** D 5
Coromandel Peninsula **81** R 8
Coronado, Bahía de **28** C 5
Coronation **14** G 4
Coronation Gulf **16** D 3
Coronel **37** B 6
Coronel Fabriciano **35** H 4
Coronel Oviedo **36** E 4
Coronel Pringles **37** D 6
Coropuna, Nevado **34** B 4
Corozal **28** B 3
Corozal **28** D 5
Corpus Christi **25** E 2
Corquin **28** B 4
Corrente **35** GH 3
Correntes, Cabo das **63** F 4
Correntina **35** GH 3
Corrientes **36** E 4
Corrientes, Cabo **32** C 2
Corse **45** E 3
Corse, Cap **45** E 3
Corsica **45** E 3
Corsicana **25** G 5
Cortez (U.S.A.) **20** E 4
Çoruh **47** F 2
Çoruh Dağları **47** F 2
Çorum **50** E 2
Corumbá **34** E 4
Corunna **44** B 3
Corvallis **20** B 3
Cosamaloapan **25** E 4
Cosenza **45** G 4
Coshocton **22** D 2
Cosmoledo Group **61** H 6
Costa Blanca **44** C 4
Costa Brava **44** D 3
Costa de la Luz **44** B 4
Costa del Azahar **44** D 3
Costa del Sol **44** C 4
Costa de Mosquitos **28** C 4
Costa Dorada **44** D 3
Costa Rica **28** BC 5
Costa Verde **44** B 3
Cotabato **75** F 2
Cotagaita **34** CD 5

Coteau du Missouri **21** FG 2
Côte d'Argent **44** C 3
Côte d'Azur **45** E 3
Cotonou **58** E 4
Cotopaxi **32** C 4
Cottbus **41** F 4
Cotulla **25** E 2
Council **12** E 3
Council Bluffs **21** GH 3
Courland **43** H 4
Courtennai **14** D 5
Coventry **40** C 4
Covington (GA, U.S.A.) **22** D 4
Covington (KY, U.S.A.) **22** D 3
Covington (TN, U.S.A.) **22** C 3
Covington (VA, U.S.A.) **22** E 3
Cowell **79** F 5
Cowra **79** H 5
Coxim **35** F 4
Cox's Bazar **73** F 3
Coyame **24** C 2
Coyotitan **24** C 3
Cradock **62** D 6
Craig (AK, U.S.A.) **13** L 4
Craig (CO, U.S.A.) **20** E 3
Craiova **46** B 2
Crakow **41** H 4–5
Cranbrook (U.S.A.) **14** F 5
Cranbrook (Austr.) **78** B 5
Crary Mountains **85**
Cratère du Nouveau-Québec
    17 M 4
Crater Lake **20** B 3
Cratéus **35** HJ 2
Crato **35** J 2
Crawford **21** F 3
Crawfordsville **22** C 2
Crazy Peak **20** D 2
Cree **14** H 3
Creel **24** C 2
Cree Lake **14** H 3
Creil **44** D 2
Cremona **45** F 2
Cres **45** F 3
Crescent City **20** B 3
Creston **21** H 3
Crestview **22** C 4
Crete **46** C 3
Creus, Cabo de **44** D 3
Creuse **44** D 2
Criciúma **36** G 4
Crimea **47** D 1
Cristmas Island **83** E 2
Cristóbal, Colón Pico **32** D 1
Croatia **45** G 2
Crockett **25** G 5
Croker, Cape **78** E 1
Croker Island **78** E 1
Crooked Creek **12** F 3
Crooked Island **29** E 2
Crooked Island Passage
    27 FG 4
Crookston **21** G 2
Crosby (N.D., U.S.A.) **21** F 2

Cross, Cape **62** A 4
Cross City **27** E 3
Crossett **21** H 5
Cross Lake **15** K 4
Cross Sound **13** K 4
Crotone **45** G 4
Crow Agency **20** E 2
Crowell **21** G 5
Crow Lake **15** L 5
Crowley **21** H 5
Crowley Ridge **21** H 4
Crown Prince Frederik Island **16** J 3
Crowsnest Pass **14** FG 5
Cruz, Cabo **28** D 3
Cruz Alta **36** F 4
Cruz del Eje **36** CD 5
Cruzeiro do Oeste **35** F 5
Cruzeiro do Sul **32** D 5
Cruz Grande (Mexico) **25** E 4
Crystal Brook **79** F 5
Cuamba **63** F 2
Cuando Cubango **62** BC 3
Cuango **62** B 1
Cuanza **62** B 1–2
Cuanza Norte **62** AB 1
Cuanza Sul **62** AB 2
Cuauhtémoc **24** C 2
Cuba **27** E 4
Cubango **62** B 3
Cuchumatanes, Sierra de los **25** F 4
Cucurpe **20** D 5
Cúcuta **32** D 2
Cuddalore **72** CD 5
Cuddapah **72** C 5
Cudi Dağı **47** F 3
Cuenca (Ecuador) **32** C 4
Cuenca (Spain) **44** C 3–4
Cuencamé de Ceniceros **24** D 3
Cuernavaca **25** DE 4
Cuero **25** E 2
Cuiabá **34** E 4
Cuilapa **25** F 5
Cuito Cuanavale **62** B 3
Cu Lao Hon **73** JK 5
Culiacán **24** C 3
Cullman **22** C 4
Cumaná **33** F 1
Cumbal **32** C 3
Cumberland **22** E 3
Cumberland, Lake (KY, U.S.A.) **22** C 3
Cumberland Lake (Sask., Can.) **15** J 4
Cumberland Peninsula **17** NO 3
Cumberland Plateau **22** CD 3
Cumberland River **22** C 3
Cumberland Sound **17** N 3
Cunani **33** H 3
Cunene (Angola) **62** A 3
Cunene (Angola) **62** B 3

Cuneo **45** E 3
Cunnamulla **79** H 4
Cupica **32** C 2
Curaçao, Isla **32** E 1
Curacautin **37** B 6
Curdimurka **79** F 4
Curiapo **29** G 5
Curicó **37** B 5–6
Curimatá **35** H 2–3
Curitiba **36** FG 4
Curtis **82** D 5
Curtis Island **79** J 3
Curuça **33** J 4
Curumu **33** H 4
Curupuru **33** K 4
Curvelo **35** H 4
Cushing **21** G 4
Cushing, Mount **14** D 3
Cuttack **72** E 3
Cuvette **59** H 6
Cuxhaven **41** E 4
Cuya **34** B 4
Cuyo Islands **75** F 1
Cuyuni **29** GH 5
Cuzco **34** B 3
Cyangugu **60** D 5
Cyclades **46** BC 3
Cypress Hills **14** GH 5
Cyprus **47** D 3
Cyprus **48** AB 2
Cyrenaica **55** JK 3
Cyrus Field Bay **17** O 4
Czechoslovakia **41** G 5
Częstochowa **41** GH 4

D

Dabajuro **29** E 4
Dabat **61** F 2
Dabbāgh, Jabal **48** B 4
Dabeiba **28** D 5
Dabola **58** B 3
Dacca **72** E 3
Dadali **82** B 3
Dadanawa **33** G 3
Daet **75** F 1
Dafeng **71** H 4
Dagabur **61** G 3
Dagana **59** H 3
Dagi **69** Q 5
Dagur **70** C 3
Dahabān **66** B 6
Da Hinggan Ling **71** GH 1–2
Dahlak Archipelago **61** FG 1
Dahonglidian **67** KL 3
Dahra **58** AB 2
Dahūk (Iraq) **48** D 1
Daintree River National Park **79** G 2
Dairen **71** H 3
Daitō-shotō **71** K 5
Dajarra **79** F 3
Dakar **58** A 3
Dakha **72** F 3

Dakhla **54** B 4
Dakovica **46** B 2
Dákura **28** C 4
Dala **62** BC 2
Dalälven **43** G 3
Dalaman **46** C 3
Dalandzadgad **70** DE 2
Dalarna **43** F 3
Da Lat **73** J 5
Dalby **79** J 4
Dale Hollow Lake **22** CD 3
Dalhart **21** F 4
Dalhousie **19** G 4
Dalhousie, Cape **13** L 1
Dali **70** D 5
Dali **13** L 5
Dallas **21** G 5
Dall Lake **12** E 3
Dalma' **49** F 4
Dal'negorsk **71** L 2
Dal'nerechensk **71** KL 1
Dal'nyaya **69** Q 6
Daloa **58** C 4
Dalsland **43** F 4
Dalstroy **69** P 3
Dalton **22** D 4
Daltonganj **72** DE 3
Dalwallinu **78** B 5
Daly Bay **15** M 2
Daly River **78** E 1
Daly Waters **78** E 2
Daman **72** B 3
Damanhūr **56** DE 2
Damara **60** B 3
Damaraland **62** B 4
Damascus **56** F 2
Damascus (Syria) **48** B 2
Damāvand **49** F 2
Dame Marie, Cap **29** E 3
Dāmghan **49** FG 1
Damoh **72** C 3
Dampier **78** B 3
Danakil Plain **61** G 2
Danané **58** C 4
Da Nang **73** J 4
Danba **70** D 4
Dandarah **56** E 3
Dandong **71** H 2–3
Danforth **23** G 2
Danghe Nanshan **70** CD 3
Dangjin Shankou **70** BC 3
Dangshan **71** G 4
Daniel **20** D 3
Daniel's Harbour **19** J 3
Danlí **28** B 4
Danmark **43** E 4
Danmarks Havn **84**
Dan Sai **73** H 4
Danube **46** C 1
Danville (IL, U.S.A.) **22** C 2
Danville (KY, U.S.A.) **22** D 3
Danville (VA, U.S.A.) **22** E 3
Dan Xian **70** E 7

Dao Xian **70** F 5
Dapoli **72** B 4
Da Qaidam **70** C 3
Dar'ā **48** B 2
Dārāb **66** E 5
Dāran **49** F 2
Darāw **48** A 4
Darband **66** F 4
Darbhanga **72** E 2
Dardanelle Lake **21** H 4
Dardanelles **46** C 3
Dar el Beida **54** C 2
Dar es Salaam **61** F 6
Dārfūr **56** C 6
Darganata **67** G 2
Dargaville **81** Q 8
Darién **32** C 2
Darjeeling **72** E 2
Darlag **70** CD 4
Darling Downs **79** H 4
Darling Range **78** B 5
Darling River **79** G 5
Darlington **40** C 4
Darmstadt **41** E 5
Darnah **55** K 2
Darnley, Cape **85**
Darnley Bay **16** B 3
Dar Rounga **60** C 2–3
Dartmoor **40** C 4
Dartmouth **23** H 2
Darvaza **66** F 2
Darweshan **67** G 4
Darwin **78** E 1
Daryācheh-ye Bakhtegān **49** FG 3
Daryācheh-ye Namak **49** F 2
Daryācheh-ye Orūmīyeh **49** D 1
Daryācheh-ye Tashk **49** FG 3
Daryā-ye Māzandarān **66** E 3
Dasht-e Kavīr **49** FG 2
Dasht-e Lūt **49** G 2
Dasht-e Naomid **66–67** G 4
Date **71** M 2
Datia **72** C 2
Datong (Qin. China) **70** D 3
Datong (Ziz. China) **70** F 2
Datta **69** Q 6
Dāuarzan **66** F 3
Daugava **43** H 4
Daugav'pils **43** J 4
Daung Kyun **73** G 5
Dauphin **15** J 4
Dauphiné **45** E 3
Dauphin Lake **15** K 4
Daurskoye **68** F 4
Davangere **72** C 5
Davao **75** G 2
Dāvar Panāh **67** G 5
Dāvarzan **49** G 1
Davenport **21** HJ 3
David **32** B 2
Davidson Mountains **13** J 2
Davis (Antarctica) **85**

Davis (CA, U.S.A.) 20 B 4
Davis Inlet 19 H 2
Davis Sea 85
Davis Strait 17 O 3
Dawḥat as Salwā 49 F 4
Dawson 13 K 3
Dawson Creek 14 E 3
Dawson Inlet 15 L 2
Dawson Range 13 K 3
Dawu 70 D 4
Dayangshu 69 M 6
Dayong 70 EF 5
Dayr az Zawr 48 C 2
Dayrūt 56 DE 3
Dayton 22 D 3
Daytona Beach 27 E 3
Dazhu 70 E 4
Dazjā 49 G 2
De Aar 62 C 6
Deadhorse 12 GH 1
Dead Sea 85
Dead Sea (Jordan) 48 B 3
Dean 13 M 5
Deán Funes 36 CD 5
Dease 13 M 4
Dease Arm 13 N 2
Dease Lake 13 L 4
Dease Strait 16 E 3
Death Valley 20 C 4
Death Valley National
  Monument 20 C 4
Débo, Lac 58 D 2
Deboyne Island 81 F 4
Debra Birhan 61 F 3
Debra Markos 61 F 2
Debra Zeit 61 F 3
Debrecen 46 B 1
Decatur (AL, U.S.A.) 22 C 4
Decatur (IL, U.S.A.) 22 C 3
Deccan 72 CD 3–5
Decelles, Réservoir 18 E 4
Decepción 85
Dechang 70 D 5
Dédougou 58 D 3
Dedza 63 E 2
Deering 12 E 2
Deering, Mount 78 D 3
Deer Lake 19 J 4
Deer Lake (Ontario, Can.)
  15 L 4
Deer Lodge 20 D 2
Dêgê 70 C 4
de Gras, Lac 14 G 2
Deh Bid 49 F 3
Deh Bid 66 E 4
Dehdez 49 F 3
Dehlorān 66 D 4
Dehra Dun 72 C 1
Deh Shū 67 G 4
Dej 46 B 1
De Kalb 22 C 2
De Land 27 E 3
Delarof Islands 12 B 6
Delaware 22 E 3

Delaware Bay 22 E 3
Delaware River 22 E 2
Del Campillo 36 D 5
Del City 21 G 4
Delegate 79 H 6
Delgado, Cabo 63 G 2
Delgerhaan 68 HJ 6
Delgerhet 70 F 1
Delgertsogt 70 E 1
Delhi 72 C 2
Deličal Dağı 46 C 2–3
Delicias 24 C 2
Delijān 49 F 2
Del Norte 21 E 4
De Long Mountains 12 E 2
Delorme, Lac 19 G 3
Delphi 46 B 3
Del Rio 25 D 2
Delta (CO, U.S.A.) 20 E 4
Delta (UT, U.S.A.) 20 D 4
Delta Dunării 46 CD 1
Delta Junction 12 H 3
Demavend, Mount 49 F 2
Demba 60 C 6
Dembia 60 C 3
Deming 20 E 5
Demopolis 22 C 4
Dempo, Gunung 74 B 4
Dem'yanovka 51 N 5
Dem'yanskoye 51 N 4
Denali 12 H 3
Denali National Park and
  Preservative 12 GH 3
Denau 67 H 3
Den Helder 40 D 4
Denio 20 C 3
Denison (IA, U.S.A.) 21 G 3
Denison (TX, U.S.A.) 21 G 5
Denison, Mount 12 G 4
Denizli 46 C 3
Denkou 70 E 2
Denmark 43 E 4
Denmark Strait 84
Dennison, Cape 85
Denpasar 74 D 5
Denton 21 G 5
D'Entrecasteaux Islands
  81 F 3
Denver 21 F 4
Deogarh 72 D 3
Deoghar 72 E 3
Deolali 72 B 4
De Peré 22 C 2
Depoe Bay 20 B 3
Depósita 33 F 3
Depréssion del Balsas
  25 DE 4
Deqing 70 F 6
De Queen 21 H 5
Derbent 66 D 2
Derby (Australia) 78 C 2
Derby (U.K.) 40 C 4
Derdap 46 B 2
Dergachi 50 J 5

De Ridder 25 H 5
Dermott 21 H 5
Derudeb 56 F 5
Deryabino 51 Q 1
Derzhavinsk 51 N 5
Désappointement, Îles du
  83 F 3
Deschambault Lake 15 J 4
Desengaño, Punta 37 C 8
Desert Center 20 C 5
Desierto de Atacama 34 C 5
Desierto de Sechura 32 B 5
Desierto de Vizcaíno 24 B 2
Des Moines 21 H 3
Des Moines River 21 H 3
Desolación, Isla 37 AB 9
Desrouches, Île 61 J 6
Dessau 41 F 4
Dessye 61 FG 2
Destruction Bay 13 K 3
Detroit 22 D 2
Détroit de Jaques-Cartier
  19 H 4
Détroit d'Honguedo 19 H 4
Detroit Lakes 21 G 2
Deutsche Bucht 41 E 4
Deutsche Demokratische
  Republik (D.D.R.) 41 F 4
Deva 46 B 1
Devil's Island 33 H 2
Devils Lake 21 G 2
Devils Paw 13 L 4
Devon Island 84
Devonport 82 A 5
Devrez 47 D 2
Dexter 22 D 4
Deyang 70 D 4
Dezfūl 49 E 2
Dez Gerd 49 F 3
Dezhneva, Mys 12 D 2
Dezhou 71 G 3
Dhahab 48 B 3
Dhamār 57 G 6
Dhamtari 72 D 3
Dharwar 72 B 4
Dhaulagiri 72 D 2
Dhelfoí 46 B 3
Dhíavlos Zakínthou 46 B 3
Dhirfis Óros 46 B 3
Dhoraji 72 B 3
Dhule 72 B 3
Diable, Île du 33 H 2
Diablo Range 20 B 4
Diaca 63 F 2
Diamante, Punta del 25 E 4
Diamantina (Minas Gerais,
  Brazil) 35 H 4
Diamantina (Queensland,
  Austr.) 79 G 3
Diamantina Lakes 79 G 3
Diamond Jenness Peninsula
  16 CD 2
Diamond Peak 20 C 4
Diana, Baie 17 N 4

Dianjiang 70 E 4
Dibrugarh 73 FG 2
Dickinson 21 F 2
Dicle 66 C 3
Didiéni 58 C 3
Didyma 46 C 3
Diéma 58 C 3
Dieppe 44 D 2
Digby 23 G 2
Dihang 70 C 5
Dijlah 49 D 2
Dijon 45 E 2
Dıkmen Dağı 47 D 2
Dikson 84
Dilaram 67 G 4
Di Linh 74 C 1
Dilj 45 G 2
Dilling 56 D 6
Dillingham 12 F 4
Dillon 20 D 2
Dilolo 62 C 2
Dimashq 48 B 2
Dimbokro 58 D 4
Dimitrovgrad 46 C 2
Dimitrovgrad (U.S.S.R.)
  50 JK 5
Dimona 48 B 3
Dinagat 75 G 1
Dinajpur 72 E 2
Dinara Planina 45 G 3
Dinder National Park 56 F 6
Dindigul 72 C 5
Dingbian 70 E 3
Dingxi 70 DE 3
Dingxian 70 FG 3
Dinokwe 62 D 4
Diomida, Ostrova 12 D 2
Dionísio Cerqueira 36 F 4
Diourbel 58 B 2
Dipkarpas 48 B 2
Dipolog 75 F 2
Diré 58 D 2
Diredawa 61 G 3
Dirico 62 C 3
Dirk Hartog Island 78 A 4
Disappointment, Lake 78 C 3
Dishnā 48 A 4
Disko 84
Disko Bugt 84
Disna 43 J 4
District of Columbia (D.C.,
  U.S.A.)22 E 3
District of Fort Smith 14 G 2
District of Inuvik 13 LM 2
District of Keewatin 16 L 1–2
Distrito Federal 35 G 4
Diu 72 B 3
Divändareeh 49 E 1
Divinopolis 35 GH 5
Divo 58 C 4
Dixon Entrance 13 L 5
Diyālā 49 D 2
Diyarbakır 47 F 3
Djanet 55 G 4

Djelfa 55 F 2
Djibouti 61 G 2
Djibouti 61 G 2
Djougou 58 E 4
Dneprodzerzhinsk 47 D 1
Dnepropetrovsk 47 E 1
Dneprovskiy Liman 46 D 1
Dnestr 46 C 1
Doba 59 H 4
Dobreta Turnu Severin 46 B 2
Dobrogea 46 C 2
Dobrowolski 85
Dobrudžansko Plato 46 C 2
Doctor Arroyo 25 D 3
Dodecanese 46 C 3
Dodge City 21 F 4
Dodoma 61 FG 6
Dog Creek 14 E 4
Dogger Bank 40 D 4
Dogondoutchi 59 EF 3
Doguéraoua 59 F 3
Doğu Karadeniz Dağlari
    47 EF 2
Doha 49 F 4
Dohad 72 B 3
Doi Inthanon 73 G 4
Doilungdêqen 73 F 1–2
Dolbeau 18 F 4
Dôle 45 E 2
Dolo 61 G 4
Dolores 37 E 6
Dolphin and Union Strait
    16 CD 3
Doma Peaks 80 D 3
Dom Aquino 35 F 4
Dominica 29 G 3
Dominican Republic 29 F 2–3
Dominica Passage 29 G 3
Dominion, Cape 17 L 3
Domino 19 J 3
Dompu 75 E 5
Don (Mexico) 24 C 2
Don (U.S.S.R.) 50 H 6
Don Benito 44 B 4
Dondo 63 EF 3
Dondra Head 72 D 6
Donegal Bay 40 B 4
Donegal Mountains 40 B 4
Donetsk 47 E 1
Donetskiy Kryazh 47 EF 1
Dongara 78 B 4
Dongchuan 70 D 5
Dongfang 70 E 7
Dong Hai 71 HJ 5
Dongning 71 JK 2
Dongo 62 B 2
Dongoura 58 BC 3
Dongping 71 G 3
Dongsheng 70 EF 3
Dongting Hu 70 F 5
Dong Ujimqin Qi 71 G 1
Dongxiang 70 FG 5
Donjek 13 K 3
Dönna 42 F 2

Doonerak, Mount 12 H 2
Door Peninsula 22 C 2
Doramarkog 70 C 4
Dorchester, Cape 17 L 3
Dordrecht 40 D 4
Dore Lake 15 H 4
Dori 58 D 3
Dornogovĭ 70 EF 2
Döröö Nuur 68 F 6
Dortmund 41 E 4
Dosso 58 E 3
Dothan 22 C 4
Douala 59 FG 5
Douentza 58 D 3
Douglas (AK, U.S.A.) 13 L 4
Douglas (AZ, U.S.A.) 20 E 5
Douglas (U.K.) 40 C 4
Douglas (WY, U.S.A.) 21 EF 3
Doumbouene 59 J 3
Dourados 35 F 5
Douro 44 B 3
Dover 40 D 4
Dover (DE, U.S.A.) 22 E 3
Dovrefjell 42 E 3
Dowlatābād 66 F 5
Dow Rūd 49 E 2
Dow Sar 49 E 2
Dozois, Réservoir 18 E 4
Drain 20 B 3
Drakensberg 62 D 5–6
Drake Passage 85
Drake Strait 37 CD 10
Dráma 46 B 2
Drammen 43 F 4
Drau 45 F 2
Drava 45 G 2
Drayton Valley 14 F 4
Dresden 41 F 4
Dreux 44 D 2
Drini 46 B 2
Drumheller 14 G 4
Drummnod 20 D 2
Drummondville 18 F 4
Druzhnaya 85
Druzhnaya II 85
Dryden 15 L 5
Drysdale River National Park
    78 D 2
Dry Tortugas 27 E 3
Dschang 59 F 4
Duaringa 79 HJ 3
Dubawnt 15 J 2
Dubawnt Lake 15 J 2
Dubayy 49 G 4
Dubbo 79 H 5
Dublin 40 B 4
Dublin (GA, U.S.A.) 22 D 4
Dubna 50 G 4
Dubno 43 J 5
Du Bois 22 E 2
Dubovskoye 47 F 1
Dubrovitsa 43 J 5
Dubrovnik 45 G 3
Dubrovnoye 51 NO 4

Dubuque 21 H 3
Duc de Gloucester, Îles du
    83 F 4
Duchesne 20 D 3
Ducie 83 G 4
du Couedic, Cape 79 F 6
Dudhi 72 D 3
Dudinka 51 R 2
Dudley 40 C 4
Duékoué 58 C 4
Duero 44 C 3
Duff Islands 82 C 3
Dugi Otok 45 F 3
Duisburg 40 E 4
Duitama 32 D 2
Dukān 49 D 2
Duke of York Bay 16 JK 3
Dukhān 49 F 4
Dukou 70 D 5
Dukwe 62 D 4
Dulan 70 C 3
Dulce, Bahia 25 E 4
Dulce, Golfo 28 C 5
Dulga-Kyuyel' 68 K 3
Duluth 21 H 2
Dūmā 48 B 2
Dumaguete 75 F 2
Dumfries 40 C 3
Dumont d'Urville 85
Dumpu 82 A 3
Dumyāt 56 E 2
Duna 46 A 1
Dunántúl 46 A 1
Dunaujváros 46 A 1
Dunav 46 B 2
Dunbar (Australia) 79 G 2
Dunbar (U.K.) 40 C 3
Duncan 21 G 5
Dundalk 40 B 4
Dundalk Bay 40 B 4
Dundee 40 C 3
Dundgovĭ 70 E 1
Dunedin 81 Q 10
Dunhua 71 J 2
Dunhuang 70 B 2
Dunkerque 44 D 1
Dunkirk 22 E 2
Dunkwa 58 D 4
Dún Laoghaire 40 B 4
Dunmarra 78 E 2
Dunqulah al 'Ordi 56 DE 5
Dunrankin 18 D 4
Dunsmuir 20 B 3
Duolun 71 G 2
Durack Range 78 D 2
Dura Europos 48 C 2
Durance 45 E 3
Durango (CO, U.S.A.) 20 E 4
Durango (Mexico) 24 CD 3
Durant 21 G 5
Duratón 44 C 3
Durban 63 E 5
Durg 72 D 3
Durgapur 72 E 3

Durham (N.C., U.S.A.) 22 E 3
Durmä 49 E 4
Duroy 68 L 5
Durresi 46 A 2
D'Urville Sea 85
Dushan 70 E 5
Dushanbe 67 H 3
Düsseldorf 40 E 4
Dutch Harbor 12 D 5
Duwayhin 66 E 6
Duye 60 D 4
Düzce 46 D 2
Dvina, Severnaya 50 H 3
Dwarka 72 A 3
Dworshak Reservoir 20 C 2
Dyadmo 68 J 4
Dyersburg 22 C 3
Dyrhólaey 42 B 3
Dyurmen'tobe 67 GH 1
Dzerzhinsk 50 H 4
Dzhagdy, Khrebet 69 O 5
Dzhalinda 69 M 5
Dzhambul 67 J 2
Dzhankoy 47 D 1
Dzhanybek 50 J 6
Dzhelinde 68 K 1
Dzhetygara 51 M 5
Dzhezkazgan 67 H 1
Dzhigudzhak 69 ST 3
Dzhirgatal' 67 J 3
Dzhugdzhur, Khrebet 69 OP 4
Dzhunkun 68 K 3
Dzhusaly 67 GH 1
Dzibalchén 28 B 3
Dziuche 28 B 3

E

Eagle (Seychelles) 13 J 3
Eagle Lake (CA, U.S.A.) 20 B 3
Eagle Lake (Ontario, Can.)
    15 L 5
Eagle Pass 25 DE 2
Eagle Peak 20 C 3
Eagle River 12 H 3
Eagle Summit 12 H 2
Ear Falls 15 L 4
Easley 22 D 4
East Antarctica 85
East Bay 16 K 4
East Cape 81 R 8
East China Sea 71 HJ 5
Eastend 15 H 5
Easter Island 83 H 4
Eastern Ghats 72 CD 3–5
East Falkland 37 E 9
East London 62 CD 6
Eastmain 18 E 3
Eastman 22 D 4
Easton 22 E 2
East Point 22 CD 4
Eastport 23 G 3
East Siberian Sea 84
Eatonville 20 B 2

Eau Claire **21** H 3
Eau-Claire, Lac à l' **18** F 2
Eauripik **82** A 2
Ebano **25** E 3
Ebe **69** Q 3
Eberswalde **41** F 4
Eboli **45** G 3
Ebolowa **59** G 5
Ebon **82** C 2
Ebyakh **69** S 2
Ech Cheliff **55** F 1
Echmiadzin **47** F 2
Echo Bay **13** O 2
Écija **44** B 4
Ecuador **32** B 4
E'cueils, Pointe aux **18** E 2
Edéa **59** FG 5
Edel Land **78** A 4
Edenton **22** E 3
Edgell **17** O 4
Edgemont **21** F 3
Edgeöya **84**
Edina **21** H 3
Edinburgh **40** C 3
Edirne **46** C 2
Edmonds **20** B 2
Edmonton **14** G 4
Edmundston **19** G 4
Edremit **46** C 3
Edson **14** F 4
Eduni, Mount **13** M 3
Edward, Lake **60** D 5
Edwards Plateau **24**
Edzo **14** F 2
Eek **12** E 3
Efaté **81** J 5
Efes **46** C 3
Effingham **22** C 3
Egan Range **20** CD 4
Egegik **12** F 4
Egersund **43** E 4
Egilsstaðir **42** C 2
Eglab Dersa **54** E 3
Egmont, Mount **81** Q 8
Eğridir Gölü **46** D 3
Egvekinot **12** B 2
Egypt **48** A 4
Egypt **56** DE 4
Eiao **83** F 3
Eidfjord **43** E 3
Eifel **40** E 4
Eights Coast **85**
Eighty Mile Beach **78** BC 2
Eire **40** B 4
Eirunepé **32** D 5
Eisenach **41** F 4
Eisenhüttenstadt **41** FG 4
Ejin Qi **70** D 2
Ekibastuz **51** P 5
Ekoli **60** C 5
Ekwan **18** D 3
El Aaiún **54** C 3
El Adeb Larache **55** G 3
El Álamo **20** C 5

Elat **48** B 3
Elâzığ **47** E 3
Elba **45** F 3
El'ban **69** P 5
El Banco **32** D 2
Elbasani **46** B 2
El Baul **29** F 5
El Bayadh **55** F 2
Elbe **41** F 4
Elbert, Mount **20** E 4
Elbeyli **47** E 3
Elbląg **41** G 4
Elbow **15** H 4
Elbrus **47** F 2
'El Bur **61** H 4
El Buro **25** D 2
Elburz Mountains **66** EF 3
Elburz Mountains (Iran) **49** F 1
El Cajon **20** C 5
El Callao **29** G 5
El Canelo **25** DE 3
El Carmen (Colombia) **28** D 5
El Casco **24** D 2
El Centro **20** C 5
El Cerro **34** D 4
Elche **44** C 4
El Cuy **37** C 6
Elda **44** C 4
'El Dère **61** H 4
El Descanso **20** C 5
El Difícil **32** D 2
El Diviso **32** C 3
El Djouf **54** CD 4
El Dorado (AR, U.S.A.) **21** H 5
Eldorado (Argentina) **36** EF 4
El Dorado (KS, U.S.A.) **21** G 4
El Dorado (Mexico) **24** C 3
El Dorado (Venezuela) **33** F 2
Eldoret **60** EF 4
Elektrostal' **50** GH 4
Elemi Triangle **60** EF 4
El Encanto **32** D 4
Elephant Butte Reservoir
  20 E 5
Elephant Island **85**
Elesbão Veloso **35** H 2
El Escorial **44** C 35
Eleuthera Island **27** F 3
El Fasher **56** CD 6
El Ferrol del Candillo **44** B 3
El Fuerte **24** D 3
El'gakan **69** M 4
Elghena **61** F 1
Elgin (OR, U.S.A.) **20** C 2
El Goléa **55** F 2
Elgon, Mount **60** EF 4
'El Hamurre **61** H 3
El Homr **55** F 3
Elim **12** E 3
Elisabethtown **22** C 3
Elisenvaara **42** JK 3
Elista **47** F 1
Elizabeth **79** F 5
Elizabeth City **22** E 3

Elizabeth Falls **15** HJ 3
El Jadida **54** D 2
El Jicaral **28** B 4
Elk **41** H 4
Elk City **21** G 4
El Kharga → Al Khārijah
  56 DE 3
Elkhart **22** C 2
Elkhorn River **21** G 3
Elkins **22** E 3
Elko **20** D 3
Ellef Ringnes Island **84**
Ellendale **21** G 2
Ellensburg **20** B 2
Ellesmere Island **84**
Ellice Islands **82** C 3
Elliot (Australia) **78** E 2
Elliot (South Africa) **62** D 6
Elliot, Mount **79** H 2
Ellisburg **22** E 2
Ellsworth Land **85**
Ellsworth Mountains **85**
El Maestrazgo **44** CD 3
El Maitén **37** B 7
El Medo **61** G 3
El Messir **59** H 2
Elmhurst **22** C 2
Elmira **22** E 2
El Mirador **28** B 3
El Mreiti **54** D 4
El Novillo **24** BC 2
El Obeid **56** DE 6
Elorza **29** F 5
El Oued **55** G 2
Eloy **20** D 5
El Palmito **24** C 2
El Paso **24** E 5
El Porvenir (Panamá) **28** D 5
El Porvenir (Venezuela) **29** F 5
El Potosi (Mexico) **25** D 3
El Progreso **28** B 3
El Puerto **24** B 2
El Puerto de Santa Maria
  44 B 4
El Real **28** D 5
El Reno **21** G 4
El Salto **24** C 3
El Salvador **25** FG 5
El Sauca **24** B 3
El Sáuz **24** C 2
El Seibo **29** F 3
El Sueco **24** C 2
El Tajin **25** E 3
El Tigre **33** F 2
El Tocuyo **29** F 5
El Tránsito **36** B 4
El Triumfo **24** B 3
El Tuito **24** C 3
El Tunal **36** D 3–4
Eluru **72** D 4
El Valle **32** C 2
Elvas **44** B 4
El Vigía **29** E 5
Elvira **32** D 5

Ely (MN, U.S.A.) **21** H 2
Ely (NV, U.S.A.) **20** D 4
Emamrud **49** G 1
Emamshar **66** F 3
Emba **66** F 1
Embalse de Alcántara **44** B 4
Embalse de Almendra **44** B 3
Embalse del Ebro **44** C 3
Embalse del Guárico **29** F 5
Embalse de Mequinenza
  44 C 3
Embarcación **34** D 5
Embarras Portage **14** G 3
Emden **41** E 4
Emel'dzak **69** N 4
Emerald **79** H 3
Emerson **15** K 5
Emi **68** G 5
Emi Koussi **59** HJ 2
Emiliano Zapata **25** F 4
Emmett **20** C 3
Emmonak **12** E 3
Emory Peak **24** D 2
Empalme **24** B 2
Empedrado **36** E 4
Emporia (KS, U.S.A.) **21** G 4
Emporia (VA, U.S.A.) **22** E 3
Ems **41** E 4
Encarnación **36** E 4
Encinal **25** E 2
Encontrados **29** E 5
Enda Salassie **61** F 2
Ende **75** F 5
Enderbury **82** D 3
Enderby Land **85**
Endicott Mountains **12** G 2
Endwell **22** E 2
Engaño, Cabo **29** F 3
Engaño, Cape **75** J 1
Engel's **50** J 5
Enggano, Pulau **74** B 5
England **40** D 4
English Channel **40** BC 4–5
Engozero **42** K 2
Enid **21** G 4
Eniwetok **82** B 2
Enkan **69** Q 4
Enköping **43** G 4
Enmore **33** G 2
Ennadai **15** J 2
Ennadai Lake **15** J 2
Ennedi **59** J 2
Enontekiö **42** H 2
Enrekang **75** EF 4
Enschede **41** E 4
Ensenada **20** C 5
Enshi **70** EF 4
Entebbe **60** E 4
Enterprise (N.W.T., Can.)
  14 F 2
Enterprise (OR, U.S.A.) **20** C 2
Entre Rios **33** H 5
Enugu **59** F 4
Enugu Ezike **59** F 4

Enurmino 12 C 2
Envigado 32 CD 2
Envira 32 D 5
Épernay 44 D 2
Ephesus 46 C 3
Epi 81 J 5
Épinal 45 E 2
Équateur 60 BC 4
Equatoria 60 DE 3–4
Equatorial Guinea 59 F 5
Erbil 48 D 1
Érd 46 A 1
Erechim 36 F 4
Ereentsav 68 L 6
Ereğli 47 D 3
Erenhot 70 F 2
Eresma 44 C 3
Erfurt 41 F 4
Erg Brusset 59 FG 2
Erg Chech 54 E 3–4
Erg de Ténéré 59 FG 2
Erg Iguidi 54 DE 3
Ergun He 68 M 5
Ergun Zuoqi 69 M 5
Eriba 56 F 5
Eric 19 G 3
Erichsen Lake 17 K 2
Erie 22 D 2
Erie, Lake 22 D 2
Erie Canal 22 E 2
'Erigābo 61 H 2
Erikub 82 C 2
Erimbet 67 G 2
Eritrea 61 FG 2
Ermelo 62 DE 5
Ernest Legouvé 83 E 5
Erode 72 C 5
Erongo 62 B 4
Erongo Mountains 62 B 4
Erozionnyy 69 R 2
Errego 63 F 3
Erromanga 82 C 4
Erromango 81 J 5
Ertai 67 N 1
Erzgebirge 41 F 4
Erzincan 47 E 3
Erzurum 47 F 3
Erzurum-Kars Yaylâsı 47 F 2
Esbjerg 43 E 4
Escalante 20 D 4
Escalón 24 D 2
Escanaba 22 C 1
Eschan 69 R 3
Escondido 20 C 5
Escuintla 25 F 5
Esfahan 49 F 2
Eskilstuna 43 G 4
Eskimo Lakes 13 L 2
Eskimo Point 15 L 2
Eskişehir 46 D 3
Eslamabad 49 E 2
Eslöv 43 F 4
Esmeralda, Isla 37 A 8
Esmeraldas 32 BC 3

España 44 C 4
Espanola 21 E 4
Esperance Bay 78 C 5
Esperanza (Antarctica) 85
Esperanza (Mexico) 24 C 2
Espinal (Bolivia) 34 E 4
Espinal (Colombia) 32 D 3
Espinar 34 B 3
Espinazo del Diablo, Sierra 24 C 3
Espírito Santo 35 HJ 4
Espiritu Santo 82 BC 4
Esplanada 35 J 3
Espoo 43 H 3–4
Esquel 37 B 7
Esquinapa de Hidalgo 24 C 3
Essaouira 54 CD 2
Essen 41 E 4
Essendon, Mount 78 C 3
Essex Mountain 20 E 3
Estados, Isla de los 37 D 9
Estância 35 J 3
Estelí 28 B 4
Estero de Agiabampo 24 C 2
Esteros 34 D 5
Estevan 15 J 5
Estherville 21 GH 3
Estoniya 43 HJ 4
Estrecho de Gibraltar 44 B 4
Estrecho de le Maire 37 CD 9–10
Estrecho de Magallanes 37 B 9
Estrêla, Serra de 44 B 3
Estremadura 44 B 4
Estrondo, Serra do 33 J 5
Esztergom 46 A 1
Ethiopia 61 FG 3
Ethiopian Plateau 61 FG 3
Etna 45 FG 4
Etolin 13 L 4
Etolin Strait 12 DE 3–4
Etosha Namib Desert Park 62 B 3
Etosha Pan 62 B 3
Etzná Tixmucuy 25 F 4
Eudora 21 H 5
Eufaula 22 C 4
Eufaula Lake 21 G 4
Eugene 20 B 3
Eugenia, Punta 24 A 2
Eugmo 42 H 3
Eungella National Park 79 HJ 3
Euphrates 47 FG 2–3
Euphrates (Iraq) 47 FG 2–4
Euphrates (Iraq) 48 C 2
Eureka (CA, U.S.A.) 20 B 3
Eureka (NV, U.S.A.) 20 C 4
Evans, Lac 18 E 3
Evans Strait 16 K 4
Evanston (IL, U.S.A.) 22 C 2
Evanston (WY, U.S.A.) 20 D 3
Evansville 22 C 3

Everest, Mount 72 E 2
Everett 20 B 2
Everett Mountains 17 N 4
Everglades City 27 E 3
Everglades National Park 27 E 3
Evergreen 22 C 4
Évora 34 B 4
Evreux 44 D 2
Evvoia 46 B 3
Ewasse 81 F 3
Excelsior Springs 21 H 4
Executive Committee Range 85
Exeter 40 C 4
Exeter Sound 17 O 3
Exmouth 78 A 3
Extremadura 44 B 4
Exuma Cays 27 F 4
Exuma Sound 27 F 4
Eyre 78 D 5
Eyre Peninsula 79 F 5
Eysturoy 40 A 1
Ezop, Gora 69 S 3

F

Fabala 58 C 4
Fabens 24 E 5
Faber Lake 14 F 2
Fabriano 45 F 3
Fada 59 J 2
Faenza 45 F 3
Færingehavn 17 Q 4
Faeroe Islands 40 A 1
Fâgâraş 46 BC 1
Fairbanks 12 H 3
Fair Bluff 22 E 4
Fairborn 22 D 3
Fairfield 20 B 4
Fair Isle 40 C 3
Fairmont (MN, U.S.A.) 21 H 3
Fairmont (W.V., U.S.A.) 22 E 3
Fair Ness 17 M 4
Fairview 79 G 2
Fairweather, Mount 13 K 4
Faisalabad 67 J 4
Faith 21 F 2
Faizabad (Afghanistan) 67 J 3
Faizabad (India) 72 D 2
Fakaina 83 F 4
Fakaofo 82 D 3
Fakarava 83 F 4
Faku 71 H 2
Falagh 60 E 3
Falfurrias 25 E 2
Falkenberg 43 F 4
Falkland Islands 37 DE 9
Falkland Sound 37 DE 9
Fallon 20 C 4
Fall River 23 F 2
Falls City 21 G 3
Falmouth 40 B 4
False Pass 12 E 5

Falster 43 G 4
Falun 43 G 3
Famagusta 47 D 3
Fana 58 C 3
Fangataufa 83 F 4
Fangzheng 71 JK 1
Faraday 85
Faradje 60 D 4
Farafangana 63 H 4
Farah 67 G 4
Farallon de Medinilla 82 A 1
Farallon de Pajaros 82 A 1
Faranah 58 B 3
Faraulep 82 A 2
Farewell 12 G 3
Farewell, Cape 81 Q 9
Fargo (GA, U.S.A.) 22 D 4
Fargo (N.D., U.S.A.) 21 G 2
Faribault, Lac 18 F 2
Faridpur 72 E 3
Färjestaden 43 G 4
Farmington (MN, U.S.A.) 23 F 2
Farmington (N.M., U.S.A.) 20 E 4
Fårö 43 G 4
Faro (Brazil) 33 G 4
Faro (N.W.T., Can.) 13 L 3
Faro (Portugal) 44 B 4
Farquhar Group 61 J 6
Fårs 49 F 3
Fartak, Ra's 57 J 5
Fasâ 49 F 3
Fasano 45 G 3
Fastov 50 E 6
Fataka 82 C 3
Fatehgarh 72 CD 2
Father Lake 18 EF 4
Fâurei 46 C 1
Faxaflói 42 A 2
Faxälven 42 G 3
Faya-Largeau 59 HJ 2
Fayetteville (AR, U.S.A.) 21 H 4
Fayetteville (N.C., U.S.A.) 22 E 4
Faysh Khâbur 48 D 1
Fayu 82 B 2
Fazilka 72 B 1
Fdérik 54 C 4
F. D. Roosevelt Lake 20 C 2
Fear, Cape 22 E 4
Feathertop, Mount 79 H 6
Federal Republic of Germany 41 E 4
Federated States of Micronesia 82 AB 2
Fehmarn 41 F 4
Feijó 32 D 5
Feira de Santana 35 J 3
Feklistova, Ostrov 69 P 4–5
Felipe Carrillo Puerto 28 B 3
Felix, Cape 16 G 3
Fengcheng 71 HJ 2

Fengjie 70 EF 4
Fengqing 70 CD 6
Fengshui Shan 69 M 5
Feni Islands 81 F 2
Fenoarivo Atsinanana
    63 HJ 3
Fensfjorden 42 DE 3
Fenyang 70 F 3
Feodosiya 47 DE 1
Fer, Cap de 55 G 1
Ferfer 61 H 3
Fergana 67 J 2
Fergus Falls 21 G 2
Ferguson Lake 16 E 3
Fergusson 81 F 3
Ferjukot 42 A 3
Ferkéssédougou 58 C 4
Fernando de Noronha Island
    31 G 3
Fernandópolis 35 F 5
Fernando Póo → Bioko 59 F 5
Ferrara 45 F 3
Ferreira Gomes 33 H 3
Ferriday 25 H 5
Fès 54 E 2
Festus 21 H 4
Fethiye 46 C 3
Feuilles, Baie aux 19 G 2
Feuilles, Rivière aux 18 F 2
Fezzan 55 HJ 3
Fianarantsoa 63 H 4
Fierras 42 G 2
Fiji 82 C 4
Fiji Islands 82 C 4
Filadélfia 34 E 5
Filchner Ice Shelf 85
Fimbul Ice Shelf 85
Fimi 60 B 5
Findlay 22 D 2
Finisterre, Cabo de 44 B 3
Finke 78 E 4
Finke, Mount 78 E 5
Finke Gorge National Park
    78 E 3
Finland 42 J 3
Finland, Gulf of 43 H 4
Finland, Gulf of 43 H 4
Finlay 14 DE 3
Finlay Forks 14 E 3
Finnie Bay 17 L 3
Finnmark 42 H 2
Finnmarksvidda 42 H 2
Finnsnes 42 G 2
Finnveden 43 F 4
Finspång 43 G 4
Fiordland National Park
    80 P 9–10
Fırat 47 E 3
Firenze 45 F 3
Firminy 44 D 2
Firozabad 72 CD 2
Firth of Forth 40 C 3
Firūzābād 66 E 5
Firūz Kūh 49 F 2

Fisher Strait 16 K 4
Fishguard 40 B 4
Fiskenæsset 17 Q 4
Fitzcarrald 34 B 3
Fitzgerald 14 G 3
Fitzgerald River National Park
    78 B 5
Fitzroy Crossing 78 CD 2
Fitzroy River (Queensland,
    Austr.) 79 HJ 3
Fitzroy River (Western
    Australia) 78 C 2
Fizi 60 D 5
Flagler Beach 27 E 3
Flagstaff 20 D 4
Flamenco 36 B 4
Flaming Gorge Reservoir
    20 E 3
Flasher 21 F 2
Flåsjön 42 G 3
Flat 12 F 3
Flathead Lake 20 D 2
Flattery, Cape (WA, U.S.A.)
    20 A 2
Flensburg 41 E 4
Flinders Chase National Park
    79 F 6
Flinders Passage 79 H 2
Flinders Range 79 F 5
Flinders Ranges National Park
    79 FG 5
Flinders River 79 G 2
Flin Flon 15 J 4
Flint (Kiribati) 83 E 3
Flint (MI, U.S.A.) 22 D 2
Flint Hills 21 G 4
Flint River 22 D 4
Flisa 43 F 3
Floraville (Queensland,
    Austr.) 79 F 2
Florence (AL, U.S.A.) 22 C 4
Florence (Italy) 45 F 3
Florence (OR, U.S.A.) 20 B 3
Florence (S.C., U.S.A.)
    22 DE 4
Florencia 32 CD 3
Flores (Guatemala) 28 B 3
Flores (Indonesia) 75 F 5
Flores, Laut 75 E 5
Flores Sea 75 EF 5
Floriano 35 H 2
Floriano Peixoto 32 E 5
Florianópolis 36 G 4
Florida (Cuba) 27 F 4
Florida (U.S.A.) 27 E 3
Floridablanca 32 D 2
Florida Keys 27 E 3
Fluk 75 G 4
Fly River 80 D 3
Foci del Po 45 F 3
Focşani 46 C 1
Foggia 45 G 3
Fogo 19 K 4
Fogo 58 B 7

Foley (N.W.T., Can.) 17 L 3
Foleyet 18 D 4
Folkston 22 D 4
Folkstone 40 D 4
Fond du Lac 15 HJ 3
Fond du-Lac (Sask., Can.)
    15 H 3
Fond du Lac (WI, U.S.A.)
    22 C 2
Fonseca, Golfo de 28 B 4
Fontas 14 E 3
Fonte Boa 32 E 4
Fonte do Pau-d'Agua 34 E 3
Fonualei 82 D 4
Foraker, Mount 12 G 3
Forbes 79 H 5
Ford City 20 C 4
Forest 22 C 4
Forestville 19 G 4
Forêt d'Ecouves 44 C 2
Forín Linares 34 D 5
Forkas 58 E 3
Forli 45 F 3
Formentera 44 D 4
Formentor, Cabo de 44 D 3–4
Formosa 35 G 4
Formosa (Taiwan) 71 H 6
Formosa, Serra 35 EF 3
Formosa Strait 71 GH 5–6
Formoso 36 E 4
Fornæs 43 F 4
Forrest 78 D 5
Forrest City 21 H 5
Forsayth 79 G 2
Forsnäs 42 G 2
Forssa 43 H 3
Fort Albany 18 D 3
Fortaleza 35 J 1
Fort Assiniboine 14 FG 4
Fort Benton 20 D 2
Fort Black 15 H 3
Fort Bragg 20 B 4
Fort Bridger 20 D 3
Fort Chimo 19 G 2
Fort Chipewyan 14 G 3
Fort Collins 21 F 3
Fort Collinson 16 C 2
Fort-de-France 29 G 4
Fort Dodge 21 H 3
Fort Edward 23 F 2
Fort Frances 15 L 5
Fort Franklin 13 N 2
Fort George 18 E 3
Fort Good Hope 13 M 2
Forth, Firth of 40 C 3
Fort Hope 18 C 3
Fortin Coronel Eugenio Garay
    34 D 5
Fortín Ingavi 34 DE 4
Fortín Madrejón 34 E 5
Fortín Ravelo 34 D 4
Fortín Suárez Arana 34 D 4
Fort Kent 19 G 4
Fort Knox 22 C 3

Fort Lauderdale 27 F 3
Fort Liard 13 N 3
Fort Mackay 14 G 3
Fort Macleod 14 G 5
Fort Madison 21 H 3
Fort McMurray 14 G 3
Fort McPherson 13 L 2
Fort Miribel 55 F 3
Fort Morgan 21 F 3
Fort Myers 27 E 3
Fort Nelson 13 N 4
Fort Nelson 14 E 3
Fort Norman 13 M 3
Fort Peck 20 E 2
Fort Peck Dam 21 E 2
Fort Peck Lake 20 E 2
Fort Pierce 27 EF 3
Fort Portal 60 DE 4
Fort Providence 14 F 2
Fort Qu'Appelle 15 J 4
Fort Randell Dam 21 G 3
Fort Resolution 14 FG 2
Fort Rupert 18 E 3
Fort Saint James 14 E 4
Fort Saint John 14 E 3
Fort Saskatchewan 14 G 4
Fort Scott 21 H 4
Fort Severn 15 M 3
Fort Shevchenko 66 E 2
Fort Simpson 13 N 3
Fort Smith (Alb., Can.) 14 G 3
Fort Smith (OK, U.S.A.) 21 H 4
Fort Stockton 24 F 5
Fort Sumner 21 F 5
Fortune Bay 19 J 4
Fort Vermilion 14 F 3
Fort Walton Beach 22 C 4
Fort Wayne 22 C 2
Fort Wellington 33 G 2
Fort William 40 BC 3
Fort Worth 21 G 5
Fort Yukon 12–13 HJ 2
Forveaux Strait 82 C 6
Foshan 70 F 6
Fosna 42 F 3
Foso 58 D 4
Fossano 45 E 3
Fossil Bluff 85
Foster, Mount 13 K 4
Fougamou 59 G 6
Fougères 44 C 2
Fouladou 58 AB 3
Foumban 59 G 4
Fourmies 44 D 1
Four Mountains, Islands of
    12 CD 6
Fouta Djallon 58 B 3
Fouta Ferlo 58 B 2
Foveaux Strait 80 P 10
Fowlers Bay 78 F 5
Foxe Basin 17 KL 3
Foxe Channel 17 L 4
Foxe Peninsula 17 L 4
Fox Islands 12 D 5

Fox River **22** C 2
Foz do Breu **32** D 5
Franca **35** G 5
France **44** CD 2
Frances **13** M 3
Francés, Cabo **27** E 4
Franceville **59** G 6
Francis Case, Lake **21** G 3
Francisco de Orellana **32** D 4
Francisco de Orellana
  (Ecuador) **32** C 4
Francisco Escárcega **25** F 4
Francistown **62** D 4
Francs Peak **20** E 3
Frankfort (KY, U.S.A.) **22** C 3
Frankfort (MI, U.S.A.) **22** C 2
Frankfurt am Main **41** E 4
Franklin Bay **16** A 2–3
Franklin Lake **16** G 3
Franklin Mountains
  13 MN 2–3
Franklin Strait **16** G 2
Franz **18** D 4
Franz Josef Land **84**
Fraser **14** E 4
Fraserdale **18** D 4
Fraser or Great Sandy Island
  79 J 4
Fraser Plateau **14** E 4
Fredericia **43** EF 4
Fredericksburg **22** E 3
Fredericton **19** G 4
Frederik IX-Land **17** Q 3
Frederikshavn **43** EF 4
Frederiksted **29** F 3
Frederik VI-Coast **84**
Fredrika **42** G 3
Fredrikstad **43** F 4
Freels, Cape **19** K 4
Freeport (IL, U.S.A.) **22** C 2
Freeport (TX, U.S.A.) **25** EF 2
Freeport City **27** F 3
Freetown **58** B 4
Freiburg **41** E 5
Fréjus **45** E 3
French Guiana **33** H 3
Frenchman **15** H 5
French Polynesia **83** EF 4
Fresnillo **24** D 3
Fresno **20** B 4
Freycinet Peninsula **80** L 9
Fria, Cape **62** A 3
Friesland **40–41** E 4
Frio, Cabo **35** H 5
Frisian Islands **40** E 4
Frobisher Bay **17** N 4
Frobisher Lake **15** H 3
Frolovo **50** H 6
Fronteiras **35** H 2
Frontera **25** F 4
Fronteras **24** E 5
Front Range **21** E 3–4
Fröya **42** E 3
Frozen Strait **16** K 3

Frunze **67** J 2
Fu'an **71** G 5
Fuding **71** H 5
Fuerte Olimpo **34** E 5
Fuerteventura **54** C 3
Fujian **71** G 5
Fujin **69** O 6
Fukui **71** L 3
Fukuoka **71** JK 4
Fukushima **71** LM 2
Fukushima **71** M 3
Fukuyama **71** K 3–4
Funafuti **82** CD 3
Funchal **54** B 2
Fundación **29** E 4
Fundy, Bay of **23** G 2
Funiu Shan **70** F 4
Funtua **59** F 3
Fuqing **71** GH 5
Furancungo **63** E 2
Furmanovka **67** J 2
Furmanovo **50** JK 6
Furneaux Group **82** A 5
Fürth **41** F 5
Fury and Hecla Strait
  16 K 2–3
Fusagasugá **32** D 3
Fushun **71** HJ 2
Fusong **71** J 2
Fuxin **71** H 2
Fuyang **70** G 4
Fuyuan **70** D 5
Fuyun **67** M 1
Fuzhou **71** GH 5
Fyn **43** F 4

G

Gabbs **20** C 4
Gabela **62** A 2
Gabès **55** H 2
Gabon **59** FG 6
Gaborone **62** CD 4
Gabriel Strait **17** N 4
Gach Sārān **49** F 3
Gadag **72** C 4
Gadame **60** E 3
Gadsden **22** C 4
Gaeta **45** F 3
Gaferut **82** A 2
Gaffney **22** D 3
Gagnoa **58** C 4
Gagnon **19** G 3
Gahkom **49** G 3
Gaimán **37** C 7
Gainesville (FL, U.S.A.) **27** E 3
Gainesville (GA, U.S.A.)
  22 D 4
Gainesville (TX, U.S.A.)
  21 G 5
Gairdner, Lake **79** F 5

Gakarosa **62** C 5
Gakona **12** H 3
Galán, Cerro **36** C 4
Galanino **68** F 4
Galápagos Islands **32** B 6
Galathea Deep **82** D 5
Galaţi **46** C 1
Galatina **45** G 3
Galdhøpiggen **42** E 3
Galeana **20** E 5
Galeana (Mexico) **25** E 3
Galena **12** F 3
Galesburg **21** H 3
Galicia (Poland) **41** H 5
Galicia (Spain) **44** B 3
Galimyy **69** ST 3
Gâlka'yo **61** H 3
Galle **72** CD 6
Gallinas, Punta **32** D 1
Gällivare **42** H 2
Gallo, Capo **45** F 4
Gallo Mountains **20** E 5
Gallup **20** E 4
Galole **61** F 5
Galveston **25** F 2
Galveston Bay **25** F 2
Galvez **36** D 5
Galway **40** B 4
Gamba **59** F 6
Gambell **12** C 3
Gambia **58** AB 3
Gambier Islands **83** FG 4
Gamboma **59** H 6
Gamboola **79** G 2
Gamvik **42** J 1
Ganāveh **49** F 3
Ganāveh **66** E 5
Gandadiwata, Bukit **75** EF 4
Gander **19** K 4
Gandhi Sagar Dam **72** C 3
Gandía **44** CD 4
Ganetti **56** E 5
Ganga **72** E 2
Ganga, Mouths of the
  72–73 EF 3
Gangan **37** C 7
Gangapur **72** C 2
Gangdisê Shan **72** DE 1
Ganges **72** E 3
Ganina Gar' **68** F 4
Gannett Peak **20** DE 3
Gansu **70** DE 3
Ganta **58** C 4
Ganzhou **70** FG 5
Gao **58** D 2
Gao'an **70** FG 5
Gaona **36** D 4
Gaoping **70** F 3
Gaoua **58** D 3
Gaoual **58** B 3
Gaozhou **70** EF 6
Gap **45** E 3
Garachiné **28** D 5
Garanhuns **35** J 2

Garberville **20** B 3
Garbokaray **68** G 5
Garbosh, Küh-e **49** EF 2
Garda, Lago di **45** F 2
Gardaneh-ye Ávej **49** E 2
Gardaneh-ye Kandovän
  49 F 1
Gardaneh-ye Khâneh Sorkh
  49 G 3
Gardemoen **43** F 3
Garden City **21** F 4
Gardiner **20** D 2
Gareloi **12** B 6
Gargano, Promontorio del
  45 G 3
Garissa **61** FG 5
Garmisch-Partenkirchen
  41 F 5
Garmsar **49** F 2
Garnett **21** G 4
Garonne,44 D 3
Garoua **59** G 4
Garoua Boulai **59** GH 4
Garöwe **61** H 3
Garri, Küh-e **49** E 2
Garrison Dam **21** F 2
Garry Bay **16** J 3
Garry Lake **16** G 3
Garwa **72** D 3
Gary **22** C 2
Garze **70** C 4
Gascogne **44** CD 3
Gascoyne Junction **78** B 3–4
Gashagar **59** G 3
Gashua **59** G 3
Gaspé **19** H 4
Gaspé, Cap de **19** H 4
Gaspé, Péninsule de **19** G 4
Gassi Touil **55** G 2
Gastello, Iméni **69** R 3
Gastonia **22** D 3
Gästrikland **43** G 3
Gata, Sierra de **44** B 3
Gatchina **43** JK 4
Gateshead (N.W.T., Can.)
  16 G 2
Gates of the Arctic National
  Park and Preserve **12** G 2
Gatineau Park **18** E 4
Gauhati **73** F 2
Gauja **43** H 4
Gausta **43** E 4
Gavanka **69** T 4
Gávdhos **46** B 4
Gave de Pau **44** C 3
Gävle **43** G 3
Gävlebukten **43** G 3
Gaya **72** E 3
Gaylord **22** D 2
Gayndah **79** J 4
Gaza Strip **48** AB 3
Gazelle Peninsula **81** F 2
Gaziantep **47** E 3
Gaziantep Yaylası **47** E 3

Gazimurskiy Zavod **68** L 5
Gazıpaşa **48** A 1
Gbarnga **58** C 4
Gdańsk **41** G 4
Gdynia **41** G 4
Gearhart Mountain **20** B 3
Gedi **61** F 5
Gediz **46** C 3
Geelong **79** G 6
Geigar **56** E 6
Geikie **15** J 3
Gejiu **70** D 6
Gela **45** F 4
Gelendzhik **47** E 2
Gelsenkirchen **41** E 4
Gemena **60** B 4
Gemsbok National Park **62** C 4–5
General Acha **37** D 6
General Alvear **37** C 6
General Belgrano II **85**
General Belgrano III **85**
General Bernardo O'Higgins **85**
General Bravo **25** E 2
General Madariaga **37** E 6
General Pico **37** D 6
General Roca **37** C 6
General San Martin **85**
General Santos **75** G 2
General Treviño **25** E 2
General Trias **24** C 2
Geneva (N.Y., U.S.A.) **22** E 2
Genève **45** E 2
Gengma **70** C 6
Genoa **45** E 3
Genova **45** E 3
Genova, Golfo di **45** E 3
Gent **40** D 4
George (Quebec, Can.) **19** G 2
George, Lake (FL, U.S.A.) **27** E 3
George, Lake (N.Y., U.S.A.) **23** F 2
Georgetown (Cayman Is.) **28** C 3
Georgetown (Gambia) **58** B 3
Georgetown (Guyana) **33** G 2
George Town (Malaysia) **74** AB 2
Georgetown (Queensland, Austr.) **79** G 2
Georgetown (S.C., U.S.A.) **22** E 4
George Town (Tasmania, Austr.) **82** A 5
Georgetown (The Bahamas) **27** F 4
Georgetown (TX, U.S.A.) **25** G 5
George V Coast **85**
George VI Sound **85**
George West **25** E 2
Georgia (U.S.A.) **22** D 4

Georgia (U.S.S.R.) **47** F 2
Georgian Bay **18** D 4
Georgiu-Dezh **50** G 5
Georgiyevka **51** Q 6
Georgiyevsk **47** F 2
Georg von Neumayer **85**
Gera **41** F 4
Geraldton **78** A 4
Geraldton (Ontario, Can.) **18** C 4
Gerås, Serra do **44** B 3
Gerasimovka **51** O 4
Gering **21** F 3
German Democratic Republic **41** F 4
Germi **49** G 2
Gerona **44** D 3
Gêrzê **72** D 1
Gesoa **80** D 3
Getafe **44** C 3
Gettysburg **21** G 2
Getz Ice Shelf **85**
Geyik Dağı **47** D 3
Ghadāmis **55** G 2
Ghana **58** D 4
Ghanzi **62** C 4
Ghardaïa **55** F 2
Gharib, Ra's **48** A 3
Gharyān **55** H 2
Ghazzah **48** B 3
Gheorghe Gheorghiu-Dej **46** C 1
Ghimbi **60** F 3
Ghudāf, Wādī al **48** D 2
Gibara **27** F 4
Gibraltar **44** B 4
Gibraltar, Estrecho de **44** BC 4
Gibraltar, Strait of **44** B 4
Gibson Desert **78** C 3
Giddings **25** G 5
Gift Lake **14** F 3
Gifu **71** L 3
Giganta, Sierra de la **24** B 2
Giglio **45** F 3
Gijon **44** B 3
Gila Bend **20** D 5
Gila River **20** D 5
Gilbert Islands **82** C 2–3
Gilbert River **79** G 2
Gilbués **33** J 5
Giles **78** D 4
Gilgandra **79** H 5
Gillam **15** L 3
Gillette **20** E 3
Gillian, Lake **17** L 3
Gilroy **20** B 4
Gimli **15** K 4
Gingin **78** B 5
Ginir **61** G 3
Gioia **45** G 3
Giresun **47** E 2
Girne **47** D 3
Gironde **44** C 2
Gisborne **81** R 8

Gitarama **60** DE 5
Giuba → Juba **61** G 4
Giza **56** DE 3
Gizhiga **69** U 3
Gizhiginskaya Guba **69** T 3
Gjiri i Vlorå **46** A 2
Gjoa Haven **16** G 3
Gjögur **42** B 2
Gjövik **43** F 3
Glace Bay **19** J 4
Glacier Bay **13** K 4
Glacier Bay National Park and Preserve **13** K 4
Glacier National Park (MT, U.S.A.) **20** D 2
Glacier Peak **20** B 2
Gladstone **22** C 1
Gladstone **79** J 3
Glasgow **40** C 3
Glasgow (KY, U.S.A.) **22** C 3
Glasgow (MT, U.S.A.) **20** E 2
Glazov **50** K 4
Glen Canyon National Recreation Area **20** D 4
Glendale **20** D 5
Glendive **21** F 2
Glenhope **81** Q 9
Glennallen **12** H 3
Glenrock **21** E 3
Glenrothes **40** C 3
Glens Falls **23** F 2
Glenwood Springs **20** E 4
Glittertind **42** E 3
Gliwice **41** G 4
Globe **20** D 5
Głogów **41** G 4
Glottof, Mount **12** G 4
Gloucester (MA, U.S.A.) **23** F 2
Gloucester (U.K.) **40** C 4
Glubokoye **43** J 4
Glukhov **50** F 5
Goa **72** B 4
Gobabis **62** B 4
Gobi **70** EF 2
Gochas **62** B 4
Godär-e Sorkh **49** G 2
Godar-i-Shah **67** G 5
Godavari **72** D 4
Gods Lake **15** L 4
Gods Mercy, Bay of **15** M 2
Gods River **15** L 3
Godthåb **17** Q 4
Godthåbfjord **17** Q 4
Godwar **72** B 2
Goéland, Lac au **18** E 3
Goélands, Lac aux **19** H 2
Gogebic Range **22** C 1
Goiânia **35** FG 4
Goiás (Brazil) **35** G 3
Goiás (Brazil) **35** F 4
Goksu **47** D 3
Göksu **47** E 3
Golan Heights **48** B 2

Golconda **20** C 3
Golcuk **46** C 2
Gold Coast (Australia) **79** J 4
Gold Coast (Ghana) **58** DE 5
Golden **14** F 4
Golden Gate **20** B 4
Golden Hinde **14** D 5
Goldfield **20** C 4
Gold Rock **15** L 5
Goldsboro **22** E 3
Goldsworthy **78** BC 3
Golets Skalistyy, Gora **69** O 4
Golf de Lion **44–45** D 2
Golfe de la Gonâve **29** E 3
Golfe de Saint-Malo **44** C 2
Golfito **28** C 5
Golfo de Ana María **27** F 4
Golfo de Cadiz **44** B 4
Golfo de California **24** DE 5–7
Golfo de Chiriquí **32** B 2
Golfo de Fonseca **28** B 4
Golfo de Guacanayabo **27** F 4
Golfo de Guayaquil **32** B 4
Golfo de Honduras **28** B 3
Golfo del Batabano **27** E 4
Golfo del Darién **28** D 5
Golfo de los Mosquitos **32** B 2
Golfo del Papagayo **28** B 4
Golfo de Nicoya **28** C 5
Golfo de Panamá **32** C 2
Golfo de Paria **29** G 4
Golfo de Penas **37** AB 8
Golfo de Tehuantepec **25** F 4
Golfo de Valencia **44** D 4
Golfo de Venezuela **32** D 1
Golfo di Genova **45** E 3
Golfo di Salerno **45** F 3
Golfo di Squillace **45** G 4
Golfo di Taranto **45** G 3
Golfo Dulce **28** C 5
Golfo San Jorge **37** C 8
Golfo San Matías **37** D 7
Gölgeli Dağları **46** C 3
Golmud **70** B 3
Golovin **12** E 3
Golovnino **71** MN 2
Golubovka **51** O 5
Goma **60** D 5
Gombe **59** G 3
Gomel **50** F 5
Gomera **54** B 3
Goméz Palacio **24** D 2
Gonäbäd **66** F 4
Gonaïves **29** E 3
Gonam **69** O 4
Gonâve, Golfe de la **29** E 3
Gonâve, Ile de la **29** E 3
Gonbad-e Qåbus **66** EF 3
Gonda **72** D 2
Gondar **61** F 2
Gondia **72** CD 3
Gongbo' gyamda **70** BC 5
Gonghe **70** D 3

Gongpoquan 70 C 2
Gonzales 25 E 3
Good Hope, Cape of 62 B 7
Gooding 20 CD 3
Goodland 21 F 4
Goodnews Bay 12 E 4
Goondiwindi 79 HJ 4
Goose Bay 19 H 3
Goose Lake 20 B 3
Gora Denezhkin Kamen'
   51 LM 3
Gora Ezop 69 S 3
Gora Fisht 47 E 2
Gora Golets-Inyaptuk 68 K 4
Gora Golets-Skalistyy
   68 LM 4
Gora Golets Skalistyy 69 O 4
Gora Kamen 68 FG 2
Gora Khil'mi 69 S 1
Gora Khoydype 51 N 2
Gorakhpur 72 D 2
Gora Konzhakovskiy Kamén
   51 LM 4
Gora Kovriga 50 J 2
Gora Kuytun 51 R 6
Gora Medvezh'ya 69 P 6
Gora Munku-Sardyk 68 GH 5
Gora Narodnaya 51 LM 3
Gora Nelkuchan 69 P 3
Gora Pobeda 69 R 2
Gora Sokhor 68 J 5
Gora Syuge-Khaya 69 OP 2
Gora Taklaun 69 Q 3
Gora Tel'pos-Iz 51 LM 3
Gora Yamantau 51 L 5
Góra Zamkowa 41 H 4
Gorda 20 B 4
Gordion 47 D 3
Gordon (NE, U.S.A.) 21 F 3
Gordon (WI, U.S.A.) 21 H 2
Gordon Downs 78 D 2
Gordon Lake 14 G 2
Gorgän 49 G 1
Gori 47 F 2
Gorki 51 N 2
Gor'kiy 50 H 4
Görlitz 41 F 4
Gorlovka 47 E 1
Gorna Oryakhovitsa 46 C 2
Gorno-Altaysk 51 QR 5
Gornozavodsk 69 Q 6
Gor·iyak 51 Q 5
Goroka 80 E 3
Goromay 69 Q 5
Gorongosa 63 E 3
Gorongosa National Park
   63 EF 3
Gorontalo 75 F 3
Gory Byrranga 68 GH 1
Goryn' 43 J 5
Gory Putorana 68 FH 2
Gory Ulutau 67 H 1
Gory Ushkanîy 12 B 2
Gorzów Wielkopolski 41 G 4

Goshogawara 71 LM 2
Gossi 58 D 2
Göta kanal 43 F 4
Götaland 43 FG 4
Göteborg 43 F 4
Gothenburg 43 F 4
Gothenburg (NE, U.S.A.)
   21 FG 3
Gotland 43 G 4
Gotska Sandön 43 GH 4
Göttingen 41 EF 4
Goulburn 79 H 5
Goulimime 54 C 3
Gouré 59 G 3
Gourma 58 E 3
Gourma-Rarous 58 D 2
Gouro 59 H 2
Gove Peninsula 79 F 1
Governador Valadares 35 H 4
Governor's Harbour 27 F 3
Goya 36 E 4
Gozo 45 F 4
Graaff Reinet 62 C 6
Gračac 45 G 3
Gracias a Dios, Cabo 28 C 4
Gradaús, Serra dos 33 H 5
Grafton 79 J 4
Grafton (N.D., U.S.A.) 21 G 2
Graham (Br. Col., Can.) 13 L 5
Graham (Ontario, Can.) 15 L 5
Graham Land 85
Grahamstown 62 D 6
Grain Coast 58 BC 4–C 5
Grajaú 33 J 5
Grampian Mountains 40 C 3
Granada (Nicaragua) 28 B 4
Granada (Spain) 44 C 4
Granby 18 F 4
Gran Canaria 54 BC 3
Gran Chaco 34 D 5
Grand Bahama Island 27 F 3
Grand Bank 19 J 4
Grand Bassam 58 D 4
Grand Canyon 20 D 4
Grand Canyon National Park
   20 D 4
Grand Cayman 28 C 3
Grand Coulee 20 C 2
Grand Coulee Dam 20 C 2
Grande, Bahía 37 C 9
Grande, Sierra(Mexico)
   24 D 2
Grande Cache 14 F 4
Grande Comore 63 GH 2
Grande Prairie 14 F 3
Grand Erg de Bilma 59 GI 2
Grand Erg Occidental
   54–55 EF 2–3
Grand Erg Oriental 55 G 2–3
Grande Rivière de la Baleine
   18 E 2–3
Grande Ronde River 20 C 2
Grand Falls 19 J 4
Grand Forks 21 G 2

Grandin, Lake 14 F 2
Grand Island 21 G 3
Grand Junction 20 E 4
Grand Lake 19 G 4
Grand Lake 19 J 4
Grand Manan 23 G 2
Grand Marais (MN, U.S.A.)
   21 HJ 2
Grand Passage 81 H 5
Grand Portage 22 C 1
Grand Rapids (Man., Can.)
   15 K 4
Grand Rapids (MI, U.S.A.)
   22 C 2
Grand Rapids (MN, U.S.A.)
   21 H 2
Grand River 22 C 2
Grand Teton 20 D 3
Grand Traverse Bay
   22 CD 1–2
Grand Turk 29 E 2
Grand Valley 20 E 4
Grangeville 20 C 2
Granite City 21 H 4
Granite Peak 20 C 3
Granite Peak (MT, U.S.A.)
   20 E 2
Granja 35 H 1
Gran Morelos 20 E 5
Granön 42 G 3
Gran Sasso d'Italia 45 F 3
Grant 21 F 3
Grants 20 E 4
Grants Pass 20 B 3
Granville Lake 15 J 3
Gräsö 43 G 3
Grave, Pointe de 44 C 2
Gravelbourg 15 H 5
'S-Gravenhage 40 D 4
Gravina 45 G 3
Grayling 22 D 2
Grays Harbor 20 B 2
Graz 45 FG 2
Great Abaco Island 27 F 3
Great Artesian Basin
   79 G 3–4
Great Australian Bight
   78 DE 5
Great Barrier 82 C 5
Great Barrier Island 81 R 8
Great Barrier Reef 79 H 1–2
Great Basin 20 C 3–4
Great Bear 13 N 2
Great Bear Lake 13 NO 2
Great Bend 21 G 4
Great Dividing Range
   79 HJ 3–4
Greater Antilles 28–29 DF 3
Great Exuma Island 27 F 4
Great Falls 20 D 2
Great Fisher Bank 40 D 3
Great Inagua Island 29 E 2
Great Indian Desert 72 B 2
Great Karroo 62 C 6

Great Nicobar 73 F 6
Great Pee Dee River 22 E 4
Great Plain of the Koukdjuak
   17 M 3
Great Plains 14 FH 3–4
Great Plains 21 F 2–4
Great Salt Lake 20 D 3
Great Salt Lake Desert 20 D 3
Great Sandy Desert 78 C 3
Great Sitkin 12 B 6
Great Slave Lake 14 G 2
Great Victoria Desert 78 DE 4
Greece 46 B 3
Greeley (CO, U.S.A.) 21 F 3
Greeley (NE, U.S.A.) 21 G 3
Green (OR, U.S.A.) 20 B 3
Green Bay (WI, U.S.A.)
   22 C 1–2
Green Coast 85
Green Islands 82 B 3
Greenland 84
Greenland Sea 42 A 2
Greenland Sea 84
Greenock 40 BC 3
Green River (KY, U.S.A.)
   22 C 3
Green River (Papua New
   Guinea) 80 D 2
Green River (UT, U.S.A.)
   20 D 4
Green River (UT, U.S.A.)
   20 DE 4
Green River (WY, U.S.A.)
   20 DE 3
Greensboro (GA, U.S.A.)
   22 D 4
Greensboro (N.C., U.S.A.)
   22 E 3
Greenvale 79 GH 2
Greenville 23 G 2
Greenville (AL, U.S.A.) 22 C 4
Greenville (Liberia) 58 C 5
Greenville (MS, U.S.A.) 21 H 5
Greenville (N.C., U.S.A.)
   22 E 3
Greenville (S.C., U.S.A.)
   22 D 4
Greenville (TX, U.S.A.) 21 G 5
Greenwood 22 D 4
Gregory, Lake 79 F 4
Gregory Range 79 G 2
Greifswald 41 F 4
Grenada 29 G 4
Grenada (MS, U.S.A.) 22 C 4
Grenadine Islands 29 G 4
Grenoble 45 E 2
Grey Islands 19 JK 3
Greymouth 81 Q 9
Grey Range 79 G 4
Griffin 22 D 4
Grim, Cape 80 K 9
Grimsby 40 CD 4
Grímsey 42 B 2
Grimshaw 14 F 3

Grímsstaðir 42 B 2
Grimstad 43 E 4
Grindavik 42 A 3
Grinnel 21 H 3
Griquatown 62 C 5
Grmeč 45 G 3
Grodno 43 H 5
Gröndalen 42 F 3
Grong 42 F 3
Groningen 40 E 4
Groote Eylandt 79 F 1
Grootfontein 62 B 3
Groot Vloer 62 BC 5
Groot Winter Berg 62 D 6
Gros Morne 19 J 4
Grosseto 45 F 3
Groswater Bay 19 J 3
Group, Actaeon 83 F 4
Groznyy 47 G 2
Grudziądz 41 G 4
Grünau 62 B 5
Grundy 22 D 3
Gruñidera 24 D 3
Gruziya 47 F 2
Grytviken 85
Guacanayabo, Golfo de
   27 F 4
Guacara 29 F 4
Guadalajara (Mexico) 24 D 3
Guadalajara (Spain) 44 C 3
Guadalcanal 81 G 3
Guadalquivir 44 C 4
Guadalupe 44 B 4
Guadalupe (Mexico) 24 D 3
Guadalupe (Mexico) 25 E 2
Guadalupe, Isla de 24 A 2
Guadalupe, Sierra de 44 B 4
Guadalupe Bravos 24 E 5
Guadalupe Mountains
   24 EF 5
Guadalupe River 25 E 2
Guadeloupe (Lesser Antilles)
   29 G 3
Guadeloupe Passage 29 G 3
Guadiana 44 B 4
Guajará Mirim 34 CD 3
Gualeguaychú 36 E 5
Guam 82 A 2
Guaminí 37 D 6
Guamo 27 F 4
Guamúchil 24 C 2
Guanajuato 25 D 3
Guanare 29 F 5
Guanare 32 E 2
Guanarito 29 F 5
Guandacol 36 C 4
Guane 26 E 4
Guangde 71 GH 4
Guangdong 70 F 6
Guanghua 70 F 4
Guangshan 70 G 4
Guangxi Zhuangzu Zizhiqu
   70 EF 6
Guangyuan 70 E 4

Guangzhou 70 F 6
Guantánamo 29 E 3
Guan Xian 70 D 4
Guapí 32 C 3
Guaporé 34 D 3
Guaqui 34 C 4
Guarapuava 36 F 4
Guarda 44 B 3
Guardal 44 C 4
Guarenas 32 E 1
Guárico 29 F 5
Guasipati 33 F 2
Guatemala 25 F 4
Guatemala City 25 FG 5
Guaviare 32 E 3
Guayabal 32 E 2
Guayaquil 32 C 4
Guayaquil, Golfo de 32 B 4
Guayaramerin 34 C 3
Guaymallén 36 C 5
Guaymas 24 B 2
Guba 62 D 2
Guba (U.S.S.R.) 50 F 3
Guba Buorkhaya 69 NO 1
Gubakha 51 L 4
Gubkin 50 G 5
Gudermes 47 G 2
Gudur 72 CD 5
Guelph 22 D 2
Guelta Zemmur 54 C 3
Guéné 58 E 3
Güera 54 B 4
Guéra 59 H 3
Guéréda 59 J 3
Guernsey 40 C 5
Guerrero 25 D 4
Gügerd, Küh-e 49 F 2
Gughe 61 F 3
Guguan 82 A 1
Guiana Highlands 33 FH 3
Guiding 70 E 5
Guidjiba 59 G 4
Guijá 63 E 4
Guildford 40 C 4
Guilin 70 F 5
Guillaume Delisle, Lac 18 E 2
Guinan 70 D 3
Guinea 58 BC 3
Guinea, Gulf of 59 EF 5
Guinea-Bissau 58 AB 3
Guinea Equatorial 59 F 5
Güines 27 E 4
Guiratinga 35 F 4
Guiria 29 G 4
Guisanbourg 33 H 3
Guixi 71 G 5
Gui Xian 70 EF 6
Guiyang 70 E 5
Guizhou 70 E 5
Gujarat 72 B 3
Gujranwala 67 J 4
Gujrat 67 J 4
Gulbarga 72 C 4
Gulf of Aden 57 H 6

Gulf of Alaska 12–13 HJ 4
Gulf of Boothia 16 H 2
Gulf of Bothnia 42 GH 3
Gulf of Carpentaria 79 F 1
Gulf of Chihli 71 GH 3
Gulf of Finland 43 H 4
Gulf of Guinea 59 EF 5
Gulf of Khambhat 72 B 3–4
Gulf of Kutch 72 A 3
Gulf of Maine 23 G 3
Gulf of Mannar 72 C 6
Gulf of Martaban 73 G 4
Gulf of Mexico 25 FG 2
Gulf of Oman 66 F 5–6
Gulf of Papua 80 DE 3
Gulf of Riga 43 H 4
Gulf of Saint Lawrence 19 H 4
Gulf of Sirt 55 J 2
Gulf of Suez 48 A 3
Gulf of Thailand 73 H 5
Gulf of Tonkin 73 J 3–4
Gulf of Venice 45 F 2–3
Gulfport 22 C 4
Gulf Saint Vincent 79 F 5–6
Gulgong 79 HJ 5
Gulin 70 E 5
Gulistan 67 H 2
Gulkana 12 H 3
Gull Lake 15 H 4
Gulu 60 E 4
Guna 72 C 3
Güneydoğu Toros lar 47 EF 3
Gungu 60 B 6
Gunnar 15 H 3
Gunnison 20 E 4
Guntersville Lake 22 C 4
Guntur 72 CD 4
Gunung Abong Abong 74 A 3
Gunung Besar 74 E 4
Gunung Binaiya 75 G 4
Gunung Dempo 74 B 4
Gunung Kerinci 74 B 4
Gunung Kinabalu 74 E 2
Gunung Kwoka 75 H 4
Gunung Leuser 74 A 3
Gunung Lokilalaki 75 F 4
Gunung Maling 75 F 3
Gunung Mulu 74 DE 3
Gunung Mutis 75 F 5
Gunung Saran 74 D 4
Gunung Sorikmerapi 74 A 3
Gunung Tahan 74 B 3
Guoyang 70 G 4
Gurban Obo 70 F 2
Gurbantünggüt Shamo
   67 M 1–2
Gurgan 49 G 1
Guri Dam 29 G 5
Gürlevik Dağı 47 E 3
Gurskoye 69 P 5
Gurupá 33 H 4
Gurupi 35 G 3
Gurvanbulag 68 HJ 6
Gur'yev 66 E 1

Gusau 59 F 3
Gusave 24 C 2
Gustavus 13 K 4
Guthrie (OK, U.S.A.) 21 G 4
Guthrie (TX, U.S.A.) 21 F 5
Guyana 33 G 3
Guyenne 44 C 3
Guzar 67 H 3
Güzelhisar 46 C 3
Gwalior 72 C 2
Gwelo 62 D 3
Gya La 72 DE 2
Gyangzê 72 E 2
Gydanskiy Poluostrov
   51 P 1–2
Gympie 79 J 4
Gyöngyös 46 B 1
Győr 46 A 1
Gypsum Point 14 F 2
Gypsumville 15 K 4
Gyula 46 B 1

H

Haanja Kõrgustik 43 J 4
Ha'apai Group 82 D 4
Haapsalu 43 H 4
Haarlem 40 D 4
Habay (Alb., Can.) 14 F 3
Hábbániyah 48 D 2
Hachinohe 71 M 2
Hadd, Ra's al 57 KL 4
Hadejia 59 F 3
Hadejia 59 G 3
Hadera 48 B 2
Hadilik 67 M 3
Hadley Bay 16 E 22
Hadramawt 57 H 5
Hafar al Bāṭin 57 H 3
Hafirat al 'Aydā 48 C 4
Hafit 49 G 4–5
Hāfūn, Ra's 61 J 2
Hagemeister 12 E 4
Hagerstown 22 E 3
Hagfors 43 F 3
Hague, Cap de la 44 C 2
Haicheng 71 H 2
Haifa 48 B 2
Haifeng 70 G 6
Haikang 70 EF 6
Haikou 70 F 6–7
Ha'il 48 C 4
Hailar 68 L 6
Hailin 71 J 2
Hailun 69 N 6
Hailuoto 42 H 2
Hainan Dao 70 F 7
Haines 13 K 4
Haines Junction 13 K 3
Hai Phong 73 J 3
Haïti 29 E 3
Hajārah, Saḥrā' al
   57 GH 2–H 3
Hājjīābād 66 F 5

Haj – Her

Hajjiabād-e Māsileh **49** F 2
Hakkâri Dağları **47** F 3
Hakodate **71** M 2
Halab **48** B 1
Ḩalā'ib **56** F 4
Ḩalbā **48** B 2
Halden **43** F 4
Hale, Mount **78** B 4
Ḩali **57** G 5
Halifax **23** H 2
Halkett, Cape **12** G 1
Hall **12** C 3
Halland **43** F 4
Hallat' Ammār **48** B 3
Hall Beach **16** K 3
Halle **41** F 4
Hallettsville **25** E 2
Halley Bay **85**
Hallingskarvet **43** E 3
Hall Islands **82** B 2
Hall Lake **16** K 3
Hall Peninsula **17** N 4
Halls Creek **78** D 2
Halmahera, Laut **75** G 4
Halmstad **43** F 4
Hälsingeskogen **42** G 3
Hälsingland **42** G 3
Halti **42** H 2
Ḩālūl **49** F 4
Hamadān **49** E 2
Hamāh **48** B 2
Hamamatsu **71** L 4
Hamar **43** F 3
Hamburg **41** F 4
Häme **42** HJ 3
Hämeenlinna **42** HJ 3
Hamelin Pool **78** A 4
Hamersley Range **78** B 3
Hamersley Range National
  Park **78** B 3
Hamhŭng **71** J 2–3
Hami **70** B 2
Hamilton (Bermuda Is.) **23** H 4
Hamilton (MT, U.S.A.) **20** D 2
Hamilton (New Zealand)
  81 R 8
Hamilton (Ontario, Can.)
  22 E 2
Hamilton (Victoria, Austr.)
  79 G 6
Hamm **41** E 4
Hammar, Hawr al **49** E 3
Hammond (IN, U.S.A.) **22** C 2
Hammond (LA, U.S.A.) **25** H 5
Hammur Koke **61** F 3
Hampden **81** Q 10
Hamrīn, Jabal **48–49** D 2
Hamuku **75** HJ 4
Hanahan **22** E 4
Hanak **48** B 4
Hanang **60** EF 5
Hanceville **14** E 4
Hanchuan **70** F 4
Handan **70** F 3

Handeni **61** F 6
Hanegev **48** B 3
Hanggin Houqi **70** E 2
Hangu **71** G 3
Hangzhou **71** H 4
Hanko **43** H 4
Hankoniemi **43** H 4
Hanksville **20** D 4
Hanna **14** G 4
Hannah Bay **18** DE 3
Hannibal **21** H 4
Hannover **41** E 4
Hanöbukten **43** FG 4
Ha Noi **73** HJ 3
Hanover **62** C 6
Hanover, Islas **37** AB 9
Hanstholm **43** E 4
Hantzsch **17** M 3
Hao **83** F 4
Haparanda **42** H 2
Hara **68** J 6
Haradh **49** E 4
Harar **61** G 3
Harare **63** E 3
Hararge **61** GH 3
Harazé **59** J 4
Harbin **71** J 1
Harbor Beach **22** D 2
Harbour Breton **19** J 4
Harbour Grace **19** K 4
Hardangerfjorden **43** E 3–4
Hardangerjökulen **43** E 3
Hardangervidda **43** E 3
Hardin **20** E 2
Hargeysa **61** G 3
Hari, Batang **74** B 4
Ḩarib **57** H 6
Hari Kurk **43** H 4
Ḩārim **48** B 1
Härjedalen **42** F 3
Harlingen (TX, U.S.A.) **25** E 2
Harney Basin **20** BC 3
Harney Lake **20** C 3
Harney Peak **21** F 3
Härnösand **42** G 3
Harrat al 'Uwayrid **48** B 4
Harrat Ithnayn **48** C 4
Harricana **18** E 3
Harrington Harbour **19** J 3
Harrisburg **22** E 2
Harrismith **62** DE 5
Harrison **21** H 4
Harrison, Cape **19** J 3
Harrison Bay **12** G 1
Harrisonburg **22** E 3
Harrisville **22** D 2
Harry S. Truman Reservoir
  21 H 4
Harsvik **42** E 3
Hartford **23** F 2
Hartlepool **40** C 4
Hartwell Lake **22** D 4
Hartz Mountains National
  Park **80** KL 9

Har Us Nuur **68** F 6
Harvey (N.D., U.S.A.) **21** G 2
Haryana **72** C 2
Harz **41** F 4
Hasalbag **67** K 3
Hassan **72** C 5
Hassi Bel Guebbour **55** G 3
Hassi Messaoud **55** G 2
Hastings (MN, U.S.A.) **21** H 3
Hastings (NE, U.S.A.) **21** G 3
Hastings (New Zealand)
  81 R 8
Hat Hin **73** H 3
Ha Tinh **73** J 4
Hatteras, Cape **22** E 3
Hatteras Island **22–23** EF 3
Hattiesburg **22** C 4
Hatutu **83** F 3
Hat Yai **73** H 6
Hauberg Mountains **85**
Haugesund **43** DE 4
Haukipudas **42** J 2
Hauraki Gulf **81** QR 8
Hauterive **19** G 4
Haut-Zaïre **60** CD 4
Havana **27** E 4
Haverhill (MA, U.S.A.) **23** F 2
Havern **42** G 3
Havre **20** E 2
Havre-Saint-Pierre **19** H 3
Hawaii **83** E 1
Hawaiian Islands **83** E 1
Hawalli **49** E 3
Hawke Harbour **19** J 3
Hawr al Hammar **49** E 3
Ḩawrān, Wādī **48** C 2
Hawr as S'adīyah **49** E 2
Hawthorne **20** C 4
Hay (U.S.A.) **14** F 3
Hay (Austr.) **79** G 5
Hayes **15** L 3
Hayes, Mount **12** H 3
Hay River (N.W.T., Can.)
  14 F 2
Hays **21** G 4
Hayward **20** B 4
Haywood, Mount **13** N 3
Hayyā **56** F 5
Hazarajat **67** H 4
Hazard **22** D 3
Hazar Gölü **47** E 3
Hazelton **13** M 4
Hazlehurst **22** D 4
Hazleton **22** E 2
Hearne **25** G 3
Hearst **18** D 4
Hebei **71** G 3
Hebel **79** H 4
Hebi **70** F 3
Hebrides, Inner **40** B 3
Hebrides, Outer **40** B 3
Hebron (Newfoundl., Can.)
  19 H 2
Hecate Strait **13** L 5

Hechi **70** E 6
Hechuan **70** E 4–5
Hedmark **42** F 3
Hefa **48** B 2
Hefei **71** G 4
Hegang **69** O 6
Heidelberg **41** E 5
Heidenheim **41** F 5
Heilbronn **41** E 5
Heilong Jiang **69** O 6
Heilongjiang **71** JK 1
Heimaey **42** A 3
Heimahe **70** C 3
Hejaz (Saudi Arabia) **48** B 4
Hekla **42** B 3
Helagsfjället **42** F 3
Helena (AR, U.S.A.) **21** H 5
Helena (MT, U.S.A.) **20** D 2
Hellas **46** B 3
Hells Canyon **20** C 2
Helmeringhausen **62** B 5
Helong **71** JK 2
Helsingborg **43** F 4
Helsingör **43** F 4
Helsinki **43** J 3–4
Henan **70** F 4
Henbury **78** E 3
Henderson **20** C 4
Henderson **83** G 4
Henderson (N.C., U.S.A.)
  22 E 3
Henderson (TX, U.S.A.)
  21 H 5
Hendersonville (N.C., U.S.A.)
  22 D 3
Hendersonville (TN, U.S.A.)
  22 C 3
Hendijan **49** E 3
Hengduan Shan **70** CD 5
Heng Xian **70** E 6
Hengyang **70** F 5
Henik Lakes **15** K 2
Henrietta Maria, Cape **18** D 2
Henryetta **21** G 4
Henry Kater Peninsula **17** N 3
Henzada **73** FG 4
Heraklia **48** C 1
Herat **67** G 4
Herbert **15** H 4
Herberton **79** H 2
Heredia **28** C 4
Hereford **40** C 4
Hereford (TX, U.S.A.) **21** F 5
Herlen He **68** L 6
Hermanas **25** D 2
Hermiston **20** C 2
Hermit Islands **82** A 3
Hermon, Mount **48** B 2
Hermosillo **24** B 2
Herning **43** E 4
Heroica Alvarado **25** E 4
Heroica Tlapacoyan **25** E 4
Herschel **13** K 2
Herzliyya **48** B 2

Hess 13 L 3
He Xian 70 F 6
Heydaràbàd 49 D 1
Heze 70 FG 3
Hialeah 27 E 3
Hibbing 21 H 2
Hidalgo 25 E 3
Hidalgo del Parral 24 C 2
Hidcolândia 35 FG 4
Hierro 54 B 3
High Level 14 F 3
High Point 22 E 3
High Prairie 14 F 3
High River 14 G 4
Highrock Lake (Man., Can.) 15 JK 3
Highrock Lake (Sask., Can.) 15 H 3
Higuerote 32 E 1
Higüey 29 F 3
Hiiumaa 43 H 4
Hill Bank 28 B 3
Hillcrest Center 20 C 4
Hill Island Lake 14 H 2
Hillsboro (IL, U.S.A.) 21 HJ 4
Hillsboro (TX, U.S.A.) 25 G 5
Hilo 83 E 1
Himachal Pradesh 72 C 1
Himâ Dariyah, Jabal 48 C 4
Hims 48 B 2
Hinchin Brook 12 H 3
Hinchinbrook Island 79 H 2
Hindu Kush 67 HJ 3–4
Hinganghat 72 C 3
Hingol 67 H 5
Hinnöya 42 G 2
Hinton 14 F 4
Hirara 71 J 6
Hirfanlı Baraji 47 D 3
Hirhafok 55 G 4
Hirosaki 71 LM 2
Hiroshima 71 K 4
Hirtshals 43 E 4
Hismâ 48 B 3
Hispaniola 29 E 3
Hitachi 71 M 3
Hite 20 D 4
Hitra 42 E 3
Hiva Oa 83 F 3
Hjälmaren 43 G 4
Hjelmsöya 42 H 1
Hmeenselk 42 H 3
Ho 58 E 4
Hoa Binh 73 HJ 3
Hoachanas 62 B 4
Hoare Bay 17 O 3
Hobart 80 L 9
Hobart (OK, U.S.A.) 21 G 4
Hobbs 21 F 5
Hoburgen 43 G 4
Hobyå 61 H 3
Ho Chi Minh 73 J 5
Hodda 61 J 2
Hodeida 57 G 6

Hodh 54 D 5
Hofsá 42 B 2
Hofsjökull 42 B 2
Höfu 71 K 4
Hogback Mountain 20 D 3
Hoggar 55 F 4
Hohhot 70 F 2
Hoima 60 E 4
Hokitika 82 C 5
Hokkaidö 71 M 2
Hokmäbåd 66 F 3
Holanda 34 C 3
Holbox, Isla 26 D 4
Holbrook 20 D 5
Holdenville 21 G 4
Holdrege 21 G 3
Holguín 27 F 4
Holitna 12 F 3
Holland 22 C 2
Hollick-Kenyon Plateau 85
Holly Springs 21 HJ 5
Hollywood (CA, U.S.A.) 20 C 5
Hollywood (FL, U.S.A.) 27 F 3
Holman Island 16 C 2
Holstebro 43 E 4
Holsteinsborg 17 Q 3
Holy Cross 12 E 3
Holyhead 40 C 4
Holyoke (CO, U.S.A.) 21 F 3
Holyoke (MA, U.S.A.) 23 F 2
Homäyünshahr 49 F 2
Homäyünshahr 66 E 4
Hombori Tondo 58 D 3
Home Bay 17 N 3
Homer 12 G 4
Homestead (FL, U.S.A.) 27 E 3
Homewood 22 C 4
Homosassa 27 E 3
Honavar 72 B 5
Honduras 28 B 4
Hönefoss 43 F 3
Honey Lake 20 B 3
Hong Kong 70 FG 6
Hongliuhe 70 BC 2
Hongor 70 F 1
Honguedo, Détroit d' 19 H 4
Hongyuan 70 D 4
Honiara 81 G 3
Honolulu 83 E 1
Hon Panjang 73 H 6
Honshü 71 KL 3
Hood, Mount 20 B 2
Hood Point 78 BC 5
Hood River 20 B 2
Hoonah 13 K 4
Hooper, Cape 17 N 3
Hooper Bay 12 D 3
Hoover Dam 20 D 4
Hope (AR, U.S.A.) 21 H 5
Hope (AZ, U.S.A.) 20 D 5
Hope, Cape 16 C 3
Hope, Point 12 E 1
Hopedale 19 H 2
Hopes Advance, Cap 17 N 4

Hopewell Islands 18 E 2
Hopin 73 G 3
Hopkinsville 22 C 3
Hoquiam 20 B 2
Hordaland 43 E 3
Horizon Deep 82 D 4
Horlick Mountains 85
Hormuz, Strait of 49 G 4
Horn, Cape 37 CD 10
Hornavan 42 G 2
Hornby Bay 13 O 2
Hörnefors 42 G 3
Hornell 22 E 2
Hornepayne 18 C 4
Horn Islands 82 D 3
Hornos, Cabo de 37 CD 10
Horn Plateau 14 F 2
Horqin Youyi Qianqi 71 H 1
Horsens 43 EF 4
Horsham 79 G 6
Horton 13 N 2
Hosalay 47 D 2
Hose Mountains 74 D 3
Hoseynïyeh 49 E 3
Hospet 72 C 4
Hospitalet 44 D 3
Hoste, Isla 37 C 10
Hotagen 42 F 3
Hotan 67 K 3
Hotazel 62 C 5
Hoting 42 G 3
Houghton 22 C 1
Houghton Lake 22 D 2
Houlton 23 G 2
Houma (China) 70 F 3
Houma (LA, U.S.A.) 25 F 2
Houston 25 G 5
Hovd (Mongolia) 68 F 6
Hovd (Mongolia) 70 D 2
Hövsgöl Nuur 68 H 5
Howe, Cape 79 J 6
Howland 82 D 2
Howland (ME, U.S.A.) 23 G 2
Howrah 72 E 3
Hoxud 70 A 2
Hox Xil Shan 70 AB 3–4
Hoy 40 C 3
Hrvatska 45 G 2
Hsinchu 71 H 6
Huachinango 25 E 3
Huacho 32 C 6
Hua Hin 73 GH 5
Huahuapén 24 C 3
Huaibin 70 FG 4
Huainan 71 G 4
Huairen 70 F 3
Huajuapan de León 25 E 4
Huallaga 32 C 5
Huambo (Angola) 62 B 2
Huanan 71 K 1
Huancabamba 32 C 5

Huancavelica 34 A 3
Huancayo 34 A 3
Huangchuan 70 G 4
Huang Hai 71 H 3
Huangshi 70 F 4
Huang Xian 71 GH 3
Huangyan 71 H 5
Huangzhong 70 D 3
Huánuco 32 C 5–6
Huara 34 C 4
Huaral 34 A 3
Huaraz 32 C 5
Huarmey 32 C 6
Huascarán, Nevado 32 C 5
Huasco 36 B 4
Huashixia 70 C 3
Huatabampo 24 C 2
Huautla 25 E 3
Huayllay 34 A 3
Hubbart Point 15 L 3
Hubei 70 F 4
Hubli 72 C 4–5
Huckitta 78 F 3
Hudat 61 F 4
Huddur Hadama 61 G 4
Huder 69 M 6
Hudiksvall 42 G 3
Hudson Bay 15 MN 2–3
Hudson Bay (Sask., Can.) 15 J 4
Hudson River 23 F 2
Hudson's Hope 14 E 3
Hudson Strait 17 M 4
Hue 73 J 4
Huehuetenango 25 F 4
Huelva 44 B 4
Huesca 44 C 3
Hughenden 79 G 3
Hughes (AK, U.S.A.) 12 G 2
Hugo 21 G 5
Huicholes, Sierra de los 24 D 3
Hüich'on 71 J 2
Huihe 68 L 6
Huíla (Angola) 62 AB 2
Huila (Colombia) 32 C 3
Huilai 70 G 6
Huili 70 D 5
Huimin 71 G 3
Huixtla 25 F 4
Huize 70 D 5
Hulayfa' 48 C 4
Huld 70 E 1
Hull 18 E 4
Huma 69 N 5
Humaitá (Amazonas, Brazil) 33 F 5
Humaitá (Paraguay) 36 E 4
Humay 34 A 3
Humboldt (Sask., Can.) 15 J 4
Humboldt (TN, U.S.A.) 22 C 3
Humboldt River 20 C 3
Húnaflói 42 A 2
Hunan 70 F 5

Hunchun 71 K 2
Hunedoara 46 B 1
Hungary 46 A 1
Hüngnam 71 J 3
Hunjiang 71 J 2
Hunsur 72 C 5
Hunter 82 C 4
Huntington 22 D 3
Huntsville (AL, U.S.A.) 22 C 4
Huntsville (Ontario, Can.)
   18 E 4
Huntsville (TX, U.S.A.) 25 G 5
Hunyuan 70 F 3
Huocheng 67 KL 2
Huon 82 B 4
Huon Gulf 80 E 3
Huo Xian 70 F 3
Huron 21 G 3
Huron, Lake 22 D 2
Huron Mountains 22 C 1
Hurricane 20 D 4
Hurst 21 G 5
Huslia 12 F 2
Husum 41 E 4
Hutag 68 H 6
Hutchinson (KS, U.S.A.)
   21 G 4
Hutchinson (MN, U.S.A.)
   21 GH 3
Hvar 45 G 3
Hveragerði 42 A 3
Hyannis 23 FG 2
Hyargas Nuur 68 F 6
Hyden 78 B 5
Hyderabad (India) 72 CD 4
Hyderabad (Pakistan) 67 H 5
Hyères, Iles d' 45 E 3
Hyesan 71 J 2
Hysham 20 E 2
Hyvinkää 43 H 3

I

Iaçu 35 H 3
Ialomiţa 46 C 2
Iaripo 33 H 3
Iaşi 46 C 1
Ibadan 59 E 4
Ibagué 32 C 3
Ibaiti 35 FG 5
Ibarra 32 C 3
Iberville, Lac d' 18 F 2
Ibestad 42 G 2
Ibi 59 F 4
Ibitiara 35 H 3
Ibiza (Spain) 44 D 4
Íbiza (Spain) 44 D 4
Ibotirama 35 H 3
Ibrim 56 E 4
Icá (Amazonas, Brazil) 32 E 4
Ica (Peru) 34 A 3
Icana 32 E 3
İçel 47 D 3
Iceland 42 A 2

Iceland 42 A 3
Ichera 68 J 4
Ichinskaya Sopka 69 ST 4
Ico 35 J 2
Icy Cape 12 E 1
Idabel 21 H 5
Idaho 20 CD 3
Idaho Falls 20 D 3
Idfû 56 E 4
Idhân Awbâri 55 H 3
Idhân Murzuq 55 H 4
Ídhi Óros 46 BC 3
Ídhra 46 B 3
Idlib 48 B 2
Idre 42 F 3
Ifalik 82 A 2
Ifanadiana 63 H 4
Ife 59 E 4
Ifjord 42 J 1
Igarka 51 R 2
Iglesias 45 E 4
Ignace 15 L 5
Ignashino 69 M 5
İğneada 46 C 2
Iguaçu 36 F 4
Iguala 25 E 4
Iguassú Falls 36 F 4
Iguatu 35 J 2
Iguigik 12 F 4
Ihosy 63 H 4
Ihtamir 68 H 6
Iisalmi 42 J 3
Iivaara 42 J 2
Ijebu Ode 59 EF 4
Ijsselmeer 40 E 4
Ijuí 36 F 4
Ikaría 46 C 3
Ikerre 59 F 4
Ikot Ekpene 59 F 4
Ilaferh 55 F 4
Ilagan 75 J 1
Ilam 49 E 2
Ilbenge 69 M 3
Ile-à-la-Crosse 15 H 3
Île à Vache 29 E 3
Ilebo 60 C 5
Île d'Anticosti 19 H 4
Ile de France 44 D 2
Ile de la Gonâve 29 E 3
Île de la Madeleine
   19 H 4
Ile de la Tortue 29 E 2
Ile de Ré 44 C 2
Ile des Noefs 61 J 6
Ile des Pins 81 J 6
Ile d'Oléron 44 C 2
Ile d'Ouessant 44 B 2
Île du Diable 33 H 2
Ile d'Yeu 44 C 2
Iles Chesterfield 82 B 4
Îles de Los 58 B 4
Iles d'Hyères 45 E 3
Îles du Désappointement
   83 F 3

Îles du Duc de Gloucester
   83 F 4
Îles du Roi Georges 83 F 3
Iles Glorienses 63 H 2
Îles Palliser 83 F 4
Ile Tidra 54 B 5
Ilford 15 K 3
Ilha de Maracá 33 HJ 3
Ilha de Marajó 33 HJ 4
Ilha Grande 32 E 4
Ilha Santa Carolina 63 F 4
Ilhéus 35 J 3
Iliamna 12 G 4
Iliamna Lake 12 F 4
Ilichevsk 46 D 1
Ilimsk 68 H 4
Ilinskiy 69 Q 6
Illapel 36 B 5
Illimani, Nevado 34 C 4
Illinois 22 C 2–3
Illinois River 21 H 4
Illizi 55 G 3
Ilo 34 B 4
Iloilo 75 F 1
Ilots de Bass 83 F 4
Ilubabor 60 EF 3
Ilyichovsk 46 D 1
Ima 68 L 4
Imâm al Hamzah 49 D 3
Imandra, Ozero 42 K 2
Imatra 42 J 3
Imbituba 36 G 4
Iméni Gastello 69 R 3
Iméni Mariny 69 QR 3
Imgytskoye Boloto 51 O 4
Imperatriz 33 J 5
Imphal 73 F 3
Imtonzha 69 NO 2
Inagua Island, Great 29 E 2
Inagua Island, Little 29 E 2
Inarijarvi 42 J 2
In Azaoua 59 F 1
İnce Burnu 47 D 2
Inch'ŏn 71 J 3
Inchôpe 63 E 3
Independence (KS, U.S.A.)
   21 G 4
Independence (MO, U.S.A.)
   21 H 4
India 72 CD 3
Indiana 22 C 2
Indianapolis 22 C 3
Indian Harbour 19 J 3
Indian Ocean 87
Indian Springs 20 C 4
Indias Occidentales 29 E 2
Indigirka 69 R 2
Indigirskaya Nizmennost'
   69 QR 2
Indispensable Reefs 82 B 3
Indispensable Strait 81 H 3–4
Indonesia 74–75 OG 4
Indore 72 C 3
Indus 67 H 6

İnegöl 46 C 2
In Gall 59 F 2
Ingoda 68 K 5
Ingrid Christensen Coast 85
Ingul 47 D 1
Inhambane 63 F 4
Inharrime 63 F 4
Inhumas 35 FG 4
Inirida 32 E 3
Inkerman 79 G 2
Inklin 13 L 4
Inn 41 F 5
Inner Mongolia 70 E 2–3
Innisfail 79 H 2
Innokent'yevka 69 P 6
Innsbruck 45 F 2
Inoucdjouac 18 E 2
In Salah 55 F 3
Insulă Sacalin 46 CD 2
Inta 51 L 2
Intletovy 51 P 3
Inuvik 13 L 2
Inuvik, District of 13 LM 2
Invercargill 80 P 10
Inverness 40 C 3
Investigator Strait 79 F 6
Inya 51 R 5
Iolotan 67 G 3
Iona National Park 62 A 3
Ionian Islands 46 A 3
Ionian Sea 46 A 3
Ionioi Nísoi 46 A 3
Iónion Pélagos 46 AB 3
Íos 46 C 3
Iowa 21 H 3
Iowa City 21 H 3
Ipameri 35 G 4
Ipatinga 35 H 4
Ipiales 32 C 3
Ipiaú 35 J 3
Ípiros 46 B 3
Ipixuna 32 D 5
Ipoh 74 B 3
Iporá 35 F 4
Ipswich (Australia) 79 J 4
Ipswich (U.K.) 40 D 4
Ipu 35 H 4
Iquapé 35 G 5
Iquique 34 B 5
Iquitos 32 D 4
Iracoubo 33 H 2
Irafshan 67 G 5
Iráklion 46 C 3
Iran 66 EF 4
Iran, Pegunungan 74 D 3
Irapa 29 G 4
Irapuato 25 D 3
Iraq 48 D 2
Irbid 48 B 2
Irbit 51 M 4
Irebu 60 B 5
Irecê 35 H 3
Irgiz 67 G 1
Irian Jaya 75 HJ 4

Iriba 59 J 2
Iringa 61 F 6
Iriomote-jima 71 HJ 6
Iriona 28 BC 3
Iriri 33 H 4
Irish Sea 40 BC 4
Irkutsk 68 HJ 5
Iron gate → Portile de Fier 46 B 2
Iron Knob 79 F 5
Iron Mountain 22 C 1
'Irq al Idrisi 55 K 4–5
'Irq al Maẓhur 48 D 4
Irrawaddy 73 G 3–4
Irrawaddy, Mouths of the 73 FG 4
Irtuia 33 J 4
Irtysh 51 N 4
Irtysh 51 O 5
Irún 44 C 3
Irving 21 G 5
Isa, Mount 79 F 3
Isabel 21 F 2
Isabela 32 B 6
Isangi 60 C 4
Ischia 45 F 3
Iscia Baidoa → Isha Bayḏabo 61 G 4
Iseyin 58 E 4
Isfendiyar Daǧları 47 D 2
Isherton 33 G 3
Ishigaki 71 HJ 6
Ishikhly 66 D 3
Ishim 51 O 4
Ishimskaya Step' 51 O 5
Ishinomaki 71 M 3
Işıklar Daǧı 46 C 2
Isil'kul 51 O 5
Isinga 68 K 5
Isiro 60 D 4
Iskamen', Khrebet 12 B 2
İskenderun 47 E 3
İskenderun Kßrfezi 47 E 3
Iskitim 51 Q 5
Iskut River 13 L 4
Isla Ángel de la Guarda 24 B 2
Isla Aruba 32 E 1
Isla Bonaire 29 F 4
Isla Campana 37 A 8
Isla Carmen 24 B 2
Isla Cedros 24 A 2
Isla Cerralvo 24 C 3
Isla Curaçao 32 DE 1
Isla de Altamura 24 C 3
Isla de Aves 29 G 3
Isla de Chiloé 37 B 7
Isla de Coiba 28 C 5
Isla de Cozumel 26 D 4
Isla de Guadelupe 24 A 2
Isla de la Juventud 27 E 4
Isla del Maíz 28 C 4
Isla de los Estados 37 D 9
Isla de Margarita 29 G 4

Isla de Ometepe 28 BC 4
Isla de Providencia 28 C 4
Isla de San Ignacio 24 C 2
Isla de Santa Margarita 24 B 3
Isla Desolación 37 AB 9
Isla de Vieques 29 FG 3
Isla Esmeralda 37 A 8
Isla Grande de Tierra del Fuego 37 C 9
Isla Holbox 26 D 4
Isla Hoste 37 C 10
Islamabad 67 J 4
Isla Magdalena (Mexico) 24 B 3
Isla Malpelo 32 B 3
Isla Maria Madre 24 C 3
Isla Maria Magdalena 24 C 3
Isla Mona 29 F 3
Isla Montague 20 D 5
Ísland 42 A 3
Island Lake 15 L 4
Island Lake 15 L 4
Islands, Bay of 19 J 4
Islands of Four Mountains 12 CD 6
Isla San José 24 BC 2
Isla San Marcos 24 B 2
Isla Santa Inés 37 B 9
Islas Baleares 44 D 3–4
Islas Canarias 54 B 3
Islas de Barlovento 29 GH 3
Islas de la Bahía 28 B 3
Islas del Cisne (Honduras) 28 C 3
Islas de Sotavento 29 FG 4
Islas Hanover 37 AB 9
Islas las Aves 29 F 4
Islas los Hermanos 29 G 4
Islas los Monjes 29 E 4
Islas los Testigos 29 G 4
Islas Marias 24 C 3
Isla Tiburon 24 B 2
Isla Tobago 33 F 1
Isla Trinidad 33 F 1
Islay 40 B 3
Isle of Man 40 C 4
Isle of Wight 40 C 4
Isle Royale 22 C 1
Isles of Scilly 40 B 5
Isole Eolie o Lipari 45 F 4
Isole Ponziane 45 F 3
Isosyöte 42 J 2
Isparta 46 D 3
Israel 48 B 3
Issano 33 G 2
İstanbul 46 C 2
İstanbul Boǧazı 46 C 2
Isteren 42 F 3
Isthmus of Kra 73 G 5
Istmo de Panamá 28 D 5
Istmo de Tehuantepec 25 F 4
Isto, Mount 13 J 2
Istra 45 F 2

Itaberaba 35 H 3
Itabira 35 H 4
Itabuna 35 J 3
Itagüí 32 C 2
Itaituba 33 G 4
Itajaí 36 G 4
Italia 45 FG 3
Italy 45 F 3
Itambé 35 H 4
Itaperucu Mirim 35 H 1
Itaperuna 35 H 5
Itapetinga 35 J 4
Itapipoca 35 J 1
Itapiranga 33 G 4
Itapiúna 35 J 1
Itarsi 72 C 3
Itaúnas 35 J 4
Itbäy 48 AB 4
Itbäy 56 EF 3–4
Itchen Lake 16 D 3
Iténez 34 D 3
Ithaca 22 E 2
Itháki 46 B 3
Ithnayn, Harat 48 C 4
Itivdleg 17 Q 3
Ituberá 35 J 3
Ituiutaba 35 FG 4
Itumbiara 35 FG 4
Iturama 35 F 4
Iturbe 34 C 5
Itzehoe 41 EF 4
Iul'tin 12 B 2
Ivalo 42 J 2
Ivalojoki 42 J 2
Ivanhoe 79 GH 5
Ivano-Frankovsk 50 D 6
Ivanovo 50 H 4
Ivory Coast 58 CD 4
Ivory Coast 58 CD 5
Ivrea 45 E 2
Ivujivik 17 L 4
Iwaki 71 M 3
Iwo 59 E 4
Iwo Jima 65 R 7
Iwŏn 71 J 2
Ixiamas 34 C 3
Izamal Balankanche 26 D 4
Izhevsk 50 K 4
İzmir 46 C 3
İzmir Körfezi 46 C 3
İzmit 46 CD 2
Izu-shotō 71 M 4–5

J

Jabal Abadab 56 EF 5
Jabal' Abd al 'Aziz 47 E 3
Jabal al Bishri 56 F 1
Jabal al Humara 56 E 5
Jabal al Lawz 56 F 3
Jabal an Nabī Shu' ayb 57 G 5
Jabal as Hasāwinah 55 H 3
Jabal ash Shaykh 48 B 2
Jabal at Tubayq 48 B 3

Jabal Dabbāgh 48 B 4
Jabal Hajhir 61 J 2
Jabal Hamátah 48 B 4
Jabal Hamoyet 56 F 5
Jabal Hamrīn 48–49 D 2
Jabal Ḥimä Dariyah 48 C 4
Jabal Ibrâhîm 57 G 4
Jabal Kâtrïna 48 AB 3
Jabal Katul 56 D 6
Jabal Lotuke 60 E 4
Jabal Lubnân 48 B 2
Jabal Marrah 56 CD 6
Jabal Oda 56 F 4
Jabalpur 72 CD 3
Jabal Ṣabir 57 G 6
Jabal Shä'ib al Banät 48 A 4
Jabal Shammar 48 CD 4
Jabal Ṭuwayq 49 D 4
Jabâlyah 48 B 3
Jablah 48 B 2
Jablanica 45 G 3
Jabung, Tanjung 74 B 4
Jacareacanga 33 G 5
Jaciara 35 F 4
Jaciparaná 33 F 5
Jack Mountain 20 B 2
Jackpot 20 D 3
Jacksboro 21 G 5
Jackson (MI, U.S.A.) 22 D 2
Jackson (MS, U.S.A.) 21 H 5
Jackson (TX, U.S.A.) 22 C 3
Jackson, Mount 85
Jackson Lake 20 D 3
Jacksonville (FL, U.S.A.) 22 D 4
Jacksonville (IL, U.S.A.) 22 C 3
Jacksonville (N.C., U.S.A.) 22 E 4
Jacksonville (TX, U.S.A.) 25 GH 5
Jacksonville Beach 22 D 4
Jacobabad 67 H 5
Jacobina 35 H 3
Jacob Lake 20 D 4
Jacona 24 D 4
Jacques Cartier, Détroit de 19 H 4
Jadal 59 E 2
Jādū 55 H 2
Jaén 44 C 4
Jaffa, Cape 79 F 6
Jaffa → Tel Aviv-Yafo 56 E 2
Jaffna 72 D 6
Jagdalpur 72 D 3
Jaguarão 36 F 5
Jaguarari 35 J 3
Jaguariaíva 35 FG 5
Jaguaribe 35 J 2
Jahrom 49 F 3
Jaina 25 F 3
Jaipur 72 C 2
Jakarta 74 C 5
Jakobshavn 84

Jakobstad **42** H 3
Jalaid Qi **71** H 1
Jalapa **28** B 4
Jalapa Enríquez **25** E 4
Jalgaon **72** BC 3
Jalībah **49** E 3
Jalisco **24** D 3
Jalón **44** C 3
Jalostotitlán **24** D 3
Jalpa **24** D 3
Jaluit **82** C 2
Jalūlā' **49** D 2
Jama **32** B 4
Jamaica **28** D 3
Jamaica Channel **28–29** DE 3
Jamāme **61** G 4
Jamari **33** F 5
Jambi **74** B 4
James **21** G 3
James Bay **18** D 3
James River (VA, U.S.A.) **22** E 3
James Ross Strait **16** G 2–3
Jamestown (N.D., U.S.A.) **21** G 2
Jamestown (N.Y., U.S.A.) **22** E 2
Jamiltepec **25** E 4
Jammu **67** K 4
Jammu and Kashmir **67** K 4
Jamnagar **72** AB 3
Jamsah **48** A 4
Jamshedpur **72** DE 3
Jämtland **42** F 3
Jandaia **35** FG 4
Jandaq **66** EF 4
Janesville **22** C 2
Janjira **72** B 4
Jan Mayen Island **84**
Janos **24** E 5
Januária **35** H 4
Japan **71** L 3
Japurá **32** E 4
Jaqué **28** D 5
Jarābulus **48** C 1
Jaramillo **37** C 8
Jarbah **55** H 2
Jardine River National Park **79** G 1
Jardines de la Reina, Archipiélago de los **27** EF 4
Jarrahdale **78** B 5
Jarud Qi **71** H 2
Jarvis **83** E 3
Jasikan **58** E 4
Jasper **14** F 4
Jasper (AL, U.S.A.) **22** C 4
Jasper (TX, U.S.A.) **25** H 5
Jasper National Park **14** F 4
Jastrzebie Zdrój **41** G 5
Jászberény **46** AB 1
Jataí **35** F 4
Jatobal **33** HJ 4
Jaú **35** G 5

Jauja **34** A 3
Jaumave **25** E 3
Java Sea **74** CD 5
Jawa **74** CD 5
Jaya, Puncak **75** J 4
Jayapura **80** D 2
Jazā'ir Farasān **57** G 5
Jazā'ir Khurīyā Murīya **57** K 5
Jazirat **48** B 4
Jbel Toubkal **54** D 2
Jeci **63** F 2
Jefferson, Mount (NV, U.S.A.) **20** C 4
Jefferson, Mount (OR, U.S.A.) **20** B 3
Jefferson City **21** H 4
Jefferson River **20** D 2
Jēkabpils **43** J 4
Jekkevarre **42** GH 2
Jelenia Góra **41** G 4
Jelgava **43** H 4
Jelow Gir **49** E 2
Jenny Lind Island **16** G 3
Jens Munk Island **17** K 3
Jequié **35** H 3
Jequitinhonha **35** HJ 4
Jerada **54** E 2
Jérémie **29** E 3
Jeremoabo **35** J 3
Jerez de Garcia Salinas **24** D 3
Jerez de la Frontera **44** B 4
Jerome **20** D 3
Jersey **40** C 5
Jerusalem **56** F 2
Jesup **22** D 4
Jesus Carranza **25** E 4
Jeypore **72** D 4
Jhang Sadar **67** J 4
Jhansi **72** C 2
Jhelum **67** J 4
Jiamusi **71** K 1
Jiang'an **70** DE 5
Jianghua **70** F 5
Jiangmen **70** F 6
Jiangsu **71** GH 4
Jiangxi **70** FG 5
Jiangyou **70** D 4
Jianyang **71** G 5
Jiaozuo **70** F 3
Jiayu **70** F 5
Jiayuguan **70** C 3
Jicarón, Isla **28** C 5
Jiddah **57** FG 4
Jieyang **70** G 6
Jigzhi **70** D 4
Jijiga **61** G 3
Jilib **61** G 4
Jilin **71** HJ 2
Jimāl, Wādi **48** B 4
Jiménez **24** D 2
Jimma **61** F 3
Jinan **71** G 3
Jincheng **70** F 3

Jingdezhen **71** G 5
Jingning **70** E 3
Jing Xian **70** E 5
Jingyuan **70** DE 3
Jinhua **71** GH 5
Jining **71** G 3
Jinja **60** E 4
Jinkouhe **70** D 5
Jinotega **28** B 4
Jinotepe **28** B 4
Jinping **70** D 6
Jinsha **70** E 5
Jinsha Jiang **70** D 5
Jinshan **71** H 4
Jin Xian **71** H 3
Jinxiang **71** G 3–4
Jinzhou **71** H 2
Jiparaná **33** F 5
Jipijapa **32** B 4
Jishou **70** EF 5
Jisr ash Shughūr **48** B 2
Jiu **46** B 2
Jiujiang **70** G 5
Jiuquan **70** C 3
Jixi **71** K 1
João Pessoa **35** K 2
Jodhpur **72** B 2
Joensuu **42** JK 3
Jõetsu **71** L 3
Johannesburg **62** DE 5
John Day **20** C 3
John Day River **20** C 3
John O'Groat's **40** C 3
Johnson **21** F 4
Johnsonburg **22** E 2
Johnson City (TN, U.S.A.) **22** D 3
Johnson City (TX, U.S.A.) **25** G 5
Johnsons Crossing **13** L 3
Johnston **82** D 1
Johnstown **22** E 2
Johor Baharu **74** B 3
Joinvile **36** G 4
Joinville Island **85**
Jokkmokk **42** H 2
Joliette **18** F 4
Jolo **75** F 2
Jones, Cape **15** L 2
Jonesboro **21** H 4
Jonglei **60** E 3
Jönköping **43** FG 4
Jonquière **19** F 4
Jonuta **25** F 4
Joplin **21** H 4
Jordan **48** B 2–3
Jordan **48** B 3
Jordan (MT, U.S.A.) **20** E 2
Jordan Valley **20** C 3
Jorhat **73** F 2
Jos **59** F 4
Joseph Bonaparte Gulf **78** D 1
Joseph Lake **19** G 3

Joshua Tree National Monument **20** C 5
Jos Sodarso, Pulau **75** J 5
Jostedalsbreen **42** E 3
Jotunheimen **42** E 3
Juan Aldama **24** D 3
Juan de Nova **63** G 3
Juan Fernández Islands **31** B 6
Juárez **37** E 6
Juarez, Cuidad **20** E 5
Juarez, Sierra de **20** C 5
Juàzeiro **35** H 2
Juàzeiro do Norte **35** J 2
Jūbā **60** E 4
Jubayl **48** B 2
Jubayt **56** F 5
Júcar **44** C 4
Juchitan de Zaragoza **25** F 4
Juigalpa **28** B 4
Juiz de Fora **35** H 5
Juktån **42** G 2
Juliaca **34** B 4
Julia Creek **79** G 3
Julianatop **33** G 3
Julimes **24** C 2
Jumanggoin **70** C 4
Junagadh **72** B 3
Jun Bulen **71** G 1
Junction **25** G 5
Junction City **21** G 4
Jundiaí **35** G 5
Juneau **13** L 4
Junee **79** H 5
Junggar Pendi **67** M 1
Junín **36** D 5
Jūniyah **48** B 2
Jun Xian **70** F 4
Juoksengi **42** H 2
Jura **40** B 3
Jurado **32** C 2
Jurien Bay **78** A 5
Jürmala **43** H 4
Juruá **32** E 4
Juruena **34** E 3
Juruti **33** G 4
Jutaí **32** E 4
Jutiapa **28** B 4
Juticalpa **28** B 4
Jutland **43** E 4
Juva **42** J 3
Juventud, Isla de la **27** E 4
Ju Xian **71** G 3
Jüyom **49** F 3
Juzur Qarqannah **55** H 2
Jylland **43** EF 4
Jyväskylä **42** J 3

K

Kabaena, Pulau **75** F 5
Kabalo **60** D 6
Kaban'ya **69** P 6
Kabba **59** F 4

Kåbdalis 42 G 2
Kabinakagami Lake 18 D 4
Kabinda 60 CD 6
Kabīr Kūh 49 E 2
Kabo 60 B 3
Kabompo 62 C 2
Kabondo Dianda 60 D 6
Kabud Rāhang 49 E 2
Kabul 67 HJ 4
Kabwe 62 D 2
Kachikattsy 69 NO 3
Kachin 73 G 2
Kachug 68 J 5
Kadirli 47 E 3
Kadiyevka 47 E 1
Kadoka 21 F 3
Kadoma 62 D 3
Kädugli 56 D 6
Kaduna 59 F 3
Kaédi 54 C 5
Kafue 62 D 3
Kafue National Park 62 D 3
Kafue (River) 62 D 2
Kafura 60 E 5
Kagalaska 12 B 6
Kagaluk 19 H 2
Kagoshima 71 JK 4
Kagul 46 C 1
Kahemba 60 B 6
Kahoolawe 83 E 1
Kahramanmaras 47 E 3
Kai, Kepulauan 75 H 5
Kaifeng 70 FG 4
Kaikoura 81 Q 9
Kaili 70 E 5
Kailu 71 H 2
Kaimur Range 72 D 3
Kainantu 80 E 3
Kainji Dam 59 EF 4
Kainji Reservoir 59 E 3
Kaintragarh 72 DE 3
Kairouan → Al Qayrawän
   55 GH 1
Kaiserslautern 41 E 5
Kai Xian 70 E 4
Kaiyuan 70 D 6
Kaiyuh Mountains 12 F 3
Kajaani 42 J 3
Kajaki Dam 67 H 4
Kakhonak 12 G 4
Kakhovka 47 D 1
Kakhovskoye Vodokhrani-
   lishche 47 DE 1
Käkï 49 F 3
Kakinada 72 D 4
Kakisa 14 F 2
Kakisa Lake 14 F 2
Kaktovik 13 J 1
Kalabagh 67 J 4
Kalach 50 H 5
Kalachinsk 51 OP 4
Kalahari 62 C 4
Kalahari Gemsbok National
   Park 62 BC 5

Kalai-Khumb 67 J 3
Kalajoki 42 H 3
Kalámai 46 B 3
Kalamazoo 22 C 2
Kalaong 75 F 2
Kalbarri National Park 78 A 4
Kaldbakur 42 A 2
Kalehe 60 D 5
Kalemie 60 CD 6
Kalevala 42 K 2
Kalewa 73 F 3
Kalga 68 L 5
Kalgoorlie 78 C 5
Kalimantan 74 DE 3
Kalinin 50 FG 4
Kaliningrad 43 H 5
Kalispell 20 D 2
Kalisz 41 G 4
Kalixälven 42 H 2
Kallsjön 42 F 3
Kalmar 43 G 4
Kalmykovo 66 E 1
Kaloko 60 D 6
Kalole 60 D 5
Kalskag 12 E 3
Kalsubai 72 B 4
Kaltag 12 F 3
Kaluga 50 FG 5
Kamaishi 71 M 3
Kamanjab 62 B 3
Kamarän 57 G 5
Kamaria Falls 33 FG 2
Kambal'naya Sopka 69 T 5
Kamchatka 69 T 4
Kamenets-Podolskiy 46 C 1
Kamenjak, Rt 45 F 3
Kamen-na-Obi 51 PQ 5
Kamensk-Ural'skiy 51 M 4
Kamet 72 D 1
Kamina 60 D 6
Kaminak Lake 15 K 2
Kaminuriak Lake 15 K 2
Kamkaly 67 J 2
Kamloops 14 E 4
Kamnrokan 68 K 4
Kampala 60 E 4–5
Kampar 74 B 3
Kampar, Sungai 74 B 3
Kampot 74 B 1
Kampuchea 73 HJ 5
Kamsack 15 J 4
Kamyshin 50 HJ 5
Kanaaupscow 18 E 3
Kanab 20 D 4
Kanaga 12 B 6
Kanairiktok 19 H 3
Kanal 43 E 5
Kananga 60 C 6
Kanangra Boyd National Park
   79 HJ 5
Kanazawa 71 KL 3
Kanchipuram 72 CD 5
Kandagach 66 F 1
Kandahar 67 H 4

Kandalaksha 42 K 2
Kandalakshskaya Guba
   42 K 2
Kandangan 74 DE 4
Kandvu 82 C 4
Kande 58 E 4
Kandi 58 E 3
Kandy 72 D 6
Kandychan 69 RS 3
Kanem 59 GH 3
Kangalassy 69 N 3
Kangāmiut 17 Q 3
Kangan 49 F 4
Kangar 74 B 2
Kangaroo Island 79 F 6
Kangävar 49 E 2
Kangchenjunga 72 E 2
Kangding 70 D 5
Kangean, Kepulauan 74 E 5
Kangeeak Point 17 O 3
Kanggye 71 J 2
Kangmar 72 DE 1
Kangnüng 71 JK 3
Kango 59 G 5
Kangping 71 H 2
Kangynin 12 B 2
Kaniama 60 C 6
Kaniet Islands 82 A 3
Kanin 50 K 4
Kankakee 22 C 2
Kankan 58 C 3
Kankesanturai 72 D 5–6
Kanmaw Kyun 73 G 5
Kannapolis 22 DE 3
Kano 59 F 3
Kanovlei 62 B 3
Kanpur 72 D 2
Kansas 21 G 4
Kansas City 21 H 4
Kansk 68 FG 4
Kantang 73 G 6
Kantaralak 73 HJ 5
Kantchari 58 E 3
Kantishna 12 G 3
Kanye 62 CD 4
Kaohsiung 71 GH 6
Kaolack 58 A 3
Kaoma 62 C 2
Kaouar 59 G 2
Kapanga 60 C 6
Kapatu 63 E 1
Kap Brewster 84
Kapchagay 67 K 2
Kapchagayskoye Vodokhrani-
   lishche 67 K 2
Kapfenberg 45 G 2
Kapingamarangi 82 B 2
Kapiri Moposhi 62 DE 2
Kapisigdlit 17 QR 4
Kapiskau 18 D 3
Kapona 60 D 6
Kaposvár 46 A 1
Kapsukas 43 H 5

Kapuskasing 18 D 4
Kapustoye 42 K 2
Kaquencgue 62 C 2
Karabekaul 67 GH 3
Karabük 47 D 2
Karabutak 66 F 1
Karachi 67 H 6
Kara Dağ 47 D 3
Karaga 69 U 4
Karaganda 51 OP 6
Karagüney Dağları 47 DE 2
Karaikkudi 72 C 6
Karaj 49 F 2
Kara-Kala 66 F 3
Karakelong, Pulau 75 G 3
Karakoram 67 JK 3–4
Karakorum Shankou
   67 JK 3–4
Karaköse 47 F 3
Karalundi 78 B 4
Karam 68 J 4
Karamagay 67 M 1
Karaman 47 D 3
Karamay 67 LM 1
Karasburg 62 B 5
Kara Sea 84
Karasjåkka 42 H 2
Karasu (Turkey) 47 F 2–3
Karasu-Aras Dağları 47 F 3
Karasuk 51 P 5
Karatal 51 P 6
Karatau 67 J 2
Karathuri 73 G 6
Karatogay 66 F 1
Karaton 66 E 1
Karaul 51 Q 1
Karaulkel'dy 66 EF 1
Karazhingil 51 O 6
Karbalá' 48 D 2
Kardhitsa 46 B 3
Kärdla 43 H 4
Kareliya 42 K 3
Karen 73 G 4
Karesuando 42 H 2
Karganay 69 X 2
Kargat 51 Q 4
Kargopol'50 G 3
Kari 59 G 3
Kariba, Lake 62 D 3
Kariba Dam 62 D 3
Karibib 62 B 4
Karikal 72 CD 5
Karimata, Selat 74 C 4
Karimganj 73 F 2
Karisimbi 60 D 5
Karjala 42 K 3
Karkär 80 E 2
Karkas, Küh-e 49 F 2
Karkinitskiy Zaliv 47 D 1
Karleby 42 H 3
Karlik Shan 70 BC 2
Karl-Marx-Stadt 41 F 4
Karlovac 45 G 2
Karlovy Vary 41 F 4

Kar – Kha

Karlshamn 43 FG 4
Karlskoga 43 FG 4
Karlskrona 43 G 4
Karlsruhe 41 E 5
Karlstad (MN, U.S.A.) 21 G 2
Karlstad (Sweden) 43 F 4
Karluk 12 FG 4
Karmöy 43 DE 4
Karnataka 72 BC 4
Karong 73 F 2
Karonga 63 E 1
Kárpathos 46 C 3
Kars 47 F 2
Karsakpay 67 H 1
Karshi 67 H 3
Karskiye Vorota, Proliv
  50–51 L 1
Karskoye More 51 LM 1
Kars Platosu 47 F 2
Kartal 46 C 2
Kartaly 51 LM 5
Karufa 75 H 4
Karwar 72 B 5
Kasai 60 B 5
Kasai Occidental 60 C 6
Kasai Oriental 60 C 5–6
Kasaji 62 C 2
Kasama 63 E 2
Kasba Lake 15 J 2
Kāshān 49 F 2
Kashi 67 K 3
Kashken Teniz 51 O 6
Kāshmar 66 F 3
Kasimov 50 H 5
Kaskaskia River 22 C 3
Kaskelen 67 K 2
Kas Kong 73 H 5
Kasongo 60 D 5
Kásos 46 C 3
Kaspiyskiy 47 G 1
Kaspiyskoye More 66 D 1
Kassalá 56 F 5
Kassándra 46 B 2
Kassel 41 E 4
Kastamonu 47 D 2
Kasungu 63 E 2
Katako-Kombe 60 CD 5
Katangli 69 Q 5
Katawaz 67 H 4
Katerini 46 B 2
Katherine 78 E 1
Katherine Gorge National
  Park 78 E 1
Kathiawar 72 B 3
Kathiri 57 H 5
Kathmandu 72 E 2
Katihar 72 E 2
Katmai, Mount 12 FG 4
Katmai National Park
  and Preserve 12 G 4
Katowice 41 G H 4
Kātrina, Jabal 48 AB 3
Katrineholm 43 G 4
Katsina 59 F 3

Kattaktoc, Cape 19 G 2
Kattegat 43 F 4
Katyl'ga 51 P 4
Kauai 83 E 1
Kaufbeuren 41 F 5
Kaunas 43 H 5
Kauno Marios 43 H 5
Kavalerovo 71 KL 2
Kaválla 46 B 2
Kavar 49 F 3
Kavendou, Mont 58 B 3
Kavir, Dasht-e 49 FG 2
Kavir-e Abarqu 49 F 3
Kavir-e Namak 49 G 1
Kawa 56 E 5
Kawich Peak 20 C 4
Kawm Umbū 48 A 4
Kawm Umbū 56 E 4
Kaya 58 D 3
Kayah 73 G 4
Kayak (AK, U.S.A.) 13 J 4
Kayala 42 K 3
Kayan 74 E 3
Kayenta 20 D 4
Kayes 58 B 3
Kaynar 51 P 6
Kayseri 47 DE 3
Kazachinskoye 68 J 4
Kazakhskiy Melkosopochnik
  51 NP 6
Kazakhstan 67 FH 1
Kazan'50 JK 4
Kazan (N.W.T., Can.) 15 K 2
Kazan Islands (Japan)
  65 QR 7
Kazanlŭk 46 C 2
Kazanskoye 51 NO 4
Kazbek 47 F 2
Kaz Daği 46 C 3
Kāzerūn 49 F 3
Kazymskaya 51 N 3
Kazymskiy Mys 51 MN 3
Kazzān ar Ruşayris 56 E 6
Keams Canyon 20 D 4
Kearney 21 G 3
Kearns 20 D 3
Keban Gölü 47 E 3
Kebbi 59 E 3
Kebnekaise 42 G 2
Kediat Idjil 54 C 4
Kediri 74 D 5
Kédougou 58 B 3
Keele 13 M 3
Keele Peak 13 LM 3
Keetmanshoop 62 B 5
Keewatin 15 KL 5
Keewatin, District of 16 L 1–2
Kefa 61 F 3
Kefallinia 46 B 3
Kégashka 19 H 3
Keimoes 62 C 5
Keitele 42 J 3
Keith 79 FG 6
Keith Arm 13 N 2

Keketa 80 D 3
Kelang 74 B 3
Keli Hāji Ibrāhim 49 D 1
Kelkit 47 E 2
Kellett, Cape 16 A 2
Kellog (U.S.S.R.) 51 R 3
Kellogg (ID, U.S.A.) 20 C 2
Kelloselkä 42 J 2
Kelowna 14 F 5
Kelsey 15 K 3
Kelsey Bay 13 M 5
Kelso (WA, U.S.A.) 20 B 2
Keluang 74 B 3
Kem' 42 K 3
Ké Macina 58 CD 3
Kemerovo 51 QR 4
Kemi 42 HJ 2
Kemijärvi 42 J 2
Kemijoki 42 J 2
Kemkra 69 P 4
Kemp, Lake 21 G 5
Kempendyayi 68 LM 3
Kemps Bay 27 F 4
Kempsey 79 J 5
Kempt, Lac 18 F 4
Kenai 12 G 3
Kenai Fjords National Park
  12 H 4
Kenai Mountains 12 G 4
Kenai Peninsula 12 GH 4
Kencha 69 PQ 3
Kendall, Cape 15 M 2
Kendallville 22 CD 2
Kendari 75 F 4
Kenhardt 62 C 5
Kenitra 54 D 2
Keniut 69 X 3
Kenmare (N.D., U.S.A.) 21 F 2
Kennedy Range National Park
  78 B 3
Kennett 21 H 4
Kennewick 20 C 2
Kenogami 18 C 3
Keno Hill 13 K 3
Kenora 15 L 5
Kentau 67 H 2
Kent Peninsula 16 E 3
Kentucky 22 C 3
Kentucky Lake 22 C 3
Kentucky River 22 D 3
Kenya 61 F 4–5
Kenya, Mount 61 F 5
Keokuk 21 H 3
Kepe 42 K 2
Kepulauan Anambas 74 C 3
Kepulauan Aru 75 HJ 5
Kepulauan Babar 75 GH 5
Kepulauan Banggai 75 F 4
Kepulauan Kai 75 H 5
Kepulauan Kangean 74 E 5
Kepulauan Leti 75 G 5
Kepulauan Lingga 74 BC 3–4
Kepulauan Mentawai 74 AB 4
Kepulauan Natuna 74 C 3

Kepulauan Riau 74 B 3
Kepulauan Sangihe 75 G 3
Kepulauan Sula 75 FG 4
Kepulauan Talaud 75 G 3
Kepulauan Tanimbar 75 H 5
Kepulauan Tenggara 75 G 5
Kepulauan Togian 75 F 4
Kepulauan Tukangbesi 75 F 5
Kerama-rettō 71 J 5
Kerch 47 E 1
Kerchenskiy Proliv 47 E 1–2
Kerekhtyakh 69 N 3
Kerema 80 E 3
Kerempe Burnu 47 D 2
Keren 61 F 1
Keret', Ozero 42 K 2
Keriske 69 O 2
Kerki 67 GH 3
Kérkira 46 AB 3
Kermadec Islands 82 D 4–5
Kermān 66 F 4
Kermanshāh 49 E 2
Kermānshāhān 49 G 3
Kerme Körfezi 46 C 3
Kermit 24 F 5
Kerrobert 14 GH 4
Kerrville 25 G 5
Kerzaz 54 E 3
Kesagami Lake 18 D 3
Kestenga 42 K 2
Ketchikan 13 L 4
Ketchum Mountain 24 F 5
Ketoy, Ostrov 69 S 6
Kettle River Range 20 C 2
Keul' 68 H 4
Keurusselkä 42 HJ 3
Kew 29 E 2
Kewagama 18 E 4
Kewanee 22 C 2
Keweenaw Peninsula 22 C 1
Keyano 18 F 3
Key Largo 27 EF 3
Keystone Lake 21 G 4
Key West 27 E 3
Kezhma 68 H 4
Khabarovsk 69 P 6
Khabr, Kūh-e 49 G 3
Khabur 47 F 3
Khachmas 66 D 2
Khafji, Ra's al 49 E 3
Khaipur 67 H 5
Khairpur 67 J 5
Khakhea 62 C 4
Khakriz 67 GH 4
Khalesavoy 51 PQ 3
Khalij al 'Aqabah 48 B 3
Khalij al 'Aqabah 56 E 3
Khalij as Suways 48 A 3
Khalij as Suways 56 E 3
Khalij Maşirah 57 K 5
Khalij Qābis 55 H 2
Khálki 46 C 3
Khalkidhiki 46 B 2
Khalkis 46 B 3

Khambhat, Gulf of **72** B 3–4
Khamgaon **72** C 3
Khampa **68** L 3
Khampa **69** M 3
Khamseh **49** E 1
Khanabad **67** HJ 3
Khandwa **72** C 3
Khandyga **69** P 3
Khanglasy **51** M 3
Khanh Hung **73** HJ 6
Khani **68** M 4
Khánia **46** B 3
Khanpur **67** J 5
Khān Shaykhūn **48** B 2
Khantau **67** J 2
Khanty-Mansiysk **51** NO 3
Khanyangda **69** Q 4
Khanyardakh **69** N 3
Khao Lang **73** G 6
Khao Luang **73** G 6
Khao Sai Dao Tai **73** H 5
Khappyrastakh **69** M 4
Khara **68** G 5
Kharagpur **72** E 3
Kharan **67** GH 5
Kharānaq **49** G 2
Kharānaq, Kūh-e **49** G 2
Kharik **68** H 5
Khārk **49** F 3
Kharkov **50** G 5
Kharoti **67** H 4
Kharstan **69** Q 1
Khasavyurt **47** G 2
Khash (Afghanistan) **67** G 4
Khāsh (Iran) **67** G 5
Khash Desert **67** G 4
Khashm Mishraq **66** D 6
Khaskovo **46** C 2
Khatanga **68** H 1
Khatangskiy Zaliv **68** JK 1
Khataren **69** T 3
Khatyrka **69** X 3
Khawr al Fakkān **49** G 4
Khaybar **48** C 4
Khaybar, Harrat **48** C 4
Khazzān Jabal al Awliyā'
  56 E 5–6
Khe Bo **73** HJ 4
Khenifra **54** D 2
Kherpuchi **69** P 5
Khersan **49** F 3
Kherson **47** D 1
Kheta **68** G 1
Kheta **68** H 1
Kheyrābād **66** EF 5
Khibiny **42** K 2
Khíos **46** C 3
Khirbat Isriyah **48** BC 2
Khmel'nitskiy **50** E 6
Khodzheyli **66** F 2
Khoe **69** P 6
Khok Kloi **73** G 6
Kholmsk **69** Q 6
Khomeyn **49** F 2

Khongo **69** S 3
Khon Kaen **73** H 4
Khor Anghar **61** G 2
Khorāsān **66** F 4
Khorat Plateau **73** H 4
Khordogoy **68** L 3
Khoronnokh **68** LM 2
Khorramābād **49** E 2
Khorramshahr **49** E 3
Khorsābād **48** D 1
Khosrowābād **49** E 3
Khrebet Bureinskiy **69** O 5
Khrebet Chayatyn **69** P 5
Khrebet Cherskogo **69** P 1–2
Khrebet Dzhagdy **69** O 5
Khrebet Dzhugdzhur **69** OP 4
Khrebet Iskamen' **12** B 2
Khrebet Khugdyunda **68** G 2
Khrebet Kolymskiy **69** SU 3
Khrebet Koryakskiy **69** VW 3
Khrebet Nuratau **67** H 2
Khrebet Pay-Khoy **51** M 2
Khrebet Sette Daban
  69 PQ 3–4
Khrebet Suntar Khayata
  69 PQ 3
Khrebet Turana **69** O 5
Khudzhakh **69** R 3
Khugdyungda, Khrebet
  68 G 2
Khulkhuta **47** G 1
Khulna **72** E 3
Khurays **49** E 4
Khurayt **56** D 6
Khurr, Wādī al **48** C 3
Khurramshahr **49** E 3
Khursanīyah **49** E 4
Khuzdar **67** H 5
Khūzestān **49** E 3
Khvāf **66** FG 4
Khvojeh, Kūh-e **49** E 2
Khvor **49** G 2
Khvormūj **49** F 3
Khvoy **66** D 3
Kiambi **60** D 6
Kiana **12** E 2
Kiantajärvi **42** J 2
Kibangou **59** G 6
Kibwezi **61** F 5
Kichi Kichi **59** H 2
Kicking Horse Pass **14** F 4
Kidal **58** E 2
Kidira **58** B 3
Kiel **41** F 4
Kielce **41** H 4
Kieta **81** G 3
Kiffa **54** C 5
Kigali **60** E 5
Kigilyakh **69** P 1
Kigoma **60** D 5
Kihnu **43** H 4
Kikiakki **51** Q 3
Kikladhes **46** BC 3
Kikori **82** A 3

Kikwit **60** B 6
Kilambé **28** B 4
Kilbuck Mountains **12** F 3
Kilchu **71** J 2
Kil'din, Ostrov **42** K 2
Kili **82** C 2
Kılıç Dağları **46** C 3
Kilimanjaro **61** F 5
Kilindini **61** F 5
Kilis **47** E 3
Kiliya **46** C 2
Killarney **40** AB 4
Killeen **25** G 5
Killinek **17** N 4
Killini Óros **46** B 3
Kilmarnock **40** C 3
Kilmez **50** K 4
Kil'mez' **50** K 4
Kilosa **61** F 6
Kilpisjärvi **42** H 2
Kilp-Javr **42** K 2
Kilwa **60** D 6
Kilwa Masoko **61** F 6
Kimball **21** G 3
Kimball, Mount **13** J 3
Kimbe Bay **81** F 3
Kimberley **14** F 5
Kimberley (South Africa)
  62 CD 5
Kimberley (Western
  Australia) **78** D 2
Kimberley Plateau **78** D 2
Kimch'aek **71** JK 2
Kimito **43** H 3
Kimparana **58** CD 3
Kinabalu, Gunung **74** E 2
Kincheqa National Park
  79 G 5
Kinda **60** C 6
Kinder **25** H 5
Kindersley **14** H 4
Kindia **58** B 4
Kindu **60** D 5
King **80** K 8
King Christian IX Land **84**
King Christian X Land **84**
King City **20** B 4
King Frederik VIII Land **84**
King George Islands **18** E 2
Kingissepp (Estoniya,
  U.S.S.R.)**43** H 4
King Leopold Ranges **78** CD 2
Kingman (AZ, U.S.A.) **20** D 4
Kingman (Pacific Ocean,
  U.S.A.) **82** C 2
Kingoonya **79** F 5
Kingsmill Group **82** C 3
King Sound **78** C 2
Kings Peak (CA, U.S.A.)
  20 B 3
Kings Peak (UT, U.S.A.)
  20 D 3
Kingsport **22** D 3
Kingston **22** E 2

Kingston (Jamaica) **28** D 3
Kingston (Norfolk Is., Austr.)
  82 C 4
Kingston (N.Y., U.S.A.) **23** F 2
Kingston Peak **20** C 4
Kingston-upon-Hull **40** C 4
Kingstown **29** G 4
Kingsville **25** E 2
King William Island **16** G 3
King Williams Town **62** D 6
Kinkala **59** G 6
Kinmaw **73** F 4
Kinnairds Head **40** C 3
Kinoosao **15** J 3
Kinshasa **60** B 5
Kinston **22** E 3
Kipaka **60** D 5
Kipawa, Lac **18** E 4
Kipnuk **12** E 4
Kipushi **62** D 2
Kirakira **82** B 3
Kirbey **68** H 2
Kirbey **68** K 2
Kirensk **68** J 4
Kirgiziya **67** JK 2
Kirgiz Step' **66–67** FH 1
Kiribati **82** DE 3
Kırıkhan **47** E 3
Kırıkkale **47** D 3
Kirillovka **47** E 1
Kirimati **83** E 2
Kirishi **43** K 4
Kirkenes **42** J 2
Kirkjubæjarklaustur **42** B 3
Kirkland Lake **18** D 4
Kırklareli **46** C 2
Kirkpatrick, Mount **85**
Kirksville **21** H 3
Kirkūk **48** D 2
Kirkwall **40** C 3
Kirov (MO, U.S.A.) **21** H 4
Kirov **50** JK 4
Kirov **50** FG 5
Kirovabad **66** D 2
Kirovakan **47** FG 2
Kirovo Chepetsk **50** K 4
Kirovograd **47** D 1
Kirovsk **42** K 2
Kırşehir **47** D 2–3
Kiruna **42** H 2
Kisangani **60** D 4
Kishinev **46** C 1
Kisii **60** E 5
Kısılırmak **47** D 2
Kiska **12** A 6
Kiska Volcano **12** A 6
Kislovodsk **47** F 2
Kismāyu **61** G 5
Kisoro **60** DE 5
Kissidougou **58** BC 4
Kisumu **60** E 5
Kita **58** C 3
Kitakyūshū **71** JK 4
Kitale **60** F 4

Kit – Kra

Kitami **71** M 2
Kitchener **22** D 2
Kitgum **60** E 4
Kithira **46** B 3
Kithnos **46** B 3
Kitimat **13** M 5
Kitimat Ranges **13** M 5
Kittanning **22** DE 2
Kitwe **62** D 2
Kiunga **80** D 3
Kivak **12** C 3
Kivalina **12** E 2
Kivijärvi **42** HJ 3
Kiviôli **43** J 4
Kivu **60** D 5
Kiyev **50** F 5
Kizel **51** L 4
Kızıl Dağ **47** D 3
Kızılırmak **50** E 3
Kizlyar **47** G 2
Kizlyarskiy Zaliv **47** G 2
Kizyl-Arvat **66** F 3
Kizyl-Atrek **66** E 3
Klagenfurt **45** FG 2
Klaipėda **43** H 4
Klamath Falls **20** B 3
Klamath Mountains **20** B 3
Klamath River **20** B 3
Klarälven **43** F 3
Klerksdorp **62** D 5
Klintsy **50** F 5
Klit **43** E 4
Kłodzko **41** G 4
Klondike Plateau **13** K 3
Klotz, Lac **17** M 4
Klotz, Mount **13** K 2
Kluane Lake **13** K 3
Kluane National Park **13** K 3
Klukhorskiy Pereval **47** K 2
Klyuchr **69** U 4
Knosós **46** C 3
Knox, Cape **13** L 5
Knox Coast **85**
Knoxville (IA, U.S.A.) **21** H 3
Knoxville (TN, U.S.A.) **22** D 3
Knud Rasmussen Land **84**
Koartac **17** M 4
Kōbe **71** KL 3–4
Kóbenhavn **43** F 4
Kobenni **54** CD 5
Koblenz **41** E 4
Koboldo **69** O 5
Kobrin **43** H 5
Kobroor, Pulau **75** H 5
Kobuk **12** EF 2
Kobuk **12** F 2
Kobuk Valley National Park
  12 F 2
Koca Çal **47** D 3
Kocaeli **46** CD 2
Kocasu **46** C 3
Koch **17** L 3
Ko Chang **73** H 5
Kōchi **71** K 4

Kochikha **68** G 1
Kodi **75** E 5
Kodiak **12** G 4
Kodiak Island **12** G 4
Kodima **50** H 3
Kodžha Balkan **46** C 2
Köes **62** B 5
Koforidua **58** D 4
Kohistan **67** J 3
Kohlu **67** H 5
Kohtla-Järve **43** J 4
Kohunlich **28** B 3
Kokalaat **67** GH 1
Kokand **67** HJ 2
Kokchetav **51** N 5
Kokkola **42** H 3
Kokomo **22** C 2
Kokpekty **51** Q 6
Koksoak **19** G 2
Kokstad **62** D 6
Koktuma **51** Q 6
Ko Kut **73** H 5
Kola **42** K 2
Kolai **67** J 3
Kola Peninsula **50** G 2
Kolar **72** C 5
Kolar Gold Fields **72** C 5
Kolbachi **69** M 5
Kolbio **61** G 5
Kolding **43** E 4
Kolesovo **69** S 1
Kolhapur **72** B 4
Koli **42** J 3
Koliganek **12** F 4
Kolkasrags **43** H 4
Kollumúli **42** C 2
Köln **41** E 4
Kołobrzeg **41** G 4
Kolombangara **81** G 3
Kolomna **50** GH 4
Kolomyya **46** C 1
Kolpakovsky **69** T 5
Kolpashevo **51** QR 4
Koluton **51** N 5
Kolwezi **62** D 2
Kolyma **69** TU 2
Kolymskaya **69** UV 2
Kolymskaya Nizmennost'
  69 ST 2
Kolymskiy, Khrebet **69** SU 3
Kolymskoye Nagor'ye **69** S 3
Kolyuchinskaya Guba **12** C 2
Kolyvan' **51** Q 5
Komárno **41** G 5
Komba **60** C 4
Kombolchia **61** FG 2
Komelek **69** O 3
Kommunarsk **47** E 1
Komoé, Parc National de la
  58 D 4
Komotini **46** C 2
Kompas Berg **62** C 6
Kompong Cham **73** J 5
Kompong Chhnang **73** HJ 5

Kompong Som **73** H 5
Kompot **75** F 3
Komsomol'sk-na-Amure
  69 P 5
Kona **58** D 3
Kondakova **69** T 2
Kondinin **78** B 5
Kondoa **61** F 5
Kondon **69** P 5
Kondut **78** B 5
Konevo **50** GH 3
Kongola **62** C 3
Kongolo **60** D 6
Kongor **60** E 3
Konin **41** G 4
Konkan **72** B 4
Konkudera **68** K 4
Konosha **50** H 3
Konotop **50** F 5
Konstantinovka **47** E 1
Konstanz **41** E 5
Kontagora **59** F 3
Kontcha **59** G 4
Kontiomäki **42** J 3
Konya **67** D 3
Konya Ovası **47** D 3
Kooch Bihar **72** E 2
Kootenay **14** F 4–5
Kootenay National Park
  14 F 4
Kópasker **42** B 2
Kopeysk **51** M 5
Ko Phangan **73** H 6
Ko Phuket **73** G 6
Köping **43** G 4
Koppang **42** F 3
Korba **72** D 3
Korça **46** B 2
Korčula **45** G 3
Kordestän **49** E 2
Kord Kūy (Iran) **49** G 1
Korea Strait **71** J 4
Korenovsk **47** E 1
Korfovskiy **69** P 6
Korhogo **58** C 4
Korinthiakos Kólpos **46** B 3
Kórinthos **46** B 3
Koriolei **61** G 4
Kōriyama **71** M 3
Korkodon **69** ST 3
Korla **67** M 2
Köroğlu Dağları **47** D 2
Korosten **43** J 5
Koro Toro **59** H 2
Korovin Volcano **12** C 6
Korsakov **69** Q 6
Korsfjorden **43** DE 3
Korshunovo **68** K 4
Koryakskiy Khrebet **69** VW 3
Koryresk **69** TU 4
Kos **46** C 3
Kosa Fedotova **47** E 1

Kosciusko **22** C 4
Košice **41** H 5
Kosŏng **71** J 3
Kosovska Mitrovica **46** B 2
Kossou, Lac de **58** CD 4
Kostino **51** R 2
Kostroma **50** H 4
Koszalin **41** G 4
Kota **72** C 2
Kotabumi **74** BC 4
Kota Kinabalu **74** DE 2
Kotel'nich **50** J 4
Kotel'nikovo **47** F 1
Kotel'nyy, Ostrov **69** P 1
Kotikovo **69** QR 6
Kotka **43** J 3
Kotlas **50** J 3
Kotlik **12** E 3
Kotovsk **46** CD 1
Kotu Group **82** D 4
Kotuy **68** H 1
Kotzebue **12** E 2
Kotzebue Sound **12** E 2
Koudougou **58** D 3
Koukdjuak **17** M 3
Koulen **73** HJ 5
Koumac **81** H 6
Koumbi-Saleh **54** D 5
Koundara **58** B 3
Koundian **58** B 3
Koungheul **58** AB 3
Kourou **33** H 2
Koutous **59** FG 3
Kouvola **42** J 3
Kova **68** H 4
Kovac **46** A 2
Kovel' **43** H 5
Kovrizhka **69** U 3
Kovrov **50** GH 4
Kowloon **70** FG 6
Kowt-e-Ashrow **67** H 4
Koyuk **12** E 3
Koyukuk **12** F 2
Koyukuk **12** FG 2
Kozáni **46** B 2
Kozlu **47** D 2
Kra, Isthmus of **73** G 5
Kragujevac **46** B 2
Kralendijk **29** F 4
Kraljevo **46** B 2
Kramfors **42** G 3
Kranj **45** F 2
Krasino **50** K 1
Krasnaya Yaranga **12** C 2
Krašnik **41** H 4
Krasnodar **47** EF 1–2
Krasnogorsk **69** Q 6
Krasnoje Selo **43** JK 4
Krasnokamsk **50** KL 4
Krasnotur'insk **51** M 4
Krasnoural'sk **51** M 4
Krasnovodsk **66** E 2
Krasnoyarsk **68** F 4
Krasnoyarskiy **51** L 5

172

Krasnyy Chikoy 68 J 5
Krasnyy Luch 47 E 1
Kremenchug 50 FG 6
Kremmling 20 E 3
Kresta, Zaliv 12 B 2
Kresti 50 F 4
Krestovka 50 K 2
Krestovskaye 69 P 4
Kresty 68 E 1
Kribi 59 F 5
Krichev 50 F 5
Krishna 72 C 4
Kristiansand 43 E 4
Kristianstad 43 F 4
Kristiansund 42 E 3
Kristineberg 42 G 2
Kristinehamn 43 F 4
Kristinestad 42 H 3
Kriti 46 B 3
Kritikón Pélagos 46 BC 3
Krivoy Rog 47 D 1
Krivoy Rog 47 D 1
Krk 45 F 2
Krnov 41 G 4
Krokom 42 F 3
Kronotsi 69 U 5
Kronotskaya Sopka 69 TU 5
Kronshtadt 43 J 4
Kroonstad 62 D 5
Kropotkin 47 F 1
Krosno 41 H 5
Krotoszyn 41 G 4
Kruger National Park 63 E 4
Krugersdorp 62 D 5
Krung Thep 73 H 5
Kruševac 46 B 2
Krutinka 51 O 4
Kruzof 13 K 4
Kryazh Kula 69 O 2
Krym (Ukraine, U.S.S.R.)
    47 D 1
Krymsk 47 E 1
Krymskiye Gory 47 D 2
Ksabi 54 E 3
Ksar Chellala 55 F 1
Ksar el Boukhari 55 F 1
Ksar Torchane 54 C 4
Ksen'yevka 68 L 5
Kuala Lumpur 74 B 3
Kuala Terengganu 74 B 2
Kuamut 74 E 2
Kuantan 74 B 3
Kuban' 47 E 1–2
Kubenskoye, Ozero 50 G 4
Kudus 74 D 5
Kudymkar 50 Kl 4
Kufstein 45 F 2
Kugmallit Bay 13 L 2
Küh-e 'Aliābād 49 F 2
Küh-e Alijūq 49 F 3
Küh-e Alvano 49 E 2
Küh-e Būl 49 F 3
Küh-e Dīnār 49 F 3
Küh-e Garbosh 49 EF 2

Küh-e Garri 49 E 2
Küh-e Gügerd 49 F 2
Küh-e Karkas 49 F 2
Küh-e Khabr 49 G 3
Küh-e Khāīz 49 F 3
Küh-e Kharānaq 49 G 2
Küh-e Khvojeh 49 E 2
Küh-e Kükalär 49 F 3
Küh-e Masāhīm 49 G 3
Küh-e Safīd 49 E 2
Küh-e Sorkh 49 G 2
Kühestak 66 F 5
Küh-e Tābask 49 F 3
Kühhā-ye Qorūd 49 F 2–3
Kühhā-ye-Sabalān 66 D 3
Kühha ye Zagros 49 EF 2–F 3
Kuhmo 42 J 3
Kuikkavaara 42 J 3
Kui Nua 74 AB 1
Kuito 62 B 2
Kuiu 13 L 4
Kuivaniemi 42 J 2
Kujani Game Reserve 58 D 4
Kuji 71 M 2
Kula Kangri 73 F 2
Kulakshi 66 EF 1
Kulaneh 67 G 5
Kul'chi 69 P 5
Kulgera 78 E 4
Kulinda 68 J 3
Kullen 43 F 4
Kul'sary 66 E 1
Kulundinskaya Step' 51 P 5
Kulyab 67 HJ 3
Kuma (Russia, U.S.S.R.)
    47 G 2
Kumai, Teluk 74 D 4
Kumamoto 71 K 4
Kumanovo 46 B 2
Kumasi 58 D 4
Kumba 59 F 5
Kumbakonam 72 CD 5
Kumdah 57 H 4
Kumertau 50 KL 5
Künas 67 L 2
Kunda Hills 72 C 5
Kunduz 67 H 3
Kunene 62 A 3
Kunes 42 J 1
Kungälv 43 F 4
Kungrad 66 F 2
Kungu 60 B 4
Kungur 50 L 4
Kunlun Shan 67 KM 3
Kunlun Shankou 70 B 3
Kunming 70 D 5
Kunsan 71 J 3
Kuntuk 69 R 4
Kununurra 78 D 2
Kunwak 15 K 2
Kuop 82 B 2
Kuopio 42 J 3
Kuoqiang 70 A 3
Kuorboaivi 42 J 2

Kuoyka 68 LM 1
Kupang 75 F 6
Kupashi 71 N 2
Kupreanof 13 L 4
Kupyansk 50 G 6
Kuqa 67 L 2
Kura 47 G 2
Kurashiki 71 K 3–4
Kurdufân 56 DE 6
Kürdžhali 46 C 2
Kure 71 K 4
Kurgan 51 N 4
Kurgan-Tyube 67 H 3
Kuria 82 C 2
Kuria Muria Islands 57 K 5
Kurilovka 50 J 5
Kuril'skiye Ostrova (U.S.S.R)
    69 RS 6
Kurmuk 56 E 6
Kurnool 72 C 4
Kursk 50 G 5
Kurşunlu Dağı 47 E 3
Kuruman (South Africa)
    62 C 5
Kuruman (South Africa)
    62 C 5
Kurunegala 72 D 6
Kurupka 12 C 3
Kurzeme 43 H 4
Kuşada Körfezi 46 C 3
Kusaie 82 B 2
Kushchevskaya 47 E 1
Kushiro 71 MN 2
Kushka 67 G 3
Kushmurun 51 MN 5
Kuskokwim 12 E 3
Kuskokwim Bay 12 E 4
Kuskokwim Mountains 12 F 3
Kustanay 51 M 5
Küsti 56 E 6
Kut 49 E 3
Kütahya 46 C 3
Kutai, Sungai 74 E 4
Kutaisi 66 C 2
Kutch 72 AB 3
Kutch, Gulf of 72 A 3
Kutch, Rann of 72 AB 3
Kutno 41 G 4
Kuumamo 42 J 2
Kuvango 62 B 2
Kuwait 49 E 3
Kuwait 49 E 3
Kuwait 57 H 3
Kuybyshev 50 K 5
Kuybyshev 51 PQ 4
Kuybyshevo 69 R 6
Kuybyshevskoye Vodokhrani-
    lishche 50 J 5
Kuygan 51 O 6
Küysanjaq 66 C 3
Kuytun, Gora 51 R 6
Kuyucuk Dağı 46 D 3
Kuyumba 68 G 3
Kuz'mouka 68 F 4

Kuznetsk 50 J 5
Kvænangen 42 H 1
Kvalöy 42 G 2
Kvalöya 42 H 1
Kvarner 45 F 2–3
Kvarnerič 45 F 3
Kverkfjol 42 B 3
Kvichak 12 F 4
Kvichak Bay 12 F 4
Kvikkjokk 42 G 2
Kvinesdal 43 E 4
Kviteseid 43 E 4
Kwajalein 82 C 2
Kwakoegron 33 G 2
Kwangju 71 J 3
Kwethluk 12 E 3
Kwigillingok 12 E 4
Kwoka, Gunung 75 H 4
Kyakhta 68 J 5
Kyancutta 79 F 5
Kyaukme 73 G 3
Kyeintali 73 F 4
Kyle of Lochalsh 40 B 3
Kynnefjell 43 F 4
Kyoga, Lake 60 E 4
Kyōto 71 KL 3
Kyrbykan 69 N 3
Kyren 68 H J 5
Kyrgyday 69 M 3
Kyrta 50 L 3
Kyrynniky 69 L 3
Kyshtovka 51 P 4
Kyshtym 51 M 4
Kystatam 68 M 2
Kytalyktakh 69 OP 2
Kyushe 66 F 1
Kyūshū 71 K 4
Kyustendil 46 B 2
Kyusyur 69 N 1
Kyzas 51 RS 5
Kyzyl 68 FG 5
Kyzyldyykan 67 H 1
Kyzylkum, Peski 67 G 2
Kyzyltau 67 J 2
Kyzyluy 67 H 1
Kzyl-Orda 67 H 2
Kzyltu 51 O 5

L

La Asunción 29 G 4
La Babia 24 D 2
La Banda 36 D 4
La Barca 24 D 3
La Barge 20 DE 3
Labbezenga 58 E 2
Labé 58 B 3
Labelle 18 F 4
Labengke, Pulau 75 F 4
Laberge, Lake 13 K 3
Labinsk 47 F 2
La Blanquilla, Isla 29 G 4

Lab – Lak

Labrador **18–19** FG 2
Labrador, Coast of **19** HJ 2–3
Labrador City **19** G 3
Labrador Sea **17** PQ 4–5
Lábrea **33** F 5
Labrieville **19** G 4
Labuhanbajo **75** EF 5
Labytnangi **51** N 2
La Cadena **24** D 2
Lac Alaotra **63** H 3
Lac Albanel **18** F 3
Lac à l'Eau-Claire **18** EF 2
Lac Allard **19** H 3
Lacantún, Rio **25** F 4
La Carlota **36** D 5
Lac au Goéland **18** E 3
Lac aux Goélands **19** H 2
Lac Belot **13** M 2
Lac Bermen **19** G 3
Lac Bienville **18** F 2
Lac Brochet **15** J 3
Lac Burton **18** E 3
Laccadive Islands **72** B 5
Lac Caniapiscau **19** G 3
Lac Champdoré **19** G 2
Lac Chibougamau **18** F 4
Lac Couture **17** M 4
Lac Débo **58** CD 2
Lac de Gras **14** G 2
Lac de Kossou **58** CD 4
Lac Delorme **19** G 3
Lac des Bois **13** N 2
Lac d'Iberville **18** F 2
La Ceiba (Honduras) **28** B 3
Lacepede Bay **79** F 6
Lac Evans **18** E 3
Lac Faribault **19** F 2
Lac Guillaume Delisle **18** E 2
Lachlan River **79** GH 5
La Chorrera **32** BC 2
Lackawanna **22** E 2
Lac Kempt **18** F 4
Lac Kipawa **18** E 4
Lac Klotz **17** M 4
Lac La Biche **14** G 4
Lac la Martre **14** F 2
Lac la Martre **14** F 2
Lac la Ronge **15** J 3
Lac Léman **45** E 2
Lac Le Moyne **19** G 2
Lac Mai-Ndombe **60** B 5
Lac Manouane **19** F 3
Lac Maunoir **13** MN 2
Lac Mégantic **19** F 4
Lac Minto **18** F 2
Lac Mistassini **18** F 3
Lac Moero **60** D 6
Lac Musquaro **19** H 3
Lac Nantais **17** M 4
Lac Naococane **19** FG 3
Lac Nichicum **19** F 3
La Colorada **24** B 2
Lacombe **14** G 4
La Concepción **29** E 4

Lac Opiscotéo **19** G 3
La Coronilla **36** F 5
La Coruña **44** B 3
Lac Payne **18** F 2
Lac Peribonca **19** F 3
Lac Plétipi **19** F 3
La Crosse **21** H 3
La Cruz (Costa Rica) **28** B 4
La Cruz (Mexico) **24** C 3
Lac Sakami **18** E 3
Lacs des Loups Marins **18** F 2
Lac Seul **15** L 4
Lac Tassialouc **18** F 2
La Cuesta **24** D 2
Lac Upemba **60** D 6
Lac Wakuach **19** G 2
La Digue **61** K 5
Ladoga, Lake **42** K 3
La Dorada **32** D 2
Ladozhskoye Ozero **42** K 3
Ladysmith **62** D 5
Lae (Marshall Is.) **82** C 2
Lae (Papua New Guinea)
80 E 3
Læsö **43** F 4
La Estrada **44** B 3
Lafayette (IN, U.S.A.) **22** C 2
Lafayette (LA, U.S.A.) **25** H 5
Lafia **59** F 4
Lafiagi **59** EF 4
La Flor **28** C 4
La Fría **29** D 4
La Fría **32** D 2
Lagarto **35** J 3
Laghouat **55** F 2
La Glória **29** E 5
Lagoa dos Patos **36** F 5
Lago Agrio **32** C 4
Lagoa Mangueira **36** F 5
Lagoa Mirim **36** F 5
Lago Buenos Aires **37** B 8
Lago Cabora Bassa **63** E 3
Lago Chilwa **63** F 3
Lago de Chapala **24** D 3
Lago de Managua **28** B 4
Lago de Maracaibo **32** D 1–2
Lago de Nicaragua **28** B 4
Lago de Poopó **34** C 4
Lago de Yojoa **28** B 4
Lago di Bolsena **45** F 3
Lago Maggiore **45** E 2
Lago O'Higgins **37** B 8
Lago Posadas **37** B 8
Lago Rogagua **34** C 3
Lagos **58** E 4
Lagos de Moreno **24–25** D 3
Lago Titicaca **34** C 4
Lago Viedma **37** B 8
La Grande **20** C 2
La Grande Rivière **18** EF 3
La Grange **22** C 4
La Gran Sabana **33** F 2–3
La Guaira **29** F 4
Laguna **36** G 4

Laguna de Brus **28** C 3
Laguna de Caratasca **28** C 3
Laguna de Chiriquí **28** C 5
Laguna de Perlas **28** C 4
Laguna de Santa Maria **24** E 5
Laguna de Tamiahua **25** E 3
Laguna de Términos **25** F 4
Laguna Madre (Mexico)
25 E 2–3
Laguna Madre (TX, U.S.A.)
25 E 2
Laguna Mar Chiquita **36** D 5
Laguna Merín **36** F 5
Laguna Morales **25** E 3
Lagunas (Chile) **34** BC 5
Lagunas (Peru) **32** C 5
Lagune Ndogo **59** G 6
Lagune Nkomi **59** F 6
Lagunillas **29** E 4
Lagunillas **34** D 4
La Habana **27** E 4
Lähijän **49** F 1
Lähijän **66** E 3
Lahore **67** J 4
Lahti **42** J 3
La Huacan **24** D 4
Lai **59** H 4
Lainioälven **42** H 2
Lajes **36** F 4
La Junta (Bolivia) **34** D 4
La Junta (CO, U.S.A.) **21** F 4
La Junta (Mexico) **24** C 2
Lake Abaya **61** F 4
Lake Abitibi **18** E 4
Lake Albert (OR, U.S.A.)
20 BC 3
Lake Albert (Zaire/Uganda)
60 E 4
Lake Amadeus **78** E 3
Lake Argyle **78** D 2
Lake Athabasca **14** GH 3
Lake Aubry **13** M 2
Lake Austin **78** B 4
Lake Ballard **78** C 4
Lake Bangweulu **62** D 2
Lake Barkley **22** C 3
Lake Barlee **78** B 4
Lake Berryessa **20** B 4
Lake Big Sand, **15** K 3
Lake Birch, **15** L 4
Lake Brown, **16** H 3
Lake Buchanan (TX, U.S.A.)
25 G 5
Lake Carey **78** C 4
Lake Carnegie **78** C 4
Lake Chad **59** G 3
Lake Champlain **23** F 2
Lake Charles **25** H 5
Lake Chelan **20** B 2
Lake Chippewa **21** H 2
Lake City (FL, U.S.A.) **22** D 4
Lake City (N.C., U.S.A.) **22** E 4
Lake Claire **14** G 3
Lake Clark **12** G 3

Lake Clark National Park and
Preserve **12** G 3
Lake Cumberland **22** CD 3
Lake Disappointment **78** C 3
Lake Edward **60** D 5
Lake Erie **22** D 2
Lake Eyasi **60** E 5
Lake Eyre **79** F 4
Lake Eyre Basin **79** F 4
Lake Francis Case **21** G 3
Lake Gairdner **79** F 5
Lake George (FL, U.S.A.)
27 E 3
Lake George (N.Y., U.S.A.)
23 F 2
Lake Gillian **17** L 3
Lake Gordon, **14** G 2
Lake Grandin **14** F 2
Lake Gregory **79** FG 4
Lake Harbour **17** N 4
Lake Havasu City **20** D 5
Lake Highrock, **15** H 3
Lake Hill Island, **14** H 2
Lake Huron **22** D 2
Lake Itchen, **16** D 3
Lake Jackson **25** E 2
Lake Kariba **62** D 3
Lake Kemp **21** G 5
Lake Kivu **60** D 5
Lake Koocanusa **20** D 2
Lake Kyoga **60** E 4
Lake Laberge **13** K 3
Lakeland **27** E 3
Lake Lefroy **78** C 5
Lake Mackay **78** D 3
Lake Malawi (Lake Nyasa)
63 EF 2
Lake Manitoba **15** K 4
Lake Marion **22** D 4
Lake Maurice **78** E 4
Lake Mc Leod **78** A 3
Lake Mead **20** D 4
Lake Mead National Recrea-
tion Area **20** CD 4
Lake Melville **19** J 3
Lake Michigan **22** C 2
Lake Minchumina **12** G 3
Lake Missisa, **18** C 3
Lake Moore **78** B 4
Lake Moultrie **22** D 4
Lake Murray (S.C., U.S.A.)
22 D 4
Lake Mweru **60** D 6
Lake Nash **79** F 3
Lake Nasser **48** A 5
Lake Nasser (Egypt) **56** E 4
Lake Natron **61** F 5
Lake Nipigon **18** C 4
Lake Nipissing **18** DE 4
Lake Nyesa **63** EF 2
Lake Oahe **21** F 2
Lake of the Ozarks **21** H 4
Lake of the Woods **15** K 5
Lake Okeechobee **27** E 3

Lake Ontario 22 E 2
Lake O' The Cherokees 21 H 4
Lake Owyhee 20 C 3
Lake Oxford 15 K 3–4
Lake Pend Oreille 20 C 2
Lake Peter, 15 L 2
Lake Placid 23 F 2
Lake Pontchartrain 25 HJ 5
Lake Powell 20 D 4
Lake Rebecca 78 C 4–5
Lake River 18 D 3
Lake Rosa 29 E 2
Lake Rukwa 60 E 6
Lakes, Eskimo 13 L 2
Lake Saint-Jean, 18 F 4
Lake Saint Joseph 15 L 4
Lake Saint Lucia 63 E 5
Lake Sakakawea 21 F 2
Lake Scugog 22 E 2
Lake Shibogama, 18 C 3
Lake Simcoe 22 E 2
Lake Stefanie 61 F 4
Lake Superior 22 C 1
Lake Tahiryuak, 16 D 2
Lake Tahoe 20 C 4
Lake Tana 61 F 2
Lake Tanganyika 60 DE 6
Lake Taupo 81 R 8
Lake Timagami 18 D 4
Lake Timiskaming 18 E 4
Lake Torrens 79 F 5
Lake Turkana (Lake Rudolf) 61 F 4
Lake Victoria 60 E 5
Lakeview 20 BC 3
Lake Volta 58 DE 4
Lake Willow, 14 F 2
Lake Winnebago 22 C 2
Lake Winnibigoshish 21 H 2
Lake Winnipeg 15 K 4
Lake Winnipegosis 15 JK 4
Lake Winnipesaukee 23 F 2
Lakewood (CO, U.S.A.) 20 E 4
Lakewood (OH, U.S.A.) 22 D 2
Lake Worth 27 F 3
Lakon 81 J 4
Lakonikos Kólpos 46 B 3
Lakselv 42 J 1–2
Lakshadweep 72 B 5
Lalara 59 G 5
Lâleli Geçidi 47 E 3
La Libertad 28 B 4
La Ligua 36 B 5
La Linea 44 B 4
Lalitpur 72 C 3
La Loche 14 H 3
La Malbaie 19 F 4
La Mancha 44 C 4
La Manche 40 CD 4
Lamar 21 F 4
La Mariscala 36 F 5
La Marmora 45 E 4
La Marque 25 E 2
Lamarque 37 C 6

Lamas 32 C 5
La Mauricie National Park 18 F 4
Lambaréné 59 F 6
Lambayeque 32 B 5
Lambert, Cape 81 F 2
Lambert Glacier 85
Lamberts Bay 62 B 6
La Merced 36 C 4
Lamesa 21 F 5
Lamezia Terme 45 G 4
Lamía 46 B 3
Lamington National Park 79 J 4
Lamont 22 D 4
La Montaña 34 B 2–3
La Mosquitia 28 C 3–4
Lamotrek 82 A 2
Lampang 73 G 4
Lampasas 25 G 5
Lampazos de Naranjo 25 DE 2
Lamu 61 G 5
Lancang Jiang 70 C 6
Lancaster 40 C 4
Lancaster (CA, U.S.A.) 20 C 5
Lanciano 45 F 3
Lander 20 E 3
Land's End 40 B 4
Landshut 41 F 5
Landskrona 43 F 4
Landsort 43 G 4
Landsortsdjupet 43 G 4
Langdon 21 G 2
Langjökull 42 AB 3
Langkon 74 E 2
Langlade 18 E 4
Langöya 42 F 2
Langry 69 Q 5
Lang Son 73 J 3
Langzhong 70 E 4
Lansdowne House 18 C 3
Lansing (MI, U.S.A.) 22 CD 2
Lansing (N.W.T., Can.) 13 L 3
Lantini 45 G 4
Lanzarote 54 C 3
Lanzhou 70 DE 3
Laoag 75 J 1
Laon 44 D 2
La Orchila, Isla 29 F 4
La Oroya 34 A 3
Laos 73 HJ 4
Laouni 55 G 4
Lapa 36 G 4
La Palma 32 C 2
La Palma (Canary Islands) 54 B 3
La Paragua 33 F 2
La Paz (Argentina) 36 C 5
La Paz (Bolivia) 34 C 4
La Paz (Mexico) 24 B 3
La Paz, Bahia de 24 B 3
La Perouse Strait 71 M 2
La Pesca 25 E 3

La Piedad 24–25 D 3
La Pine 20 B 3
Lapland 42 H 2
La Plata 36 E 5–6
Lappajärvi 42 H 3
Lappi 42 J 2
Laptev Sea 84
Lapua 42 H 3
La Quemada 24 D 3
La Rioja (Argentina) 36 C 4
La Rioja (Spain) 44 C 3
Lárisa 46 B 3
Larkana 67 H 5
Larlomkriny 51 O 4
Larnaca 48 A 2
Larne 40 B 4
Larned 21 G 4
La Rochelle 44 C 2
La Roche-sur-Yon 44 C 2
La Romana 29 F 3
La Ronge 15 H 3
Larrey Point 78 B 2
Larsen Ice Shelf 85
La Salina 20 D 5
La Salle 22 C 2
Läs 'Ánôd 61 H 3
La Sarre 18 E 4
Las Bonitas 29 F 5
Las Cejas 36 D 4
Las Cruces 20–21 E 5
La Serena (Chile) 36 B 4
La Serena (Spain) 44 B 4
La Seyne-sur-Mer 45 E 3
Las Flores 37 E 6
Läsh-e Joveyn 67 G 4
Lashio 73 G 3
Lashkar Gâh 67 GH 4
Las Lajas 37 BC 6
Las Mestenas 24 D 2
Las Palmas 54 BC 3
Las Palomas 24 E 5
La Spezia 45 EF 3
Las Plumas 37 C 7
Lassen Peak 20 B 3
Las Tablas 32 B 2
Last Mountain Lake 15 J 4
Las Vegas (N.M., U.S.A.) 21 F 4
Las Vegas (NV, U.S.A.) 20 C 4
Latady Island 85
Latakia 48 B 2
Lätäseno 42 H 2

Latgales Augstiene 43 J 4
La Tortuga, Isla 29 F 4
La Tuque 18 F 4
Latviya 43 J 4
Laughlin Peak 21 F 4
Lau Group 82 D 4
Lauhanvuori 42 H 3
Launceston 82 A 5
La Unión 37 B 7
La Union (El Salvador) 28 B 4
La Union (Mexico) 24 D 4
La Urbana 29 F 5
Laurel (MS, U.S.A.) 22 C 4
Laurel (MT, U.S.A.) 20 E 2
Laurentian Scarp 18 E 4
Lauria 45 G 3
Laurie River 15 J 3
Lausanne 45 E 2
Laut, Pulau 74 E 4
Laut Arafura 75 HJ 5
Laut Bali 74 E 5
Laut Banda 75 GH 5
Laut Flores 75 E 5
Laut Halmahera 75 G 4
Laut Jawa 74 CD 4
Laut Seram 75 G 4
Laut Sulawesi 75 EF 3
Laut Timor 75 GH 5
Laval (France) 44 C 2
Laval (Quebec, Can.) 18 F 4
Lävän 49 F 4
La Vega 29 E 3
La Venta 25 F 4
La Ventana 25 D 3
La Ventura 25 D 3
Lavka Integralsoyuza 69 VW 2
Lavrentiya 12 C 2
Lawra 58 D 3
Lawrence 21 G 4
Lawrenceburg 22 C 3
Lawton 21 G 5
Laydennyy, Mys 50 J 2
Layton 20 D 3
La Zarca 24 D 2
Lazarev 69 Q 5
Läzeh 49 F 4
Leadville 21 E 4
Leavenworth 21 GH 4
Lebanon 56 EF 2
Lebanon (Lebanon) 48 B 2
Lebanon (MO, U.S.A.) 21 H 4
Lebanon (PA, U.S.A.) 22 E 2
Lebedin 50 F 5
Lebu 37 B 6
Lebyazh'ye 51 P 5
Lecce 45 G 3
Lechang 70 F 5
Le Creusot 45 D 2
Leduc 14 G 4
Leeds 40 C 4
Leeuwarden 40 DE 4
Leeward Islands (French Polynesia) 83 E 4

Leeward Islands (West Indies) 29 G 3
Leganés 44 C 3
Legaspi 75 F 1
Legnago 45 F 2
Legnano 45 E 2
Legnica 41 G 4
Legune 78 D 2
Le Havre 44 CD 2
Lehi 20 D 3
Leicester 40 C 4
Leichardt River 79 F 2
Leiden 40 DE 4
Leipzig 41 F 4
Leiyang 70 F 5
Leka 42 F 2
Lëkana 59 G 6
Leksozero, Ozero 42 K 3
Le Lamentin 29 G 4
Leleque 37 B 7
Le Maire, Estrecho de 37 CD 9–10
Léman, Lac 45 E 2
Le Mans 44 D 2
Le Mars 21 G 3
Lemieux Islands 17 O 4
Lemmenjoki 42 J 2
Lemmon 21 F 2
Lemmon, Mount 20 D 5
Lemoro 75 F 4
Le Moyne, Lac 19 G 2
Lempa, Rio 28 B 4
Lena 68 J 4
Lendery 50 F 3
Leninabad 67 HJ 2–3
Leninakan 47 F 2
Leningrad 43 K 4
Leningradskaya 85
Leninogorsk 50 K 5
Leninogorsk 51 Q 5
Leninsk-Kuznetskiy 51 QR 5
Len'ki 51 Q 5
Lenkoran' 66 D 3
Lensk 68 K 3
Leon (Mexico) 25 D 3
León (Nicaragua) 28 B 4
León (Spain) 44 B 3
Leonardville 62 B 4
León Nuevo (Mexico) 25 E 2
Leonora 78 C 4
Leopold and Astrid Coast 85
Leorla 70 A 2
Lepsy 51 P 6
Le Puy 44 D 2
Lerfroy, Lake 78 C 5
Lérida (Colombia) 32 D 3
Lérida (Spain) 44 D 3
Leronotski 69 V 4
Léros 46 C 3
Lerum 43 F 4
Lerwick 40 C 2
Les Cayes 29 E 3
Les Escoumins 19 G 4
Leskovac 46 B 2

Les Landes 44 C 3
Lesnaya 69 U 4
Lesosibirsk 68 F 4
Lesotho 62 D 5
Lesozavodsk 71 KL 1
L'Esperance Rock 82 D 5
Lesser Antilles 29 G 3–4
Lesser Slave Lake 14 FG 3
Lestijoki 42 H 3
Lésvos 46 C 3
Leszno 41 G 4
Lethbridge 14 G 5
Lethem 33 G 3
Leti, Kepulauan 75 G 5
Leticia 32 D 4
Letsok-aw Kyun 73 G 5
Leuser, Gunung 74 A 3
Levante, Riviera di 45 E 3
Levis 19 F 4
Levkás 46 B 3
Lewis 40 B 3
Lewiston (ID, U.S.A.) 20 C 2
Lewiston (ME, U.S.A.) 23 G 3
Lewistown (MI, U.S.A.) 22 D 2
Lewistown (MT, U.S.A.) 20 E 2
Lewistown (PA, U.S.A.) 22 E 2
Lexington 22 DE 3
Lhari 70 B 4
Lhasa 73 F 2
Lhazhong 72 E 1
Liancheng 70 G 5
Lianjiang 70 EF 6
Lian Xian 70 F 6
Lianyin 69 M 5
Lianyungang 71 GH 4
Liao He 71 H 2
Liaoning 71 H 2
Liaoyuan 71 HJ 2
Liard 13 N 3
Liard River 14 D 3
Libby 20 C 2
Liberal 21 F 4
Liberia 58 BC 4
Liberia (Costa Rica) 28 B 4
Libya 55 HK 3
Libyan Desert 56 CD 3–4
Licata 45 F 4
Lichinga 63 F 2
Lida (U.S.S.R.) 43 J 5
Lidköping 43 F 4
Liechtenstein 45 EF 2
Liege 40 E 4
Lieksa 42 K 3
Lienart 60 D 4
Lienz 45 F 2
Liepäja 43 H 4
Lievestuoreenjärvi 42 J 3
Lievre 18 E 4
Lifou 81 J 6
Ligurian Sea 45 E 3
Lihir Group 82 B 3
Lihou Reef and Cays 79 J 2
Lijiang 70 D 5

Likasi 62 D 2
Likiep 82 C 2
Likouala 59 H 5
Lille 44 D 1
Lilloet 14 E 4
Lilongwe 63 E 2
Lima (MT, U.S.A.) 20 D 3
Lima (OH, U.S.A.) 22 D 2
Lima (Peru) 34 A 3
Lima (Portugal) 44 B 3
Limassol 47 D 4
Limay Mahuida 37 C 6
Limerick 40 B 4
Limfjorden 43 E 4
Limningen 42 F 3
Limnos 46 C 3
Limoeiro 35 JK 2
Limoges 44 D 2
Limon (CO, U.S.A.) 21 F 4
Limón (Costa Rica) 28 C 4
Limousin 44 D 2
Limpopo 63 E 4
Linakamen 42 K 2
Linares (Chile) 37 B 6
Linares (Mexico) 25 E 3
Linares (Spain) 44 C 4
Lincang 70 CD 6
Lincoln (IL, U.S.A.) 22 C 2
Lincoln (NE, U.S.A.) 21 G 3
Lincoln (U.K.) 40 C 4
Lincoln City 20 B 2
Lincoln Sea 84
Lindau 41 EF 5
Linden 33 G 2
Lindesnes 43 E 4
Lindi 61 F 6–7
Line Islands 83 E 2–3
Linfen 70 F 3
Lingayen 75 H 1
Lingga, Kepulauan 74 B 3–4
Lingomo 60 C 4
Lingyuan 71 G 2
Linhares 35 J 4
Linhe 70 E 2
Linhpa 73 G 2
Linjanti 62 C 3
Linköping 43 G 4
Linkou 71 JK 1
Linosa 45 F 4
Lins 35 G 5
Lintao 70 D 3
Linton 21 G 2
Linxi 71 G 2
Linxia 70 D 3
Linyi 71 G 3
Linz 45 F 2
Lipa 75 F 1
Lipari 45 F 4
Lipetsk 50 GH 5
Lipin Bor 50 G 3
Lisala 60 C 4
Lisboa 44 B 4
Lisbon (N.D., U.S.A.) 21 G 2
Lisbon (Portugal) 44 B 4

Lisburn 40 B 4
Lisburne, Cape 12 D 2
Lishui 71 GH 5
Lisichansk 50 G 6
Lisieux 44 D 2
Lithinon, Ákra 46 B 4
Lithuania 43 H 4
Litke 69 Q 5
Litovko 69 P 6
Little Abaco Island 27 F 3
Little Andaman 73 F 5
Little Cayman 28 C 3
Little Colorado River 20 D 4
Little Desert National Park 79 G 6
Little Falls 21 H 2
Littlefield 21 F 5
Little Grand Rapids 15 KL 4
Little Inagua Island 29 E 2
Little Missouri River 21 F 2
Little Nicobar 73 FG 6
Little Rock 21 H 5
Little Sitkin 12 A 6
Little Smoky River 14 F 4
Little Tanaga 12 BC 6
Littleton 21 E 4
Litva 43 H 4
Liuzhou 70 EF 6
Livengood 12 H 2
Liverpool 40 C 4
Liverpool (Nova Scotia, Can.) 23 H 2
Liverpool Bay 13 LM 1–2
Livingston (MT, U.S.A.) 20 D 2
Livingston (Newfoundl., Can.) 19 G 3
Livingstone 62 D 3
Livingstone Falls 59 G 7
Livoniya 43 J 4
Livorno 45 EF 3
Liwale 61 F 6
Liwonde 63 F 2–3
Li Xian (Hunan China) 70 F 5
Li Xian (Sichuan China) 70 D 4
Lizard 40 BC 5
Lizarda 33 J 5
Ljubeli 45 F 2
Ljungby 43 F 4
Ljusnan 42 F 3
Llallagua 34 C 4
Llano Estacado 21 F 5
Llano River 25 G 5
Llanos 32 DE 2–3
Llanos de Moxos 34 CD 4
Llanos de Tabasco y Campeche 25 F 4
Llanos de Tamaulipas 25 E 2
Llullaillaco, Volcán 34 C 5
Lobito 62 A 2
Locarno 45 E 2
Loch Lomond 40 C 3
Loch Ness 40 C 3

Lockhart River Mission 79 G 1
Lod 48 B 3
Lodja 60 C 5
Lodwar 60 F 4
Łodz 41 G 4
Lofoten 42 F 2
Logan 20 D 3
Logan, Mount 13 J 3
Logan Mountains 13 M 3
Logansport 22 C 2
Logroño 44 C 3
Lohjanjärvi 43 H 3
Lohjanselkä 43 H 3
Loholoho 75 F 4
Loire, Val de 44 D 2
Loja 32 C 4
Lokan tekojärvi 42 J 2
Lokilalaki, Gunung 75 F 4
Lökken 42 E 3
Lokshak 69 O 5
Loks Land 17 O 4
Lolland 43 F 5
Loma Bonita 25 E 4
Lomami 60 C 4–5
Loma Mountains 58 B 4
Lomas 34 B 4
Lomas de Zamora 36 DE 6
Lomblen, Pulau 75 F 5
Lombok 74 E 5
Lomé 58 E 4
Lomonosov 43 J 4
Lompoc 20 B 5
Łomz'a 41 H 4
Loncoche 37 B 6
London 22 D 2
London (U.K.) 40 CD 4
Londonderry (Chile)
    37 B 10
Londonderry (U.K.) 40 B 3
Londonderry, Cape 78 D 1
Londrina 35 F 5
Lone Pine 20 C 4
Long Bay 22 E 4
Long Beach (CA, U.S.A.)
    20 C 5
Long Beach (N.Y., U.S.A.)
    23 F 2
Long Beach (WA, U.S.A.)
    20 B 2
Long Island (Papua New
    Guinea) 80 E 2–3
Long Island (Quebec, Can.)
    18 E 3
Long Island (The Bahamas)
    27 F 4
Longjiang 69 M 6
Longlac 18 C 4
Long Lake 18 C 4
Longmont 21 F 3
Long Range Mountaines
    19 J 3–4
Longreach 79 G 3
Longs Peak 21 E 3–4
Long Valley 20 D 5

Longview (TX, U.S.A.)
    21 GH 5
Longview (WA, U.S.A.) 20 B 2
Longxi 70 D 3
Long Xian 70 E 4
Long Xuyen 73 J 5
Longyan 70 G 5
Longzhou 70 E 6
Lookout, Cape 22 E 4
Lookout Ridge 12 F 2
Lopatka 69 T 5
Lop Buri 73 H 5
Lopcha 69 M 4
Lop Nur 70 B 2
Lopphavet 42 H 1
Lopydino 50 K 3
Lorca 44 C 4
Lord Howe Island 79 K 5
Lord Mayor Bay 16 HJ 3
Lordsburg 20 E 5
Lorestan 49 E 2
Loreto 24 B 2
Loreto (Colombia) 32 D 4
Loreto (Maranhão, Brazil)
    33 JK 5
Loreto (Mexico) 24 D 3
Lorica 28 D 5
Lorient 44 C 2
Lorraine 45 E 2
Los Alamos 20 E 4
Los Angeles 20 BC 5
Los Ángeles (Chile) 37 B 6
Losap 82 B 2
Los Blancos 34 D 5
Los Gatos 20 B 4
Lošinj 45 F 3
Los Lagos 37 B 6
Los Lavaderos 25 E 3
Los Mochis 24 C 2
Los Palacios 27 E 4
Lospalos 75 G 5
Los Reyes de Salgado 24 D 4
Los Roques, Islas 29 F 4
Los Teques 29 F 4
Los Teques 32 E 1
Lost Trail Pass 20 D 2
Los Vilos 36 B 5
Lot 44 D 3
Lota 37 B 6
Lotta 42 J 2
Loubomo 59 G 6
Louga 58 A 2
Louisa 22 D 3
Louisiade Archipelago 79 J 1
Louisiana 25 H 5
Louis Trichardt 62 D 4
Louisville 22 C 3
Loukhi 50 F 2
Loum 59 FG 5
Loup River 21 G 3
Loups Marins, Lacs des
    18 F 2
Lövånger 42 H 3
Lovech 46 B 2

Loveland 21 E 3
Lovell 20 E 3
Lovelock 20 C 3
Loviisa 43 J 3
Lovington 21 F 5
Lovozero 42 L 2
Low, Cape 15 MN 2
Lowa 60 D 5
Lowell 23 F 2
Lower California 24 B 2
Lower Post 13 M 4
Lower Red Lake 21 H 2
Lowestoft 40 D 4
Loyalty Islands 81 J 6
Loyalty Islands 82 C 4
Loyoro 60 E 4
Luacano 62 C 2
Lualaba 60 D 5
Luanda 62 A 1
Luando (Angola) 62 B 2
Luando (Angola) 62 B 2
Luando Reserve 62 B 2
Luang Prabang 73 H 4
Luangwa 63 E 2
Luangwa Valley Game
    Reserve 63 E 2
Luanshya 62 D 2
Luapala 62 D 2
Luba 59 F 5
Lubalo 62 B 1
Lubang Islands 75 EF 1
Lubango 62 A 2
Lubao 60 D 6
Lubbock 21 F 5
Lübeck 41 F 4
Lubefu 60 CD 5
Lublin 41 H 4
Lubnān, Jabal 48 B 2
Lubny 50 F 6
Lubumbashi 62 D 2
Lucania, Mount 13 J 3
Lucas 34 E 3
Lucea 28 D 3
Lucena 44 C 4
Lučenec 41 G 5
Lucera 45 G 3
Lucero 24 E 5
Lüchun 70 D 6
Lucknow 72 D 2
Lucusse 62 C 2
Lüda 71 H 3
Ludhiana 72 BC 1
Ludington 22 C 2
Ludogorie 46 C 2
Ludvika 43 G 3
Ludwigshafen 41 E 5
Luebo 60 C 6
Lüeyang 70 E 4
Lufeng 70 G 6
Luga 43 J 4
Lugano 45 E 2
Luganville 82 C 4
Lugenda 63 F 2
Lugnvik 42 G 3

Lugo 44 B 3
Lugoj 46 B 1
Lugovoy 67 J 2
Luhuo 70 D 4
Luiana 62 C 3
Luimneach 40 B 4
Luís Correia 35 H 1
Luiza 60 C 6
Lukashin Yar 51 PQ 3
Lukeville 20 D 5
Lukolela 60 B 5
Luleå 42 H 2
Luleälven 42 H 2
Lüleburgaz 46 C 2
Lumbala Kaquengue 62 C 2
Lumbala N'guimbo 62 C 2
Lumberton 22 E 4
Lumding 73 F 2
Lumsden 80 P 10
Lunda Norte 62 BC 1
Lunda Sul 62 C 2
Lundazi 63 E 2
Lüneburg 41 EF 4
Lunkho 67 J 3
Luochuan 70 E 3
Luofu 60 D 5
Luoisiade 82 B 3
Luoyang 70 F 4
Luoyuan 71 GH 5
Lupane 62 D 3
Lupeni 46 B 1
Luperón 29 E 3
Luputa 60 C 6
Lüq 61 G 4
Lusaka 62 D 3
Lusambo 60 C 5
Lushui 70 C 5
Lusk 21 F 3
Lüt, Dasht-e 49 G 2
Luton 40 C 4
Lutsk 43 J 5
Luxembourg 40 DE 5
Luxi (Junnan China) 70 C 6
Luxi (Junnan China) 70 D 6
Luxor 48 A 4
Luza 50 J 3
Luza 50 J 3
Luzern 45 E 2
Luzhai 70 E 6
Luzhou 70 E 5
Luzhskaya Vozvyshennost'
    43 HJ 4
L'vovka 51 P 4
Lyakhovskiye Ostrova 69 P 1
Lynchburg 22 E 3
Lynd 79 G 2
Lynn Canal 13 K 4
Lynn Lake 15 J 3
Lynx Lake 15 H 2
Lyon 45 E 2
Lyon Inlet 16 K 3
Łyso Gory 41 H 4
Lytton 14 E 4
Lyubertsy 50 G 4

M

Ma'ān 48 B 3
Maarianhamina (Mariehamn) 43 H 3–4
Ma'arrat an Nu'mān 47 E 3–4
Maastricht 40 E 4
Mabaruma 33 G 2
Mabote 63 E 4
Ma'būs Yūsuf 55 K 3
Macadam Plains 78 B 4
Macaíba 35 J 2
MacAlpine Lake 16 G 3
Macao 70 F 6
Macapá 33 H 3
Macará (Peru) 32 C 4
Macas 32 C 4
Macau 35 J 2
Macauley 82 D 4–5
Macaya, Pic de 29 E 3
Macdonnell Ranges 78 E 3
Maceió 35 JK 2
Macerata 45 F 3
Machala 32 C 4
Machevna 69 W 3
Machilipatnam 72 D 4
Machiques 29 E 4
Machupicchu 34 B 3
Macia 63 E 5
Mackay, Lake 78 D 3
Mackenzie 13 LM 2
Mackenzie 13 N 3
Mackenzie Bay 13 K 2
Mac Kenzie Bay 85
Mackenzie King Island 84
Mackenzie Mountains 13 LM 2–3
Mackenzie River 79 H 3
Mackinaw City 22 D 2
Macmillan 13 L 3
Macmillan Pass 13 L 3
Macocola 62 B 1
Macomia 63 FG 2
Mâcon (France) 45 DE 2
Macon (GA, U.S.A.) 22 D 4
Macon (MS, U.S.A.) 22 C 4
Macquarie Island 85
Mac Robertson Land 85
Madagascar 63 H 3
Madā'in Şālih 66 B 5
Madang 80 E 3
Madaoua 59 F 3
Mac'awaska Highlands 18 E 4
Madd, Ra's Abū 48 B 4
Madeira (Brazil) 33 F 4–5
Madeira (Portugal) 54 B 2
Madeleine, Île de la 19 H 4
Madeniyet 51 P 6
Madera 20 B 4
Madetkoski 42 J 2
Madhya Pradesh 72 CD 3
Madimba 60 B 5
Madingo-Kayes 59 G 6
Madison (IN, U.S.A.) 22 C 3
Madison (MN, U.S.A.) 21 G 2

Madison (WI, U.S.A.) 22 C 2
Madison River 20 D 2
Madisonville (KY, U.S.A.) 22 C 3
Madisonville (TX, U.S.A.) 25 G 5
Madiun 74 D 5
Madoi 70 C 4
Madrakah 66 BC 6
Madrakah, Ra's al 57 K 5
Madras 72 D 5
Madras (OR, U.S.A.) 20 B 3
Madre, Sierra 25 F 4
Madre de Dios 34 C 3
Madre del Sur, Sierra 24 D 4
Madre Oriental, Sierra 25 DE 2–3
Madrid 44 C 3
Madrona, Sierra 44 C 4
Madura, Pulau 74 D 5
Madurai 72 C 6
Madyan 48 B 4
Maebashi 71 L 3
Maevatanana 63 H 3
Maéwo 81 J 5
Mafeteng 62 D 5
Mafia Island 61 G 6
Magadan 69 S 4
Magallanes, Estrecho de 37 B 9
Magangue 32 D 2
Magaria 59 F 3
Magdagachi 69 N 5
Magdalena 32 D 1–2
Magdalena (Mexico) 24 D 5
Magdalena, Bahia 24 B 3
Magdalena, Isla (Mexico) 24 B 3
Magdeburg 41 F 4
Magellan, Strait of 37 BC 9
Magerøya 42 J 1
Maggiore, Lago 45 E 2
Magnitogorsk 51 L 5
Magnolia 21 H 5
Magpie 19 H 3
Magyarország 46 A 1
Mahābād 49 D 1
Mahābād 66 D 3
Mahabharat Range 72 E 2
Mahabo 63 GH 4
Mahadday Wèyne 61 H 4
Mahajan 72 B 2
Mahajanga 63 H 3
Mahalapye 62 D 4
Mahanoro 63 H 3
Maharashtra 72 BC 4
Maha Sarakham 73 H 4
Mahatsanary 63 G 5
Mahbés 54 CD 3
Mahbubnagar 72 C 4
Mahd adh Dhahab 66 C 6
Mahḍah 49 G 4
Mahdia 33 G 2
Mahenge 61 F 6

Mahesana 72 B 3
Mahia Peninsula 81 R 8
Mahkene 42 F 3
Mahmūdābād 49 F 1
Mahmud-Raqi 67 H 4
Mahnomen 21 G 2
Mahón 44 D 4
Mahuva 72 B 3
Maiana 82 C 2
Maicao 29 E 4
Maiduguri 59 G 3
Maimana 67 GH 3
Main Channel 22 D 2
Mai-Ndombe, Lac 60 B 5
Maine 23 G 2
Mainland (Orkney Is., U.K.) 40 C 1
Mainland (Shetland Is., U.K.) 40 C 2
Maintirano 63 G 3
Mainz 41 E 5
Maio 58 B 6
Maipú 37 E 6
Maipuco 32 D 4
Maisi, Punta 29 E 2
Maitengwe 62 D 4
Maitland 79 J 5
Maíz, Isla del 28 C 4
Majagual 29 E 5
Majuro 82 C 2
Makale 61 FG 2
Makambako 60 EF 6
Makarikari 62 CD 4
Makarikha 51 LM 2
Makarov 82 Q 6
Makat 66 E 1
Makaw 70 C 5
Makedhonía 46 B 2
Makedonia 46 B 2
Makeyevka 47 E 1
Makgadikgadi Pan 62 CD 4
Makhachkala 66 D 2
Makinsk 51 O 5
Makkah 57 G 4
Makkovik 19 J 2
Makó 46 B 1
Makokou 59 G 5
Makran 66–67 G 5
Makri 72 D 4
Maksimovka 71 L 1
Mäkü 47 F 3
Makurdi 59 F 4
Makushino 51 N 4
Makushin Volcano 12 D 5
Makuyuni 61 F 5
Makwa 82 BC 3
Malabar Coast 72 BC 5–6
Malabo 59 F 5
Malacca, Strait of 74 B 3
Malad City 20 D 3
Málaga 44 C 4
Malagasy Republic 63 H 3
Malaimbandy 63 H 4
Malaita 81 H 3

Malakāl 60 E 3
Malakula 81 J 5
Malang 74 D 5
Malanje 62 B 1
Malao 81 J 5
Mälaren 43 G 4
Malargue 37 C 6
Malaspina 37 C 7
Malaspina Glacier 13 J 4
Malatya 47 E 3
Malatya Dağları 47 E 3
Malāwi 49 E 2
Malawi 63 E 2
Malawi, Lake 63 EF 2
Malawi National Park 63 E 2
Malaybalay 75 FG 2
Malåyer 49 E 2
Malaysia 74 BD 2
Malden 83 E 3
Maldives 72 B 6
Maldonado 36 F 5
Malegaon 72 BC 3
Malei 63 F 3
Malek 60 E 3
Malekula 82 C 4
Maleyevo 68 G 4
Malhada 35 H 3
Malheur Lake 20 C 3
Mali 58 CD 2–3
Mali Kyun 73 G 5
Malindi 61 G 5
Maling, Gunung 75 F 3
Malin Head 40 B 3
Mallaig 40 B 3
Mallani 72 B 2
Mallery Lake 15 K 2
Mallorca 44 D 4
Malmö 43 F 4
Maloelap 82 C 2
Malozemel'skaya Tundra 50 JK 2
Malpelo, Isla 32 B 3
Malta 45 F 4
Malta (MT, U.S.A.) 20 E 2
Maluku 75 G 4
Maluku, Laut 75 G 3
Malung 43 F 3
Maly Kavkaz 47 FG 2
Malyy Lyakhovskiy, Ostrov 69 Q 1
Malyy Yenisey 68 FG 5
Mama 68 K 4
Mamagota 81 FG 3
Mambasa 60 D 4
Mambéré 60 B 3–4
Mammamattawe 18 D 3
Mamoré 34 C 3
Mamou 58 B 3
Mamuju 75 E 4
Mamuno 62 C 4
Man 58 C 4
Manacapuru 33 F 4
Manado 75 F 3
Managua 28 B 4

Managua, Lago de **28** B 4
Manaka **81** Q 9
Manakara **63** H 4
Manama **49** F 4
Mananara **63** H 3
Manapouri **82** C 6
Manas **67** M 2
Manaus **33** FG 4
Manchester **40** C 4
Manchuria **71** HJ 2
Máncora **32** B 4
Mand **49** F 3
Mandalay **73** G 3
Mandal-Ovoo **70** D 2
Mandan **21** F 2
Mandasor **72** B 3
Mandera **61** G 4
Mandeville **28** D 3
Mandiana **58** C 3
Mandimba **63** F 2
Mandinga **28** D 5
Mandji **59** G 6
Mandla **72** CD 3
Mandor **74** C 3
Mandvi **72** A 3
Manfredonia **45** G 3
Manga (Minas Gerais, Brazil)
    35 H 3
Manga (Niger/Chad) **59** GH 3
Mangaia **83** E 4
Mangalore **72** B 5
Mangnai **70** B 3
Mangoky **63** G 4
Mangole, Pulau **75** G 4
Mangueira, Lagoa **36** F 5
Mangut **68** K 6
Manhan **68** F 6
Manhattan **21** G 4
Manicaland **63** E 3
Manicore **33** F 5
Manicouagan **19** G 3
Manicouagan, Réservoir
    19 G 3
Maniganggo **70** CD 4
Manihi **83** F 3
Manipur **73** F 3
Manisa **46** C 3
Manistique **22** C 1
Manitoba **15** K 4
Manitoba, Lake **15** K 4
Manitoulin Island **18** D 4
Manitou Springs **21** F 4
Manitowoc **22** C 2
Maniwaki **18** E 4
Manizales **32** C 2
Manjil **49** E 1
Mankato **21** H 3
Manlay **70** E 2
Manley Hot Springs **12** G 2
Manmad **72** BC 3
Mannheim **41** E 4–5
Manning **14** F 3
Manoa **32** E 5
Manono **60** D 6

Manouane **18** F 4
Manouane, Lac **19** F 3
Manra **82** D 3
Manresa **44** D 3
Mansa **62** D 2
Mansel Island **17** K 4
Mansfield (OH, U.S.A.) **22** D 2
Manta **32** B 4
Mantecal **32** E 2
Manteo **22** E 3
Mantova **45** F 2
Manú **34** B 3
Manuae **83** E 4
Manuangi **83** F 4
Manuel Benavides **24** D 2
Manuel Urbano **32** DE 5
Manukau **82** C 5
Manus **80** E 2
Manychskaya Vpadina **47** F 1
Manyoni **60** E 6
Manzanillo (Cuba) **27** F 4
Manzanillo (Mexico) **24** D 4
Manzhouli **68** L 6
Manzil Bū Ruqaybah **55** G 1
Manzurka **68** J 5
Mao **29** E 3
Maoke, Pegunungan **75** J 4
Maoming **70** F 6
Mapaga **75** EF 4
Mapai **63** E 4
Mapi **75** J 5
Mapire **29** G 5
Maple Creek **14** H 5
Mapuera **33** G 4
Maputo **63** E 5
Maquela do Zombo **62** B 1
Maquinchao **37** C 7
Maraá **32** E 4
Marabá **33** HJ 5
Maracá, Ilha de **33** HJ 3
Maracaibo **32** D 1
Maracaibo, Lago de **32** D 1–2
Maracaju **35** F 5
Maracay **32** E 1
Marádah **55** J 3
Maradi **59** F 3
Marágheh **66** D 3
Marahuaca, Cerro **32** E 3
Marajó, Ilha de **33** HJ 4
Maramba **62** D 3
Maránd **66** D 3
Maranhão **35** GH 2
Marañón **32** C 4
Marão, Serra do **44** B 3
Marathon (Ontario, Can.)
    18 C 4
Marathon (TX, U.S.A.) **24** F 5
Marawi **56** E 5
Marbella **44** C 4
Marble Canyon **20** D 4
Marcala **28** B 4
March **45** G 2
Marche **45** F 3
Marche, Plateaux de la **44** D 2

Mar Chiquita, Laguna **36** D 5
Marcus Baker, Mount **12** H 3
Mar del Plata **37** E 6
Mardin **47** F 3
Mardin Eşigi **47** F 3
Maré **81** J 6
Marēg **61** H 4
Marfa **24** F 5
Marganets **47** D 1
Margaret River **78** A 5
Margaritovo **71** KL 2
Margie **14** G 3
Margilan **67** J 2
Margyang **72** E 1–2
Mari (Burma) **73** G 2
Mari (Papua New Guinea)
    80 D 3
Maria (Tuamotu Is.) **83** F 4
Maria (Tubai Is.) **83** E 4
Mariana Islands **82** A 1
Marianao **27** E 4
Marias River **20** D 2
Maria Theresa **83** E 5
Mariato, Punta **32** B 2
Maria van Diemen, Cape
    81 D 7
Maribor **45** FG 2
Maricourt **17** M 4
Marie Byrd Land **85**
Marie-Galante **29** G 3
Mariental **62** B 4
Mariestad **43** F 4
Marietta **22** D 4
Mariinsk **51** R 4
Mariinskoye **69** Q 5
Marília **35** G 5
Marinette **22** C 1
Maringa **35** F 5
Mariny, Iméni **69** R 3
Marion (IA, U.S.A.) **21** H 3
Marion (IL, U.S.A.) **22** C 3
Marion (IN, U.S.A.) **22** C 2
Marion (OH, U.S.A.) **22** D 2
Marion, Lake **22** D 4
Marion Reef **79** J 2
Maripa **29** FG 5
Mariu **80** D 3
Mariyyah **49** F 5
Märjamaa **43** HJ 4
Marka **61** GH 4
Markha **68** M 3
Markham Bay **17** M 4
Marko **42** G 2
Markovo **51** R 3
Marlin **25** G 5
Marmara **46** C 2
Marmara, Sea of **46** C 2
Marmara Denizi **46** C 2
Marmaris **46** C 3
Marne **44** D 2
Maroa **32** E 3
Maroni **33** H 3
Maroua **59** GH 3
Marovoay **63** H 3

Marowijne **33** H 3
Marquadah **47** F 3
Marquesas Islands **83** F 3
Marquette **22** C 1
Marrakech **54** D 2
Marree **79** F 4
Marrero **25** F 2
Marrupa **63** F 2
Marsa al' Alam **48** B 4
Marsabit National Reserve
    61 F 4
Marsala **45** F 4
Marsa 'Umm Ghayj **48** B 4
Marseille **45** E 3
Marsfjllet **42** G 2
Marshall (AK, U.S.A.) **12** E 3
Marshall (MN, U.S.A.) **21** G 3
Marshall (TX, U.S.A.) **21** H 5
Marshall Islands **82** BC 2
Marshalltown **21** H 3
Marshfield **22** C 2
Marsh Harbour **27** F 3
Marsh Island **25** F 2
Marta **45** F 3
Martaban, Gulf of **73** G 4
Martigues **45** DE 3
Martin (U.S.A.) **21** F 3
Martínez de la Torre **25** E 3
Martinique **29** G 4
Martinique Passage **29** G 4
Martinsburg **22** E 3
Martinsville **22** DE 3
Martin Vaz Islands **31** H 5
Martre, Lac la **14** F 2
Marutea **83** F 4
Mary **67** G 3
Maryborough **79** J 4
Maryland **22** E 3
Marystown **19** K 4
Marysville (CA, U.S.A.) **20** B 4
Marysville (KS, U.S.A.) **21** G 4
Maryville **21** H 3
Masāhīm, Kūh-e **49** G 3
Masai Steppe **61** F 5
Masaka **60** E 5
Masākin **55** H 1
Masan **71** J 3
Masasi **63** F 2
Masaya **28** B 4
Masbate **75** F 1
Mascarene Islands **63** K 6
Mascota **24** D 3
Maseru **62** D 5
Mashhad **66** FG 3
Mashiz **49** G 3
Mashonaland **63** E 3
Masindi **60** E 4
Maşīrah **57** K 4
Masjed Soleymān **49** E 3
Maskanah **48** B 2
Masoala, Cap **63** J 3
Masohi **75** G 4
Mason City **21** H 3
Masqat **57** K 4

Mas – Men

Massachusetts **23** F 2
Massafra **45** G 3
Massangena **63** E 4
Massau **81** EF 2
Massava **51** M 3
Massawa **61** FG 1
Massena **23** F 2
Masset **13** L 5
Massif Central **44** D 2–3
Massif du Pelvoux **45** E 2
Massif du Tsaratanana **63** H 2
Massinga **63** F 4
Masteksay **66** E 1
Mastuj **67** J 3
Mastung **67** H 5
Mastūrah **66** B 6
Masvingo **63** E 4
Maşyāf **48** B 2
Matabeleland **62** D 3–4
Matachewan **18** D 4
Matachic **24** C 2
Matadi **60** A 6
Matador **21** F 5
Matagalpa **28** B 4
Matagalpa, Rio Grande de **28** C 4
Matagami **18** E 4
Matagorda Island **25** E 2
Mataiva **83** F 3
Matamı **58** B 2
Matamoros **24** D 2
Matamoros **25** E 2
Matancita **24** B 2
Matane **19** G 4
Matanzas **27** E 4
Matara **72** CD 6
Matarani **34** B 4
Mataranka **78** E 1
Matatiele **62** D 6
Matatila Dam **72** C 2
Mata-Utu **82** D 3
Matay **51** P 6
Matehuala **25** D 3
Matera **45** G 3
Matheson **18** D 4
Mathura **72** C 2
Matla **72** E 3
Mato Grosso **34–35** EF 3
Mato Grosso (Mato Grosso, Brazil) **34** E 3
Matozinhos **44** B 3
Mátra **46** A 1
Matrüh **56** D 2
Matsudo **71** M 3
Matsue **71** K 3
Matsuyama **71** K 4
Matterhorn (Switzerland) **45** E 2
Matterhorn(U.S.A.) **20** C 3
Matthew **82** C 4
Matthew Town **29** E 2
Mattoon **22** C 3
Matu **74** D 3
Matua, Ostrov **69** S 6

Maturín **33** F 2
Matyushkinskaya **51** PQ 4
Maubeuge **44** D 1
Maués **33** G 4
Maui **83** E 1
Mauke **83** E 4
Maun **62** C 4
Mauna Kea **83** E 1
Maunoir, Lac **13** MN 2
Maupihaa **83** E 4
Maupin **20** B 2
Mauralasan **74** E 3
Maurice, Lake **78** E 4
Mauritania **54** BD 5
Mauritius **63** K 5
Mavasjaure **42** G 2
Mawson **85**
Mawson Coast **85**
Maxcanu **25** FG 3
Mayaguana Island **29** E 2
Mayaguana Passage **29** E 2
Mayagüez **29** F 3
Mayámey **49** G 1
Maya Mountains **28** B 3
Mayapán **26** D 4
Mayd **61** H 2
Maydān **49** D 2
Maykop **47** F 2
Maymakan **69** P 4
Mayna **68** F 5
Maynas **32** C 4
Mayo **13** K 3
Mayo, Mountains of **40** B 4
Mayor-Krest **69** Q 2
Mayotte **63** H 2
May Pen **28** D 3
Maysk **51** P 4
Maysville **22** E 4
Mayumba **59** FG 6
Mayya **69** O 3
Mazabuka **62** D 3
Mazar **67** K 3
Mazar-i-Sharif **67** H 3
Mazatenango **25** F 5
Mazatlán **24** C 3
Mazomeno **60** D 5
Mazong Shan **70** C 2
Mazowsze **41** H 4
Mazury **41** H 4
Mbabane **63** E 5
Mbakaou Reservoir **59** G 4
Mbala **63** E 1
Mbale **60** E 4
Mbalmayo **59** G 5
Mbamba Bay **63** E 2
Mbandaka **60** B 4
Mbanga **59** FG 5
M'banza Congo **62** AB 1
Mbanza-Ngungu **60** B 6
Mbeya **60** E 6
Mbinda **59** G 6
Mbini **59** F 5
Mbokou **60** D 3
Mbour **58** A 3

Mbuji-Mayi **60** CD 6
McAlester **21** G 5
McAllen **25** E 2
McBeth Fjord **17** N 3
McCamey **24** F 5
McCammon **20** D 3
McCarthy **13** J 3
McComb **25** H 5
McCook **21** F 3
McDame **13** M 4
McDermitt **20** C 3
McGill **20** D 4
Mc Grath **12** F 3
McGregor **21** H 4
McKean **82** D 3
McKeand **17** N 4
McKeesport **22** E 2
McKenzie Island **15** L 4
McKinley, Mount **12** G 3
McKinley Park **12** H 3
McKinney **21** G 5
Mc Leod, Lake **78** A 3
McLeod Bay **14** G 2
Mc Leod Lake **14** E 4
M'Clintock **15** L 3
M'Clintock Channel **16** F 22–3
McLoughlin, Mount **20** B 3
M'Clure Strait **16** C 2
Mc Murdo **85**
Mc Murdo Sound **85**
McPherson **21** G 4
McVicar Arm **13** O 2
Mead, Lake **20** D 4
Meade **12** F 1–2
Meade Peak **20** D 3
Meadow Lake **15** H 4
Mealy Mountains **19** J 3
Meander River **14** F 3
Meaux **44** D 2
Mecca **57** D 4
Mechigmenskiy Zaliv **12** C 2
Mecklenburg **41** F 4
Mecklenburger Bucht **41** F 4
Medan **74** A 3
Medanosa, Punta **37** CD 8
Medellín **32** CD 2
Medelpad **42** G 3
Medford **20** B 3
Medgidia **46** C 2
Mediaş **46** B 1
Medical Lake **20** C 2
Medicine Bow **20–21** E 3
Medicine Hat **14** G 4
Medicine Lodge **21** G 4
Medigan **51** R 5
Medina **48** C 4
Medina **57** G 4
Mediterranean Sea **44** CE 4
Mednogorsk **51** L 5
Medvezhiy Var **68** F 1
Meekatharra **78** B 4
Meeker **20** E 3
Meerut **72** C 2
Mega (Ethiopia) **61** F 4

Mega (Indonesia) **75** H 4
Megasani Hill **72** E 3
Meghalaya **73** F 2
Megra **50** H 2
Meguinenza, Embalse de **44** CD 3
Mehriz **49** G 3
Meiganga **59** G 4
Meissen **41** F 4
Mei Xian **70** G 6
Mejillones **34** BC 5
Mékambo **59** G 5
Meknès **54** D 2
Mekong **73** HJ 4–5
Mekong, Mouths of the **73** J 6
Mekongga, Gunung **75** F 4
Mekoryuk **12** D 3
Melaka **74** B 3
Melanesia **81** FJ 2–3
Melanesia **82** BC 3
Melbourne **79** G 6
Melbourne (FL, U.S.A.) **27** EF 3
Melchor Múzquiz **25** D 2
Melchor Ocampo **24** D 4
Melendiz Dağı **47** D 3
Meletsk **68** F 4
Meleuz **50** KL 5
Mélèzes, Rivière aux **18** F 2
Melfort **15** H 4
Melilla **54** E 1
Melimoyo, Monte **37** B 7
Melitopol' **47** E 1
Mellen **21** H 2
Melo **36** F 5
Melrose (U.S.A.) **20** D 2
Meltaus **42** H 2
Melun **44** D 2
Melville **15** J 4
Melville, Cape **79** G 1
Melville, Lake **19** J 3
Melville Bay **84**
Melville Hills **13** B 3
Melville Island **78** E 1
Melville Island **84**
Melville Peninsula **16** K 3
Melville Sound **16** E 3
Melyuveyem **69** W 3
Memmingen **41** EF 5
Memphis (Egypt) **56** E 3
Memphis (TN, U.S.A.) **22** C 3
Mena **50** F 5
Mena (AR, U.S.A.) **21** H 5
Ménaka **58** E 2
Mendocino, Cape **20** B 3
Mendoza (Argentina) **36** C 5
Mendoza (Peru) **32** C 5
Mene Grande **29** E 5
Mengcheng **71** G 4
Mengene Dağı **47** F 3
Menghai **70** CD 6
Mengzi **70** D 6
Menihek Lakes **19** G 3
Meningie **79** FG 6

Menkere **68** M 2
Menominee **22** C 1
Menongue **62** B 2
Menorca **44** D 3
Mentasta Lake **13** J 3
Mentawai, Kepulauan **74** A 4
Mentese **46** C 3
Menyuan **70** D 3
Menza **68** J 6
Menzies **78** C 4
Menzies, Mount **85**
Meoqui **24** C 2
Mepistskaro **47** F 2
Meppen **41** E 4
Meråker **42** F 3
Merano **45** F 2
Merced **20** B 4
Mercedes (Argentina) **36** E 4
Mercedes (Argentina) **36** C 5
Mercedes (Uruguay) **36** E 5
Merchants Bay **17** O 3
Mercy, Cape **17** O 4
Mercy Bay **16** C 2
Meredith, Cape **37** D 9
Merefa **50** G 6
Merenga **69** ST 3
Mergui **73** G 5
Mergui Archipelago **73** G 5
Meriç **46** C 2
Mérida (Mexico) **26** D 4
Mérida (Spain) **44** B 4
Mérida (Venezuela) **32** D 2
Meridian **22** C 4
Mérignac **44** C 2
Merikarvia **42** H 3
Merín, Laguna **36** F 5
Merredin **78** B 5
Merril **22** C 1
Merriman **21** F 3
Merritt **14** E 4
Merritt Island **27** EF 3
Merseburg **41** F 4
Mersin **47** D 3
Meru Game Reserve **61** F 4–5
Merzifon **47** E 2
Mesabi Range **21** H 2
Mesa de San Carlos **24** AB 2
Mescalero **21** E 5
Meseta Central **24** D 3
Meseta de Chiapas **25** F 4
Mesopotamia **48–49** D 2–3
Mesopotamia **57** GH 2
Mesquite **21** G 5
Messina **45** FG 4
Messiniakós Kolpós **46** B 3
Messo **51** P 2
Mesters Vig **84**
Meta **32** DE 2
Meta Incognita Peninsula
  17 N 4
Metairie **25** H 5–6
Metán **36** D 4
Metangula **63** EF 2
Metapan **28** B 4

Meteghan **23** G 2
Metemma **60** F 2
Metéora-monastery **46** B 3
Metlakatla **13** L 4
Metu **60** F 3
Metz **45** E 2
Meuse **45** E 2
Mexicali **20** CD 5
Mexican Hat **20** E 4
Mexico **25** E 3
Mexico (MO, U.S.A.) **21** H 4
Mexico, Gulf of **25** FG 2
México City **25** DE 4
Meymeh **49** F 2
Mezcalapa, Rio **25** F 4
Mezen' **50** H 2
Mezhdurechenskiy **51** N 4
Miami (AZ, U.S.A.) **20** D 5
Miami (FL, U.S.A.) **27** E 3
Miami (OK, U.S.A.) **21** H 4
Miami Beach **27** F 3
Miändowāb **49** D 1
Mianeh (Iran) **49** E 1
Mianyang **70** DE 4
Miarinarivo **63** H 3
Miazz **51** LM 5
Michelson, Mount **12** H 2
Michigan **22** CD 1–2
Michigan, Lake **22** C 2
Michigan City **22** C 2
Michipicoten Bay **18** C 4
Michipicoten Island **18** C 4
Michoacán **24** D 4
Michurinsk **50** G 5
Micronesia **82** BC 2
Middelburg **62** DE 5
Middle Alkali Lake **20** C 3
Middle Andaman **73** F 5
Middlesboro **22** D 3
Middletown **22** CD 3
Midi, Canal du **44** D 3
Midland (MI, U.S.A.) **22** D 2
Midland (Ontario, Can.) **22** E 2
Midland (TX, U.S.A.) **24** F 5
Midwest **21** E 3
Midžor **46** B 2
Miekojärvi **42** HJ 2
Mielec **41** H 4
Mieres **44** B 3
Migiurtinia **61** HJ 2
Mijdahah **57** H 6
Mikha Tskhakaya **47** F 2
Mikhaylovgrad **46** B 2
Mikhaylovka **50** H 5
Mikinai **46** B 3
Mikindani **63** FG 2
Mikino **69** U 3
Míkonos **46** C 3
Milagro **32** C 4
Milan **45** E 2
Milâs **46** C 3

Milazzo **45** FG 4
Milcan Tepe **47** E 3
Mildura **79** G 5
Mile **70** D 6
100 Mile House **14** E 4
Miles **79** HJ 4
Miles City **21** E 2
Milford **20** D 4
Milford Haven **40** B 4
Milgun **78** B 3–4
Mili **82** C 2
Milk River **20** E 2
Mill **17** L 4
Millau **44** D 3
Milledgeville **22** D 4
Mille Lacs Lake **21** H 2
Millevaches, Plateau de
  44 D 2
Millington **22** C 3
Mills Lake **14** F 2
Millwood Lake **21** H 5
Mílos **46** B 3
Milparinka **79** G 4
Milton (N.C., U.S.A.) **22** E 3
Milwaukee **22** C 2
Milwaukie **20** B 2
Mina **68** F 5
Minä' 'Abd Allāh **49** E 3
Minahassa Peninsula **75** F 3
Minas **36** F 5
Minas, Sierra de las **28** B 3
Minä' Sa'üd **49** E 3
Minas Gerais **35** GH 4
Minas Novas **35** H 4
Minatitlán **25** F 4
Minbya **73** F 3
Mincha **36** B 5
Mindanao **75** FG 2
Mindelo **58** B 6
Minden (LA, U.S.A.) **21** H 5
Mindoro **75** F 1
Mindoro Strait **75** EF 1
Mineiros **35** F 4
Mineral'nyye Vody **47** F 2
Mineral Wells **21** G 5
Minerva Reefs **82** D 4
Minfeng **67** L 3
Mingan **19** H 3
Mingary **79** G 5
Mingechaur **66** D 2
Mingo Lake **17** M 4
Mingshui **71** J 1
Mingteke **67** K 3
Minho **44** B 3
Ministro João Alberto **35** F 3
Minna **59** F 4
Minneapolis (KS, U.S.A.)
  21 G 4
Minneapolis (MN, U.S.A.)
  21 H 3
Minnedosa **15** K 4
Minnesota **21** GH 2
Minnesota River **21** G 2–3
Minot **21** F 2

Minqin **70** D 3
Minqing **71** G 5
Minsin **73** G 2
Minsk **43** J 5
Minto **13** K 3
Minto **82** B 2
Minto, Lac **18** F 2
Minto Inlet **16** C 2
Minusinsk **68** F 5
Min Xian **70** D 4
Miquelon **18** E 4
Miquelon **19** J 4
Miquelon et Saint Pierre
  19 J 4
Mirabad **67** G 4
Miramichi Bay **19** H 4
Miranda **34** E 5
Miranda de Ebro **44** C 3
Miravalles, Volcán **28** C 4
Miri **74** D 3
Miriam Vale **79** J 3
Mirim, Lagoa **36** F 5
Mirnyy **85**
Mirpur Khas **67** H 5
Mirtóon Pélagos **46** B 3
Mirzapur **72** D 2–3
Mish'āb, Ra's al **49** E 3
Mishan **71** K 1
Miskitos, Cayos **28** C 4
Miskolc **46** AB 1
Misool, Pulau **75** H 4
Mişr **56** DE 4
Mişrātah **55** H 2
Mişrātah, Ra's **55** J 2
Missinaibi **18** D 3
Missisa Lake **18** C 3
Mississippi **21** HJ 5
Mississippi Delta **25** F 2
Mississippi River **25** H 5
Missoula **20** D 2
Missouri **21** H 4
Missouri River **21** H 4
Mistassini, Lac **18** F 3
Misti, Volcán **34** B 4
Misty Fjords National Monu-
  ment **13** L 4
Mitchell **21** G 3
Mitchell, Mount **22** D 3
Mitchell River **79** G 2
Mitilíni **46** C 3
Mitla **25** E 4
Mitra **59** F 5
Mitú **32** D 3
Mitumba, Monts **60** D 5–6
Miyako **71** M 3
Miyakonojō **71** K 4
Miyako-rettō **71** H 6
Miyaly **66** E 1
Mizdah **55** H 2
Mizoram **73** F 3
Mizusawa **71** M 3
Mjölby **43** G 4

Mjösa **43** F 3
Mkata **61** F 6
Mkomazi **61** F 5
Mkomazi Game Reserve **61** F 5
Mkushi **62** DE 2
Mladá Boleslav **41** FG 4
Mljet **45** G 3
Moab **20** E 4
Moamba **63** E 5
Moba **60** D 6
Mobaye **60** C 4
Moberly **21** H 4
Mobile **22** C 4
Mobile Bay **22** C 4
Mobridge **21** F 2
Moçambique **63** G 3
Mochudi **62** D 4
Mocímboa da Praia **63** G 2
Moctezuma **24** C 2
Moctezuma **25** D 3
Mocuba **63** F 3
Modena (Italy) **45** F 3
Modena (U.S.A.) **20** D 4
Modesto **20** B 4
Moero, Lac **60** D 6
Mogadouro, Serra do **44** B 3
Mogaung **73** G 2
Mogilev **43** JK 5
Mogilev Podol'skiy **46** C 1
Mogogh **60** E 3
Mogoyn **68** G 6
Mogoytui **68** KL 5
Moguqi **69** M 6
Mohall **21** F 2
Mohe **69** M 5
Moheli **63** G 2
Mohikan, Cape **12** D 3
Mohon Peak **20** D 5
Mohoro **61** F 6
Mohtar-Lam **67** H 4
Mointy **51** O 6
Mo i Rana **42** F 2
Moise **19** G 3
Moisie **19** G 3
Moitaco **29** G 5
Mojave **20** C 4
Mojave Desert **20** C 4
Mojiang **70** D 6
Mokp'o **71** J 4
Mokra Gora **46** AB 2
Molagno **25** E 3
Moldava **46** C 1
Moldava **46** C 1
Moldaviya **46** C 1
Moldefjorden **42** E 3
Mole Game Reserve **58** D 4
Molepolole **62** CD 4
Moline **21** H 3
Mollendo **34** B 4
Molodechno **43** J 5
Molodezhnaya **85**
Molokai **83** E 1
Molopo **62** C 5

Mombasa **61** FG 5
Mombetsu **71** M 2
Momboyo **60** B 5
Mompós **29** E 5
Momskiy Khrebet **69** QR 2
Mona, Canal de la **29** F 3
Mona, Isla **29** F 3
Monaco **45** E 3
Monaghan **40** B 4
Monahans **24** F 5
Monapo **63** G 2
Monarch Mountain **13** M 5
Monashee Mountains **14** F 4
Monasterio de Montserrat **44** D 3
Monastery of Saint Catherine **48** AB 3
Monchegorsk **42** K 2
Mönchen-Gladbach **40** E 4
Monclova **24** D 2
Moncton **19** G 4
Mondo **59** H 3
Mondragone **45** F 3
Monfalcone **45** F 2
Monga **60** C 4
Mong Hpayak **73** G 3
Monghyr **72** E 2–3
Mongolia **68** GJ 6
Mongolia **68** GJ 6
Mongolo **68** J 2
Mongu **62** C 3
Mönhhaan **70** F 1
Monkey River **28** B 3
Monkira **79** G 3
Mono Lake **20** C 4
Monou **59** J 2
Monreal del Campo **44** C 3
Monroe (LA, U.S.A.) **21** H 5
Monroe (MI, U.S.A.) **22** D 2
Monroe (N.C., U.S.A.) **22** D 4
Monrovia **58** B 4
Mons **40** D 4
Mont Afao **55** G 3
Montagne Pelée **29** G 4
Montague **12** H 4
Montague, Isla **20** D 5
Montana **20** DE 2
Montauban **44** D 3
Montbeliard **45** E 2
Mont Blanc **45** E 2
Mont Cameroon **59** F 5
Montceau-les-Mines **44** D 2
Mont-de-Marsan **44** C 3
Monte Alban **25** E 4
Monte Alegre **33** H 4
Monte Binga **63** E 3
Monte Carlo **45** E 3
Monte Cinto **45** E 3
Monte Claros **35** H 4
Montecristi **29** E 3
Monte Cristo **34** D 3
Montecristo **45** F 3
Monte d'Oro **45** E 3
Montego Bay **28** D 3

Montejinnie **78** E 2
Monte Melimoyo **37** B 7
Montemoreos **25** E 2
Monte Negro Falls **62** A 3
Montepuez **63** F 2
Monte Quemado **36** D 4
Monterado **74** C 3
Monterey **20** B 4
Monterey Bay **20** B 4
Monteria **32** C 2
Monteror **34** D 4
Monterrey **25** DE 2
Montes Altos **33** J 5
Montes de Toledo **44** C 4
Montesilvano **45** F 3
Montes Universales **44** C 3
Montevideo **36** EF 5–6
Montgomery **22** C 4
Monticello **20** E 4
Monti di Ala **45** E 3
Montijo, Golfo de **29** C 5
Mont Jacques-Cartier **19** GH 4
Mont Joli **19** G 4
Mont Kavendou **58** B 3
Mont Lozère **44** D 3
Montluçon **44** D 2
Montmagny **19** FG 4
Mont Panié **81** H 6
Mont Pelat **45** E 3
Montpelier (ID, U.S.A.) **20** D 3
Montpelier (VT, U.S.A.) **23** F 2
Montpéllier **44** D 3
Montréal **18** F 4
Montreal Lake **15** HJ 4
Montreux **45** E 2
Montrose (U.S.A.) **20** E 4
Monts Chic-Chocs **19** G 4
Monts d'Aubrac **44** D 3
Montserrat **29** G 3
Monts Mitumba **60** D 5–6
Monts Nimba **58** C 4
Monts Notre-Dame **19** G 4
Monts Otish **19** F 3
Monts Tamgak **59** F 2
Monts Timétrine **58** DE 2
Mont Tahat **55** G 4
Mont Tembo **59** G 5
Mont Ventoux **45** E 3
Monza **45** E 2
Moonie **79** J 4
Mooraberree **79** G 4
Moore, Lake **78** B 4
Moorhead **21** G 2
Moorlands **79** FG 6
Moose **18** D 3
Moosehead Lake **23** G 2
Moose Jaw **15** H 4
Moose Pass **12** H 3
Moosomin **15** J 4
Moosonee **18** D 3
Mopti **58** D 3
Moquegua **34** BC 4
Mora **43** F 3

Moradabad **72** CD 2
Moramanga **63** H 3
Moran **20** D 3
Morane **83** F 4
Morant Cays **28** D 3
Moratuwa **72** CD 6
Morava (Czechoslovakia) **41** G 5
Morava (Western Australia) **78** B 4
Morava (Yugoslavia) **46** B 2
Morawhanna **33** G 2
Moray Firth **40** C 3
Morden **15** K 5
Moree **79** H 4
Morehead City **22** E 4
More Laptevykh **68** MN 1
Morelia **24** D 4
Morelos **25** E 4
Morena, Sierra **44** BC 4
Morenci **20** E 5
Moreno **32** C 5
Möre og Romsdal **42** E 3
Moresby **13** L 5
Morgan City **25** F 2
Morganton **22** D 3
Mori **70** B 2
Moriarty **21** E 4
Morioka **71** M 3
Morne Diablotin **29** G 3
Mornington Island **79** F 2
Morobe **82** A 3
Morocco **54** D 2
Morogoro **61** F 6
Moro Gulf **75** F 2
Moroleón **25** D 3
Morombe **63** G 4
Mörön **68** H 6
Morón (Cuba) **27** F 4
Morón (Spain) **44** B 4
Morón (Venezuela) **32** E 1
Morondava **63** G 4
Moroni **63** G 2
Moroshechnoye **69** T 4
Morotai, Pulau **75** G 3
Morozovsk **47** F 1
Morris **15** K 5
Morro de Môco **62** AB 2
Mors **43** E 4
Morshansk **50** H 5
Mörsil **42** F 3
Mortlock Islands **82** B 2
Morwell **79** H 6
Moscow (ID, U.S.A.) **20** C 2
Moselle **45** E 2
Moses Lake **20** C 2
Moses Point **12** E 3
Moshi **61** F 5
Mosjöen **42** F 2
Moskal'vo **69** Q 5
Moskenesöya **42** F 2
Moskva **50** FG 4
Mosquera **32** C 3
Mosquito, Baie **17** L 4

Mosquitos, Costa de **28** C 4
Mosquitos, Golfo de los
32 B 2
Moss **43** F 4
Mosselbaai **62** C 6
Mossendjo **59** G 6
Mossoró **35** J 2
Mostaganem **54** EF 1
Mostar **45** G 3
Mosul **57** G 1
Motala **43** G 4
Motihari **72** DE 2
Motril **44** C 4
Motul **26** D 4
Motykleyka **69** RS 4
Moudjéria **54** C 5
Moul **59** G 2
Moulins **44** D 2
Moulmein **73** G 4
Moultrie **22** D 4
Moundou **59** H 4
Mount Adam **37** DE 9
Mountain Grove **21** H 4
Mountain Home **20** C 3
Mountains of Mayo **40** B 4
Mountain Village **12** E 3
Mount Airy **22** D 3
Mount Aspiring **80** P 9
Mount Assiniboine **14** F 4
Mount Augustus **78** B 3
Mount Balbi **81** F 3
Mount Bangeta **80** E 3
Mount Blackburn **13** J 3
Mount Bona **13** J 3
Mount Brassey **78** E 3
Mount Bruce **78** B 3
Mount Brukkaros **62** B 5
Mount Carter **79** G 1
Mount Catherine **20** D 4
Mount Clark **13** N 3
Mount Cleveland **20** D 2
Mount Columbia **14** F 4
Mount Cook **81** Q 9
Mount Cushing **14** D 3
Mount Dalrymple **79** H 3
Mount Deering **78** D 3
Mount Demavend **49** F 2
Mount Denison **12** G 4
Mount Doonerak **12** H 2
Mount Douglas **79** H 3
Mount Eduni **13** M 3
Mount Egmont **81** Q 8
Mount Elbert **20** E 4
Mount Elgon **60** EF 4
Mount Elliot **79** H 2
Mount Essendon **78** C 3
Mount Everest **72** E 2
Mount Fairweather **13** K 4
Mount Feathertop **79** H 6
Mount Finke **78** E 5
Mount Foraker **12** G 3
Mount Forel **84**
Mount Forest **22** D 2
Mount Foster **13** K 4

Mount Gambier **79** FG 6
Mount Gimie **29** G 4
Mount Glottof **12** G 4
Mount Godwin Austin **67** K 3
Mount Hale **78** B 4
Mount Harper **13** J 3
Mount Hayes **12** H 3
Mount Haywood **13** N 3
Mount Hermon (Lebanon)
48 B 2
Mount Hood **20** B 2
Mount Hutton **79** H 4
Mount Isa **79** F 3
Mount Isto **13** J 2
Mount Jackson (Antarctica)
85
Mount Jackson (Australia)
78 BC 5
Mount Jefferson (NV, U.S.A.)
20 C 4
Mount Jefferson (OR, U.S.A.)
20 B 3
Mount Katmai **12** G 4
Mount Kenya **61** F 5
Mount Kimball **13** J 3
Mount Kirkpatrick **85**
Mount Klotz **13** K 2
Mount Lemmon **20** D 5
Mount Livermore **24** F 5
Mount Logan **13** J 3
Mount Lucania **13** J 3
Mount Magnet **78** B 4
Mount Marcus Baker **12** H 3
Mount McKinley **12** G 3
Mount McLoughlin **20** B 3
Mount Menzies **85**
Mount Michelson **12** H 2
Mount Mitchell **22** D 3
Mount Morgan **79** J 3
Mount Mowbullan **79** J 4
Mount Nurri **79** H 5
Mount Nyiru **61** F 4
Mount Oglethorpe **22** D 4
Mount Olympus **20** B 2
Mount Omatako **62** B 4
Mount Ord **78** D 2
Mount Ossa **80** L 9
Mount Palomar **20** C 5
Mount Pattullo **13** LM 4
Mount Pinos **20** C 4–5
Mount Pleasant (MI, U.S.A.)
22 C 2
Mount Pleasant (UT, U.S.A.)
20 D 4
Mount Pulog **75** J 1
Mount Queen Bess **14** E 4
Mount Rainier **20** B 2
Mount Ratz **13** L 4
Mount Ritter **20** C 4
Mount Robson **14** EF 4
Mount Roosevelt **14** D 3
Mount Saint Elias **13** J 3
Mount Saint Helens **20** B 2
Mount Sanford **13** J 3

Mount Shasta **20** B 3
Mount Shenton **78** C 4
Mount Sir Alexander **14** E 4
Mount Sir James MacBrian
13 M 3
Mount Smythe **14** DE 3
Mount Springer **18** F 4
Mount Sunflower **21** F 4
Mount Tama **62** A 2
Mount Taylor **20** E 4
Mount Tipton **20** D 4
Mount Tom White **13** J 3
Mount Torbert **12** G 3
Mount Trumbull **20** D 4
Mount Veniaminof **12** EF 4
Mount Vernon (IL, U.S.A.)
22 C 3
Mount Vernon (KY, U.S.A.)
22 D 3
Mount Vernon (OH, U.S.A.)
22 D 2
Mount Vernon (WA, U.S.A.)
20 B 2
Mount Victoria **73** F 3
Mount Vsevidof **12** D 5
Mount Waddington **13** M 5
Mount Washington **23** F 2
Mount Whitney **20** C 4
Mount Wilhelm **80** D 3
Mount Wilson **20** E 4
Mount Wrightson **20** D 5
Moura **33** F 4
Moussoro **59** H 3
Mouths of the Amazon **33** J 3
Mouths of the Danube
46 CD 1–2
Mouths of the Ganges
72–73 EF 3
Mouths of the Indus **72** A 3
Mouths of the Irrawaddy
73 FG 4
Mouths of the Mekong
73 J 5–6
Mouths of the Orinoco
33 FG 2
Movas **24** C 2
Mowbullan, Mount **79** J 4
Moxico **62** BC 2
Moxos, Llanos de **34** CD 4
Moyahua **24** D 3
Moyale **61** F 4
Moyobamba **32** C 5
Mozambique **63** EF 3
Mozambique Channel
63 FG 2–4
Mozdok **47** FG 2
Mozharka **68** F 5
Mozyr' **43** J 5
Mpanda **60** E 6
Mpika **63** E 2
Msata **61** F 6
Mtsensk **50** G 5
Mtwara **63** G 2
Muang Nan **73** H 4

Muang Ngao **73** GH 4
Muang Phrae **73** H 4
Muang Ubon **72** H 4
Muar **74** B 3
Muaraenim **74** B 4
Muara Teweh **74** D 4
Mubarak **49** G 4
Mubi **59** G 3
Muchinga Escarpment **63** E 2
Mucojo **63** G 2
Mudanjiang **71** JK 2
Muddy Gap **20** E 3
Mufulira **62** D 2
Muganskaya Step' **66** D 3
Muhagiriya **56** D 6
Muhammad, Ra's **48** B 4
Muhammad Qawl **56** F 4
Mühlhausen **41** F 4
Mühlig-Hofmann Mountains
85
Muhulu **60** D 5
Mui Bai Bung **73** H 6
Muite **63** F 2
Mukachevo **46** B 1
Mukur **66** EF 1
Mukur **67** H 4
Mulan **71** J 1
Mulanje **63** F 3
Mulata **61** G 3
Mulchatna **12** F 3
Mulchén **37** B 6
Mulegé **24** B 2
Mulegé, Sierra de **24** B 2
Mulgrave Island **80** D 4
Mulhacén **44** C 4
Mulhouse **45** E 2
Mull **40** B 3
Mullaittivu **72** D 6
Mullaley **79** HJ 5
Muller, Pegunungan **74** D 3
Mullet Peninsula **40** A 4
Mullewa **78** B 4
Mulligan River **79** F 4
Mulobezi **62** D 3
Multan **67** J 5
Multanovy **51** O 3
Mulu, Gunung **74** DE 3
Mulym'ya **51** N 3
Mumra **66** D 1
Muna, Pulau **75** F 5
München **41** F 5
Muncho Lake **14** D 3
Muncie **22** CD 2
Mundar **69** R 2
Munday **21** G 5
Münden **41** E 4
Munhango **62** B 2
Munich **41** F 5
Munkhafad al Qaţţārah **56** D 3
Munster **40** B 4
Münster **41** E 4
Muntii Rodnei **46** B 1
Munugudzhak **69** TU 3
Munzur Silsilesi **47** EF 3

Muojärvi **42** J 2
Muong Hiem **73** H 3
Muong Khoua **73** H 3
Muong Sing **73** H 3
Mupa National Park **62** B 3
Mura **45** G 2
Murallón, Cerro **37** B 8
Murana **75** H 4
Muranga **61** F 5
Murashi **50** J 4
Murat **47** F 3
Murchison River **78** AB 4
Murcia **44** C 4
Murdo **21** F 3
Mureş **46** B 1
Murfreesboro **22** C 3
Muriaé **35** H 5
Murilo **82** B 2
Murjek **42** H 2
Murmansk **42** K 2
Murmashi **42** K 2
Murom **50** H 4
Muromtsevo **51** P 4
Muroran **71** M 2
Murphysboro **22** C 3
Murray (KY, U.S.A.) **22** C 3
Murray (UT, U.S.A.) **20** D 3
Murray, Lake **22** D 4
Murray Bridge **79** F 6
Murray River **79** G 5
Murrumbidgee River **79** H 5
Murta **68** F 5
Murukta **68** H 2
Mururoa **83** F 4
Murwara **72** D 3
Muş **47** F 3
Musala **46** B 2
Musan **71** JK 2
Musandam Peninsula **49** G 4
Muscat **57** K 4
Musgrave **79** G 1
Musgrave Ranges **78** E 4
Mushāsh al 'Ashāwī **49** E 4
Müsiān **49** E 2
Muskegon **22** C 2
Muskegon River **22** C 2
Muskogee **21** GH 4
Musquaro, Lac **19** H 3
Musselshell River **20** E 2
Mussende **62** B 2
Mustafa **69** P 3
Müṭ **56** D 3
Mutanda **62** D 2
Mutarara **63** F 3
Mutare **63** E 3
Mutoray **68** H 3
Mutshatsha **62** CD 2
Mutsu-wan **71** M 2
Mu Us Shamo **70** E 3
Muynak **66** F 2
Muzaffarnagar **72** CD 2
Muzaffarpur **72** DE 2
Muzhi **51** M 2
Muztag **67** L 3

Muztag **67** M 3
Mvomero **61** F 6
Mwanza **60** E 5
Mweka **60** C 5
Mwinilunga **62** CD 2
Myakit **69** S 3
Myaundzha **69** R 3
Mycenae **46** B 3
Myingyan **73** G 3
Myitkyina **73** G 2
Myitta **73** G 5
Myittha **73** G 3
Mymensingh **73** F 3
Mýrdalsjökull **42** B 3
Myrtle Beach **22** E 4
Mys Aniva **69** Q 6
Mys Buorkhaya **69** O 1
Mys Chukotskiy **12** C 3
Mys Dezhneva **12** D 2
Mys Duga-Zapadnaya **69** R 4
Mys Kanin Nos **50** H 2
Mys Kril'on **69** Q 6
Mys Kronotskiy **69** U 4–5
Mys Kurgalskiy **43** J 4
Mys Laydennyy **50** J 2
Mys Lopatka **69** T 5
Mys Navarin **69** X 3
Mys Olyutorskiy **69** VW 4
Mysore **72** C 5
Mysovaya **69** T 2
Mys Peschanyy **66** E 2
Mys Pitsunda **47** F 2
Mys Sarych **47** D 2
Mys Shipunskiy **69** TU 5
Mys Svatoy Nos **69** P 1
Mys Svyatoy Nos **50** GH 2
Mys Taran **43** GH 4–5
Mys Tarkhankut **47** D 1
Mys Taygonos **69** U 3
Mys Terpeniya **69** QR 6
Mys Tolstoy **69** T 4
Mys Uengan **51** MN 1
Mys Yelizavety **69** Q 5
Mys Yuzhnyy **69** ST 4
My Tho **73** J 5

N

Naandi **60** D 3
Naba **73** G 3
Na Baek **73** H 4
Nabk al Gharbī **48** B 3
Nābul **55** H 1
Nābulus **48** B 2
Nachana **72** B 2
Nachvak Fiord **19** H 2
Nacozari **24** E 5
Nadiad **72** B 3
Nador **54** E 1
Nadym **51** O 2
Nærbö **43** E 4
Næstved **43** F 4
Naftshahr **49** D 2
Nafuce **59** F 3

Nafūd al 'Urayq **48** D 4
Nafūd as Sirr **66** CD 5–6
Nafūd as Surrah **66** C 6
Naga **75** F 1
Naga Hills **73** FG 2
Nagai **12** E 5
Nagaland **73** FG 2
Nagano **71** L 3
Nagaoka **71** L 3
Nagasaki **71** J 4
Nagaur **72** B 2
Nagda **72** C 3
Nagercoil **72** C 6
Nago **71** J 5
Nagornyy **69** N 4
Nagoya **71** L 4
Nagpur **72** C 3
Nagqu **70** B 4
Nagykanizsa **46** A 1
Naha **71** J 5
Nahanni Butte **13** N 3
Nahanni National Park **13** M, N 3
Nahariyya **48** B 2
Nahāvand **49** E 2
Nahr an Nīl **48** A 4
Nain **19** H 2
Nā'īn **49** F 2
Nairobi **61** F 5
Najafābād **49** F 2
Najd **48** CD 4
Najin **71** K 2
Najrān **57** GH 5
Nakhichevan' **66** CD 3
Nakhodka **71** K 2
Nakhon Ratchasima **73** H 5
Nakhon Sawan **73** G 4
Nakhon Si Thammarat **73** GH 6
Nakina **18** C 3
Naknek **12** F 4
Nakuru **61** F 5
Nalayh **68** J 6
Nal'chik **47** F 2
Nālūt **55** H 2
Namak, Kavir-e **49** G 1
Namanga **61** F 5
Namangan **67** J 2
Namapa **63** G 2
Namaqualand **62** B 5
Namatanai **81** F 2
Nambour **79** J 4
Nam Can **73** J 6
Nam Dinh **73** HJ 3
Nametil **63** F 3
Namib Desert **62** AB 4–5
Namib Desert Park **62** AB 4
Namibe **62** A 3
Namibe Reserve **62** A 3
Namibia **62** AB 4
Namiquipa **24** C 2
Namjagbarwa Feng **70** C 5
Namkham **73** G 3
Namlea **75** G 4

Namling **72** E 2
Namoi River **79** H 5
Namoluk **82** B 2
Namonuito **82** A 2
Namorik **82** C 2
Nampa **20** C 3
Nampala **58** C 2
Nampula **63** FG 3
Namru **72** D 1
Namsang **73** G 3
Namsen **42** F 2–3
Namsos **42** F 3
Namtsy **69** NO 3
Namu **82** C 2
Namuli **63** F 3
Namur **40** E 4
Namy **69** O 2
Nanaimo **14** DE 5
Nancha **69** NO 6
Nanchang **70** G 5
Nanchong **70** E 4
Nancy **45** E 2
Nanda Devi **72** D 1
Nander **72** C 4
Nandyal **72** C 4
Nanfeng **70** G 5
Nanga Parbat **67** J 3–4
Nangatayap **74** D 4
Nangong **70** FG 3
Nang Xian **70** B 5
Nanjiang **70** E 4
Nanjing **71** GH 4
Nan Ling **70** EF 5
Nanning **70** E 6
Nanping (Fujian, China) **71** G 5
Nanping (Gansu, China) **70** DE 4
Nansei-shotō **71** J 5
Nantais, Lac **17** M 4
Nantes **44** C 2
Nanton **14** G 4
Nantong **71** H 4
Nantucket Island **23** G 3
Nantucket Sound **23** FG 2
Nanumanga **82** C 3
Nanumea **82** C 3
Nanuque **35** HJ 4
Nanyang **70** F 4
Nanyuki **61** F 4
Nanzhang **70** F 4
Naococane, Lac **19** F 3
Napassoq **17** Q 3
Napata **56** E 5
Napier **81** R 8
Napier Mountains **85**
Naples **45** F 3
Naples (FL, U.S.A.) **27** E 3
Napo **32** D 4
Napoli **45** F 3
Nara (Japan) **71** L 4
Nara (Mali) **58** C 2
Naranjos **25** E 3
Narasun **68** K 5

Narathiwat 73 H 6
Narayanganj 73 F 3
Narbonne 44 D 3
Nares Strait 84
Narew 41 H 4
Narmada 72 C 3
Närpes 42 H 3
Narrabri 79 HJ 5
Narrogin 78 B 5
Narsinghgarh 72 C 3
Narssaq 17 Q 4
Narva 43 J 4
Narvik 42 G 2
Narwietooma 78 E 3
Naryn 68 G 5
Näsåker 42 G 3
Nashville 22 C 3
Näsijärvi 42 H 3
Nasik 72 B 3
Näşir 60 E 3
Naskaupi 19 H 3
Nass 13 M 4
Nassau (The Bahamas) 27 F 3
Nasser, Birkat 56 E 4
Nasser, Lake 48 A 5
Nässjö 43 FG 4
Nastapoka Islands 18 E 2
Nata 62 D 4
Natal (Brazil) 35 JK 2
Natal (South Africa) 62–63 E 5
Natashquan 19 H 3
Natchez 25 H 5
Natchitoches 25 H 5
Natitingou 58 E 3
Natividade 35 G 3
Natkyizin 73 G 5
Natron, Lake 61 F 5
Natuna, Kepulauan 74 C 3
Nauja Bay 17 L 3
Naupe 32 C 5
Nauru 81 J 2
Naushki 68 J 5
Nauta 32 D 4
Nava 25 D 2
Navajo Reservoir 20 E 4
Navarino 37 C 10
Navarra 44 C 3
Navassa 28 D 3
Navia 44 B 3
Navojoa 24 C 2
Navolato 24 C 3
Navolok 50 G 3
Nawabshah 67 H 5
Náxos 46 C 3
Nayarit 24 D 3
Nayarit, Sierra 24 D 3
Nåy Band 49 F 4
Nåy Band, Ra's-e 49 F 4
Nayoro 71 M 2
Nazaré 44 B 4
Nazareth 32 C 5
Nazas 24 D 2
Nazca 34 A 3

Naze 71 J 5
Nazerat 48 B 2
Nazilli 46 C 3
Ndali 58 E 4
Ndélé 60 C 3
Ndendé 59 G 6
N'Djamena 59 H 3
Ndola 62 D 2
Neagh, Lough 40 B 4
Néapolis 46 B 3
Near Islands 12 A 5–6
Nebit-Dag 66 E 3
Nebolchi 50 F 4
Nebraska 21 FG 3
Nebraska City 21 G 3
Nechako 14 E 4
Nechako Plateau 14 E 4
Nechako Reservoir 13 M 5
Nechi 29 E 5
Necochea 37 E 6
Nédéley 59 H 2
Nedong 73 F 2
Needles 20 CD 5
Neftelensk 68 J 4
Nefteyugansk 51 O 3
Negage 62 AB 1
Neganili Lake 15 K 3
Negelli 61 F 3
Negombo 72 C 6
Negonengo 83 F 4
Negra, Punta 32 B 5
Negrais, Cape 73 F 4
Negritos 32 B 4
Negros 75 F 1–2
Nehåvand 49 E 2
Nehe 69 MN 6
Neijiang 70 DE 5
Neilton 20 B 2
Nei Monggol Zizhiqu 70 DG 2
Neiva 32 CD 3
Nejd (Saudi Arabia) 48 CD 5
Nekemt 61 F 3
Nelemnoye 69 S 2
Nel'kan 69 P 4
Nelkuchan, Gora 69 P 3
Nellore 72 D 5
Nel'ma 69 P 6
Nelson 81 Q 9
Nelson (Br. Col., Can.) 14 F 5
Nelson (Man., Can.) 15 K 4
Nelson Head 16 B 2
Nelson Island 12 D 3
Nelspruit 63 E 5
Néma 54 D 5
Némiscau 18 E 3
Nemunas 43 H 4
Nemuro 71 N 2
Nenana 12 H 3
Nenana 12 H 3
Nendo 81 J 4
Nenjiang 69 MN 6
Nepa 68 J 4
Nepal 72 DE 2
Nepeña 32 C 5

Nephi 20 D 4
Nerchinsk 68 L 5
Nerekhta 50 H 4
Neringa-Nida 43 H 4
Neriquinha 62 C 3
Nesbyen 43 E 3
Néstos 46 B 2
Netanya 48 B 2
Netherlands 40 D–E 4
Netherlands Antilles 29 G 3
Nettilling Lake 17 M 3
Nettuno 45 F 3
Neuchâtel 45 E 2
Neuquén 37 C 6
Nevada (MO, U.S.A.) 21 H 4
Nevada (U.S.A.) 20 C 4
Nevada, Sierra (Spain) 44 C 4
Nevada, Sierra (U.S.A.)
   20 BC 4
Nevado Ausangate 34 B 3
Nevado Cololo 34 C 4
Nevado Coropuna 34 B 4
Nevado de Cachi 34 C 5
Nevado de Colima 24 D 4
Nevado Huascarán 32 C 5
Nevado Illimani 34 C 4
Nevado Sajama 34 C 4
Nevado Salluyo 34 C 3
Nevado Yerupajá 34 A 3
Never 69 M 5
Nevers 44 D 2
Nevinnomyssk 47 F 2
Nevis 29 G 3
Nevşehir 47 D 3
Nev'yansk 51 M 4
New Albany 22 C 3
New Amsterdam 33 G 2
Newark 22 D 2
Newark (N.J., U.S.A.) 23 F 2
Newark (OH, U.S.A.) 22 D 2
New Bedford 23 F 2
New Bern 22 E 3
Newberry 22 C 1
New Braunfels 25 E 2
New Britain 81 F 3
New Brunswick (Canada)
   19 G 4
New Brunswick (N.J., U.S.A.)
   23 F 2
New Buffalo 22 C 2
Newburgh (N.Y., U.S.A.)
   23 F 2
New Caledonia 81 H 6
Newcastle 19 G 4
New Castle 22 D 2
Newcastle (N.S.W., Austr.)
   79 J 5
Newcastle (WY, U.S.A.) 21 F 3
Newcastle-upon-Tyne 40 C 3
Newcastle Waters 78 E 2
New England 23 FG 2
Newenham, Cape 12 E 4
Newfoundland 19 J 3
Newfoundland 19 J 4

New Georgia 81 G 3
New Glasgow 19 H 4
New Guinea 75 J 4
New Hampshire 23 F 2
New Hampton 21 H 3
New Hanover 81 F 2
New Haven 23 F 2
New Hebrides 81 J 5
New Hebrides 82 C 4
New Iberia 25 F 2
New Ireland 81 F 2
New Ireland 82 AB 3
New Jersey 22–23 EF 3
New Liskeard 22 D 2
New London 23 F 2
Newman 78 B 3
New Meadows 20 C 2
New Mexico 20–21 E 5
New Orleans 22 C 4–5
New Plymouth 81 Q 8
Newport (AR, U.S.A.) 21 H 4
Newport (OR, U.S.A.) 20 B 3
Newport (U.K.) 40 C 4
Newport (VT, U.S.A.) 23 F 2
Newport (WA, U.S.A.) 20 C 2
Newport Beach 20 C 5
New Providence Island 27 F 4
New Richmond 19 G 4
New River (W.V., U.S.A.)
   22 D 3
New Rockford 21 G 2
Newry 78 D 2
New Siberian Islands 84
New Smyrna Beach 27 EF 3
New South Wales 79 GH 5
New Stuvahok 12 F 4
Newton 21 H 3
Newtonabbey 40 B 4
New Ulm 21 H 3
New Westminster 14 E 5
New York 22 E 2
New York (N.Y., U.S.A.) 23 F 2
New Zealand 81 RS 9
New Zealand 82 C 5
Neya 50 H 4
Neyriz 49 G 3
Neyshābūr 66 F 3
Nezhin 50 F 5
Ngamiland 62 C 3
Ngamring 72 E 2
Ngangla Ringco 72 DE 1
Nganglong Kangri 72 D 1
Ngatik 82 B 2
Ngidinga 60 B 6
Ngoc Linh 73 J 4
Ngoko 59 H 5
Ngoring 70 C 3
Nguara 59 H 3
Nhambiquara 34 E 3
Nha Trang 73 JK 5
Niagara Falls 22 E 2
Niagara River 22 E 2
Niamey 58 E 3
Niamtougou 58 E 3

Niangara **60** D 4
Nia-Nia **60** D 4
Nianzishan **69** M 6
Nias, Pulau **74** AB 3
Niassa **63** F 2
Nicaragua **28** BC 4
Nicaragua, Lago de **28** B 4
Nice **45** E 3
Nichalakh **69** QR 1
Nichicum, Lac **19** F 3
Nicholas Channel **27** F 4
Nicholls Town **27** F 3
Nicobar Islands **73** F 6
Nicocli **32** C 2
Nicosia **47** D 3
Nicosia (Cyprus) **48** A 2
Nicoya **28** B 4
Nicoya, Golfo de **28** C 5
Nicoya, Península de **28** B 5
Nicuadala **63** F 3
Nidelva **43** E 4
Nido, Sierra del **24** C 2
Niedersachsen **41** EF 4
Niedre Tauern **45** F 2
Niellé **58** C 3
Niemba **60** D 6
Nieuw Amsterdam **33** H 2
Nieuw Nickerie **33** G 2
Nieuwoudtville **62** BC 6
Niğde **47** DE 3
Niger **59** FG 2
Niger Delta **59** F 5
Nigeria **59** EG 4
Nihau **83** E 1
Nihiru **83** F 4
Niigata **71** L 3
Nijmegen **40** E 4
Nikel **42** K 2
Nikk **58** E 4
Nikolayev **46** D 1
Nikolayevka **51** N 5
Nikolayevsk-na-Amure **69** PQ 5
Nikoleyeva **43** JK 4
Nikol'sk **50** J 4
Nikolski **12** D 5
Nikol'skiy **67** H 1
Nikopol **47** D 1
Nikpey **49** E 1
Nikšic **46** A 2
Nikumaroro **82** D 3
Nile (Egypt) **48** A 4
Niles **22** C 2
Nimba, Monts **58** C 4
Nimbe **59** F 5
Nimes **44** D 3
Nimule **60** E 4
Nincheng **71** G 2
Ninety Mile Beach **79** H 6
Nineveh **48** D 1
Ningbo **71** H 5
Ningde **71** G 5
Ningdu **70** G 5
Ningxia Huizu Zizhiqu **70** E 3

Ninigo Group **82** A 3
Niobrara River **21** FG 3
Niokolo Koba, Parc
   National du **58** B 3
Nioro du Sahel **58** C 2
Niort **44** C 2
Niout **54** D 5
Nipa **29** G 5
Nipawin **15** J 4
Nipigon **18** C 4
Nipigon, Lake **18** C 4
Nipissing, Lake **18** DE 4
Nippur **57** H 2
Nis **46** B 2
Nisâb **57** H 6
Nísoi **46** B 3
Nitchequon **19** F 3
Niterói **35** H 5
Nitiya **69** P 4
Nitiya **69** P 4
Nitra **41** G 5
Niuafo'ou **82** D 4
Niuato Putapu **82** D 4
Niue **82** D 4
Niugini **81** E 4
Niulakita **82** C 3
Niutao **82** C 3
Nizamabad **72** C 4
Nizhneangarsk **68** JK 4
Nizhne-Ozernaya **69** UV 4
Nizhneudinsk **68** G 5
Nizhnevartovskoye **51** PQ 3
Nizhneye Karelina **68** J 4
Nizhniy Pyandzh **67** H 3
Nizhniy Tagil **51** M 4
Nizhnyaya Omka **51** O 4
Nizhnyaya Poyma **68** G 4
Nizhnyaya Tunguska **68** F 3
Nizhnyaya Voch' **50** K 3
Nizhnyaya Zolotitsa
   (Nizhnyaya) **50** H 2
Nizina Podlaska **41** H 4
Nizip **48** B 1
Njunes **42** G 2
Njutånger **42** G 3
Nkayi **59** G 6
Nkhata Bay **63** E 2
Nkolabona **59** G 5
Nkomi, Lagune **59** F 6
Nkongsamba **59** G 4–5
Nkurenkuru **62** B 3
Noatak **12** E 2
Noatak **12** EF 2
Noatak National Preserve
   12 F 2
Nobel **18** D 4
Noefs, Ile des **61** J 6
Nogales **20** D 5
Nogales **24** D 5
Nogayskiye Step' **47** G 2
Noginsk **50** G 4
Nokrek Peak **73** F 2
Nomad **82** A 3
Nombre de Dios **24** D 3

Nome **12** D 3
Nonacho Lake **15** H 2
Nong Khai **73** H 4
Nonoava **24** C 2
Nonouti **82** C 3
Noorvik **12** E 2
Nordaustlandet **84**
Nordfriesische Inseln
   41 E 3–4
Norðoyar **40** A 1
Nordkapp **42** J 1
Nordkinn **42** J 1
Nord-Kvaloy **42** G 1
Nordland **42** EF 2
Nordostrundingen **84**
Nordöyane **42** E 3
Nordreisa **42** H 2
Nordre Strømfjord **17** Q 3
Nordsjßn **43** E 4
Nord-Trondelag **42** F 3
Nordvik **68** K 1
Norfolk (NE, U.S.A.) **21** G 3
Norfolk (VA, U.S.A.) **22** E 3
Norfolk Islands **82** C 4
Norfolk Lake **21** H 4
Norge **42** EF 2
Nori **51** O 2
Noril'sk **51** R 2
Normal **22** C 2
Norman **21** G 4
Normanby Island **79** J 1
Normandie **44** CD 2
Normanton **79** G 2
Norra Storfjället **42** G 2
Norrbotten **42** GH 2
Norris Lake **22** D 3
Norrköping **43** G 4
Norrland **42** FG 3
Norrtälje **43** G 4
Norseman **78** C 5
Norsjö **42** G 3
Norsk **69** O 5
Norte, Canal do **33** H 3
North, Cape (Nova Scotia,
   Can.) **19** H 4
North Adams **23** F 2
Northam **78** B 5
Northampton **40** C 4
North Andaman **73** F 5
North Arm **14** G 2
North Aulatsivik Island **19** H 2
North Battleford **15** H 4
North Bay **18** E 4
North Belcher Islands **18** D 2
North Bend **20** B 3
North Canadian River **21** G 4
North Cape **82** C 5
North Caribou Lake **15** L 4
North Carolina **22** E 3
North Cascades National Park
   20 B 2
North Channel **18** D 4
North Channel **40** B 3–4
North Dakota **21** FG 2

Northeast Cape **12** D 3
Northeast Providence
   Channel **27** F 3
Northern Cook Islands **82** E 3
Northern Indian Lake **15** K 3
Northern Ireland **40** B 4
Northern Mariana Islands
   82 B 1
Northern Territory **78** E 2–3
Northfield **21** H 3
North Fork Pass **13** K 3
North Geomagnetic Pole **84**
North Highlands **20** B 4
North Island **81** Q 8
North Island **82** C 5
North Korea **71** K 2
North Korea **71** K 2
North Lakhimpur **73** F 2
North Las Vegas **20** C 4
North Little Rock **21** H 5
North Loup River **21** F 3
North Magnetic Pole **84**
North Minch **40** B 3
North Platte **21** F 3
North Platte **21** F 3
North Platte River **20–21** E 3
North Point **80** L 8
North Pole **84**
North River **15** L 3
North Saskatchewan **14** GH 4
North Sea **40** D 3
North Slope **12** FH 2
North Thompson **14** F 4
North Uist **40** B 3
Northumberland Islands
   79 J 3
Northumberland Strait **19** H 4
Northway Junction **13** J 3
North West Cape **78** A 3
North West Highlands
   40 BC 3
North West River **19** H 3
Northwest Territories
   (Canada) **16** BH 3
Norton (KS, U.S.A.) **21** F 4
Norton (VA, U.S.A.) **22** D 3
Norton Bay **12** E 3
Norton Sound **12** E 3
Norvegia, Cape **85**
Norwalk **22** D 2
Norway **42** F 2
Norway (WI, U.S.A.) **22** C 1
Norway Bay **16** F 2
Norway House **15** K 4
Norwegian Sea **42** DE 2–3
Norwich **40** D 4
Noshiro **71** L 2
Nosovaya **50** K 2
Nosratâbâd **66** F 5
Nossob **62** BC 5
Nosy-Bé **63** H 2
Noteć **41** G 4
Nótioi Sporádhes **46** C 3
Notodden **43** E 4

Noto-hantō **71** L 3
Notre Dame, Monts **19** G 4
Notre Dame Bay **19** JK 4
Nottawasaga Bay **22** D 2
Nottaway **18** E 3
Nottingham **40** C 4
Nottingham (Ontario, Can.)
  17 L 4
Nouadhibou **54** B 4
Nouakchott **54** B 5
Nouméa **81** J 6
Nouveau Comptoir **18** E 3
Nouvelle-Calédonie **81** H 6
Nouvelle France, Cap de
  17 M 4
Nova Cruz **35** JK 2
Nova Iguaçu **35** H 5
Nova Mambone **63** F 4
Novara **45** E 2
Nova Scotia **23** H 2
Nova Vida **34** D 3
Novaya Kakhovka **47** D 1
Novaya Kazanka **50** J 6
Novaya Zemlya **50** KL 1
Novgorod **43** K 4
Novgorodka **43** J 4
Novi Ligure **45** E 3
Novillero **24** C 3
Novi Pazar **46** AB 2
Novi Sad **46** A 1
Novoaltaysk **51** QR 5
Novobiryusinskiy **68** G 4
Novograd-Volynskiy **43** J 5
Novo Hamburgo **36** FG 4
Novokazalinsk **67** G 1
Novokocherdyk **51** M 5
Novokuznetsk **51** R 5
Novolazarevskaya **85**
Novomoskovsk **50** G 5
Novopavlovskoye **68** K 5
Novopokrovskaya **47** F 1
Novopolotsk **43** J 4
Novorossiysk **47** E 2
Novorybnoye **68** HJ 1
Novoshakhtinsk **50** H 6
Novosibirsk **51** QR 4
Novosibirskiye Ostrova
  → New Siberian Islands
  49 QR 2
Novotroitskoye **67** JK 2
Novoyeniseysk **68** FG 4
Novoye Ust'ye **69** Q 4
Novvy Bug **47** D 1
Novy Uzen' **66** E 2
Novyy Karymkary **51** N 3
Novyy Port **51** O 2
Novyy Tanguy **68** H 4
Nowa Sól **41** FG 4
Nowbarān **49** E 2
Nowdesheh **49** E 2
Nowgong **73** F 2
Nowitna **12** FG 3
Nowra **79** J 5
Now Shahr **49** F 1

Nowy Sacz **41** H 5
Nsukka **59** F 4
Ntui **59** G 5
Nuatja **58** E 4
Nūbiyah **56** DE 5
Nueces River **25** E 2
Nueltin Lake **15** K 2
Nueva Esperanza **34** CD 4
Nueva Galia **37** CD 6
Nueva Gerona **27** E 4
Nueva León **25** DE 2
Nueva Lubecka **37** BC 7
Nueva Rosita **25** D 2
Nueva San Salvador **25** FG
Nueve de Julio **37** D 6
Nuevitas **27** F 4
Nuevo Casas Grandes **20** E
Nuevo Laredo **25** DE 2
Nuevo Mundo, Cerro **34** C 5
Nuevo Rocafuerte **32** C 4
Nugāl **61** H 3
Nuguria Islands **82** B 3
Nui **82** C 3
Nuiqsut **12** G 1
Nukey Bluff **79** F 5
Nukhayb **48** D 2
Nuku'alofa **82** D 4
Nukufetau **82** C 3
Nuku Hiva **83** F 3
Nukulaelae **82** D 3
Nukumanu Islands **82** B 3
Nukunau **82** C 3
Nukunonu **82** D 3
Nukuoro **82** B 2
Nukus **66** FG 2
Nulato **12** F 3
Nullarbor Plain **78** DE 5
Numan **59** G 4
Numbulwar Mission **78** EF 1
Numfor, Pulau **75** H 4
Numto **51** O 3
Nungnain Sum **71** G 1
Nunivak Island **12** D 3
Nunlygran **12** B 3
Nuntherungie **79** G 5
Nunyamo **12** C 2
Nuoro **45** E 3
Nuqrah **48** C 4
Nuratau, Khrebet **67** H 2
Nuremberg **41** F 5
Nurhak Daği **47** E 3
Nūri **56** E 5
Nuristan **67** J 3
Nürnberg **41** F 5
Nurri, Mount **79** H 5
Nushagak **12** F 4
Nushki **67** H 5
Nutak **19** H 2
Nuupas **42** J 2
Nuwaybi'al Muzayyinah
  48 B 3
Nyabéssan **59** G 5
Nyakanazi **60** E 5
Nyaksimvol' **51** M 3

Nyala **56** CD 6
Nyamlell **60** D 3
Nyandoma **50** H 3
Nyasa, Lake **63** EF 2
Nyazepetrovsk **51** L 4
Nyda **51** O 2
Nyika Plateau **63** E 2
Nyima **72** E 1
Nyíregyháza **46** B 1
Nyiru, Mount **61** F 4
Nyköbing **43** F 5
Nyköping **43** G 4
Nylstroom **62** D 4
Nymagee **79** H 5
Nyssa **20** C 3
Nyurba **68** L 3
Nzega **60** E 5
Nzerékoré **58** C 4

O

Oahe, Lake **21** F 2
Oahe Dam **21** F 3
Oahu **83** E 1
Oakbank **79** G 5
Oakland (CA, U.S.A.) **20** B 4
Oakland (MD, U.S.A.) **22** E 3
Oakley **21** F 4
Oakridge **20** B 3
Oak Ridge **22** D 3
Oakville **22** E 2
Oasis **20** D 3
Oates Coast **85**
Oaxaca **25** E 4
Oaxaca de Juárez **25** E 4
Oba **18** D 4
Obala **59** G 5
Oban **40** B 3
Obeh **67** G 4
Óbidos **33** GH 4
Obihiro **71** M 2
Obil'noye **47** FG 1
Obluch'ye **69** O 6
Obodovka **46** C 1
Obruk Platosu **47** D 3
Obshchiy Syrt **50** K 5
Obskaya Guba **51** O 1–2
Ocala **27** E 3
Ocampo **24** C 2
Ocaña **32** D 2
Occidental, Cordillera
  32 C–3
Ocean City **22** E 3
Ocean Falls **13** M 5
Ocmulgee River **22** D 4
Oconee **22** D 4
Oconee River **22** D 4
Ocotlán **24** D 3
Ocotlán de Morelos **25** E 4
Ocumare del Tuy **29** F 4
Odawara **71** L 3–4
Ödemis **46** C 3
Odendaalsrus **62** D 5
Odense **43** EF 4

Oder **41** F 4
Odessa (TX, U.S.A.) **24** F 5
Odessa (U.S.S.R.) **46** D 1
Odienné **58** C 4
Odorheiu Secuiesc **46** C 1
Odra **41** FG 4
Odzala National Park **59** GH 5
Oeiras **35** H 2
Oelwein **21** H 3
Oeno **83** G 4
Offenbach **41** E 4–5
Oficina **33** F 2
Ogaden **61** GH 3
Ogbomosho **59** EF 4
Ogden **20** D 3
Ogdensburg **22**–23 EF 2
Ogilvie Mountains **13** JK 2
Oglat Beraber **54** E 2
Ogoki **18** C 3
Ogoki Reservoir **18** C 3
Ogooué **59** G 6
Ograzden **46** B 2
O'Higgins, Lago **37** B 8
Ohio **22** D 2
Ohio River **22** D 3
Ohopoho **62** A 3
Ohrid **46** B 2
Oiapoque **33** H 3
Ōita **71** K 4
Ojinaga **24** D 2
Ojo de Agua **36** D 4
Ojos del Salado, Cerro **36** C 4
Okaba **75** J 5
Okahandja **62** B 4
Okak Islands **19** H 2
Okanagan Lake **14** EF 5
Okapa **80** E 3
Okara **67** J 4
Okavango **62** C 3
Okavango Swamp **62** C 3
Okavarumendu **62** B 4
Okayama **71** K 3–4
Okeanskoye **69** T 5
Okeechobee, Lake **27** E 3
Okha (U.S.S.R.) **69** Q 5
Okhotsk **69** Q 4
Okhotskiy Perevoz **69** P 3
Okhotskoye More **69** QS 4
Okinawa-jima **71** JK 5
Oki-shotō **71** K 3
Oklahoma **21** G 4
Oklahoma City **21** G 4
Okondja **59** G 6
Okonogan **14** F 5
Okstindan **42** F 2
Oktemberyan **47** F 2
Oktyabrskiy **50** KL 5
Oktyabr'skiy (U.S.S.R.) **68** F 5
Oktyabr'skiy (U.S.S.R.) **69** N 4
Oktyabr'skoye **51** N 3
Olancha **20** C 4
Olanchito **28** B 3

Öland **43** G 4
Olanga **42** JK 2
Olathe **21** H 4
Olavarría **37** DE 6
Olbia **45** E 3
Old Bahama Channel **27** F 4
Old Crow **13** K 2
Oldenburg **41** E 4
Old Harbor **12** G 4
Olds **14** G 4
Old Wives Lake **15** H 4
Oleaborg **42** J 3
Olenegorsk **42** K 2
Olenëk **68** M 1
Olenëk **68** K 2
Olenëkskiy Zaliv **68** LM 1
Olenevod **69** WX 3
Oléron, Ile d' **44** C 2
Ölgiy **68** F 6
Olifants **63** E 4
Olimarao **82** A 2
Olimbia **46** B 3
Olimbos **46** B 2–3
Olinda **35** K 2
Ollagüe, Volcán **34** C 5
Olmos **32** C 5
Olomouc **41** G 5
Olonets **42** K 3
Oloyskiye Gorg **69** U 2
Oloyskiye Gory **69** U 2
Olsztyn **41** H 4
Olt **46** B 2
Olympia (U.S.A.) **20** B 2
Olympia → Olimbia (Greece) **46** B 3
Olympic National Park **20** B 2
Olympus **46** B 3
Olympus, Mount **20** B 2
Olyutorka **69** V 3
Olyutorskiy **69** VW 3
Omaha **21** G 3
Oman **49** G 5
Oman **57** JK 4–5
Oman, Gulf of **57** K 4
Oman, Gulf of **66** F 5–6
Omatako, Mount **62** B 4
Omboué **59** F 6
Omchali **66** E 2
Ometepe, Isla de **28** B 4
Ometepec **25** E 4
Omineca Mountains **14** D 3
Ommanney Bay **16** F 2
Ömnögovĭ **70** DE 2
Omolon **69** T 2
Omolon **69** U 2
Omsk **51** O 4
Omutinskiy **51** N 4
Omutninsk **50** K 4
Onamia **21** H 2
Onawa **21** G 3
Ondangwa **62** B 3
Ondo **59** E 4
Öndörhaan **68** K 6
Onega **50** G 3

Onega **50** G 3
O'Neill **21** G 3
Oneonta **23** F 2
Ongole **72** D 4
Onilahy **63** G 4
Onitsha **59** F 4
Onkuchakh **68** KL 2
Ono-i-Lau Islands **82** CD 4
Onon **68** L 5
Onotoa **82** C 3
Onslow **78** B 3
Onslow Bay **22** E 4
Ontario (Canada) **18** BD 3
Ontario (OR, U.S.A.) **20** C 3
Ontario, Lake **22** E 2
Ontojärvi **42** J 3
Ontong Java **82** B 3
Oodnadatta **79** F 4
Ooldea **78** E 5
Oologah Lake **21** G 4
Oostende **40** D 4
Opasatika **18** D 4
Opelousas **25** H 5
Ophir **12** F 3
Opis **48** D 2
Opiscotéo, Lac **19** G 3
Opobo **59** F 5
Opole **41** G 4
Oporto **44** B 3
Opp **22** C 4
Oppland **42** E 3
Opportunity **20** C 2
Oputo **24** E 5
Oradea **46** B 1
Oran **54** E 1
Orange (France) **45** D 3
Orange (TX, U.S.A.) **25** H 5
Orange, Cabo **33** H 3
Orange Free State **62** D 5
Orange Park **22** D 4
Orange Walk **28** B 3
Oranje **62** B 5
Orapa **62** D 4
Ora Tyube **67** H 3
Orcadas **85**
Ord, Mount **78** D 2
Ord River **78** D 2
Ordu **47** E 2
Ordynskoye **51** Q 5
Ordzhonikidze **47** FG 2
Örebro **43** FG 4
Oregon **20** BC 3
Oregon Inlet **22** E 3
Orel **50** G 5
Orem **20** D 3
Orenburg **50** K 5
Orense **44** B 3
Öresund **43** F 4
Organ Peak **21** E 5
Organ Pipe Cactus National Monument **20** D 5
Orgeyev **46** C 1
Orhon Gol **68** HJ 6
Orick **20** B 3

Oriental, Cordillera (Bolivia) **34** CD 3–5
Oriental, Cordillera (Colombia) **32** CD 2–3
Orihuela **44** C 4
Orillia **22** E 2
Orinduik **33** F 3
Orinoco (Colombia) **32** E 3
Orinoco (Venezuela) **32** E 2
Orissa **72** DE 3
Orissaare **43** H 4
Oristano **45** E 3–4
Orivesi **42** J 3
Oriximiná **33** G 4
Orizaba **25** E 4
Orkanger **42** E 3
Orkney **62** D 5
Orkney Islands **40** C 3
Orlando **27** E 3
Orléans **44** D 2
Ormara **67** GH 5
Ormoc **75** FG 1
Ornö **43** G 4
Örnsköldsvik **42** G 3
Oro, Monte d' **45** E 3
Orocué **32** D 3
Orofino **20** C 2
Orogrande **21** E 5
Oroluk **82** B 2
Oromocto **19** G 4
Orona **82** D 3
Oroqen Zizhiqi **69** M 5
Oroquieta **75** F 2
Oroville (CA, U.S.A.) **20** B 4
Oroville (WA, U.S.A.) **20** C 2
Orr **21** H 2
Orsa **42** F 3
Orsa Finnmark **42** F 3
Orsha **43** JK 5
Orsk **51** L 5
Ortegal, Cabo **44** B 3
Ortiz **24** B 2
Orto-Ayan **69** NO 1
Ortonville **21** G 2
Orümïyeh **47** F 3
Oruro **34** C 4
Osa **68** H 5
Osa, Península de **28** C 5
Ōsaka **71** L 4
Osakarovka **51** O 5
Osborne **21** G 4
Osceola **21** H 3
Osen **42** F 3
Osh **67** J 2
Oshakati **62** AB 3
Oshawa **22** E 2
Oshkosh **22** C 2
Oshogbo **59** EF 4
Oshtoran Küh **49** E 2
Osijek **45** G 2
Osinovka **51** Q 6
Oskaloosa **21** H 3
Oskarshamn **43** G 4
Oskoba **68** H 3

Oslo **43** F 4
Oslofjorden **43** F 4
Osmanabad **72** C 4
Osmaneli **46** D 2
Osmaniye **47** E 3
Osnabrück **41** E 4
Osorno **37** B 7
Osoyoos **14** EF 5
Ospito **29** F 5
Ost Berlin **43** F 5
Österdalälven **42** F 3
Österdalen **42** F 3
Östergötland **43** G 4
Östersund **42** FG 3
Östhavet **42** JK 1
Ostrava **41** G 5
Ostroda **41** GH 4
Ostroleka **41** H 4
Ostrov (Russia, U.S.S.R.) **43** J 4
Ostrova Chernyye Brat'ya **69** S 6
Ostrova Diomida **12** D 2
Ostrov Bol'shoy Begichev **68** KL 1
Ostrov Bol'shoy Shantar **69** P 4–5
Ostrov Feklistova **69** P 4–5
Ostrov Iturup **69** R 6–7
Ostrov Ketoy **69** S 6
Ostrov Kil'din **42** KL 2
Ostrov Kolguyev **50** J 2
Ostrov Kotel'nyy **69** P 1
Ostrov Malyy Lyakhovskiy **69** Q 1
Ostrov Matua **69** S 6
Ostrovnoye (U.S.S.R.) **69** U 2
Ostrovnoye (U.S.S.R.) **69** TU 5
Ostrov Onekotan **69** ST 6
Ostrov Paramushir **69** ST 5
Ostrov Rasshua **69** S 6
Ostrov Shiashkotan **69** S 6
Ostrov Simushir **69** S 6
Ostrov Urup **69** S 6
Ostrov Vaygach **51** L 1–2
Ostrov Zav'yalova **69** RS 4
Ostrowiec Świetokrzyski **41** H 4
Ostrow Wielkopolski **41** G 4
Ōsumi-shotō **71** JK 4
Oswego **22** E 2
Otaru **71** M 2
Otavalo **32** C 3
Otavi **62** B 3
Otepää Kõrgustik **43** J 4
Otish, Monts **18** F 3
Otjozondu **62** B 4
Otoskwin **15** LM 4
Otradnoye **69** T 5
Ottawa **18** EF 4
Ottawa (KS, U.S.A.) **21** G 4
Ottawa Islands **18** D 2
Ottawa River **18** E 4

Otter Creek 27 E 3
Ottumwa 21 H 3
Otway, Cape 79 G 6
Otwock 41 H 4
Ouachita Mountains 21 GH 5
Ouadane 54 C 4
Ouadda 60 C 3
Ouaddaï 59 J 3
Ouad Naga 54 BC 5
Ouagadougou 58 DE 3
Ouahigouya 58 D 3
Oualam 58 E 3
Ouanda-Djallé 60 C 3
Ouangolodougou 58 D 4
Ouargla 55 G 2
Ouarzazate 54 D 2
Oubangui 59 H 5
Oudtshoorn 62 C 6
Oued Zem 54 D 2
Ouessant, Ile de 44 B 2
Ouesso 59 H 5
Ouezzane 54 DE 2
Ouham 59 H 4
Ouiriguó 28 B 3
Oujda 54 E 2
Oulu 42 J 2
Oulujärvi 42 J 3
Oum Chalouba 59 J 2
Oum Hadjer 59 H 3
Ounianga 59 J 2
Ouricuri 35 J 2
Ourinhos 35 G 5
Outaouais 18 E 4
Outapi 62 A 3
Outardes, Rivière aux
  19 G 3–4
Outjo 62 B 4
Outlook 15 H 4
Outokumpu 42 J 3
Ouvéa 81 J 6
Ouyen 79 G 5–6
Ovalle 36 B 5
Ovamboland 62 AB 3
Overland Park 21 H 4
Oviedo 44 B 3
Oviedo (Haiti) 29 E 3
Owatonna 21 H 3
Owensboro 22 C 3
Owen Sound 22 D 2
Owerri 59 F 4
Owo 59 F 4
Owosso 22 D 2
Owyhee 20 C 3
Owyhee, Lake 20 C 3
Owyhee River 20 C 3
Oxford 40 C 4
Oxford (MS, U.S.A.) 22 C 4
Oxford Lake 15 K 3–4
Oyem 59 G 5
Oyo 58 E 4
Oyón 34 A 3
Oysurdakh 69 S 2
Ozamiz 75 F 2
Ozark 22 C 4

Ozark Plateau 21 H 4
Ozarks, Lake of the 21 H 4
Ózd 46 B 1
Ozernovskiy 69 T 5
Ozero Balkhash 51 OP 6
Ozero Baykal 68 J 5
Ozero Chany 51 P 5
Ozero Chervonoye 43 J 5
Ozero Dadynskoye 47 FG 1
Ozero Il'men 43 K 4
Ozero Imandra 42 K 2
Ozero Keret' 42 K 2
Ozero Kubenskoye 50 G 4
Ozero Leksozero 42 K 3
Ozero Manych Gudilo 47 F 1
Ozero Nyuk 42 K 3
Ozero Osvejskoje 43 J 4
Ozero Pyaozero 42 K 2
Ozero Sasykkol' 51 Q 6
Ozero Segozero 42 K 3
Ozero Seletyteniz 51 O 5
Ozero Sevan 47 G 2
Ozero Syamozero 42 K 3
Ozero Taymyr 68 H 1
Ozero Tengiz 51 N 5
Ozero Verkhneye Kuyto
  42 K 3
Ozero Zaysan 51 Q 6
Ozona 24 F 5

P

Paarl 62 B 6
Paavola 42 J 3
Pacaraima, Sierra 33 F 3
Pacasmayo 32 BC 5
Pachiza 32 C 5
Pachuca 25 E 3–4
Pacific Ocean 86
Pacific Ranges 13 M 5
Pacora 28 D 5
Padang 74 B 4
Padang, Pulau 74 B 3
Padangpanjang 74 AB 4
Padangsidempuan 74 A 3
Paddle Prairie 14 F 3
Paderborn 41 E 4
Padilla 34 D 4
Padova 45 F 2
Padre Island 25 E 2
Paducah 22 C 3
Pag 45 FG 3
Pagan 82 A 1
Page 20 D 4
Pago-Pago 82 D 3
Pagosa Springs 20 E 4
Pagri 72 E 2
Päijänne 42 J 3
Painesville(OH, U.S.A.) 22 D 2
Painted Desert 20 D 4
Paisley 40 B 3
Paita 32 B 4–5
Pekin 82 B 2
Pakistan 67 H 5

Pakokku 73 FG 3
Pak Phanang 73 H 6
Pakse 73 J 4
Pakwach 60 E 4
Palacios 25 E 2
Palangkaraya 74 D 4
Palanpur 72 B 3
Palapye 62 D 4
Palatka 69 RS 3
Palauk 73 G 5
Palaw 73 G 5
Palawan 74–75 E 2
Palawan Passage 74–75 E 1–2
Palca 34 C 4
Palembang 74 BC 4
Palencia 44 C 3
Palenque 25 F 4
Palermo 45 F 4
Palestine 48 B 2–3
Palestine (TX, U.S.A.) 25 G 5
Paletwa 73 F 3
Pali 72 B 2
Paljakka 42 J 3
Palk Strait 72 C 5–6
Pallastunturit 42 H 2
Palliser, Cape 81 R 9
Palma 44 D 4
Pal Malmal 81 F 3
Palmares 35 JK 2
Palmarito 29 EF 5
Palmar Sur 28 C 5
Palmas Bellas 28 C 5
Palma Soriano 27 F 4
Palm Bay 27 EF 3
Palmeira dos Indios 35 J 2
Palmeirais 35 H 2
Palmer 85
Palmer (AK, U.S.A.) 12 H 3
Palmer Archipelago 85
Palmer Land 85
Palmerston 82 E 4
Palmerston North 81 R 9
Palmira 32 C 3
Palm Springs 20 C 5
Palmyra (Pacific Ocean,
  U.S.A.) 82 E 2
Palmyra (Syria) 48 C 2
Palmyras Point 72 E 3
Palo Alto 20 B 4
Paloich 56 E 6
Palomar, Mount 20 C 5
Palopo 75 F 4
Palo Santo 36 E 4
Paltamo 42 J 3
Palu (Indonesia) 75 E 4
Palu (Turkey) 47 EF 3
Pamekasan 74 D 5
Pamir 67 JK 3
Pamlico Sound 22 E 3
Pampa 21 F 4
Pampas 36–37 D 5–6
Pamplona 44 C 3
Pamplona (Colombia) 29 E 5
Pan, Tierra del 44 B 3

Panaji 72 B 4
Panama 32 C 2
Panamá, Golfo de 32 C 2
Panama Canal 32 B 2
Panama City (FL, U.S.A.)
  22 C 4
Panay 75 F 1
Pandamatenga 62 D 3
Pandharpur 72 BC 4
Pandivere Kõrgustik 43 J 4
Panevežys 43 HJ 4
Panggoe 82 B 3
Pangnirtung 17 NO 3
Panhandle 21 F 4
Panjao 67 H 4
Panjgur 67 G 5
Panorama 35 F 5
Pantanal de São Lourénço
  34 E 4
Pantanal do Río Negro 34 E 4
Pantelleria 45 F 4
Panuco 25 E 3
Panuco, Rio 25 E 3
Pan Xian 70 DE 5
Paoua 60 B 3
Pápa 46 A 1
Papagayo, Golfo del 28 B 4
Papantla de Olarte 25 E 3
Papeete 83 F 4
Papenburg 41 E 4
Papey 42 C 3
Paphos 47 D 4
Papua, Gulf of 80 DE 3
Papua New Guinea 80 E 2–3
Papua New Guinea 82 AB 3
Pará 33 GH 5
Parabel 51 Q 4
Paracatu 35 G 4
Paracel Islands 73 K 4
Paragould 21 H 4
Paraguai 34 E 5
Paraguarí 36 E 4
Paraguay 34 DE 5
Paraguay 36 E 4
Paraíba 35 J 2
Parakou 58 E 4
Paramaribo 33 GH 2
Paramillo 28 D 5
Paramirim 35 H 3
Paraná (Argentina) 36 DE 5
Paraná (Brazil) 35 F 5
Paranaguá 36 G 4
Paranam 33 G 2
Paranavaí 35 F 5
Parangaba 35 J 1
Paraoa 83 F 4
Paratinga 35 H 3
Parbig 51 Q 4
Parc National de la Boucle De
  Baoule 58 C 3
Parc National de la Komoé
  58 D 4
Parc National de Sinianka-
  Minia 59 H 3

189

Parc National de Taï **58** C 4
Parc National de Wonga
  Wongué **59** F 6
Parc National de Zakouma
  59 H 3
Parc National du Bamingui-
  Ban-goran **60** BC 3
Parc National du Niokolo
  Koba **58** B 3
Parcs Nationaux du "W"
  58 E 3
Pardo **35** H 4
Pardubice **41** G 4
Parecis, Serra dos **34** D 3
Parent **18** F 4
Parepare **75** E 4
Paricutín, Volcán **24** D 4
Parima, Sierra **33** F 3
Parinari **32** D 4
Pariñas, Punta **32** B 4
Parintins **33** G 4
Paris (France) **44** D 2
Paris (IL, U.S.A.) **22** C 3
Paris (TN, U.S.A.) **22** C 3
Paris (TX, U.S.A.) **21** G 5
Parismina **28** C 4
Parkano **42** H 3
Parker **20** D 5
Parkersburg **22** D 3
Parkland **20** B 2
Park Rapids **21** H 2
Parlakimidi **72** D 4
Parlakote **72** D 4
Parma **45** F 3
Parma (OH, U.S.A.) **22** D 2
Parnaíba **35** H 1
Parnamirim **35** J 2
Parnarama **35** H 2
Parnassós Óros **46** B 3
Pärnu **43** H 4
Parpaillon **45** E 3
Parque Nacional Símon
  Bolívar **29** E 5
Parral **37** B 6
Parras, Sierra de **24** D 2
Parras de la Fuente **24** D 2
Parrita **28** C 5
Parry Bay **16** K 3
Parry Islands **84**
Parry Peninsula **16** AB 3
Partille **43** F 4
Partizansk **71** K 2
Paryang **72** D 2
Parys **62** D 5
Pasadena **20** C 5
Pascagoula **22** C 4
Pasni **67** G 5
Paso de Indios **37** C 7
Paso del Limay **37** BC 7
Paso de los Libres **36** E 4
Paso de los Vientos **29** E 2–3
Paso de San Francisco **36** C 4
Paso Río Mayo **37** B 8

Passau **41** F 5
Passo Fundo **36** F 4
Passos **35** G 5
Pastos Bons **35** H 2
Pasto **32** C 3
Patagonia **37** BC 7–9
Patan (India) **72** B 3
Patan (Nepal) **72** DE 2
Paterson **23** F 2
Pathankot **72** C 1
Pathfinder Reservoir **20** E 3
Patiala **72** C 1–2
Pativilca **32** C 6
Patkaglik **67** M 3
Patna **72** E 2
Patnagarh **72** D 3
Patos **35** J 2
Patos, Lagoa dos **36** F 5
Patos de Minas **35** G 4
Pátrai **46** B 3
Patras **46** B 3
Patríkos Kólpos **46** B 3
Patrocínio **35** G 4
Pattullo, Mount **13** LM 4
Patuca, Rio **28** C 3
Pau **44** C 3
Pau d'Arco **33** J 5
Paulatuk **13** B 3
Paulina Peak **20** B 3
Paulistana **35** H 2
Paulo Afonso **35** J 2
Pauls Valley **21** G 5
Pavlodar **51** P 5
Pavlof Islands **12** E 5
Pavlof Volcano **12** E 4
Pavlovka **51** O 5
Paxson **12** H 3
Payakumbuh **74** B 3–4
Payne, Baie **19** G 2
Payne, Lac **18** F 2
Paynes Find **78** B 4
Paysandú **36** E 5
Payson **20** D 4
Payturma **68** F 1
Pazardžik **46** B 2
Peace Point **14** G 3
Peace River **14** F 3
Peace River **14** G 3
Peach Springs **20** D 4
Peacock Hills **16** DE 3
Peaked Mountain **23** G 2
Pearl **22** C 4
Pearsall **25** E 2
Pearsoll Peak **20** AB 3
Peary Land **84**
Pebane **63** F 3
Pebas **32** D 4
Peć **46** B 2
Pechora **50** K 2
Pechorskoye More **50** KL 2
Pecos **24** F 5
Pecos Plains **21** F 5
Pecos River **21** F 5
Pécs **46** A 1

Pedernales **33** F 2
Pedernales (Venezuela)
  29 G 5
Pedriceña **24** D 2
Pedro Afonso **33** J 5
Pedro Cays **28** D 3
Pedro de Valdivia **34** BC 5
Pedro Juan Caballero **34** E 5
Peel (N.W.T., Can.) **13** L 2
Peera Peera Poolanna Lake
  79 F 4
Pegu **73** G 4
Pegunungan Barisan **74** B 4
Pegunungan Maoke **75** J 4
Pegunungan Muller **74** D 3
Pegunungan Schwaner
  74 D 4
Pegu Yoma **73** G 3–4
Pehuajó **37** D 6
Peixe **35** G 3
Pekalongan **74** CD 5
Pekanbaru **74** B 3
Pekin **21** H J 3
Peking **71** G 3
Pelat, Mont **45** E 3
Pelican **13** K 4
Pelican Narrows **15** J 3
Peljesac **45** G 3
Pelly **13** L 3
Pelly Bay **16** H 3
Pelly Bay **16** J 3
Pelly Crossing **13** K 3
Pelly Mountains **13** L 3
Peloponnese **46** B 3
Pelopónnisos **46** B 3
Pelotas **36** F 5
Pelvoux, Massif du **45** E 3
Pemangkat **74** C 3
Pematangsiantar **74** A 3
Pemba **63** G 2
Pemba Island **61** FG 6
Pembina **21** G 2
Pembroke (Ontario, Can.)
  18 E 4
Pembroke, Cape (N.W.T.,
  Can.) **17** K 4
Penas, Golfo de **37** AB 8
Pendembu **58** B 4
Pendleton **20** C 2
Pend Oreille **20** C 2
Pend Oreille, Lake **20** C 2
Penedo **35** J 3
Penglai **71** GH 3
Península Brecknock **37** B 9
Península de Azuero **28** C 5
Península de Guajira **29** E 4
Península de Nicoya **28** B 5
Península de Osa **28** C 5
Península de Paraguaná
  29 EF 4
Península de Paria **29** G 4
Península de Taitao **37** AB 8
Península de Yucatán →
  Yucatán Peninsula **26** D 4–5

Península Valdés **37** D 7
Péninsule de Gaspé **19** G 4
Peninsule d'Ungava **18** EF 2
Penisola Salentina **45** G 3
Pénjamo **25** D 3
Penn Hills **22** E 2
Penninechain **40** C 4
Pennsylvania **22** E 2
Penny Ice Cap **17** N 3
Penobscot Bay **23** G 3
Peñón Blanco **24** D 3
Penong **78** E 5
Penonomé **28** C 5
Penrhyn **83** E 3
Pensacola **22** C 4
Pensacola Mountains **85**
Pentecoste **82** C 4
Pentecôte **81** J 5
Penticton **14** F 5
Penza **50** H 5
Penzhinskaya Guba **69** U 3
Penzhinskiy Khrebet **69** U 3
Peoria **22** C 2
Percé **19** H 4
Perche, Collines du **44** D 2
Pereira **32** C 3
Pereval Yablonitse **46** BC 1
Pergamino **36** D 5
Pergamon **46** C 3
Péribonca **19** F 4
Peribonca, Lac **18** F 3
Pericos **24** C 2
Périgueux **44** CD 2
Perlas, Laguna de **28** C 4
Perm **50** L 4
Pernambuco **35** J 2
Perote **25** E 4
Perpignan **44** D 3
Perry **22** D 4
Perry Island **16** G 3
Perryton **21** F 4
Perryville **12** F 4
Persepolis **49** F 3
Perseverancia **34** D 3
Persia **49** F 2
Persia **66** EF 4
Persian Gulf **49** F 4
Persian Gulf → The Gulf
  57 J 3
Perth **40** C 3
Perth (Australia) **78** B 5
Perth-Andover **19** G 4
Perthus, Col de **44** D 3
Peru **32** C 5
Perugia **45** F 3
Pervomaysk (Ukraine,
  U.S.S.R.) **46** D 1
Pervomayskiy **50** H 3
Pervoural'sk **51** L 4
Pesaro **45** F 3
Pescara **45** F 3
Peschanyy, Mys **66** E 2
Peshawar **67** J 4
Peski Karakumy **66–67** FG 3

Peski Kyzylkum **67** GH 2
Peski Sary Ishikotrau **51** P 6
Peski Taukum **67** JK 2
Pessac **44** C 3
Petacalco, Bahia de **24** D 4
Petaluma **20** B 4
Petare **32** E 1
Petatlán **25** D 4
Petauke **63** E 2
Petén **25** F 4
Petenwell Lake **22** C 2
Peterborough (Ontario, Can.)
22 E 2
Peterborough (South
Australia) **79** F 5
Peter I Island **85**
Peter Lake **15** L 2
Peter Pond Lake **14** GH 3
Petersburg (AK, U.S.A.) **13** L 4
Petersburg (VA, U.S.A.) **22** E 3
Petites Pyrénées **44** D 3
Petit-Mécatina, Rivière du
19 HJ 3
Petitot **14** E 3
Petitsikapau Lake **19** G 3
Peto **26** D 4
Petorca **36** B 5
Petra **56** F 2
Petra Azul **35** H 4
Petrel **85**
Petrila **46** B 1
Petrodvorets **43** J 4
Petrolina **35** H 2
Petropavlovsk **51** NO 4–5
Petropavlovsk-Kamchatskiy
69 ST 5
Petrópolis **35** H 5
Petrova Gora **45** G 2
Petrovsk **50** J 5
Petrovsk-Zabaykal'skiy **68** J 5
Petrozavodsk **50** FG 3
Peureulak **74** A 3
Pevek **84**
Pforzheim **41** E 5
Phalodi **72** B 2
Phaltan **72** BC 4
Phatthalung **73** H 6
Phenix City **22** C 4
Phet Buri **73** G 5
Philadelphia **23** F 3
Philae **56** E 4
Philippines **75** G 1
Philip Smith Mountains
12 H 2
Phillipsburg **21** G 4
Phitsanulok **73** H 4
Phnom Aural **74** B 1
Phnom Penh **73** H 5
Phoenix (AZ, U.S.A.) **20** D 5
Phoenix Islands **82** D 3
Phuket **73** G 6
Phuoc Le **73** J 5
Phu Set **73** J 4
Phu Vinh **73** J 5–6

Piacenza **45** EF 2–3
Piara Açu **33** H 5
Piatra Neamţ **46** C 1
Piauí **35** H 2
Pibor Post **60** E 3
Picacho del Centinela
24–25 D 2
Picardie **44** D 2
Pic Boby **63** H 4
Pic de la Selle **29** E 3
Pic de Macaya **29** E 3
Pichanal **34** D 5
Pichilemu **37** B 5
Pichilingue **24** BC 3
Pickle Lake **15** L 4
Pickwick Lake **22** C 3
Pico Bolívar **29** E 5
Pico Bonito **28** B 3
Pico Cristóbal Colón **32** D 1
Pico de Aneto **44** D 3
Pico Rondón **33** F 3
Picos **35** H 2
Pico San Juan **27** E 4
Pico Tamacuarí **32** E 3
Pictou **19** H 4
Pidurutalagala **72** D 6
Piedecuesta **29** E 5
Piedmont (MO, U.S.A.) **21** H 4
Piedras Negras **25** D 2
Piedra Sola **36** E 5
Pielinen **42** J 3
Pierre **21** FG 3
Piešťány **41** G 5
Pietarsaari **42** H 3
Pietermaritzburg **62** DE 5
Pietersburg **62** D 4
Pigué **37** D 6
Pihtipudas **42** J 3
Pikangikum **15** L 4
Pikelot **82** A 2
Pikes Peak **21** E 4
Pikhtovka **51** Q 4
Pik Kommunizma **67** J 3
Pik Pobedy **67** KL 2
Piła **41** G 4
Pilão Arcado **35** H 3
Pilar (Alagoas, Brazil) **35** J 2
Pilar (Paraguay) **36** E 4
Pilcomayo **34** DE 5
Piloncillo Mountains **20** E 5
Pilot Peak **20** D 3
Pilot Rock **20** C 2
Pil'tun **69** Q 5
Pim **51** O 3
Pimenta Bueno **34** D 3
Pimental **33** G 4
Pimentel **32** B 5
Pinaki **83** F 4
Pínar del Rio **26–27** E 4
Pincher Creek **14** G 5
Pindaíba **35** F 3
Pindaré Mirim **33** J 4
Pindhos Óros **46** B 2–3
Pine Bluff **21** H 5

Pine Bluffs **21** F 3
Pine Falls **15** K 4
Pine Island Bay **85**
Pine Pass **14** E 3
Pine Point **14** G 2
Pine Ridge **21** F 3
Pinerolo **45** E 2–3
Pinetown **63** E 5
Pingdingshan **70** FG 4
Pingdu **71** H 3
Pingelap **82** B 2
Pingle **70** EF 6
Pingliang **70** E 3
Pingluo **70** E 3
Pingquan **71** G 2
Pingtung **71** H 6
Pingwu **70** DE 4
Pingxiang (China) **70** E 6
Pingxiang (Jiangxi, China)
70 F 5
Pingyang **71** H 5
Pingyao **70** F 3
Pinheiro **33** J 4
Pink Mountain **14** E 3
Pinnaroo **79** G 6
Pinos, Mount **20** C 4–5
Pinrang **75** E 4
Pins, Île des **82** C 4
Pinsk **43** J 5
Pinyug **50** J 3
Piotrków Trybunalski **41** G 4
Pipestone **21** G 3
Pipmouacan, Réservoir **19** F 4 ⟨
Piracaiba **35** G 5
Piracuruca **35** H 1
Piraiévs **46** B 3
Pirapora **35** H 4
Pires do Río **35** G 4
Pirin **46** B 2
Piripiri **35** H 1
Pirot **46** B 2
Piru **75** G 4
Pisa **45** F 3
Pisac **34** B 3
Pisagua **34** B 4
Pisco **34** A 3
Písek **41** F 5
Pishan **67** K 3
Pisté **26** D 4
Pitaga **19** G 3
Pitalito **32** C 3
Pitcairn **83** G 4
Piteå **42** H 2
Piteşti **46** B 2
Pit-Gorodoko **68** FG 4
Pitkyaranta **42** K 3
Pitt **82** D 5
Pitt Banks Island (Br. Col.,
Canada) **13** L 5
Pittsburg (KS, U.S.A.) **21** H 4
Pittsburgh (PA, U.S.A.) **22** E 2
Pittsfield (IL, U.S.A.) **21** H 4
Pittsfield (MA, U.S.A.) **23** F 2
Pium **35** G 3

Pjorga **42** B 3
Placentia **19** K 4
Placentia Bay **19** K 4
Placetas **27** F 4
Plaine des Flandres **44** D 1
Plainview **21** F 5
Planalto Central **35** G 4
Planalto do Brasil **35** H 4
Planalto do Mato Grosso
34–35 EF 3–4
Planeta Rica **28** D 5
Plasencia **44** B 3–4
Plateau de Millevaches **44** D 2
Plateau du Djado **59** G 1
Plateau du Tademaït **55** F 3
Plateau Laurentien **19** FJ 3
Plateau of Tibet **72** DE 1
Plateaux **59** GH 6
Plateaux de la Marche **44** D 2
Plato **29** E 5
Plato Ustyurt **66** EF 2
Platte River **21** F 3
Platterville **21** H 3
Plattsburg **23** F 2
Plattsmouth **21** G 3
Playa Azul **24** D 4
Playgreen, Lake **15** K 4
Playitas **29** E 5
Plaza Huincul **37** C 6
Pleasanton **25** E 2
Pleiku **73** J 5
Plentywood **21** EF 2
Plétipi, Lac **18** F 3
Pleven **46** BC 2
Ploče **45** G 3
Płock **41** GH 4
Ploieşti **46** C 2
Plovdiv **46** B 2
Plymouth **40** C 4
Plymouth (Montserrat)
29 G 3
Plzeň **41** F 5
Po **45** F 3
Pobedy, Pik **67** KL 2
Pocatello **20** D 3
Pocklington Reef **81** G 4
Poconé **34** E 4
Pocono Mountains **23** F 2
Poços de Caldas **35** G 5
Podgornoye **51** Q 4
Podgornyy **69** R 6
Podol'sk **50** G 4
Podosinovets **50** J 3
Podresovo **51** N 4
Pod'yelanka **68** H 4
Pofadder **62** BC 5
Pogibi **69** Q 5
Pohjanmaa **42** J 3
Poinsett, Cape **85**
Point Arena **20** B 4
Point Baker **13** L 4
Point Barrow **12** F 1
Point Conception **20** B 5
Point Culver **78** CD 5

Point D'Entrecasteaux **78** AB 5
Pointe-à-Pitre **29** G 3
Pointe aux E'cueils **18** E 2
Pointe de Grave **44** C 2
Pointe de l'Est **19** H 4
Pointe de Penmarch **44** BC 2
Pointe des Monts **19** G 4
Pointe Louis-XIV **18** D 3
Pointe Noire **59** G 6
Point Hope **12** D 2
Point Hope **12** D 2
Point Lake **16** D 3
Point Pleasant **23** F 3
Poitiers **44** D 2
Poitou **44** CD 2
Pojeierze Pomorskie **41** G 4
Pojezierze Mazurskie **41** H 4
Pokrovsk **69** N 3
Pola de Siero **44** B 3
Poland **41** G 4
Polar Plateau **85**
Polatlı **47** D 3
Pole of Inaccessibility **85**
Polesie Lubelskie **41** H 4
Polesye **43** J 5
Polgovskoye **51** N 4
Polist' **43** K 4
Pollensa **44** D 4
Polotsk **43** J 4
Polska **41** G 4
Polson **20** D 2
Poltava **50** FG 6
Poluostrov Buzachi **66** F 1
Poluostrov Kamchatka **69** S 4–5
Poluostrov Kanin **50** HJ 2
Poluostrov Kol'skiy **50** G 2
Poluostrov Koni **69** S 4
Poluostrov Rybachiy **42** K 2
Poluostrov Taymyr **68** FH 1
Poluostrov Yamal **51** NO 1
Polyarnik **12** B 2
Polyarnyy Ural **51** MN 2
Polynesia **83** EG 2–4
Pombal **35** J 3
Pomerania **41** FG 4
Pomio **82** B 3
Pommersche Bucht **41** F 4
Pomona **20** C 5
Pompei **45** F 3
Pompeyevka **69** O 6
Ponape **82** B 2
Ponca City **21** G 4
Ponce **29** F 3
Pondicherry **72** CD 5
Ponente, Rivera di **45** E 3
Ponoy **50** H 2
Ponta da Baleia **35** J 4
Ponta do Padrão **62** A 1
Ponta Grossa **36** F 4
Ponta Porã **35** EF 5
Pontchartrain, Lake **21** H 5

Ponte Nova **35** H 5
Pontevedra **44** B 3
Pontiac (IL, U.S.A.) **22** C 2
Pontianak **74** C 4
Pontine Mountains **47** EF 2
Poochera **78** E 5
Pool **59** H 6
Poole **40** C 4
Poopó **34** C 4
Poopó, Lago de **34** C 4
Poorman **12** F 3
Popar Hill **15** L 4
Popayán **32** C 3
Poplar Bluff **21** H 4
Popokabaka **60** B 6
Popondetta **80** E 3
Poptún **28** B 3
Porangatu **35** FG 3
Porbandar **72** A 3
Porco **34** C 4
Porcupine **13** J 2
Porcupine Plain **13** K 2
Pori **42** H 3
Porirua **81** R 9
Porjus **42** H 2
Porlamar **33** F 1
Porpoise Bay **85**
Porsangerhalvöya **42** HJ 1
Porsgrunn **43** EF 4
Portage la-Prairie **15** K 4
Port Alberni **14** E 5
Portales **21** F 5
Port Alice **13** M 5
Port Angeles **20** B 2
Port Antonio **28** D 3
Port Arthur (Tasmania,
   Austr.) **80** L 9
Port Arthur (TX, U.S.A.) **25** F 2
Port Augusta **79** S 5
Port au Prince **29** E 3
Port Blair **73** F 5
Port Blandford **19** K 4
Port Burwell **17** O 4
Port-Cartier **19** G 3
Port Charlotte **27** E 3
Port Darwin (Falkland Is.,
   U.K.) **37** E 9
Port Darwin (N.T., Austr.)
   78 DE 1
Port Elgin **22** D 2
Port Elizabeth **62** D 6
Porterville **20** C 4
Port Gentil **59** F 6
Port Graham **12** G 4
Port Harcourt **59** F 4–5
Port Hardy **13** M 5
Port Hawkesbury **19** H 4
Port Hedland **78** B 3
Port Heiden **12** F 4
Port Hope Simpson **19** JK 3
Port Huron **22** D 2
Port Keats **78** DE 1
Port Láirge **40** B 4
Portland (ME, U.S.A.) **23** G 3

Portland (OR, U.S.A.) **20** B 2
Portland (Victoria, Austr.)
   79 G 6
Portlaoise **40** B 4
Port Lavaca **25** E 2
Port Lincoln **79** F 5
Port Loko **58** B 4
Port-Louis **63** K 6
Port-Louis (Guadeloupe)
   29 G 3
Port Menier **19** H 4
Port Moller **12** E 4
Port Moresby **80** E 3
Port Nelson **15** L 3
Port Nolloth **62** B 5
Port-Nouveau-Québec **19** G 2
Pôrto Alegre **36** FG 5
Porto Amboim **62** A 2
Pôrto Artur **35** F 3
Portobelo (Panamá) **28** D 5
Pôrto de Moz **33** H 4
Pôrto Esperidião **34** E 4
Port of Spain **33** F 1
Pôrto Gránde **33** H 3
Pôrto Jofre **34** E 4
Pörtom **42** H 3
Pôrto Murtinho **34** E 5
Pôrto Nacional **35** G 3
Porto Novo **58** E 4
Port Ontario **22** E 2
Pôrto Santana **33** H 4
Pôrto Santo **54** B 2
Pôrto Seguro **35** J 4
Pôrto Valter **32** D 5
Pôrto Velho **33** F 5
Portoviejo **32** BC 4
Portree **40** B 3
Port Said **48** A 3
Port Saint Joe **25** F 2
Port Saint Johns **62** DE 6
Port Saunders **19** J 3
Port Simpson **13** L 5
Portsmouth (N.H., U.S.A.)
   23 F 2
Portsmouth (OH, U.S.A.)
   22 D 3
Portsmouth (U.K.) **40** C 4
Portsmouth (VA, U.S.A.)
   22 E 3
Port Sulphur **25** F 2
Portugal **44** B 3
Portugalete **44** C 3
Port Wakefield **79** F 5
Porvenir **37** BC 9
Porvoo **43** J 3
Posadas **36** E 4
Posht-e Badam **49** G 2
Positos **34** D 5
Posse **35** G 3
Postavy **43** J 4
Poste-de-la-Baleine **18** E 2
Poste Maurice Cortier **55** F 4
Postmasburg **62** C 5

Posto Cunambo **32** CD 4
Postville **169** J 3
Potapovo **51** R 2
Potenza **45** G 3
Potgietersrus **62** D 4
Potholes Reservoir **20** C 2
Poti (Gruziya, U.S.S.R.)
   47 F 2
Potiskum **59** G 3
Potomac River **22** E 3
Potosí **34** C 4
Potrerillos **36** BC 4
Potsdam **41** F 4
Pottstown **22** E 2
Pou Bia **73** H 4
Povenets **50** F 3
Póvoa de Varzim **44** B 3
Povungnituk **17** L 4
Powassan **18** E 4
Powder River **21** E 2
Powell, Lake **20** D 4
Powell River **14** E 5
Pożarevac **46** B 2
Poza Rica de Hidalgo **25** E 3
Poznan **41** G 4
Pozo Almonte **34** C 5
Prado **35** J 4
Praha → Prague **41** FG 4–5
Praia **58** B 7
Prainha **33** FG 5
Prairie du Chien **21** H 3
Praslin **61** K 5
Prato **45** F 3
Pratt **21** G 4
Praya **74** E 5
Prentice **21** H 2
Prepansko jezero **46** B 2
Presa de la Boquilla **24** CD 2
Presa Falcon **25** E 2
Presa Miguel Alemán **25** E 4
Presa Netzahualcyótl **25** F 4
Prescott **20** D 5
Presidencia Roque Sáenz-
   Peña **36** D 4
Presidente Dutra **35** H 2
Presidente Prudente **35** F 5
Presnogor'kovka **51** N 5
Presque Isle **23** G 2
Preston **20** D 3
Preston **40** C 4
Prestonburg **22** D 3
Pretoria **62** D 5
Priazovskaya Vozvyshennost'
   47 E 1
Pribilof Islands **12** D 4
Příbram **41** F 5
Price **20** D 4
Prichard **22** C 4
Prichernomorskaya
   Nizmennost' **47** D 1
Prieska **62** C 5
Prieta, Sierra **20** D 5
Prikaspiyskaya Nizmennost
   66 DE 1

Prikubanskaya Nizmennost' 47 E 1
Prilep 46 B 2
Priluki 50 H 3
Primavera 85
Primeira Cruz 35 H 1
Primorsk 43 J 3
Primorsko-Akhtarsk 47 E 1
Primrose Lake 14 H 3
Prince Albert 15 H 4
Prince Albert Mountains 85
Prince Albert National Park 15 H 4
Prince Albert Peninsula 16 C 2
Prince Albert Sound 16 CD 2
Prince Alfred, Cape 16 A 2
Prince Charles Island 17 L 3
Prince Charles Mountains 85
Prince-de-Galles, Cap 17 M 4
Prince Edward Island (Canada) 19 H 4
Prince Edward Islands (Antarctica) 85
Prince George 14 E 4
Prince of Wales, Cape 12 D 2
Prince of Wales Island 16 G 2
Prince of Wales Island (AK, U.S.A.) 13 L 4
Prince of Wales Island (Queensland, Austr.) 79 G 1
Prince of Wales Strait 16 C 2
Prince Patrick Island 84
Prince Rupert 13 L 5
Princess Astrid Coast 85
Princess Charlotte Bay 79 G 1
Princess Martha Coast 85
Princess Ragnhild Coast 85
Princess Royal Island 13 M 5
Princeton 14 E 5
Princeton (IN, U.S.A.) 22 C 3
Princeton (MO, U.S.A.) 21 H 3
Prince William Sound 12 H 3
Príncipe 59 F 5
Prineville 20 B 3
Prinzapolka 28 C 4
Pripet Marshes 43 J 5
Pripyat' 43 J 5
Pristina 46 B 2
Prizren 46 B 2
Progreso 26 D 4
Prokhladnyy 47 F 2
Prokhorkino 51 P 4
Prokop'yevsk 51 R 5
Proliv Karskiye Vorota 50–51 L 1
Proliv Nevel'skogo 69 Q 5
Prome 73 G 4
Promontoire Portland 18 DE 2
Promontorio del Gargano 45 G 3
Propria 35 J 3
Prosser 20 B 2
Protochnoye 51 N 3

Provence 45 E 3
Providence (R.I., U.S.A.) 23 F 2
Providence, Cape 80 P 10
Providencia, Isla de 28 C 4
Provideniya 12 C 3
Provincetown 23 G 3
Provo 20 D 3
Prudhoe Bay 12 H 1
Prut 46 C 1
Prydz Bay 85
Przheval'sk 67 K 2
Pshish 47 E 2
Pskov 43 J 4
Pskovskoye Ozero 43 J 4
Ptich 43 J 5
Pucallpa 32 D 5
Pucheng 71 G 5
Pudasjärvi 42 J 2
Puebla 25 E 4
Pueblo 21 F 4
Pueblo Hundido 36 C 4
Puelches 37 CD 6
Puente Alto 36 BC 5
Puente-Genil 44 C 4
Puerto Aisén 37 B 8
Puerto Angel 25 E 4
Puerto Arista 25 F 4
Puerto Armuelles 28 C 5
Puerto Asis 32 C 3
Puerto Ayacucho 32 E 2
Puerto Baquerizo Moreno 32 B 6
Puerto Barrios 28 B 3
Puerto Cabello 32 E 1
Puerto Cabezas 28 C 4
Puerto Carreño 32 E 2
Puerto Chicama 32 BC 5
Puerto Coig 37 C 9
Puerto Colombia 32 C 1
Puerto Cortés 28 B 3
Puerto Cumarebo 32 E 1
Puerto Deseado 37 CD 8
Puerto de Somport 44 C 3
Puerto de Villatoro 44 B 3
Puerto Escondido 25 E 4
Puerto Esperanza 36 F 4
Puerto Estrella 32 D 1
Puerto Heath 34 C 3
Puerto Juárez 26 D 4
Puerto la Cruz 33 F 1
Puerto Leguizamo 32 D 4
Puerto Lempira 28 C 3
Puerto Libertad 24 B 2
Puerto Limón 32 D 3
Puertollano 44 C 4
Puerto Madero 25 F 5
Puerto Madryn 37 C 7
Puerto Magdalena 24 B 3
Puerto Maldonado 34 C 3
Puerto Montt 37 B 7
Puerto Natales 37 B 9
Puerto Nuevo 32 E 2
Puerto Padilla 34 B 3

Puerto Páez 32 E 2
Puerto Patillos 34 B 5
Puerto Patiño 34 C 4
Puerto Plata 29 EF 3
Puerto Portillo 32 D 5
Puerto Princesa 75 E 2
Puerto Rico (Argentina) 36 F 4
Puerto Rico (U.S.A.) 29 F 3
Puerto Rondón 32 D 2
Puerto Siles 34 C 3
Puerto Suárez 34 E 4
Puerto Vallarta 24 C 3–4
Puerto Varas 37 B 7
Puerto Verlarde 34 D 4
Puerto Villamizar 32 D 2
Puerto Villazón 34 D 3
Puerto Wilches 29 E 5
Puerto Wilches 32 D 2
Puerto Williams 37 BC 9–10
Pugachev 50 JK 5
Puget Sound 20 B 2
Pukapuka (Cook Is.) 82 DE 3
Pukapuka (French Polynesia) 83 F 3
Pukaruha 83 FG 4
Pukaskwa National Park 18 C 4
Pukatawagan 15 J 3
Pukch'ŏng 71 J 2
Puksoozero 50 H 3
Pula 45 F 3
Pulap 82 A 2
Pulau Alor 75 F 5
Pulau Bacan 75 G 4
Pulau Bangka 74 C 4
Pulau Belitung 74 C 4
Pulau Biak 75 J 4
Pulau Bintan 74 B 3
Pulau Enggano 74 B 5
Pulau Jos Sodarso 75 J 5
Pulau Kabaena 75 F 5
Pulau Kai Besar 75 H 5
Pulau Karakelong 75 G 3
Pulau Kobroor 75 H 5
Pulau Labengke 75 F 4
Pulau Laut 74 E 4
Pulau Lomblen 75 F 5
Pulau Madura 74 D 5
Pulau Mangole 75 G 4
Pulau Misool 75 H 4
Pulau Morotai 75 G 3
Pulau Muna 75 F 5
Pulau Nias 74 A 3
Pulau Numfor 75 H 4
Pulau Padang 74 B 3
Pulau Roti 75 F 6
Pulau Salawati 75 H 4
Pulau Selaru 75 H 5
Pulau Selayar 75 F 5
Pulau Siberut 74 A 4
Pulau Simeulue 74 A 3
Pulau Taliabu 75 F 4
Pulau Trangan 75 H 5

Pulau Waigeo 75 H 3
Pulau Wetar 75 G 5
Pulau Wokam 75 H 5
Pulau Yamdena 75 H 5
Pulau Yapen 75 J
Puławy 41 H 4
Pullman 20 C 2
Pulog, Mount 75 J 1
Pulozero 42 K 2
Pulusuk 82 A 2
Puna de Atacama 34 C 5–6
Puncak Jaya 75 J 4
Pune 72 B 4
Punjab 67 J 4
Punkaharju 42 J 3
Puno 34 B 4
Punta, Cerro de 29 F 3
Punta Alegre 27 F 4
Punta Alta 37 D 6
Punta Arenas 37 B 9
Punta Burica 28 C 5
Punta del Diamante 25 DE 4
Punta de Mata 29 G 5
Punta Desengaño 37 C 8
Punta Eugenia 24 A 2
Punta Fijo 32 D 1
Punta Gallinas 32 D 1
Punta Gorda (Belize) 28 B 3
Punta Gorda (Nicaragua) 28 C 4
Punta Gorda, Bàhía de 28 C 4
Punta Maisí 29 E 2
Punta Mariato 28 C 5
Punta Medanosa 37 CD 8
Punta Negra 32 B 5
Punta Pariñas 32 B 4
Punta Prieta 24 B 2
Puntarenas 28 BC 5
Punta Rieles 34 E 5
Punta Verde 28 C 4
Puqi 70 F 7
Pur 51 P 2
Purcell Mountains 14 F 4
Purdy Islands 82 A 3
Purnia 72 E 2
Purtuniq 17 M 4
Purus 33 F 4
Puruvesi 42 J 3
Pusan 71 JK 3
Pushchino 69 T 5
Pushkin 43 K 4
Pushkino 50 J 5
Pustoretsk 69 U 3
Putao 73 G 2
Putla de Guerrero 25 E 4
Putorana, Gory 68 FH 2
Putumayo 32 D 4
Puulavesi 42 J 3
Puyang 70 G 3
Puy de Sancy 44 D 2
Puyo 32 C 4
Pweto 60 D 6
Pyaozero, Ozero 42 K 2
Pyatigorsk 47 F 2

Pyatistennoy **69** TU 2
Pyawbwe **73** G 3
Pyhäjoki HJ 3
Pyhätunturi **42** J 2
Pyinmana **73** G 4
P'yŏngyang **71** HJ 3
Pyramid Lake **20** C 3–4
Pyrénées **44** CD 3
Pyshchug **50** J 4

Q

Qâbis **55** H 2
Qâ'emshahr **49** F 1
Qafşah **55** G 2
Qagcaka **72** D 1
Qahremânshahr **49** E 2
Qaidam Pendi **70** BC 3
Qala-Nau **67** G 3
Qâlat **67** H 4
Qal' at Dīzah **49** D 1
Qal'at Şâliḥ **49** E 3
Qal' at Sukkar **49** E 3
Qalīb ash Shuyūkh **49** E 3
Qamalung **70** CD 4
Qamdo **70** C 4
Qamīnis **55** J 2
Qanât as Suways **48** A 3
Qapqal **67** L 2
Qarah Dagh **47** F 3
Qardo **61** H 3
Qasr-e Shīrīn **49** DE 2
Qasr-e Shīrīn **66** D 4
Qaşr Farâfirah **56** D 3
Qatar **49** F 4
Qatrūyeh **49** G 3
Qâyen **66** F 4
Qayyârah **48** D 2
Qazvīn **66** DE 3
Qeshm **49** G 4
Qeshm **49** G 4
Qeys **49** F 4
Qezel Owzan **49** E 1
Qezi'ot **48** B 3
Qian'an **71** H 2
Qiaowan **70** C 2
Qidong **71** H 4
Qiemo **67** M 3
Qift **48** A 4
Qijiang **70** E 5
Qijiaojing **70** B 2
Qila Saifullah **67** H 4
Qilian Shan **70** CD 3
Qimen **71** G 5
Qinâ **48** A 4
Qina, Wâdī **48** A 4
Qingdao **71** H 3
Qinggang **71** HJ 1
Qinghai **70** C 3
Qinghai Hu **70** D 3
Qingjiang (Jiangsu, China)
    71 GH 4
Qingjiang (Jiangxi, China)
    70 FG 5

Qing Zang Gaoyuan **72** DE 1
Qinhuangdao **71** GH 3
Qinling Shan **70** E 4
Qinzhou **70** E 6
Qionghai **70** F 7
Qionglai **70** D 4
Qiqiar **68** M 5
Qiqihar **69** MN 6
Qira **67** L 3
Qirjat Yam (Israel) **48** B 2
Qitai **70** AB 2
Qitaihe **71** K 1
Qiyang **70** F 5
Qog UI **71** G 2
Qolleh-ye Damâvand **49** F 2
Qom **49** F 2
Qomsheh **49** F 2–3
Qôrnoq **17** Q 4
Qorud, Kuhha-ye **49** F 2–3
Qoşbeh-ye Nassâr **49** E 3
Qotbâbâd **49** G 4
Quang Ngai **73** J 4
Quanhov **70** E 5
Quan Phu Quoc **73** H 5
Quanzhou **71** GH 6
Qu'Appelle **15** J 4
Quartu Sant' Elena **45** E 4
Quartz Mountain **20** B 3
Quartzsite **20** D 5
Quatro Ciénegas **24** D 2
Qûchân **66** F 3
Québec **18–19** F 3
Québec **19** F 4
Quebracho Coto **36** D 4
Queen, Cape **17** L 4
Queen Charlotte Islands
    13 KL 5
Queen Charlotte Sound
    13 LM 5
Queen Elizabeth Islands **84**
Queen Fabiola Mountains **85**
Queen Mary Coast **85**
Queen Maud Gulf **16** G 3
Queen Maud Land **85**
Queen Maud Mountains **85**
Queensland **79** GH 3
Queenstown (South Africa)
    62 D 6
Queenstown (Tasmania,
    Austr.) **80** L 9
Quelimane **63** F 3
Quemado **20** E 5
Quembo **62** B 2
Quen Bess, Mount **14** E 4
Que Que **62** D 3
Querétaro **25** DE 3
Quesada **28** C 4
Queshan **70** F 4
Quesnel **14** E 4
Quesnel Lake **14** E 4
Quetta **67** H 4
Quevedo **32** C 4
Quezaltenango **25** F 5
Quibala **62** B 2

Quibdó **32** C 2
Quiçama National Park
    62 A 1–2
Quiculungo **62** B 1
Quila **24** C 3
Quillabamba **34** B 3
Quillacollo **34** C 4
Quillaicillo **36** B 5
Quillota **36** B 5
Quilmili **36** D 4
Quilon **72** C 6
Quimper **44** C 2
Quincy **21** H 4
Quines **36** C 5
Quinhagak **12** E 4
Qui Nhon **73** JK 5
Quiñones **24** B 3
Quintana Roo **26** D 4–5
Quitasueño, Banco **28** C 4
Quito **32** C 4
Quixadá **35** J 1
Qujing **70** D 5
Qulansiyah **61** J 2
Qulbân Layyah **49** E 3
Quoich **15** L 2
Quorn **80** B 5
Qusaybah **66** C 4
Qusum **70** B 5
Qu Xian **71** GH 5

R

Raab **45** G 2
Raahe **42** H 3
Rába (Hungary) **46** A 1
Raba (Indonesia) **75** E 5
Rabak **56** E 6
Rabat **54** D 2
Rabaul **82** B 3
Rabyânah **55** K 4
Race, Cape **19** K 4
Rach Gia **73** HJ 5–6
Racine **22** C 2
Radhanpur **72** B 3
Radisson **18** E 3
Radom **41** H 4
Radomsko **41** G 4
Radville **15** J 5
Rae **14** F 2
Ra's-e Nây Band **49** F 4
Raevavae **83** F 4
Rafaela **36** D 5
Rafah **48** B 3
Rafha' **48** D 3
Rafsanjân **49** G 3
Raga **60** D 3
Ragged Island Range **27** F 4
Rahimyar Khan **67** J 5
Raiatea **83** E 4
Raichur **72** C 4
Raiganj **72** E 2
Raigarh **72** D 3
Rainbow Peak **20** C 3

Rainier, Mount **20** B 2
Rainy Lake **15** L 5
Raipur **72** D 3
Rajada **35** H 2
Rajahmundry **72** D 4
Rajakoski **42** J 2
Rajapalaiyam **72** C 6
Rajasthan **72** BC 2
Rajgarh **72** C 3
Rajkot **72** AB 3
Raj Nandgaon **72** D 3
Rajshahi **72** E 3
Rakahanga **82** E 3
Rakitnoye **43** J 5
Rakulka **50** HJ 3
Raleigh **22** E 3
Raleigh Bay **22** E 4
Ralik Chain **82** C 2
Rama **28** C 4
Ramâdah **55** H 2
Ramapo Deep **65** R 6
Ramea **19** J 4
Râmhormoz **49** E 3
Ramlat Hagolan **48** B 2
Ramlat Rabyânah **55** JK 4
Rampart **12** G 2
Rampur **72** CD 2
Ramree **73** F 4
Ramsey **18** D 4
Ramsgate **40** D 4
Rancagua **36** B 5
Ranchi **72** DE 3
Randers **43** F 4
Randijaure **42** G 2
Ranger **25** G 5
Rangoon **73** FG 4
Rangpur **72** E 2
Rankin Inlet **15** L 2
Rann of Kutch **72** AB 3
Rantauprapat **74** AB 3
Ranua **42** J 2
Raoul **82** D 4
Rapa **83** F 4
Rapa Nui **83** H 4
Raper, Cape **17** N 3
Rapid City **21** F 3
Raraka **83** F 4
Rarotonga **83** E 4
Ra's Abū Madd **48** B 4
Ra's Abū Qumayyis **49** F 4
Ra's al Abyad **48** BC 5
Ra's al Abyad **55** G 1
Ra's al Khafji **49** E 3
Ra's al Khaymah **49** G 4
Ra's al Madrakah **57** K 5
Ra's al Mish'âb **49** E 3
Ra's ash Shaykh **48** B 3
Ra's Asir **61** J 2
Ra's as Saffânīyah **49** E 3
Ra's aţ Ţīb **55** H 1
Ra's az Zawr **49** E 4
Ra's Ba'labakk **48** B 2
Ra's Banâs **48** B 5
Ra's Barīdī **48** B 4

Ras Dashan 61 F 2
Ra's Fartak 57 J 5
Ra's Ghārib 48 A 3
Ra's Ḥāfūn 61 J 2
Rasht 66 D 3
Raskoh 67 GH 5
Ra's Miṣrātah 55 J 2
Ra's Muhammad 48 B 4
Rasmussen Basin 16 GH 3
Rasshua, Ostrov 69 S 6
Rasskazovo 50 H 5
Rastigaissa 42 J 1
Råstojaure 42 H 2
Rat 12 A 6
Ratak Chain 82 C 2
Ratangarh 72 B 2
Rat Buri 73 G 5
Rat Islands 12 A 6
Ratlam 72 BC 3
Ratnagiri 72 B 4
Ratnapura 72 D 6
Raton 21 F 4
Ratta 51 Q 3
Ratz, Mount 13 L 4
Raufarhöfn 42 BC 2
Raukela 72 DE 3
Raúl Leoni, Represa 33 F 2
Rauma 42 H 3
Raupelyan 12 C 2
Ravahere 83 F 4
Ravānsar 49 E 2
Rävar 49 G 3
Ravenna 45 F 3
Ravenshoe 79 GH 2
Rāwah 66 C 4
Rawaki 82 D 3
Rawalpindi 67 J 4
Rawāndūz 66 C 3
Rawlinna 78 D 5
Rawlins 20 E 3
Rawson 37 D 7
Ray, Cape 19 J 4
Raychikhinsk 69 NO 6
Raymond 20 B 2
Raymondville 25 E 2
Rayón 25 E 3
Rāzān 49 E 2
Razdan 47 F 2
Razgrad 46 C 2
Ré, Ile de 44 C 2
Read 16 D 3
Reading 40 C 4
Real, Cordillera 32 C 4
Realico 36 D 5
Reao 83 G 4
Reata 25 D 2
Rebbenesöy 42 G 1
Rebecca, Lake 78 C 5
Reboly 50 F 3
Recife 35 K 2
Récifs d'Entrecasteaux 82 B 4
Reconquista 36 DE 4
Red Bank 22 C 3

Red Bay (Newfoundl., Can.) 19 J 3
Red Bluff 20 B 3
Red Cloud 21 G 3
Red Deer 14 G 4
Red Deer River (Alb., Can.) 14 G 4
Red Deer River (Sask., Can.) 15 J 4
Red Devil 12 F 3
Redding 20 B 3
Redenção da Gurguéia 35 H 2
Redfield 21 G 3
Red Hills 21 G 4
Red Lake 15 L 4
Redlands 20 C 5
Red Lodge 20 E 2
Red Oak 21 GH 3
Redoubt Volcano 12 G 3
Red River (LA, U.S.A.) 25 H 5
Red River (MN, U.S.A.) 21 G 2
Red Rock River 20 D 3
Red Sea 48 B 4
Red Sea 56–57 FG 4–5
Red Water 14 G 4
Red Wing 21 H 3
Reef Islands 82 BC 3
Regensburg 41 F 5
Reggane 54 EF 3
Reggio di Calabria 45 G 4
Reggio nell'Emilia 45 EF 3
Reghin 46 B 1
Regina 15 J 4
Regina 33 H 3
Registan 67 GH 4
Regocijo 24 CD 3
Rehoboth 62 B 4
Reims 44 D 2
Reina Adelaida, Archipiélago-de la 37 A 9
Reindeer 15 J 3
Reindeer Lake 15 J 3
Reinoksfjellet 42 G 2
Reitoru 83 F 4
Rekinniki 69 U 3
Reliance 15 H 2
Remanso 33 HJ 4
Remanso 35 H 2
Rembang 74 D 5
Renascença 32 E 4
Renfrew 18 E 4
Rengo 36 B 5
Rennell 81 H 4
Rennes 44 C 2
Rennie Lake 15 H 2
Reno (U.S.A.) 20 B 4
Renton 20 B 2
Replot 42 H 3
Represa Raúl Leoni 33 F 2
Republic 20 C 2
Republican River 21 G 3
Republic of Ireland 40 B 4
Repulse Bay 16 J 3
Repulse Bay 16 J 3

Requena 32 D 5
Réservoir Baskatong 18 EF 4
Réservoir Cabonga 18 E 4
Réservoir Decelles 18 E 4
Réservoir Dozois 18 E 4
Réservoir Gouin 18 EF 4
Réservoir Manicouagan 19 G 3
Réservoir Pipmouacan 19 F 4
Reshteh-ye Kühhä-ye Alborz 49 F 1
Resistencia 36 DE 4
Reşiţa 46 B 1
Resolution Island 17 O 4
Retalhuleu 25 F 5
Réunion 63 HK 6
Reus 44 D 3
Revelstoke 14 F 4
Revilla Gigedo 13 L 4
Revilla Gigedo Islands 11 G 8
Rewari 72 C 2
Rexburg 20 D 3
Rey 49 F 2
Reykjahlð 42 B 2
Reykjanes 42 A 3
Reykjavik 42 A 3
Reynosa 25 E 2
Rezé 44 C 2
Rēzekne 43J 4
Rhein 40 E 4
Rhinelander 22 C 1
Rhinmal 72 B 2
Rhode Island 23 F 2
Rhodes 46 C 3
Rhodope Mts 46 BC 2
Rhondda 40 C 4
Rhône 45 D 3
Rías Altas 44 B 3
Rías Bajas 44 B 3
Riau, Kepulauan 74 B 3
Ribeirão Prêto 35 G 5
Riberalta 34 C 3
Richard Collinson Inlet 16 D 2
Richard's Bay 63 E 5
Richardson Mountains 13 K 2
Richfield 20 D 4
Richland 20 C 2
Richmond (CA, U.S.A.) 20 B 4
Richmond (Queensland, Austr.) 79 G 3
Richmond (VA, U.S.A.) 22 E 3
Richmond Hill 22 E 2
Riding Mountain National-Park 15 J 4
Rietavas 43H 4
Riga 43 H 4
Riggins 20 C 2
Rigolet 19 J 3
Rihand Dam 72 D 3
Riikimäki 43 H 3
Riiser-Larsen Ice Shelf 85
Riiser-Larsen Peninsula 85
Rijau 59 F 3
Rijeka 45 F 2

Riley 20 C 3
Rimatara 83 E 4
Rimini 45 F 3
Rimnicu Sãrat 46 C 1
Rîmnicu Vîlcea 46 B 1–2
Rimouski 19 G 4
Rinchinlhümbe 68 G 5
Rinconada 34 C 5
Ringgold Isles 82 D 4
Ringvassöy 42 G 2
Rio Balsas 24 D 4
Riobamba 32 C 4
Río Branco (Acre, Brazil) 32 E 5
Río Branco (Roraima, Brazil) 33 F 3
Río Bravo del Norte24 EF 5–6
Río Bravo del Norte 25 E 2
Río Chico 37 C 8
Río Chico (Venezuela) 29 F 4
Río Claro 35 G 5
Rio Coco o Segovia 28 C 4
Río Colorado 37 D 6
Rio Conchos 24 CD 2
Río Cuarto 36 CD 5
Rio das Mortes 35 F 3
Río de Janeiro 35 H 5
Río de la Plata 36 E 5–6
Rio de Oro 54 BC 4
Río Gallegos 37 C 9
Rio Grande 25 E 2
Río Grande (Argentina) 37 C 9
Río Grande (Bahía, Brazil) 35 H 3
Río Grande (Brazil) 35 G 4–5
Rio Grande (Río Grande do Sul, Brazil) 36 F 5
Rio Grande de Matagalpa 28 C 4
Rio Grande de Santiago 24 D 3
Río Grande do Norte 35 J 2
Río Grande do Sul 36 EF 4
Río Grande o'Guapay 34 D 4
Ríohacha 29 E 4
Rioja 32 C 5
Rio Lacantún 25 F 4
Río Lagartos 26 D 4
Rio Lempa 28 B 4
Riom 44 D 2
Río Mezcalapa 25 F 4
Río Mulatos 34 C 4
Rio Negro (Argentina) 37 D 6–7
Río Negro (Brazil) 33 F 4
Río Patuca 28 C 3
Rio San Juan 28 C 4
Rio Siquia 28 C 4
Rio Sonora 24 B 2
Ríosucio 32 C 2
Río Turbio Mines 37 B 9
Rio Usumacinta 25 F 4
Río Verde 35 F 4

Rioverde (Mexico) 25 DE 3
Río Verde de Mato Grosso
35 F 4
Rio Viejo 28 B 4
Rio Yaqui 24 C 2
Ripley (N.Y., U.S.A.) 22 E 2
Ripley (W.V., U.S.A.) 22 D 3
Ritter, Mount 20 C 4
Ritzville 20 C 2
Rivadavia 36 BC 4
Rivas 28 B 4
Rivera (Argentina) 37 D 6
Rivera (Uruguay) 36 E 5
Riverside 20 C 5
Rivers Inlet 13 M 5
Riverton (Man., Can.) 15 K 4
Riverton (WY, U.S.A.) 20 E 3
Riviera di Levante 45 E 3
Riviera di Ponente 45 E 3
Rivière à la Baleine 19 G 2
Rivière aux Feuilles 18–19 F 2
Rivière aux Mélèzes
18–19 F 2
Rivière aux Outardes 19 G 3
Rivière-du-Loup 19 G 4
Rivière du Petit-Mécatina
19 HJ 3
Rivoli 45 E 2
Riwoqê 70 C 4
Riyâdh 49 E 4
Rize 47 F 2
Rizhao 71 GH 3
Rizhskiy Zaliv 43 H 4
Rjuven 43 E 4
Rkiz 54 B 5
Road Town 29 G 3
Roanne 44 D 2
Roanoke 22 E 3
Roanoke Rapids 22 E 3
Roanoke River 22 E 3
Roan Plateau 20 E 4
Roatán 28 B 3
Robât-e Khân 49 G 2
Robert Butte 85
Robert Lee 24 F 5
Robinson River 79 F 2
Robore 34 E 4
Robson, Mount 14 F 4
Robstown 25 E 2
Rocha 36 F 5
Rocha de Galé, Barragem da
44 B 4
Rochefort 44 C 2
Rocher River 14 G 2
Rocher Thomasset 83 F 3
Rochester (MN, U.S.A.) 21 H 3
Rochester (N.H., U.S.A.)
23 F 2
Rochester (N.Y., U.S.A.)
22 E 2
Rockefeller Plateau 85
Rockford 22 C 2
Rockhampton 79 HJ 3
Rock Hill 22 D 4

Rockingham (N.C., U.S.A.)
22 E 4
Rock Island 21 H 3
Rockport (CA, U.S.A.) 20 B 4
Rockport (TX, U.S.A.) 25 E 2
Rock River 22 C 2
Rock Springs 20 E 3
Rockville 22 E 3
Rocky Mount 22 E 3
Rocky Mountain House 14 F 4
Rocky Mountain National-
Park 20–21 E 3
Roddickton 19 J 3
Rodeo (AZ, U.S.A.) 20 E 5
Rodeo (Mexico) 24 D 2
Rodez 44 D 3
Ródhos (Greece) 46 C 3
Ródhos (Greece) 46 C 3
Rodina 68 FG 4
Rodney, Cape 80 E 4
Rodopi 46 BC 2
Roebourne 78 B 3
Roebuck Bay 78 C 2
Roes Welcome Sound
16 J 3–4
Rogagua, Lago 34 C 3
Rogaland 43 E 4
Rogers City 22 D 2
Rogers Peak 20 D 4
Rogue River 20 B 3
Rohtak 72 C 2
Rojo, Cabo 29 F 3
Rolla (MO, U.S.A.) 21 H 4
Rolla (N.D., U.S.A.) 21 G 2
Rolleston 79 H 3
Roma (Italy) 45 F 3
Roma (Queensland, Austr.)
79 H 4
Romaine 19 H 3
Roman 46 C 1
Romania 46 BC 1
Romanovka 68 K 5
Romans-sur-Isère 45 E 2
Romanzof, Cape 12 D 3
Romanzof Mountains 13 J 2
Rome (GA, U.S.A.) 22 C 4
Rome (Italy) 45 F 3
Rome (N.Y., U.S.A.) 22 E 2
Rome (OR, U.S.A.) 20 C 3
Romny 50 F 5
Romsdal 42 E 3
Roncador, Cayos de 28 D 4
Roncador, Serra do 35 F 3
Ronda 44 C 4
Rondane 42 EF 3
Rondón, Pico 33 F 3
Rondônia (Brazil) 34 D 3
Rondonia (Brazil) 34 D 3
Rondonópolis 35 F 4
Rongan 70 E 5
Ronge, Lac la 15 J 3
Rongelap 82 C 2
Rongerik 82 C 2
Rongjiang 70 E 5

Rong Xian 70 F 6
Rönne 43 F 4
Ronneby 43 G 4
Ronne Ice Shelf 85
Roosevelt, Mount 14 D 3
Roosevelt Island 85
Roper River 78 E 1
Roraima (Brazil) 33 F 3
Roraima (Venezuela) 33 F 2
Röros 42 F 3
Rosa, Lake 29 E 2
Rosamorada 24 C 3
Rosario 24 C 3
Rosario (Argentina) 36 D 5
Rosário (Maranhão, Brazil)
35 H 1
Rosario, Bahía 24 A 2
Rosario de Lerma 36 C 4
Rosarito 24 B 2
Roseau 29 G 3
Roseburg 20 B 3
Rosenberg 25 E 2
Rosenheim 41 F 5
Rosetown 15 H 4
Rosignol 33 G 2
Roşiori de Vede 46 C 2
Roskilde 43 F 4
Roslavl' 50 F 5
Roslyn 20 B 2
Ross (Canada) 13 L 3
Rossano 45 G 4
Ross Ice Shelf 85
Ross Island 85
Rosslare 40 B 4
Rosso 54 B 5
Rossosh 50 GH 5
Ross River 13 L 3
Ross Sea 85
Rosthern 15 H 4
Rostock 41 F 4
Rostov 50 G 4
Rostov-na-Donu 47 EF 1
Roswell 21 F 5
Rota 82 A 2
Rothera 85
Roti, Pulau 75 F 6
Rotorua 81 R 8
Rotterdam 40 D 4
Rotuma 82 C 3
Rouen 44 D 2
Rouyn 18 E 4
Rovaniemi 42 J 2
Rovdino 50 H 3
Rovereto 45 F 2
Rovigo 45 F 2
Rovno 43 J 5
Rowley 17 L 3
Roxas 75 F 1
Roy 21 F 4
Roy Hill 78 C 3
Rozhdestvenskoye 50 J 4
Roztocze 41 H 4
Rtishchevo 50 H 5
Rt Ploča 45 G 3

Ruacana Falls 62 AB 3
Ruaha National Park 60 E 6
Ruapehu 81 R 8
Rubio 29 E 5
Rubtsovsk 51 Q 5
Ruby 12 F 3
Ruby Mountains 20 C 3
Rudall River National Park
78 C 3
Rudbar 67 G 4–5
Rudnyy 51 M 5
Rudyard 20 D 2
Rufiji 61 F 6
Rufino 36 D 5
Rufisque 58 A 3
Rugby (N.D., U.S.A.) 21 G 2
Rügen 41 F 4
Ruhr 41 E 4
Ruijin 70 G 5
Rujm al Mudhari 66 B 4
Rukwa, Lake 60 E 6
Rumädah 57 G 6
Rum Cay 29 E 2
Rum Jungle 78 E 1
Rumphi 63 E 2
Rundu 62 B 3
Rungwa 60 E 6
Rupert (ID, U.S.A.) 20 D 3
Rupert (Quebec, Can.) 18 E 3
Rupert, Baie de 18 DE 3
Rurrenabaque 34 C 3
Rururtu 83 E 4
Rusakovo 69 U 4
Ruse 46 C 2
Rushan (U.S.S.R.) 67 J 3
Russas 35 J 1
Russell 15 J 4
Russellville (AL, U.S.A.)
22 C 4
Russellville (AR, U.S.A.)
21 H 4
Russkaya (Antarctica) 85
Russkaya (U.S.S.R.) 71 L 1
Rustavi 47 G 2
Rustenburg 62 D 5
Ruston 21 H 5
Rutenga 63 E 4
Ruvuma 63 FG 2
Ruwenzori National Park
60 DE 5
Ruzayevka 50 H 5
Ružomberok 41 GH 5
Rwanda 60 DE 5
Ryan 21 G 5
Ryazan' 50 GH 5
Ryazhsk 50 GH 5
Rybachiy, Poluostrov 42 K 2
Rybach'ye 67 K 2
Rybnik 41 G 4
Rybnitsa 46 C 1
Ryegate 20 E 2
Ryn Peski 50 J 6
Ryukyu Islands 71 J 5
Rzeszów 41 H 4

S

Sa'ādatābād **49** F 3
Saalfeld **41** F 4
Saarbrücken **41** E 5
Saaremaa **43** H 4
Saariselkä **42** J 2
Šabac **46** A 2
Sabadell **44** D 3
Sabah **74** E 2
Sabanalarga **32** C 1
Sabaya **34** C 4
Sabhā **55** H 3
Sabinas **25** D 2
Sabinas Hidalgo **25** D 2
Sabine **25** H 5
Sabkhat al Bardawīl **48** A 3
Sable, Cape **23** G 2
Sable, Cape **27** E 3
Sable Island **23** H 2
Sabonkafi **59** F 3
Sabrina Coast **85**
Sabzevār **66** F 3
Sacajawea Peak **20** C 2
Sachsen **41** F 4
Sachs Harbour **16** B 2
Saco **20** E 2
Sacramento **20** B 4
Sacramento Mountains
   21 E 5
Sacramento Valley **20** B 3–4
Şa'dah **57** G 5
Sad Bi'Ar **48** B 2
Saddlede **42** F 3
Sa Dec **74** C 1
Sadiya **73** G 2
Sad Kharv **49** G 1
Sadon **66** C 2
Sado-shima **71** L 3
Sæböl **42** A 2
Şafāqis **55** GH 2
Saffānīyah, Ra's as **49** E 3
Safford **20** E 5
Safi **54** D 2
Safid, Kūh-e **49** E 2
Safonovo (U.S.S.R.) **50** J 2
Safonovo (U.S.S.R.) **50** F 4
Safonovo (U.S.S.R.) **69** X 3
Şafwān **49** E 3
Saga **72** DE 2
Sagaing **73** FG 3
Sagar **72** C 3
Sagastyr **69** N 1
Sagavanirktok **12** H 2
Sage **20** D 3
Saginaw **22** D 2
Saginaw Bay **22** D 2
Saglek Bay **19** H 2
Saglouc **17** L 4
Sagres **44** B 4
Saguache **21** E 4
Sagua de Tánamo **29** E 2
Sagua la Grande **27** F 4
Saguenay **19** FG 4
Sagunto **44** C 4

Sagwon **12** H 2
Sahagún **32** CD 2
Sahara **54–55** HK 4
Saharanpur **72** C 2
Sahiwal **67** J 4
Sahlābad **66** F 4
Şaḥrā' al Hajārah **48–49** D 3
Sahuaripa **24** C 2
Sahuayo de Diaz **24** D 4
Sa'idābād **49** G 3
Said Bundas **60** CD 3
Saigon **73** JK 5
Saihan Toroi **70** CD 2
Saiki **71** KL 4
Saimaa **42** J 3
Sain Alto **24** D 3
Saindak **67** G 5
Sāin Dezh **49** E 1
Saint Alban's (Newfoundl.,
   Can.) **19** J 4
Saint Albans (VT, U.S.A.)
   23 F 2
Saint Albert **14** G 4
Saint-André, Cap **63** G 3
Saint Ann's Bay **28** D 3
Saint Anthony **19** JK 3
Saint Arnaud **79** G 6
Saint Augustine **27** E 3
Saint Augustin Saguenay
   19 J 3
St. Austell **40** BC 4
Saint-Barthélemy **29** G 3
Saint-Brieuc **44** C 2
Saint Christopher **29** G 3
Saint Clair River **22** D 2
Saint Cloud **21** H 2
Saint Croix **29** FG 3
Saint-Denis (France) **44** D 2
Saint-Denis (Réunion)
   63 HK 6
Saint-Dizier **45** E 2
Sainte Genevieve **21** H 4
Saint Elias, Mount **13** J 3
Saint Elias Mountains **13** K 3
Saint-Elie **33** H 3
Sainte Lucie, Canal de **29** G 4
Saintes **44** C 2
Sainte-Thérèse **18** EF 4
Saint-Étienne **44** D 2
Saint Félicien **18** F 4
Saint Francis **21** F 4
Saint Francis, Cape **62** CD 6
Saint Francois Mountains
   21 H 4
St. Gallen **45** E 2
Saint George (AK, U.S.A.)
   12 D 4
Saint George (Queensland,
   Austr.) **79** H 4
Saint George (UT, U.S.A.)
   20 D 4
Saint George, Cape **19** HJ 4
Saint George, Cape **81** F 2
Saint-Georges **19** FG 4

Saint George's **29** G 4
Saint George's Bay **19** J 4
Saint George's Channel
   (Papua New Guinea) **81** F 2–3
Saint George's Channel
   (Un. Kingdom) **40** B 4
Saint Helena **52** B 6
Saint Helens, Mount **20** B 2
Saint Ignace **22** D 2
Saint Ignace Island **18** C 4
Saint Jean **18** F 4
Saint-Jean, Lake **18** F 4
Saint Jérôme **18** F 4
Saint-John (Canada) **19** G 4
Saint John River **19** G 4
Saint John's (Antigua) **29** G 3
Saint Johns (AZ, U.S.A.)
   20 E 5
Saint John's (Canada) **19** K 4
Saint Johnsbury **23** F 2
Saint Johns River (FL, U.S.A.)
   22 D 4–5
Saint Joseph (MI, U.S.A.)
   22 C 2
Saint Joseph (MO, U.S.A.)
   21 H 4
Saint Joseph, Lake **15** L 4
Saint Kitts-Nevis **29** G 3
Saint Kitts [Saint Christopher]
   29 G 3
Saint Lawrence, Gulf of
   19 H 4
Saint Lawrence Island **12** C 3
Saint Lawrence River **19** G 4
Saint Léonard **19** G 4
Saint Louis (MO, U.S.A.)
   21 H 4
Saint-Louis (Senegal) **58** A 2
Saint Lucia **29** G 4
Saint Lucia, Lake **63** E 5
Saint-Malo **44** C 2
Saint-Marc **29** E 3
St. Marks **22** D 4
Saint-Martin **29** G 3
Saint Marys **80** L 9
St. Marys (AK, U.S.A.) **12** E 3
Saint Mary's Bay **19** K 4
Saint Matthew **12** C 3
Saint Matthias Group **81** EF 2
Saint Maurice **18** F 4
Saint Michael **12** E 3
Saint Michaels **20** E 4
St. Moritz **45** F 2
Saint-Nazaire **44** C 2
Saint Paul (AK, U.S.A.)
   12 D 4
Saint Paul (Alb., Can.) **14** G 4
Saint Paul (MN, U.S.A.)
   21 H 3
Saint-Paul (Réunion) **63** HK 6
St. Peter and St. Paul Rocks
   31 G 2
Saint Petersburg **26–27** E 3
Saint Pierre **19** J 4

Saint Pierre et Miquelon
   19 J 4
Saint-Quentin **44** D 1–2
St. Roch Basin **16** GH 3
Saint Stephen **19** G 4
Saint-Thomas (Ontario, Can.)
   22 D 2
Saint-Thomas (Puerto Rico)
   29 FG 3
Saint Vincent **29** G 4
Saint Vincent, Gulf **79** F 6
Saint Vincent Passage **29** G 4
St. Walburg **14** H 4
Saipan **82** A 1
Sajama, Nevado **34** C 4
Sakākah **48** C 3
Sakami **18** E 3
Sakami, Lac **18** E 3
Sakami River **18** F 3
Sakaraha **63** G 4
Sakarya **46** D 2
Sakata **71** L 3
Såkevare **42** G 2
Sakhalin **69** QR 5
Sakhalinskiy Zaliv **69** Q 5
Sakht Sar **49** F 1
Saksaul'skiy **67** G 1
Salaca **43** HJ 4
Salada **24** D 2
Salado **36** D 4
Salado **37** C 6
Salaga **58** D 4
Salālah **57** J 5
Salamá **25** F 4
Salamanca **44** B 3
Salamanca (Mexico) **25** D 3
Salamat **59** J 3
Salar de Atacama **34** C 5
Salar de Uyuni **34** C 5
Salavat **50** KL 5
Salaverry **32** C 5
Salawati, Pulau **75** H 4
Sala y Gómes **83** H 4
Saldanha **62** B 6
Sale (Australia) **79** H 6
Salé (Morocco) **54** D 2
Şālehābād **49** E 2
Salekhard **51** N 2
Salem **72** C 5
Salem (IL, U.S.A.) **22** C 3
Salem (OR, U.S.A.) **20** B 3
Salerno **45** F 3
Saletekri **72** D 3
Salida **21** E 4
Salihli **46** C 3
Salina (KS, U.S.A.) **21** G 4
Salina (UT, U.S.A.) **20** D 4
Salinas **20** B 4
Salinas (Ecuador) **32** B 4
Salinas de Hidalgo **25** D 3
Salinas Grandes **36** CD 4–5
Salinas Peak **20–21** E 5
Salinópolis **33** J 4
Salisbury (Canada) **17** L 4

Salisbury (MD, U.S.A.) **22** E 3
Salling **43** E 4
Salluyo, Nevado **34** C 3
Salmas **47** F 3
Salmon **20** D 2
Salmon Arm **14** F 4
Salmon Mountains **20** B 3
Salmon River **20** CD 2
Salmon River Mountains
  20 CD 2–3
Salo **43** H 3
Salon-de-Provence **45** E 3
Salonga National Park **60** C 5
Salonica **46** B 2
Salpausselkä **42** J 3
Salsbruket **42** F 3
Sal'sk **47** F 1
Salso **45** F 4
Salta **34** CD 5
Saltdalselva **42** G 2
Salt Fork Brazos **21** FG 5
Saltillo **25** D 2
Salt Lake **79** F 3
Salt Lake City **20** D 3
Salto **36** E 5
Salton Sea **20** C 5
Salt Range **67** J 4
Salt River **20** D 5
Salumbar **72** B 3
Salvador **35** J 3
Salvatierra (Mexico) **25** D 3
Salwá **49** F 4
Salwá Baḩrī **48** A 4
Salween **73** G 4
Salzach **45** F 2
Salzburg **45** F 2
Salzgitter **41** F 4
Sa Madre Occidental
  24 CD 2–3
Samagaltay **68** G 5
Samak, Tanjung **74** C 4
Samalga Pass **12** D 5
Samaná **29** F 3
Samangan **67** H 3
Samar **75** G 1
Samarkand **67** H 3
Sāmarrā' **48** D 2
Samarskoye **51** Q 6
Samaūma **32** E 5
Sambaliung **74–75** E 3
Sambalpur **72** DE 3
Sambava **63** J 2
Sambor **74** C 1
S. Ambrosio Island **31** C 5
Samfya **62** DE 2
Samka **73** G 3
Sam Neua **73** H 3
Samoa Islands **82** D 3
Samokov **46** B 2
Sámos **46** C 3
Samothraki **46** C 2
Sampit **74** D 4
Sam Rayburn Reservoir
  25 H 5

Samsang **72** D 1
Samsun **47** E 2
Samthar **72** C 2
Samus' **51** QR 4
San'ā' **57** GH 5
Sanae **85**
Sanaga **59** G 5
Sanak Islands **12** E 5
Sanandaj **49** E 2
San Andres Mountains **20** E 5
San Andrés Tuxtla **25** F 4
San Angelo **24** F 5
San Antonia de Cortés
  28 B 3–4
San Antonio **25** E 2
San Antonio (Chile) **36** B 5
San Antonio, Cabo
  (Argentina) **37** E 6
San Antonio, Cabo (Cuba)
  26 E 4
San Antonio Bay **25** E 2
San Antonio de Caparo
  29 E 5
San Antonio del Tachira
  29 E 5
San Antonio Oeste **37** D 7
Sanāw **57** J 5
San Bernardino **20** C 5
San Bernardo **36** BC 5
San Bernardo (Mexico) **24** B 2
San Blas **24** C 2
San Blas **24** C 3
San Blas **25** D 2
San Blas, Cape **25** F 2
San Borja **34** C 3
San Borjas, Sierra de **24** B 2
San Buenaventura **25** D 2
San Carlos **29** F 5
San Carlos (Mexico) **25** E 3
San Carlos (Nicaragua) **28** C 4
San Carlos (Philippines)
  75 F 1
San Carlos (Venezuela) **29** F 5
San Carlos de Bariloche
  37 BC 7
San Carlos del Zulia **32** D 2
San Casme **36** E 4
Sánchez **29** F 3
San Clemente **20** C 5
San Clemente Island **20** C 5
San Cristóbal (Argentina)
  36 D 5
San Cristóbal (Dominican
  Rep.) **29** EF 3
San Cristóbal (Solomon Is.)
  81 H 4
San Cristóbal (Venezuela)
  32 D 2
San Cristobal, Isla **32** B 6
San Cristóbal de las Casas
  25 F 4

Sancti Spíritus **27** F 4
Sand **43** E 4
Sandakan **74** E 2
Sandaré **58** B 3
Sandefjord **43** EF 4
Sanderson **24** F 5
Sand Hills **21** F 3
San Diego **20** C 5
San Diego, Cabo **37** C 9
San Dimitri Point **45** F 4
Sandnes **43** DE 4
Sandoa **60** C 6
Sandon **47** F 2
San Dona di Piave **45** F 2
Sandoy **40** A 1
Sand Point **12** EF 4
Sandspit **13** L 5
Sandstone (MN, U.S.A.)
  21 H 2
Sandusky **22** D 2
Sandviken **43** G 3
Sandwich Bay (Newfoundl.,
  Can.) **19** J 3
Sandykachi **67** G 3
Sandy Lake **15** L 4
San Felípe (Chile) **36** B 5
San Felípe (Colombia) **32** E 3
San Felipe (Mexico) **20** D 5
San Felipe (Mexico) **25** D 3
San Felipe (Venezuela) **32** E 1
San Fernando (Chile) **37** B 5
San Fernando (Mexico)
  25 E 3
San Fernando (Spain) **44** B 4
San Fernando (Trinidad and
  Tobago) **29** G 4
San Fernando (Trinidad and
  Tobago) **33** F 1
San Fernando de Apure
  32 E 2
San Fernando de Atabapo
  32 E 3
Sanford, Mount **13** J 3
San Francisco **20** B 4
San Francisco (Argentina)
  36 D 5
San Francisco, Paso de **36** C 4
San Francisco de Arriba
  24 D 2
San Francisco del Oro **24** C 2
San Francisco del Rincón
  24 D 3
San Francisco de Macorís
  29 EF 3
Sangar **69** N 3
Sangatolon **69** R 3
Sanger **20** C 4
Sangha **59** GH 5
Sangihe, Kepulauan **75** G 3
Sangli **72** BC 4
Sangre de Cristo Mountains
  21 E 4
San Gregorio **37** B 9
Sangre Grande **29** G 4

Sanhe **68** M 5
San Hilario **24** B 3
San Ignacio (Belize) **28** B 3
San Ignacio (Bolivia) **34** C 3
San Ignacio (Mexico) **24** B 2
San Ignacio (Paraguay) **36** E 4
San Ignacio, Isla de **24** C 2
Sanikiluaq **18** E 2
San Isidro **36** DE 5
San Isidro (Costa Rica) **28** C 5
San Jacinto **32** C 2
San Javier **34** D 4
Sanjawi **67** H 4
San Joaquín **34** D 3
San Joaquin River **20** BC 4
San Joaquin Valley **20** BC 4
San Jorge, Bahia de **20** D 5
San Jorge, Golfo **37** C 8
San Jose (CA, U.S.A.) **20** B 4
San José (Costa Rica) **28** C 5
San José (Guatemala) **25** F 5
San José, Isla **24** BC 2
San José de Amacuro **29** G 5
San José de Chiquitos
  34 DE 4
San José de Gracia **24** C 2
San José de Guanipa **29** G 5
San José de Jáchal **36** C 5
San José del Cabo **24** C 3
San José del Guaviare **32** D 3
San José de Mayo **36** E 5
San Juan (Argentina) **36** C 5
San Juan (Dominican Rep.)
  29 E 3
San Juan (Peru) **34** A 4
San Juan (Puerto Rico) **29** F 3
San Juan, Pico **27** E 4
San Juan, Rio **28** C 4
San Juan Bautista Tuxtepec
  25 E 4
San Juan de Guadalupe
  25 D 3
San Juan del Norte **28** C 4
San Juan de los Cayos **29** F 4
San Juan del Rio **24** D 3
San Juan del Rio **25** DE 3
San Juan de Payara
  (Venezuela) **178** E 2
San Juan Mountains **20** E 4
San Julián **37** C 8
San Justo **36** D 5
Sankt Gotthard-Pass **45** E 2
Sankt Pölten **45** G 2
Sankt Veit an der Glan **45** F 2
Sankuru **60** C 5
San Lázaro, Sierra de **24** C 3
San Lorenzo **32** C 3
San Lorenzo (Mexico) **24** C 3
Sanlúcar de Barrameda
  44 B 4
San Lucas (Mexico) **24** B 3
San Lucas, Cabo **24** C 3
San Luis (Argentina) **36** C 5
San Luis (Mexico) **24** B 2

San Luís (Venezuela) **32** E 1
San Luis de la Paz **25** DE 3
San Luis Gonzaga, Bahía **24** B 2
San Luis Obispo **20** B 4
San Luis Peak **20** E 4
San Luis Potosi **25** D 3
San Luis Rio Colorado **20** D 5
San Marcos (Colombia) **28** D 5
San Marcos (Mexico) **24** D 3
San Marcos (Mexico) **25** E 4
San Marcos (TX, U.S.A.) **21** G 5–6
San Marcos, Isla **24** B 2
San Marino **45** F 3
San Martín (Colombia) **32** D 3
San Martín de los Andes **37** BC 7
San Mateo **20** B 4
San Matías **34** E 4
San Matías, Golfo **37** D 7
San Miguel (Bolivia) **34** D 3
San Miguel (El Salvador) **28** B 4
San Miguel de Allende **25** DE 3
San Miguel de Horcasitas **24** B 2
San Miguel de Huachi **34** C 4
San Miguel del Padrón **27** E 4
San Miguel de Tucumán **36** C 4
San Miguel Sole de Vega **25** E 4
Sannär **56** E 6
San Nicolás (Argentina) **36** DE 5
San Nicolás (Mexico) **25** D 2
Sannikova **84**
Sanok **41** H 5
San Onofre **32** C 2
San Pablo **37** C 9
San Pedro (Argentina) **34** D 5
San Pedro (Dominican Rep.) **29** F 3
San Pedro (Mexico) **24** D 2
San Pedro (Paraguay) **34** E 5
San Pedro de Arimena **32** D 3
San Pedro de las Bôcas **29** G 5
San Pedro Pochutla **25** E 4
San Pedro Sula **28** B 3
San Quintin **24** C 5
San Quintin, Bahia de **24** C 5
San Rafael **36** C 5
San Rafael (Mexico) **25** D 2
San Rafael, Cabo **29** F 3
San Rafael Mountains **20** BC 4–5
San Remo **45** E 3
San Salvador (El Salvador) **28** B 4

San Salvador (Watling Is.) **27** FG 4
San Salvador de Jujuy **34** C 5
Sansanding **58** C 3
San Sebastian (Argentina) **37** C 9
San Sebastián (Spain) **44** C 3
San Severo **45** G 3
San Silvestre **29** E 5
Santa Ana **24** D 5
Santa Ana (CA, U.S.A.) **20** C 5
Santa Ana (El Salvador) **25** FG 5
Santa Ana (Solomon Is.) **81** H 4
Santa Barbara (CA, U.S.A.) **20** B 5
Santa Barbara (Mexico) **24** C 2
Santa Barbara Channel **20** B 5
Santa Bárbara do Sul **36** F 4
Santa Catalina **36** C 4
Santa Catalina Island (CA, U.S.A.) **20** C 5
Santa Catarina **36** FG 4
Santa Clara (CA, U.S.A.) **20** B 4
Santa Clara (Cuba) **27** E 4
Santa Clara (Mexico) **24** C 2
Santa Clotilde **32** D 4
Santa Cruz (Argentina) **37** C 9
Santa Cruz (Bolivia) **34** D 4
Santa Cruz (CA, U.S.A.) **20** B 4
Santa Cruz (Costa Rica) **28** B 4
Santa Cruz, Isla (Ecuador) **32** B 6
Santa Cruz del Sur **27** F 4
Santa Cruz de Mudela **44** C 4
Santa Cruz de Tenerife **54** BC 3
Santa Cruz do Sul **36** F 4
Santa Cruz Island **20** C 5
Santa Cruz Islands **81** J 4
Santa Elena **32** B 4
Santa Elena, Bahía de **28** B 4
Santa Elena, Cabo **28** B 4
Santa Fé (Argentina) **36** DE 5
Santa Fe (N.M., U.S.A.) **21** E 4
Santa Filomena **33** J 5
Santa Helena **33** JK 4
Santa Ines, Bahía **24** B 2
Santa Inés, Isla **37** B 9
Santa Isabel **82** B 3
Santa Isabel (Argentina) **37** C 6
Santa Isabel (Solomon Is.) **81** G 3
Santa Juana **29** F 5
Santa Lucia Range **20** B 4
Santa Margarita, Isla de **24** B 3
Santa Maria (CA, U.S.A.) **20** B 4
Santa Maria (Portugal) **54** A 1

Santa María (Río Grande do Sul, Brazil) **36** F 4
Santa Maria, Bahia de **24** C 2
Santa Maria, Cabo de **44** B 4
Santa María de Ipire **29** F 5
Santa María del Oro **24** C 2
Santa Maria del Río **25** D 3
Santa Maria di Leuca, Capo **45** G 4
Santa Maria dos Marmelos **33** F 5
Santa Marta **32** D 1
Santana do Livramento **36** EF 5
Santander (Colombia) **32** C 3
Santander (Spain) **44** C 3
Sant' Antioco **45** E 4
Santarém **33** H 4
Santaren Channel **27** F 4
Santa Rita (Colombia) **32** D 3
Santa Rita (N.M., U.S.A.) **20** E 5
Santa Rita (Venezuela) **32** E 2
Santa Rosa (Argentina) **37** CD 6
Santa Rosa (CA, U.S.A.) **20** B 4
Santa Rosa (N.M., U.S.A.) **21** F 5
Santa Rosa (Río Grande do Sul, Brazil) **36** F 4
Santa Rosa de Copán **28** B 3–4
Santa Rosa Island **20** B 5
Santa Rosalia **24** B 2
Santa Sylvina **36** DE 4
Santa Teresa **35** G 3
Santee River **22** E 4
San Telmo **24** C 5
Santiago (Chile) **36** BC 5
Santiago (Haiti) **29** E 3
Santiago (Panamá) **32** B 2
Santiago, Cerro **29** C 5
Santiago, Rio Grande de **24** C 3
Santiago da Cacém **44** B 4
Santiago de Compostela **44** B 3
Santiago de Cuba **28** D 3
Santiago del Estero **36** CD 4
Santiago de Papasquiaro **24** CD 2
Santo André **35** G 5
Santo Ângelo **36** F 4
Santo Antão **58** A 6
Santo António de Jesus **35** HJ 3
Santo Antônio do Icá **32** E 4
Santo Domingo (Cuba) **27** E 4
Santo Domingo (Dominican Rep.) **29** F 3
Santo Domingo (Mexico) **24** B 2
Santos **35** G 5

Santo Tomás (Nicaragua) **28** C 4
Santo Tomé de Guayana **33** F 2
San Valentin, Cerro **37** B 8
San Vicente (Mexico) **20** C 5
São Borja **36** E 4
São Carlos **35** G 5
São Domingos **35** G 3
São Felix **35** F 3
São Felix do Xingu **33** H 5
São Francisco **35** HJ 2
São Francisco do Sul **36** G 4
São João **35** G 5
São João del Rei **35** GH 5
São João do Piauí **35** H 2
São José do Río Prêto **35** FG 5
São José dos Campos **35** FG 5
São Leopoldo **36** FG 4
São Luís **35** H 1
São Mateus **35** J 4
São Miguel **54** A 1
São Miguel do Araguaia **35** FG 3
Saône **45** D 2
São Nicolau **58** B 6
São Paulo (Brazil) **35** FG 5
São Paulo (Brazil) **35** G 5
São Paulo de Olivença **32** E 4
São Raimundo Nonato **35** H 2
São Romão **35** G 4
São Roque, Cabo de **35** HJ 2
São Sebastião **35** GH 5
São Tiago **58** B 6
São Tomé **59** F 5
São Tomé and Principe **59** F 5
São Vicente (Cape Verde) **58** A 6
São Vicente (São Paulo, Brazil) **35** G 5
São Vicente, Cabo de **44** B 4
Sape **75** E 5
Sapele **59** F 4
Sapporo **71** LM 2
Sapulpa **21** G 4
Sapulut **74** E 3
Sàqand **49** G 2
Saqqez **49** E 1
Sara Buri **73** H 5
Sarafjagär **49** F 2
Sarajevo **45** G 3
Saraktash **50** L 5
Saralzhin **66** E 1
Saran' **51** O 6
Saran, Gunung **74** D 4
Saranpaul' **51** M 3
Saransk **50** J 5
Sarapul **50** KL 4
Sarasota **27** E 3
Saratok **74** D 3
Saratov **50** HJ 5

Sarawak 74 D 3
Saraya 47 E 3
Sarco 36 B 4
Sar Dasht 49 D 1
Sardegna 45 E 3
Sardinia 45 E 3
Sarek National Park 42 G 2
Sarektjåkkå 42 G 2
Sargasso Sea 27 GH 3
Sargodha 67 J 4
Sarh 59 H 4
Sârî 66 E 3
Sarigan 82 A 1
Sarıoğlan 47 E 3
Sarîr Tibisti 55 J 4
Sariwon 71 HJ 3
Sarkand 51 P 6
Sarmi 75 J 4
Sarmiento 37 C 8
Sarnia 18 D 5
Saroako 75 F 4
Saronikos Kólpos 46 B 3
Saros Körfezi 46 C 2
Saroto 51 NO 2
Sarpinskaya Nizmennost'
  47 G 1
Sartyn'ya 51 M 3
Sarva 46 A 2
Sarvestän 49 F 3
Saryassiya 67 H 3
Saryg-Sep 68 G 5
Sary-Ozek 67 K 2
Sary-Tash 67 J 3
Sasaram 72 D 3
Sasebo 71 J 4
Saskatchewan 15 H 4
Saskatchewan 15 J 4
Saskatoon 15 H 4
Saskylakh 68 KL 1
Saslaya 28 C 4
Sason Dağları 47 F 3
Sasovo 50 H 5
Sassari 45 E 3
Sassuolo 45 F 3
Sastre 36 D 5
Sasykkol', Ozero 51 Q 6
Satara (U.S.S.R.) 69 NO 2
Satawal 82 A 2
Satawan 82 B 2
Satipo 34 B 3
Satka 51 L 4
Satna 72 D 3
Satpura Range 72 BC 3
Sattahip 74 B 1
Satu Mare 46 B 1
Sauce 36 E 5
Sauceda Mountains 20 D 5
Saucillo 24 CD 2
Sauda Nathil 49 F 4
Saudi Arabia 48–49 CD 4
Saudi Arabia 57 GH 4
Sauk Centre 21 H 2
Sault Sainte Marie 18 D 4
Saumarez Reef 79 J 3

Saurimo 62 BC 1
Sava 46 AB 2
Savai'i 82 D 3
Savannah 22 D 4
Savannah River 22 D 4
Savannakhet 73 HJ 4
Savanna la Mar 28 D 3
Savanne 18 C 4
Savant Lake 15 LM 4
Save 63 E 4
Säve 49 F 2
Savo 42 J 3
Savoie 45 E 2
Savonlinna 42 J 3
Savonselkä 42 J 3
Savoonga 12 C 3
Sawäkin 56 F 5
Sawbä 60 E 3
Sawdiri 56 D 6
Sawhäj 56 E 3
Sawmill Bay 13 O 2
Sawtooth Mountains 21 H 2
Sawu Laut 75 F 5
Sayan Vostochnyy 68 G 5
Saydä 48 B 2
Sayhüt 57 J 5
Saynshand 70 F 2
Saywün 57 H 5
Sazin 67 J 3
Sbaa 54 E 3
Scafell Pike 40 C 4
Scaife Mountains 85
Scammon Bay 12 D 3
Scarborough 40 C 4
Scarborough (Trinidad and
  Tobago) 29 G 4
Schefferville 19 G 3
Schenectady 23 F 2
Schleswig 41 EF 4
Schleswig-Holstein 41 E 4
Schouten Islands 80 DE 2
Schultz Lake 15 K 2
Schurz 20 C 4
Schwaner, Pegunungan
  74 D 4
Schwarzwald 41 E 5
Schwatka Mountains
  12 F 2
Schwedt 41 F 4
Schweinfurt 41 F 4
Schwenningen 41 E 5
Schwerin 41 F 4
Sciacca 45 F 4
Scicli 45 F 4
Scilly, Isles of 40 B 5
Scioto River 22 D 3
Scoresby Sound 84
Scoresbysund 84
Scotia Sea 85
Scotland 40 C 3
Scotlandville 25 H 5
Scott 15 H 4
Scott (Antarctica) 85
Scott, Cape 13 M 5

Scott, Cape (N.T., Austr.)
  78 D 1
Scott City 21 F 4
Scott Island 85
Scottsbluff 21 F 3
Scottsdale 20 D 5
Scottsdale (Tasmania, Austr.)
  80 L 9
Scottsville 22 C 3
Scranton 22 E 2
Scugog, Lake 22 E 2
Seabra 35 H 3
Seahorse Point 16 K 4
Sea Islands 22 D 4
Seal 15 K 3
Sea of Azov 47 E 1
Sea of Crete 46 BC 3
Sea of Japan 71 KL 3
Sea of Marmara → Marmara-
  Denizi 46 C 2
Seaside 20 B 2
Seattle 20 B 2
Sebastián Vizcaino, Bahía
  24 B 2
Sebewaing 22 D 2
Sebkha Azzel Matti 54 EF 3
Sebkha Mekerrhane 55 F 3
Sebkha Oumm ed Droûs Telli
  54 CD 4
Sebkha Tah 54 C 3
Sebkhet Oumm ed Droûs-
  Guebli 54 C 4
Sebring 27 E 3
Sechura 32 B 5
Sechura, Desierto de 32 B 5
Sedalia 21 H 4
Sedan 45 D 2
Sedanka 12 D 5
Seddenga 56 DE 4
Sedona 20 D 5
Seeheim 62 B 5
Sefadu 58 B 4
Sefrou 54 E 2
Segesta 45 F 4
Segezha 42 K 3
Ségou 58 C 3
Segovia 44 C 3
Segozero, Ozero 42 K 3
Segre 44 D 3
Seguam 12 C 6
Seguin 25 E 2
Segula 12 A 6
Segura 44 C 4
Seiland 42 H 1
Seinäjoki 42 J 3
Seine 44 D 2
Seke 60 E 5
Sekkemo 42 H 2
Sekoma 62 C 4
Sekondi-Takoradi 58 D 5
Selaru, Pulau 75 H 5
Selassi 75 H 4
Selatan, Tanjung 74 D 4
Selat Karimata 74 C 4

Selat Mentawai 74 A 4
Selat Salue Timpaus 75 F 4
Selawik 12 F 2
Selawik Lake 12 F 2
Selayar, Pulau 75 F 5
Selby 21 G 2
Seldovia 12 G 4
Selemdzhinsk 69 O 5
Selenge (Mongolia) 68 HJ 6
Selenge (Zaire) 60 B 5
Selgon 69 P 6
Selinunte 45 F 4
Selizharovo 50 F 4
Selkirk Mountains 14 F 4
Selle, Pic de la 29 E 3
Selma (AL, U.S.A.) 22 C 4
Selma (CA, U.S.A.) 20 C 4
Selous Game Reserve 61 F 6
Selvagens, Ilhas 54 B 2
Selvänä 47 F 3
Selvas 32–33 EF 5
Selwyn Lake 15 J 2–3
Selwyn Mountains 13 LM 3
Semarang 74 D 5
Sembé 59 G 5
Semichi Islands 12 A 6
Semiozernoye 51 M 5
Semipalatinsk 51 Q 5
Semisopochnoi 12 AB 6
Semitau 74 D 3
Semmering 46 A 1
Semnän 49 F 2
Semporna 75 E 3
Senador Pompeu 35 HJ 2
Sena Madureira 32 E 5
Sendai 71 M 3
Sêndo 70 C 4
Sénégal 58 B 2
Senegal 58 AB 3
Seney 22 C 1
Senftenberg 41 F 4
Senhor do Bonfim 35 H 3
Senja 42 G 2
Senjavin Grop 82 B 2
Senneterre 18 E 4
Sens 44 D 2
Senta 46 A 1
Sentinel Peak 14 E 4
Seoni 72 C 3
Seoul 71 J 3
Separation Point 19 J 3
Sepik 82 A 3
Sepik River 80 D 2
Sept-Îles 19 G 3
Sequoia National Park 20 C 4
Şerafettin Dağları 47 F 3
Serakhs 67 G 3
Seram 75 G 4
Seram, Laut 75 GH 4
Serang 74 C 5
Serdobsk 50 HJ 5
Seremban 74 B 3
Serengeti National Park
  60 EF 5

Sergino **51** N 3
Sergipe **35** J 3
Seroglazovka **47** G 1
Serov **51** M 4
Serowe **62** D 4
Serpa **44** B 4
Serpukhov **50** G 5
Serra Acarai **33** G 3
Serra Bonita **35** G 4
Serra da Estrêla **44** B 3
Serra do Cachimbo **33** G 5
Serra do Estrondo **33** J 5
Serra do Marao **44** B 3
Serra do Mogadouro **44** B 3
Serra do Navio **33** H 3
Serra do Roncador **35** F 3
Serra dos Carajás **33** H 4–5
Serra dos Gradaús **33** H 5
Serra dos Parecis **34** D 3
Serra do Tombador **34** E 3
Serra Formosa **35** EF 3
Serrai **46** B 2
Serrana, Banco de **28** D 4
Serranía de Imataca **29** G 5
Serranías Turagua **29** G 5
Serranilla, Banco **28** D 3
Serra Talhada **35** J 2
Serrezuela **36** C 5
Serrinha **35** J 3
Serrota **44** BC 3
Seruai **75** J 4
Serule **62** D 4
Seseganaga Lake **18** C 3
Sesfontein **62** A 3
Sesheke **62** CD 3
Sesibi **56** DE 4
Seskarö **42** H 2
Sestroretsk **43** JK 3
Séte **44** D 3
Sete Lagoas **35** H 4
Sétif **55** G 1
Settat **54** D 2
Sette Daban, Khrebet **69** P 3
Setúbal **44** B 4
Setúbal, Baía de **44** B 4
Seumanyam **74** A 3
Sevarujo **34** C 4
Sevastopol' **47** D 2
Sever **69** V 3
Severnaya Dvina **50** H 3
Severnaya Zemlya **84**
Severn Lake **15** LM 4
Severnoye **51** P 4
Severn River (Ontario, Can.)
   15 M 3
Severnyy Anyuyskiy Khrebet
   69 UW 2
Severodvinsk**50** G 3
Severomorsk **42** KL 2
Severo Sibirskaya
   Nizmennost' **68** FK 1
Sevier **20** D 4
Sevier Desert **20** D 4
Sevilla **44** B 4

Sevrey **70** D 2
Seward (AK, U.S.A.) **12** H 3
Seward (NE, U.S.A.) **21** G 3
Seward Peninsula **12** E 2
Sewell **36** BC 5
Seychelles **61** J 6
Seyhan **47** E 3
Seymchan **69** S 3
Seymour (IN, U.S.A.) **22** C 3
Sfax **55** GH 2
S. Félix Island **31** B 5
Shaanxi **70** EF 4
Shaba **60** CD 6
Shache **67** K 3
Shackleton Ice Shelf **85**
Shackleton Range **85**
Shaddādi **47** F 3
Shadrinsk **51** MN 4
Shaffhausen **45** E 2
Shageluk **12** F 3
Shahdol **72** D 3
Shahhāt **55** K 2
Shahjahanpur **72** CD 2
Shahmīrzad **49** F 2
Shahr Kord **49** F 2
Shahtinsk **51** O 6
Shā'ib al Banāt, Jabal **48** A 4
Sha'ib Hasb **48** D 3
Shakhrisyabz **67** H 3
Shakhterskiy **69** XY 3
Shakhty **47** F 1
Shaki **58** E 4
Shaktinsk **67** J 2
Shaktoolik **12** E 3
Shaler Mountains **16** D 2
Shalgiya **51** O 6
Shalkar **50** K 5
Shām, Jabal ash **57** K 4
Shamattawa **15** L 3
Shambe **60** E 3
Shāmīyah **48** C 2
Shammar, Jabal **48** CD 4
Shamokin **22** E 2
Shamrock **21** F 4
Shams **49** G 3
Shan **73** G 3
Shandan **70** D 3
Shandī **56** E 5
Shandong **71** GH 3
Shandong Bandao **71** H 3
Shangcheng **70** FG 4
Shangdu **70** F 2
Shanghai **71** H 4
Shanghang **70** G 5–6
Shangqiu **70** G 4
Shangrao **71** G 5
Shangzhi **71** J 1–2
Shanh **68** H 6
Shankou **70** B 2
Shannon **40** B 4
Shannon, Mouth of the
   40 A 4
Shanshan **70** B 2
Shantarskiye Ostrova **69** P 4

Shantou **70** G 6
Shanxi **70** F 3
Shaoguan **70** F 6
Shaowu **71** G 5
Shaoxing **71** GH 5
Shaoyang **70** F 5
Shaqrā' **57** H 6
Sharāf **66** C 4
Shark Bay **78** A 4
Sharm ash Shaykh **48** AB 4
Shary **66** C 5
Shashamanna **61** F 3
Shashi **70** F 4
Shasta, Mount **20** B 3
Shasta Lake **20** B 3
Shatt al Arab **49** E 3
Shatt al Jarīd **55** G 2
Shaunavon **15** H 5
Shaviklde **47** G 2
Shawinigan **18** F 4
Shawnee **21** G 4
Shaybārā **48** B 4
Shaykh, Ra's ash **48** B 3
Shaykh Sa'd **49** E 2
Shaykh 'Uthmān **57** H 6
Shchara **43** J 5
Shchel'yayur **50** KL 2
Shchuchinsk **51** N 5
Sheboygan **22** C 2
Shedin Peak **13** M 4
Sheenjek **13** J 2
Sheet Harbour **23** H 2
Sheffield **40** C 4
Sheffield (AL, U.S.A.) **22** C 4
Shekhawati **72** C 2
Sheki **66** D 2
Shelburne **23** GH 2
Shelby **20** D 2
Sheldon Point **12** D 3
Shelikof Strait **12** G 4
Shellbrook **15** H 4
Shellharbour **79** J 5
Shenandoah National Park
   22 E 3
Shendam **59** F 4
Shenmu **70** F 3
Shenton, Mount **78** C 4
Shenyang **71** HJ 2
Shepetovka **43** J 5
Sherbro Island **58** B 4
Sherbrooke **18–19** F 4
Sheridan **20** E 3
Sherman **21** G 5
Sherman Station **23** G 2
Sherridon **15** J 3
Shetland Islands **40** CD 2
Shevchenko **66** E 2
Shevli **69** O 5
Sheya **68** L 3
Sheyang **71** H 4
Sheyenne River **21** G 2
Shibarghan **67** GH 3
Shibazhan **69** MN 5
Shīb Kūh **49** F 3–4

Shibogama Lake **18** C 3
Shijiazhuang **70** FG 3
Shikarpur **67** H 5
Shikoku **71** K 4
Shilka **68** L 5
Shilkan **69** R 4
Shilla **72** C 1
Shillong **73** F 2
Shimanovsk **69** N 5
Shimizu **71** L 4
Shimoga **72** BC 5
Shingshal **67** JK 3
Shiping **70** D 6
Shippegan **19** H 4
Shipunovo **51** Q 5
Shiquanhe **72** C 1
Shirabad **67** H 3
Shirase Glacier **85**
Shīrāz **49** F 3
Shire **63** E 3
Shirikrabat **67** G 2
Shir Kūh **49** FG 3
Shirley Mountains **21** E 3
Shishaldin Volcano **12** E 5
Shishmaref **12** D 2
Shishou **70** F 5
Shiveluch, Sopka **69** U 4
Shivpuri **72** C 2
Shizuoka **71** L 4
Shkodra **46** AB 2
Sholapur **72** C 4
Shoptykul' **51** P 5
Shorawak **67** H 4–5
Shoshone **20** D 3
Shoshone Peak **20** C 4
Shoshoni **20** E 3
Shouguang **71** G 3
Showa **85**
Show Low **20** E 5
Shqiperia **46** AB 2
Shreveport **21** H 5
Shrewsbury **40** CD 4
Shuangliao **71** H 2
Shuangyashan **71** K 1
Shucheng **71** G 4
Shuicheng **70** DE 5
Shule **67** K 3
Shumagin Islands **12** F 4–5
Shumerlya **50** J 4
Shungnak **12** F 2
Shuo Xian **70** F 3
Shurinda **68** K 4
Shūshtar **66** D 4
Shuwak **56** F 6
Shuyak **12** G 4
Siahan Range **67** GH 5
Siah-Chashmeh **47** F 3
Siargao **75** G 2
Šiauliai **43** H 4
Sibay **51** L 5
Šibenik **45** G 3
Siberut, Pulau **74** A 4
Sibirskoa **45** F 4
Sicilia, Canale di **45** F 4

Sicily **45** F 4
Sicuani **34** B 3
Siderno **45** G 4
Sidi-bel-Abbès **54** EF 1–2
Sidney **14** E 5
Sidney (MT, U.S.A.) **21** F 2
Sidney (NE, U.S.A.) **21** F 3
Sidney (OH, U.S.A.) **22** D 2
Sidon **48** B 2
Siedlce **41** H 4
Siegen **41** E 4
Siena **45** F 3
Sierra Alamos **24** D 2
Sierra Blanca **24** E 5
Sierra Cimaltepec **25** E 4
Sierra Colorada **37** C 7
Sierra de Agalta **28** B 3
Sierra de Alcaraz **44** C 4
Sierra de Aracena **44** B 4
Sierra de Coalcoman **24** D 4
Sierra de Gata **44** B 3
Sierra de Gredos **44** B 3
Sierra de Guadarrama **44** C 3
Sierra de Gúdar **44** C 3
Sierra de Juarez **20** C 5
Sierra de la Cabrera **44** B 3
Sierra de la Encantada **24** D 2
Sierra de la Giganta **24** B 2
Sierra de las Minas **28** B 3
Sierra de las Tunas **24** C 2
Sierra de la Tasajera **24** C 2
Sierra del Cadí **44** D 3
Sierra del Nido **24** C 2
Sierra de los Alamitos **24** D 2
Sierra de los Cuchumatanes
  25 F 4
Sierra de los Huicholes
  24 D 3
Sierra de Mulegé **24** B 2
Sierra de Parras **25** D 2
Sierra de Perijá **29** E 4–5
Sierra de San Borjas **24** B 2
Sierra de San Lázaro **24** C 3
Sierra Espinazo del Diablo
  24 C 3
Sierra Grande (Mexico)
  24 D 2
Sierra Leone **58** B 4
Sierra Madre (Mexico) **25** F 4
Sierra Madre del Sur **25** DE 4
Sierra Madre Oriental
  25 DE 2–3
Sierra Madrona **44** C 4
Sierra Maestra **27** F 4
Sierra Mojada **24** D 2
Sierra Morena **44** BC 4
Sierra Nayarit **24** D 3
Sierra Nevada (Spain) **44** C 4
Sierra Nevada (U.S.A.)
  20 BC 3–4
Sierra Pacaraima **33** F 3
Sierra Parima **33** F 3
Sierra Prieta **20** D 5
Sierra Tarahumara **24** C 2

Sierra Vizcaíno **24** B 2
Sífnos **46** B 3
Sighetu Marmaţiei **46** B 1
Signal Peak **20** D 5
Signy Island **85**
Siguiri **58** C 3
Siirt **47** F 3
Sikanni Chief **14** E 3
Sikar **72** C 2
Sikasso **58** C 3
Sikerin **69** Q 2
Sikeston **22** C 3
Sikkim **72** E 2
Siktyakh **69** N 2
Silchar **73** F 3
Silesia **41** G 4
Silet **55** F 4
Silifke **47** D 3
Siliguri **72** E 2
Silistra **46** C 2
Siljan **43** FG 3
Silkleborg **43** E 4
Siloam Springs **21** H 4
Siltou **59** H 2
Silver Bank Passage **29** EF 2
Silver City **20** E 5
Silverton **20** E 4
Sil'yeyaki **69** Q 1
Simanggang **74** D 3
Simav **46** C 2–3
Simcoe, Lake **22** E 2
Simenga **68** J 3
Simeulue, Pulau **74** A 3
Simferopol' **47** D 2
Simla **72** C 1
Simojärvi **42** J 2
Simojovel de Allende **25** F 4
Simplicio Mendes **35** H 2
Simpson Desert **79** F 3
Simpson Desert National Park
  79 F 4
Simpson Peninsula **16** J 3
Simrishamn **43** FG 4
Sinā' **48** A 3
Sinai (Egypt) **48** A 3
Sinaloa **24** C 2–3
Sinamaica **29** E 4
Sināwan **55** H 2
Sincé **28** D 5
Sincelejo **32** C 2
Sind **67** H 5
Sinda **69** P 6
Singapore **78** B 3
Singaraja **74** E 5
Singida **60** E 5
Singleton **79** J 5
Sinianka-Minia, Parc
  National du **59** H 3
Sinjaja **43** J 4
Sinjär **47** F 3
Sinkiang Uighur **67** L 3
Sinnamary **33** H 2
Sinop **47** E 2
Sinskoye **69** N 3

Sintang **74** D 3
Sinüiju **71** HJ 3
Sioux City **21** G 3
Sioux Falls **21** G 3
Sioux Lookout **15** L 4
Siping **71** H 2
Sipiwesk **15** K 3
Sipiwesk Lake **15** K 3
Siple Station **85**
Siquia, Rio **28** C 4
Siquisique **29** EF 4
Siracusa **45** G 4
Sir Alexander, Mount **14** E 4
Sir Edward Pellew Group
  79 F 2
Sireniki **12** C 3
Siret **46** C 1
Sirgän **67** G 5
Sirino **45** G 3
Sir James MacBrian, Mount
  13 M 3
Sirsa **72** C 2
Sirt **55** J 2
Sisak **45** G 2
Siskiyou Mountains **20** B 3
Sisophon **73** H 5
Sisseton **21** G 2
Sistema Iberico **44** C 3
Sistemas Béticos **44** C 4
Sistig-Khem **68** G 5
Sitapur **72** D 2
Sitka **13** K 4
Sitkalidak **12** G 4
Sittwe **73** F 3
Siuna **28** C 4
Sivaki **69** N 5
Sivas **47** E 3
Sivash **47** DE 1
Siverek **47** E 3
Siwah **56** D 3
Siwalik Range **72** CD 1–2
Siwan **72** D 2
Si Xian **71** G 4
Sjælland **43** F 4
Sjövegan **42** G 2
Skagen **43** F 4
Skagern **43** F 4
Skagerrak **43** EF 4
Skagway **13** K 4
Skara **43** F 4
Skarsöy **42** E 3
Skarstind **42** E 3
Skarżysko-Kamienna **41** H 4
Skeena **13** M 5
Skeena Mountains **13** M 4
Skeldon **33** G 2
Skeleton Coast Park **62** A 3
Skellefteå **42** H 3
Skellefteälven **42** G 2
Skidegate **13** L 5
Skien **43** E 4
Skierniewice **41** H 4
Skiftet **43** H 3
Skikda **55** G 1

Skikotsu **71** N 2
Skiros **46** B 3
Sklad **68** M 1
Skópelos **46** B 3
Skopi **46** C 3
Skopje **46** B 2
Skövde **43** F 4
Skowhegan **23** F 2
Skwentna **12** G 3
Skye **40** B 3
Slantsy **43** J 4
Śląsk **41** G 4
Slatina **46** B 2
Slave Coast **58** E 4
Slave Lake **14** F 3
Slave River **14** G 2–3
Slavgorod **51** P 5
Slavonski Brod **45** G 2
Slavuta **43** J 5
Slavyansk **50** G 6
Sleeper Islands **18** D 2
Sligo **40** B 4
Sliven **46** C 2
Slobodka **46** C 1
Slobodskoy **50** K 4
Slocum Mountain **20** C 4
Slonim **43** J 5
Slovakia **41** H 5
Slovechno **43** J 5
Slovensko **41** H 5
Sluch' **43** J 5
Słupşk **41** G 4
Slutsk **43** J 5
Småland **43** G 4
Smallwood Réservoir **19** H 3
Smidovich **84**
Smirnykh **69** Q 6
Smith **14** G 3
Smith Arm **13** N 2
Smith Bay **12** G 1
Smithers **13** M 5
Smith Falls **22** E 2
Smokey Dome **20** CD 3
Smoky Cape **79** J 5
Smoky Falls **18** D 3
Smoky Hill River **21** F 4
Smoky Hills **21** G 4
Smoky River **14** F 4
Smöla **42** E 3
Smolensk **50** F 5
Smooth Rock Falls **18** D 4
Smythe, Mount **14** DE 3
Snag **13** J 3
Snake River **20** C 2
Snake River Plain **20** D 3
Snare **14** F 2
Snezhnoye **69** W 2
Snoul **74** C 1
Snowbird Lake **15** J 2
Snowdon **40** C 4
Snowdrift **14** G 2
Snow Lake **15** J 4
Snow Mountain **20** B 4
Snowville **20** D 3

Snyder **21** F 5
Sobolevo **69** T 5
Sobral **35** HJ 1
Sochi **47** E 2
Society Islands **83** EF 4
Socorro (N.M., U.S.A.) **20** E 5
Sodankylä **42** J 2
Soddu **61** F 3
Söderhamn **42** G 3
Södermanland **43** G 4
Södertälje **43** G 4
Sofia → Sofiya **46** B 2
Sofiysk **69** O 5
Sofiysk **69** PQ 5
Sofporog **42** K 2
Sogamoso **32** D 2
Sogndalsfjöra **42** E 3
Sogn og Fjordane **42** E 3
Sog Xian **70** B 4
Söke **46** C 3
Sokhor, Gora **68** J 5
Sokodé **58** E 4
Sokótka **41** H 4
Sokolov **41** F 4
Sokosti **42** J 2
Sokoto **59** EF 3
Solberg **42** G 3
Soldatovo **69** V 3
Soldotna **12** G 3
Soledad **32** D 1
Soledad (Venezuela) **29** G 5
Soligorsk **43** J 5
Solikamsk **50** KL 4
Sol'-Iletsk **50** L 5
Solimões **32** E 4
Solita **29** E 5
Solitaire **62** B 4
Solomon Islands **81** G 3
Solomon Islands **82** B 3
Solomon Islands **82** BC 3
Solomon Sea **81** F 3
Solomon Sea **82** B 3
Solov'yevsk **68** L 5
Solyanka **68** M 3
Somalia **61** GH 3–4
Sombrerete **24** D 3
Somerset (Australia) **79** G 1
Somerset (KY, U.S.A.) **22** D 3
Somme **44** D 1
Somoto **28** B 4
Sonakh **69** P 5
Söndre Strömfjord **17** Q 3
Söndre Strömfjord **17** QR 3
Songea **63** F 2
Song Hong **73** H 3
Songhua Jiang **71** J 1
Songkhla **73** H 6
Songnim **71** J 3
Songo **63** E 3
Sonid Youqi **70** F 2
Sonid Zuoqi **70** F 2
Sonmiani Bay **67** H 5
Sonneberg **41** F 4
Sonoita **20** D 5

Sonoma Peak **20** C 3
Sonora (Mexico) **24** B 2
Sonora (TX, U.S.A.) **24** F 5
Sonora, Rio **24** B 2
Sonoran Desert **20** D 5
Songor **66** D 4
Sonsonate **25** FG 5
Sopka Shiveluch **69** U 4
Sopochnaya Karga **68** DE 1
Sopron **46** A 1
Sopur **67** J 4
Sora **45** F 3
Sorel **18** F 4
Soria **44** C 3
Sorikmerapi, Gunung **74** A 3
Sorkh, Küh-e **49** G 2
Sorkheh **49** F 2
Sor Mertvyy Kultuk **66** E 1
Sorong **75** H 4
Soroti **60** E 4
Söröya **42** H 1
Sör Rondane Mountains **85**
Sorsatunturi **42** J 2
Sorsele **42** G 2
Sorsogon **75** F 1
Sortavala **42** K 3
Sör-Tröndelag **42** F 3
Sosnogorsk **50** KL 3
Sosnovyy Bor **51** Q 3
Sosyka **47** EF 1
Sotra **43** D 3
Sotsial **51** P 6
Souanké **59** GH 5
Soudan **79** F 3
Soufrière (Guadeloupe)
  29 G 3
Soufrière (St. Vincent) **29** G 4
Söul **71** HJ 3
Soumenselkä **42** H 3
Soure **33** J 4
Souris **15** J 5
Souris **19** H 4
Souris River **15** J 5
Sousa **35** J 2
Sousse → Süsah **55** H 1
South Africa **62** BD 6
Southampton **40** C D 4
Southampton, Cape **15** MN 2
Southampton Island **15** MN 2
South Andaman **73** F 5
South Aulatsivik **19** H 2
South Australia **78–79** E 4
South Bay **16** K 4
South Bend (IN, U.S.A.)
  22 C 2
South Bend (WA, U.S.A.)
  20 B 2
South Carolina **22** D 4
South China Sea **74** CD 2
South Dakota **21** FG 3
South East Cape **80** L 9
Southend **15** J 3
Southend-on-Sea **40** D 4
Southern Alps **82** C 5

Southern Cook Islands **83** E 4
Southern Cross **78** B 5
Southern Indian Lake **15** K 3
Southern Uplands **40** C 3
Southern Yemen **57** HJ 5–6
South Geomagnetic Pole **85**
South Georgia **85**
South Indian Lake **15** K 3
South Island **80** P 9
South Island **82** C 5
South Korea **71** JK 3
South Lake Tahoe **20** C 4
South Magnetic Pole **85**
South Nahanni **13** M 3
South Orkney Islands **85**
South Platte River **21** F 3
South Pole **85**
South Sandwich Islands **85**
South Saskatchewan **14** GH 4
South Shetland Islands **85**
South Shields **40** C 3
South Sioux City **21** G 3
South Uist **40** B 3
South Wellesley Islands
  79 FG 2
Southwest Cape **80** P 10
South Yolla Bolly Mountains
  20 B 4
Soven **36** C 5
Sovetsk **50** J 4
Sovetskaya Gavan' **69** PQ 6
Sovetskaya Rechka **51** QR 2
Soya Strait **65** R 5
Soyatita **24** C 2
Sozimskiy **50** K 4
Spain **44** BC 4
Spanish Fork **20** D 3
Spanish Town **28** D 3
Sparks **20** C 4
Spartanburg **22** D 4
Sparti **46** B 3
Spassk Dal'niy **71** K 2
Spearfish **21** F 3
Spenard **12** G 3
Spence Bay **16** H 3
Spencer **21** G 3
Spencer Gulf **79** F 5
Spicer Islands **17** L 3
Spirit River **14** F 3
Spitsbergen **84**
Split **45** G 3
Split Lake **15** K 3
Spokane **20** C 2
Spooner **21** H 2
Springbok **62** B 5
Springdale **19** J 4
Springdale (AR, U.S.A.)
  21 H 4
Springer **21** F 4
Springer, Mount **18** F 4
Springfield (CO, U.S.A.)
  21 F 4
Springfield (IL, U.S.A.)
  21 HJ 4

Springfield (MA, U.S.A.)
  23 F 2
Springfield (MO, U.S.A.)
  21 H 4
Springfield (OR, U.S.A.)
  20 B 3
Springfield (S.D., U.S.A.)
  21 G 3
Springfield (TN, U.S.A.)
  22 C 3
Springhill **19** H 4
Springs **62** D 5
Squamish **14** E 5
Square Islands **19** JK 3
Squillace, Golfo di **45** G 4
Srbija **46** B 2
Sredinnyy Khrebet **69** TU 4–5
Sredna Gora **46** BC 2
Srednekolymsk **69** S 2
Sredne Sibirskoye
  Ploskogor'ye **68** FK 2–3
Sredniy **69** S 4
Srednyaya Itkana **69** U 3
Sremska Mitrovica **46** A 1–2
Srikakulam **72** DE 4
Sri Lanka (Ceylon) **72** D 6
Srinagar **67** K 4
Staaten River National Park
  79 G 2
Stadlandet **42** D 3
Stafford **40** C 4
Stalowa Wola **41** H 4
Stamford (CT, U.S.A.) **23** F 2
Stamford (TX, U.S.A.) **21** G 5
Standerton **62** D 5
Stanke Dimitrov **46** B 2
Stanley **37** E 9
Stanley (N.D., U.S.A.) **21** F 2
Stanley Falls **60** D 4
Stanley Mission **15** J 3
Stanovka **51** O 4
Stanovoy Khrebet **68** LN 4
Stanovoy Nagor'ye **68** KL 4
Stara Planina **46** BC 2
Staraya Russa **43** K 4
Staraya Vorpavla **51** N 3
Stara Zagora **46** C 2
Starbuck **83** E 3
Stargard Szczecinski **41** G 4
Starodub **50** F 5
Starogard Gdanski **41** G 4
Staryy Oskol **50** G 5
State College **22** E 2
Staten Island **37** D 9–10
Statesboro **22** D 4
Statesville **22** D 3
Staunton **22** E 3
Stavanger **43** DE 4
Stavropol' **47** F 1
Stavropolka **51** N 5
Stavropol'skaya
  Vozvyshennost' **47** F 1
Steen River **14** F 3
Steensby Inlet **17** L 2

Stefanie, Lake **61** F 4
Stefansson Island **16** E 2
Steinbach **15** K 5
Steinkopf **62** B 5
Stellenbosch **62** BC 6
Stenon **46** C 3
Stepanakert **66** D 3
Stephens Passage **13** L 4
Stephenville **19** J 4
Stephenville (TX, U.S.A.)
   25 G 5
Sterling **21** F 3
Sterlitamak **50** KL 5
Stettler **14** G 4
Steubenville **22** D 2
Stevenson Entrance **12** G 4
Stevens Point **21** HJ 3
Stewart **13** KL 3
Stewart (AK, U.S.A.) **13** M 4
Stewart (New Zealand)
   80 P 10
Stewart Crossing **13** K 3
Stewart Island (New Zeeland)
   80 P 10
Stewart Island (Solomon
   Islands) **82** B 3
Stewart River **13** K 3
Steyr **45** F 2
Stikine **13** L 4
Stikine Ranges **13** L 4
Stillwater **21** G 4
Stip **46** B 2
Stirling Range National Park
   78 B 5
Stjördal **42** F 3
Stockholm **43** G 4
Stockton **20** B 4
Stockton Lake **21** H 4
Stockton Plateau **24** F 5
Stöde **42** G 3
Stoke-on-Trent **40** C 4
Stokksnes **42** BC 3
Stony **12** F 3
Stony Rapids **15** H 3
Stony River **12** F 3
Storån **42** G 3
Storavan **42** G 2
Stord **43** E 4
Storis Passage **16** G 3
Storkerson Bay **16** A 2
Storkerson Peninsula **16** E 2
Stornoway **40** B 3
Storsjßn **42** F 3
Storuman **42** G 2
Storvigelen **42** F 3
Stöttingfjället **42** G 3
Strait of Belle Isle **19** J 3
Strait of Bonifacio **45** E 3
Strait of Canso **19** H 4
Strait of Dover **40** D 4
Strait of Gibraltar **44** B 4
Strait of Hormuz **49** G 4
Strait of Hormuz **57** K 3
Strait of Juan de Fuca **14** D 5

Strait of Magellan **37** BC 9
Strait of Makassar **74** E 4
Strait of Malacca **74** B 3
Straits of Florida **27** EF 3
Straits of Mackinac **22** C 1
Stralsund **41** F 4
Strand **62** B 6
Stranraer **40** B 4
Strasbourg **45** E 2
Stratford **22** D 2
Stratford (TX, U.S.A.) **21** F 4
Straubing **41** F 5
Strawberry Mountain **20** C 3
Streaky Bay **78** E 5
Strelka-Chunya **68** H 3
Stretto de Messina **45** G 4
Streymoy **40** A 1
Strömfjord, Norde **17** Q 3
Strömfjord, Söndre **17** Q 3
Strömsund **42** G 3
Stuart **12** E 3
Stuart, Lake **14** DE 4
Stung Treng **73** J 5
Sturgeon Lake **15** L 5
Sturt Desert **79** G 4
Sturt National Park **79** G 4
Stuttgart **41** E 5
Styr' **43** J 3
Subayhah **66** B 5
Sublette **21** F 4
Suceava **46** C 1
Sucre **34** D 4
Sudan **56** DE 6
Sudbury **18** D 4
Suddie **33** G 2
Sudety **41** G 4
Suðuroy **40** A 1
Suez **48** A 3
Suez Canal (Egypt) **48** A 3
Şuhãr **57** K 4
Sühbaatar **70** F 1
Suhl **41** F 4
Suide **70** EF 3
Suining **71** G 4
Suir **50** F 3
Suizhong **71** H 2
Sukaraja **74** D 4
Sukhana **68** L 2
Sukhona **50** H 4
Sukhumi **47** F 2
Sukkertoppen **17** Q 3
Sukkur **67** H 5
Suksukan **69** S 3
Sula, Kepulauan **75** FG 4
Sulaimãniya **49** D 2
Sulaiman Range **67** H 4–5
Sulanheer **70** E 2
Sulawesi **75** EF 4
Sulawesi, Laut **75** F 3
Sulb **56** DE 4
Sulima **58** B 4
Sulitjelma **42** G 2
Sullana **32** BC 4
Sulphur **25** H 5

Sulphur Springs **21** G 5
Sultan Dağları **46–47** D 3
Sulu Archipelago **75** EF 2–3
Sulu Sea **75** EF 2
Sumarokovo **51** R 3
Sumatera **74** AB 3–4
Sumaúma **33** G 5
Šumava **41** F 5
Sumba **75** EF 5
Sumbawa **74** E 5
Sumbawanga **60** E 6
Sumbe **62** A 2
Sümber **70** E 1
Sumburgh Head **40** C 3
Sumgait **66** DE 2
Summel **47** F 3
Summer Lake **20** BC 3
Summit Lake **14** E 3
Sumperk **41** G 5
Sumter **22** DE 4
Sumy **50** G 5
Suna **60** EF 6
Sunbury **22** E 2
Sunderland **40** C 4
Sündiren Dağları **46** D 3
Sundsvall **42** G 3
Sunflower, Mount **21** F 4
Sungai Barito **74** D 4
Sungai Kampar **74** B 3
Sungai Kutai **74** E 4
Sungai Mamberamo **75** J 4
Sunnan **42** F 3
Sunndalsfjorden **42** E 3
Suntar Khayata, Khrebet
   69 PQ 3
Sun Valley **20** D 3
Suokonmäki **42** H 3
Suolahti **42** J 3
Suomenselkä **42** J 3
Suomi **42** J 3
Suoyarvi **50** F 3
Superior (MT, U.S.A.) **20** D 2
Superior (WI, U.S.A.) **21** H 2
Superior, Lake **22** C 1
Süphan Dağı **47** F 3
Suquṭrã **61** J 2
Şür **48** B 2
Surabaya **74** D 5
Surakarta **74** CD 5
Surat (India) **72** B 3
Surat (Queensland, Austr.)
   79 H 4
Suratgarh **72** B 2
Surat Thani **73** GH 6
Surendranagar **72** AB 3
Surgut **51** O 3
Surgutikha **51** R 3
Surin **73** H 5
Surinam **33** G 3
Sürìyah **48** BC 2
Surud Ad **61** H 2
Survey Pass **12** G 2
Susa **49** E 2
Susanville **20** B 3

Susitna **12** G 3
Susquehanna River **22** E 2
Susques **34** C 5
Sussex **19** G 4
Susuman **69** R 3
Sutlej **67** J 4–5
Sutton (AK, U.S.A.) **12** H 3
Sutton (W.V., U.S.A.) **22** D 3
Sutun'ya **69** NO 2
Sutwik **12** F 4
Suva **82** C 4
Suva Gora **46** B 2
Suva Planina **46** B 2
Suvorov **82** E 3
Suwałki **41** H 4
Suways, Qanat as **48** A 3
Suwon **71** J 3
Suzhou **71** GH 4
Suzun **51** Q 5
Svalbard **84**
Svartisen **42** F 2
Svealand **43** FG 4
Sveg **42** F 3
Svendborg **43** F 4–5
Sverdlovsk **51** M 4
Sverige **42** G 3
Svetlogorsk (Belorussiya,
   U.S.S.R.) **43** J 5
Svetlograd **47** F 1
Svetlyy **69** N 4
Svetozarevo **46** B 2
Svobodnyy **69** N 5
Swain Reefs **79** J 3
Swains **82** D 3
Swakopmund **62** A 4
Swan Islands → Islas del
   Cisne **28** C 3
Swan Range **20** D 2
Swan River **15** J 4
Swansea **40** C 4
Swaziland [Ngwane] **63** E 5
Sweden **42** G 3
Sweet Home **20** B 3
Sweetwater **21** F 5
Sweetwater River **20** E 3
Swellendam **62** C 6
Świdnik **41** H 4
Swift Current **15** H 4
Swift River **13** L 4
Swinburne, Cape **16** FG 2
Swinoujście **41** FG 4
Switzerland **45** E 2
Syadaykharvuta **51** OP 2
Syalakh **69** MN 2
Syangannakh **69** R 2
Syðri-Hagangur **42** B 2
Sydney **19** H 4
Sydney (N.S.W., Austr.)
   79 J 5
Sydney Mines **19** HJ 4
Syktyvkar **50** JK 3
Sylacauga **22** C 4
Sylhet **73** F 3
Syracuse (KS, U.S.A.) **21** F 4

Syracuse (N.Y., U.S.A.) **22** E 2
Syr-Dar'ya **67** H 2
Syria **48** BC 2
Syria **56** F 2
Syrian Desert **48** C 2
Syuge-Khaya, Gora **69** P 2
Syurkum **69** Q 5
Syzran **50** J 5
Szczecin **41** F 4
Szczecinek **41** G 4
Szeged **46** A 1
Székesféhérvár **46** A 1
Szekszárd **46** A 1
Szentes **46** AB 1
Szolnok **46** B 1
Szombathely **46** A 1

T

Taarom **79** HJ 4
Tabacal **34** D 5
Tabaqah **48** C 2
Tabarqah **47** E 3
Tabas **49** G 2
Tabasco **25** F 4
Tabatinga **32** E 4
Tabelbala **54** E 3
Tabelbalet **55** G 3
Tabeng **73** HJ 5
Taber **14** G 5
Tabiteuea **82** C 3
Tabla **58** E 3
Table Mountain **62** B 6
Table Rock Lake **21** H 4
Tábor **41** F 5
Tabor (U.S.S.R.) **69** R 1
Tabora **60** E 6
Tabou **58** C 5
Tabriz **66** D 3
Tabuaeran **83** E 2
Tabük **48** B 3
Tacámbaro **24** D 4
Tacheng **67** L 1
Tacloban **75** F 1
Tacna **34** B 4
Tacoma **20** B 2
Tacuarembó **36** EF 5
Tademaït, Plateau du **55** F 3
Tadoule Lake **15** K 3
Tadzhikistan **67** HJ 3
Taegu **71** J 3
Taejŏn **71** J 3
Tagama **59** F 2
Taganrog **47** E 1
Taganrogskiy Zaliv **47** E 1
Tagish Lake **13** L 3
Tagounite **54** D 3
Taguatinga **35** G 3
Taguenout Haggueret **58** D 1
Tagula Island **79** J 1
Tahan, Gunung **74** B 3
Tahat, Mont **55** G 4
Tahiryuak Lake **16** D 2
Tahiti **83** EF 4

Tahoe, Lake **20** C 4
Tahoua **59** EF 3
Tahrüd **66** F 5
Tahtali Dağlari **47** E 3
Tahuata **83** F 3
Taibus Qi **70** FG 2
Taichung **71** H 6
Tailai **71** H 1
Taimba **68** G 3
Tainan **71** GH 6
Taipei **71** H 6
Taiping **74** B 3
Taipu **35** J 2
Taitao, Península de **37** AB 8
Taitung **71** H 6
Taivalkoski **42** J 2
Taiwan **71** H 6
Taiyuan **70** F 3
Ta'izz **57** G 6
Tajito **20** D 5
Tájo **44** B 4
Tajrish **49** F 2
Tajumulco, Volcán **25** F 4
Tak **73** G 4
Takãb **49** E 1
Takamatsu **71** KL 4
Takatshwane **62** C 4
Takeo **74** B 1
Takestan **49** E 1
Takhta-Bazar **67** G 3
Takht-e Soleiman **49** F 1
Takijuq Lake **16** D 3
Takla Lake **13** M 4
Takla Landing **14** D 3
Takla Makan **67** L 3
Taklaun, Gora **69** Q 3
Taklimakan Shamo **67** LM 3
Takua Pa **74** A 2
Tala **24** D 3
Talak **59** EF 2
Talakan **69** O 6
Talandzha **69** O 6
Talara **32** B 4
Talaud, Kepulauan **75** G 3
Talavera de la Reina **44** C 3–4
Talawdi **56** E 6
Talaya (U.S.S.R.) **68** G 4
Talaya (U.S.S.R.) **69** S 3
Talca **37** B 6
Talcahuano **37** B 6
Taldy-Kurgan **51** PQ 6
Talence **44** C 3
Tålesh **66** D 3
Taliabu, Pulau **75** FG 4
Talimardzhan **67** H 3
Taliqan **67** HJ 3
Taliwang **74** E 5
Talkalakh **48** B 2
Talkeetna **12** G 3
Talkeetna Mountains **12** H 3
Tall Afar **48** D 1
Tallahassee **22** D 4
Tallapoosa River **22** C 4
Tall aş Şuwār **48** C 2

Tallinn **43** J 4
Tall Kayf **48** D 1
Tall Küshik **48** C 1
Tallulah **21** H 5
Talo **61** F 2
Taltal **36** B 4
Taltson **14** G 2
Taltson **15** H 2
Tama, Mount **62** A 2
Tamale **58** D 4
Tamanrasset **55** G 4
Tamaulipas **25** E 3
Tamazunchale **25** E 3
Tambacounda **58** B 3
Tambalan **74** E 3
Tambisan **75** E 2
Tambo **79** H 3
Tambov **50** H 5
Tamch **68** F 6
Tamchaket **54** C 5
Tame **32** D 2
Tamel Aike **37** BC 8
Tamgak, Monts **59** F 2
Tamil Nadu **72** C 5
Tampa **27** E 3
Tampa Bay **27** E 3
Tampere **42** H 3
Tampico **25** E 3
Tamu **73** F 3
Tamuin **25** E 3
Tamworth **79** J 5
Tana (Kenya) **61** F 5
Tana (Norway) **42** J 1
Tana (Vanuatu) **82** C 4
Tana, Lake **61** F 2
Tanacross **13** J 3
Tanaga **12** B 6
Tanam, Cape **15** L 3
Tanami **78** DE 2
Tanami Desert **78** E 2
Tanami Desert Wildlife
   Sanctuary **78** E 3
Tanana **12** G 2
Tanana River **12** H 3
Tanch'ŏn **71** JK 2
Tandaho **61** G 2
Tandil **37** E 6
Tane-ga-shima **71** K 4
Tanga **61** F 5–6
Tanganyika, Lake **60** DE 6
Tang-e Karam **49** F 3
Tanger **54** D 1
Tanggula Shan **70** AB 4
Tanggula Shankou **70** B 4
Tanghe **70** F 4
Tangmai **70** C 4
Tangshan **71** G 3
Tangyuan **71** J 1
Tanimbar, Kepulauan **75** H 5
Tanjung, Jabung **74** C 4
Tanjung, Api **74** C 3
Tanjungbalai **74** AB 3
Tanjung Samak **74** C 4
Tanjung Selatan **74** D 4

Tanjungselor **74** E 3
Tanjung Vals **75** J 5
Tannu Ola **68** F 5
Tanțā **56** E 2
Tan Tan **54** C 3
Tantoyuca **25** E 3
Tanzania **60** EF 6
Tao'an **71** H 1–2
Taolanaro **63** H 5
Taoudenni **58** D 1
Taoyuan **71** H 5
Tapachula **25** F 5
Tapajós **33** GH 4
Tappahannock **22** E 3
Tapurucuara **32** E 4
Taquari (Brazil) **34** E 4
Taquari (Brazil) **35** F 4
Tara (U.S.S.R.) **51** OP 4
Tarãbulus (Lebanon) **48** B 2
Tarãbulus (Libya) **55** HJ 2
Taracua **32** E 3
Tarahumara, Sierra **24** C 2
Tarakan **74** E 3
Tarakki **67** H 4
Taranto **45** G 3
Taranto, Golfo di **45** G 3–4
Tarapoto **32** C 5
Tarasovo **50** J 2
Tarata **34** C 4
Tarauacá **32** D 5
Tarawa **82** C 2
Tarbes **44** D 3
Taree **79** J 5
Tareya **68** F 1
Tarif **49** F 4
Tarija **34** D 5
Tarim Liuchang **70** A 2
Tarin Kowt **67** GH 4
Tarko-Zale **51** PQ 3
Tarkwa **58** D 4
Tarlac **75** J 1
Tarma **34** A 3
Tarn **44** D 3
Tarnobrzeg **41** H 4
Tarnów **41** H 4
Taroudant **54** D 2
Tarpon Springs **27** E 3
Tarragona **44** D 3
Tarrasa **44** D 3
Tarsūs Müsä **55** J 4
Tarsus **48** B 1
Tart **70** B 3
Tartagal **34** D 5
Tartu **43** J 4
Tartus **48** B 2
Tarutung **74** A 3
Tasajera, Sierra de la **24** C 2
Tashakta **51** R 6
Tashauz **66** F 2
Tashk, Daryächeh-ye **49** FG 3
Tashkent **67** H 2
Tashtagol **51** R 5
Tasman Bay **81** Q 9
Tasmania **80** KL 9

Tas – Tic

Tasman Sea **80** NO 8
Tasman Sea **82** B 5
Tassialouc, Lac **18** F 2
Tassili N-Ajjer **55** G 3
Tas-Tumus **69** O 1
Tasüj **47** G 3
Tatabánya **46** A 1
Tatakoto **83** F 4
Tatarbunary **46** C 1
Tatarsk **51** P 4
Tatarskiy Proliv **69** Q 6
Tathlina Lake **14** F 2
Tatry **41** H 5
Taubaté **35** GH 5
Taumaturgo **32** D 5
Taunggon **73** G 3
Taungup **73** F 4
Taunton **40** C 4
Tauranga **81** R 8
Taurus Mountains (Turkey)
  48 A 1
Taurus Mountains → Toros
  Dağlari **47** DE 3
Tavatuma **69** T 3
Tavda **51** N 4
Taverner Bay **17** M 3
Tavolara **45** E 3
Tavoy **73** G 5
Tawas City **22** D 2
Tawau **74** E 3
Tawitawi Group **75** F 2
Ţawūq **48** D 2
Tawzar **55** G 2
Taxco de Alarcón **25** E 4
Taxkorgan **67** K 3
Tayga **51** QR 4
Taylor **12** DE 2
Taylorville **22** C 3
Taymä' **48** C 4
Taymyr **68** F 2
Taymyr, Ozero **68** H 1
Tayshet **68** G 4
Taytay **75** E 1
Taz **51** P 2
Taza **54** E 2
Tāzah Khurmātū **48** D 2
Tazovskoye **51** P 2
Tazumal **25** FG 5
Tbilisi **47** FG 2
Tcholliré **59** G 4
Teapa **25** F 4
Teba **75** J 4
Tébessa **55** G 1
Tebingtinggi **74** A 3
Tebulos Mta **47** G 2
Tecalitlán **24** D 4
Tecate **20** C 5
Tecer Dağlari **47** E 3
Tecka **37** B 7
Tecomán **24** D 4
Tecuala **24** C 3
Tecuci **46** C 1
Tedzhen **66** FG 3
Teeside **40** C 4

Tefé **33** F 4
Tegal **74** C 5
Tegre **61** FG 2
Tegucigalpa **28** B 4
Tegyul'te-Tërde **69** O 3
Teheran → Tehrän **66** DE 3
Tehuacán **25** E 4
Tehuantepec **25** E 4
Teiga Plateau **56** D 5
Tejo **44** B 4
Tekeli **67** K 2
Tekes **67** L 2
Tekirdağ **46** C 2
Telanaipura **74** B 4
Tel Aviv-Yafo **48** B 2–3
Telegraph Creek **13** L 4
Telemaco Borba **35** FG 5
Telemark **43** E 4
Telén **37** C 6
Telescope Peak **20** C 4
Teles Pires **33** G 5
Teli **68** F 5
Tell al 'Amärna **56** E 3
Teller **12** D 2
Tello **36** C 5
Telok Anson **74** B 3
Teloloapan **25** E 4
Tel'pos-Iz, Gora **51** L 3
Telukbatang **74** CD 4
Teluk Berau **75** H 4
Teluk Bone **75** F 4
Teluk Cendrawasih **75** HJ 4
Teluk Kumai **74** D 4
Teluk Tomini **75** F 4
Témacine **55** G 2
Tematangi **83** F 4
Tembenchi **68** G 3
Temblador **29** G 5
Tembo **60** B 6
Tembo, Mont **59** G 5
Temirtau **51** O 5
Temiscaming **18** E 4
Temoe **83** G 4
Tempa **84**
Tempe **20** D 5
Temple **25** G 5
Temuco **37** B 6
Tena **32** C 4
Tenali **72** D 4
Tenasserim **73** G 4–5
Tenere **59** FG 1–2
Ténéré, Erg de **59** G 2
Tenerife **54** B 3
Ténès **55** F 1
Tengchong **70** C 5
Tenggara, Kepulauan **75** G 5
Tengiz, Ozero **51** N 5
Teniente Marsh **85**
Teniente Matienzo **85**
Tenke (U.S.S.R.) **68** L 3
Tennant Creek **78** EF 2
Tennessee **22** C 3
Tennessee River **22** C 3
Tenojoki **42** J 2

Tenosique de Pino Suárez
  25 F 4
Teocaltiche **24** D 3
Teófilo Otoni **35** H 4
Teotihuacan **25** E 4
Tepache **24** C 2
Tepatitlán **24** D 3
Tepic **24** D 3
Tepoca, Bahia de **20** D 5
Tequila **24** D 3
Teraina **83** E 2
Teramo **45** F 3
Tercan **47** F 3
Terceira **54** A 1
Terek **47** G 2
Teresina **35** H 2
Teressa **73** F 6
Terhazza **54** D 4
Termez **67** H 3
Terni **45** F 3
Ternopol' **50** E 6
Terpugovo **51** N 4
Terrace **13** M 5
Terracina **45** F 3
Terracy Bay **18** C 4
Terrebonne Bay **25** F 2
Terre Haute **22** C 3
Teshekpuk Lake **12** G 1
Teslin **13** L 3
Teslin **13** L 3
Teslin Lake **13** L 3–4
Tesocoma **24** C 2
Tessalit **58** E 1
Tessenei **61** F 2
Testa, Capo **45** E 3
Tete **63** E 3
Teton Peak **20** D 2
Tétouan **54** D 1
Tetovo **46** B 2
Tevere **45** F 3
Teverya **48** B 2
Tëwo **70** D 4
Texarkana **21** H 5
Texas (U.S.A.) **24** FG 5
Texas City **25** F 2
Teya **68** F 3
Teykovo **50** GH 4
Teyuareh **67** G 4
Teziutlán **25** E 4
Tezpur **73** F 2
Tha-anne **15** K 2
Thailand **73** H 4
Thailand, Gulf of **73** H 5
Thakhek **73** HJ 4
Thames **40** C 4
Thana **72** B 4
Thangoo **78** C 2
Thanh Hoa **73** HJ 4
Thanjavur **72** CD 5
Thap Sakae **73** GH 5
Thar Desert **72** B 2
Thargomindah **79** G 4
Tharthär, Wädī ath **48** D 2
Thásos **46** BC 2

Thaton **73** G 4
The Alps **45** EF 2
The Bahamas **27** FG 3
Thebes **48** A 4
The Dalles **20** B 2
Thedford **21** F 3
The Everglades **27** E 3
The Gambia **58** A 3
The Granites **78** DE 3
The Gulf **49** EF 3–4
The Gulf **57** J 3
The Hague **40** D 4
Thehran **49** F 2
The Johnston Lakes **78** BC 5
Thelon **15** K 2
The Pas **15** J 4
Thermaïkos Kólpos **46** B 2–3
Thermopolis **20** E 3
Thesiger Bay **16** AB 2
Thessalía **46** B 2
Thessaloníki **46** B 2
Thetford Mines **19** F 4
The Valley **29** G 3
The Wash **40** D 4
Thief River Falls **21** G 2
Thiès **58** A 3
Thimphu **72** E 2
Thio (Ethiopia) **61** G 2
Thio (New Caledonia) **81** J 6
Thíra **46** C 3
Thlewiaza **15** K 2
Thomasville (AL, U.S.A.)
  22 C 4
Thomasville (GA, U.S.A.)
  22 D 4
Thompson **15** K 3
Thompson Falls **20** C 2
Thon Buri **73** GH 5
Thonon **45** E 2
Thraki **46** BC 2
Thrakion Pélagos **46** BC 2
Three Forks **20** D 2
Three Kings Islands **81** PQ 7
Three Pagodas Pass **73** G 4
Thule **84**
Thunder Bay (Canada) **18** C 4
Thunder Bay (MI, U.S.A.)
  22 D 2
Thung Song **73** GH 6
Thurston Island **85**
Thy **43** E 4
Tiandong **70** E 6
Tiangua **35** H 1
Tianjin **71** G 3
Tianjun **70** CD 3
Tianmen **70** F 4
Tiantai **71** H 5
Tiaret **55** F 1
Tiber **45** F 3
Tibesti **59** H 1
Tibet **72** E 1
Tiburon, Isla **24** B 2
Tichla **54** B 4
Ticul **26** D 4

Tidjkdja **54** C 5
Tidra, Ile **54** B 5
Tieli **71** J 1
Tielongtan **67** K 4
Tientsin **71** G 3
Tierra Blanca **25** E 4
Tierra Colorada **25** E 4
Tierra de Campos **44** BC 3
Tierra del Fuego, Isla
  Grande de **37** C 9
Tierra del Pan **44** B 3
Tifton **22** D 4
Tigalda **12** E 5
Tigil **69** T 4
Tigris **48** D 2
Tiguent **54** B 5
Tihâmat **57** G 5
Tijuana **20** C 5
Tikal **28** B 3
Tikchik Lakes **12** F 3
Tikhoretsk **47** F 1
Tikhvin **50** FG 4
Tilburg **40** DE 4
Tilichiki **69** V 3
Tillabéri **58** E 3
Tillamook **20** B 2
Timagami, Lake **18** D 4
Timanskiy Kryazh **50** J 2–K 3
Timaru **81** Q 9
Timashevskaya **47** EF 1
Timbauba **35** J 2
Timétrine **58** D 2
Timétrine, Monts **58** D 2
Timia **59** F 2
Timir-Atakh-Tas **69** S 2
Timiskaming, Lake **18** E 4
Timişoara **46** B 1
Timkapaul' **51** M 3
Timmins **18** D 4
Timmoudi **54** E 3
Timor **75** G 5
Timor, Laut **75** G 6
Timor Sea **75** GH 5
Timote **37** D 6
Tinaca Point **75** G 2
Tinaco **29** F 5
Tin City **12** D 2
Tindouf **54** D 3
Tinfouchy **54** DE 3
Tingri **72** E 2
Tinian **82** A 2
Tini Wells **56** C 6
Tinogasta **36** C 4
Tínos **46** C 3
Tinsukia **73** G 2
Ti-n Zaouâtene **55** F 4
Tipton, Mount **20** D 4
Tiquisate **25** F 5
Tirán **48** B 4
Tirana **46** AB 2
Tiraspol' **46** CD 1
Tire **46** C 3
Tîrgovişte **46** C 1–2
Tîrgu Jiu **46** B 1

Tîrgu Mureş **46** BC 1
Tîrnăveni **46** B 1
Tirol **45** F 2
Tirso **45** E 3
Tiruchchirappalli **72** CD 5
Tirunelveli **72** C 6
Tirupati **72** CD 5
Tiruvannamalai **72** C 5
Tisdale **15** J 4
Tisza **46** B 1
Tiszántúl **46** B 1
Titicaca, Lago **34** C 4
Titograd **46** A 2
Titovo Užice **46** AB 2
Titov Veles **46** B 2
Titusville **27** E 3
Tiveden **43** F 4
Tizatlan **25** E 4
Tizimín **26** D 4
Tiznit **54** CD 3
Tjåhumas **42** G 2
Tkhach **47** F 2
Tkvarcheli **47** F 2
Tlalnepantla **25** E 4
Tlapa de Comonfort **25** E 4
Tlaxcala **25** E 4
Tlemcen **54** E 2
Toamasina **63** HJ 3
Tobago, Isla **33** F 1
Toba & Kakar Ranges **67** H 4
Tobermorey **79** F 3
Tobermory **18** D 4
Tobol **51** N 4
Tobol **51** M 5
Tobol'sk **51** NO 4
Tobseda **50** K 2
Tocantinia **33** J 5
Tocantins **33** J 4
Tocapilla **34** B 5
Tocorpuri, Cerro de **34** C 5
Todos Santos **24** B 3
Tofino **14** D 5
Togiak **12** E 4
Togian, Kepulauan **75** F 4
Togni **56** F 5
Togo **58** E 4
Togtoh **70** F 2
Togyz **67** G 1
Tohma **47** E 3
Toijala **42** H 3
Tok (AK, U.S.A.) **13** J 3
Tokara-rettō **71** J 4–5
Tokat **47** E 2
Tokelau Islands **82** D 3
Tokko **68** L 4
Tokmak (U.S.S.R.) **47** E 1
Tokmak (U.S.S.R.) **67** K 2
Toksun **67** M 2
Toktogul **67** J 2
Toku-no-shima **71** J 5
Tokur **69** O 5
Tokushima **71** KL 4
Tōkyō **71** L 3
Tolbukhin **46** C 2

Toledo **44** C 4
Toledo(OH, U.S.A.) **22** D 2
Toledo, Montes de **44** C 4
Toledo Bend Reservoir
  25 H 5
Tolga **42** F 3
Toli **67** L 1
Toliara **63** G 4
Tolima **32** CD 3
Toltén **37** B 6
Toluca **25** E 4
Tol'yatti **50** J 5
Tomakomai **71** M 2
Toman **21** H 3
Tomaszów Mazowiecki
  41 H 4
Tomatlán **24** C 4
Tombador, Serra do **34** E 3
Tombigbee River **22** C 4
Tombouctou **58** D 2
Tomé **37** B 6
Tomelloso **44** C 4
Tomini, Teluk **75** F 4
Tomkinson Ranges **78** D 4
Tomma **42** F 2
Tommot **69** N 4
Tompa **68** JK 4
Tomsk **51** R 4
Tom White, Mount **13** J 3
Tonantins **32** E 4
Tonasket **20** BC 2
Tondano **75** G 3
Tonekābon **49** F 1
Tonga **82** D 4
Tonga (Sudan) **60** E 3
Tonga Islands **82** D 4
Tongariro National Park
  81 QR 8
Tongatapu Group **82** D 4
Tongchuan **70** E 3
Tonghai **70** D 6
Tonghe **71** J 1
Tonghua **71** J 2
Tongliao **71** H 2
Tongoy **36** B 5
Tongren (Guizhou, China)
  70 E 5
Tongren (Qinghai, China)
  70 D 3
Tongtian He **70** C 4
Tongue of the Ocean **27** F 4
Tongyu **71** H 2
Tonichí **24** C 2
Tonj **60** D 3
Tonk **72** C 2
Tonle Sap **73** H 5
Tonopah **20** C 4
Tonstad **43** E 4
Tooele **20** D 3
Toompine **79** G 4
Toowoomba **79** J 4
Topeka **21** G 4
Topolinyy **69** P 3
Topolobampo **24** C 2

Topolobampo, Bahia de
  24 C 2
Topozero, Ozero **42** K 2
Toppenish **20** B 2
Toraya **34** B 3
Torbat-e Heydarīyeh
  66 FG 2–3
Torbay **40** C 4
Torbino **50** F 4
Torey **68** H J 5
Tori **60** E 3
Torino **45** E 2
Torneälven **42** H 2
Torneträsk **42** GH 2
Torngat Mountains **19** H 2
Tornio **42** H 2
Toro, Cerro del **36** C 4
Torom **69** P 5
Toronto **22** E 2
Toropets **50** F 4
Tororo **60** E 4
Toros Dağlari **47** D 3
Torquato Severo **36** F 5
Torrelavega **44** C 3
Torrens, Lake **79** F 5
Torrens Creek **79** H 3
Torrente **44** C 4
Torreón **24** D 2
Torres Strait **79** G 1
Torrington **21** F 3
Tortkuduk **51** O 5
Tortola **29** G 3
Tortosa **44** D 3
Tortue, Ile de la **29** E 2
Tortuguero **28** C 4
Torud **49** G 2
Toruń **41** G 4
Toscana **45** F 3
Tosontsengel **68** G 6
Tostuya **68** K 1
Totma **50** H 4
Totness **33** G 2
Totonicapan **25** F 4–5
Totoras **36** D 5
Totten Glacier **85**
Tottori **71** K 3
Touggourt **55** G 2
Toulon **45** E 3
Toulouse **44** D 3
Toungoo **73** G 4
Touraine **44** D 2
Tourcoing **44** D 1
Tourine **54** C 4
Tours **44** D 2
Towakaima **33** G 2
Towanda **22** E 2
Townsend **20** D 2
Townsville **79** H 2
Towson **22** E 3
Toyama **71** L 3
Toygunen **12** C 2
Toyohashi **71** L 4
Toyota **71** L 3
Trabzon **47** E 2

Trafalgar, Cabo **44** B 4
Trāghan **55** HJ 3
Trail **14** F 5
Trang **73** G 6
Trangan, Pulau **75** H 5
Transantarctic Mountains **85**
Transilvania **46** B 1
Transkei **62** D 6
Transtrandsfjällen **42** F 3
Transvaal **62** D 5
Trapani **45** F 4
Traun **45** F 2
Traverse City **22** C 2
Travesia **28** B 3
Treinta y Tres **36** EF 5
Trelew **37** CD 7
Trelleborg **43** F 4
Tremonton **20** D 3
Trenčin **41** G 5
Trenel **37** D 6
Trenque Lauquen **37** D 6
Trento **45** F 2
Trenton (MO, U.S.A.) **21** H 3
Trenton (N.J., U.S.A.) **23** F 2
Trepassey **19** K 4
Tres Arroyos **37** D 6
Tres Cerros **37** C 8
Tres Esquinas **32** CD 3
Três Lagoas **35** F 5
Tres Picos **25** F 4
Tres Puentes **36** BC 4
Tres Zapotes **25** EF 4
Treviso **45** F 2
Triabunna **80** L 9
Trialetskiy Khrebet **47** F 2
Trichur **72** C 5
Trier **40** E 5
Trieste **45** F 2
Trikala **46** B 3
Trincomalee **72** D 6
Trindade Island **31** G 5
Trinidad (Bolivia) **34** D 3
Trinidad (CA, U.S.A.) **20** B 3
Trinidad (CO, U.S.A.) **21** F 4
Trinidad (Colombia) **32** D 2
Trinidad (Cuba) **27** F 4
Trinidad (Uruguay) **36** E 5
Trinidad, Isla **33** F 1
Trinidad and Tobago **33** FG 1
Trinity Bay **19** K 4
Trinity Islands **12** G 4
Trinity River **25** G 5
Trinkitat **56** F 5
Tripoli **48** B 2
Tripoli (Libya) **55** H 2
Tripolitania **55** HJ 2
Tripura **73** F 3
Trivandrum **72** C 6
Trnava **41** G 5
Trobriand or Kiriwina Islands **81** F 3
Trois-Pistoles **19** G 4
Trois Rivières **18** F 4
Troitsk (U.S.S.R.) **51** M 5

Troitsk (U.S.S.R.) **68** F 4
Troitsko-Pechorsk **50** KL 3
Trollhättan **43** F 4
Trollhetta **42** E 3
Tromelin **53** H 6
Troms **42** G 2
Tromsö **42** G 2
Trona **20** C 4
Trondheim **42** F 3
Troodos **47** D 4
Trout Lake (N.W.T., Can.) **13** N 3
Trout Lake (Ontario, Can.) **15** L 4
Trout Peak **20** E 3
Trout River **19** J 4
Troy (AL, U.S.A.) **22** C 4
Troy (Turkey) **46** C 3
Troyan **46** BC 2
Troyez **44** D 2
Troy Peak **20** C 4
TrucialCoast **57** KJ 3–4
Trucial Coast (United Arab Emirates) **49** FG 4
Trujillo (Honduras) **28** B 3
Trujillo (Peru) **32** C 5
Trujillo (Venezuela) **32** D 2
Truk Islands **82** B 2
Trumbull, Mount **20** D 4
Truro **19** H 4
Trust Territory of the Pacific Islands **82** AB 2
Truth or Consequences (Hot Springs) **20** E 5
Truva **46** C 3
Trysilfjellet **42** F 3
Tsavo National Park **61** F 5
Tselinograd **51** NO 5
Tsenhermandal **68** JK 6
Tsenogora **50** J 3
Tsentralno Tungusskoye Plato **68** H 3–4
Tsetseg **68** F 6
Tsetserleg **68** G 6
Tshane **62** C 4
Tshesebe **62** D 4
Tshikapa **60** C 6
Tsiafajavona **63** H 3
Tsimlyanskoye Vodokhranilishche **47** F 1
Tsingtao **71** H 3
Tsipanda **69** OP 4
Tsjokkarassa **42** HJ 2
Tskhinvali **47** F 2
Tsodilo Hills **62** C 3
Tsuchiura **71** M 3
Tsumeb **62** B 3
Tsumkwe **62** C 3
Tsuruoka **71** L 3
Tuamotu Archipelago **83** FG 4
Tuan **73** H 3
Tuapse **47** E 2
Tuba **68** H 4

Tuba City **20** D 4
Tubal, Wādī aţ **48** C 2
Tubarão **36** G 4
Tubayq, Jabal at **48** B 3
Tubruq **55** K 2
Tubuaï **83** F 4
Tubuai Islands **83** EF 4
Tucacas **29** F 4
Tucano **35** J 3
Tucson **20** D 5
Tucumcari **21** F 4
Tucupita **29** G 5
Tucuruí **33** HJ 4
Tufi **82** A 3
Tuguegarao **75** J 1
Tugur **69** P 5
Tukangbesi, Kepulauan **75** F 5
Tuktoyaktuk **13** L 2
Tukzar **67** H 3
Tula (Mexico) **25** E 3
Tula (Mexico) **25** E 4
Tula (U.S.S.R.) **50** G 5
Tulancingo **25** E 4
Tulare **20** C 4
Tulbagh **62** B 6
Tulcán **32** C 3
Tulcea **46** C 1
Tulchin **46** C 1
Tulemalu Lake **15** JK 2
Tullahoma **22** C 3
Tuloma **42** K 2
Tulsa **21** G 4
Tuluá **32** C 3
Tuluksak **12** E 3
Tulum **26** D 4
Tulun **68** H 5
Tumaco **32** C 3
Tumany **69** T 3
Tumat **69** PQ 1
Tumbes **32** B 4
Tumd Youqi **70** F 2
Tumeremo **33** F 2
Tümü **55** H 4
Tunas **35** G 5
Tunas, Sierra de las **24** C 2
Tunduru **63** F 2
Tunga **59** F 4
Tungsten **13** M 3
Tunguska, Nizhnyaya **68** F 2
Tungus-Khaya **69** N 3
Tūnis **55** G 1
Tunisia **55** GH 1
Tunja **32** D 2
Tununak **12** D 3
Tunungayualok **19** H 2
Tunxi **71** G 5
Tuöroyri **40** A 1
Tuostakh **69** P 2
Tuotuo Heyan **70** B 4
Tupā **35** F 5
Tupelo **22** C 4
Tupiza **34** C 5

Tuquan **71** H 1
Tura (U.S.S.R.) **68** H 3
Turakh **68** MN 1
Turana, Khrebet **69** O 5
Turanskaya **66** F 2
Turanskaya Nizmennost **66–67** FG 2
Turbaco **28** D 4
Turbo **32** C 2
Türeh **49** E 2
Tureia **83** F 4
Turen **29** F 5
Turgay **67** G 1
Turgayskaya Dolina **51** M 5–6
Turgayskaya Stolovaya Strana **51** M 5
Türgen Uul **68** F 6
Türgovishte **46** C 2
Turgutlu **46** C 3
Turhal **47** E 2
Turin **45** E 2–3
Turkana, Lake **61** F 4
Turkestan **67** H 2
Turkey **47** DE 3
Turkey **48** AB 1
Türkiiye **47** DE 3
Turkmeniya **66** F 3
Turks and Caicos Islands **29** EF 2
Turks Island Passage **29** E 2
Turks Islands **29** E 2
Turku **43** H 3
Turneffe Islands **28** B 3
Turnu Măgurele **46** BC 2
Turpan **70** A 2
Tursha **50** J 4
Turukhansk **51** RS 2
Turukta **68** L 3
Tuscaloosa **22** C 4
Tuticorin **72** C 6
Tutonchany **68** FG 3
Tuttle Creek Lake **21** G 4
Tutubu **60** E 6
Tutuila **82** D 3
Tuvalu **82** D 3
Tuwayq, Jabal **49** D 4
Tuxpán **24** C 3
Tuxpan de Rodríguez Cano **25** E 3
Tuxtla Gutiérrez **25** F 4
Tuz Gölü **47** D 3
Tüz Khurmātū **49** D 2
Tuzla **45** G 3
Twin Falls (ID, U.S.A.) **20** D 3
Twin Falls (Newfoundl., Can.) **19** H 3
Twin Islands **18** D 3
Twisp **20** C 2
Two Harbors **21** H 2
Tyan'-Shan' **67** JK 2
Tychy **41** G 4
Tygda **69** N 5
Tyler **21** G 5
Tynda **69** M 4

Tyrma 69 O 5
Tyrrell Lake 15 H 2
Tyrrhenian Sea 45 F 3–4
Tyubelyakh 69 Q 2
Tyukalinsk 51 O 4
Tyumen' 51 MN 4
Tyungulyu 69 O 3
Tzaneen 62 DE 4

U

Uad el Jat 54 C 3
Ua Huka 83 F 3
Uatumá 33 G 4
Uauá 35 J 2
Uaupés 32 E 4
Uaxactún 25 F 4
Ubá 35 H 5
Ubangi 60 B 4
'Ubayyid, Wādī al 48 CD 2
Ubeda 44 C 4
Uberaba 35 G 4
Uberlândia 35 G 4
Ubolratna Dam 73 H 4
Ubombo 63 E 5
Ubort' 43 J 5
Ucayali 32 D 5
Uch-Aral 51 Q 6
Uch Kuduk 67 GH 2
Udachnaya 68 K 2
Udaipur 72 B 3
Udanna 69 Q 2
Uddevalla 43 F 4
Uddjaure 42 G 2
Udgir 72 C 4
Udine 45 F 2
Udipi 72 B 5
Udon Thani 73 H 4
Udskoye 69 O 5
Udzha 68 L 1
Uele 60 C 4
Uelen 12 CD 2
Uel'kal' 12 AB 2
Uelzen 41 F 4
Ufa 50 L 4–5
Ugalla 60 E 6
Ugalla River Game Reserve 60 E 6
Uganda 60 E 4
Ugashik 12 F 4
Uglegorsk 69 Q 6
Ugoyan 69 N 4
Ugulan 69 T 3
Ugumun 68 L 2
Ugun 69 N 4
Uherské Hradiště 41 G 5
Uil 66 E 1
Uinta Mountains 20 DE 3
Uis Mine 62 AB 4
Uitenhage 62 DE 6
Ujae 82 C 2
Ujarrás 28 C 5
Ujelang 82 B 2
Ujiji 60 D 6

Ujjain 72 C 3
Ujung 75 E 5
Ujung Pandang 75 E 4–5
Uka 69 U 4
Ukelayat 69 WX 3
Ukhta 50 K 3
Ukiah (CA, U.S.A.) 20 B 4
Ukiah (OR, U.S.A.) 20 C 2
Ukmergė 43 HJ 4
Ukraina (U.S.S.R.) 46–47 D 1
Ukrainka 42 K 5–6
Uktym 50 J 3
Ukwaa 60 E 3
Ulaanbaatar 68 J 6
Ulaga 69 O 2
Ulan Bator 68 J 6
Ulan-Ude 68 J 5
Ularunda 79 H 4
Ulety 68 K 5
Ulhasnagar 72 B 4
Uliastay 68 G 6
Uliga 82 C 2
Ullapool 40 B 3
Ulovo 69 S 1
Ulsan 71 JK 3
Ulster 40 B 4
Ulu 56 E 6
Uludağ 46 C 3
Ulutau, Gory 67 H 1
Ul'yanovsk 50 J 5
Uma 68 M 5
Uman' 46 D 1
Umanak 84
Umari 75 J 4
Umba 42 K 2
Umboi 80 E 3
Umbria 45 F 3
Umeå 42 H 3
Umiat 12 G 2
Umm al Qaywayn 49 G 4
Umm Durmān 56 E 5
Umm Lajj 48 B 4
Umm Ruwābah 56 E 6
Umm Urūmah 48 B 4
Umnak 12 D 5
Umtata 62 D 6
Umuarama 35 F 5
Umvuma 63 E 4
Unadilla 22 D 4
Unaí 35 G 4
Unalakleet 12 E 3
Unalaska 12 D 5
Unayzah (Jordan) 48 B 3
'Unayzah (Saudi Arabia) 48 D 4
Unga 12 E 4
Ungava, Peninsule d' 18 EF 2
Ungava Bay 19 G 2
União do Vitória 36 F 4
Unimak 12 E 5
Unimak Pass 12 E 5
Union City 22 C 3
United Arab Emirates 49 FG 5
United Kingdom 40 DC 3

United States 20–21
Unity 14 H 4
Universales, Montes 44 C 3
University City 21 H 4
Unst 40 C 2
Uoyan 68 K 4
Upata 33 F 2
Upemba, Lac 60 D 6
Upemba National Park 60 D 6
Upernavik 84
Upington 62 C 5
Upolu 82 D 3
Upper Arlington 22 D 2
Upper Klamath Lake 20 B 3
Upper Red Lake 21 H 2
Uppland 43 G 3
Uppsala 43 G 4
Uracoa 29 G 5
Urak 69 Q 4
Ural 50 K 5
Ural 66 E 1
Ural Mountains 51 LM 2–4
Ural'sk 50 K 5
Urandangie 79 F 3
Urandi 35 H 3
Uranium City 15 H 3
Uraricoera 33 F 3
Urayq, Natud al 48 D 4
Urbandale 21 H 3
Urbano Santos 35 H 1
Uren 50 J 4
Urewera National Park 81 R 8
Urfa (Turkey) 47 E 3
Urfa Platosu 47 E 3
Urgench 66 FG 2
Uribia 32 D 1
Uromi 59 F 4
Ur Suq ash Shuyūkh 49 DE 3
Ursus 41 H 4
Uruaçu 35 G 3
Uruapan 24 D 4
Urucará 33 G 4
Uruçuí 35 H 2
Uruguaiana 36 E 4–5
Uruguay 36 EF 5
Urumchi 67 M 2
Ürümqi 67 M 2
Uruqnay 36 E 5
Uryupinsk 50 H 5
Uşak 46 C 3
Usevoloizsk 42 K 3
'Ushayrah 49 DE 4
Ushuaia 37 C 9
Üsküdar 46 C 2
Ussuriysk 71 K 2
Ust'-Bol'sheretsk 69 ST 5
Ust'-Chayka 68 J 3
Ust'-Ilimsk 68 H 4
Ust-Kada 68 H 5
Ust'-Kamchatsk 69 U 4
Ust'-Kamenogorsk 51 QR 5–6
Ust'-Karenga 68 L 5
Ust'-Karsk 68 L 5
Ust'-Khayryuzovo 69 ST 4

Ust'-Kulom 50 K 3
Ust'-Kut 68 J 4
Ust-Labinsk 47 EF 1
Ust'-Nera 69 Q 3
Ust'-Olenёk 68 LM 1
Ust'-Ozernoye 51 RS 4
Ust'-Pit 68 F 4
Ust'-Port 51 Q 2
Ust'-Sugoy 69 S 3
Ust'-Tatta 69 O 3
Ust'-Tym 51 Q 4
Ust'-Ura 50 H 3
Ust'-Urgal 69 O 5
Ust'-Us 68 F 5
Ust'-Usa 50 L 2
Ust'-Uyskoye 51 M 5
Ustuyurt, Plato 66 F 2
Ust'-Vyyskaya 50 J 3
Ust'Yuribey 51 NO 2
Usu 67 L 2
Usulután 28 B 4
Usumacinta, Rio 25 F 4
Utah 20 D 4
Utah Lake 20 D 3
Utatá 68 H J 5
Utёs 51 P 5
Utesiki 69 W 2
Utiariti 34 E 3
Utica 23 F 2
Utirik 82 C 2
Utrecht 40 DE E 4
Utrera 44 B 4
Uttyakh 69 O 2
Utukok 12 E 2
Uuldza 68 K 6
Uusikavpunki 43 GH 3
Uusimaa 43 J 3
Uvalde 25 E 2
Uvarovo 50 H 5
Uvinza 60 DE 6
Uvs Nuur 68 F 5
Uwayrid, Harrat al 48 B 4
Uxituba 33 G 4
Uxmal 26 D 4
Uyaly 67 G 2
Uyandi 69 Q 2
Uyega 69 Q 3
Uyuni 34 C 5
Uyuni, Salar de 34 C 5
Uzbekistan 67 GH 2
Uzbel Shankou 67 J 3
Uzhgorod 46 B 1
Uzhur 51 R 4
Uzunköprü 46 C 2

V

Vaal 62 C 5
Vaasa 42 H 3
Vác 46 A 1
Vacaria 36 FG 4
Vadodara 72 B 3
Vaduz 45 E 2
Vágar 40 A 1

Vaghena 81 G 3
Vairaatea 83 F 4
Vaitupu 82 C 3
Vakarevo 69 W 3
Valachia 46 BC 2
Valcheta 37 C 7
Valday 50 F 4
Val de Loire 44 D 2
Valdepeñas 44 C 4
Valdés, Península 37 D 7
Valdez 12 H 3
Valdivia 37 B 6
Valdivia (Colombia) 28 D 5
Val-d'Or 18 E 4
Valdosta 22 D 4
Valença 35 J 3
Valenca do Piauí 35 H 2
Valence 45 DE 2–3
Valencia (Spain) 44 CD 4
Valencia (Venezuela) 32 E 2
Valentine 21 F 3
Valera 32 D 2
Valga 43 J 4
Valjevo 46 AB 2
Valladolid (Mexico) 26 D 4
Valladolid (Spain) 44 C 3
Vall de Uxó 44 C 4
Valle de la Pascua 32 E 2
Valle de Topia 24 C 2
Valle de Zaragoza 24 C 2
Valledupar 32 D 1
Valle Grande 34 D 4
Valle Hermoso 25 E 2
Vallenar 36 BC 4
Valle Salado 24 D 3
Valletta 45 F 4
Valley City 21 G 2
Valleyfield 18 F 4
Valley Station 22 C 3
Valleyview 14 F 3
Valparaíso 36 B 5
Valparaíso (Mexico) 24 D 3
Vals, Tanjung 75 J 5
Vammala 42 H 3
Van 47 F 3
Vanavara 68 H 3
Van Buren 21 H 4
Vancouver 14 E 5
Vancouver Island 14 D 5
Vanda 85
Vanderbijlpark 62 D 5
Vanderhoof 14 E 4
Van Diemen, Cape 78 D 1
Van Diemen Gulf 78 E 1
Vanduzi 63 E 3
Vänern 43 F 4
Van Gölü 47 F 3
Vangunu 81 G 3
Van Horn 24 F 5
Vanikolo Islands 81 J 4
Vanikoro Island 82 C 3
Vankarem 12 B 2
Vannes 44 C 2
Vanoua Lava 81 J 4

Vanrhynsdorp 62 B 6
Vansittart 16 K 3
Vantaa 43 HJ 3
Vanua Levu 82 C 4
Vanuatu 81 J 5
Vanuatu 82 B 3
Van Wert 22 D 2
Vanzhil'kynak 51 QR 3
Varanasi 72 D 2
Varangerfjorden 42 K 1–2
Varangerhalvöya 42 JK 1
Varaždin 45 G 2
Varberg 43 F 4
Vardofjällen 42 FG 2
Varginha 35 GH 5
Varkaus 42 J 3
Värmland 43 F 4
Varna (Bulgaria) 46 C 2
Värnamo 43 F 4
Varsinais Suomi 43 H 3
Var'yegan 51 P 3
Vashnel 51 N 3
Vasiss 51 O 4
Vassdalsegga 43 E 4
Västerås 43 G 4
Västerbotten 42 G 3
Västergötland 43 F 4
Västervik 43 G 4
Vasto 45 F 3
Västra Granberget 42 H 2
Vasyugan 51 P 4
Vaticano, Citta Del 45 F 3
Vatnajökull 42 B 3
Vatoa 82 D 4
Vättern 43 F 4
Vatyna 69 W 3
Vaughn 21 E 5
Vaupés 32 D 3
Vava'u Group 82 D 4
Växjö 43 FG 4
Vayvida 68 FG 3
Vazhgort 50 J 3
Veadeiros 35 G 3
Vefsna 42 F 2
Vega 42 F 2
Vegreville 14 G 4
Vejle 43 E 4
Velež 45 G 3
Vélez-Málaga 44 C 4
Velikiye Luki 43 K 4
Velikiy Ustyug 50 HJ 3
Veliko Türnovo 46 C 2
Vella Lavella 81 G 3
Vellore 72 CD 5
Velsk 50 H 3
Vel't 50 K 2
Vemor'ye 69 Q 6
Venado Tuerto 36 D 5
Venda 63 E 4
Venetie 12 H 2
Venezia 45 F 2
Venezuela 32–33 EF 2
Venezuela, Golfo de 32 D 1
Vengerovo 51 P 4

Venice 45 F 2
Venta 43 H 4
Ventoux, Mont 45 E 3
Ventspils 43 H 4
Ventura 20 C 5
Venustiano Carranza 25 F 4
Vera 36 DE 4
Veracruz (Mexico) 25 E 4
Veraval 72 AB 3
Verbania 45 E 2
Verdalsöra 42 F 3
Verde 20 D 5
Verdun 45 E 2
Vereeniging 62 D 5
Verkhn'aya Salda 51 M 4
Verkhneimbatskoye 51 RS 3
Verkhneural'sk 51 LM 5
Verkhnevilyuysk 68 LM 3
Verkhneye Kuyto,Ozero
      42 K 3
Verkhnyaya Amga 69 NO 4
Verkhnyaya Vol'dzha 51 PQ 4
Verkhoyansk 69 O 2
Verkhoyanskiy Khrebet
      69 N 2–P 3
Vermilion Bay 15 L 4
Vermont 23 F 2
Vernal 20 E 3
Vernon (Canada) 14 F 4
Vernon (TX, U.S.A.) 21 G 5
Vero Beach 27 EF 3
Verona 45 F 2
Vérroia 46 B 2
Versailles 44 D 2
Vershina 51 M 3
Vershino-Shakhtaminskiye
      68 L 5
Vest-Agder 43 E 4
Vesterålen 42 FG 2
Vestfirðir 42 A 2
Vestfjorden 42 F 2
Vestvågöy 42 F 2
Vesuvio 45 F 3
Vetlanda 43 G 4
Vetrenyy 69 R 3
Viacha 34 C 4
Viborg 43 E 4
Vibo Valentia 45 G 4
Vicecommodoro Marambio
      85
Vicenza 45 F 2
Vichada 32 E 3
Vichy 44 D 2
Vicksburg 21 H 5
Victoria (Australia) 79 G 6
Victoria (Canada) 14 E 5
Victoria (Chile) 37 B 6
Victoria (Hong Kong) 70 F 6
Victoria (Seychelles) 61 JK 5
Victoria (TX, U.S.A.) 25 E 2
Victoria, Lake 60 E 5
Victoria, Mount 82 A 3
Victoria, Mount (Burma)
      73 F 3

Victoria de Durango 24 D 3
Victoria de las Tunas 27 F 4
Victoria Falls 62 D 3
Victoria Island 16 DE 2
Victoria Land 85
Victoria River 78 E 2
Victoria Strait 16 G 3
Victoriaville 18 F 4
Victoria West 62 C 6
Victorville 20 C 5
Vicuña Mackenna 36 D 5
Vidin 46 B 2
Vidisha 72 C 3
Vidsel 42 H 2
Viduša 45 G 3
Vidzemes Augstiene 43 J 4
Viedma 37 D 7
Viedma, Lago 37 B 8
Viejo, Rio 28 B 4
Vieng Pou Kha 73 H 3
Vienna 45 G 2
Vienna (W.V., U.S.A.) 22 D 3
Vienne 45 DE 2
Vientiane 73 H 4
Vientos, Paso de los 29 E 2–3
Vieques, Isla de 29 FG 3
Vierzon 44 D 2
Viesca 24 D 2
Vietnam 73 JK 5
Vieux-Fort 19 J 3
Vifosa 46 B 2
Vigan 75 J 1
Vigevano 45 E 2
Vigo 44 B 3
Viiala 42 H 3
Vijayawada 72 D 4
Viking 14 G 4
Vikna 42 F 3
Vila 81 J 5
Vila Conceição 33 F 3
Vilanculo 63 F 4
Vila Nova de Gaia 44 B 3
Vila Velha (Amapá, Brazil)
      33 H 3
Vila Velha (Espírito Santo,
      Brazil) 35 HJ 5
Vildiz Dağlari 46 C 2
Vilhena 34 D 3
Villa Abecia 34 CD 5
Villa Ahumada 24 E 5
Villa Bella 34 C 3
Villach 45 F 2
Villa Constitución 36 D 5
Villa Coronado 24 D 2
Villa de Cos 24 D 3
Villa de Guadalupe 25 D 3
Villa del Rosario (Venezuela)
      29 E 4
Villa de Reyes 25 D 3
Villa Dolores 36 C 5
Villa Flores 25 F 4
Villa Frontera 25 D 2
Villagarcía de Arosa 44 B 3
Villaguay 36 E 5

Villahermosa 25 F 4
Villa Hidalgo 24 D 2
Villa Huidobro 36 D 5
Villa Ingavi 34 D 5
Villaldama 25 D 2
Villalonga 37 D 6
Villa María 36 D 5
Villa Mazán 36 C 4
Villa Montes 34 D 5
Villanova y Geltrú 44 D 3
Villanueva 24 D 3
Villa Ocampo 24 CD 2
Villareal de las Enfants 44 CD 4
Villa Regina 37 C 6
Villarreal de los Infantes 44 CD 4
Villarrica (Chile) 37 B 6
Villarrica (Paraguay) 36 E 4
Villatoro, Puerto de 44 B 3
Villa Unión 36 C 4
Villa Union (Mexico) 24 C 3
Villavicencio 32 D 3
Villazón 34 C 5
Villefranche 45 DE 2
Villena 44 C 4
Vilnius 43 J 5
Vilyuy 69 MN 3
Vilyuyskoye Plato 68 J 2
Vilyuyskt 68 M 3
Viña del Mar 36 B 5
Vincennes 22 C 3
Vindhya Range 72 BC 3
Vineland 23 F 3
Vinh 73 J 4
Vinh Giat 73 JK 5
Vinh Linh 73 J 4
Vinh Loi 73 J 6
Vinkovci 45 G 2
Vinnitsa 50 E 6
Vinson Massif 85
Virac 75 F 1
Virandozero 50 FG 3
Viranşehir 47 F 3
Virden 15 J 5
Virgem da Lapa 35 H 4
Virginia (MN, U.S.A.) 21 H 2
Virginia (South Africa) 62 D 5
Virginia (U.S.A.) 22 E 3
Virginia Beach 22–23 E 3
Virginia Falls 13 N 3
Virgin Islands 29 G 3
Virrat 42 H 3
Virtsu 43 H 4
Virtul Gutii 46 B 1
Visalia 20 C 4
Visayan Sea 75 F 1
Visby 43 G 4
Viscount Melville Sound 16 D 2
Vishakhapatnam 72 DE 4
Vista Alegre 33 F 3
Vistula 41 G 5
Vitebsk 43 K 4

Vitiaz Strait 80 E 3
Viti Levu 82 C 4
Vitim 68 K 4–5
Vitimskoye Ploskogor'ye 68 K 5
Vitória (Espírito Santo, Brazil) 35 HJ 5
Vitória (Pará, Brazil) 33 H 4
Vitoria (Spain) 44 C 3
Vitória da Conquista 35 H 3
Vittorio Veneto 45 F 2
Vivorata 37 E 6
Vizcaino, Sierra 24 B 2
Vizianagaram 72 D 4
Vladimir 50 H 4
Vladimir 71 L 2
Vladimirovka 50 K 5
Vladimir-Volynskiy 43 H 5
Vladivostok 71 K 2
Vlissingen 40 D 4
Vlorë 46 A 2
Vltava 45 F 2
Vogan 58 E 4
Voghera 45 E 2
Voi 61 F 5
Voinjama 58 C 4
Volcán Ceboruco 24 D 3
Volcán Citlaltépetl 25 E 4
Volcan Irazu 28 C 4
Volcán Las Tres Virgenes 24 B 2
Volcán Llullaillaco 34 C 5
Volcán Miravalles 28 BC 4
Volcán Misti 34 B 4
Volcán Ollagüe 34 C 5
Volcán Paricutín 24 D 4
Volcán Popocatéptl 25 E 4
Volcán San Juan 24 CD 3
Volcán Tajumulco 25 F 4
Volga 50 J 5
Volgo-Balt (I.V. Lenin) Kanal 50 FG 3
Volgodonsk 47 F 1
Volgograd 50 H 6
Volkhau 42 K 4
Volkhov 43 K 4
Volochayevka 69 O 6
Vologda 50 GH 4
Volokon 68 J 4
Volos 46 B 3
Vol'sk 50 J 5
Volta 58 E 4
Volta, Lake 58 DE 4
Volta Redonda 35 GH 5
Volynskoye Polesye 43 J 5
Volzhsk 50 J 4
Volzhskiy 50 J 6
Von Frank Mountain 12 G 3
Vopnafjörður 42 C 2
Vórioi Sporádhes 46 B 3
Vorkuta 51 MN 2
Vormsi 43 H 4
Voronezh 50 GH 5
Voroshilovgrad 47 EF 1

Võrts Järv 43 J 4
Võru 43 J 4
Vosges 45 E 2
Vostochnaya Litsa 50 G 2
Vostochnyy Sayan 68 G 5
Vostok (Antarctica) 85
Vostok (Kiribati) 83 E 3
Votkinsk 50 K 4
Voyampolka 69 T 4
Vozhega 50 H 3
Voznesensk 46 D 1
Vozvyshennost' Karabil' 67 G 3
Vran 45 G 3
Vranje 46 B 2
Vratsa 46 B 2
Vršac 46 B 1
Vryburg 62 C 5
Vryheid 63 E 5
Vsetin 41 G 5
Vsevidof, Mount 12 D 5
Vsevolozhsk 43 K 3
Vukovar 45 G 2
Vung Tau 73 J 5
Vuoksa 42 J 3
Vyaltsevo 50 H 4
Vyatskiye Polyany 50 K 4
Vyazemskiy 69 OP 6
Vyaz'ma 50 F 4
Vyborg 42 J 3
Vychegda 50 J 3
Vygozero, Ozero 50 G 3
Vyksa 50 H 4
Vyngapur 51 P 3
Vysotsk 43 J 3
V'yuny 51 Q 4

W

"W", Parcs Nationaux, du 58 E 3
Wabana 19 K 4
Wabasca 14 G 3
Wabasca River 14 F 3
Wabash River 22 C 3
Wabowden 15 K 4
Wabrah 66 D 5
Waco (Quebec, Can.) 19 G 3
Waco (TX, U.S.A.) 25 G 5
Waconda Lake 21 G 4
Wad 67 H 5
Waddān 55 J 3
Waddington, Mount 13 M 5
Wādī al 'Arabah 48 B 3
Wādī al Bātin 49 DE 3
Wādī al Ghudāf 48 D 2
Wādī al Khurr 48 C 3
Wādī al 'Ubayyid 48 CD 2
Wādī ath Tharthār 48 D 2
Wādī at Tubal 48 C 2
Wādī Halfa' 56 E 4
Wādī Hawrān 48 C 2
Wādī Jimāl 48 B 4
Wādī Qina 48 A 4

Wadley 22 D 4
Wad Madanī 56 EF 6
Wadsworth 20 C 4
Wafrah 66 D 5
Wager Bay 16 J 3
Wagga Wagga 79 H 6
Wagin 78 B 5
Wagoner 21 G 4
Wagon Mound 21 F 4
Wah 67 J 4
Wahai 75 G 4
Wahpeton 21 G 2
Waigeo, Pulau 75 H 4
Waingapu 75 F 5
Wainwright (AK, U.S.A.) 12 E 1
Wainwright (Alb., Can.) 14 G 4
Wajir 61 G 4
Wakayama 71 L 4
Wake 82 C 1
Wa Keeney 21 F 4
Wakkanai 71 M 1
Wakuach, Lac 19 G 2
Wałbrzych 41 G 4
Walden 21 E 3
Waldia 61 F 2
Waldo 27 E 3
Waldport 20 B 3
Wales 40 C 4
Wales (AK, U.S.A.) 12 D 2
Wales Island (N.W.T., Can.) 16 J 3
Walewale 58 D 3
Walgett 79 H 4–5
Walker Lake 20 C 4
Wall 21 F 3
Wallaceburg 18 D 5
Wallaroo 79 F 5
Walla Walla 20 C 2
Wallis 82 D 3
Wallis and Futuna 82 CD 3
Walnut Ridge 21 H 4
Walrus Islands 12 EF 4
Walsenburg 21 F 4
Walsingham, Cape 17 O 3
Walt Disney World 27 E 3
Walterboro 22 D 4
Walvis Bay 62 A 4
Wanaaring 79 G 4
Wanaka 82 C 5
Wandel Sea 84
Wanganui 81 R 8
Wangka 73 G 5
Wangqing 71 J 2
Wan Hsa-la 73 G 3
Wankie 62 D 3
Wankie National Park 62 D 3
Wanxian 70 E 4
Warangal 72 CD 4
Warbumi 75 H 4
Warburton Bay 14 G 2
Warburton Mission 78 D 4

Ware **14** D 3
Waren **75** J 4
Warm Springs **20** C 4
Warner Mountains **20** B 3
Warner Peak **20** C 3
Warner Robins **22** D 4
Warragul **79** H 6
Warren (MI, U.S.A.) **22** D 2
Warrenton **62** C 5
Warri **59** F 4
Warrnambool **79** G 6
Warrumbungle Range **79** H 5
Warszawa → Warsaw **41** H 4
Warta **41** G 4
Warwick **79** J 4
Wasatch Range **20** D 3–4
Wasco **20** C 4
Washburn **21** F 2
Washburn Lake **16** E 3
Washington (D.C., U.S.A.)
    22 E 3
Washington (IN, U.S.A.)
    22 C 3
Washington (U.S.A.) **20** BC 2
Washington Court House
    22 D 3
Washita River **21** G 4
Waspám **28** C 4
Wasua **80** D 3
Wasum **81** E 3
Watampone **75** F 4
Waterberg **62** B 4
Waterbury **23** F 2
Waterford **40** B 4
Waterloo (IA, U.S.A.) **21** H 3
Watersmeet **22** C 1
Waterton Lakes National Park
    14 FG 5
Watertown (N.Y., U.S.A.)
    22 E 2
Watertown (S.D., U.S.A.)
    21 G 2
Watertown (WI, U.S.A.) **22** C 2
Waterville **23** G 3
Watford City **21** F 2
Watheroo **78** B 5
Watrous **15** H 4
Watrous **21** F 4
Watsa **60** D 4
Watson Lake **13** M 3
Watts Bar Lake **22** D 3
Wauchope **79** J 5
Waukegan **22** C 2
Waukesha **22** C 2
Wausau **22** C 2
Wave Hill **78** E 2
Waverly **21** H 3
Wāw **60** D 3
Wawa **18** D 4
Wawotobi **75** F 4
Waycross **22** D 4
Wayland **22** D 3
Wayne **22** D 3
Weagamow Lake **15** L 4

Webbe Shibeli **61** G 3
Webster **21** G 2
Webster City **21** H 3
Weddel Sea **85**
Weeki Wachee **27** E 3
Weichang **71** G 2
Weiden **41** F 5
Weifang **71** GH 3
Weimar **41** F 4
Weining **70** D 5
Weipa **79** G 1
Weirton **22** D 2
Weiser **20** C 3
Wejherowo **41** G 4
Welkom **62** D 5
Wellesley Islands **79** F 2
Wellington (KS, U.S.A.)
    21 G 4
Wellington (New Zealand)
    81 R 9
Wellington (NV, U.S.A.)
    20 C 4
Wellington, Isla (Chile)
    37 AB 8
Wells (NV, U.S.A.) **20** C 3
Wells (VT, U.S.A.) **23** F 2
Wellsboro **22** E 2
Wellton **20** D 5
Wels **45** F 2
Wenatchee **20** C 2
Wendeng **71** H 3
Wendover (NV, U.S.A.) **20** D 3
Wenshan **70** DE 6
Wentworth **79** G 5
Wenzhou **71** H 5
Wepener **62** D 5
Weser **41** E 4
Weslaco **25** E 2
Wesleyville **19** K 4
Wessel, Cape **79** F 1
Wessington Springs **21** G 3
West Allis **22** C 2
West Antarctica **85**
Westbank **48** B 2
West Bend **22** C 2
West Berlin **43** F 5
Westbrook **23** F 2
West Cape **82** C 6
West Elk Mountains **20** E 4
Western Australia **78** C 3–4
Western Ghats Kerala
    72 BC 4–5
Western Sahara **54** C 4
Western Samoa **82** D 3
West Falkland **37** D 9
West Ice Shelf **85**
West Indies **27** F 4
Westlock **14** G 4
West Memphis **21** H 4
Weston **22** D 3
West Palm Beach **27** F 3
West Plains **21** H 4
West Point **22** C 4
Westport **81** Q 9

Westree **18** D 4
West Wirginia **22** D 3
Westwood **20** B 3
West Wyalong **79** H 5
West Yellowstone **20** D 3
Wetar, Pulau **75** G 5
Wetaskiwin **14** G 4
Wete **61** FG 5
Wewak **80** D 2
Weyburn **15** J 5
Whale Cove **15** L 2
Whangarei **81** Q 8
Wharton Lake **15** J 2
Wheatland **21** F 3
Wheeler (OR, U.S.A.) **20** B 2
Wheeler (Quebec, Can.)
    19 G 2
Wheeler Park **21** E 4
Wheeler Peak (NV, U.S.A.)
    20 D 4
Wheeling **22** D 2
White Bay **19** J 3
White Bear Lake **21** H 2
White Butte **21** F 2
Whitecourt **14** F 4
Whitefish Bay **22** D 2
Whitefish Point **22** C 1
Whitehaven **40** C 4
Whitehorse **13** L 3
White Island **16** JK 3
White Mountain (AK, U.S.A.)
    12 E 3
White Mountain Peak **20** C 4
White Mountains **12** H 2
White Nile **56** E 6
White Pass **13** L 4
White River (AR, U.S.A.)
    21 H 4–5
White River (IN, U.S.A.)
    22 C 3
White River (N.W.T., Can.)
    13 J 3
White River (Ontario, Can.)
    18 D 4
White River (S.D., U.S.A.)
    21 F 3
White Russia **43** J 5
White Sulphur Springs **20** D 2
Whitewater Bay **27** E 3
Whitewood **79** G 3
Whitmore Mountains **85**
Whitney **18** E 4
Whitney, Mount **20** C 4
Whittier **12** H 3
Wholdaia Lake **15** HJ 2
Wibaux **21** F 2
Wichita **21** G 4
Wichita Falls **21** G 5
Wick **40** C 3
Wickenburg **20** D 5
Wien **45** G 2
Wiener Neustadt **45** G 2
Wieprz **41** H 4
Wiesbaden **41** E 4

Wilbur **20** C 2
Wilhelm, Mount **80** D 3
Wilhelmshaven **41** E 4
Wilkes-Barre **22** E 2
Wilkes Land **85**
Willamette River **20** B 3
Willapa Bay **20** B 2
Willard **20** E 5
Willcox **20** E 5
Willemstad **32** E 1
Willeroo **78** E 2
William Lake (Man., Can.)
    15 J 4
Williams (AZ, U.S.A.) **20** D 4
Williamsburg (KY, U.S.A.)
    22 D 3
Williamsburg (VA, U.S.A.)
    22 E 3
Williams Lake **14** E 4
Williamsport **22** E 2
Williston (South Africa) **62** C 6
Williston (U.S.A.) **21** F 2
Williston Lake **14** E 3
Willow **12** G 3
Willow Bunch **15** H 5
Willow Lake **14** F 2
Willows **20** B 4
Willow Springs **21** H 4
Wilmington (DE, U.S.A.)
    22 E 3
Wilmington (N.C., U.S.A.)
    22 E 4
Wilowmore **62** C 6
Wilson **22** E 3
Wilson, Cape **16** K 3
Wilson, Mount **20** E 4
Wilson Bluff **78** D 5
Wilson Lake **22** C 4
Wilsons Promontory **79** H 6
Winchester (KY, U.S.A.)
    22 D 3
Windhoek **62** B 4
Wind River **20** E 3
Wind River Range **20** E 3
Windsor (MI, U.S.A.) **18** D 5
Windsor (Nova Scotia, Can.)
    23 H 2
Windsor Forest **22** D 4
Windsor Locks **23** F 2
Windward Islands (French
    Polynesia) **83** F 4
Windward Islands (Lesser
    Antilles) **29** H 3–4
Winfield (AL, U.S.A.) **22** C 4
Winfield (KS, U.S.A.) **21** G 4
Winisk **15** M 3
Winisk Lake **18** C 3
Winisk River **18** C 3
Winnebah **58** D 4
Winnebago, Lake **22** C 2
Winnemucca **20** C 3
Winnfield **25** H 5
Winnibigoshish, Lake **21** H 2
Winnipeg **15** L 4

Winnipeg **15** K 5
Winnipeg, Lake **15** K 4
Winnipegosis **15** J 4
Winnipegosis, Lake **15** JK 4
Winnipesaukee, Lake **23** F 2
Winona **21** H 3
Winslow **20** D 4
Winslow (Kiribati) **82** D 3
Winston-Salem **22** D 3
Winter Park **27** E 3
Winterthur **45** E 2
Wisconsin **21** HJ 2
Wiseman **12** H 2
Wisła **41** G 4
Wismar **41** F 4
Wittenberg **41** F 4
Wittenberge **41** F 4
Włocławek **41** G 4
Wokam, Pulau **75** H 5
Woleai **82** A 2
Wolf **22** C 2
Wolf Creek **20** D 2
Wolf Point **21** E 2
Wollastone Lake **15** J 3
Wollaston Lake **15** J 3
Wollaston Peninsula **16** CD 3
Wollongong **79** J 5
Wolseley **15** J 4
Wolstenholme, Cap **17** L 4
Wolverhamton **40** C 4
Wonga Wongué, Parc
 National de **59** F 6
Wonju **71** J 3
Wŏnsan **71** J 3
Wonthaggi **79** GH 6
Woodall Mountain **22** C 4
Wood Buffalo National Park
 14 FG 3
Woodland **20** B 4
Woodlark **81** F 3
Wood River Lakes **12** F 4
Woods, Lake of the **15** K 5
Woodstock (New Brunsw.,
 Can.) **19** G 4
Woodstock (Queensland,
 Austr.) **79** G 2
Woodstock (VT, U.S.A.) **23** F 2
Woodville **25** H 5
Woodward **21** G 4
Woomera **79** F 5
Wooramel **78** A 4
Worcester (South Africa)
 62 BC 6
Worcester (U.K.) **40** C 4
Worchester (MA, U.S.A.)
 23 F 2
Worland **20** E 3
Worthington **21** G 3
Wosi **75** G 4
Wotho **82** BC 2
Wotje **82** C 2
Wrangel Island **84**
Wrangell **13** L 4
Wrangell Mountains **13** J 3

Wrangell–Saint Elias National
 Park and Preserve **13** J 3
Wright Patman Lake **21** H 5
Wrightson, Mount **20** D 5
Wrigley **13** N 3
Wrocław **41** G 4
Wrottesley, Cape **16** B 2
Wuchuan **70** E 5
Wudaoliang **70** B 3
Wudu **70** D 4
Wugang **70** F 5
Wugong **70** E 4
Wuhai **70** E 3
Wuhan **70** FG 4
Wuhu **71** G 4
Wüjang **72** D 1
Wukari **59** F 4
Wuliang Shan **70** D 6
Wunnummin Lake **18** C 3
Wun Rog **60** D 3
Wuppertal **41** E 4
Wurung **79** G 2
Würzburg **41** F 5
Wutunghliao **70** D 5
Wuvulu **82** A 3
Wuwei **70** D 3
Wuxi **71** H 4
Wuxing **71** H 4
Wuyiling **69** N 6
Wuyuan **70** E 2
Wuzhi Shan **70** E 7
Wuzhong **70** E 3
Wuzhou **70** F 6
Wynbring **78** E 5
Wyndham **78** D 2
Wynniatt Bay **16** D 2
Wynyard **15** J 4
Wyoming (MI, U.S.A.) **22** C 2
Wyoming (U.S.A.) **20–21** E 3
Wyoming Peak **20** DE 3
Wyperfeld National Park
 79 G 6
Wysoczyzna Ciechanowska
 41 GH 4

X

Xainza **72** E 1
Xai-Xai **63** E 5
Xalapa → Jalapa Enríquez
 25 E 4
Xambioá **33** J 5
Xangongo **62** AB 3
Xánthi **46** B 2
Xanthos **46** C 3
Xapecó **36** F 4
Xapuri **34** C 3
Xayar **67** L 2
Xenia **22** D 3
Xiaguan **70** D 5
Xiamen **71** G 6
Xi'an **70** EF 4
Xiangfan **70** F 4
Xiangshan **71** H 5

Xiangtan **70** F 5
Xiangyin **70** F 5
Xianju **71** H 5
Xianyang **70** E 4
Xiao'ergou **69** M 6
Xiao Hinggan Ling **69** N 5–6
Xiapu **71** H 5
Xichang **70** D 5
Xicoténcatl **25** E 3
Xigazê **72** E 2
Xiliao He **71** H 2
Ximiao **70** D 2
Xin Barag Zuoqi **68** L 6
Xingcheng **71** GH 2
Xingdi **70** A 2
Xingren **70** E 5
Xingtai **70** F 3
Xingu **33** H 4
Xing Xian **70** EF 3
Xingxingxia **70** C 2
Xingyi **70** D 5–6
Xining **70** D 3
Xinjiang Uygur Zizhiqu
 67 KM 2
Xinjin (Liaoning, China)
 71 H 3
Xinjin (Sichuan, China) **70** D 4
Xinlitun **69** N 5
Xin Xian **70** F 3
Xinxiang **70** FG 3
Xinyang **70** F 4
Xinyi **71** G 4
Xinyuan **67** L 2
Xique-Xique **35** H 3
Xiushui **70** F 5
Xiuyan **71** H 2
Xiwu **70** C 4
Xixiang **70** E 4
Xizang Zizhiqu **72** DE 1
Xpuhil **28** B 3
Xuanhan **70** E 4
Xuanhua **70** F 2
Xuanwei **70** D 5
Xuchang **70** FG 4
Xuguit Qi **68** LM 6
Xümatang **70** C 4
Xuwen **70** F 6
Xuyong **70** DE 5
Xuzhou **71** G 4

Y

Yablonovyy Khrebet **68** JL 5
Yabrūd **48** B 2
Yacuiba **34** D 5
Yadgir **72** C 4
Yagoua **59** GH 3
Yagradagze Shan **70** C 3
Yakima **20** B 2
Yakmach **67** G 5
Yakoma **60** C 4
Yakrik **67** L 2
Yakumo **71** LM 2
Yakutat **13** K 4

Yakutat Bay **13** J 4
Yakutsk **69** N 3
Yala (Sri Lanka) **72** D 6
Yala (Thailand) **73** H 6
Yale Point **20** E 4
Yalgoo **78** B 4
Yalnızçam Dağları **47** F 2
Yalong Jiang **70** D 4–5
Yalta **47** D 2
Yalutorovsk **51** MN 4
Yamagata **71** LM 3
Yambio **60** D 4
Yambol **46** C 2
Yamburg **51** OP 2
Yamdena, Pulau **75** H 5
Yamoussoukro **58** C 4
Yamuna **72** D 2
Yana **69** P 1
Yan'an **70** E 3
Yanartaş Dağları **46** CD 3
Yanbu' **48** C 4
Yanchang **70** EF 3
Yandrakinot **12** C 3
Yangambi **60** CD 4
Yangjiang **70** F 6
Yangquan **70** F 3
Yangtze Leiang **71** G 4
Yang Xian **70** E 4
Yanhe **70** E 5
Yanhuqu **72** D 1
Yankton **21** G 3
Yano-Indigirskaya
 Nizmennost **69** PR 1
Yanov Stan **51** Q 2
Yanqi Huizu Zizhixian
 67 LM 2
Yanshou **71** J 1
Yanskiy Zaliv **69** OP 1
Yantai **71** H 3
Yaoundé **59** G 5
Yapen, Pulau **75** J 4
Yapura **32** D 4
Yaqui, Rio **24** B 2
Yaraka **79** G 3
Yaranga **69** X 3
Yaransk **50** J 4
Yari **32** D 3
Yaritagua **29** F 4
Yarlung Zangbo Jiang **70** B 5
Yarmouth **23** G 2
Yaroslavl' **50** G 4
Yarram **79** H 6
Yarroto **51** O 2
Yartsevo **51** RS 3
Yarumal **32** CD 2
Yashkino **69** P 5
Yasnyy **69** N 5
Yaté-Village **81** J 6
Yathkyed Lake **15** K 2
Yatsushiro **71** JK 4
Yavi, Cerro **32** E 2
Yawng-hwe **73** G 3
Yaxchilán **25** F 4
Ya Xian **70** E 7

Yazd 49 G 3
Yazdān 67 G 4
Yaz-ed Khvāst 49 F 3
Yazoo 21 HJ 5
Yazoo City 21 H 5
Yecheng 67 K 3
Yedoma 50 H 3
Yeeda River 78 C 2
Yefremov 50 G 5
Yegorlykskaya 47 F 1
Yei 60 E 4
Yelabuga 50 K 4
Yelets 50 G 5
Yelizarovo 51 N 3
Yelizovo 69 T 5
Yellowhead Pass 14 F 4
Yellowknife 14 G 2
Yellow Sea 71 H 4
Yellowstone Lake 20 D 3
Yellowstone National Park 20 D 3
Yellowstone river 21 EF 2
Yelovka 69 U 4
Yelvertoft 79 F 3
Yemanzhelinsk 51 M 5
Yematan 70 C 3
Yemen 57 GH 5
Yengisar 67 K 3
Yengo 59 H 5
Yengue 59 F 5
Yenice 47 E 3
Yenisey 51 R 2
Yenisey 68 F 4
Yenisey, Malyy 68 FG 5
Yeniseyskiy Kryazh 68 F 3–4
Yepoko 51 OP 2
Yercha 69 R 2
Yerema 68 J 3
Yerevan 47 FG 2
Yergeni 47 F 1
Yermak 51 P 5
Yermo 24 D 2
Yerofey-Pavlovich 69 M 5
Yeropol 69 V 2
Yertom 50 J 3
Yerupajá, Nevado 34 A 3
Yerushalayim 48 B 3
Yesil 51 N 5
Yeşilırmak 47 E 2
Yessentuki 47 F 2
Yetman 79 J 4
Yeu, Ile d' 44 C 2
Yevpatoriya 47 D 1
Yeya 47 E 1
Yeysk 47 E 1
Yi'an 69 N 6
Yibin 70 D 5
Yichang 70 F 4
Yichun 69 N 6
Yidu 70 F 4
Yıldız Dağı 47 E 2
Yilehuli Shan 69 MN 5
Yiliang 70 D 6
Yinchuan 70 E 3

Yingde 70 F 6
Yingkou 71 H 2
Yining 67 L 2
Yirga Alem 61 F 3
Yitulihe 69 M 5
Yiyang 70 F 5
Ylikitka 42 J 2
Yllastuntun 42 H 2
Yoboki 61 G 2
Yogyakarta 74 CD 5
Yojoa, Lago de 28 B 4
Yokohama 71 LM 3–4
Yokosuka 71 LM 3–4
Yokote 71 LM 3
Yola 59 G 4a
Yolombo 60 C 5
Yonago 71 K 3
Yŏngan 71 JK 2
Yongchang 70 D 3
Yong deng 70 D 3
Yongren 70 D 5
Yonkers 23 F 2
Yonne 44 D 2
York (NE, U.S.A.) 21 G 3
York (PA, U.S.A.) 22 E 3
York (U.K.) 40 C 4
York (Western Australia) 78 B 5
Yorke Peninsula 79 F 5
Yorkton 15 J 4
Yoro 28 B 3
Yosemite National Park 20 C 4
Yoshkar Ola 50 J 4
Yŏsu 71 J 4
Young 79 H 5
Youngstown 22 DE 2
Yozgat 47 D 3
Yreka 20 B 3
Ytyk-Kel' 69 O 3
Yuanping 70 F 3
Yucatán Peninsula 26 D 4–5
Yucheng 71 G 3
Yuci 70 F 3
Yudoma 69 P 4
Yuexi 70 D 5
Yueyang 70 F 5
Yugorskiy Poluostrov 51 M 2
Yugoslavia 45 G 3
Yukagirskoye Ploskogor'ye 69 ST 2
Yukon 12 E 3
Yukon, Fort 12 H 2
Yukon-Charley Rivers National Preserve 13 J 2–3
Yukon Flats 12 H 2
Yukon Flats National Monument 12 HJ 2
Yukon Plateau 13 K 3
Yukon Territory 13 KL 3
Yulin (China) 70 EF 6
Yulin (Shaanxi, China) 70 E 3
Yuma (AZ, U.S.A.) 20 D 5
Yuma (CO, U.S.A.) 21 F 3

Yumari, Cerro 32 E 3
Yumen 70 C 3
Yumenzhen 70 C 2
Yunaska 12 C 6
Yunling Shan 70 C 5
Yunnan 70 D 6
Yunxiao 71 G 6
Yuriby 51 P 1
Yurimaguas 32 C 5
Yurty 69 U 4
Yushan (China) 71 G 5
Yushan (Taiwan) 71 H 6
Yushnoye 69 Q 6
Yuxi 70 D 6
Yu Xian 70 FG 2–3
Yuzhno-Sakhalinsk 69 Q 6
Yuzhnyy Bug 46 CD 1

Z

Zabarjad 48 B 5
Zabol 67 G 4
Zabrze 41 G 4
Zacapa 28 B 4
Zacapu 24 D 4
Zacatecas 24 D 3
Zacatepec 25 E 4
Zadar 45 G 3
Zadetkale Kyun 73 G 5
Zadran 67 H 4
Za'faranah 48 A 3
Zag 54 D 3
Zägheh-ye Bālā 49 E 2
Zagorsk 50 G 4
Zagreb 45 G 2
Zagros, Kūhha ye 49 EF 2
Zagros Mountains (Iran) 49 F 3
Zagros Mountains (Iran) 66 E 5
Zāhedān 67 G 5
Zāhirah 49 G 5
Zahlah 48 B 2
Zahlah 56 F 2
Zaire 60 BD 5
Zaire (Angola) 62 A 1
Zakamensk 68 H J 5
Zakharov 69 O 3
Zākhū 66 C 3
Zákinthos 46 B 3
Zakouma, Parc National de 59 H 3
Zalābiyah (Syria) 48 C 2
Zalaegerszeg 46 A 1
Zalim 57 G 4
Zaliv Akademii 69 P 5
Zaliv Kara-Bogaz Gol 66 E 2
Zaliv Kresta 12 B 2
Zaliv Shelikhova 69 T 3–4
Zaliv Terpeniya 69 Q 6
Zallah 55 J 3
Zamakh 57 H 5
Zambeze 63 E 3
Zambezi 62 C 2

Zambia 62 D 2
Zamboanga 75 F 2
Zamkowa, Góra 41 H 4
Zamora (Ecuador) 32 C 4
Zamora (Spain) 44 B 3
Zamora de Hidalgo 24 D 4
Zamość 41 H 4
Zanesville 22 D 3
Zanjān 66 D 3
Zanthus 78 C 5
Zanul'e 50 K 3
Zanzibar 61 FG 6
Zanzibar Island 61 FG 6
Zaouatallaz 55 G 4
Zaoyang 70 F 4
Zaozernyy 68 FG 4
Zaozhuang 71 G 4
Zapadnaya Dvina 43 J 4
Zapadno 51 OP 3
Zapala 37 B 6
Zapata 25 E 2
Zaporosh'ye 47 E 1
Zaragoza 44 C 3
Zaragoza (Colombia) 29 E 5
Zaragoza (Mexico) 25 D 2
Zarand (Iran) 49 F 2
Zarand (Iran) 49 G 3
Zárate 36 E 5
Zaraza 32 E 2
Zard Kūh (Iran) 49 F 2
Zarechensk 42 K 2
Zarghun 67 H 4
Zaria 59 F 3
Zaruma 32 C 4
Zaskar Mountains 67 K 4
Zastron 62 D 6
Zatish'ye 69 T 2
Zatoka Gdańska 41 G 4
Zav'yalova, Ostrov 69 RS 4
Zāwiyat Masūs 55 K 2
Zawr, Ra's az 49 E 4
Zayū 70 C 5
Zduńska Wola 41 G 4
Zeehan 82 A 5
Žêkog 70 D 4
Zelenoborskiy 42 K 2
Zelenodol'sk 50 JK 4
Zelenokumsk 47 F 2
Zell am See 45 F 2
Žemaičiu Aukštuma 43 H 4
Žemaitija 43 H 4
Zemgale 43 HJ 4
Zemio 60 D 3
Zenica 45 G 3
Zeya 69 N 5
Zêzere 44 B 4
Zhag'yab 70 C 4
Zhailma 51 M 5
Zhaksylyk 51 O 6
Zhanabas 67 H 1
Zhanabek 51 P 6
Zhangjiakou 70 FG 2
Zhangping 71 G 5
Zhangwu 71 H 2

Zhangye **70** CD 3
Zhangzhou **71** G 5–6
Zhangzi **70** F 3
Zhanjiang **70** F 6
Zhantekets **51** Q 6
Zhao'an **70** G 6
Zhaodong **71** HJ 1
Zhaojue **70** D 5
Zhaotong **70** D 5
Zhaoyuan **71** J 1
Zhaozhou **71** HJ 1
Zharkamys **66** F 1
Zharkova **51** R 4
Zharlykamys **51** P 6
Zharma **51** Q 6
Zharyk **51** O 6
Zhdanov **47** E 1
Zhejiang **71** GH 5
Zhelaniya, Cape **84**
Zhel'dyadyr **67** H 1
Zhelezinka **51** P 5
Zheleznodorozhnyy
 50 K 3

Zheleznogorsk **50** FG 5
Zhenghe **71** G 5
Zhengzhou **70** F 4
Zhenjiang **71** GH 4
Zhenlai **71** H 1
Zhenning **70** DE 5
Zhenxiong **70** D 5
Zhenyuan **70** E 5
Zhigalovo **68** J 5
Zhijiang **70** E 5
Zhitomir **43** J 5
Zhlatyr **51** P 5
Zhmerinka **46** C 1
Zhongba **72** D 2
Zhongning **70** E 3
Zhongwei **70** DE 3
Zhong Xian **70** E 4
Zhongxiang **70** F 4
Zhoukouzhen **70** FG 4
Zhovtnevoye **47** D 1
Zhuanghe **71** H 3
Zhuo Xian **70** G 3
Zhupanovo **69** TU 5

Zhurban **69** N 5
Zhushan **70** EF 4
Zhuzhou **70** F 5
Zibā **48** B 4
Zielona Góra **41** G 4
Zigong **70** DE 5
Ziguinchor **58** A 3
Zihuatanejo **25** D 4
Zilair **51** L 5
Zile **50** E 2
Žilina **41** G 5
Zima **68** H 5
Zimatlán de Alvarez **25** E 4
Zimba **62** D 3
Zimbabwe **62–63** DE 3
Zimbabwe **63** E 4
Zimi **58** B 4
Zimovniki **47** F 1
Zincirli **47** E 3
Zinder **59** F 3
Zitacuaro **25** DE 4
Zlatoust **51** L 4
Zlatoustovsk **69** OP 5

Znamenka **47** D 1
Znojmo **41** G 5
Zoigê **70** D 4
Zolotaya Gora **69** N 5
Zomba **63** F 3
Zonga **60** B 4
Zonguldak **47** D 2
Zorritos **32** B 4
Zrenjanin **46** B 1
Zufār **57** J 5
Zugdidi **47** F 2
Zugspitze **45** F 2
Zújar **44** B 4
Zunyi **70** E 5
Zurbāṭīyah **49** D 2
Zurich **45** E 2
Zurmat **67** H 4
Zuwārah **55** H 2
Zvolen **41** G 5
Zwickau **41** F 4
Żyrardów **41** H 4
Zyryanka **69** S 2
Zyryanovsk **51** Q 6

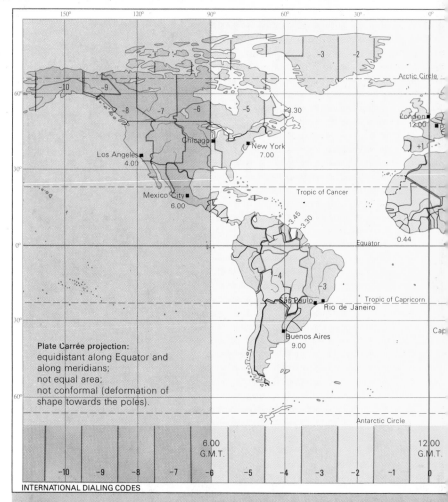

Plate Carrée projection:
equidistant along Equator and
along meridians;
not equal area;
not conformal (deformation of
shape towards the poles).

INTERNATIONAL DIALING CODES

To make an international call it is necessary to dial first the dialing-out code (011 in USA), then the dialing-in code followed by the subscriber number
including the city code.

Country	Code	Country	Code	Country	Code	Country	Code
Algeria	213	Greece	30	Mexico	52	Spain	34
Argentina	54	Hong Kong	852	Netherlands	31	Sweden	46
Australia	61	India	91	New Zealand	64	Switzerland	41
Belgium	32	Iraq	964	Nigeria	234	Taiwan	886
Brazil	55	Ireland	353	Norway	47	Trinidad/Tobago	309
Canada	1	Israel	972	Pakistan	92	Turkey	90
Chile	56	Italy	39	Panama	507	United Arab Emirates	971
Denmark	45	Jamaica	809	Philippines	63	United Kingdom	44
Dominican Republic	809	Japan	81	Portugal	351	USA	1
Finland	358	Kuwait	965	Saudi Arabia	966	USSR	7
France	33	Libya	218	Singapore	35	Venezuela	58
Germany	49	Malaysia	60	South Africa	27	Yugoslavia	38

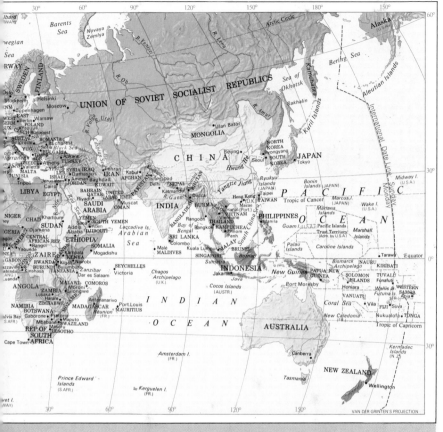

Country	Page	Country	Page	Country	Page	Country	Page
Malawi	63	Oman	57	Sierra Leone	58	Tunisia	55
Malaysia	74	Pakistan	67	Singapore	74	Turkey	47
Maldives	72	Panama	28	Solomon Islands	81	Tuvalu	82
Mali	54	Papua New Guinea	80	Somalia	61	Uganda	60
Malta	45	Paraguay	36	South Korea	71	Union of Soviet	50,68
Mauritania	54	Peru	32,33	South Yemen	57	Socialist Republics	
Mauritius	62	Philippines	75	Spain	44	(U.S.S.R)	
Mexico	24	Poland	41	Sri Lanka	72	United Arab Emirates	49
Monaco	45	Portugal	44	Sudan	56,60	United Kingdom and	
Mongolia	68,70	Qatar	48	Surinam	33	Northen Ireland	40
Morocco	54	Republic of Ireland	40	Swaziland	63	United States	12,20-25
Mozambique	63	Republic of South Africa	62	Sweden	42	Uruguay	36
Namibia	62	Romania	46	Switzerland	45	Vanuatu	82
Nauru	82	Rwanda	60	Syria	48	Vatican State	45
Nepal	72	Saint Kitts- Nevis	29	Taiwan	71	Venezuela	32
Netherlands	40	Saint Lucia	29	Tanzania	60	Vietnam	73
New Zealand	81	Saint Vincent	29	Thailand	73	Western Samoa	82
Nicaragua	28	San Marino	45	The Bahamas	27	Yemen	57
Niger	55	São Tomé and Principe	59	The Gambia	54	Yugoslavia	46
Nigeria	59	Saudi Arabia	48,57	Togo	58	Zaire	60
North Korea	71	Senegal	54	Tonga	82	Zambia	62
Norway	42	Seychelles	61	Trinidad and Tobago	29	Zimbabwe	62

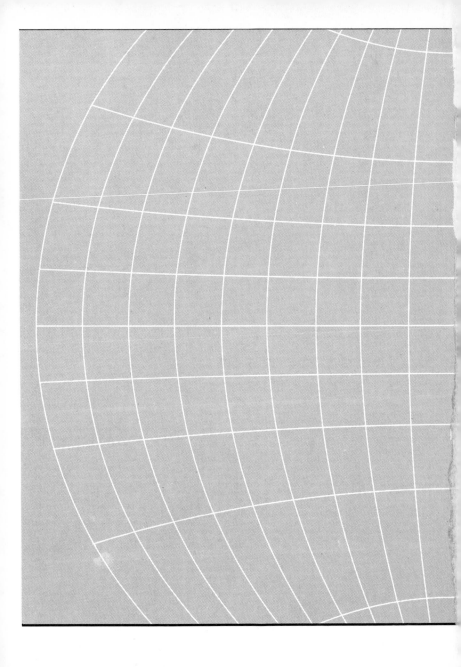